2000 MOST CHALLENGING & OBSCURE WORDS

2000
MOST CHALLENGING
and OBSCURE WORDS

by Norman Schur

Galahad Books • New York

First Galahad Books edition published in 1994.

Galahad Books
A division of BBS Publishing Corporation
386 Park Avenue South
New York, NY 10016

Galahad Books is a registered trademark of BBS Publishing Corporation.

Published by arrangement with Facts on File, Inc.

Library of Congress Catalog Card Number: 93–80460

ISBN: 0-88365-848-8

Printed in the United States of America.

CONTENTS

Part I

▼▼▼▼

1000
MOST CHALLENGING
WORDS

Latine is now of equal use become
To Englishmen, as was the Greek to Rome:
It guides our language, nothing is exprest
Gracefull or true but by the Roman test.

—Dryden

These are the opening lines of a poem signed "J. Drydon (a contemporary spelling of *Dryden*), one of two poems prefacing a 17-century manuscript Latin grammar by Lewis Maidwell (1650-1715), a schoolteacher and minor author. The poem, forty lines long, goes on to praise Maidwell, through whose work

Grammer, which was before the ungratefull part
Of our green yeares, is made a pleasing Art . . .

and

. . . as it teaches words it moulds the mind.

* * * * * *

Beside, 'tis known he could speak Greek
As naturally as pigs squeak:
That Latin was no more difficile,
Than to a black-bird 'tis to whistle.

—Samuel Butler (*Hudibras*)

(Note: *Difficile* has to be pronounced *dih FIS uhl* to rhyme with *whistle*.)

* * * * * *

He Greek and Latin speaks with greater ease
Than hogs eat acorns, and tame pigeons peas.
—Lionel Cranfield, Earl of Middlesex
(Panegyric on Tom Coriate)

(Note: Cranfield's couplet preceded Butler's *Hudibras* by a good many years.)

And to any who may object to the plenitude of space devoted to derivation, remember that none other than Dr. Johnson defined *lexicographer* as "a harmless drudge, that busies himself in *tracing the original*, and detailing the signification of words."

For Marjorie

Preface

"Americans today," says Bryan A. Garner in volume X, No. 3, of *Verbatim*, *The Language Quarterly*, "are as averse as any nation to unfamiliar words, which seem to proclaim intellectual pretension, flaunted knowledge, or cultural snobbery—and this if they are used well! Yet hard words have a reputable literary tradition . . . But sesquipedalophobia ('hatred or fear of big words') has prevailed, even among men of learning . . . " (See **sesquipedalian**.)

There are more than 400,000 words in today's unabridged dictionaries, and supplements appear from time to time. They include entries like *you, me, it, is, to, how, why*, etc.—words that are part of every English-speaking person's vocabulary—and others like *abelmosk, benzophenone, holoblastic, leptoprosopic, mylohyoideus, zingiberaceous*, words that, a thousand to one, you'll never run into except perhaps in word games, and can live without. In between, there is a third lot: words not in common use, but ones you may well run into.

Within this third lot, there are certain groupings: words based on the names of people, real (*Lucullan, gerrymander, jeremiad, Roscian*) or fictional (*Gargantuan, Pantagruelian, rodomontade*), or on place names, geographical (*brummagem*) or literary (*Brobdingnagian, Lilliputian*); others that have been taken over intact from foreign languages (*a cappella, bivouac, bravura, chiaroscuro, legerdemain, louche, nous, tzigane, Zeitgeist*). The majority by far, though they owe their origin in the main to classical Latin and Greek, are perfectly good English words that might lurk around any corner of literature, waiting to jump out and perhaps puzzle you, and therefore challenge you. Hence the title of this book.

Compilations of difficult words are nothing new. Philetas of Cos in ancient Greece (b.c. 320 B.C.) produced such a work, known in English as "Miscellaneous Difficult Words," consisting of a collection explaining rare words found in Homer and certain dialects, and technical terms. His pupil. Zenodotus of Ephesus (b.c. 325 B.C.), the first head of the celebrated Library of Alexandria, wrote a Homeric glossary, known in English as "Difficult Words." He was responsible for a great innovation: he listed his entries in alphabetical order! Aristophanes of Byzantium (c. 257-180 B.C.—not to be confused wiht the earlier Aristophanes, c. 445-c. 385 B.C., the foremost writer of Greek comedy) became head of the great library c. 194 B.C. and followed up with an exhaustive compilation bearing the simple title "Words" that included, in addition to obscure terms from poetry, difficult words from prose writings as well. This book follows a tradition established a very long time ago.

Pronunciation is indicated in parentheses immediately following the headword.

"a"	for "a" as in "hat"
"ay" or "a—e"	for "a" as in "hate"
"ah"	for "a" as in "bah," "o" as in gone
"air"	for "a" as in "dare," "ai" as in "air"
"ar"	for "a" as in "art"
"aw"	for "a" as in "awe," "ou" as in "ought"
"e" or "eh"	for "e" as in "met"
"ee"	for "ee" as in "meet"
"i" or "ih"	for "i" as in "bit"
"(e)ye" or "i—e"	for "i" as in "bite"
"o"	for "o" as in "got"
"oh" or "o—e"	for "o" as in "go"
"oo"	for "oo" as in "look"
"ooh"	for "oo" as in "boot," "u" as in "lute"
"or"	for "o" as in "or"
"oy"	for "o" as in "boy" or "void"
"ou"	for "ou" as in "out"
"u" or "uh"	for "u" as in "but," and for schwa (an indefinite "uh?" sound of an unaccented syllable, like the "a" in "woman," the "i" in "pencil," the "u" in "focus," etc.)
"u(r)"	for "u" as in "fur"

In demonstrating meaning by example, I have at times seen fit to amplify my own concoctions with quotations from literature, with the dual purpose of showing such exquisitely apposite and dramatic choices of words by great writers as might serve to fix their meanings in the mind, and that of introducing readers to the masters and their writings in the hope that closer acquaintance might be sought. Foreign authors are, of course, quoted in translation, and here it is the translators whose choice of words is the model.

Wherever *Fowler* is quoted or mentioned in the text, I refer to *Fowler's Modern English Usage* (Second Edition Revised by Sir Ernest Gowers, Oxford University Press). *Latin* and *Greek* in the text mean the classical forms; *Late Latin* is that of A.D. 300-700; *Middle Latin* or *Medieval Latin* that of A.D. 700-1500; *New Latin* that which came into use circa 1500. *Old English* is the English of A.D. 450-1150; *Middle English* that of 1150-1475. *Old French* is the French of A.D. 1000-1400; *Middle French* that of 1500-1700.

Parts of speech are abbreviated thus: *n.* noun; *vb.* verb; *adj.* adjective; *adv.* adverb; *conj.* conjunction; *pl.* plural.

My criteria in the selection of the 1000 words have necessarily been subjective. They are, without exception, words that I have come across myself, words that have challenged me by giving me pause or somehow exciting my interest and inviting investigation. I have not resorted to plucking words out of dictionaries.

Any "challenging" word that appears in the explanatory comment under another entry is set in boldface. If you find an unfamiliar word set in ordinary type, look for it in my *1000 Most Important Words* or *1000 Most Practical Words*. If that doesn't work, find it in your unabridged and meet the challenge head on!

Norman W. Schur
Hawkhurst, Kent, England
Weston, Connecticut, U.S.A

a fortiori (ay for shee OR eye) *adj, adv*. This Latin phrase meaning, literally, "from the stronger [point]" is used quite frequently in English to introduce a statement that, assuming a previous statement is accepted as true, must *all the more so* be true. What *a fortiori* really means, in arguing a point, is "all the more so." If statement A is true, then *a fortiori*, i.e., all the more so, statement B must be true. If a certain job can't be done by a certain crew in a week, *a fortiori* a similar job can't be done by a similar crew in five days. If a man isn't rich enough to stay a night at a second-rate hotel, *a fortiori* he can't afford to put up at the Ritz. This is a useful expression in arguing, to prove a weaker point from a stronger one—i.e., *a fortiori*.

a posteriori, see **a priori**

a priori (ay pree OR eye) *adj.*; *adv.*; **a posteriori** (ay poh steer ee OR eye) (The vowels can be pronounced in different ways depending on one's system of pronunciation of Latin) *adj.*; *adv*. Both these expressions are Latin but are freely used in English, especially in argument. They mean, literally and respectively, "from the one before" and "from the one behind," and apply as follows: An *a priori* conclusion or judgment is one reached by reference to self-evident truths, deductively, not based on prior examination, experimentation or analysis. Thus, the American critic and editor Norman Cousins (born 1912) spoke of the "*a priori* acceptance of the greatness of a book," reasoning not from an examination of its merits but from deductions based on surrounding circumstances, such as the greatness of its author and the influence the book has had. In *a priori* reasoning, one works from a known premise or premises to an effect. An *a posteriori* conclusion is one reached by examination and analysis of the specific facts, as happens in a science laboratory, where one reasons inductively from actual observation of data and derives a conclusion or theory from the observed facts. In short, an *a priori* conclusion is based upon presumptions; an *a posteriori* conclusion is based upon observations. Fowler ingeniously gives *God's in his heaven—all's right with the world* as either an *a priori* inference if it means: "We know there is a god; therefore the state of the world must be right," or an *a posteriori* inference if it means: "The world is so right that there must be a god in heaven."

abatis (AB uh tee, -tis, uh BAT ee, -is) *n*. A term describing a primitive form of military barricade; an obstruction against the foe consisting of felled trees with sharpened branches, sometimes interlaced with barbed wire. In these days of extremely long-range artillery, to say nothing of bombers (shall we remain silent about the A- and H- variety?), the *abatis* seems as naive as the classical military phalanx, but in its day the *abatis* was very effective. Incidentally, the hedges of today that serve to mark land boundaries, embellish landscapes, or provide residential privacy are descendants of another piece of old-time military construction, a defense used by the Roman army: its military hedges (*saepes* or *saepimenta*), as thick as 30 feet, very tall, a line of living trees with their branches interwoven, were quite impenetrable by the enemy. The noun *abatis* was taken from the French, a variant of *abattis*, the word used generally to denote any materials thrown down, based on the verb *abbatre* (throw down), but more specifically the label given to felled trees used as a barricade. You won't find *abatis* in today's military dispatches, but there are always those 1,184-page historical novels.

abecedarian (ay bee see DAR ee un) *n.*, *adj.* This amusing word, obviously based on the first four letters of the alphabet (*abecedarianus* in Middle Latin, *abecedarius* in Late Latin), applies to a beginner, anyone learning the rudiments in any field of learning. The "ABC" or "ABCs" of anything is a term denoting the rudiments of that subject. The Russian physiologist Ivan Petrovich Pavlov (1849-1936) told the youth of his country who were going into science to "learn the ABC of science before you try to ascend its summit." As an adjective, *abecedarian*, apart from its literal use to describe anything pertaining to the alphabet or arranged in alphabetical order, means "rudimentary, elementary." The Wright brothers (Orville, 1871-1948, and Wilbur, 1867-1912) were the *abecedarians* of aeronautics. Spelt with an upper case *A, Abecedarian* was the title of an Anabaptist sect founded in 1520 that rejected human learning as a hindrance, on the ground that only the guidance of the Holy Spirit was needed for the interpretation of the Bible. (It wasn't so long ago that evolution was a taboo subject in the schools of certain American states.)

a-biblion, see **bibliopole**

abigail (AB uh gale) *n.* We are familiar with *Abigail* as a girl's given name, quite popular in past generations, like so many other Biblical names. Abigail was the wife of Nabal, and later one of David's wives (1 Samuel 25); her name in Hebrew meant "My father is joy." When she first met David, she "fell at his feet" and called herself "thine handmaid." So it came to pass that when Beaumont and Fletcher (Francis Beaumont, 1584-1616, and John Fletcher, 1575-1625, who collaborated on a number of comedies) wrote a part for a "waiting gentlewoman" in their 1620 play *The Scornful Lady*, they named her *Abigail.* Whence, with a lower case *a*, the proper noun became a common noun for "lady's maid." There aren't many *Abigails* or *abigails* around these days, but at least now you know what they mean.

abiosis (ab ee OH sis, ay bye-) *n.* *Abiosis* is the absence of life; the related adjective *abiotic* (ay by OT ik) describes any state or condition marked by the absence of life. Extensive tests were made by a satellite controlled from earth to determine whether life existed on Mars. It was found that that planet was characterized by *abiosis.* The moon has likewise been found to be *abiotic.* *Abiosis* is formed from the Greek prefix *a-* (the "alpha privative," indicating negation, as in *apolitical, asymmetrical, asexual*) plus *bio-* (the Greek prefix meaning "life," as in *biography, biology—bios* is the Greek word for *life*) plus

-sis (the Greek suffix used to form nouns denoting state or condition, as in *paralysis, peristalsis, stasis*). The condition of Pompeii and Herculaneum after the eruption of Mt. Vesuvius in A.D. 79 was one of complete destruction of life and resulting *abiosis*. The defoliation program of the American forces in Vietnam, to deprive the foe of cover, resulted in botanical *abiosis* over wide areas of the jungle. When, in office elevators, stony-faced passengers seem not to dare even look at one another, *abiosis* seems to have set in.

abjure (ab JOOHR) *vb*. To *abjure* something is to renounce it, retract, repudiate, forswear it. *Abjure* comes from the Latin verb *abjurare* (to deny under oath); *abjuration* from Late Latin *abjuratio* (recantation); both are based on *ab-* (away) plus *jurare* (to swear). Reformed sinners *abjure* the errors of their ways. A number of American communists *abjured* their allegiance to the Communist Party and informed on their former colleagues. The noun *abjuration* (ab joo RAY shuhn) implies renunciation upon oath, or at least some measure of solemnity and formality, something more than a mere change of mind. Born again Christians *abjure* their former unbelief. The English poet John Donne (1572-1631) wrote:

> The heavens rejoice in motion, why should I
> *Abjure* my so much loved variety?

In *Paradise Lost*, the English poet John Milton (1608-1674) says:

> I waked
> To find her, or for ever to deplore
> Her loss, and other pleasures all *abjure*.

ablation (ab LAY shun) *n*. *Ablation* has several usages. In surgery, *ablation* is the removal of growths from the body. In meteorology, *ablation* is the reduction of snow or ice through melting or evaporation. In rocketry, *ablation* is the falling off of parts of a nose cone melted away by the heat generated in reentry. It will be seen that, whatever the context, *ablation* involves the removal or taking away of something. There is a verb, to *ablate* (a BLATE), that covers all these senses. Both noun and verb are derived from Latin *ablatus*, past participle of *auferre* (to carry away). Do not confuse *ablation* with **ablution**, which has an entirely different derivation and meaning. *Ablation* is etymologically related to *ablative* (A bluh tiv), a grammatical case (in Latin and other inflected languages) involving changes in noun endings to indicate (inter alia) "place from which," i.e., removal.

ablaut (AB lout) *n*. In philology and grammar, *ablaut* is the term for vowel changes in related words and suffixes, especially in indicating a change in tense, part of speech or other grammatical function. Examples: *get, got*; *bid, bade* or *bad*; *ride, rode, ridden*; *sing, sang, sung, song*; *choose, chose*. *Ablaut* is from the

German, based on the prefix *ab-* (off) plus *Laut* (sound). It is synonymous with *apophony* (uh POF uh nee), based on the Greek prefix *apo-* (away, different from) plus suffix *-phone*, combining form of *phone* (sound).

ablution   (ab LOOH shun, uh BLOOH-) *n. Ablution* is the washing of one's hands or body. To perform one's *ablutions* is to cleanse oneself. The British use "have a wash" as a polite euphemism for *urinate*, and jocularly speak of "attending to their *ablutions*" in the same connection. Fowler has some strong words to say on this subject: "Pedantic Humour . . . " is the "only fitting place outside religious ceremonial" for *ablutions*. "[We] do not need monstrosities like *ablution facilities, ablution cubicles*, and *mobile ablution centres." Ablution*, in religious terminology, is the ritual cleansing of the body, as in a *mikvah*, the public bathing establishment where orthodox Jews go for purification on certain occasions (notably, the bride, prior to the wedding). The English poet John Keats (1795-1821) used the term *ablution* in a special poetic sense in his sonnet *Bright Star*, writing of

> The moving waters at their priestlike task
> Of pure *ablution* round earth's human shores.

This sonnet was found written on a blank page in Keats' copy of Shakespeare's *Poems*. The word comes from the Latin *ablutio*, related to *ablutus*, the past participle of the verb *abluere*, based on the prefix *ab-* (away) and the verb *luere* (to wash). Do not confuse *ablution* with **ablation**, which is a very different story.

aborticide   (uh BOR tih side) *n. Aborticide* is defined as the destruction of the fetus in the womb. *Feticide* (FEE tih side) is given as a synonym. *Aborticide* can also be used of a drug or other substance that produces abortion; in this sense, it is a synonym of *abortifacient* (uh bor tuh FAY shunt). *Aborticide* is a peculiar word and seems incorrectly formed. In the run of *-cide* words, derived from Latin *-cida*, based on *caedere* (to kill), the *-cide* is attached to the victim, and the word denotes the killing of that victim, as well, in some cases, as the killer or destructive agent. In the following examples, the identification of the victim follows the *-cide* word in parentheses: *deicide* (god—must have been a rare occurrence and perpetrated by another god); *fratricide* (brother); *fungicide* (fungi); *genocide* (national or racial group); *germicide* (germs); *herbicide* (weeds); *homicide* (person); *infanticide* (infant); *mariticide* (spouse); *matricide* (mother); *parasiticide* (parasites); *parricide* (close relative); *pediculicide* (lice); *regicide* (king); *sororicide* (sister); *spermatocide* or *spermicide* (spermatozoa); *suicide* (oneself); *tyrannicide* (tyrant); *uxoricide* (wife); *viricide* (viruses). Thus, under this system, *aborticide* would logically mean "killing of an abortion," which is what it doesn't mean. The logical form is *feticide*, the killing of a fetus. Kindly note that we have dealt exclusively with the linguistic side of this matter, carefully avoiding the physiological, medical, ethical, and religious aspects so much in the news these days.

abri (uh BREE, ah-) *n.* An *abri* is a place of shelter or refuge, especially a dugout. It is a word taken over intact from the French, who, the authorities say, got it from the Latin *apricum* (open place), that being the neuter form of the adjective *apricus* (open to the sun), related to the verb *aperire* (to lay bare, to expose). Somewhere along the etymological line, someone or something must have gone off the track, else how could *apricum* (open place), of all things, have given rise to *abri* (shelter)? It would seem that the last place one would repair to in flight from the foe, for shelter or refuge, would be an *apricum*!

abruption, see **aposiopesis**

abscission (ab SIZH uhn, -SISH-) *n.* An *abscission* is a cutting off, a sudden termination. The verb *abscind* (ab SIND) means "sever, cut off." These are general terms, but the related verb *abscise* (ab SIZE) is a botanical term, used, for example, in the separation of a leaf from its stem. *Abscission* would be resorted to in an advanced case of gangrene, where the patient's life could be saved only by *abscission* of the affected member. *Abscission* has a special use in rhetoric, as a figure of speech in which words that would normally be demanded by the sense are left unspoken, the speaker suddenly stopping short. Example: War, when one thinks of its indescribable and endless horrors—! *Abscission* is from Latin *abscissio*; *abscind* from the related verb *abscindere* (to tear off) and *abscise* from *abscissus*, past participle of *abscidere* (to cut off). *Abscissio* and *abscindere* are based on prefix *ab-* (away) plus *scindere* (to cut) and its past participle *scissus*, which help to explain the *c* in *scissors*. *Abscise* happens to come from a different Latin verb: *abscidere* (to cut off), based on prefix *abs-*, a variant of *ab-*, plus *caedere* (to cut), which changes its *-ae-* to *-i-* in combination form. Thus, *abscidere* and its past participle *abscissus* do not help to explain the *s* in *scissors*. In any event, *scissors* came by its *c* honestly.

absquatulate (ab SKWAH chuh late) *vb.* This amusing, vivid, and expressive word is a bit of jocular, contrived slang. To *absquatulate* is to decamp, to scram, to take off in a hell of a hurry like a fugitive heading into the woods; sometimes, to abscond, like a cashier running off with the contents of the till. The term, invented in America in the 1830s and adopted by the English in the 1870s, is an example of supposed derivation from factitious mock-Latin, based on a combination of parts of *abscond*, *squat*, *perambulate* and heaven knows what else. A certain J. Lamont, in an old book entitled *Seahorses*, wrote of a grizzled bull-walrus who "heard us, and lazily awakening, raised his head and prepared to *absquatulate*." You may not run across this little item nowadays, but it's a picturesque word whose revitalization should be encouraged, though it may be used to describe a practice that should be discouraged.

abulia (uh BYOOH lee uh) *n. Abulia* is a term used mostly in psychiatry to denote a type of mental disorder causing the loss of willpower or volition, or at least its serious weakening. The word comes, via New Latin, from the Greek noun *aboulia* (lack of resolution; *a-* is the Greek prefix signifying negation and *boule* is Greek for "will"); it is often spelt *aboulia*, closer to its Greek origin. Hamlet is probably the best known sufferer from *abulia*; the entire "To be or not to be" soliloquy is a study in that disorder.

> The native hue of resolution
> Is sicklied o'er with the pale case of thought
> And enterprises of great pith and moment. . .
> lose the name of action. (Act III, Scene 1)

To depart from the sublime (but not to the ridiculous), there is also the memory of the late Jimmy Durante (1893-1980), ambivalent in the extreme, sitting at the piano and singing: "Didja evah have the feelin' that ya wanted to go, and yet had the feelin' ya wanted to stay, go, stay, go, stay," etc. With each "go" he grabbed his battered fedora off the piano and started up; with each "stay" he darted back and dumped it back on the piano. Poor Hamlet and Jimmy both suffered from *abulia*—and not a psychiatrist in sight.

academe   (AK uh deem) *n. Academe* (sometimes capitalized) is the equivalent of "school," any place where instruction is given, but it is more commonly used to denote college or university ambience or environment. College professors often choose their careers because they look forward to the alleged peace and quiet of *academe*, as a refuge from the hurly-burly of the marketplace, but they sometimes despair at the internecine rivalries that embitter life in *academe*. Capitalized, *Academe* is the name of the garden or grove in ancient Athens, open to the public, where the Greek philosopher Plato (427-347 B.C.) taught. The place was named for Akademos, a Greek who lived in the mountainous region of Arkadia (see **Arcadian**), on whose property the philosophers of Athens used to meet. The Roman poet Horace (65-8 B.C.) wrote, in his *Epistles*, of those who "seek for truth in the groves of *Academe*" (translation from the Latin), and the English poet John Milton (1608-1674) wrote, in *Paradise Regained*, of

> The olive grove of *Academe*,
> Plato's retirement, where the Attic bird
> Trills her thick-warbled notes the summer long.

Academe gave rise to the word *academic* (ak uh DEM ik), which, in its literal sense, describes anything or anyone having to do with higher education, but has been expanded to include the figurative meanings of "theoretical, not practical" (any discussion of man's travel to other galaxies is of *academic* interest only) and "conventional" (the impressionists got away from the *academic* school of painting). *Academic* is sometimes used as a noun to signify a college teacher or student. In the opening speech of Shakespeare's *Love's Labour's Lost*, Ferdinand,

King of Navarre, outlining his three-year plan of ascetic life and study at his court, says:

> Our court shall be a little *academe*,
> Still and contemplative in living art.

acarine, see **accipitrine**

acarophobia, see **acrophobia**

accidence   (AK sih dens) *n. Accidence* has nothing (except derivation) to do with its **homophone** *accidents*. In grammar, it is the part that deals with inflection (variations in the forms of words, like *go, goes, going, gone, went* or *boys, boy's, boys'*) and word order. *Accidence* sets the rules that govern word order and inflection. We don't say "I goes" or "Go I," but "I go," using the rules of *accidence*. Children who grow up in literate families get these things right by imitation (no *me and my friend are hungry* or *between you and I*) and only later, in school, learn the rules of *accidence*. It comes from Latin *accidentia*, neuter plural of *accidens*, present participle of the verb *accidere* (to happen), based on prefix *ac-* (to or towards; a variant of *ad-* before *c*) plus *cadere* (to fall).

accipitrine   (ak SIP ih trin, -trine) *adj.* This adjective, formed from the noun *accipiter* (ak SIP ih tuhr), which means "hawk," as it does in Latin, is applicable to the Accipitrinae family, one that includes certain types of hawk and other birds of prey. Apart from its scientific meaning, it may be used figuratively as the equivalent of "predatory." There is a large group of adjectives ending in *-ine* that designate zoological or entomological families but are susceptible of figurative use as well, in certain cases. Thus, *bovine*, which in its literal sense means "of or pertaining to the ox family," is commonly applied to people or their behavior to mean "dull, stolid, listless," and is undoubtedly used more often in that sense than as a zoological term. In the same way, the technical meaning of *asinine* is "pertaining to the ass family," but its more frequent use is to describe people or their acts as stupid or inane. *Aquiline* (relating to eagles) is most often found as a description of noses, like Julius Caesar's who gave his name to a gynecological operation rather than a nose; and *leonine* (pertaining to the lion family) is a favorite dramatic representation of massive heads, particularly those with sweeping hairdos, like Beethoven's. *Feline* (relating to cats) is used, quite unfairly, to describe sly, stealthy, and even treacherous persons and their behavior. *Elephantine* has been used as a vivid description of ponderous, clumsy movements of people, and has also been applied to awkward, insensitive humor. The use of *accipitrine* might well be extended to describe predatory people and their acts, evoking the image of a hawk swooping down on its prey. It is unlikely that secondary, figurative uses will be found for a good many of the *-ine* words mentioned below (items like *alectoridine, charadrine, herpestine, oscine*). But, for the benefit of those who may run into *-ine* adjectives new to them and, even more importantly, for those who may wish to invent figurative uses of some of them, we append a list (not exhaustive, and, for convenience, inclusive of some words already discussed), and leave it to the reader to dream up figurative, even fanciful uses and thus enrich our beautiful language.

	Relates to:
acarine	mites
accipitrine	hawks, eagles
alaudine	skylarks
alci(di)ne	auks, puffins
alectoridine	cranes, rails
anatine	ducks
anguine	snakes
anopheline	mosquitoes
anserine	geese
antelopine	antelopes
aquiline	eagles
asinine	asses
aspine	asps
avine	birds
bisontine	bisons
bombycine	silkworms
bubaline	antelopes, hartebeests
buteonine	buzzards
caballine	horses
cameline	camels
canine	dogs
capreoline	roe, deer
caprine	goats
cathartine	vultures
cervine	deer
charadrine	plovers
ciconi(i)ne	storks
colubrine	king-, gartersnakes
columbine	doves
corvine	crows
cricetine	hamsters
crocodiline	crocodiles
crotaline	rattlesnakes
cuculine	cuckoos
culicine	mosquitoes
cygnine	swans
cyprine	carp
dacelonine	kingfishers
daysurine	daysures
delphi(ni)ne	dolphins
didelphine	opossums
didine	dodos
elephantine	elephants

equine	horses
falconine	falcons
feline	cats
formicine	ants
fringilline	finches
fulciline	coots
fuliguline	eider ducks
galline	domestic fowl
garruline	magpies, jays
gazelline	gazelles
giraffine	giraffes
herpestine	mongooses
hippopotamine	hippopotami
hippotigrine	zebras
hirudine	leeches
hirundine	swallows
homarine	lobsters
hominine	man
hyenine	hyenas
hylobatine	gibbons
hystricine	porcupines
ibidine	ibises
lacertine	lizards
lapine	rabbits
lari(di)ne	gulls
lemurine	lemurs
leonine	lions
leporine	hares
lumbricine	earthworms
lupine	wolves
lutrine	otters
lyncine	lynxes
macropine	kangaroos
macropodine	kangaroos, wallabies
manatine	manatees
megapterine	humpback whales
meleagrine	turkeys
mephitine	skunks
milvine	kites
moschine	musk deer
murine	mice, rats
musteline	weasel, mink
nestorine	keas, kakas
noctilionine	bats
octopine	octopi
oscine	songbirds
ostracine	oysters
ovibovine	musk ox
ovine	sheep

pantherine	panthers
pardine	leopards
passerine	songbirds
pavonine	peacocks
phasianine	pheasants
phocaenine	porpoises
phocine	seals
picine	woodpeckers
piscine	fish
porcine	pigs
procyonine	raccoons, kinkajous
psittacine	parrots
pteropine	bats
ralline	rails
rangiferine	caribous, reindeer
ranine	frogs
rhinocerine	rhinoceroses
rucervine	Indian swamp deer
rupicaprine	chamoix
sabelline	sables
salamandrine	salamanders
sciurine	squirrels
serpentine	serpents
soricine	shrews
strigine	screech-owls
sturnine	swallows
suilline	hogs
talpine	moles
tapirine	tapirs
taurine	bulls
tetraonine	grouse, ptarmigans
tigrine	tigers
tolypeutine	armadillos
tringine	sandpipers
trochili(di)ne	hummingbirds
turdine	thrushes
ursine	bears
vaccine	cows
vespine	wasps
viperine	vipers
vituline	calves
viverrine	civets
volucrine	birds
vulpine	foxes
vulturine	vultures
zebrine	zebras

accouterment   (uh KOOH truh muhnt) *n. Accouterment* is equipment, outfit, trappings. This word, taken over from the French *accoutrement* (which is the way the British sometimes spell it), has a specific application in military circles, where it denotes a soldier's outfit, as in a line by the English poet and dramatist Ambrose Philips (1675-1749):

> How gay with all the *accouterments* of war!

In Shakespeare's *Taming of the Shrew* (Act III, Scene 2), Petruchio shows up for his wedding in unseemly clothes and is chided by Tranio about his "irreverent robes." Petruchio answers:

> To me she's married, not unto my clothes.
> Could I repair what she will wear in me
> As I can change these poor *accoutrements*,
> 'Twere well for Kate and better for myself.

The verb is *accouter*   (uh KOO tuhr). To *accouter* someone is to equip or outfit him. In *Julius Caesar* (Act I, Scene 2), Shakespeare has Cassius tell how he accepted Caesar's dare to jump into the raging Tiber with him:

> Upon the word
> *Accoutred* as I was, I plunged in.

In *The Merchant of Venice* (Act III, Scene 4), Portia boasts to Nerissa:

> When we are both *accoutred* like young men,
> I'll prove the prettier fellow of the two.

These are all quotations from works of many a yesterday, but there is no reason why we should abandon these expressive words, or why we can't *accouter* ourselves today in whatever *accouterments* we wish, and saunter on *accoutered* as we choose.

acedia   (uh SEE dee uh) *n. Acedia* is sloth, one of the seven deadly sins. It is more commonly known as *laziness. Acedia* was taken intact from Middle Latin, which took it from the Greek *akedeia*, based on negative prefix *a-* plus *kedos* (care). A specialized meaning of *acedia* is "indifference" (i.e., no care or concern), particularly in matters of religion. This word can be found in another form, *accidie* (AK sih dee), Middle English taken from Middle Latin *accidia*, a variant of *acedia*. Sloth, or *acedia*, was considered deadly enough to be included among the seven deadly sins. In *Proverbs* 6:6 we read: "Go to the ant, thou sluggard; consider her ways, and be wise." Such was the Biblical condemnation of sloth, *acedia*, or *accidie*! In an engaging letter to *The Times* (London - issue of August 2, 1986), from the Rev. G.S. Luff, mention is made of *accidie*, and this sentence follows: "Hard to define, it has been described as 'dont-care-ishness' and 'torpor', though the latter is more appropriate to the time after lunch."

acronical   (uh KRAHN ih kuhl) *adj.* Also *acronykal.* This adjective applies to phenomena occurring at sunset, as opposed to *cosmical* (KOZ mih kul), applicable to things that occur at or near sunrise. Both terms are used in astronomy with respect to the rising and setting of certain stars; but they can be used figuratively of other events, like the chirping of some birds and insects that become active and make their sounds as the sun rises or sets. *Acronical* is not synonymous with *vespertine* (VES puhr tin, -tine), but comes close: *vespertine*, like **crepuscular**, covers things that happen in the early evening, at dusk, just after sunset, and is used of birds and insects that fly, or flowers that open, or, like nicotiana (flowering tobacco), begin to give off their scent at that time. *Vespertine* is a poetic word, especially in a phrase like *vespertine calm* or *stillness. Acronical* comes from Greek *akronychos* (at nightfall), based on *akros* (at the edge) plus *nyx* (night). *Cosmical*, a variant of *cosmic*, is based on Greek *kosmikos* (of the world), related to *kosmos* (world). *Vespertine* is from Latin *vespertinus*, based on *vesper* (evening), which gave us *Vesper*, evening star, particularly Venus, and *vespers* (evensong). *Vesper* is also called *Hesperus* (HES puhr uhs); based on Greek *hesperos* (evening).

acrophobia   (ak ruh FOH bee uh) *n. Acrophobia* is morbid dread of heights. The word is taken from New Latin, based on two Greek words that do a lot of service in the formation of English words: *akros* (highest, topmost) and *phobos* (fearing). The prefix *acro-* shows up in words like *acrobat, acronym, acropolis*; the suffix *-phobia* is likewise common: *agrophobia, claustrophobia, xenophobia*. People who suffer from *acrophobia* shouldn't climb mountains or live in penthouses. They would make good spelunkers unless they were also claustrophobic. A psychiatrist friend of the author refers to patients in the arts who fear success as "acrophobes," those who dread the dizzying heights of fame and the consequent exposure. The insertion of an *a* between the first two syllables of this word produces *acarophobia* (ak uh ruh FO bee uh), a morbid fear of skin parasites. Here we have the familiar *-phobia* attached to the combining form of *acaris* (AK uhr uhs), meaning "mite," from which we get *acarology* (ak uh ROL uh jee), the study of mites, ticks, and the like. It is quite possible to suffer from both these phobias (as well as others we have not sufficient space to enumerate).

acuity   (uh KYOOH ih tee) *n. Acuity* is a synonym of *acuteness, keenness, sharpness*, whether the sharpness applies to a physical object such as a nail or a needle, or, more commonly, to keenness of mind, understanding, or the senses. The word comes from Middle Latin *acuitas*, based on Latin *acus* (needle) and *acuere* (to sharpen). We get *acute* from *acutus*, past participle of *acuere*. Our noun *acumen* was taken over intact from Latin, where it means "anything sharp," and figuratively, "sharpness of mind," as in English. *Visual acuity* is a term in ophthalmology denoting sharpness of vision with respect to one's ability to resolve detail. The main use of *acuity* is in the field of understanding and perception. A person lucky enough to be endowed with *acuity* is quick to comprehend, to get the point. Getting back to *acus* (needle) for a moment: *In Rudens*, a play by the Roman comic poet and dramatist Plautus (254-184 B.C.), Gripus says to Labrax, "Then you are a beggar?" Labrax answers, "Tetegisti *acu*," literally "You've touched [it] with a needle" (*acu* being a form of *acus*), and freely translated: "You've hit the nail on the head."

adduce   (uh DOOHS, -DYOOHS) *vb.* To *adduce* is to cite as proof, to present as an argument or as evidence in order to support one's point. *Adduce* is from Latin *adducere* (to bring or lead [a person] to [a place]). Lawyers *adduce* as much evidence and as many arguments as they can muster to persuade judge or jury. The authors of almanacs *adduce* past weather records to support their predictions for the coming year. Such theories or arguments as are considered pertinent are *adducible* (uh DOOHS uh bul, -DYOOHS-).

adeem, see **ademption**

ademption   (uh DEMP shun) *n.* If someone leaves you a specific object (as opposed to a sum of money, or a share of the estate) in his will, and after he dies, it turns out that it no longer belongs to the estate (he gave it away, sold it or lost it), the bequest fails. This failure is called an *ademption*, from Latin *ademptio* (a taking away), based on *ademere* (to take away). A related verb is *adeem* (uh DEEM), to cancel a bequest not by changing the will but by selling or otherwise disposing of the thing bequeathed. A will is "ambulatory," which in law means "alterable" or "revocable" at will. (This is a special meaning of *ambulatory* having nothing to do with patients walking around in hospitals). Since a will can "walk around," as it were, and "speaks" only as of the date of the testator's death, then any specific object the will may bequeath to you, if it's not to be found after the testator's death, has been *adeemed* and you have become the victim of an *ademption*. So don't count your Rembrandts or your Stradivariuses before they're hatched.

ad hoc   (ad hok) *adj., adv.* This phrase, taken over intact from the Latin, means "for this special purpose" or "with respect to this particular subject or occasion." The Latin phrase *ad hoc* means, literally, "for this (thing)," *hoc* being the neuter form of the demonstrative adjective *hic* (this) here used as a noun, as neuters often are in Latin. *Ad hoc* can apply to a body, such as a committee, or to a decision or an argument, to limit general application. It can sometimes have the disparaging effect of implying hurried improvisation, but this is not its usual sense. The expression can be used adjectivally or adverbially: one can speak of an *ad hoc* committee, or a committee formed *ad hoc*. An *ad hoc* decision is one applicable to a particular problem or state of affairs, often an emergency, without setting a binding precedent. An *ad hoc* committee is one formed for the particular occasion requiring study or decision and action. Such a committee disbands as soon as its work is completed.

adiaphorous   (ad ee AF ur us) *adj*. This is a term that describes anything that neither benefits nor harms, like a placebo that is medically neuter. In a more general sense, *adiaphorous* means "neutral," "indifferent," "neither right nor wrong." The word is from the Greek *adiaphoros*, based on negative prefix *a-* plus *diaphoros* (different), i.e., making no difference, of no consequence. An *adiaphoron* (ad ee AF uhr on), a word taken intact from the Greek, is a matter of indifference in morals or ethics or religion: to each his own, *de gustibus*, etc.—providing it doesn't affect anyone else. These words have nothing to do with *adiaphoresis* (uh dy uh for EE sis), meaning "absence of sweat," or *adiaphoretic* (uh dy uh for ET ik), sweat-preventing, like all those beautifully packaged underarm sprays and sticks for sale in drugstores. For *diaphoresis*, see **sudorific**.

adulate   (AJ uh late) *vb*. To *adulate* someone is to fawn upon, exhibit an excess of devotion to, express one's admiration obsequiously for, or make a disproportionate fuss over him or her. An *adulator* (AJ uh lay tuhr) is a sycophant. *Adulation* (aj uh LAY shuhn) is the noun for "abject adoration." The verb is a back formation from the noun, which comes from Latin *adulatio* (fawning), related to *adulatus*, past participle of *adulari* (to fawn). *Adulatory* (AJ uh luh tor ee, -tohr-) is the adjective. Courtiers, in the old days, *adulated* their sovereigns to a sickening degree. When foreign heads of state meet, there is a tendency to exchange *adulatory* addresses, full of platitudes and insincerity. *Adulation* seems to be an essential ingredient in the introductions of guests on talk shows. "The man who ..." is an inevitable cliché in *adulatory* introductions at political rallies and conventions. After an *adulatory* introduction by the chairperson at a women's club during a political campaign, the American politician Adlai Stevenson (1900-1965) rose and said (in effect): "After hearing all the wonderful things Mrs. Smith [?] has said about me, I can hardly wait to hear myself begin."

adumbrate   (ad UM brate) *vb*. To *adumbrate* something is to foreshadow it, to give a hint of what is coming to pass. The activities of Hitler in the late 1930s *adumbrated* the coming of World War II. The facility and poise of the child Mozart *adumbrated* the majestic career to come. There is another sense of *adumbrate*: to "outline" or sketch," as when a faint indication of something is given. It is in this sense that the theologians say the invisible God is *adumbrated* in the vastness and richness of the visible world. The noun is *adumbration* (ad um BRAY shuhn), meaning "faint sketch" or "outline." The English prelate Samuel Horsley (1733-1806), a noted scientist who became a bishop, wrote of the visible phenomena of the universe as "elegant *adumbrations* of sacred truth." In a section entitled "Formal words," Fowler lists "adumbrate (outline)" as one of those words used by people subject to the "prevalent notion that the commoner synonyms . . . ought to be translated into them"; then, in the section headed "French words," he cautions the speaker against excessive care in producing the exact pronunciation of a French term in the middle of an English sentence, and says: " . . . there are some French sounds so obviously alien to the English mouth that words containing them . . . should either be eschewed by English speakers, or have these sounds *adumbrated* [i.e., suggested, or hinted at]." Fowler, in this instance, didn't follow his own advice, but we love him all the more for this sign of human frailty. *Adumbrate* and *adumbration* are from Latin *adumbratus* (sketched; by extension, shadowy, imperfect), past participle of *adumbrare* (to sketch, especially in words), based on prefix *ad-* (towards) plus *umbra* (shade, shadow), from which we get, among other things, *umbrella*.

adventitious (ad ven TISH uhs) *adj.* Anything described as *adventitious* (do not confuse with *advantageous*) is associated with something else as a matter of happenstance, not intentionally as an integral part; something accidental, fortuitous, extraneous, foreign to the main purpose. The word comes from Latin *adventicius* (extraneous). Narrow, winding lanes lend an *adventitious* charm to the English countryside. Stone walls and hedges have long been used in various parts of the world as boundary markers; their proliferation in rural areas affords *adventitious* variety to what might otherwise have been uninteresting terrain. The hurly-burly of large centers adds *adventitious* excitement to city life. The sudden hush as the lights dim just before the curtain goes up in the theater produces an *adventitious* thrill of anticipation. Many painstaking efforts (the most elaborate picnic preparations) go unrewarded and soon forgotten, while *adventitious* occurrences (sudden thunderstorms with pelting showers) often make the most memorable impressions and best-remembered experiences.

aeonian (ee OH nee un) *adj.* An *aeon* (EE uhn, -ahn) is an immeasurable period of time, an eternity. Anything described as *aeonian* is everlasting, eternal. The source of *aeon* is, via Latin *aeon*, the Greek noun *aion* (age, period of time); *aeonian* comes from the Greek *aionios*. *Eon* and *eonian* are variant spellings, as so often happens with *e* taking the place of the diphthong *ae* in English. Both *aeon* and *aeonian* can be used literally or metaphorically. The English poet Rudyard Kipling (1865-1936) used *aeon* figuratively and dramatically in his poem *When Earth's Last Picture*:

> When Earth's last picture is painted and the tubes are
>   twisted and dried,
> When the oldest colours have faded, and the youngest
>   critic has died,
> We shall rest, and, faith, we shall need it — lie down
>   for an *aeon* or two,
> Till the Master of All Good Workmen shall put us to
>   work anew.

Not one of Rudyard's best, and his *aeon* had to be figurative; you can't, literally, have more than one eternity. All he meant by *aeon* was *one helluva long time*, as in: "Where have you been, dear? I've been waiting here for *aeons*!" *Aeonian* is far from common; one would not expect to hear: "My love for you is *aeonian*," but it might be a nice way to put it.

aerie, **aery**, **eyrie**   (AIR ee; EER ee) *n*. Literally, an *aerie* is a nest built by a bird of prey, especially an eagle, but the term can be applied to the nest of any bird that builds high in the air. Figuratively, *aerie* is used to denote a human residence perched high on a hill or mountainside. Hitler's mountaintop house in Garmisch-Partenkirchen, often referred to as "Hitler's *aerie*," was blown up by the allied forces after the war. Wealthy owners or occupants of city penthouses, and the society columnists who celebrate such denizens of the metropolis, sometimes refer to those lofty dwellings as "aeries." *Aerie* is traced to Old French *aire*, origin unknown.

afflatus   (uh FLATE us) *n*. An *afflatus* is an inspiration, especially a prophetic one coming from a divine source, imparting special knowledge or power. The word sometimes implies, as well, an overpowering supernatural impulse. *Afflation* (uh FLAY shuhn) is a variant, and *afflated* (uh FLAY tid) means "inspired," with all the connotations attached to the noun. *Afflatus* was taken over intact from Latin, where it means, literally, a "breathing on," based on prefix *ad-* (to, toward) plus *flatus*, past participle of *flare* (to breathe). The American writer Max Eastman (1883-1969), who in his younger days was the editor of radical periodicals like *New Masses* but later attacked communism (and was famous, also, for engaging in fisticuffs with the American writer Ernest Hemingway [1899-1961]), wrote: "We imagine that a great speech is caused by some mysterious *afflatus* that descends into a man from on high." The teachings of the great religious figures of the past—Moses, Jesus, Confucius, Mohammed—all issued from divine *afflatus*. There are more recent individuals who have laid claim to the same source—Father Divine (1882-1965), Billy Sunday (1863-1935), Aimee Semple McPherson (1890-1944)—to say nothing of certain present-day evangelists who shall remain nameless and dateless.

agape   (ah GAH pay, AH guh pay, AG uh pay) *n*. *Agape*, however you pronounce it, taken over from the Greek, was the name given to a love-feast practiced by early Christians in connection with the Lord's Supper. It came to signify God's love of mankind, and then, in a more general sense, brotherly love without sexual implications, as opposed to *eros* (EER ohs, AIR ohs), meaning, with a lower case *e*, "sexual desire." (Eros, with an upper case *E*, was, as we all know, the ancient Greek god of love, whom we know also as *Cupid*.) While we're on the subject, *platonic love* is a purely spiritual relationship free from sexual desire, especially between a man and a woman. "We are just good friends" is often heard in media interviews. Plato (427-347 B.C.) was responsible for the concept of platonic love as a striving toward love of spiritual beauty.

agitprop (AJ it prop) *n. Agitprop* is, as the word suggests, the combined activities of *agit*ation (in the political sense) and *prop*aganda, particularly in the cause of communism. The USSR. maintains an office with the rather frightening name of "Agitpropbyuro," based on Russian *agitaisiya* (agitation) plus *propaganda* (same word as ours) plus *byuro* (bureau). *Agit* is from Latin *agitatus*, past participle of *agitare* (to set in motion, stir up, shake—as in "Shake well before using"; *agit*, in doctors' prescriptions, means just that, and *stirring* is, of course, the business of *agitators*). *Prop* is short for *propaganda*, a form of the Latin verb *propagare* (to propagate, spread, disseminate), and means, literally, "things to be spread," like the joys of the workers' paradise. *Byuro* is simply a Russianization of *bureau*, taken, as we took it, from the French. In one way or another, we extol and propagandize the virtues of our system, and in one way or another, we (particularly the CIA) do a bit of agitating, but thus far we have avoided the formation of an official *byuro* combining the *agit* and the *prop*.

aglet (AG lit) *n.* Also *aiglet* (AY glit) and *aiguillette* (ay gwih LET). An *aglet* is the metal end of a lace, e.g., of a shoelace or of a piece of string. The term can also be applied to any metallic ornament of a dress. In the form *aiguilette*, it usually denotes the metal point of shoulder-braid on certain costumes or uniforms. *Aiguilette*, later shortened to *aglet* or *aiglet*, was taken over intact from the French, where it is the diminutive of *aiguille* (needle), from the Latin *acucula*, diminutive of *acus* (needle). In Shakespeare's *Taming of the Shrew* (Act I, Scene 2), Grumio, Petruchio's servant, tells the latter's friend Hortensio that his master will marry any woman for her money: " . . . why, give him gold enough and marry him to a puppet or an *aglet*-baby, or an old trot [crone] woth ne'er a tooth in her head . . . " An *aglet-baby* was a small ornamental figure serving as the tag of lace.

agnate (AG nate) *n., adj.* An *agnate* is a relative on the paternal side. A *cognate* (KOG nate) is a relative descended from any common ancestor. An *enate* (EE nate) is a relative on the maternal side. All three words serve as adjectives as well. Your father's brother is your *agnate*, or an *agnate* uncle. Your mother's brother is an *enate*, or an *enate* uncle. Both are your *cognates*, or *cognate* uncles. These three words come from Latin: *agnatus*, *cognatus*, and *enatus*, all formed from prefixes plus *natus*, past participle of *nasci* (to be born). *Cognate* has a special meaning in philology: words in different languages descended from a common ancestor are *cognate* words, or *cognates*. English *father*, German *vater*, Latin *pater* are *cognates*; so are English *frigid*, Spanish *frio*, French *froid*, Italian *freddo*, Latin *frigidus*; and English *cold*, German *kalt*, Dutch *koud*, Latin *gelidus*.

agnomen (ag NOH mun) *n.* An *agnomen* is a nickname. It is from Late Latin, composed of the prefix *ag-*, developed from *ad-* (toward—indicating addition) under the influence of *agnoscere* (to recognize), plus *nomen* (name). In olden days, the Romans formed the custom of tacking an additional name onto the names of famous persons as an indication of a great achievement or special characteristic. Thus, the Roman satirist Gaius Petronius (died A.D. 66) was the official in charge of entertainments and the authority on matters of taste and elegance at the court of Nero (37-68; see **arbiter**), and acquired the title of *arbiter elegantiae*. He gained the *agnomen* "arbiter" and became known as "Petronius Arbiter" (Petronius the Arbiter). Quintus Fabius Maximus Verrucosus, a Roman general of the second century B.C. (see **cunctator**), became famous for his successful delaying strategy against the Carthaginians in the Second Punic War. He acquired the *agnomen* "Cunctator" (Delayer, Postponer), and was popularly knows as "Fabius Cunctator" (Fabius the Delayer). There were two Roman generals who distinguished themselves in Africa, Publius Cornelius Scipio Major (Scipio the Elder—Scipio Sr., c. 234-183 B.C.), victorious over Hannibal, and his adopted grandson, Publius Cornelius Scipio Aemilianus Minor (Scipio the Younger—Scipio Jr., c. 185-129 B.C.), who destroyed Carthage. To each, the Romans attached the *agnomen* "Africanus," to commemorate their African exploits, and each was known as "Scipio Africanus" (Scipio of Africa). In more recent times, we have invented sobriquets of the type of "Honest Abe," "Lucky Lindy," and "Tricky Dick," preferring to put our *agnomina* before the familiar form of the given name. From these customs begun in ancient Rome, *agnomen* had gained the force of "nickname" generally. For a fuller list of *agnomina*, see also **antonomasia**. *Cognomen* (kog NO muhn) is related but different. Its principal meaning is "surname," but it, too, has acquired the additional meaning of "nickname." In ancient Rome, the *cognomen* was the third (usually the last) name or surname of an individual. In the name Publius Cornelius Scipio, *Scipio* was the *cognomen*. The full name of the poet Virgil (70-19 B.C.) was Publius Vergilius Maro; *Maro* was his *cognomen*. His contemporary Horace (65-8 B.C.)—full name Quintus Horatius Flaccus—had the *cognomen Flaccus*. He was, so to speak, Mr. Flaccus; but who would ever think of T.S. Eliot as *Mr.* Eliot, or W.H. Auden as *Mr.*A.?

agon (AG on, -ohn) *n. Agon* is a literary term for "conflict," especially between the protagonist (hero) and the antagonist (adversary) in a drama or novel. The plots of Shakespeare's tragedies center around clear-cut *agones* (uh GO neez), e.g., those between Hamlet and Claudius, Macbeth and Macduff, Othello and Iago, Richard III and Henry Tudor. The same goes for all those cowboys-and-Indians and cops-and-robbers shows. Note the *-agon-* in both *protagonist* and *antagonist. Agon* was taken over intact from the Greek, where it means "struggle, conflict" generally, and in ancient Greek was the term for a "contest" in which prizes were given in athletic events and the arts, including poetry, drama and music. Via Late Latin *agonia*, the Greek *agon* is the source of our words *agony, agonize, agonist* (one engaged in a contest or conflict, or beset by inner conflict; also short for *protagonist*); and it figures as well in the adjective *agonistic* (combative). *Agonistes* is Greek for "champion," as in *Samson Agonistes* of the English poet John Milton (1608-1674) and *Sweeney Agonistes* of the British poet T.S. Eliot (American born: 1888-1965). *Agon* has nothing to do with *agonic* (ay GON ik), an adjective meaning "not forming an angle," from the Greek negative prefix *a-* plus *gonia* (angle).

agonic, see **agon**

agoraphobia   (ag ur uh FOH bee uh) *n. Agoraphobia* is the morbid dread of being in or crossing an open space. One suffering from this pathological fear would hardly feel at Home on the Range, where the buffalo roam. *Agora* is Greek for "marketplace" or "public square"; *phobia* is based on Greek *phobos* (fearing), and has itself become an English word by extraction from words like *agoraphobia, acrophobia, claustrophobia*, etc. There are those who admire the sight of the wide open fields of the countryside, but who are presented by *agoraphobia* from walking through them. *Claustrophobia* would disqualify a person from becoming an astronaut; *agoraphobia* would certainly disqualify him from indulging in a space walk. See also *agromania*.

agrestic   (uh GRES tik) *adj. Agrestic* means "rustic" or "rural," but is also used in its figurative sense of "uncouth, awkward, unpolished, boorish," in the description of the behavior of a clumsy country lout or oaf. *Agrestic* is derived from Latin *agrestis* (literally, rustic; figuratively, countrified, boorish), based on *ager* (land, field). *Agrestic* is quite distinct from *agrarian* (uh GRAIR ee un), which describes things related to land, like laws, tenure, political or social movements, a type of society, and has nothing to do with behavior, loutish or other. *Agrarian* is from Latin *agrarius*, also based on *ager*. One would never talk of "agrarian behavior" or, conversely, "an agrestic society." Both words go back to the basic Latin *ager*, but go off in entirely different directions.

agromania   (ag ruh MAY nee uh, -MAYN yuh) *n. Agromania* is the morbid desire to live in open spaces, or in isolation. *Agromania* is not quite the opposite of *agoraphobia*, the abnormal dread of open places. People suffering from *agoraphobia* dread being in, or crossing open spaces; those with *agromania* not only do not fear open spaces, they actually have to live in them. Can you imagine a Mr. and Mrs. Sprat suffering from these respective psychological disturbances? *Agromania* is based on Greek *agros* (tilled land; *agro-* is found in *agrology, agronomics*, etc.) plus Greek or Latin *mania* (madness; *-mania* is found in words like *megalomania, monomania*, etc.). See **agoraphobia**.

ailurophile   (eye LOOHR uh file) *n*. There is a group of *ailuro-* words, all of which can be written *ailouro-* as well, based on *ail(o)uros*, the Greek noun for "cat." These words add familiar Greek suffixes. An *ailurophile* is a cat fancier, a lover of cats, as everybody should be (suffix from *-philos*, dear, beloved). *Ailurophilia* is love of cats, an obvious mark of distinction (adding *-philia*, loving). An *ailurophobe* is a cat hater, or one who suffers from a dread of cats, obviously a pathological condition (*-phobos* fearing). *Ailurophobia* is dread of cats, a condition already characterized (*-phobia*, fear, dread, abnormal aversion or hate). It must by now be clear where the author's sympathies lie. After all, in ancient Rome the cat was a symbol of liberty and in ancient Egypt the cat was held so sacred that, according to the Sicilian historian Diodorus (d. c. 21 B.C.), the killing of a cat, even though accidental, was a capital offense. So much for *ailurophobes!*

akimbo   (uh KIM boh) *adj., adv.* Hand(s) on hip(s) and elbow(s) extended outwards. *With arms akimbo* is the usual expression. *There he was, standing with arms akimbo*, evokes the image of someone standing there with legs apart, somewhat like Henry VIII later in life, or just anyone looking straight ahead and saying, "Well?" *Arms akimbo* suggests moods ranging from simple contemplation to expectation to defiance. The English novelist John Galsworthy (1867-1933) wrote of people standing "*akimbo*, surveying their little plots of land." The word is said to be derived from Middle English *in kene bowe* (in keen bow), i.e., in the position of a tautly drawn bow; and to be related to the Icelandic word for "crooked," *kengboginn*, which is reflected in the derivation of our word *kink*. In a column entitled "Jostling With Elbows" (*New York Times*, June 22, 1984), William Safire discusses *akimbo*:

> On occasion, the elbows still go a bit too far. In "Caveat," the memoirs of nuance-ridden Alexander Haig, he captions a picture of himself with hands on hips, elbows prominent: "The 'take-charge' image had taken hold . . . My photograph (jaw jutting, arms *akimbo*), had been on the cover of *Time* magazine . . . "

alaudine, see **accipitrine**

albeit   (ahl BEE it) *conj.* This conjunction is short for *all though it be that*, via the shorter form *all be it (that)*. It means "although, though, even though, even if," and is a pleasant substitute (if not overdone). Not so many years ago, it was considered archaic by some authorities; indeed, it was so labeled in the first edition of Fowler, which now says, "it has since been picked up and dusted . . . " So now we can say, for instance, that Columbus was a great navigator *albeit* without success in his search for a westward passage to Asia, or that virtue is its own reward, *albeit* often a skimpy one. *Albeit* is a useful word, *albeit* somewhat literary. As we have said, don't overdo it.

alci(di)ne, see **accipitrine**

aleatory   (AY lee uh tor ee) *adj.* An *aleatory* event is one that depends on luck or chance or contingencies, and is therefore unpredictable. *Aleatory* has certain special uses: in law, a contract is *aleatory* if the obligations of the parties depend on a contingent event; in music and the other arts, where the form *aleatoric* (ay lee uh TOR ik) is more common, the adjective indicates that the performance involves random choices of notes or other elements rather than a fixed score or rigid directions. The origin of the word is found in the Latin noun *aleator* (gambler), based on *alea* (dice game; by extension, chance, uncertainty). For a famous use of *alea*, remember "Jacta est alea!" ("the die is cast!"), the cry of Julius Caesar in 49 B.C. when he crossed the Rubicon, invading Italy from his allotted province of Gaul, defying the Roman senate and launching civil war.

alectoridine, see **accipitrine**

alexia (uh LEK see uh) *n*. *Alexia* is a disorder of the brain that deprives the sufferer of the ability to read; also known as word blindness. *Alexia* is derived from the Greek negative prefix *a-* (not) plus *lexis* (speech), based on the Greek verb *legein* (to speak), as a result of confusion with the Latin verb *legere* (to read). The pathologist who concocted the term *alexia* suffered from a confusion of the classical tongues, a condition for which no medical term has as yet been dreamt up. Suggestion for a word to describe confusion of the classical tongues: *dysetymologia*. This is a condition that has to do with a defect in the educational system. *Alexia* is complete word blindness, while the related, and probably more familiar word *dyslexia* (dis LEK see uh) covers only partial inability to read, also resulting from a brain defect. (*Dyslexia* is from the Greek prefix *dys-* (bad, ill), plus *lexis* and the same confusion.) Those affected with *alexia* cannot read at all; *dyslexia* sufferers have great difficulty learning to read or spell. Neither of these conditions has to do with intelligence, and their cause has not been discovered.

alfresco, al fresco (al FRES ko) *adj., adv*. The Italian source is *al fresco*, meaning "in the open air." *Fresco* is Italian for "cool," but *al fresco* means "out of doors," whatever the temperature. When you eat at a sidewalk café, you are eating *alfresco*. Picnics are *alfresco* outings, complete with ants and rain. The open-air theater is an *alfresco* entertainment. Street musicians perform *alfresco*. Many people prefer old-fashioned *alfresco* football stadia to those newfangled domes and dromes.

algesia (al JEE zee uh, -see-) *n*. Most people are familiar with *analgesic* (an al JEE zik) as an adjective meaning "pain-relieving" and a noun for "pain-reliever," perhaps less so with the noun *analgesia* (an al JEE zee uh) meaning "relief of pain." The underlying terms *algesia* (al JEE zee uh) for "sensitivity to pain" and *algesis* (al JEE sis) for "sensation of pain" are much less familiar than the ones beginning with the Greek negative prefix *an-*. All these words involve as a source, via Late Latin, the Greek noun *algos* (pain) and verb *algein* (to suffer). Strange as it may seem, it is a common phenomenon in the English language that the negative of a word is in much more common use than the positive from which it is formed; e.g., *impeccable/peccable*; *unalterable/alterable*; *irreproachable/reproachable*—and the list is a long one. The measure of one's *algesia* or sensitivity to pain is often referred to as "threshold of pain," i.e., the point at which a person begins to feel pain. This is also known in the trade as one's *limen* (LYE muhn), a word taken over intact from the Latin meaning "threshold." In any event, the higher the *limen* the better, though bad for the procaine—$C_6H_4NH_2COOCH_2CH_2N(C_2H_5)_2$—business. *Limen* shows up in the formation of the adjective *subliminal* (sub LIM uh nuhl, -LYE muh-), describing stimuli that operate below the *threshold* of consciousness, from Latin prefix *sub-* (under) plus *limen*.

algid   (AL jid) *adj*. *Algid* means "cold, chill, chilly," especially to describe the feeling of chill one has in certain illnesses. It is from the Latin *algidus* (cold), related to the verb *algere* (to be cold), and the verb *algescere* (to catch cold). The related noun *algor* designates the kind of chill that hits one at the onset of fever; it was taken over intact from the Latin noun *algor* (cold), and has nothing to do with **algorism** or **algorithm**, or for that matter, **algolagnia**.

algolagnia   (al guh LAG nee uh) *n*. *Algolagnia* is a term used in psychiatry for sadomasochism, the derivation of sexual enjoyment from undergoing or inflicting pain. There are other *algo-* words (see *algor*, discussed under **algid**, and **algorism**). *Algolagnia* is derived from the combination of Greek *algos* (pain) and *lagneia* (lust, coitus), a very different derivation from those of the other *algo-* words.

algorism   (AL guh riz um) *n*. This is the name of the Arabic numbering system, using the figures 1 to 9 plus the zero. The derivation is from Middle Latin *algorismus*, from the Arabic *al* (the) plus *Khuwarizmi*, the surname of a ninth-century Arabic mathematician. *Algorithm* is sometimes used as a synonym, but is also used to designate a set of rules for the solution of a mathematical problem in a finite number of steps. These words are entirely unrelated to **algolagnia**, with its very different meaning and derivation.

algorithm, see **algorism**

aliment   (AL uh munt) *n*. *Aliment* is nourishment, nutriment, anything that feeds or sustains. *Alimentum* is Latin for "food," based on the verb *alere* (to nourish). The related adjective is *alimentary* (al uh MENT uh ree), often found in the term *alimentary canal*, the passage from mouth to anus involved in the digestive process. Sherlock Holmes did not say, "*Alimentary*, my dear Watson," but the American humorist and drama critic Robert Benchley (1889-1945) said, in one of his side-splitting short films entitled *Through the Alimentary Canal with Gun and Camera*, "We now come to the stomach [Benchley using a pointer and a diagram on an easel], which we will call 'Prince Charming.'" *Enteron* (EN tuh ron) is another term for *alimentary canal*; it comes, via New Latin, from the Greek, where it means "intestine." A further Latin word for "nourishment" is *alimonia* (also based on *alere*, nourish), from which we get *alimony*, provision for food, and usually lots more.

aliquant, see **aliquot**

aliquot (AL i kwut), *adj.*; **aliquant** (AL i kwunt) *adj. Aliquot* is usually found in the term *aliquot part*, and describes a quantity that is contained in a larger quantity an even or integral number of times. Example: 3 and 5 are *aliquot parts* of 15. Less often met with is *aliquant*, also usually coupled with *part*. An *aliquant part* is a quantity contained in a larger quantity an uneven number of times. Example: 3 and 5 are *aliquant parts* of 16. *Aliquot parts* are exact divisors; *aliquant parts* are not. *Aliquot* was taken intact from Latin, where it means "some, several"; *aliquant* is from Latin *aliquantus*, meaning "of some size, more or less great." The English uses seem somewhat arbitrary, considering their ancestry, but there's often many a slip 'twixt the Latin or the Greek and the English.

allochthonous, see **autochthon**

alpha and omega (AL fuh and oh MEE guh, -ME-) *Alpha* and *omega* are the first and last letters of the Greek alphabet. The phrase the *alpha and omega* is used to mean "the beginning and the end" in the *Revelation of St. John* 1:8. The *New English Bible* version:

> "I am the *Alpha and Omega*," says the Lord God, who is and who was and who is to come, the sovereign Lord of all.

The *King James* version:

> "I am *Alpha and Omega*, the beginning and the ending," saith the Lord, which is, and which was, and which is to come, the Almighty.

In P.D. James's *Innocent Blood* (Charles Scribner's Sons, New York, 1980), the troubled protagonist Philippa, in the Minster at York (England), gazes at the medieval stained glass image of God the Father. "Before him was an open book. *Ego sum alpha et omega.* How simple life must be for those who could both lose and find identity in that magnificent assurance." *Alpha and omega* has another figurative use, to mean "the principal element, the all-important feature." Rice is the *alpha and omega* of the diet of many far eastern people. Planning is the *alpha and omega* of a successful enterprise. The Greek alphabet comes in handy in other ways: *iota*, the ninth Greek letter, is used to mean "a very small amount, a jot." Example: That man is a dunce; he hasn't an *iota* of common sense! Other Greek letters are used as symbols in the sciences: *pi*, for example, is the ratio between the size of the circumference of a circle and its diameter (3.141592 +), and then there are all those college fraternities.

amaranthine (am uh RAN thin, -thine), *adj.* It is the figurative use of this lovely word meaning "everlasting, unfading" that we run into in literature. Thus, in *Siegfried's Journey 1916-1920* (Faber and Faber Limited, London, 1945) the

English poet and writer Siegfried Sassoon (1886-1967) refers to the "*amaranthine* essays" of the English critic, essayist and caricaturist Max Beerbohm (1872-1956). And the English poet William Cowper (1731-1800), in *The Garden*, wrote:

> The only *amaranthine* flower on earth
> Is virtue. . .

Literally, *amaranthine* means "resembling the *amaranth*" (AM uh ranth), a legendary flower that never dies. In botany, *amaranth* is the name given to plants of the genus *Amaranthus* that bear beautiful blossoms and showy foliage. That name came from the Greek *amaranton*, formed from the neuter form of *amarantos* (unfading), based on the negative prefix *a-* (un-) plus the stem of the verb *marainein* (to fade). The unfading flower has given us an unfading word.

ambagious (am BAY jus) *adj.* An *ambagious* path is a circuitous or roundabout one. *Ambages* (am BAY jeez) *n. pl.*, should you run into it in an ancient tome, is an archaic word for "winding paths." *Ambagious* comes from Latin *ambagiosus*, based on Latin prefix *ambi-* (both—as found, e.g., in *ambidextrous, ambiguous*, etc.) plus *ag-*, stem of the verb *agere* (to move). The expression *to go round Robin Hood's barn* is to reach the correct conclusion by an *ambagious* route. There is also a French expression that describes the taking of an *ambagious* or roundabout way: *prendre le chemin des écoliers*, literally, to take the schoolboys' route, evoking the image of the loitering schoolboy, getting to school by the most circuitous route, to delay the agony of the classroom. Whether it's the schoolboys' route or the one round Robin Hood's barn, it's the *ambagious* way to get there.

ambulatory see **ademption**

amerce (uh MURS) *vb.* To *amerce* a person convicted of a crime is to impose a fine in an amount fixed by the court in its discretion rather than one set by statute, or to impose any other discretionary penalty. In old Anglo-French, *a merci* meant "at (someone's) mercy," and from that phrase the Middle English verb *amercy* developed and gave us the verb *amerce*. An arbitrary or discretionary fine or jail term or other penalty is called an *amercement* (uh MURS munt). *Amerce* can be used in the general sense of "punish," without reference to a discretionary, as opposed to a fixed, penalty, but the usual implication is that of a fine or other sentence determined by the court in its sole discretion. Shakespeare used the verb in *Romeo and Juliet* (Act III, Scene 1), when the Prince, learning of the death of his kinsman Mercutio, killed by Tybalt, and the killing of Tybalt by Romeo, imposes the sentence of exile on poor Romeo:

> And for that offence
> Immediately we do exile him from hence;

. . . My blood for your rude brawls doth lie a-bleeding;
But I'll *amerce* you with so strong a fine
That you shall all repent the loss of mine.

Exile was the *amercement* imposed by the Prince, acting judicially, in his discretion. What with the disparity of sentences in the criminal courts of the United States nowadays, it would appear that *amercement*, with the implication of arbitrariness, is the order of the day.

amicus curiae (uh MEEK us KYOOR ee ee). Literally, in New Latin, "a friend of the court," an *amicus curiae* is a disinterested adviser to the court in a litigation, a person or organization not a party to a lawsuit, that nonetheless volunteers, or, on occasion, is invited by the court to advise it in pending litigation. The *amicus curiae*, with no financial interest in the outcome, is nevertheless concerned because of the principle or public policy involved. There can be more than one *amicus curiae* in a given case; the plural of *amicus* is *amici* (uh MEEK ee), and the *curiae* stays unchanged. The *amicus curiae* may submit a brief expressing an opinion, or supply information, or do both.

ampersand (AM pur sand, am pur SAND) *n.* The symbol for *and*, written &, or, in the italic form &. The word *ampersand* is a corruption of *and per se and*, i.e., *and by itself and* (*per se* is Latin for "by itself" or "in and of itself"). A close examination of the italic form of the symbol reveals an *e* and the cross of the *t*, thus spelling *et*, Latin for "and." Well into the 18th century, children were given hornbooks, lightweight boards about nine by five inches serving as a backing to a single sheet of paper containing the alphabet, the Lord's Prayer, a table of Roman numerals and the formula for exorcism. The sheet was covered by a thin piece of transparent horn (the bony substance of which certain animal growths are composed). Shakespeare mentions the hornbook in *Love's Labour's Lost* (Act V, Scene 1), when Armado asks Holofernes, "Monsieur, are you not lettered?" and Moth, the page boy, interjects, "Yes, yes, he teaches boys the hornbook." All this by way of introducing the fact that at the end of the alphabet in the hornbook an *ampersand* was added (. . . x, y, z, &). In this little essay we have learned about *ampersands* & hornbooks & a tiny bit of Shakespeare & an even tinier bit of Latin.

amphibology (am fuh BOL uh jee) *n.* *Amphiboly* (am FIB uh lee) is a variant. An *amphibology* is a sentence or a phrase that is ambiguous because of its uncertain construction, allowing of two interpretations. *Amphibology*, generally, is ambiguous writing. The problem most often arises because of the misuse of pronouns and the resulting uncertainty about their antecedents. William Safire, in his "On Language" column in *The New York Times Magazine* of November 4, 1984, furnishes an excellent example of *amphibology*: "Joe and Mike took his sister and her friend to the disco, but they didn't want to dance." Safire goes on to ask: "Who (sic) does *his* refer to, Joe or Mike? And who are *they*, the two girls or all four of the confused wallflowers?" Fowler gives an example that has nothing to do with pronouns or antecedents. After the definition "a statement so expressed as to admit of two grammatical constructions each yielding a different sense," we read: *"Stuff a cold and starve a fever* appears to be two sentences containing directions for two maladies, but may also be a conditional sentence meaning if you are fool enough to stuff a cold you will produce and have to starve a fever." *Amphibology* comes from Late Latin *amphibologia*; *amphiboly* from Latin *amphibolia*. *Amphibolic* (am fuh BOL ik) is the adjective. All these words go back to the Greek *amphibolos* (ambiguous).

amphigory (AM fuh gohr ee) *n*. Also **amphigouri** (am fuh GOOR ee). An *amphigory* is a senseless concoction or rigamarole, usually of meaningless verse; often a parody. From the French *amphigouri*, composed of the familiar Greek prefix *amphi-* (both) plus *gouri*, of unknown derivation. The verses of an *amphigory* may sound well, but on inspection, prove to make no sense whatever. The English poet Swinburne (1837-1909) was known for his sensuous, musical style, as in his verse drama *Atalanta in Calydon*, and his collection *Poems and Ballads*. He wrote a parody of his own style entitled *Nephelidia. Brewer's Phase and Fable* gives the opening lines, an excellent example of an *amphigory*:

> From the depth of the dreamy decline of the dawn
>   through a notable nimbus of nebulous noonshine,
> Pallid and pink as the palm of the flag-flower
>   that flickers with fear of the flies as they float,
> Are they looks of our lovers that lustrously lean
>   from a marvel of mystic miraculous moonshine? *etc.*

Beyond question, the best known *amphigory* in all English literature is *The Jabberwocky*, the poem found on a table by Alice, the heroine of *Through the Looking-Glass* (1872), the sequel of *Alice's Adventures in Wonderland* (1865), by the English writer and mathematician Lewis Carroll (pseudonym of Charles Lutwidge Dodgson, 1832-1898), about which poor Alice remarked: " . . . it's all in some language I don't know." The opening quatrain reads:

> 'Twas brillig, and the slithy toves
>   Did gyre and gimble in the wabe:
> All mimsy were the borogroves,
>   And the mome raths outgrabe.

Later in the poem, there are the lines:

> Come to my arms, my beamish boy!
> O frabjous day! Calloof! Callay!

and Alice says: "It seems very pretty, but it's *rather* hard to understand! . . . Somehow it seems to fill my head with ideas—only I don't exactly know what they are . . . !" What a marvelous comment on an *amphigory*!

anabasis (uh NAB uh sis) *n.* In its most general sense, an *anabasis* is a military expedition in the nature of an advance. Its antonym, or opposite, is a *katabasis* (kuh TAB uh sis), a retreat, in military terms. More narrowly, an *anabasis* is a military march from a coast to the interior of a country. One of the most famous *anabases* in classical history is that of Cyrus the Younger (c. 424-401 B.C.), the Persian prince who marched against his brother Ataxerxes II, as related by the Greek historian and essayist Xenophon (c. 434-385 B.C.) in his classical account *The Anabasis*, the schoolboy text in the teaching of classical Greek that is the counterpart of Caesar's *Gallic War* in the Latin course. *Anabasis* is a Greek word whose literal meaning is "stepping up," from the prefix *ana-* (up) plus the noun *basis* (stepping). A *katabasis* is a march from the interior to the coast. It is a Greek word with the literal meaning of "stepping down," from the prefix *kata-* (down—a variant of *cata-*; and *katabasis* can be spelt *catabasis*) plus our old friend *basis*. Ten-thousand Greeks, hired as mercenaries by Cyrus the Younger for his *anabasis*, in a famous retreat after the battle of Cunaxa and the death of Cyrus, marched northward *to* the coast in the *katabasis* also reported by Xenophon in his *Anabasis*. The retreat of over 300,000 Allied troops from Dunkirk in 1940 completed their *katabasis* from the coast of France when they were rescued by a catch-as-catch-can fleet of British ships and boats.

anacoluthia (an uh kuh LOO thee uh) *n.* This is a grammatical term denoting the lack of syntactical sequence or want of coherence in a case where the latter part of a sentence is rhetorically out of keeping with the earlier part; in short, the juxtaposition in one sentence of two grammatically incomplete and incompatible constructions. *Anacoluthia* is derived from the Greek *anakolouthia*, based on the negative prefix *an-* plus the adjective *akalouthos* (marching together). An *anacoluthon* (an uh kuh LOO thon) is an instance of this; for example: "If you go on flouting the basic rules of social behavior—well, what do you think will happen?" The "if" clause (see **apodosis** and the discussion of *protasis* in that entry) should grammatically be followed by a "then" clause, a conclusion: "If you go on flouting the basic rules of social behavior, (then) you'll find yourself in lots of trouble (or words to that effect). So you'd better behave; if you don't—well—what more can I say?"

analects (AN uh lekts) *n. pl.* Sometimes *analecta* (an uh LEK tuh). *Analects* or *analecta* are collected fragments or passages from the works of an author (sometimes a number of authors). The *Analects of Confucius*, for example, is a collection of his sayings and discourses from the fourth century B.C. The term is usually applied to literary gleanings from the works of a single author; in that use, *analects* differ from an anthology. Via Latin *analecta*, the word is derived from Greek *analekta* (things gathered). All we have left of the works of certain classical poets and writers, like Sappho, the foremost of the early Greek lyric poets (early sixth century B.C.), and Ennius, the father of Latin poetry (239-c.169 B.C.), are *analects*.

anamnesis   (an am NEE sis) *n*. This pleasant-sounding word serves a number of purposes. In general, *anamnesis* is reminiscence. In the field of medicine, it is a patient's recital of his medical history to his doctor. In psychiatry, an *anamnesis* is a case history. In Proustian terms, it is a remembrance of things past. In Platonic terms, it is the recollection of a previous existence. *Anamnesis* comes intact from the Greek, where it means "remembrance" generally, and is based on the prefix *ana-* (again, back) plus the verb *mimnestein* (to remind, recall to memory). Anything that recalls to mind earlier experiences may be described as *anamnestic* (an am NES tik). A scent, a tune, the timbre of a voice, a bit of landscape can have an *anamnestic* effect. Sometimes, *anamnesis* and nostalgia go hand in hand.

anaptyxis, see **epenthesis**

anastrophe   (uh NAS truh fee) *n. Anastrophe* is a rhetorical device—the inversion of the normal order of words—for dramatic effect. *Anastrophe* was taken intact from the Greek, where it means "a turning back," formed from the prefix *ana-* (against) plus *strophe* (turning about), based on the verb *strophein* (to turn). It takes a number of forms: subject after verb: "Came the dawn." "Able was I ere I saw Elba." "And damned be him who first cries, 'Hold, enough!'" And from the poem *The Old Vicarage, Grantchester* by the English poet Rupert Brooke (1887-1915):

> Stands the Church clock at ten to three?
> And is there honey still for tea?

and

> Unkempt about those hedges blows
> An English unofficial rose.

Object before subject "Me he condemned, him he acquitted." Preposition after noun: "No trace of him was found the world around." Adjective after noun, as in a play-review by the American writer and critic Dorothy Parker (1893-1967): "*The House Beautiful* is the play lousy"—two *anastrophes* at a clip! The same Dorothy gave us more examples (subject after verb) in her 1927 poem, *Enough Rope*:

> Four be the things I am wiser to know:
> Idleness, sorrow, a friend, and a foe.
> Four be the things I'd been better without:
> Love, curiosity, freckles, and doubt.

Verb after adverbial clause: "When lilacs last in the dooryard bloomed . . . ," from the poem of that title by the American poet Walt Whitman (1819-1892); and *By*

Love Possessed, title of the novel by the American novelist James Gould Cozzens (1903-1978). Preposition after noun:

> It was young David, lord of sheep and cattle
> Pursued his fate, the April fields among . . . ,

the first lines of the poem *Five Smooth Stones* by the English novelist and poet Stella Benson (1892-1933).

anatine, see **accipitrine**

anchorite (ANG kuh rite) *n*. An *anchorite* is a hermit, a recluse, particularly one who has gone to a remote place to enter upon a life of religious retreat. The older form, *anchoret* (ANG kuh rit, -ret) is rarely seen. The word is from Greek *anachoretes*, based on the verb *anachoreein* (to retire, withdraw), via Middle Latin *anachorita*. The English poet Lord Byron (1788-1824) wrote of things (*Childe Harold's Pilgrimage*) that "Might shake the saintship of an *anchorite*..." *St. Simeon Stylites* (*stylites* is Greek for "of a pillar") was a famous *anchorite*, a Syrian hermit of the fifth century who lived for more than 35 years on a tiny platform atop a high pillar. *Many anchorites*, dubbed "stylites," imitated his withdrawal into seclusion. An earlier *anchorite* was St. Anthony of Egypt (c. 251-c. 350), who became a recluse at the age of 20 and went into total seclusion when he was 35. He was the *anchorite* who resisted every temptation the devil could devise, and lived alone in the desert for the last years of his life. His life inspired *The Temptation of St. Anthony*, one of the masterpieces of the French novelist Gustave Flaubert (1821-1880). An *anchorite* is the ultimate loner.

androgynous (an DROJ un us) *adj*. An *androgyn* (AN druh gine) is an organism, human or other, that is of both sexes. *Androgynos* is Greek for "hermaphrodite," based on *andros*, genitive (possessive) form of *aner* (man) plus *gyne* (woman). *Androgynous* is used in botany to describe plants bearing both stamens and pistils in the same cluster. Applied to man and other animals, *androgynous* describes specimens having the characteristics of both sexes. This can refer to sexual organs or other physical characteristics, or to personality or temperament. The English poet and philosopher Samuel Taylor Coleridge (1772-1834) said, "The truth is, a great mind must be *androgynous.*" The noun *androgyny* (an DROJ uh nee) is a synonym of *hermaphroditism*, but can also mean "effeminacy" in men; but never confuse *androgyny* with *homosexuality*, an altogether different story. A great male ballet dancer should be *androgynous*, in the sense of combining in one body and temperament masculine strength and feminine grace.

anguine, see **accipitrine**

anile (AN ile, AY nile) *adj*. *Anile* applies only to females, meaning "like a doddering old crone," full of confusion, fussy manners, and silly, nervous questions. These all mark *anile* conduct. *Anile* comes from Latin *anilis* (pertaining to or like an old woman) and its noun *anility* (uh NIL ih tee) from *Latin anilitas* (a woman's old age), both based on *anus* (old woman). Note: There are two entirely separate Latin words spelt *a-n-u-s* (most probably pronounced differently—we don't know how classical Latin was pronounced—and declined differently), one meaning "anus," the other "old woman." It is fortunate that we do not pronounce *anile* "AN il" by analogy to one of the permissible pronunciations of *senile* (SEE nil) or to the way we pronounce *futile* in American (FYOO tul—the English say FYOO tile), else there would be confusion between *anile* and *anal* (a word popular from Freud), which comes from the other Latin *a-n-u-s*. *Anile*, restricted to women, is narrower than *senile* (SEE nile, -nil, SEN ile), which applies to both sexes, like its noun *senility* (suh NIL ih tee), indicating loss or serious decline of mental powers. *Senescent* (suh NES unt) means "growing old" and is used of either sex (from Latin *senescens*, present participle of *senescere*, to grow old). Despite the remark in *Tristram Shandy* by the English novelist and clergyman Laurence Sterne (1713-1768) about "the nonsense of the old women (of both sexes)," you can call an old woman *senile* but you can't call an old man *anile*.

animadversion   (an uh mad VUR zhun, -shun) *n. Animadversion* is the making of adverse comment or criticism, the casting of aspersions; an *animadversion* is a critical, usually censorious observation or comment. Drama and literary critics seem to find it easier to indulge in *animadversion* than to find occasion for praise. Their *animadversions* can put untimely ends to gallant efforts and, at times, cut short careers that might have flourished. The Scottish author James Boswell (1740-1795), biographer of Samuel Johnson (1709-1784), the great English lexicographer, poet, and critic, spoke of the latter's "*animadversion* upon his old acquaintance." The English poet William Cowper (1731-1800) said of a critic, "[His] *animadversions* hurt me . . . In part they appeared to me unjust, and in part ill-natured." This was a case where the *animadversions* did no lasting harm! This word is from Latin *animadversio* (observation, blame, censure), based on *animus* (mind) plus *advertere* (turn towards). Man is so ready to criticize, blame, and censure that in both Latin and English, a word that originally denoted the simple act of *turning the mind towards* someone or something has taken on the meaning of "blaming" or "censuring."

anodyne   (AN uh dine) *n.* In medical circles, an *anodyne* is a painkiller, but in general use, an *anodyne* is anything, material or nonmaterial, that relieves pain or distress, physical or emotional. *Anodyne* is also an adjective, meaning "pain-relieving" or "soothing" generally. It is from Greek *anodynos* (painless), based upon Greek prefix *an-* (not, without) plus *odyne* (pain). The Irish statesman and orator Edmund Burke (1729-1797) spoke of "the *anodyne* draught of oblivion." In medicine, opiates and narcotics are used as *anodynes*. Massages and baths are *anodyne* treatments in osteopathy. When a person is depressed or distressed, a change of scene can have an *anodyne* effect. Music (the food of love—that has charms to soothe a savage breast) can be effective as an *anodyne* to the distress of one in an emotional crisis.

anoesis (an oh EE sis) *n. Anoesis* is a feeling or sensation or emotion un-accompanied by an understanding of it; purely passive receptiveness without awareness of what's really being presented, or, as the psychologists express it, without cognitive content. *Anoesia* (an oh EE zhee uh, -zee-) or *anoia*, taken intact from the Greek, based on negative prefix *a-* plus *noos* (mind), means "want of understanding" in Greek and is used in English as a term for extreme mental deficiency or idiocy. *Anoetic* (an oh ET ik), the adjective, might come in handy as a description of the mentality that has led to the proliferation of atomic weaponry.

anomie (AN uh mee) *n.* This is the word for a situation affecting an in-dividual, a group, or a society when the usual standards of social conduct fail to operate, producing social chaos, a breakdown of all social values, a condition often found among displaced persons in this world full of refugees. *Anomie* comes from Greek *anomia* (lawlessness), based on the Greek negative prefix *a-* plus *nomos* (law). The adjective describing the condition is *anomic* (uh NOM ik). *Anomie* is characterized by a feeling of hopelessness and a loss of a sense of purpose, stemming from the breakdown of the rules of social behavior. *Anomie* was widespread among the inmates of the Nazi concentration camps. The faces and attitudes of people confined in refugee centers in war zones like Lebanon, or after natural disasters like earthquakes, indicate the state of mass *anomie*.

anopheline, see **accipitrine**

anserine, see **accipitrine**

ant(a)ean (an TEE un) *adj.* An *antaean* person is one of tremendous strength, immensely robust, sturdy and earthy, whose power is quickly and easi-ly renewed after apparent exhaustion. The adjective comes from *Antaeus*, of Greek mythology, who lived in ancient Libya in North Africa. He was a wrestler of gigantic proportions and superhuman strength, the offspring of Gaea, goddess of the earth, and Poseidon, god of the sea. He was possessed of a unique characteristic, which gave him a tremendous advantage over all other wrestlers: every time he was flung to earth, his strength was renewed—indeed, he became stronger than before. Remember: the earth was his mother. Hercules had to wrestle with him, and overcame the problem of Antaeus's ever-renewable vigor by lifting him into the air and crushing him. Clever Hercules! Antaeus's quality of drawing strength from the earth was celebrated in the poem *The Municipal Gallery Revisited* by the Irish poet William Butler Yeats (1865-1939), contain-ing these lines:

> John Synge, I and Augusta Gregory, thought
> All that we did, all that we said or sang

> Must come from contact with the soil, from that
> Contact everything *Antaeus*-like grew strong.

(Incidentally—and this has nothing whatever to do with *Antaeus* or *antaean*—that same poem has these two beautiful lines:

> Think where man's glory most begins and ends,
> And say my glory was I had such friends.

Yeats was referring to the Irish poet and dramatist John Millington Synge (1871-1909), who wrote *The Playboy of the Western World* and *Riders to the Sea*, and the Irish playwright Lady Augusta Gregory (1859-1932), the author of many plays, including *Spreading the News* and *The Full Moon*. Another incidental: in 1902, Lady Gregory, Yeats, and others founded the Irish National Theater, which became the Abbey Theater, where Synge was an associated dramatist.) To get back to our headword: It would be appropriate to say that Yeats and Synge were *antaean* figures!

antelopine, see **accipitrine**

antepartum, see **parturition**

anteprandial, see **preprandial**

antipodal   (an TIP uh dul) *adj.* As a geographical term, *antipodal* applies to places on the globe that are located diametrically opposite each other, like the United States and Australia. *Antipodal* is taken from the Greek, where it means "(those) with the feet opposite," based on the prefix *anti-* (against, opposite) plus *podes* (feet). Used figuratively, as a general term, *antipodal* means "diametrically opposite." Debating teams argue *antipodal* points of view. It has been said that a man and wife with *antipodal* temperaments supplement each other and make for a good marriage. *Antipodes* (an TIP uh deez), *n. pl.*, are, literally, places on the globe diametrically opposite to each other, or people who dwell in *antipodal* places; figuratively, the term applies to any opposites. The English poet John Keats (1795-1821) wrote:

> The poet and the dreamer are distinct,
> Diverse, sheer opposite, *antipodes*.
> The one pours out a balm upon the world,
> The other vexes it.

The American psychologist Edward Bradford Titchener (1867-1927) said: "Common sense is the very *antipodes of science*." The *Antipodes* are a small island group southeast of and belonging to New Zealand.

antonomasia   (an tuh nuh MAY zhuh) *n.* This word covers two related but distinct rhetorical devices: (1) the identification of an individual by the use of an epithet, designation, or title in place of his real name, or, conversely, (2) the use of the name of a person who is the embodiment of a particular characteristic or type of achievement—a name out of history, that has passed into the language—to designate an individual with the same characteristic or background. Examples of (1): his *lordship* or *grace* or *majesty, the gentleman from Arizona, my learned adversary, the Chief Justice, the Right Honourable Member* (of Parliament); as to particular individuals, especially historical persons, *the Great Engineer* (President Hoover), *Il Duce, Der Führer, The Unready* (Etherlred II, King of England, 978-1016; unready was a corruption of *redeless,* meaning "lacking in wisdom"), *Le Roi Soleil* or *The Sun King* (Louis XIV of France, 1638-1715), *Le Gros* or *The Fat* (applied to Charles III of France, 839-888, and Louis VI of France, 1081-1137; Alphonzo II of Portugal, 1185-1223, was also known as "The Fat"), *The Cunctator* or *Delayer* (General Quintus Fabius Maximus Verrucosus of Rome, second century B.C.—see **cunctator**). Examples of (2): a *Casanova* or *Don Juan* (a libertine), a *Hitler* (a detestable demagogue or dictator), a *Solomon* (a wise man), a *Sherlock* (an able sleuth, anyone who can unravel a mystery), a *Raffles* (a smooth, glamorous crook). For a fine example of *antonomasia*—a word taken intact from Latin, which got it from a Greek noun based on the verb *antonomazein* (to rename)—there is a tale about two eminent pianists who heard the great Polish pianist Paderewski play for the first time. "What do you think?", one of them asked the other after the concert. "Good," was the reply, "but he's no Paderewski."

apatetic   (ap uh TET ik) *adj.* This unfamiliar word looks like a misprint; it isn't—no *h* after the first *t.* It is a zoological term, describing animals or insects or creatures of the sea that can change color or form or both for purposes of camouflage, a mighty handy talent in the survival business. *Apatetic* comes from Greek *apatetikos* (deceiving), based on the verb *apateuein* (to deceive). What immediately comes to mind, of course, is the chameleon, known for its ability to change skin color to blend with its surroundings, a trait so well known that the adjective *chameleonic* (kuh mee lee ON ik), applied to persons, means "changeable, inconstant." The chameleon, it so happens, is also noted for its very slow locomotion, which makes it look apathetic as well as *apatetic.* There are *apatetic* species of moth that can fold their wings over their bodies, hang onto a branch, and make themselves look like twigs, and there are other *apatetic* insects, animals and fish capable of amazingly effective camouflage. One might be tempted to use the word in describing certain politicians.

aperçu   (ah per SEE—*ee* being approximate, somewhere between *ooh* and *ee,* the *u*-sound in French) *n.* An *aperçu* is an intuitive insight, a glimpse, an immediate appreciation, a hasty glance leading to a quick view; also used as a general survey, outline, rough outline, summary. *Aperçu* is a French word, the past participle of the verb *apercevoir* (to perceive) used as a noun; literally, something perceived. Its common use is to denote an insight that inspires one as a result of an intuitive understanding as opposed to a labored study. Striking *aperçus* spring up in old proverbs, the lines of great poets, especially

Shakespeare, and the works of the pioneers of psychology and psychiatry, particularly Freud. As to the *u*-sound in French mentioned above, see the quotation from Fowler under **fin de siècle**.

aph(a)eresis   (uh FER ih sis) *n. Apheresis* is one of three grammatical terms that deal with the omission of one or more letters from a word. The other two, as one moves through the word, are *syncope* (SIN kuh pee) and *apocope* (uh POK uh pee). *Apherisis* is omission at the beginning of a word; examples: *especial* became *special*; *adder* used to be *nadder* (*a nadder* turned into *an adder*); *cute* came from *acute*; *squire* from *esquire*; *count* from *account. Synocope* is omission from the middle; examples: *briticism* should logically be *britannicism*; *conservativism* was reduced to *conservatism*; *idololatry* became *idolatry*; *pacificist* was shortened to *pacifist*; *symbolology* to *symbology*. In poetry, an apostrophe is used, as in *ee'n* (even), *e'er* (ever), *ne'er* (never). A subdivision of *syncope* is *haplology*, where a syllable, rather than a single letter, is omitted from the middle, as in the case of *briticism*, *conservatism*, and the other examples given under *syncope. Haplology* is derived from the Greek adjective *haploos* (single, simple) plus *logos* (word). *Apocope* covers the loss of a final letter or syllable; examples: *cinematograph* went to *cinema*; *curiosity* became *curio* (in context); *mine* to *my*, *thine* to *thy*. All these grammatical terms are from the Greek: *apheresis* from *aphairesis* (taking away), based on prefix *ap-* (shortened form of *apo-*, away) plus *hairein* (to snatch); *syncope* from *synkope* (cutting short), based on prefix *syn-* (with, together) plus *koptein* (to cut); *apocope* from *apokope* (cutting off), based on prefix *apo-* (away) plus *koptein* (to cut). The *biz* in *show biz* is a case of double *apocope*, for which there is no single term. We could invent one: *diapocope*. Better not. See also **haplology**.

apocalyptic   (uh pok uh LIP tik) *adj. The Apocalypse* (uh POK uh lips) is the last book of the New Testament, the *Revelation of St. John the Divine*. An *apocalypse* (lower case *a*) is a revelation. The word is derived, via Late Latin, from Greek *apokalypsis* (revelation), based on the verb *apokalyptein* (reveal). Since so many revelations, beginning with St. John's, have dealt with imminent doom, the adjective *apocalyptic* has come to signify the prediction of disaster around the corner and the end of the world. One reads of the *apocalyptic* vision of the prophets of doom. Those who fear the end of life on earth through atomic warfare are prone to speak in *apocalyptic* terms (and who can blame them?) of the Big Bang that will end everything that began with a Big Bang, if we accept that version rather than *Genesis*.

apocope, see **aph(a)eresis**

apodictic   (ap uh DIK tik) *adj.* Also **apodeictic** (ap uh DIKE tik). A statement is *apodictic* if it is necessarily true, without need for demonstration or proof. On the third of July, the statement "Tomorrow will be the Fourth of July" is *apodictic*. An *apodictic* statement is self-evident, axiomatic, unquestionable, incontestable. *Apodictic* comes, via Latin *apodicticus*, from Greek *apodeiktikos*, formed from the prefix *apo-* (away, from, off) plus *deiknynai* (to show, demonstrate). It is true that since Einstein and relativity, "facts" once thought to be *apodictic* ("A straight line is the shortest distance between two points") have turned out to be open to question, or at least, to interpretation under certain circumstances. But the fourth dimension doesn't much enter into the lives of plain folk like you and me.

apodosis   (uh POD uh sis) *n*. A conditional sentence has two parts, one that expresses the condition, usually introduced by *if*, the other that states the consequence of the condition's being fulfilled, often introduced by *then*. The *if* clause is the *protasis* (PROT uh sis); the *then* clause is the *apodosis*. If it rains, then we'll postpone the picnic. *If it rains* is the *protasis*; *then we'll postpone the picnic* is the *apodosis*. Both words are from the Greek: *protasis* (literally, a stretching forth; by extension, a proposition); *apodosis* (literally, a turning; by extension, an answering clause). The next time someone makes you an offer based on an outrageous condition, just tell him to go away and take his *protasis* with him! If he seems puzzled, tell him to buy a copy of this book.

apogee   (AP uh jee) *n*. This is a term used in astronomy to designate the point in the orbit of a celestial body at which it is the most distant from the earth. The *perigee* (PER ih jee) is the point in the orbit at which the heavenly body is nearest the earth. *Apogee* comes from the Greek *apogaion* (off-earth), based on prefix *apo-* (from) plus *gaia*, a variant of *ge* (earth): *Perigee* is from the Greek *perigeion* (close to the earth), based on prefix *peri-* (about, around) plus *ge* (earth). Both terms are used chiefly with respect to the movements of the moon and man-made satellites. *Apogee* is used figuratively to mean "apex, highest point, climax" in any situation. Cf. the use of the astronomical terms *zenith* and *nadir*, but *perigee* does not appear to have a figurative use corresponding to that of *apogee*. It can be said that the work of the Italian sculptor, painter, and architect Michelangelo (1475-1564) was the *apogee* of Renaissance art. One might have used *zenith* in place of *apogee* in the last sentence; but in describing the opposite—the low point—use *nadir*, never *perigee*. Incidentally, *apis* (AP sis) is the inclusive term in astronomy for either of the two points in question: the *higher apsis* is the point in any eccentric orbit farthest from the center of attraction, i.e., the *apogee*; the *lower apsis* the point nearest to that center, i.e., the *perigee*. *Apsis* is from Greek *hapsis* (felloe, i.e., rim of a wheel; arch; vault; and *felloe*—also *felly*—is from Middle English *felwe*).

apolaustic   (ap uh LAW stik), *n., adj*. An *apolaustic* person is one whose aim in life is the attainment of enjoyment, who expends his energy in the search for pleasure, a *hedonist* (HEE duh nist) whose doctrine is that pleasure is the highest good; a *sybarite* (SIB uh rite) devoted to luxury. All these words relate to *la dolce vita* rather than to the lofty concept of the pursuit of happiness mentioned in our Declaration of Independence. The search for pleasure: the

Greeks had more than one word for it. *Apolaustic* comes from their adjective *apolaustikos*, related to the verb *apolauein* (to enjoy). *Hedonistic* (and *hedonism, hedonic, hedonics,* and *hedonistics*) come from the Greek noun *hedone* (pleasure). *Sybarite* we get from the ancient Greek city of Sybaris in southern Italy, famous for the luxurious life style of its inhabitants. But what's left of all that?

Appollonian, see Dionysian

apopemptic (ap uh PEMP tik) *adj. Apopemptic* describes anything addressed to one departing, whether spoken or sung, a farewell message, a valedictory. It is from Greek *apopemptikos* (pertaining to sending away), based on prefix *apo-* (away) plus *pempein* (to send). The advice of Polonius to his son Laertes in Shakespeare's *Hamlet* (Act I, Scene 3) is one of the most eloquent (if long-winded) *apopemptic* speeches in literature. Good advice, too. *Apopemptic* describes messages to, rather than from those taking leave. Thus, it does not apply to a farewell address, like George's Washington's, or to those so eloquently delivered by divas (like the Austrian-American contralto Ernestine Schumann-Heinck, 1861-1936) on their oft-repeated retirements from the operatic stage. Today's practically automatic *apopemptic* message is "Have a nice day!" to which the American columnist Russell Baker (born 1925) once thought of replying, "I will, if I can find one."

apophasis (uh POF uh sis) *n.* When you say: "It is quite unnecessary for me to mention his many valorous deeds" or "It goes without saying that . . . " or "We can omit any reference to . . . " or "Why even mention the fact that . . . ," you are indulging in *apophasis*—the art of mentioning something while declaring your intention not to mention it, denying your need to bring up a subject while you proceed to bring it up quite distinctly. This is an effective device to emphasize the subject you're "not going to go into." "I will not speak of his countless misdeeds!" "Why even mention his disloyalty to the flag?" *Apophasis* was taken over from the Greek. It is related to another rhetorical trick, *paralipsis* (par uh LIP sis), the suggestion through brief mention of a topic that there's a lot more being left out. "He's a reckless fellow—not to go into other shortcomings" or "There is hardly room in this brief space to set forth the complete record of his wanton violations of decency." This word is from Greek *paraleipsis* (omission); omission can be more effective, at times, than enumeration.

apophony, see ablaut

aporia (uh POH ree uh, -PAW-) *n. Aporia* is a term in rhetoric, for a doubt real or professed (usually the latter), about how to start, where to begin, what to say, how to go on. In the science of logic, a branch of philosophy, *aporia* is the problem of establishing the truth of a proposition where there is conflicting evidence on both sides of the question. *Aporia* has also been defined in the general sense of a "difficulty," which would embrace its special meanings in both rhetoric and logic. Its commonest use is in rhetoric. For example, "It's hard to know just where to start . . . ," says the orator, who has practiced his speech and knows perfectly well where he's going to begin. Or, "What can one say about the evils of . . . ?" (whatever the object of the attack may be), asks the speaker, whose notes contain exactly what to say about the evils of . . . (whatever it is). *Aporia* is an effective tool to appeal to the emotions of members of an audience, who are thus invited to participate in the speaker's (or writer's) professed dilemma and start thinking more actively about the subject of the discourse.

aposiopesis (ap uh sye uh PEE sis) *n.* When you suddenly break off in the middle of a sentence, leaving it unfinished, as though you are unable or unwilling to continue, you are committing an act of *aposiopesis*. Such an interruption is described as *aposiopetic* (ap uh sye uh PET ik). These words come from the Greek *aposiopaein* (to be completely silent). The breaking off is meant to be significant to the hearer, who is called upon to supply the missing words from his own imagination. An *aposiopesis* is a pregnant silence, a stopping short for rhetorical effect. "We must go on—if we should stop now—" is an example of *aposiopesis*. "If you don't leave this instant—" bespeaks a warning of a dire result. "Or else—" is a common *aposiopesis* with an ominous ring. Perhaps the commonest *aposiopesis* in all conversation (especially in the dialogue of inferior plays and novels) is "You mean—?" *Aposiopeses* are nothing new; one of the best known in classical literature is found in Book I of the *Aeneid* of the Roman epic poet Virgil (70-19 B.C.). The rebellious winds have disobeyed the commands of the sea god Neptune to afford safe passage to Aeneas, and have kicked up a bad storm that threatens the fleet. Neptune summons Eurus, the southeast wind, and Zephyrus, the west wind, and lets them have it: "Has pride of birth made you so insolent?/So, winds, you dare to mingle sky and land,/heave high such masses, without my command,/Whom I—? But no, let me first calm the restless/swell; you shall yet atone—another time . . . " (Translation of Professor Allen Mandelbaum of the City University of New York.) The words "Whom I—" are an *aposiopesis*, leaving unsaid the Latin for " . . . will punish . . . ," as clearly indicated by the " . . . you shall yet atone . . . " on the next line. In the original Latin, the words for "Whom I—" are "Quos ego—" and based on this famous passage, the phrase *Quos ego* (kwos EG o) has come to signify a threat of punishment for disobedience. Eurus and Zephyrus knew perfectly well what was meant by Neptune's unspoken words. They were going to catch hell. Neptune's *aposiopesis* spoke volumes! Another word for *aposiopesis* is *abruption* (uh BRUP shun), from the Latin *abruptio* (a breaking off), which gave us *abrupt* as well. In Shakespeare's *Troilus and Cressida* (Act III, Scene 2), Cressida invites the lovesick Troilus to enter her bedchamber. "Will you walk in, my lord?" Troilus: "O Cressida, how often have I wished me thus!" "Wished, my lord?—The gods grant—O my lord!" Troilus asks: "What should they grant? What makes this pretty *abruption*?"

apostil(le) (uh POS til); also **postil** (POS til) *n*. An *apostil* or *postil* is a marginal note, annotation, or comment, especially, in context, an explanatory marginal comment in the Bible. Via Middle Latin, Middle French, and Middle English, the term is most likely derived form the Latin phrase *post illa*, probably short for *post illa verba textus* (after those words of the text). The *a* in the form *apostil* or *apostille* is of doubtful origin. Though *apostil* sometimes refers to annotations of the Holy Scriptures, it is not to be bracketed with the noun *apostle* (one of the twelve sent forth by Christ to preach the gospel), which comes from quite another source: the Greek *apostolos* (literally, one who is sent out, from the verb *apostellein*, to send off). It is often amusing to read the *postils* of previous owners of books you have picked up in a secondhand bookshop.

apothegm (AP uh them) *n*. An *apothegm* is an aphorism, a terse, pithy saying, along instructive lines; an adage, a maxim, usually expressing a universal truth. It is from the Greek *apophthegma* (thing uttered), based on *apo-* (forth, from) plus *phthengesthai* (to speak). Some universally known *apothegms*: Man proposes, God disposes. Art is long, life is short. A bird in the hand . . . A stitch in time . . . A penny saved . . . A fool and his money . . . One good turn . . . There are those who prefer the spelling *apophthegm* with the extra *-ph-*, closer to the original Greek. You may add that *-ph-* if you wish, but don't leave out the *g*, or you'll get *apothem*, (which is pronounced the same way but is a horse of quite a different color: a perpendicular line from the center of a regular polygon to one of its sides; from the Greek *apothema*, based on the same *apo-* plus *thema* (something laid down). From such tiny omissions do great consequences flow. As Hugh Kenner so aptly put it in his review of the new "critical and **synpotic**" edition (edited by Hans Walter Gabler et al.—Garland Publishing) of James Joyce's *Ulysses*, punningly entitled "Leopold's bloom restored" (*Times Literary Supplement*, July 1, 1984): "Weighty issues, as Sherlock Holmes said, can hang upon a bootlace; likewise upon one letter of the alphabet."

apothem, see **apothegm**

apotropaic (ap uh truh PAY ik) *adj*. This adjective describes anything that wards off or is intended to ward off evil influence or ill fortune; from Greek *apotropaion* (something that turns aside evil), neuter of *apotropaios* (averting, turning away), based on prefix *apo-* (away) plus *trope* (turning). We have all heard or read about the evil eye, the widespread belief, from olden times down to this very day, that there are people able to injure or even kill with a glance. (This has nothing whatever to do with "if looks could kill," which is concerned with hatred rather than the evil eye.) The ancients used a variety of *apotropaic* charms, amulets, gestures, symbols, and votive offerings to avert the effect of the evil eye. Some of the gestures were designedly obscene. *Apotropaism* (ap uh truh PAY iz uhm) is the science and art of warding off evil, usually by rituals and incantations. Many years ago, the author himself, as an indiscreet youth, snapped a photo of an ancient white-haired crone in the Italian countryside, carrying an incredible load of faggots on her head. She promptly hurled the faggots to the ground and engaged in an obscene ritualistic sort of dance that lasted a few seconds, and then turned her head and spat over her left shoulder three times. Let's hope her *apotropaic* efforts were successful.

appanage (AP uh nij) *n.* This is the technical term for estates or income granted to a member of a royal family, usually by the sovereign to a younger relative, but since there are so few of that class around any more, the term is rarely met with in its literal sense except in histories or historical novels. More broadly, it is a term covering anything rightfully belonging to one's station, and even more generally, any natural endowment or adjunct. The English poet and essayist Coventry Patmore (1823-1896) used the term figuratively in the expression, " ... beauty, which is the natural *appanage* of happiness ... " The origin of this noun is found in Middle Latin *appanagium* (endowment), related to the verb *appanare* (literally, to supply with bread; by extension, to endow with a revenue or maintenance), based on the prefix *ap-*, used before *p* as a variant of *ad-* (to) plus *panis* (bread). The richer enjoyment of life and of the arts in particular is an *appanage* of a classical education. Do not confuse this word with *empannage* (om puh NAHZH), which is a term for the tail of an airplane, including the stabilizer, elevator, vertical fin, and rudder. *Empannage* was taken over intact from the French word for "feathering," and by extension, for those same airplane terms, and the fins or vanes of a bomb as well.

aprosexia (ay pro SEKS ee uh) *n.* This is the term for a person's inability to keep his mind on the subject, or to keep paying attention generally. This word comes from Greek negative prefix *a-* (un-, in-, non-, etc.) plus *prosexis* (heedfulness), based on the verb *prosechein* (to heed). There are those who simply cannot sustain attention; the mind wanders. They suffer from *aprosexia*. This will interfere radically, for example, with a student's ability to take proper notes. A boring lecturer can add to the problem. *Aprosexia* sufferers don't do well with nagging spouses or long-winded tellers of tales.

apsis, see **apogee**

aquiline, see **accipitrine**

arable (AR uh bul) *adj. Arable* land is capable of cultivation, suitable for farming, able to produce crops; plowable. From Latin *arabilis*, based on the verb *arare* (to plow). The Israelis converted great expanses of desert sand into *arable* soil through proper irrigation and farming. It is useless for governments to distribute land among penniless peasants unless it is *arable*.

arbiter (AR bih tur) *n.* An *arbiter* (not to be confused with *arbitrator*) is one who has the absolute power to pass judgment. He acts *arbitrarily*, and is accountable to no one. An *arbitrator* acts as an appointed judge or referee in a dispute referred to him by the parties. He may not act *arbitrarily*, but must abide by the rules of procedure and act judicially, and he is accountable to the appropriate authorities. *Arbiter* was taken over intact from Latin; *arbitrator* is from Late Latin, derived from *arbitratus*, past participle of the verb *arbitrari* (to judge, decide); and *arbitrary* and its adverb *arbitrarily* come from Latin *arbitrarius* (arbitrary, or uncertain—because dependent on an *arbiter's* decision). The Latin expression *arbiter elegantiae* (or *elegantiarum*) is the title of an *arbiter* of fashion and gracious living, an authority on elegance and matters of taste. The most famous of these was the Roman satirist Gaius Petronius (died c. 66), who, holding that position in the court of the Emperor Nero (37-68), was in charge of the imperial entertainments. He was known as Petronius Arbiter, famous for his own extravagant dinners and lavish entertainments, and for his satirical writings, chiefly the *Satyricon*, especially the story of *Trimalchio's Dinner*, a comic episode of vulgar display by a nouveau riche freed slave. See **agnomen**. The English essayist Sir Richard Steele (1672-1729), in *The Spectator*, wrote of "Fashion, the *arbiter*, and rule of right." The English poet Lord Byron (1788-1824), in his *Ode to Napoleon Bonaparte*, called him (after his exile) "The *Arbiter* of others' fate/A Suppliant for his own!" In *Paradise Lost*, the English poet John Milton (1608-1674) wrote that " . . . high *arbiter*/Chance governs all," and that " . . . overhead the moon/Sits *arbitress*," giving *arbiter* its feminine form (*-ess*), a practice now decried by ardent feminists who object to poet*ess*, sculptr*ess*, Jew*ess*, etc. (but *actress* seems to some acceptable, and *countess*, *baroness*, *mistress* must be, as well as *lioness*?). Today's *arbiters* of fashion, like the American professional hostess (another *-ess*!) Elsa Maxwell (1883-1963), "society" columnists, self-appointed and -anointed social "leaders," and proprietors of the "in" spots like the once super-exclusive Studio 54 on New York's West Side, have their brief spans of glory and soon fade away, while Petronius *Arbiter* lives on.

Arcadian (ar KAY dee un) *adj. Arcadian* (often with a lower case *a*) means "rustic, pastoral," and by extension "innocent, unspoiled." An *arcadian* life is one of simplicity and happiness, peace, and simplicity. The name, according to mythology, came from Arcas, a son of the god Zeus. It was adopted by the English poet, soldier, and statesman Sir Philip Sidney (1554-1586) for his unfinished romance *Arcadia*, written in 1578-1580 and circulated only in manuscript while he lived. A simpler and complete original version appeared in print only in 1926. *Arcadian* has become a byword for bucolic bliss. Nonetheless, in a number of early paintings, there appears a tomb inscription reading "Et in Arcadia ego" (Even in Arcadia am I [death]). But away from that gloomy observation: the *arcadian life* is one of serenity and unalloyed joy. Do not confuse *Arcadia* with *Acadia*, scene of the famous poem *Evangeline* ("This is the forest primeval . . . ") by the American poet Henry Wadsworth Longfellow (1807-1882), where life for the French settlers turned out to be anything but serene.

archetype (AR kih tipe) *n*. The *archetype* of anything is its original model, its prototype. In Latin, *archetypum* means "original," taken over from Greek *archetypon* (pattern, model), neuter of *archetypos*, based on prefix *arche-* (primitive) plus *typos* (mold). The English historian and statesman Thomas Macauley (1800-1859) called the British House of Commons "the *archetype* of all representative assemblies." The adjective is *archetypal* (AR kih tye pul) or *archetypical* (ar kih TIP ih kul). The American novelist Sinclair Lewis (1885-1951) created an *archetype* in the novel *Babbitt*, whose protagonist of that name became the *archetype* of the smug American, a devout conformist who subscribes to conventional middle-class ideas of business success and material gains (*babbitt*, with a lower case *b*, has become a common noun denoting such a person), just as Casanova is the *archetypical* rake, Sherlock Holmes the *archetypical* detective (*sherlock*, too, is now a common noun), Shylock the *archetypical* relentless moneylender (a shylock is a usurer), Lolita the *archetypical* nymphet, and Emma Bovary, the *archetypical* discontented, conceited self-glamorizing wife, whose name gave rise to the noun *bovarism* (BOH vuh riz um), signifying that type of self-delusion.

arctoid (ARK toyd) *adj*. *Arctoid* means "bearlike, ursine." There is a zoological superfamily known as the *Arctoidea* (ark TOI dee ah) that includes raccoons and weasels as well as bears. *Arctoid* is derived from the Greek noun *arktos* (bear), and an *arctophile* is a bear fancier, a lover of bears. The term has been extended to cover one who loves teddy bears, like Sebastian in *Brideshead Revisited*, by the English novelist Evelyn Waugh (1903-1966). *Teddy bears* were named after Theodore Roosevelt, whose nickname was *Teddy*. Legend has it that he spared the life of a bear cub while hunting. *Arktos* gave rise to the adjective *arktokos*, meaning "northern," literally "of the (Great) Bear," the most prominent northern constellation, whence *arctic*. *Arktos* is also the Greek name for the constellation *Ursa Major*, but in English it includes *Ursa Minor* as well. The bear is a symbol of Russia, especially the Northern Bear or "Russian Bear," beloved of political cartoonists. Trained bears figure prominently in Russian circuses. The Russians, generally speaking, are *arctophiles* (*arktos* plus *-phile*, dear, beloved). *Arktos* is also the basis of the name of the brightest star in the northern hemisphere, *Arcturus*, which you can find by following the curve of the tail of Ursa Major.

arctophile, see **arctoid**

arête (uh RATE) *n*. This is the geological term for a ridge with a very sharp crest, found in rough mountain country, especially the type that has been cut through by glaciers. *Arêtes* are common in the Alps. The word was taken from the French, which derived it from the Latin *arista*, which included among its several meanings "fish-spine." There is another word spelt the same way except for the absence of a circumflex and pronounced differently—a word that has nothing to do with ridges: *arete* (AIR uh tay, -tee), taken from the Greek, and signifying the sum of good qualities that together constitute character—courage, virtue, excellence. This word gave rise to *aretalogy* (air uh TOL uh jee), a tale of the great feats of gods and heroes. *Arete* is related to the Greek verb *areskein* (to please, satisfy).

aristology   (air is TOL uh gee) *n. Aristology* is the art and science of dining; from Greek *aristos* (breakfast, luncheon—the context, or fuller explanation, would determine which) plus *logos* (discourse). It is the gourmet, not the gourmand, who is interested in *aristology* and devotes time and effort to its practice. Petronius (see **arbiter**) and Lucullus (see **Lucullan**) were practitioners of *aristology* in ancient times; more recently, Brillat-Savarin, the French jurist, writer, and epicure (1755-1826), wrote a witty discourse on the art of dining, entitled *La Physiologie du Goût (The Physiology of Taste)*. And more recently than that, there was Auguste Escoffier (c. 1847-1935), who rose to be head chef at the Savoy in London, and invented peach Melba and other sensational dishes. All these people were *aristologists* (air is TOL uh jists); their interests and activities were *aristological* (uh ris tuh LOJ uh kul). Synonyms for *aristologist* more frequently met with are *epicure* and **gastronome**.

arras   (AIR us) *n.* An *arras* is a wall hanging, especially a tapestry. The noun comes from the town of Arras, the capital of Pas-de-Calais in northeastern France, once renowned for the manufacture of tapestries. An *arras* is a convenient thing to hide behind; Shakespeare certainly thought so, and found it convenient as a dramatic prop in a number of his plays. In *Hamlet* (Act II, Scene 2), Polonius suggests to the King that, to test Hamlet's sanity, "Be you and I behind the *arras* . . . " to see how Hamlet acts when alone with Ophelia. It was behind the *arras* in Queen Gertrude's bedroom that Polonius hid, and was stabbed for his troubles. "Polonius hides behind the *arras*," reads the stage direction in Act III, Scene 4. Further directions: Gertrude calls for help, Polonius echoes her call and Hamlet "draws" and "makes a pass through the *arras*," then "lifts up the *arras* and discovers Polonius," the "wretched, rash, intruding fool." Falstaff hides behind an *arras* in *Merry Wives of Windsor* (Act III, Scene 3). He is in Ford's house, when Mistress Page approaches. Falstaff cries, "She shall not see me: I will ensconce myself behind the *arras*." In *King John* (Act IV, Scene 1), Hubert tells the two attendants who were to put out young Arthur's eyes, "Heat me these irons hot; and look thou stand/Within the *arras* . . . " And the *arras* figures in several other Shakespeare plays as well. Apparently, the *arras* was sometimes used for purposes other than as a wall hanging. The English poet William Cowper (1731-1800) wrote of "Statliest couches with rich *arras* spread." Writing of her childhood in Knole, her vast, complex ancestral home in Sevenoaks, Kent, the English poet, novelist, and gardener extraordinary Vita Sackville-West (1892-1962) wrote a poem *To Knole* about her early wanderings around the great house on lonely days:

> My fingers ran along the tassels faded;
> My playmates moved in *arrases* brocaded;

I slept beside the canopied and shaded;
Beds of forgotten kings . . .

I contemplated long the tapestries . . .

The *arras* is hardly ever used in interior decoration nowadays, and they don't come from Arras any more, but if you do run across one, you'll know what to call it.

arriviste (air e VEEST) *n*. An *arriviste* is a very unpleasant character: an upstart, a pushy, aggressive person who manages to achieve his goal of power, money, status, or other type of what he considers success through unscrupulous methods; a self-seeker, a parvenu, always on the make. The word is taken from the French, where it is a general term for an unscrupulous careerist, whether or not he has as yet succeeded in "arriving." The American novelist John Hersey (b. 1914) wrote of "an impoverished family of high breeding and training that sneers self-consolingly at vulgar *arrivistes*." In *The English Companion* (Pavilion Books, London, 1984), the contemporary English novelist, editor, and columnist Godfrey Smith (b. 1926) writes of Winston Churchill (1874-1965): "His closest friends—Beaverbrook, Bracken and Birkenhead—were known to his wife as the three terrible Bs. All were self-made men: adventurers and *arrivistes*."

artifact (AR tuh fakt) *n*. Anything made or worked on by man is an *artifact*. A tree occurs in nature. When it is felled and the trunk is sawn into certain lengths and then one piece is carved by a sculptor and another made into a dugout canoe, both resulting objects are *artifacts*. So is a chair, a table, a rug, a lamp, a pin, a pen, a pan—obviously, the list is endless, because new *artifacts* are always being created. The term is usually applied to something relatively simple or small. One would not classify the Empire State Building or the *Queen Elizabeth II* as an artifact; they consist of a very great number of *artifacts*, including nuts and bolts. *Artifact* is derived from the Latin phrase *arte factum* (something made with skill). The dictionaries use terms like "made by man" or "product of human work," but how about a nest made by a bird or a dam made by beavers? They are certainly "made with skill." Should we not broaden the definition to include things made by any animal? Spiders' webs, bees' honeycombs? Make your own list. In any event, do not confuse *artifact* with *artifice*, which is quite a different story.

artifice (AR tuh fis) *n*. An *artifice* is a trick, a ruse, a stratagem; *artifice*, generally, is cunning, trickery, guile, craftiness. You might think, then, that an *artificer* (AR tif ih sur) is a cunning, sly, tricky fellow, but you would err. An *artificer* (not a common word) is simply an inventor, a craftsman, a person clever in devising ways of making things, and not the least bit tricky or deceitful. *Artifice*, a much commoner word than *artificer*, is nevertheless a back formation from the latter. Strange are the ways of language. We have many *art-* words: *artful, artifice,* *artifact* (with which *artifice* should never be confused), *artificial, artisan, art-less,* etc., all based on *art-,* the stem of Latin *ars,* whose principal meaning is "skill." An *artless* person is not, however, an unskillful one: he is simply straightforward, free from deceit, guileless. An *artful* person is full of guile, cunning and crafty, the opposite of *artless.* Remember the *artful* dodger in *Oliver Twist?* To get back to *artifice*: President Nixon's dirty tricks operators were masters of *artifice.* The *artifice* of the haggling casbah tradesman is a memorable experience for the artless Western tourist.

ascesis (uh SEE sis) *n. Ascesis* is self-discipline, and can be used as a synonym of *asceticism. Ascesis* is one of those cases of an unfamiliar word that underlies a familiar one, here *ascetic* (uh SET ik). An *ascetic* is one who practices *ascesis,* i.e., gives up the normal pleasures of life, preferring the rigors of self-denial to the satisfactions flowing from material gain. As an adjective, *ascetic* describes such a person, one who pledges himself to rigorous abstinence. *Ascesis* is from Greek *askesis* (exercise, training); *ascetic* from Greek *asketikos* (hardworking), and they both go back to the Greek verb *askeein* (to work hard, discipline oneself). *Ascesis* is good for the body, good for the mind, good for society, and all too rare.

ashram (AHSH rum) *n.* This a Hindi word, which you may run across in any one of today's spate of novels set in India. An *ashram* is a hermitage, a religious retreat for a colony of disciples, a place for religious instruction or exercises. *Ashrams* play an important part in the lives of millions of Hindus. The word comes from the Sanskrit *asrama* (place for religious exercises), based on prefix *a-* (towards) plus *srama* (fatigue, exertion). An *ashram* need not be a temple, but can be any meetingplace where people congregate for exercise or religious teaching.

asinine, see **accipitrine**

aspergillum (as pur JIL um) *n.* This word, not to be confused with *aspergillus* (as pur JIL us), is the name of the short-handled instrument bearing a brush or small perforated globe containing a sponge, used by clerics for sprinkling holy water. It comes from the Latin verb *spergere* (to sprinkle), the past participle of which, *aspersus,* gives us *aspersorium* (as pur SAW ree um), a synonym of *aspergillum,* and also the name for a holy water vessel. *Aspergillus,* on the other hand, is the botanical term for a fungus with a knoblike top bearing bristles that makes it resemble an *aspergillum.* It causes certain animal diseases and we certainly don't want any of those in church! On the matter of confusion between words resulting from the change of a single letter, see **formication**, and the last sentence of **apothegm**.

aspine, see **accipitrine**

asseverate (uh SEV uh rate) *vb.* To *asseverate* something is to assert it earnestly, to declare it seriously, emphatically, solemnly, and with confidence. Our language got it from the Latin *adseveratus, asseveratus,* past participle of the verb *adseverare, asseverare* (to assert confidently, strongly), the *d* of the prefix *ad-* often changing to *s* before another *s*. The *-sever-* part is based on the Latin adjective *severus* (serious). In the criminal courts, the accused often *asseverates* his innocence. Elected officials *asseverate* that they will faithfully perform the duties of their office, uphold the Constitution, etc. The author of this book *asseverates* that he has run across these 1,000 words in the course of his reading, and not simply plucked them out of an unabridged dictionary—except for a very small number that stared him in the eye while he was consulting a dictionary in connection with one that had already challenged him!

asthenic   (as THEN ik) *adj. Asthenia* (as THEE nee uh), *n.*, is debility, weakness, loss of strength or vigor. One suffering from *asthenia* is *asthenic*, weak, narrow-chested, slender. *Asthenic,* describing a physical type, denotes slightness of build, as opposed to *athletic,* designating sturdiness and well-built body structure, and to *pyknic* (PIK nik), describing squatness, overweight, a rounded build characterized by a large belly, small hands and feet, short legs and neck and a round face. *Asthenic* comes from Greek *asthenikos* (weak), based on *a-* (not) plus *sthenos* (strength); *athletic* from Greek *athletikos,* based on *athleein* (compete for a prize—*athlos* means "contest"); *pyknic* from Greek *pyknos* (thick), having nothing to do with the picnic celebrated in the play by the American dramatist William Inge (b. 1913) or the painting by the French impressionist Edouard Manet (1832-1883), that type of outing (once described by a friend of the author as "organized discomfort") being derived from German *Picknick,* which came from French *pique-nique,* which appears to have come from nowhere. These derivations are no picnic! *Asthenic* and *pyknic,* standing alone, can be used as nouns designating the respective physical types. *Athletic* is not used as a noun. It is a common adjective; the other two are not, and should be avoided in giving specifications to Hollywood Central Casting.

astride, see **bestride**

asyndeton   (uh SIN dih ton, -tun) *n.* This is the grammatical term for the omission of a copulative (connecting: see **copula**) conjunction—usually *and*—a favorite, and rather unattractive rhetorical device in advertising copy. Example: "Smoothikreme will eliminate wrinkles, make you look years younger!" It would be hateful enough *with* the conjunction, but somehow is more so with *asyndeton.* The term comes from Greek *asyndetos* (not connected), based on negative prefix *a-* and *syndetos,* past participle of the verb *syndeein* (to link). One of the best known and most effective examples of *asyndeton* is Caesar's "Veni, vidi, vici." ("I came, I saw, I conquered.") Another one—a naval message from World War II—and a fine show of alliteration in the bargain: "Sighted sub, sank same." Great stuff, even if apocryphal. Still another: "Have gun, will travel." In these cases, as opposed to its use in advertising, *asyndeton* is most effective; the insertion of *et* in Caesar's message, or *and* in the naval flash, would have destroyed the dramatic impact. The opposite of *asyndeton* is *polysyndeton* (pol ee SIN dih ton), which is the use of a string of identical conjunctions in succession: "She has everything: youth and looks and money and talent!" Quite a girl. *Polysyndeton*, modeled on *asyndeton*, was formed, via Late Latin, from Greek prefix *poly-* (many) plus the same *syndetos*.

ataraxia (at uh RAK see uh), **ataraxy** (at uh RAK see) *n.* An idyllic state, one of complete serenity, free from anxiety, the cares of the world, or any sort of emotional upset. One thinks of the inhabitants of Shangri-la as enjoying *ataraxia* in their hidden paradise. The adjectives *ataractic* (at uh RAK tik) and *ataraxic* (at uh RAKS ik) are sometimes used to denote tranquilizing drugs. All these words come, via Latin, from Greek *ataraxia* (calmness); *ataraktos* means "undisturbed," based on the negative prefix *a-* plus *tarak-*, a variant stem of the verb *tarassein* (to disturb). *Ataraxia* was the state of calm and indifference sought as a goal by the Stoics, members of a philosophical school founded by Zeno about 300 B.C., which taught the rigid suppression of passions, self-indulgence, and unjust thoughts. The teaching of indifference to pleasure or pain led to the definition of *stoical* as "impassive" with the implication of austere courage and submission without complaint to the inevitable hard knocks of life. That's *ataraxia*.

atrabilious (a truh BIL yus) *adj.* We know about *bile*, the name of the liver secretion that helps in the digestion of fats (if your liver is working properly) and its figurative meaning of "ill temper," and the adjective *bilious*, dealing with excessive secretion of the stuff and the consequent suffering, and also figuratively used for both "peevish" and "extremely distasteful." We then come to *atrabilious*, describing one who is simply dejected, or actively irritable, wrathful, bad-tempered—the context should make it clear which is meant. *Atra* is the feminine form of the Latin adjective *ater* (black—dead black, as opposed to *niger*, glossy black); add *atra* to *bilis* (bile; by extension, anger) and you get *atra bilis* (literally, black bile; metaphorically, melancholy, dejection). A variant form is *atrabiliar* (a truh BIL yur) and the condition is *atrabiliousness*. The English novelist and poet Aldous Huxley (1894-1963)—he of *Brave New World*—wrote, in *The Ninth Philosopher's Song*:

> Then brim the bowl with *atrabilious* liquor!
> We'll pledge our Empire vast across the flood:
> For Blood, as all men know, than water's thicker,
> But water's wider, thank the Lord, than Blood.

atticism (AT ih siz um) *n. Atticism* (often with a lower case *a*) is concise, superior, polished discourse and diction. The adjective *attic* describes elegant, subtle, inicisive expression and articulation, with a strong admixture of subtle wit. The English poet John Milton (1608-1674) wrote:

> What neat repast shall feast us, light and choice,
> of *Attic* taste . . .

and the Roman rhetorician Quintilian (c. 35-c. 95) praised the *Attic* style in these terms:

> The distinction between *Attic* and Asiatic orators is of great antiquity, the *Attic* being regarded as compressed and energetic in their style, the Asiatics as inflated and deficient in force.

Attica was the name of a region in the southeasterly part of ancient Greece. It was under the rule and influence of Athens, whose culture reached its height around the middle of the fifth century B.C.—the age of Pericles, the great poets, dramatists, sculptors and architects. The Roman historian Pliny the Elder (23-79) wrote of "sal atticum" (Attic wit—literally, Attic salt; *sal* (salt) was used figuratively by the Romans to mean "wit"). *Attic* wit is dry, delicate, subtle wit. The Romans had a verb *atticisare* ("atticise") to describe the imitation of Athenian diction and expression. *Atticism*, then, is the art of the elegant, well-timed expression, refined simplicity laced with sophistication and wit. In more modern times, the distinction between thest two styles has been described in a learned article by Byran A. Garner in Volume X, No. 3 of *Verbatim, The Language Quarterly*, which includes this passage:

> English inherited two strains of literary expression, both deriving ultimately from Ciceronian Latin. On the one hand is the plain style now in vogue, characterized by unadorned vocabulary, directness, unelaborate syntax, and earthiness. (This style is known to scholars as Atticism.) On the other hand we have the grand style, which exemplifies floridity, allusiveness, formal sometimes abstruse diction, and rhetorical ornament. Proponents of this verbally richer style (called Asiaticism) proudly claim that the nuances available in the "oriental profusion" of English synonyms make the language an ideal putty for the skilled linguistic craftsman to mold and shape precisely in accordance with his conceptions.

Well may you ask, what has this to do with the *attic* of a house, the room or story just under the roof? Here is the answer: In the residences of the rich in old *Attica*, there was often a small row of columns or **pilasters** placed on the roof, as a decorative feature. Neo-Grecian architecture became fashionable in England in the 17th century. In error, the top floor of a building fashioned in the *Attic* style was called the "Attic storey" (*story*, meaning "floor of a house," has an *e* before the *y* in British English). Error, because the *Attic* feature was a façade, whereas the English imitation was an enclosed floor. In time, the upper case *A* became a small *a*, the "storey" was dropped, and we wound up with, simply, *attic*.

Augean, see herculean

aulic (AW lik) *adj. Aulic* describes things pertaining to a royal court. It comes from the Greek adjective *aulikos* (courtly), based on *aule* (court, hall). The English poet and writer Walter Savage Landor (1775-1864) wrote of "Eccelesiastical wealth and *aulic* dignities." In 1501, Maximilian I of the Holy

Roman Empire established the *Aulic* Council, which acted as a supreme court. There aren't many *aulic* activities these days, because there aren't many courts any more. When Elizabeth II of England receives an ambassador, creates knights, dames, or barons, and distributes other New Year or Birthday Honours, or gives a state dinner, the goings-on can be described as *aulic* activities.

autarchy; autarky (AW tar kee) *n.* Although some authorities consider these homophonic words interchangeable, they mean different things, are differently derived, and should be kept separate. *Autarchy* is absolute sovereignty, and *an autarchy* is an autocratic government. An *autarch* (AW tark) is an absolute ruler or tyrant. *Autarky* means "self-sufficiency," and is a term applied to a nation that is economically self-sufficient, not dependent on foreign trade or help from any foreign government. Both words are derived from Greek: *autarchy* from *autarchia* (self-rule), based on the noun *archos* (ruler), *autarky* from *autarkeia* (self-sufficiency), based on the verb *arkeein* (suffice). *Autarch* is from *autarchos* (autocratic). In all these words, the prefix *aut-* is a shortened form of *auto-* (self-, a prefix we see in many English words, like *automatic*, *automobile*, etc.). Although their use is not common, it is well to understand their difference in meaning and derivation on the rare occasion of meeting one or both of them.

autism (AW tiz um) *n. Autism* (from Greek *autos*—self) is a morbid mental condition that causes withdrawal into a private world of fantasy and prevents communication with the real world. The adjective is *autistic* (aw TIS tik), often found in the term *autistic child*, because the condition appears to affect children especially; they lose contact with reality, and seem unable to respond to their environment, or to grasp objective actuality. No determination has been made of the cause of this pathological condition, nor has any cure been discovered.

autochthon (aw TOK thun) *n.* An *autochthon* is an aborigine, one of the original, or at least earliest recorded, inhabitants of a region, like the aboriginal tribes of America. In the field of ecology, the term *autochthon* covers the native flora and fauna of a region. The adjective is *autochthonous* (o TOK thuh nus), meaning "indigenous" or "native." *Autochthon* is Greek for "of the land itself," based on the prefix *auto-* (self, same) plus *chthon* (earth, land). Other *-chthonous* words are *allochthonous* (uh LOK thuh nus), using the Greek prefix *all-*, from *allos* (other), and *heterochthonous* (het uh ROK thuh nus), using the Greek prefix *hetero-*, from *heteros* (other). Both these words mean "foreign, not indigenous." *Allochthonous* is found in geological studies of minerals and rocks originating in one place but found elsewhere as a result of the movement of the earth's crust (see **tectonics**). *Heterochthonous* is often used in the field of biology, in discussions of foreign flora and fauna, not native to the region.

avifauna (ay vuh FAW nuh) *n.* The *avifauna* of an area consists of the birds native to that region. *Avi-* is a Latin prefix, from *avis* (bird), and our word *fauna*, denoting the animal life native to a given area, is from Latin *Fauna*, a goddess, sister of *Faunus*, a mythological deity of the forests. The fauna of a region (*fauna* being the wider term) includes, of course, the *avifauna*. *Piscis* is Latin for "fish," and, logically enough, the *piscifauna* is the fish life of a given region, also included in the general term *fauna*.

avine, see **accipitrine**

bacchanal (BA kuh nal) *n.* Bacchus (BAK us), also known as Dionysus (dy uh NY sus), was the god of wine in classical mythology. He lent his name to the noun *bacchanal*, which usually denotes an orgy or a drunken revel, but the word can also mean "drunken reveler," though it is not commonly used that way. *Bacchanalia* (bak uh NAY lee uh, -NALE yuh) was the name of an ancient triennal festival in honor of Bacchus, but is now used with a lower case *b* to denote any drunken party, not necessarily a sexual orgy, but accidents can happen. The adjective *bacchanalian* (bak uh NAY lee un, -NALE yun) can describe activities all the way from orgiastic or debauched to less serious goings-on, like merely uninhibitedly festive shenanigans, usually involving the consumption of large quantities of intoxicating beverages. A related word, *bacchant* (BAK unt) also means "drunken reveler," and with an *-e* added, a female of that category. The most common of all these words related to the god Bacchus is *bacchanalian*, and it usually applies to what the Sunday supplements used to call "wild parties," a term that covered a multitude of sins.

bacchant(e), see **bacchanal**

bahuvrihi (bah hooh VREE hee) *n.* A *bahuvrihi* (nice word!) is a compound noun or adjective consisting of two parts, an adjective and a noun, the combination describing someone or something characterized by what is denoted by the noun element. Complicated? Not so very; here are some examples: *bluebell* (the flower), *bonehead*, *hard-hearted*, *redcoat* (a British soldier in the American revolution), *redhead*, *yellowlegs* (an American shore bird). *Bahuvrihi* is a Sanskrit (an Indo-European Indic language that goes back to the 13th century as a literary language of India) word meaning, literally, "with much rice," based on *bohu-* (much) plus *vrihi* (rice), and is itself a model of a *bahuvrihi*. The author apologizes if this discourse seems too *heavy-handed* (another example) an exposition. The English poet Gerard Manley Hopkins (1844-1889) used a *bahuvrihi* in his poem *Felix Randal*:

> Felix Randal the farrier, O is he dead then?
> My duty all ended,
>   Who have watched his mold of man, big-boned
> and hardy-handsome,
>   Pining, pining.

Big-boned is the *bahuvrihi*; *hardy-handsome* doesn't qualify.

ballyrag   (BAL ee rag), **bullyrag** (BOOL ee rag) *vb*. To *ballyrag* or *bullyrag* someone is to harass or abuse him, in the more violent sense of the word, or less dramatically, to tease him. Fowler says that the derivation is unknown, and that *ballyrag* is the far more common and preferable form, but other dictionaries give *bullyrag* as the first choice. To *rag* someone is to tease him, in American usage, but in British usage, to do rather more than that: to persecute him with crude practical jokes, with *rag* also a noun denoting that kind of tormenting behavior. The *bullyrag* form probably has some connection with *bully*, embellished by *rag*. In any case, *bally-* or *bullyragging* is reprehensible abusive horseplay and badgering, the kind employed, for example, in the sort of fraternity hazing that is a practice now mercifully fading from the scene.

basilisk   (BAS uh lisk, baz-) *n*. This was the name, in ancient mythology, of a deadly creature, represented from time to time as a dragon or serpent, claimed by the ancients to have been hatched by a serpent from the egg of a cockatrice (of which more later). It could kill by its breath or gaze. Nowadays, the term is applied in zoology to certain tropical lizards who can run upright, even across the surface of water, at dizzying speeds, and to a species of wren, and figuratively, to an "evil eye," especially in the context of a person who can "kill" one's reputation, like a malicious critic or a lethal gossip. In *The Faerie Queene*, the English poet Edmund Spenser (c. 1552-1595) wrote that:

> The Basilisk . . .
> From powerful eyes close venim doth convey
> Into the lookers hart, and killeth farre away.

Basilisk comes, via Late Latin *basiliscus*, from Greek *basiliskos* (princeling), diminutive of *basileus* (king). There are adjectives *basciliscine* (bas uh LIS in, -ine, baz-) and *basiliscan* (bas uh LIS kuhn, baz-). There is a theory that the use of *basilisk* to denote certain animals, like the lizards and wrens (a species called "kinglets") mentioned above, all of whom have crownlike crests, harps back to the crowns of the kings and princelings of ancient times. Kin to the *basilisk* is the *cockatrice*, also a monster of fable, common in heraldic art, a composite beast endowed with wings, a dragon's tail, and the head of cock. Isaiah says (11:

6-8): "The wolf shall dwell with the lamb . . . the sucking child shall play on the hole of the asp . . . and the weaned child shall put his hand on the *cockatrice'* den . . . " (i.e., the most dangerous of creatures shall not harm the weakest of God's children). But the misogynous English dramatist John Gay (1685-1732), in *The Beggar's Opera*, warns:

> Man may escape from rope and gun;
>   Nay, some have outliv'd the doctor's pill:
> Who takes a woman must be undone,
>   That *basilisk* is sure to kill.
> The fly that sips treacle is lost in the sweets,
> So he that tastes woman, woman, woman,
>   He that tastes woman, ruin meets.

Thus, *basilisk* and *cockatrice* have been used to designate a treacherous, evil person bent on destruction. Shakespeare was keenly aware of the *cockatrice's* power, like that of the *basilisk*, to kill with a look. *In Twelfth Night* (Act III, Scene 4), Sir Toby Belch has engineered a duel (that will never occur) between the cowardly Sir Andrew Aguecheek and the terrified Viola [see reference to this in **clodpoll**] and describes each to the other as a mortally dangerous adversary. He says, "This will so fright them both that they will kill one another by the look, like *cockatrices.*" In *The Rape of Lucrece*, Shakespeare describes the ominous Tarquin as "Here with a *cockatrice'* dead-killing eye . . . "; in *Romeo and Juliet* (Act III, Scene 2), Juliet speaks of " . . . the death-darting eye of *cockatrice* . . . "; in *Richard III* (Act IV, Scene 1), the Duchess of York, King Richard's mother, cries:

> O! my accursed womb, the bed of death,
> A *cockatrice* hath thou hatch'd to the world,
> Whose unavoided eye is murderous.

Gorgons were no fun, either: their glance turned their victims to stone. Someone with a good working knowledge of the ways of *basilisks*, *cockatrices*, and Gorgons must have invented the expression, "If looks could kill . . . !"

bathysiderodromophobia   (bath ee sid uh roh droh moh PHO bee uh) *n.* This **sesquipedalian** jawbreaker denotes a subdivision of claustrophobia: the dread of subways (undergrounds, in Britain), wholly independent of the terror of the violence that has become characteristic of them. In the same way that **floccinaucinihilipilification** was built of bits and pieces of Latin, this word, was put together from a series of Greek elements. This is how it works: *bathys* (deep); *sidero-*, from *sideros* (iron); *dromo-*, from *dromos* (running); *-phobia*, from *phobos* (fearing). That is, *fear of* deep, i.e. *underground*, iron, *i.e. rail*, running, i.e., *way*. Doubtless, in view of what has been happening in the New York subways, this phobia (usually defined as "obsessive or irrational fear or anxiety") doesn't seem all that irrational any more, merely somewhat enhancéd.

battology (buh TOL uh jee) *n.* This is the word for tiresome, excessive, useless, futile repetition in speech or writing. Never, please never, and I mean never—but never!—indulge in *battalogy*. The word comes from Greek *battologia* (stuttering). To be guilty of this wearisome exercise is to *battologize* (buh TOL uh jize), which also includes the equally annoying, needless, and tiresome repetition of mannerisms. The perptrator is known as a *battologist* (buh TOL uh jist) and the adjective describing the offending person or his behavior is *battological* (bat uh LOJ ih kul). The origin of these words is said to be *Battos*, who, according to the Greek historian Herodotus (c. 484-c. 425 B.C.), implored the Delphic Oracle to tell him how to correct his stammer.

bedizened (bih DYE zund) *adj.* This word is a participal adjective, formed from the rarely encountered verb *bedizen*, to dress or adorn (someone) in a gaudy, showy, vulgar manner. To be *bedizened*, then, is to be dressed that way. The American essayist and novelist Kenneth Roberts (1885-1957) used it in that sense in describing a character as "a bold and shameless creature, *bedizened*, painted and overdressed." Although there is no logical reason why *bedizened* should not be applied to both sexes, the word seems always to evoke the image of a meretricious woman. Early movie vamps like Pola Negri, decked out in ropes of pearls and skirts of fringe and heavily made up, were prototypes of the *bedizened* woman, the shameless hussy. The American producer of musicals Florenz Ziegfield (1867-1932) bedecked his ladies of the ensemble in an exaggeratedly *bedizened* manner, utilizing lots of feathers and glittering fake jewelry in their outfits. The word has an interesting origin. We start with the common prefix *be-* used in the formation of verbs like *bedeck, befriend, belittle*, add *dizen*, an archaic verb meaning "adorn with finery," which itself comes from *dis-* (based on Low German *diesse*, meaning "bunch of flax on a distaff"—and thus we see the origin of *distaff* itself) and tack on the suffix *-en*, used to form verbs from adjectives (*fasten, shorten, sweeten*) or from nouns (*heighten, lengthen, strengthen*), and come up with *bedizen*. All that remains is to add the participial ending *-ed*, and voilà!

belated (bih LAY tid) *adj. Belated* is the adjective for anything that comes too late, that happens after the customary or expected time, like the *belated* birthday greetings you remember to send on the 14th to your friend whose 50th occurred on the 12th. You can buy cards with "Better late than never" on the outside and apologetic doggerel on the inside. A *belated* arrival at a dinner party can be very embarrassing. The adverb is *belatedly* (bih LAY tid lee). Mail often arrives *belatedly* nowadays. Shakespeare's great "seven ages" speech by Jaques in *As You Like It* (Act II, Scene 7) speaks of " . . . the whining school-boy . . . creeping like snail/Unwillingly to school," perhaps taking what the French call the "chemin des écoliers" (the roundabout way; literally, the schoolboys' route), and we get a picture of the little chap making a *belated* appearance, quailing before the angry schoolmaster. *Belated* is a combination of the prefix *be-*, used in the formation of verbs (e.g., *become, bedizen, befriend, bewitch*) plus *late* plus the *d* of the participial ending *-ed*. The verb *belate* (to delay) is itself archaic.

beldam   (BEL dum) *n.* A *beldam*, despite the look of the word (*belle dame* is "fair lady" in French) is a hag, an ugly old woman, or a shrew regardless of her age. Shakespeare used *beldam* in the now obsolete sense of "grandmother" in *The Rape of Lucrece*: "Time's glory is . . . /To show the *beldam* daughters of her daughter . . . " He used it in the modern meaning as well, in *Macbeth* (Act III, Scene 5), when the witches ask Hecate why she is angry and she answers: "Have I not reason, *beldams* as you are,/Saucy and overbold?" And in *King John* (Act IV, Scene 2), Hubert de Brugh tells the King about dreadful portents: "My Lord, they say five moons were seen tonight . . . /Old men and *beldams* in the streets/Do prophesy upon it dangerously . . ." A man should never address his fair companion as "beldam"; it means the opposite of what it appears to mean.

benighted   (bih NYE tid) *adj.* A *benighted* person is unenlightened, intellectually barren, morally ignorant. The Dark Ages (the period from 476 to the beginnings of the Renaissance in the 14th century) were replete with superstitious beliefs and barbaric practices; those were *benighted* times, and the earth was populated by *benighted* people. The word is a combination of the prefix *be-* (see **bedizened** for a discussion of *be-*), the noun *night* (in the figurative sense of 'darkness') and the common suffix *-ed*, forming participial adjectives as in *crossed swords*, *belated news*, etc. The English author and poet Rudyard Kipling (1865-1936), in his famous *Fuzzy-Wuzzy* poem, had this to say:

> So 'ere's to Fuzzy-Wuzzy at your 'ome in the Soudan;
> You're a pore *benighted* 'eathen but a first-class fightin' man . . .

In the poem *Comus*, the English poet John Milton (1608-1674) wrote:

> . . . he that hides a dark soul and foul thoughts
> *Benighted* walks under the midday sun . . .

(like mad dogs and Englishmen?). We would describe as *benighted* those poor teenagers whom the Ayatollah sends to their death in the war with Iraq, wearing the "key to heaven" around their necks.

besom   (BEE zum) *n.* A *besom* is a broom, especially the sort one sees in the European countryside, made of dried twigs tied around a stick. Its derivation is from Middle English *besem*; cf. German *Besen* (broom). In Isaiah 14: 22-23, we read of the Lord's anger against Babylon and its people: "For I will rise up against them . . . I will make it a possession for the bittern, and pools of water; and I will sweep it with the *besom* of destruction, saith the Lord . . . " *Besoms* are witches' favorite means of transportation. *Besom* sounds like a relic of bygone days, but *besoms* are by no means extinct and can be found in many an English and

European home and shop. *Besom*, in the Scottish Lowlands, is slang for "prostitute" or "slut," and *jumping the besom* is the failure to go through with the marriage ceremony after the publication of the banns in the parish church as notice of an intended marriage. To *hang out the besom* is to lead a bachelor's life and sow some belated wild oats while one's wife is away on a visit. The French use the idiom *rôtir le balai* (literally, roast the *besom*) to mean "go on a spree, lead a fast life."

bestride (bih STRIDE) *vb.* When one spreads his legs on both sides of something, he is said to be *astride* (uh STRIDE) of it. Under the headline SHOCK END TO CHARITY PARA JUMP in the May 16, 1984, edition of the (London) *Daily Telegraph*, we are advised that " . . . out of the 30 novices who descended on Northumberland from 2,000 feet, one woman broke a leg, another her ankle, and one man landed *astride* a bull." *Bestride* is the verb; *astride* a preposition, though it can also be used as an adverb or an adjective, to describe an action or a posture with legs apart, on either side of something—horse, fence, or, under certain circumstances, bull. *Bestride* is used in its literal sense when you mount and *bestride* a horse or a fence. In a figurative sense, to *bestride* is to tower over something, to dominate it. The name of Shakespeare *bestrides* the centuries. He used the word in a dramatic way, combining the literal and figurative senses. In *Julius Caesar* (Act I, Scene 2), Cassius complains to Brutus of Caesar's rise to glory:

> Why, man, he doth *bestride* the narrow world
> Like a Colossus; and we petty men
> Walk under his huge legs . . .

We find *bestride* again (in the alternative past tense *bestrid*; the usual form is *bestrode*) in *Anthony and Cleopatra* (Act V, Scene 2). Anthony is dead; Cleopatra, mourning him, laments to Dolabella:

> His legs *bestrid* the ocean; his rear'd arm
> Crested the world . . .

Remember the distinction: when you *bestride* something, you are *astride* it. Both words are based on *stride*, which comes from Middle English *striden*.

bête noire (bet nuh WAHR) *n., adj.* This is a French expression (literally, *black beast*) taken into English to describe anything that is a pet aversion, a bugbear, a thorn in one's side. A *bête noire* can be a person, an object, a chore, anyone or anything that one simply can't stand. To a child, spinach can be a *bête noire*. The caption under a Carl Rose cartoon in the December 8, 1928, issue of *The New Yorker* (mother and child) reads:

> "It's broccoli, dear."
> "I say it's spinach, and I say the hell with it."

To some, Wagner may be a *bête noire*; to others, hard rock may qualify. Contemporary painting is a *bête noire* to countless thousands, nay, millions. Choose your own: ballet, corned beef and cabbage, Liberace, politicans, wine connoisseurs; long airplane trips, missiles, New Year's Eve parties, children in TV commercials, all TV commercials, books about words . . .

bibelot   (BIB loh) *n.* A *bibelot* is a knick-knack or small curio; the word implies beauty or rarity or both. *Bibelot* is a word taken over from the French, and is not to be confused with *bauble* (BAW bul), which is a cheap, showy trinket or gewgaw (GYOOH gaw, GOOH-). *Bibelot* is the proper term for those mantel ornaments tourists pick up in their travels and like to strew around the house to remind them of their happy days in foreign and exotic places.

bibliobibulus, see **pecksniffian**

biblioclast, see **bibliopole**

bibliognost, see **bibliopole**

bibliogony, see **bibliopole**

biblioklept, see **bibliopole**

bibliomania, see **bibliopole**

bibliopegy, see **bibliopole**

bibliophage, see **bibliopole**

bibliophobe, see **bibliopole**

bibliopole   (BIB lee uh pole) *n.* Most of us are familiar with *bibliophile* (lover and collector of books) and *bibliography* (compilation of books on a given subject). There are less familiar *biblio-* words, like *bibliopole*, a bookseller, especially one who deals in secondhand and rare books, derived from Greek *bibliopoles* (bookseller), made from the common Greek prefix *biblio-*, based on *biblion* (book) and suffix *-pol*, based on *polesthai* (to sell). Since books play such an important role in our lives, it is not surprising that our language contains a large number of *biblio-* words, with suffixes based on Greek nouns or verbs. Here is a partial list: *biblioclast* (BIB lee uh klast), a mutilator of books; *bibliognost* (BIB lee og nost), an expert on books; *bibliogony* (bib lee OG uh nee), book production and publishing; *biblioklept* (BIB lee uh klept), a book thief; *bibliomania* (bib lee oh MAY nee uh), immoderate zeal in the collection of books; *bibliopegy* (bib lee OP uh jee), bookbinding; *bibliophage* (BIB lee uh faje), a bookworm; *bibliophobe* (BIB lee uh fobe), one who fears or hates books; *bibliotaph* (BIB lee uh taf), a book hoarder; *bibliotiks* (bib lee OT iks), handwriting and document analysis to authenticate authorship. The plural of Greek *biblion* is *biblia*. The English essayist Charles Lamb (1775-1834) invented the words *a-biblion*, an "unbook" or "nonbook," based on the Greek negative prefix *a-* plus *biblion*. In "Detached thoughts on Books and Reading" he wrote:

> I can read anything which I call a book. There are things in that shape which I cannot allow for such. In this catalogue of books which are no books—*biblia a-biblia*—I reckon Court Calendars [this is a reference to the Royal Court, not legal courts], Directories . . . the works of Hume, Gibbon, Robertson, Beattie, Soame Jenyns, and, generally, all those volumes which 'no gentleman's library should be without'.

He disagreed with Thomas Jefferson (1743-1826), who wrote to a friend in 1771, providing a list that should be in "a gentleman's library"—a long list, containing books on law, history, religion, and the "fine arts," including Pope, Dryden, Shakespeare, Congreve, Voltaire, Rousseau, and Molière. In any event, if you are *bibliophile* or suffer from *bibliomania*—but certainly not if you are a *biblioklept* or a *biblioclast* or a *bibliophobe*—seek out a good, reliable *bibliopole*. See also *bibliobibulus* under **pecksniffian**.

bibliotaph, see **bibliopole**

bibliotiks, see **bibliopole**

bicameral   (bye KAM ur ul) *adj.* This is a term used in government to describe a legislative system consisting of two houses, an upper and a lower, like the Senate and the House of Representatives, which together constitute the Congress of the United States. The United Kingdom has a *bicameral* system, composed of Parliament and the House of Lords, and other countries have two legislative chambers as well, but the powers of the respective houses and the relationship between them vary from nation to nation. *Unicameral* (yooh nuh KAM ur ul) applies to a system consisting of only one branch or chamber. *Bi-* and *uni-* are prefixes taken from Latin, and *camera* is Late Latin for "chamber." (Cf. *bicycle* and *unicycle.*) The *bi-* in *bicameral* is a true *bi-*, unlike the *bi* in *bikini*, which was mistaken for the prefix meaning "two," so that when daring ladies discarded the bra, the residual scanty nether covering was erroneously touted as the "monokini"!

bifurcate   (BYE fur kate) *vb.*, *adj.*; (BYE fur kit) *adj. Bifurcate*, the verb, is both transitive and intransitive: to *bifurcate* a road is to fork it into two branches; a road or stream so divided can be said to *bifurcate*. The adjective *bifurcate* describes any road or stream thus divided, and the process is *bifurcation* (bye fur KAY shun). *Bifurcate* comes from Middle Latin *bifurcatus*, past participle of *bifurcare*, based on prefix *bi-* (twice) plus *furca* (fork). Apart from use in connection with roads, there is a philosophical term, *bifurcation theory*, signifying the division of reality into two parts, the world as it exists in the mind and the external world as it exists in actuality.

billingsgate   (BIL ingz gate) *n*. *Billingsgate* is foul and abusive language, coarse invective. The word comes from Billingsgate, London, for hundreds of years the site and name of a fish market where fish sellers and porters were notorious for their foul, coarse language. The market was near a gate in the old city wall named after a property owner, Billings. To *talk billingsgate* (sometimes capitalized) is to indulge in vituperation and vilification. The women who worked there were particularly offensive; from the Middle English *fisshwyf* we get *fishwife*, a term applied to coarse, vituperative, foul-tongued women who belie the traditional gentility of their sex. These lines appear in *The Plain Dealer*, a play by the English poet and dramatist William Wycherley (c. 1640-1716):

> QUAINT: With sharp invectives—
> WIDOW: Alias, *Billingsgate*.

Birrellism, see **obiter dictum**

bisontine, see **accipitrine**

bissextile   (by SEKS til, bih-) *adj*. A *bissextile* year, commonly known as a "leap year," is one of 366 days, containing a February 29. The *bissextus* (by SEKS tus, bih-) is February 29 itself. The extra day is added to our regular calendar year every fourth year except for centenary years (those ending in -00) not evenly divisible by 400 (e.g., 1700, 1800, 1900—in this connection you might like to refer to the entry **aliquot, aliquant**). The extra day in a *bissextile* year, also known as an "intercalary" day (see **intercalate**), is added to make up for the difference of approximately one-fourth of a day between the 365-day year (also known as a "common year") and the astronomical year of approximately 365.25 (to be exact, 365.2422) days, the time it takes for the earth to travel its elliptical course around our sun. The difference between 365.25 and 365.2422 is made right by the loss of three days in the 400-year period between each pair of consecutive centenary years not evenly divided by 400. The word *bissextile* doesn't have a thing in the world to do with bisexuality. It comes from Late Latin *bissextilis*, based on *bissextus*, based in turn on Latin *bis* (twice—the French still shout "Bis!" at concerts in place of "Encore!") and *sextus* (sixth). But why? Because in the old Julian calendar (reformed by Pope Gregory XIII, 1502-1585, to become the calendar now in use, called "Gregorian" after that innovative Pope), instead of adding a day at the end of February, the Romans had two February 24s; and February 24 was the sixth day before March 1 (the Calends of March), which in their calendar was New Year's Day—which explains why our tenth, eleventh and twelfth months are named after the Latin for *eight* (octo), *nine* (novem), and *ten* (decem). The *annus bissextus* was the year (*annus*) when the sixth (*sextus*) day before March 1 occurred twice (*bis*). Hence, *bissextus* (twice sixth). If all this astronomical discussion is too complicated, just remember that leap year is the time when it is proper for ladies to propose marriage to gentlemen, and let it go at that.

bivouac   (BIV ooh ak, BIV wak) *n. Bivouac* is a military term for an improvised encampment in the open air, usually consisting of tents, exposed without protection to enemy fire. To *bivouac* is to set up such an arrangement. *Bivouac* was taken over intact from the French, which got it from Swiss German *Beiwacht*, now *Biwak* in modern German. Though *bivouac* is a technical term in military parlance, it has been used jocularly to denote any point of assembly. "Where shall we *bivouac* for tea, darling?" You may want to decline the invitation from one taking such liberties with the language. The American poet Theodore O'Hara (1820-1867) wrote *The Bivouac of the Dead* to commemorate the American soldiers fallen at the battle of Buena Vista during the Mexican War of 1847:

> On Fame's eternal camping ground
> Their silent tents are spread,
> And Glory guards, with solemn round,
> The *bivouac* of the dead.

bloviate   (BLOH vee ate) *vb.* To *bloviate* is to declaim or orate long-windedly and bombastically. Doesn't it sound that way? Blowhards *bloviate*, and doubtless the *blo-* of *bloviate* has something to do with *blowing*, as in blowing your own horn or blowing a blast on a wind instrument or blowing off, in the sense of "talking boastfully" and at great length. It was characteristic of Southern senators, old style, to *bloviate*, often to empty Senate chambers. Commencement speakers sometimes have a tendency to *bloviate*; a waggish friend has commented that the ending is preferable to the commencement. Motto for speakers: Don't *bloviate*.

bolt   (bohlt) *vb. Bolt* has a great many meanings, as a noun, a verb, both transitive and intransitive, and even as an adverb (e.g., *bolt* upright), but one meaning as a verb may be unfamiliar: to "sift," usually through fine-meshed cloth; and a *bolter*, in this context, is such a sieve. The common use of both verb and noun is in the sifting of flour or meal, where *bolt* has the force of "refine" or "purify" through the sifting process. To *bolt* can also mean to "examine" through sifting, as in a laboratory, in a situation where larger and smaller particles have to be separated. *Bolt* has been used figuratively as well, as it was by the English journalist and pamphleteer Sir Roger L'Estrange (1616-1704), who wrote: "Time and nature will *bolt* out the truth of things." This brings to mind the aphorism of the Roman philosopher and dramatist Seneca (c. 4 B.C.-A.D. 65): "Time discovers truth." The old proverb, "Truth is the daughter of time," inspired the English novelist Josephine Tey (1897-1952) to entitle her novel in defense of Richard III *The Daughter of Time*, a book that will enlighten those misled by the libels of the English chronicler Holinshed (or Hollingshead—take your choice: died c. 1580), Sir Thomas More, the English statesman (1478-1535), later canonized, and William Shakespeare. My, how far we've come from *bolt*!

bombilate (BOM buh late), also **bombinate** (BOM buh nate) *vb*. To *bombinate* or *bombilate* is to hum, buzz, drone, or boom; taken from Middle Latin *bombilare/bombinare* (to buzz), based, via Latin *bombus*, on Greek *bombos* (hum, boom, or deep, hollow sound, especially of trumpets), from which we also get *bomb*, which booms rather than hums, except that the buzz-bombs of World War II did both over England. Flies and mosquitoes annoy us by *bombilating* or *bombinating* continually, while the *bombilation* of bees, for some reason, is a rather pleasant sound. After all, the bees are extremely useful, while one wonders why flies and mosquitoes were ever put on earth. If one said that the sour d of a loud buzz-saw was an *abombinable* noise, one would un-doubtedly and perhaps deservedly be greeted with the groans that customarily accompany **paronomasias**.

bombycine, see **accipitrine**

bonhomie (BON uh mee) *n*. This word, taken from the French (where it is pronounced bo no MEE), means "geniality, straightforward good nature, openhearted friendliness." The French based *bonhomie* on the noun *bonhomme*, denoting a simple, good-natured fellow, sometimes with an im-plication that he may be too simple for his own good, overly credulous, someth-ing of a schlemiel; but there is no such implication in the English use of *bonhomie*. The related adjective *bonomous* (BON uh mus) is little used, and rightly so, for it has an unpleasant sound, though it might be helpful in a limerick involving *anonymous*. There is a very nice **clerihew** built around *bonhomie*:

> John Stuart Mill
> By a might effort of will
> Overcame his natural *bonhomie*
> And wrote 'Principles of Political Economy'.

boniface (bon uh FASE) *n*. A *boniface* is an innkeeper. *Boniface* was the name of the jovial innkeeper in *The Beaux' Stratagem*, a comedy by the Irish playwright George Farquhar (1678-1707) which was produced in the last year of his young life. Farquhar wrote in the period of the British Restoration, and was the author of a series of rather licentious comedies notable for their flowing natural dialogue. There had been a hearty innkeeper named *Bonifazio* in the comedy *La Scolastica* by the Italian poet Ludovico Ariosto (1474-1533), and there would appear to have been a connection between that Bonifazio and Farquhar's Boniface. The success of Farquhar's last comedy and masterpiece was so great that the name *Boniface*, at first associated with only hearty, jovial in-keepers, acquired a lower case *b* and was eventually applied to any innkeeper, whatever his disposition.

bonnyclabber   (BON ee klab ur) *n*. Bonnyclabber, sometimes shortened to *clabber*, is thick sour milk, naturally clotted as it turns, a kind of buttermilk, a very refreshing drink, they say. The derivation is from two Irish words: *bainne* (milk) and *claba* (thick), related to *clabair* (clapper, or churn paddle). It wasn't to the taste of the English poet Ben Jonson (c. 1573-1637), who wrote, in his poem *The New Inn*:

> It is against my freehold, my inheritance,
> My Magna Charta, *cor laetificat*,
> To drink such balderdash or *bonny-clabber*!
> Give me good wine!

The Magna Charta (or Carta) was the "Great Charter" of rights and liberties forced by the Barons from King John of England in 1215 at Runnymede; it became a symbol of civil liberties, like our Bill of Rights. *Cor laetificat* is Latin for "It gladdens my heart." *Balderdash*, which now means "nonsense, senseless twaddle," once was the name for a worthless mixture of liquors, a meaning now obsolete. To Rare Ben Jonson, *bonny(-)clabber* must have been used in the generic sense of any unpalatable potion.

bosky   (BOS kee) *adj*. When you come across a woody bit of country, covered with shrubs, you are in a *bosky* place. *Bosk* is an archaic word for a small thicket of bushes, and comes from Middle English *boske* or *buske*, from which we get *bush*. *Boskage* or *boscage* (BOS kij) means "thicket" or "grove" but is rarely used. The Scottish novelist and poet Sir Walter Scott (1771-1832, famous for *Ivanhoe*, the dreaded reading requirement of high school students), wrote of traveling "through *bosk* and dell," and the American author Henry James (1843-1916) described "long *bosky* shadows" in a country scene. The British use *bosky* in a wholly unrelated colloquial sense for "tipsy." On a hot, sunny day, it is pleasant to find a *bosky* spot and relax in the shade. If you should suggest such a maneuver to a companion who is not familiar with *bosky*, say "Tut-tut!" and refer your uncultured friend to Walter Scott and Henry James. There is a related verb, to *embosk* (em BOSK), which denotes the act of shrouding or hiding something, someone, or oneself with greenery, foliage, or plants, the way some people like to *embosk* a summerhouse with vines, or themselves in a leafy recess or arbor, or a bower intertwined with climbing vines.

boustrophedon   (booh struh FEE don; bou-, booh STRAHF eh don) *adj., adv*. Based on the Greek noun *bous* (ox) plus the verb *strephein* (to turn), this word applies to writing, as in early Greek inscriptions, where the lines run alternately in opposite directions, i.e., from right to left and left to right. That is the way an ox turns as it ploughs—in rows that alternate in direction. Nowadays, when a word processor types from a disc, the typing moves that way but in the alternate lines running from right to left, the spelling is in reverse so that it all reads left to right in the end. It works the same way in the Semitic countries where the reading is from right to left. This type of writing is referred to by name in *Justine*, the first novel in *The Alexandria Quartet*, by the English novelist Lawrence Durrell (b. 1912), as the method used by an Egyptian secret society. It is sometimes referred to as "serpentine" writing.

bovarism, see **archetype**

bowdlerize (BOHD luh rize; BOUD-) *vb*. To *bowdlerize* a writing, such as a play, a novel, a history, an essay, a speech, is to expurgate it, particularly in a priggish, prudish, squeamish way. The word, together with the related group—*bowdlerist, bowdlerizer, bowdlerization, bowdlerism*, etc.—comes from the English editor Thomas Bowdler (1754-1825), famous or, better, notorious for his ten-volume expurgated edition of Shakespeare, as well as his "cleaned-up" editions of the Bible and the monumental six-volume *History of the Decline and Fall of the Roman Empire* by the English historian Edward Gibbon (1737-1794), usually referred to as "Gibbon's Decline and Fall." Bowdler described his edition of Shakespeare as one "in which nothing is added to the original text; but those words are omitted which cannot with propriety be read aloud in a family." There have been *bowdlerizing* authorities in more recent days, like the Hays Office, which held sway over the censorship of American films, and the Lord Chamberlain's Office which did the same to English stage productions—both authorities now happily consigned to history. Over the years, there have been other censorship bodies in the form of watch and ward societies formed for the purpose of guarding the morals of communities. "Lay on, Macduff, and darned be he . . . " etc.?

brabble (BRAB ul) *n., vb. Brabble* is loud, acrimonious wrangling. To *brabble* is to engage in quarrelsome arguments, usually stubborn ones, about trifles. We get this word from the Dutch verb *brabbelen* (to wrangle). In Shakespeare's *Titus Andronicus* (Act II, Scene 1), the Moor Aaron, beloved of the evil Tamora, Queen of the Goths, comes upon her sons Demetrius and Chiron, both smitten with Lavinia, Titus's daughter, wrangling and threatening each other. Aaron exclaims:

> Away, I say!
> This petty *brabble* will undo us all . . .
> For shame, be friends . . .

And in *King John* (Act V, Scene 2), the Dauphin, after listening to the Bastard's long plea for peace, says:

> We grant thou canst outscold us: fare thee well;
> We hold our time too precious to be spent
> With such a *brabbler* . . .

Brabble has an almost onomatopoeic sound.

braggadocio   (brag uh DOH shee oh) *n. Braggadocio* is boasting, bragging, vainglorious talk; a *braggadocio* is a braggart. *Brag* goes back to the Middle English noun *brag* and verb *braggen. Braggadocio* comes from a character named *Braggadocchio* in *The Faerie Queene* of the English poet Edmund Spenser (c. 1552-1599), a braggart who is really a coward at heart. He invents all sorts of glories for himself, but is eventually unmasked and sneaks off amid jeers. Spenser formed the name from *brag*, adding the suffix *-ade*, often used in forming nouns of action, and then the Italian augmentative suffix *-occhio*. Cf. **fanfaronade, gasconade, rodomontade, thrasonical**.

brannigan   (BRAN uh gun) *n.* This word has two distinct meanings. A *brannigan* is a drinking spree. To go on a *brannigan* is to go on a bender, of the lost weekend variety. *Brannigan* is also the name for a row, a squabble, usually over a difference of opinion. Town councils sometimes get into a *brannigan* over the route to be followed by a proposed new road, or the location of the new town hall. *Brannigan* is a not unusual surname, with an Irish sound, and the likelihood is that the common noun stems from the proper one, but let's not get into a *brannigan* about the derivation of the word.

brattice   (BRAT is) *n., vb.* A *brattice* is a partition of wooden planks or strong tarred cloth, known as *brattice-cloth*, forming an air passage or shaft lining to ventilate a mine, and the verb to *brattice* is to provide a mine with such a system. The wall of separation in a mine shaft or gallery deflects air toward the locations where the miners are working. The word is from Middle Latin *bretescia* or *brittisca*. In olden times, *brattice* was the term applied to a wooden tower used in siege tactics, or a roofed gallery on the wall of a castle that commanded the wall-face below, for nice activities like pouring down boiling oil and that sort of fun.

bravura   (bruh VYOOR uh) *n.* In music, *bravura* denotes either the florid style that shows off the technical artistic skill of a virtuoso, or the showy piece or passage itself that demands tremendous spirit and dash in execution. The American novelist Washington Irving (1783-1859) wrote of "listening to a lady amateur skylark it up and down through the finest *bravura* of Rossini or Mozart." The English novelist and essayist Maurice Hewlett (1861-1923) wrote of "that careless fling of the voice, that happy rapture, that *bravura* which makes the listener's heart go near to burst with . . . joy." *Bravura* characterizes brilliant coloratura singing but can apply to brilliance and dexterity in instrumental playing as well, and the music requiring it. *Bravura* can be used as an adjective as well, as in *a bravura performance*. Apart from its technical use in music, *bravura* can apply to any daringly brilliant or dashing display, as in acting. Anyone who remembers the exploits of Douglas Fairbanks, Sr. (1883-1939) in the old movies was indeed treated to exhibitions of theatrical *bravura*. Soldiers of fortune lead lives of *bravura*, which is an Italian word meaning "skill, deftness, bravery, spirit"—the kind of performance that elicits shouts of "Bravo!" But never confuse *bravura* with *bravado*, which is an ostentatious, pretentious show of defiance and swagger, and not nearly as nice as *bravura*.

bretelle   (brih TEL) *n.* A *bretelle* is a shoulder strap, one of a pair of ornamental suspender-type attachments to the front and back of a garment. Via the French, it comes all the way from Old High German *brittil* (bridle), and one can easily trace the etymological development. *Bretelles* are sewn to the back of the garment and fastened, usually clipped rather than buttoned, to the front of the waistband. Nowadays they're called shoulder-straps or suspender-straps; "bretelles" won't get you very far in a children's shop today. They are found principally on little boys' short pants, up to age four, and little girls' skirts, up to age eight, and can be plain or ornamental.

brobdingnagian, see **lilliputian**

brummagem   (BRUM uh jum) *n., adj.* As an adjective, *brummagem* describes anything showy but shoddy, inferior, worthless; as a noun, it denotes a showy, inferior, worthless object. *Brummagem* is an old local variant of *Birmingham*, the second largest city of England, in the northwestern part of the county of Warwickshire, where inferior trinkets, toys, imitation jewelry and the like were once manufactured in quantity. The name was first applied to a counterfeit coin made in Birmingham in the 17th century, and was later applied to the miscellaneous output of shoddy articles produced there. The first syllable, *brum-*, resulted from a transposition of the letters of the first syllable of *Birmingham* and the corruption of the rest of the name. *Brum* is occasionally used as a nickname for *Birmingham*, and can also denote the Birmingham dialect, one extremely hard to follow, not only for Americans but also for Britons from other parts of the country. A limerick invented by the late Royal Ballet conductor and composer Constant Lambert (1905-1951) begins:

> There was a young lady of Birmingham
> Who paraded the streets with a dirmingham.

Those familiar with *Brum* as a slang name for *Birmingham* were meant to recognize the nonsense word *dirmingham* as a back formation (of sorts) from *drum*!

bubaline, see **accipitrine**

buteonine, see **accipitrine**

Byzantine   (BIZ un teen, -tine; bih ZAN tine), *adj.* Literally, this adjective describes anything having to do with Byzantium, an ancient Greek city on the

Bosporus, rebuilt in 330 by the Roman Emperor Constantine I (288-337), who named it Constantinople after himself; it was renamed Istanbul in 1930. Based on the complex and labyrinthine political maneuvering that surrounded old Byzantium, the adjective *Byzantine* has come to apply to any activity of a devious and surreptitious nature, or at least so intricately involved as to give that impression. The operations of the intelligence departments of governments are *Byzantine* in the extreme, so much so that it is often very difficult, if not impossible, to follow the novels about spies and counterspies and double agents which make such compelling, if not always entirely clear, television series. It is also enormously difficult to sort information out of the *Byzantine* complexity of government records. Tourists in eastern countries are familiar with the *Byzantine* tactics of the merchants of the casbah.

caballine, see **accipitrine**

cachinnate (KAK uh nate) *vb*. To *cachinnate* is to laugh raucously, immoderately, convulsively. The word comes from *cachinnatus*, past participle of the Latin verb *cachinnare* (to laugh loudly). The adjective to describe such laughter is *cachinnatory* (kak uh NATE uh ree); the noun is *cachinnation* (kak uh NAY shun). One might guess that *cachination* and *cackle* are etymologically related. Not so: *cackle* is of Middle English origin, *cackelen*, cognate with Dutch *kakelen*. The American naturalist and essayist John Burroughs wrote of someone who "*cachinnated* till his sides must have ached." *Cachinnate* is not precisely an onomatopoeic word, but there is something in the sound of it (the identity with the pronounciation of the first syllable of *cackle*?) that suggests laughter.

cacodemon, see **cacoepy**

cacodoxy, see **cacoepy**

cacoepy (kuh KOH ih pee) *n*. *Cacoepy* means "incorrect pronunciation"; *orthoepy* (or THOH ih pee) means "correct pronunciation." These words are from Greek *kak(o)epeia* and *orth(o)epeia* respectively; *kakos* (bad) gives us the prefix *caco-*, as, e.g., in *cacophony*, while *orthos* (straight) gives us the prefix *ortho-*, as in, e.g., *orthodox*. There is a group of *caco-* words that go back to *kakos*: *cacography* (kuh KOG ruh fee), bad handwriting or spelling, from *kakos* plus *graphein* (to write); *cacology* (kuh KOL uh jee), bad choice of words or incorrect pronunciation, from *kakos* plus *logos* (word). Apart from writing, spelling, and pronunciation, *cacodemon* (ka koh DEE mun) is an evil spirit or a malicious person, from *kakos* plus *daimon* (spirit); *cacadoxy* (KAK oh doks ee), wrong opinion, incorrect doctrine, from *kakos* plus *doxa* (belief); and *cacoethes* (kak oh EE theez), an irresistible urge, from *kakos* plus *ethos* (habit). There are a couple of strange hybrid (Greek-Latin) expressions: *cacoethes loquendi*, the irresistible urge to speak (*loquendi* is a form of the Latin verb *loqui*, to speak); and *cacoethes scribendi*, the irresistible urge to write (*scribendi* is a form of the Latin verb *scribere*, to write), sometimes called the "itch to scribble," an affliction that has undoubtedly played a large part in the production of this book.

cacoethes, see **cacoepy**

cacography, see **cacoepy**

cacology, see **cacoepy**

Cadmean (kad MEE un) *adj.* This adjective means, literally, "pertaining to Cadmus," a figure in Greek mythology, the Phoenician prince who introduced the alphabet to Greece. The adjective is found in the expression *Cadmean victory*, one of disastrous cost to the victor. Cadmus slew the dragon that guarded the Fountain of Dirce, near Thebes in Boeotia, and then planted its teeth, from which the Sparti, fully armed warriors, sprang intending to kill Cadmus, but he threw a precious stone into their midst, and they, fighting among themselves to gain possession of it, killed one another except for five survivors, with whom Cadmus founded Thebes. Hence, a *Cadmean victory* is one gained at tragic cost, like the costly victory won against the Romans by King Pyrrhus of Epirus at Asculum in 279 B.C., in the course of which he lost the flower of his army. "One more such victory and I am lost," cried Pyrrhus, thus originating the phrase *Pyrrhic victory*, a goal attained or a victory gained, like Cadmus's, at too great a cost. *Cadmean* and *Pyrrhic* victories aren't worth winning.

caducity (kuh DOOH sih tee, -DYOOH-) *n. Caducity* is another word for senility, the infirmity of old age, frailty. Another distantly related meaning is "transitoriness." It comes, via French *caducité* (decrepitude), based on French *caduc* (broken-down, frail, perishable—and therefore transitory), from the Latin verb *cadere* (to fall). The etymologically related adjective *caducous* (kuh DOOH kus, -DYOOH-) is a term used in branches of biology. In zoology and botany, it describes parts that tend to fall, like the leaves of deciduous trees, or to shed, like the skin of snakes; in other words, parts that are lost but are renewed in the natural cycle (and are therefore "transitory"), without reference to decrepitude or senility.

caducous, see **caducity**

calligraphy (kuh LIG ruh fee) *n*. *Calligraphy* is used in a variety of ways that relate to its Greek origin, *kalligraphia*, based on *kallos* (beautiful) and *graphein* (to write): beautiful penmanship, fancy, highly decorative handwriting with flourishes of the sort common in Victorian and earlier times—the kind seen in old deeds and other documents—and the word can denote the art of beautiful penmanship itself. In contemporary usage, however, it has one meaning that ignores the *kallos* part of its Greek origin: simply, "handwriting," as opposed to printing or typing. The *calligraphy* found in 18th-century manuscripts is often a work of art in itself. When this author was very young, one studied *calligraphy* (called "penmanship") in elementary school; the favorite system was the "Palmer method." Somewhere along the line, with a fine disregard for the etymology of *calli-*, *calligraphy* came to be used simply as a learned synonym for *handwriting*, whether beautiful or a scrawl resembling hen tracks.

callipygian (kal uh PIJ ee un), **callipygous** (kal uh PYE gus) *adj*. Both forms of this adjective describe a person (presumably female) endowed with beautiful, shapely buttocks; presumably female, at any rate, because of the fame of the *Callipygian* Venus, a marble statue of a female discovered in the Emperor Nero's Domus Aurea (Golden House) in Rome, now on show at the Museo Nazionale (National Museum) in Naples. The Greek adjective is *kallipygos* (having beautiful buttocks) based on *kallos* (beautiful) plus *pyge* (rump). It is a great asset to a woman to be *callipygian* or *callipygous*, and in this author's mind, there stirs the memory of the use of *callipygian* in some enthusiast's description of Gypsy Rose Lee (Rose Louise Hovick, 1914-1970), the ecdysiast who took her work very seriously.

calque (kawk) *vb*. Also **calk**. To *calque* is to make a copy of a drawing, plan, etc., by the following ingenious method: You rub the back of what you want to copy with a coloring substance like chalk or pastel crayon, put a piece of paper or other surface beneath it, then pass a blunt needle or stylus over the lines to be copied so as to leave a tracing on the surface you have placed beneath what you want to copy, et voilà! We get *calque*, via French *calquer* (to trace) and Italian *calcare* (to trace, to trample), from the Latin verb *calcare* (to trample). This is a process somewhat similar to the "rubbing" technique described under **frottage**—the one relating to church floors, not the second one, relating to crowded subway cars!

came, see **quarrel**

cameline, see **accipitrine**

campestral (kam PES trul) *adj*. Also **campestrian** (kam PES tree un). *Campestral* is descriptive of anything relating to open country and fields, or any crop growing in level fields. The word is derived from the Latin adjective *campester* (flat, of level country), based on *campus* (level space, field, plain). Our word *camp* also comes from *campus* (an army would not ordinarily pitch a camp on other than level ground), and *campus*, the grounds of a university or other school, is simply the adoption of the Latin noun for a specialized use.

canine, see **accipitrine**

Canossa (kuh NOS uh; in Italian, kah NAW sa) *n*. As an entry in this book, the place-name *Canossa* is one of interest only in the phrase *go to Canossa*, which is a picturesque way of saying "humble oneself, undergo humiliation, eat humble pie," or, less dramatically, "submit." Canossa, a hamlet in north central Italy in the Apennines, is the scene of a ruined castle once the home of the Canossa family who ruled over most of Tuscany in the 10th and 11th centuries. Pope Gregory VII was a guest at the castle in January 1077. He had excommunicated Holy Roman Emperor Henry IV during a political controversy between church and state. The Emperor humbled himself by going to Canossa and standing three days barefoot in the snow dressed as a penitent before being admitted into the pope's presence. The excommunication was withdrawn but the dispute soon flared up once more. Centuries later, when Chancellor of Germany Otto von Bismark (1815-1898) was involved in a state-church controversy with Pope Pius IX, he refused to bend the knee and stated in the Reichstag (German parliament) in 1872: "Nach Canossa gehen wir nicht!" ("We shall not go to Canossa!"). Bismark knew his history. A compromise was reached, and ever since, to *go to Canossa* is to yield, submit, give in, surrender, capitulate, bend the knee, throw in the towel, cry uncle. "Lay on Macduff, and damned be he who first" *goes to Canossa.*

capreoline, see **accipitrine**

caprine, see **accipitrine**

carapace (KAR uh pase) *n*. A *carapace* is the hard covering of all or part of the backs of certain animals, like the upper shell of a turtle or the armor on the dorsal part of an armadillo. It is also known in zoology as a "shield" or "test," a word that has a special use in that field designating the protective shell or other hard covering of some invertebrates like sea urchins and starfishes. *Carapace* comes from the French, which got it from the Spanish *carapacho* (origin unknown—and the usual Spanish for *seashell* is *concha*). An animal equipped with a *carapace* is said to be *carapaced*, and the covering is described as *carapacic* (kar uh PAY sik) or *carapacial* (kar uh PAY shuhl). *Test*, in this context, is from Latin *testa* (shell or tile), and gives us *testaceous* (teh STAY shus), describing any animal bearing a shell or *carapace.*

carnassial (kar NAHS ee ul) *n., adj.* This dental term describes a tooth adapted for the tearing of flesh. It is derived, via the French adjective *carnassier*, from

carn-, the stem of the Latin noun *caro* (flesh), the same *carn-* as we find in *carnal, carnivore*, etc. As a noun, *carnassial* is also known as a *scissor-tooth*. It is the largest premolar upper tooth of a carnivore. The term is used with respect to all carnivorous animals except man.

carphology, see **floccillation**

carpology, see **floccillation**

carrel (KAR ul) *n*. In olden times, a *carol* was a small enclosure in a cloister that served as a study, built against a window on the inner side. That word, now archaic, became *carole* in Middle English, and is the ancestor of our word *carrel*, which is a cubicle built into a library stack, used for individual study away from the madding, whispering, shuffling, coughing crowd in the general reading-room. It is sometimes spelt *carrell*.

cartography (kar TOG ruh fee) *n*. *Cartography* is the art of map-making, and one engaged in that activity is a *cartographer* (kar TOG ruh fur). *Cartomancy* (kar TOH muhn see) is fortune-telling based on the interpretation of playing-cards, and is as reliable as tea-leaf reading and the examination of palms. A *cartogram* (KAR toh gram) is a map in diagrammatic form showing statistical data. The first syllable of all these words is derived from the Latin *c(h)arta* and Greek *chartes* (sheet of paper); *cartograph* and *cartographer* add *-graph* and *-grapher*, respectively, from Greek *graphein* (to write). *Cartomancy* adds *-mancy*, from Greek *manteia* (**divination**). *Cartology* (kar TOL uh jee) is the science of maps, charts, etc., and adds the suffix *-logy*, common in the names of sciences (*geology, philology*, etc.), based on Greek *logos* (word, discourse).

cartomancy, see **cartography**

caryatid (kar ee AT id) *n*. This is an architectural term for a sculpture of a woman in classical Greek dress, used as a column, as in one of the porches of the Erechtheum, the beautiful temple on the Acropolis at Athens. Greek architects likewise used *atlantes* (plural of *atlas*, in architectural parlance), also known as *telamones* (plural of *telamon*), male sculptures, for the same purpose. *Caryatid* has a sad and interesting derivation. It is from Greek *Karyatides* (columns in the figure of women; literally, women of Karyae, a city of ancient Laconia), so named because Karae sided with the Persian King Xerxes I (c. 519-465 B.C.) and his army at Thermopylae in 480 B.C., and after their defeat, the Greeks sacked Karyae, massacred all the men and took the women into slavery. The Greek sculptor Praxiteles (fl. c. 350 B.C.) symbolized the disgrace by using female figures as columns.

Cassandra (kuh SAN druh) *n*. Cassandra is a figure from Greek mythology, the daughter of King Priam and Queen Hecuba of Troy, endowed by Apollo with the gift of prophecy. However, she refused his advances, and in revenge, he brought down upon her the curse that, though her prophecies invariably proved true, no one would ever believe them. Her name has become an epithet for a prophet of gloom, especially one whose dire predictions are disregarded. She is a character in Shakespeare's *Troilus and Cressida*. In Act V, Scene 3, she tells her father to hold back his son Hector from the war: "Unarm, sweet Hector," she begs and later, "Lay hold upon him, Priam . . . "

> He is thy crutch; now if you lose thy stay,
> Then on him leaning, and all Troy on thee,
> Fall all together."

Priam begs his son to go back: "Cassandra doth foresee . . . " Troilus says of Cassandra:

> This foolish, dreaming,˙ superstitious girl
> Makes all these bodements [predictions].

Cassandra predicts Hector's death and the fall of Troy; she's right; no one believes her. A *Cassandra*, then, is one who prophesies doom, usually to a heedless audience; the very antithesis of a Pollyanna, the irrepressibly optimistic heroine of the 1913 novel of that name by the American writer Eleanor Hodgman Porter (1868-1920). "Don't be a Cassandra, always looking on the dark side of things!" people will exclaim, without realizing that Cassandra's predictions of disaster and doom were right on the money.

catachresis (kat uh KREE sis) *n. Cathachresis* covers a group, if not a multitude, of sins: the misuse or wrong application of a word, attempting to give it a meaning that it does not have; stretching or straining the meaning of a term; the use of a word in an erroneous form arising from popular eytmology. Examples of misuse: a *chronic* illness when one means a *severe* one (an illness can be chronic without being severe); a *mutual* friend instead of a *common* friend (if you and someone have a friend in common, there is nothing mutual about it); *restive* when one should say *restless* (*restive* implies impatience with restraint or control, not general unquiet, unease or unsettledness). Stretching the meaning: the use of *alibi* for *excuse* (*alibi* should be confined to a defense in criminal law by way of proving that the accused was somewhere other than the scene of the crime at the time of its commission—its use for *excuse* in general is what Fowler calls "slipshod extension"). Erroneous folk etymology: *crayfish*, and its variant *crawfish*, are not fish at all, but rather, small lobster-like crustaceans, which got the name from Middle English *crevis*; a *demijohn* is not a "half-john," there being no such measure as a "john"; it is a large bottle with a short, narrow neck, named, so they say, after a certain Dame Jeanne who had that unfortunate shape; a *Jerusalem artichoke* has nothing to do with that great city, but acquired its name from the Italian *girasole articiocco*, an edible sun-flower that *turns* (in

Italian, *gira*) with the *sun* (in Italian, *sole*, as in *O sole mio!*). This type of *catachresis* is not really a wrong usage but, rather, a usage based upon a false derivation. *Catachresis* itself is derived from *katachresis*, Greek for "misuse," built from *kata* (against) and *chresis* (use).

catamite (KAT uh mite) *n.* A *catamite* is a boy kept by an older man for pederastic purposes, or, in language less clinical, as a young lover. Such a companion was known in Latin as a *catamitus*; the word was a corruption of *Ganymede*, the Greek name of the cup-bearer of Zeus. Ganymede, in classical mythology, the successor of Hebe, daughter of Zeus and his wife Hera, was the personification of youthful male beauty. A Trojan youth, he was carried up to Olympus and made immortal. A recent (1983) police raid in England upon the premises of an organization formed for the purpose of rounding up young boys for training as *catamites* netted a large group of middle-aged members. De gustibus . . . The keeper of a *catamite* is known as a *pedophile* (PEE duh file, PED-), the name for an adult having sexual desire for a child, and this condition is labeled *pedophilia* (pee duh FIL ee uh, -FEEL yuh, ped uh-). The first syllable of these words may also be spelt *paed-*; *pedo-* and *paedo-* words are based on the Greek prefix *paido-*, from *paid-*, the stem of *pais* (child)—except for a few *pedo-* words (e.g., *pedology, pedometer*) based on *ped-*, the stem of Latin *pes* (foot). The novel *Earthly Powers* (Simon & Schuster, New York, 1980) by the English writer Anthony Burgess (b. 1917), opens: "It was the afternoon of my eighty-first birthday, and I was in bed with my *catamite*, when Ali announced that the archbishop had come to see me." Some opening!

catawampus, see **goluptious**

catechumen (kat uh KYOOH mun) *n.* In church parlance, a *catechumen* is a neophyte, a person being instructed in the basic principles of Christianity. In the days of the early Christian church, the term applied to a converted heathen or Jew taking instruction preparatory to baptism. Figuratively, *catechumen* has been extended to cover anyone being taught the rudiments of any subject. *Catechumen* is derived from Late Latin *catechumenus*, taken from the Greek *katechoumenos* (a person receiving oral instruction), based on the verb *katechein* (to teach by word of mouth). We are more familiar with the word *catechism*, the question and answer book containing a summary of the principles of Christianity, or the body of questions and answers used as a test in that field. The Late Latin name for the question and answers book was the *catechismus*. To *catechize* (KAT uh kize) is to teach via the catechism, but here, too, the meaning has been extended to cover any close or excessive questioning, especially one invading the privacy of an individual.

cater-cousin (KAY tur kuz un) *n.* A *cater-cousin* is not a relative at all, but rather a close friend, an affectionate, intimate pal. The word is built from *cater* (provide food) and *cousin*, used in the extended sense in which we give that name to persons of like natures, tastes, proximity, etc., in the way we speak of our "Canadian cousins" or Harvard men refer to their "Yale cousins" (when they're not insulting them). The *cater-* part indicates the mutual assistance aspect of close and loving friendship, in which the parties *cater* to each other's needs. In Shakespeare's *Merchant of Venice* (Act II, Scene 2), Launcelot Gobbo, Shylock's servant, beseeches Bassanio to take him into service, complaining of what a hard master Shylock is. Gobbo, Launcelot's father, pleading his son's case, tells Bassanio: "His master and he, saving your worship's reverence, are scarce *cater-cousins* . . . " In other words, Shylock and Launcelot weren't what you'd call loving friends.

caterwaul   (KAT ur wol) *n.*, *vb.* To *caterwaul* is to screech or howl, like a rutting cat, or to engage in a brawl the way fighting cats do. *Caterwaul* is also used as a noun to depict any screeching session, but the form *caterwauling* is more common. This onomatopoeic word comes from Middle English *caterwawen*, based on *cater* (tomcat) plus *wawen* (to howl). The rarely seen English verbs *waul* and *wawl*, variants of *wail*, must enter into the etymological picture as well. Shakespeare was fond of the word, using it in almost identical lines in both a comedy and a tragedy. In *Twelfth Night* (Act II, Scene 3), Sir Toby Belch, Sir Andrew Aguecheek, and the Clown are carrying on, talking loudly and singing late at night in a room in Countess Olivia's house, when her maid Maria breaks in, crying: "What a *caterwauling* do you keep here!" In *Titus Andronicus* (Act IV, Scene 2), when the nurse, holding the black baby in her arms, cries to the Moor Aaron: " . . . we are all undone. Now help, or woe betide thee evermore!" he replies: "Why, what a *caterwauling* dost thou keep!" *Caterwauling* is a good word to describe the sound of a calliope, or the sound of two bands too near each other in a parade, or the screaming of the young guests at a children's birthday party. There are times when the angry exchanges between nations at the U.N. degenerate into a *caterwauling* of accusation and venom (but better to let off steam than bombs).

cathartine, see **accipitrine**

causerie   (koh zuh REE) *n.* A *causerie* is a chat or, more often, a brief, informal, or light-hearted essay or article on a literary subject or another of the arts. It is a word taken into our language from the French, where, too, it is used to mean a "chat" or "gossip," and in its other use, a "chatty essay," often in the nature of a review. *Causerie* goes back to the French verb *causer* (to chat), and that in turn stems from the Latin verb *causari* (to plead in court), based on *causa* in the sense of "lawsuit." The term originated with the "Causeries de Lundi" ("Monday Chats"), a weekly series of newspaper criticisms during the years 1851 to 1862 by Charles Augustin Sainte-Beuve (1804-1869), the French literary critic and historian. In our own day, the weekly series "On Language" by William Safire in The New York Times Magazine might well qualify as *causeries* and, though not on literature or the arts generally, so might the "Observer" columns of Russell Baker in the same newspaper. A critic friendly to this author has attached the same label to these brief dissertations on words, but that may be stretching a point or a definition.

cavil (KAV ul), *n.*, *vb.* To *cavil* is to carp or quibble, to raise picayune, inconsequential, and usually irritating objections, to offer gratuitous criticisms, to find fault for the sake of finding fault. As a noun, a *cavil* is that sort of annoying trivial objection, a bit of pointless carping, that adds nothing but irritation. In Latin, *cavillari* means to "scoff" or "jeer," the nouns *cavilla* and *cavillatio* mean "raillery," and a *cavillator* is a quibbler; *cavilla gratia cavillae* (like *ars gratia artis*, as it were). In Shakespeare's *Henry IV, Part 1* (Act III, Scene 1) there is a furious argument between Hotspur and Owen Glendower about the division of some land, and Hotspur cries:

> I do not care: I'll give thrice so much land
> To any well-deserving friend;
> But in the way of bargain, mark ye me,
> I'll *cavil* on the ninth part of a hair.

Note *cavil on*; nowadays it's *cavil at* or *cavil about*. The Irish statesman and writer Edmund Burke (1729-1797) condemned "*cavilling* pettifoggers and quibbling pleaders." Lawyers are known to *cavil* tirelessly and endlessly at the terms of an agreement.

cenotaph, see **sarcophagus**

cento (SEN toh) *n. Cento*, adopted from the Latin, which took it from the Greek *kentron* (patchwork), is the technical name for a work, usually a poem, composed by piecing together the writings of earlier writers or poets. On occasion, the meaning of *cento* has been extended to include any conglomeration or string of commonplace phrases and quotations. Sometimes the *cento* is built from the writings of one author in a way that creates a new meaning; sometimes passages from a variety of writers are used. This was a frequent practice in ancient Greece and Rome, after the golden age had passed. The Roman poet Ausonius (c. 310-c. 395), author of travel poems and family sketches, composed a marriage poem from selected verses of Virgil (70-19 B.C.), the foremost of Roman poets. Ausonius actually concocted a set of rules for the composition of *centos*. There were *Homerocentos* made up of passages from the Greek epic poet Homer (eighth century B.C.), the *Cento Virgilianus* using verses from Virgil, and hymns consisting of lines from the *Odes* of the Roman lyric poet Horace (65-8 B.C.). Nobody worried about plagiarism in those days, apparently. In any event, the exploited poets weren't around to do any complaining.

centripetal (sen TRIP ih tul) *adj. Centripetal* describes anything that is being forced inward toward a center or an axis, as opposed to *centrifugal*, describing anything being forced outward, away from a center or axis. The term *centripetal force* denotes a force moving something toward the center or axis around which it is moving, and *centrifugal force* is one directing something away from the center or axis. A boat or a swimmer unfortunate enough to be caught in an eddy would be forced toward the center and tend to be sucked down, while a penny on a turntable would be whirled off by *centrifugal force*. *Centripetal force* directs the movement of eddies and whirlpools. *Centripetal* is derived from New Latin *centripetus* (seeking the center), based on *centri-*, the combining form of Latin *centrum* (center), plus the Latin verb *petere* (to seek). *Centrifugal* uses the Latin verb *fugere* (to flee).

cerebrate   (SER uh brate) *vb*. To *cerebrate* is to use the mind, to think, or, in transitive use, to think about. *Cerebration* (ser uh BRAY shuhn) is the working of the brain. *Unconscious cerebration* is the term used in psychology to describe the reaching of mental results without conscious thoughts. The American novelist Henry James (1843-1915), in *The American*, wrote of "the deep well of *unconscious cerebration*." Both verb and noun are derived from Latin *cerebrum* (brain), which has been taken into English (SER uh brum; suh REE bruhm), to denote the front part of the brain, which controls voluntary movements and coordinates mental activity. In *The Human Comedy*, the American historian James Harvey Robinson (1863-1936) wrote: "Political campaigns are designedly made into emotional orgies which endeavor to distract attention from the real issues involved, and they actually paralyze what slight powers of *cerebration* man can normally muster." Note Robinson's date of death—many years before television served to exacerbate the situation. How timely his words are in this year of our Lord 1986!

cerulean   (suh ROOH lee un) *adj*. *Cerulean* is the color deep blue or azure, derived from Latin *caeruleus* (blue), based on *caelum* (sky). The name "bluestocking" was given, in the mid-18th century, to intellectual, literary women with scholarly interests and ability. According to the Scottish biographer James Boswell (1740-1795) in his *Life of Dr. Johnson*, there were "bluestocking clubs" which met for intellectual and literary enlightenment with leading figures of the London literary scene and were always attended by a Mr. Stillfleet, a leading conversationalist who always wore blue stockings. Some of the women affected them in place of the conventional black silk, thus giving rise to the colloquialism *bluestocking*, later often shortened to *blue*. Jocularly, *blue*, in this sense, came to be referred to as "cerulean," heaping jocularity upon jocularity—good, clean fun among the **literati**—if you can bear it. Nowadays, the term is applied merely as a color, and not too commonly at that.

cervine, see **accipitrine**

cetacean   (sih TAY shun) *n., adj*. A *cetacean* is a member of the Cetacea, an order of marine mammals that includes whales, dolphins, and porpoises; and *cetacean* is the adjective for any of those creatures. *Cetus* or *cetos*, from Greek *ketos*, is Latin for any large creature of the sea, such as whale, dolphin, seal, etc., and is the basis for the zoological order and our noun and adjective. *Cetacean* has been used in a figurative sense to describe mammoth objects, like a huge hill or mountain looming in the distant haze. A hangar of immense proportions will house one of those *cetacean* 747s whose shape suggests the humpbacked whale.

chaffer (CHAF ur) *n.*, *vb.* *Chaffer* is haggling, dickering, hard bargaining, and to *chaffer* is to engage in those activities. Anyone who ventures into a shop in a North African casbah will soon be deeply involved in *chaffer*. *Chaffer* is used as well for "chatter" or "bandying words," quite apart from the element of trading or haggling. It comes from Middle English *chaffare* derived from *chapfare* (trading journey), based on Old English *ceap* (trade, bargain—from which we get *cheap*) plus *faru* or *faran* (journey—from which we get *fare*). According to the author's *British English, A to Zed* (Facts On File, 1987), the British used to use the noun *chapman* for "peddler" (which they spell *pedlar*) and still use *cheapjack* for "hawker" at a fair, and as an adjective for "shoddy" (the kind of goods hawkers at fairs usually offer). The *chap-* in *chapman* and the *cheap-* in *cheapjack* both come from the Old English *ceap* mentioned above.

charadrine, see **accipitrine**

charivari, see **shivaree**

chiaroscuro (kyah ruh SKYOOR oh) *n.* *Chiaroscuro* is the use and effect of gradations of light and shade in a picture, especially when there is a pronounced contrast. *Chiaroscuro* can produce dramatic and emotional effects in the hands of a master like the Dutch painter Rembrandt (1609-1669), whose use of *chiaroscuro* produced a sublime effect. In his masterpiece *The Night Watch*, his genius for the production of space and form through the use of *chiaroscuro* reaches the heights of this technique. *Chiaroscuro* is an Italian word, made up of *chiaro* (light—from Latin *clarus*) and *oscuro* (dark—from Latin *obscurus*). We get *clear* and *obscure* from these Latin words as well. One can speak of the *chiaroscuro* of a scene in nature, like a forest that admits a mottled light, or mountains lit here and there through breaks in the clouds. *Chiaroscuro* has been used figuratively in discussions of literary works, as a term descriptive of the juxtaposition of contrasting moods. In another figurative use, *chiaroscuro* can be employed attributively, meaning "half-hidden, half-revealed," as in a *chiaroscuro explanation* or *report*, full of half-truths, with gradations of revelation and concealment.

chiliast, see **millenarian**

ch(e)irognomy (kih ROG nuh mee) *n.* Without stopping to discuss old familiars based on the Greek noun *cheir* (hand), like *chiropody* (*-ist*) or *chiropractic* (*-tor*), there is a group of less common *chiro-* words (the *e* is normally omitted in America, as opposed to the practice in Britain) to which we may direct our attention. *Chirognomy*, adding Greek *gnome* (understanding) is palmistry. *Chirography* (kih ROG ruh fee), drawing on the Greek verb *graphein* (to write), is handwriting or penmanship, and a *chirographist* is a handwriting expert, the type important in authenticating documents and revealing forgeries. *Chiromancy* (KIH ruh man see), using the Greek noun *manteia* (**divination**), is another word for palmistry, foretelling the future by studying the hand, often practiced in a tent by a lady in multicolored garments.

chirography, see **ch(e)irognomy**

chiromancy, see **ch(e)irognomy**

choler (KOL ur) *n. Choler* is anger, irascibility, hotheadedness, irritability, and a person exhibiting these unhappy traits is said to be *choleric* (KOL ur ik or kuh LER ik). In Middle English and Middle Latin, *choler* was *colera*, and that, via Latin *cholera*, came from Greek *cholera*, which was the name of various intestinal diseases endemic in the Far East and all too often epidemic in other parts of the world. In Shakespeare's *King Richard II* (Act I, Scene 1), Bolingbroke and Mowbray are having a furious row in the presence of the monarch, and Richard says:

> Wrath-kindled gentlemen, be rul'd by me,
> Let's purge the *choler* without letting blood.

The English essayist Joseph Addison (1672-1719), writing in *The Spectator*, has this to say: "A reader seldom peruses a book with pleasure until he knows whether the writer of it be a black man or a fair man, of a mild or *choleric* disposition, married or a bachelor." (A strange observation; it certainly doesn't hold true today!) The Swiss poet and Theologian Johann Kaspar Lavater (1741-1801), in his *Aphorisms on Man*, wrote: "Venerate four characters: the sanguine who has checked volatility and the rage for pleasure; the *choleric* who has subdued passion and pride; the phlegmatic emerged from indolence; and the melancholy who has dismissed avarice, suspicion and asperity."

chrestomathy (kres TOM uh thee) *n.* A *chrestomathy* is a book containing a collection of selected passages, usually from the works of a single author, especially in a foreign language, for use in teaching and learning that language. They are in common use in high school and college foreign language courses. The word comes from Greek *krestomatheia*, based on *krestos* (useful) plus *math-*, a variant stem of *manthanein* (to learn). *Chrestomathies* based on the works of the French poet and fabulist La Fontaine (1621-1695) and the German poet, novelist, and dramatist Goethe (1749-1832) were used during this author's schooldays.

chthonic, **chthonian**, see **gnome**

cicerone   (sis uh RONE ee, chee chuh-) *n*. A *cicerone* is a guide, especially the type that points out and explains to visitors the antiquities and history of a site. These guides are named after the Roman orator, statesman, and writer Cicero (106-43 B.C.) on the theory that a good, knowledgeable guide should have the information, education, and eloquence of a Cicero. One can hardly visit certain famous spots (the Pyramids, the Roman Forum, Fontainebleau, Pompeii) without being importuned by a host of *cicerones* (or *ciceroni*) who would be delighted, for a consideration, to show you around and tell you rather more than you wanted to know about the lore and curiosities of the place. But there are very good *cicerones* too, who do know their stuff and can really enlighten the visitor. Who can ever forget the *cicerone* of Italian origin at Fontainebleau, an ardent admirer of Louis XIV, who pointed to the fourteen busts of Louis in the Hall of Mirrors and explained that they served the purpose of supporting the king's wigs. "Dat-a Looie, he's-a change-a da wig-a fourteen-a times a day; dat-a Looie, he was-a some-a boy!" That was more dramatic than anything else this author had ever heard about Looie.

ciconi(i)ne, see **accipitrine**

Cimmerian   (sih MEER ee un) *adj. Cimmerian* is a poetic word for "dark and gloomy." In *The Odyssey* (XI, 14), Homer tells of the *Cimmerians*, a people that lived in everlasting night in a land "beyond the ocean stream" where the sun never shines. In *L'Allegro*, the English poet John Milton (1608-1674) writes of the "dark *Cimmerian* desert" where he bids loath'd Melancholy to "ever dwell." Before Milton was born, the poet Edmund Spenser (c. 1552-1599) mentioned the "Cimmerian shades" in *Virgil's Gnat*. Because of the classical myth about a *Cimmerian* people dwelling in perpetual night, their name became a symbol of darkness and gloom, and the adjective has been used in the sense of "gloomy, intensely dark, cavernous" by later writers. There was an actual Cimmerian people, who dwelt on the shores of the Black Sea in southern Russia and gave their name to Crimea. They were driven out by invaders in the 8th century and scattered, but have left us the legacy of their name, evocative of deep, eternal, cavernous gloom and darkness.

cisalpine   (sis AL pine, -pin) *adj*. This adjective, like the others discussed below, was derived from one concocted by the ancient Romans from their point of view, which was exceedingly self-centered at the height of their imperial power. *Cis* is a Latin preposition meaning "on this side of," so that *cisalpinus* described anything on "this" (the Roman, naturally) side of the Alps, i.e., the southern side, and that gave us *cisalpine*. (*Cis Tibernum* means "on this side of the Tiber," *cis Rhenum* "on this side of the Rhine," the adjective *cisrhenanus* means that as well, and so on, always from the viewer's, speaker's, or writer's point of view.) *Cisatlanticus*, which gave us *cisatlantic*, applies to anything on "this" side of that ocean, depending on which way you're looking, and *cismontanus* gave us *cismontane*, describing what's on "this" side of whatever mountains are being referred to, and in Roman times, that almost always had to do with the Alps. Likewise, the Romans used their preposition *trans* (across, to the other side of) in the formation of *transalpinus* (beyond the Alps), *transmarinus* (beyond the ocean, overseas), and *transalpine*, *transmarine* and *transmontane*, the last of these existing also in the variant form *tramontane* (the Romans didn't like three-consonant combinations). *Tra(ns)montanus* (on the other side of the mountains) eventually acquired the meaning "foreign," and not surprisingly, that came to have the effect of "barbarous" as well. *Tra(ns)montanus* was used as a noun meaning "alien," and, where xenophobia exists (and where doesn't it?), that means "barbarian." For centuries, white people were known as "white devils" in China. *Ultra* is another Latin preposition meaning "beyond, on the far side of," and that combined to form the Middle Latin adjectives *ultramarinus* (beyond the sea), which gave us *ultramarine*, and *ultramontanus* (beyond the mountains), which gave us *ultramontane*. *Ultramarine* happens also to be used as a noun for a pigment originally made of powdered lapis lazuli and later certain other substances, and is also used as an adjective for "deep blue," probably using Latin *ultra* in the sense of "more than," i.e., deeper even than the blue of the sea. (This is only a guess.) Summarizing: *cisalpine* (this side of the Alps); *transalpine* (the other side of the Alps); *cisatlantic* (this side of the Atlantic): *cismontane* (this side of the mountains); *transmontane* and *ultramontane* (the other side of the mountains—what the bear saw when he went over the mountain?); *transmarine* and *ultramarine* (the other side of the ocean). *Transatlantic*, a familiar word, has come to describe anything not only on the other side of the Atlantic, but anything crossing or reaching across that body of water, like fame, success, an idiom, custom, or other cross-cultural aspect of life.

cisatlantic, see **cisalpine**

cismontane, see **cisalpine**

clabber, see **bonnyclabber**

clamant (KLAY munt) *adj.* This adjective, derived from Latin *clamans*, the present participle of the verb *clamare* (to cry out), is synonymous with *clamorous* (KLAM ur us) in the sense of "noisy," but has the additional meanings of "urgent, pressing, insistent." Noisy, vociferous people can be described as *clamant*, but one may speak also of the *clamant* needs of the people, like those millions suffering in many parts of Africa today (1986). *Clamant* is a literary word, as is its noun *clamancy* (KLAY mun see), meaning "urgency."

clerihew (KLER ih hyooh) *n.* E. Clerihew Bentley (1875-1956), an English writer, invented a verse form consisting of a comic, usually nonsensical jingle composed of two rhyming couplets, with lines of unequal length and a complete disregard for meter. The first line is or contains the name of a notable person; the rest of the jingle tells a ludicrous tale about him, purporting, in a fanciful and often satirical way, to present the essence of his life and character. The first of these appeared in Clerihew's *Biography for Beginners*, published in 1905, and they came to be known as *clerihews*, with a lower case *c*. Two of his own favorites were:

> It was a weakness of Voltaire's
> To forget to say his prayers,
> And one which, to his shame,
>   He never overcame.

> Sir Christopher Wren
> Said "I'm going to dine with some men.
> If anyone calls,
> Say "I'm designing St. Paul's."

Here are some more:

> Henry Ford
> Has a secret hoard
> To which he adds a dime
> From time to time.

> It only irritated Brahms
> To be tickled under the arms.
> What really helped him to compose
> Was to be stroked on the nose.

> George the Third
> Ought never to have occurred.
> One can only wonder
> At so grotesque a blunder.

Others have attempted the form. A friend of the author, a specialist in difficult rhymes, came up with:

> Gilbert Keith Chesterton
> Weighs, it must be confessed, a ton.
> Too much grub,
> That's the rub.

>   —Stephen Barr, Woodstock, N.Y.

And here is an anonymous one:

> Johann Sebastian Bach
> Was fond of sighing "Ach!"
> Instead of saying "Guten Morgen"
> He'd play his Toccata and Fugue on the organ.

cleromancy, see **divination**

cloaca (kloh AY kuh) *n.* A *cloaca* is a sewer; the use of the word, taken over intact from the Latin, implies that an ancient sewer is involved. Another meaning, though rare, is "privy," and in zoology, *cloaca* is the name of the common chamber or cavity into which the intestinal, urinary, and generative canals discharge in birds, reptiles, some fish and other animals. The adjective is *cloacal* (kloh AY kul). In ancient Rome, the main sewer was known as the *Cloaca Maxima*, constructed to drain marshland at the foot of the Capitoline and Palatine hills. *Cloacina* (kloh uh SYE nuh) was the Roman goddess of sewers (sewers had gods too!). The English dramatist and poet John Gay (1685-1732), remembered today chiefly for *The Beggar's Opera*, wrote satirical mock pastorals, including *Trivia* (1716) making fun of London life. In *Trivia* we find these lines:

> Then Cloacina, goddess of the tide,
> Whose sable streams beneath the city glide,
> Indulged the modish flame: the town she roved,
> A mortal scavenger she saw, she loved.

Sable streams is pretty romantic descriptive poetry for what's involved!

clodpoll (KLOD pole), also **clodpole** and **clodpate**, *n.* All these variants mean the same thing: "blockhead, oaf, lout." A *clodhopper* is a peasant, boor, or bumpkin, though the usual meaning of the plural, *clodhoppers*, is a "pair of stout, sturdy, heavy shoes," the type you expect a *clodhopper* to wear. The first syllable, *clod-*, is itself a word: a *clod* is a lump, usually of earth or clay, and pejoratively, *clod* on its own can mean "blockhead." Its derivation is from Middle English *clodde*, and the word is related to *clot*, familiar from medical usage, but also with the primary meaning of "lump." In Britain, *clot* is a strong slang pejorative for "fool" or "jerk." ("She's suffering from marital thrombosis," quipped the English doctor, "having a *clot* for a husband." Mild British humor.) Shakespeare used *clodpole* in *Twelfth Night* (Act III, Scene 4), when Sir Toby Belch refuses to deliver Sir Andrew Aguecheek's letter challenging the supposed page to a duel, saying that the letter, "being so excellently ignorant, will breed no terror in the youth; he will find it comes from a *clodpole*." In *King Lear* (Act I, Scene 4), we find the form *clotpoll* (the Elizabethans were fairly relaxed about spelling) when he wants to hear from the exiting Oswald and says to one of his knights: "Call the *clotpoll* back." *Clodpoll* is a word that somehow, though not onomatopoeic, sounds like what it means, and is applicable, alas, to a fair number of people in the world—some of them in high places. (But please, no political discussion.)

cloistered (KLOY sturd) *adj.* A *cloistered* life is a sheltered, secluded one, far from the madding crowd. This adjective comes from the noun *cloister* (KLOY stur), the name for a place of religious seclusion, like a convent or a monastery, and in extreme cases, an **eremite's** cave, although the term has on occasion been used figuratively to include any secluded, out-of-the-way place of refuge. *Cloister* was *cloistre* in Middle English, derived from the Latin *claustrum* (barrier), which came to mean "enclosed place" in Middle Latin. Another Latin word for "enclosed place" is *clausum*, the neuter form of *clausus*, past participle of *claudere* (to shut, close). Though *cloistered* is based upon *cloister*, one does not have to dwell in a *cloister* (in its literal sense) to lead a *cloistered* life. Those fortunate enough to enjoy the serenity of the countryside, away from the hurly-burly of the crowded city, can claim the joys of a *cloistered* existence. Other participants in a *cloistered* life are ivory-tower academics and poor little rich girls, and we may as well include lighthousekeepers and oil-rig workers.

clowder (CLOU dur) *n.* A *clowder* is a group of cats. In the case of collective nouns generally (a *pride* of lions, an *exaltation* of skylarks, a *pod* of whales), the word for *group* or *collection* is followed by the name of the creature—fish, flesh, fowl, or insect. *Clowder* is an exception, in that the word by itself designates the animal in question. *Clowder* is thought to be a variant of *clutter*, utilized for this special purpose. It somehow sounds pejorative—an aspersion on that most noble of creatures (other than man?)—the cat. Perhaps on the streets of Venice, or in the Coliseum of Rome, where the cats roam about scrounging for food, a mass of them appear as a clutter, but that's not their fault. In a home, where they're cherished, they don't make a clutter, but a graceful and decorative group. *Clowder*, indeed!

clyster   (KLIS tur) *n.* A *clyster* is an enema, a liquid injected into the intestines for flushing them out. *Clyster* comes from the Greek noun *klyster*, based on the verb *klyzein* (to rinse out). A related noun is *clisis* (CLYE sis), a general medical term for the washing out of any bodily cavity. A *clyster-pipe* is a nozzle for introducing the enema into the body—not a particularly attractive bit of apparatus. In Shakespeare's *Othello* (Act II, Scene 1), the evil Iago, jealous of Cassio because Othello promoted him to be lieutenant rather than Iago, plans revenge by planting into Othello's head the belief that Cassio and Desdemona, Othello's wife, are lovers. When Cassio innocently takes Desdemona's hand during a conversation, Iago mutters, in an aside: "He takes her by the palm . . . it had been better you had not kissed your three fingers so oft . . .Yet again, your fingers to your lips? Would they were *clyster-pipes* for your sake!" Shakespeare could hardly have chosen a nastier image to portray Iago's detestable character!

cockatrice, see **basilisk**

coetaneous see **coeval**

coeval (koh EE vul) *n., adj.* As an adjective, *coeval* means "of the same age or duration" or "contemporary"; as a noun, a *coeval* is a contemporary. Another adjective, *coetaneous* (koh ih TAY nee us), is synonymous with *coeval*. Both stem from Latin; the prefix *co-* is a shortened form of *com-* (with, together) used before vowels. *Coeval* comes from Late Latin *coaevus*, based on *co-* plus Latin *aevum* (age). *Coetaneous* is from Latin *coataneus*, based on *co-* plus *aetas* (age). The American Civil War began on April 12, 1861, and ended on April 9, 1865; Abraham Lincoln died on April 15, 1865. Thus it can be said that the Civil War was practically *coeval* with the last four years of Lincoln's life. In the substantive sense, *coevals* can apply to two persons of unequal age, but who were alive at the same time—i.e., contemporaries. The Italian artists Michelangelo (1475-1564) and Da Vinci (1452-1519) can therefore be designated *coevals*, despite the difference in their actual ages. This is not a common use; they would more likely be described as "contemporaries". And it might be best to avoid the danger that *coevals* be misunderstood as "co-villains" (perish the thought!).

cognate, see **agnate**

cognomen, see **agnomen**

cognoscenti (kon yuh SHEN tee, kog nuh-) *n. pl.* The *cognoscenti* are those having special knowledge, the connoisseurs of the arts. The singular, rarely used, is *cognoscente* (same pronunciation as the plural). *Conoscente* (without the *g*) is the present participle of the Italian verb *conoscere* (to know), but the Italians went back to the original Latin *cognoscere*, inserting the *g* and producing the -yuh- sound. Bach fugues appeal principally to the *cognoscenti*. Abstract painting and contemporary music are the special province of the *cognoscenti*. At the **vernissages** of art exhibitions, you will meet the *cognoscenti* en masse. The term would not be applied to those well versed in the history and statistics of the various sports but unfamiliar with what's going on in twelve-tone music or retrospectives of Kandinsky, Arp & Co.

collective noun; **noun of multitude**; **noun of assembly**. These three mean the same thing: a noun, singular in form, but denoting a collection of persons, animals, or things, for example: an army, a crew, a herd, a family, a jury, a committee, a series. Such a noun can take a singular verb or a plural, depending on whether it implies a single entity or its individual components, thus: my family *is* my inspiration; my family *are* all tall. Some such nouns are quite familiar: a *pride* of lions; some rather exotic: an *exaltation* of skylarks. There is a legend about four dons who met at a pub once a month to report on any new specimens that might have come their way, like a *cloud* of WASPS (an *Aristophanes* of WASPS, perhaps, or even an *Aristophanes* of *Clouds*—or are we going too far?), a *plague* of Frogs (on a day's trip to Channel ports from Calais), a *Fauré* of warlike 19th century French composers? Well, while the dons were downing their first beers, three ladies of the evening happened to stroll in. "What about them?" asked one of the boys. "A trey (tray) of tarts?" ventured one of them. "A volume of Trollope's?" suggested the second. "Or a flourish of strumpets?" proffered the third. But "an anthology of pro's" put an end to the contest. See also **paronomasia**.

collocutor   (KOL uh kyooh tur) *n.* A *collocutor* is a person who participates in a conversation. Thus, the expression *my collocutor* means "the person talking to me." Fowler, in the section on PRONUNCIATION under the heading "French Words," tells us not to try to pronounce a French word in the middle of an English sentence as a Frenchman would in a French sentence. He says: "It is a feat that should not be attempted. The greater its success as a *tour de force*, the greater its failure as a step in the conversational progress; for your *collocutor*, aware that he could not have done it himself, has his attention distracted whether he admires or is humiliated." We are more familiar with the noun *colloquy* (KOL uh kwee), meaning "conversation, conversational exchange, dialogue," which can also be used in the sense of "conference." There is also the noun *colloquium* (kuh LOH kwee um) for an informal group discussion. The adjective *colloquial* (kuh LOH kwee ul) is used of informal speech or writing, and the noun *colloquialism* (kuh LOH kwee ul iz um) applies to a word or phrase used *colloquially*. *Collocutor* is less frequently met with. All these words go back to the Latin verb *loqui* (to talk), its past participle *locutus* (cf. *elocution, circumlocution,* etc.), and the prefix *con-* (together, with), which built *colloqui* (to converse) and its past participle *collocutus*.

colophon (KOL uh fon, -fun) *n.* A *colophon* is a publisher's logo or house device or imprint, like the check mark in a square on the title page of the Facts On File edition of this book. Originally, the *colophon* was a notation appearing not at the front, but at the end of a book or manuscript, setting forth the title or subject, the name of the author, the printer's name and the date and place of printing and publication, sometimes with a bit of sales talk in praise of the work. *Colophon* was taken from the Greek noun *kolophon* (summit, finishing touch). In addition, there is a legend about the horsemen of *Kolophon*, an ancient city in Asia Minor, one of the 12 in Ionia. It was famed for its cavalry, according to this version, who had the reputation for turning the tide of battle and gaining victory in war by their last charge; hence the word *kolophon* for what used to appear at the very end of the book—the finishing touch. The old idiom *add a colophon* meant "give a final stroke" and *from title-page to colophon* is a British expression for "from cover to cover."

colubrine, see **accipitrine**

columbarium (kol um BAR ee um) *n.* A *columbarium* is a burial vault with niches for the placing of cinerary urns, i.e., vessels containing the ashes of the dead. Another wholly distinct and rather more cheerful meaning is "columbary" (KOL um ber ee), which is a synonym for "dovecote." Both *columbarium* and *columbary* come from Latin *columba* (dove), and the rather strange coupling of these quite distinct structures under one label has to do with the similarity of cellular construction typical of both, with all those pigeonholes, as it were, or should they be called "doveholes"?

columbine, see **accipitrine**

comestible (kuh MES tuh bul) adj. *Comestible* means "edible," and in the plural it is used as a noun meaning "food" generally. Late Latin produced the adjective *comestibilis*, based on Latin *comestus*, past participle of *comedere* or *comesse* (to consume, eat up—the Latin infinitive had both forms). *Esculent* is another adjective for "edible," and as a noun, embraces anything edible, but appears to apply especially to vegetables. *Esculent* is derived from Latin *esculentus* (edible), based on *esca* (food), related to the verb *edere* or *esse* (to eat—again, both forms were used), the verb that gave rise to *comedere/comesse*, from which we got *comestible*. Thus, we see the etymological relationship between *comestible* and what at first seems to be a wholly different word, *esculent*, a synonym. It is more likely that you will meet up with *comestible* than run across *esculent*, but as far as your health is concerned, you needn't worry; you can eat (subject to your particular diet restriction) anything *comestible* or *esculent*.

comity (KOM ih tee) *n. Comity* is mutual civility, friendliness, and consideration. *Comity* between labor and management is essential for the success of a commercial enterprise. Our country could not have prospered or even continued to exist without *comity* among the colonies and then the states. This word is derived from the Latin noun *comitas* (courtesy, friendliness), based on the adjective *comis* (kind, courteous). In international law, the term *comity of nations* (*comitas gentium*, in New Latin) signifies international courtesy, more specifically, a nonmandatory, informal code to which the courts of a country defer in determining questions involving the interests of another country, and effect is given to the laws of one country within the territory of another.

commensal (kuh MEN sul) *n., adj.* Literally, this adjective describes people eating together at the same table. *Mensa* is *table* in Latin, and one of the meanings of our adjective **mensal** (different from the one discussed under **hedomedal**) is "relating to the table" or "used at table." The Middle Latin adjective *commensalis* led to our *commensal*. When it is used of animals or plants, *commensal* describes types living together, or a type living on or in another, without harm to either. In sociology, *commensal* describes any individual or social group living in the same area as another person or group of a different social order and having different customs, without opposition or territorial or other competition with each other. Used as a noun, *commensal* is a synonym for *messmate*. In the plant and animal world, *commensals* live without parasitism, in a type of partnership not quite so intimate as symbiosis, a mutually beneficial relationship.

commination (kom uh NAY shun) *n. Commination* is the denunciation and threat of punishment, especially of sinners, through divine vengeance ("Vengeance is mine, etc."), and any such threat is described as *comminatory* (kuh MIN uh tor ee; KOM uh-). In ecclesiastical parlance, *commination* is the recital of God's threats against sinners, read in the Anglican liturgy on the first day of Lent, Ash Wednesday, which got its name from the Roman Catholic ritual of sprinkling on penitents' heads the ashes of burnt palms from Palm Sunday, the Sunday before Easter. The Latin source is *comminatio*, from *comminatus*, past participle of *comminari*, based on the intensive prefix *com-* plus *miniari* (to threaten). To *comminate* (KOM in ate) is to threaten; a verb not to be confused with **comminute**, an entirely different affair.

comminute (KOM uh nooht, -nyooht) *vb.* To *comminute* is to crush, pulverize, reduce to *minute* particles; from Latin *comminutus*, past participle of *comminuere* (to break into pieces), based on intensive prefix *com-* plus *minuere* (to lessen), related to our words *minus* and *diminish*, and to Latin *minor* (less). A synonym of *comminute* is *triturate* (TRIT uh rate), from Late Latin *trituratus*, past participle of *triturare* (to thresh). The worst kind of bone break is a *comminuted fracture*, in which the separated parts are broken into small fragments. *Comminute* has nothing in common with *comminate*, a wholly different kettle of fish, both as to meaning and derivation.

compendious (kom PEND ee us) *adj.* A *compendious* treatment of a subject is a concise one. The noun *compendium* (com PEND ee um) denotes a brief survey, a concise treatment, an abridgement or summary, usually of a broad subject, as in a *compendium of astronomy*, or a *compendious treatise on modern physics*. For some reason, *compendium* and *compendious* seem to evoke, erroneously, the image of a fully detailed extensive treatment. On the contrary, they stress the concept of conciseness and abridgement. *Compendious* comes from the Latin *compendiosus* (brief). *Compendium* was taken as is from the Latin, where it means "shortening" or "abbreviation," and was based on the familiar prefix *con-* (together, with) plus *pend-*, the stem of the verb *pendere* (to weigh, consider). "Weighing together," by transference, came to mean "shortening." Language development never ceases to surprise.

compotation (kom puh TAY shun) *n. Potation* (poh TAY shun) is the act of drinking, or the drink itself, particularly an intoxicating quaff. It is from Latin *potatio* (a drinking), based on *potatus*, the past participle of *potare* (to drink). *Compotation* is the act of drinking in company with another or others, and here, too, the implication is that of imbibing intoxicating beverages, or group tippling. The Latin prefix *com-* (with, together—as in *combine*, *commingle*, etc.) plus *potatio* gave us *compotation*. In classical Greece it was customary among the upper classes to have an after-dinner party for drinking and conversation, known as a *symposion*, a word formed of the Greek prefix *syn-* (with, together—as in *syndrome*, *synergy*, etc.) plus *posis* (a drinking). *Compotation*, then, was a direct Latin translation of the Greek *symposion*, which became *symposium* in Latin, and later, by extension, acquired its modern meaning.

conation (koh NAY shun) *n. Conation* is the area of one's active mentality that has to do with desire, volition, and striving. The related word *conatus* (koh NAY tus) is the resulting effort or striving itself, or the natural tendency or force in one's mental makeup that produces an effort. *Conative* (KOHN uh tiv) is the term in psychology that describes anything relating to *conation*. All these words come from Latin *conatus*, past participle of the verb *conari* (to try). The Scottish philosopher Sir William Hamilton (1788-1856) considered *conation* to be one of the three divisions of the mind, the one that included desire and volition, the other two being cognition (perception, awareness) and feeling. The English theologian and philosopher William Paley (1743-1805) asked: "What *conatus* could give prickles to the porcupine or hedgehog, or to the sheep its fleece?" *Conation* differs from **velleity** (the wish without the effort).

concatenation (kon kat uh NAY shun) *n.* A *concatenation* of events is a chain or series of happenings leading, usually, to a denouement or outcome. The implication from the use of *concatenation* is that the outcome or result was interesting or dramatic or in some way significant, and that the events in the *concatenation* were in themselves fortuitous and connected chronologically rather than logically. The alarm clock failed to go off, he missed his usual train, he took a later one, he took the only seat which happened to be next to the only girl in the world, and they lived happily ever after. "In the beginning, God created the heaven and the earth . . . So God created man in his own image." No *concatenation* there; it just happened that way. There are those who differ, and ascribe the existence of the universe and the development of man to an extremely long and complicated *concatenation*. There is a verb *concatenate* (kon KAT uh nate), to link together in a series, but it is rarely met with. It comes from Late *concatenatus*, past participle of *concatenare*, based on Latin prefix *con-* (together) plus *catena* (chain). *Concatenation* is from Late Latin *concatenatio*. It was a *concatenation* of statesmen's stupid errors that led to the First World War. Ditto the Second World War. Go back over your own biography and you will discover that it is a *concatenation* of events from beginning to today. Did your grandparents (and how did they meet?) arrange your parents' marriage, or did your mummy and daddy meet in a singles bar? Etc.

concinnity (kun SIN i tee). To *concinnate* (KON suh nate) is to fit or blend elements together so skillfully and appropriately that they form a harmonious and elegant whole. The verb is derived from Latin *concinnatus*, past participle of *concinnare* (to arrange or put together with care), based on prefix *con-* (together) plus *cinnare*, related to the adjective *concinnus* (well put together, pleasing because of harmony and proportion) and the noun *concinnitas* (elegance, harmony of style). Latin *cinnus* is a mixed drink (cocktail?). *Con-*

cinnity is a term used in rhetoric to denote close harmony of tone, and, in context, of logic in discourse. *Concinnous* (kun SIN us) means "elegant, harmonious as to style." In his *Diaries 1920-1922* (Faber, London, 1981), the English poet and novelist Siegfried Sassoon (1886-1967) discusses the clavichord:

> The diminutive remoteness of the clavichord makes one realise [British spelling] how crude one's auditory palate is. The problem is how to be exquisite without lapsing into preciosity. *Concinnity* is a quality which can be acquired by collocution with a clavichord . . . The clavichord belongs to the Ultima Thule of acoustics. The notes evoke hyperphysical sweetness and sensitivity . . . Orpheus might have made such music at a special recital for glow-worms [British spelling again] and tiny moonlight-coloured [more British spelling] moths.

Phew! This passage is followed by a Sassoon poem entitled *Clavichord Recital* that starts:

> Mute were the neighboring nightingales
> When Orpheus touched his clavichord . . .

Concinnity showed up a year earlier in *"Shakespeare" Identified* (Duell, Sloan & Pearce, New York, 1920) by J. Thomas Looney (pronounced LONEY), who "identified" Shakespeare with Edward de Vere, 17th Earl of Oxford (1550-1604, a courtier at the court of Queen Elizabeth I and a lyric poet known as Lord Bulbeck—pronounced BOOL bek—until 1562) believed by the so-called Oxfordian school to have written Shakespeare's dramas. This belief was based on an appreciation of the style of de Vere's lyric poetry:

> If to these qualities we add an intense sensibility to all kinds of external impressions, and a faculty of passionate response, brought to the service of clear, intellectual perceptions, we shall have seized hold of the outstanding features of de Vere's mentality. The result is the production of poems which impress the mind with a sense of their unity. The ideas cohere, following one another in a natural sequence, and leave in the reader's mind a sense of completeness and artistic finish. That this *concinnity* is characteristic of Shakespeare's mind and work needs no insisting on at the present day.

(All of the foregoing to the contrary notwithstanding, this author agrees with the American scholar and biographer Marchette Chute [b. 1909; *Shakespeare of London*, E.F. Dutton, New York, 1957] that Shakespeare's plays were written by Mr. Shakespeare.)

concupiscence   (kon KYOOH pih suns) *n. Concupiscence* is ardent sexual desire, in any degree from sensuous longing to raw lust. The adjective is *concupiscent* (con KYOOH pih sunt). These words stem from Late Latin *concupiscentia*, formed from the Latin verb *concupiscere* (to desire ardently, covet), based in turn on the prefix *con-* (used as an intensive with the force of "completely"), plus *cupere* (to desire). A related adjective, *concupiscible* (con KYOOH pih suh bul), from Late Latin *concupiscibilis*, formerly meant "desirable," but Shakespeare used it in the sense of "lecherous"—active rather than passive in the lust department—in *Measure for Measure* (Act V, Scene 1), when Isabella tells Duke Vincentio the truth about his faithless deputy Angelo:

> . . .the vile conclusion
> I now begin with grief and shame to utter:
> He would not, but by gift of my chaste body
> To his *concupiscible* intemperate lust
> Release my brother . . .

condign (kon DINE) *adj.* This adjective is used chiefly in the expression *condign punishment*, where it means "fitting, proper, adequate, well-deserved." It comes from Latin *condignus* (very worthy). Originally, *condign* could apply to many situations, including those involving praise as well as punishment. Shakespeare used it that way in *Loves Labour's Lost* (Act I, Scene 2), in an amusing colloquy between the "fantastical" Spaniard Armado and his page, Moth, whom he praised as "pretty, and apt." Moth asks, "Speak you this in my praise, master?" and Armado answers, "In thy *condign* praise." Its application is now virtually confined to *punishment*, or, in the proper context, *fate, suffering,* and the like. *Condign* punishment is deservedly severe; it must be severe as well as deservedly so. This, of course, is just what the English poet and dramatist W.S. Gilbert (1836-1919, the "Gilbert" of Gilbert and Sullivan) had in mind when he wrote, in *The Mikado*:

> My object all sublime
> I shall achieve in time—
> To let the punishment fit the crime—
> The punishment fit the crime . . .

and what was earlier intended in *Exodus* 21, 23-25:

> . . . life for life,
> Eye for eye, tooth for tooth, hand for hand, foot for foot,
> Burning for burning, wound for wound, stripe for stripe . . .

In Roman times, this primitive penal system was known as *Lex Talionis*, the Law of Retaliation (note the *-tal-*), or in simpler terms, *tit for tat*. *Talio* is Latin for "retaliation" and is the basis for the rarely met word *talion*. Getting back to "life for life": capital punishment has much gone out of style, at least in many parts of the civilized world, though in some parts it's rearing its ugly *caput* again. And the Ayatollah Khomeini's interpretation of *condign*, whatever the word is in Iranian, is something else again, what with stoning, the cutting off of hands, and other delectable arrangements. Incidentally, stay off the booze in Saudi Arabia.

condottiere, see **grisaille**

congener   (KON juh nur) *n*. A person, animal, or thing of the same kind or nature as another is a *congener* of that other. In the world of flora and fauna, a *congener* is a member of the same genus as another. The goldfinch is a *congener* of the canary. The American elk is a *congener* of the European red deer. In both cases, one might add "and vice versa," of course. The adjectives are *congenerous* (kon JEN ur us) and *congeneric* (kon juh NER ik); also *congenetic* (kon juh NET ik), meaning "having a common origin." All these words are derived from the Latin prefix *con-* (with) plus *genus* (kind). Persons alike in nature, character, conduct, or action may be described as *congeners*. Napoleon Bonaparte (1769-1821) and Alexander the Great (356-323 B.C.), in their generalship and insatiable thirst for conquest, were *congeners*.

congeries   (kon JEER eez, kun JIR eez) *n*. Fowler says most dictionaries favor the pronunciation "kon JER ih eez"—four syllables—but later on, makes the following comment about words ending in *-ies*:

> **-ies, -ein.** Until recently the dictionaries prescribed a disyllabic pronunciation of *-ies* for words of Latin origin such as *series*, *species*, *rabies*, *caries*, *scabies*. But in fact few doctors pronounce the second syllable of *rabies* and *caries* differently from that of *herpes*, and almost everyone takes the same liberty with *series* and *species*. It is better to bow to the inevitable than to persist in a vain attempt to preserve what we suppose to have been the way the Romans pronounced these words, and the dictionaries now recognize *eez* for most of them, if only as alternatives.
>
> Words ending *ein(e)* (*protein, caffeine, codeine*) are rebelling in the same way, even though they are less commonly used; *een* is likely to establish itself; modern life is too hurried for these niceties.

A *congeries* is a disordered heap of things, a collection or aggregation piled together any old way. There can be a *congeries* of concrete objects, like documents, boxes, objets d'art, or a *congeries* of nonmaterial things, like ideas, concepts, thoughts, theories. As we walk along a beach, looking down, we see a *congeries* of pebbles and shells of all sizes. From a great height, a settlement or a parking lot looks like a *congeries* of little packages or boxes. A visit to a children's playroom usually confronts one with a *congeries* of playthings. An accused person often splutters a *congeries* of unconvincing explanations and excuses. The word was taken over intact from Latin, where it means "heap, mass, pile, accumulation," and is related to the verb *congerere* (to collect, bring together), from whose past participle, *congestus*, we get our noun *congestion* and adjective *congested*. *Congeries* doesn't change in the plural, so that an erroneous singular, *congerie* or *congery* (usually pronounced KON juh ree), has been concocted and must be avoided. This is as good a place as any to remember that *kudos*, from Greek *kydos* (praise, honor, glory), is singular, and there is no such thing as one kudo, or for that matter, one mump or one measle.

conglobate (kon GLOH bate, KONG-) *adj., vb. Conglobate*, as an adjective, describes anything formed into a ball, like a lump of clay or a pat of butter. As a verb, transitive or intransitive, to *conglobate* is to form into a ball or sphere. A variant of the verb is *conglobe* (kon GLOBE), which comes from the Latin prefix *con-* (together) plus *globus* (ball, sphere—from which we get our noun *globe*). *Conglobate* is from Latin *conglobatus*, past participle of *conglobare* (form into a ball or sphere). The Latin noun *conglobatio* has a more abstract meaning: "crowding together." We are more familiar with our word *conglomerate* (*n.*, *adj.*—kon GLOM ur it; *vb.*—kon GLOM uh rate), derived from Latin *con-* plus *glomus* (ball of yarn). The English novelist Virginia Woolf (1882-1941), in Volume V of her *Diary*, says that she keeps it for a "run of her pen," a "scribble." It is her "running ground," her "fidget ground." "I wish," she writes, "I could *conglobulate* thoughts like Gide [the French novelist and essayist (1869-1951)]." Mrs. Woolf either slipped into *conglobulate* as an echo of *conglomerate*, or casually invented it—and made a better-sounding word.

connubial (kuh NYOOH bee ul, -NOOH) *adj. Connubial* love or discord is that between spouses; *connubial* means "matrimonial" or "conjugal," describing anything relating to matrimony. It comes from Latin *conubialis*, based on *conubium* (marriage, wedlock). The English poet Lord Byron (1788-1824) wrote, in *Don Juan*:

> Romances paint at full length people's wooings,
>   But only give a bust of marriages;
> For no one cares for matrimonial cooings,
>   There's nothing wrong in a *connubial* kiss:
> Think you, If Laura had been Petrarch's wife,
> He would have written sonnets all his life?

In *Paradise Lost*, the English poet John Milton (1608-1674) wrote of Adam and Eve:

>   Into their inmost bower
> Handed they went; and eas'd the putting off
> These troublesome disguises which we wear,
> Strait side by side were laid, nor turned I ween
> Adam from his fair spouse, nor Eve the rites
> Mysterious of *connubial* love refused . . .

The English novelist Charles Dickens (1812-1870), in *Pickwick Papers*, put these words into Mr. Sam Weller's mouth:

> The wictim o' *connubiality*, as Blue Beard's domestic chaplain said, with a tear of pity, ven he buried him.

consanguinity   (kon sang GWIN ih tee) *n. Consanguinity* is blood relationship resulting from the sharing of ancestors; from Latin *consanguinitas*, based on prefix *con-* (with) plus *sanguis* (blood). People related by blood are said to be *consanguineous* (kon sang GWIN ee us). In Shakespeare's *Twelfth Night* (Act II, Scene 3), Sir Toby Belch and Sir Andrew Aguecheek are singing drunkenly late at night in a room in the house of the rich Countess Olivia. Her woman Maria breaks in: "What a *caterwauling* do you keep here!" Says Sir Toby: "My lady's a Cataian [Cathayan, i.e., Chinese]; we are politicians . . . Am I not *consanguineous*? Am I not of her blood? Tillyvally [a term of contempt], lady!" Malvolio, Olivia's steward, shows up and chastises the revelers: "My lady bade me tell you, that, though she harbours you as kinsman [there really is *consanguinity* between Sir Toby and the Countess] . . . she is very willing to bid you farewell." In other words, *consanguinity* goes only so far, and mustn't be abused. Degrees of *consanguinity* form the basis of statutory formulas for the distribution of the estates of persons dying intestate (i.e., without a will) as well as defining permissible and incestuous marriages. These formulas vary from state to state, country to country, church to church. In parts of the United States, marriages between first cousins are prohibited as involving too close a degree of *consanguinity*. The Roman Catholic Church has very strict rules on *consanguinity* as an impediment to marriage. In some cases, relatives of a deceased spouse are counted as having the same degree of *consanguinity* as the bereaved spouse's own family. Henry VIII of England married his brother Arthur's widow, Katharine of Aragon, but only pursuant to a papal dispensation. After an unsuccessful struggle with the papacy to have the dispensation declared invalid, Henry obtained a divorce when Archbishop Cranmer proclaimed the marriage invalid because it violated the law respecting *consanguinity*. Henry was excommunicated—the rest is history. (see also **sanguinary**.)

contemn   (kun TEM) *vb.* To *contemn* is to despise, regard with scorn and disdain. The person or thing so regarded may be described as *contemnible* (kun TEM nuh bul). The noun *contempt* and the adjective *contemptible* are much more common and familiar than the verb *contemn* and its adjective *contemnible*, nor has *contemn* any related active adjective like *contemptuous*. The coexistence of the *contemn* and *contempt* groups results from the inflection of the Latin verb *contemnere*, whose past participle is *contemptus*; and it is well known that we have taken our English words rather arbitrarily and often quite at random from this or that form of Latin and Greek verbs. *Ecclesiasticus* 19:1 tells us: "He that *contemneth* small things shall fall by little and little," modernized by the *New English Bible* as "Carelessness in small things leads little by little to ruin." (It was the *King James Version* that warned P.T. Barnum not to disdain Tom Thumb, no doubt.)

contumacy   (KON tooh muh see, -tyooh-) *n. Contumacy* is obstinate disobedience, stubborn and unreasonable resistance or perverseness, rebelliousness. The adjective, *contumacious* (kon tooh MAY shus, -tyooh-), describes all these disagreeable qualities. A *contumacious* person is intractable, pigheaded, or, as the British say, "bloody-minded." *Contumax* means "insolent, defiant" in Latin, based on the intensive prefix *con-* plus the verb *tumere* (to swell, to puff up), or possibly *temmere* (to despise), from which we get **contemn**, *contempt*, *contemptuous*, etc. *Contumacy* and *contumacious* often imply contemptuous opposition to lawful authority, like the attitude of some trade unions toward court decisions, as in the miners' strike in Great Britain in 1984 under the leadership of its president Arthur Scargill. Do not confuse *contumacy* with **contumely**, though both may have derivations involving the Latin verb *tumere* (to swell).

contumely (KON toohm lee, -tyooh-; kon TOOH muh lee, -TYOOH-; KON tum lee) *n.* As to this profusion of pronunciations, Fowler points out that the famous line from the "To be, or not to be" soliloquy in Shakespeare's *Hamlet* (Act III, Scene 3): "The oppressor's wrong, the proud man's *contumely*," favors something close to the first one given above, which he describes as *KO ntoom lee* (*oo* as in *boot*). *Contumely* is contemptuous language or treatment; humiliation, insult, by word or deed. It is from Latin *contumelia* (insult). The English philosopher Francis Bacon (1561-1626) wrote: "It were better to have no opinion of God at all than such an opinion as is unworthy of him; for the one is unbelief, the other is *contumely*." The adjective is *contumelious* (kon tooh MEE lee us, -tyooh-). Shakespeare was fond of it. In *Henry VI, Part 1* (Act I, Scene 4), Lord Talbot tells the Earl of Salisbury of his treatment as a prisoner of the French in these terms:

> With scoffs and scorns and *contumelious* taunts,
> In open market-place produced they me,
> To be a public spectacle to all . . .

The adverb had already shown up in Scene 3, when the Mayor of London, coming upon the brawling forces of Gloucester and Beaufort, cries:

> Fie, lords! that you, being supreme magistrates,
> Thus *contumeliously* should break the peace!

In *Henry VI, Part 2* (Act III, Scene 2), Queen Margaret describes the Earl of Warwick in these words:

> He does not calm his *contumelious* spirit . . .

And in *Timon of Athens* (Act V, Scene 1), Timon describes war as " . . . *contumelious*, beastly, mad-brained . . . ," anticipating General William Tecumseh Sherman (1820-1891) by a good many years: "War is cruelty . . . War is . . . barbarism . . . War is hell."

copacetic (koh puh SET ik) *adj.* This is a bit of slang, the origin of which is unknown according to all the dictionaries consulted. It appears in a number of forms: *copasetic, copassetic, copesetic,* as well as the spelling in the headword above. It means "fine and dandy, completely satisfactory, just great, in good order, excellent, in fine shape," and would be found in sentences like, "If only Harry were here, everything would be *copacetic*," or, "The weather was great, they all showed up on time, it was *copacetic*." As an interjection, *copacetic* means "All clear!" Despite the dictionaries' disclaimer of any knowledge of the origin of this word, it would appear to emit echoes of words like *sympathetic* and *empathetic* with a hint of *compassion* thrown in for good measure, all of which express feelings of emotional kinship, understanding, and in a sense, satisfaction. Any suggestions?

coprologic(al), see **scatalogy**

copula (KOP yuh luh) *n*. A *copula* is a link or tie, something that serves to join things together. In grammar, it is a word or phrase that links the subject and predicate in a sentence. In *John is a trustworthy friend* or *Mary is a marvelous woman* the verb *is* is the *copula*. In *Fred, poor chap, has been quite ill, but he seems a lot better now*, the *copulas* (or *copulae*, if you prefer) are *has been* and *seems*. In these examples, all the *copulas* are verbs, known as *copulative* (KOP yuh lay tiv, -luh-) verbs. *And* is a *copulative* conjunction. Conjunctions that do not link, but offer a choice or a contrast, are *disjunctive* (dis JUNGK tiv). In *poor but proud*, *but* is *disjunctive*; the same goes for *or* in *this or that*. The distinction between *copulative* and *disjunctive* conjunctions becomes important in determining the verb number after a compound subject. Sam *and* John *are* here. Sam *or* John *is* here. *Copula*, taken intact from Latin, is the basis of the Latin words *copulare* (to join together) and *copulatio* (union), and the source of our *couple* (noun and verb), and *copulate* and *copulation*, a specialized type of union. *Copula*, in the original Latin, appears in one of the odes of the Roman poet Horace (65-8 B.C.), Book I, Ode 13 (Wickham translation):

> Thrice happy they, and more than thrice
> whom an unbroken bond (*copula*) holds fast,
> and whom love, never torn asunder by foolish
> quarrelings, will not loose till life's last
> day!

And the great English poet William Butler Yeats (1865-1939), in his *News for the Delphic Oracle*, wrote of a lovely scene where

> . . . *nymphs and satyrs*
> *Copulate* in the foam . . .

In *Sweeney Agonistes*, the American-born English poet T.S. Eliot (1888-1965) wrote:

> Birth, and *copulation*, and death.
> That's all the facts when you come to brass tacks.

In Shakespeare's *King Lear* (Act IV, Scene 6), Lear rants:

> The wren goes to 't, and the small gilded fly
> Does lecher in my sight.
> Let *copulation* thrive . . .

(Does this not bring to mind the Cole Porter song *Let's Do It?*) In any case, we see that the little word *copula* and its derivatives have played a great part in literature, to say nothing of life itself!

coracle   (KOR uh kul) *n.* A *coracle* is a small oval-shaped rowboat, constructed of wickerwork or interwoven laths, covered with watertight material like tarred or oiled canvas, animal skins, etc. These are used on the inland waterways of Ireland and Wales, and here and there in the west of England. The making of *coracles* is an old and fast-becoming extinct local craft, and one rarely sees a *coracle* afloat any longer. As might be expected, the derivation is not from classical Greek or Latin, but rather from Welsh *corwgl*, related to Gaelic *curach* (boat), and has nothing whatever to do with oracles or miracles, though it seems a miracle that *coracles* remain afloat.

corban (KOR bun) *n.* A *corban* is any gift offered to God in fulfillment of a vow. In Hebrew the word is *qorban* (offering, sacrifice); its literal meaning is "drawing near." We read in Genesis 22 how God put Abraham to the test by telling him to offer his son Isaac as a sacrifice. When Isaac asked Abraham, "Where is the young beast for the sacrifice?" the father answered that God would provide it, but as Abraham took the knife to kill his son, the Angel of God stopped him and a ram was substituted. The ram, not Isaac, became the *corban*. The next time you swear to God: "If You would only . . . , I'll . . . ," and describe your *corban*, be sure you can provide it!

corvine, see **accipitrine**

cosmical, see **acronical**

cosmogony   (koz MOG uh nee) *n. Cosmogony* is a theory of the origin of the universe, not to be confused with *cosmology*, the science of the universe, its structure and evolution. Both words are based on the Greek noun *kosmos* (cosmos, universe): *cosmogony* uses the suffix *-goneia*, based on *gonos* (seed, creation), which gives us the suffix *-gony*, appearing in words denoting origination, like *monogony, theogony*, etc.; whereas *cosmology* uses the suffix *-logia*, based on *logos* (word, discourse), a suffix which gives us the suffix *-logy*, appearing in names of sciences, like *philology, theology*, etc.

cosmology, see **cosmogony**

costive (KOS tiv) *adj*. A *costive* person is one in the unfortunate state of being constipated—a member of the great TV audience watching the display of the countless remedies that leave the unhappy sufferer beaming and brimming over with health, happiness, and indomitable energy after one dose. *Costive* is never heard on the air, but "regular" regularly is. Via Middle English and Middle French, *costive* is derived from Latin *constipatus*, past participle of *constipare* (to press together). There is something about a tight anal sphincter that somehow led to the figurative use of *costive* in the sense of "niggardly." The British statesman and author Lord Chesterfield (1694-1773) used it that way in giving his Polonius-to-Laertes type of guidance (see *Hamlet*, Act I, Scene 3) to his son, advising him: "You must be . . . close, but without being *costive*."

coulisse (kooh LEES) *n*. *Coulisse* has a number of meanings. Basically, a *coulisse* is a piece of wood having a groove along which a panel can slide. The side-flats of a theater run along *coulisses*, and from that use *coulisses*, the plural, is used for the wings themselves, or the space between two wing-flats. The British use *coulisse* in the sense of "corridor" as well, and from that it came to mean a place for any informal discussion or negotiation. *Coulisse* means "groove" in French, where it also has the sense of something that slides in a groove. A *portcullis* is a heavy grating, usually in a medieval castle, that can be let down to close a gateway and prevent access. It slides along grooves in the sides of the gateway. *Portcullis* (port KUL is) is from Old French *porte coleice* (sliding door). The *-cullis* in *portcullis* is related to *coulisse*, which is based on the French verb *couler* (to flow or glide).

coup de grace (kooh duh GRAS; the *s* is sounded). This expression, taken over from the French *coup de grâce*, means, literally, "blow of mercy"—the death blow mercifully given to end suffering, as in the case of a horse with a broken leg, or a still squirming victim of a firing-squad with a poor aim. But *coup de grace* is used figuratively to denote any decisive finishing stroke that once and for all settles a matter and has nothing to do with mercy—often, quite the contrary. The resignation of a leading member of a political party might be a *coup de grace* ensuring defeat in the middle of an election campaign. The revelations on Nixon's tapes delivered the *coup de grace* that put an end to his presidency. Thus, a term originally based on the concept of compassion has taken quite a different turn, and now signifies a final, convulsive, destructive blow. Caution: sadly, all too often, the *grace* in this expression is mispronounced as *grah*, like the *gras* in *pâté de foie gras*, which has a lovely taste but a silent *s*. And remember, the *p* in *coup* is silent, and not to be confused with the *p* in *coupe*, as in *coupe Hélène* (a stewed pear with chocolate sauce), which also has a lovely taste but a sounded *p*. To come out with *coup de gras* or *coupe de grace*, or, heaven forbid, *coupe de gras* (which would mean "cup of fat") would deliver a *coup de grace* to one's hope to be taken for a man of the world.

cozen (KUZ un) *vb*. To *cozen* someone is to cheat, trick, defraud, swindle, or beguile him, and *cozenage* (KUZ uh nij) is the practice of these unseemly acts:

trickery and swindling. The origin of *cozen* is in question. It is believed by some authorities to be derived from the French verb *cousiner* (to claim kinship; by extension, to deceive through a false claim of kinship). The British statesman Oliver Cromwell (1599-1658), in a 1654 speech to Parliament, said: "Feigned necessities, imaginary necessities, . . . are the greatest *cozenage* that man can put upon the Providence of God, and make pretences to break down rules by." In Shakespeare's *Othello* (Act IV, Scene 2), Iago's wife Emilia, bewildered by Othello's accusations against Desdemona, exclaims:

> I will be hang'd, if some eternal villain,
> Some busy and insinuating rogue,
> Some cogging [i.e., tricking], *cozening* slave, to get some office,
> Have not devised this slander.

The English poet John Dryden (1631-1700) wrote these pessimistic lines:

> When I consider life, 'tis all a cheat;
> Yet, fool'd with hope, men favour the deceit;
> Trust on, and think tomorrow will repay:
> Tomorrow's falser than the former day;
> Lies worse, and, while it says we shall be blest
> With some new joys, cuts off what we possest.
> Strange *cozenage*! None would live past years again,
> Yet all hope pleasure in what yet remain;
> And, from the dregs of life, think to receive,
> What the first sprightly running could not give.

The English historian and statesman Macaulay (1800-1859) thundered against a political opponent: "He had *cozened* the world by fine phrases!" One who indulges regularly in the unwholesome practice of *cozenage* is a *cozener*.

crambo (KRAM boh) *n.* This is the name of a rhyming game, between individuals or teams. One side concocts a line of verse to which the opposing side must find a rhyme, but no word occuring in the first line must appear in the answering line. In the variation *dumb crambo*, rhymes of the given word are pantomimed or acted out in charades until guessed. In *Love for Love*, by the English dramatist Congreve (1670-1729), we hear: "Get the maids to *crambo* of an evening and learn the knack of rhyming." The word *crambo* was taken over from Latin *crambe*, based on Greek *krambe* (cabbage) and is thought to be short for *crambe repetita*, literally, *cabbage reclaimed*—cold cabbage warmed up and served again—figuratively, stale repetition, the same old story, as used by the Roman satirist Juvenal (c. 60-140), who wrote (translation of Lewis Evans): "Cabbage cooked twice wears out the master's life."

crapulent (KRAP yoo lunt, -yuh-) *adj.* The unfortunate who can properly be described as *crapulent* is one suffering the effects of imbibing too freely or eating to excess. If such overindulgence is chronic, he can be called *crapulous*

(KRAP yoo lus, -yuh-), but, in the confusing ways of our language, that term is also sometimes used as a synonym of *crapulent. Crapulent* comes from Late Latin *crapulentus*, based on Latin *crapula* (drunkenness), which was an import from Greece, where *kraipale* meant "hangover"; and the condition is *crapulence. Crapulous* is from Late Latin *crapulosus*. None of these words has anything to do with the vulgar word that forms the first syllable of each and has an altogether distinct etymology: Middle English *crappe*, from Dutch *krappe* (chaff—the husks thrown away in threshing—whence the word came to mean "worthless stuff, refuse").

crapulous, see **crapulent**

credenza (krih DEN zuh) *n*. This word, taken intact from the Italian, means "sideboard" or "buffet." In ecclesiastical parlance, a *credenza* is a "credence table," a side table or a shelf for holding the bread and wine used in the Eucharist, the Holy Communion. In olden times, credence tables were used for a different purpose: to hold food to be tasted by the host or one of his staff before being served to guests, to convince them that it wasn't poisoned (comforting thought). *Credence* comes from Middle Latin *credentia* (literally, belief, credit; later, it came to mean "sideboard, buffet"), based on the Latin verb *credere* (to believe). One had to *believe* in one's hosts in those days, especially at places like the Borgias'. *Credenzas*, nowadays, are innocent enough articles of furniture, far removed from anything so naughty as poisoning one's guests.

crepuscular (krih PUS kyuh lur) *adj*. From the Latin noun *crepusculum* (twilight), based on *crespus*, a variant of *cresper* (dark) plus the suffix -*culus*, attached to diminutives, we get *crepuscule* (krih PUS kyoohl, KREP uh skyoohl), meaning "twilight, dusk." The adjective *crepuscular*, in its literal sense, is applied to anything resembling twilight, and as a zoological term, to animals and insects that come out at dusk. Figuratively, *crepuscular* can be used to describe things dim or indistinct. The Russian novelist Turgenev (1818-1883), in the Harry Stevens translation of *Fathers and Sons*, made dramatic and moving use of the term in the sense of "indistinct":

> That vague, *crepuscular* time, the time of regrets that resemble hopes, of hopes that resemble regrets, when youth has passed, but old age has not yet arrived.

crescive (KRES iv) *adj. Crescive* describes anything that is increasing, growing. The Latin verb *crescere* means "to grow," and the form *increscere* gave us *increase*. A rare meaning of *crescent*, based on *crescens*, present participle of *crescere*, is "increasing, growing." The *crescent moon* is one in its first quarter and gains its name because it is bound to *increase*. The *croissants* we eat are not going to grow; quite the contrary—but the literal meaning of *croissant* is "growing," that word being the present participle of the French verb *croître* (to grow). As a noun in French *croissant* means "new moon" and many other things, including the delectable *crescent*-shaped roll.

cresset (KRES it) *n*. A *cresset* is a metal basket mounted on a pole for use as a torch, or hung on a chain and used as a lantern, containing oil, pitch-soaked wood, or any slow-burning combustible whose fire will serve as an illuminant or beacon. *Cressets* were placed in courtyards, on wharves and lighthouses and the like. There is doubt about its derivation: it is either from Old French *craisset*, which gave rise to French *graisse* (grease), or from Old French *creuset* or *crasset*, from which modern French *creuset* (crucible) was derived. The English poet John Milton (1608-1674) wrote of

> . . .Blazing *cressets* fed
> With naphtha and asphaltus . . . ,

and later, his countryman, the poet Shelley (1792-1822), used *cresset* in the figurative sense of any illumination in writing of

> A *cresset* shaken from the constellations . . .

In Shakespeare's *Henry IV, Part 1* (Act III, Scene 1), in an angry exchange between Hotspur and Owen Glendower, the latter, boasting of his powers, says:

> . . . at my nativity
> The front of heaven was full of fiery shapes,
> Of burning *cressets*, and at my birth
> The frame and huge foundation of the earth
> Shak'd like a coward.

And Hotspur answers:

> Why, so it would have done
> At the same season, if your mother's cat
> Had but kitten'd, though yourself had ne'er been born.

cricetine, see **accipitrine**

criticaster, see **poetaster**

crocket (KROK it) *n*. This is an architectural term, denoting a decorative feature of certain structures of the Middle Ages. A *crocket* is an ornament, usually in the form of curled leaves, buds, or flower petals, on the inclined sides of a pediment, spire or pinnacle of a building, or on capitals or the coping of gables. They curve up and away from the surface to which they are attached and turn down part of the way upon themselves, with a knob at the end. One would find *crockets* on medieval cathedrals, palaces, and other public buildings. *Crocket* comes from Middle English *croket* (hook), and is not to be confused with **crotchet**, which is quite a different matter.

crocodiline, see **accipitrine**

cromlech, see **dolmen**

crotaline, see **accipitrine**

crotchet (KROCH it) *n*. This word has a number of distinct meanings: a small hook; any hooked tool or instrument; in British English, a quarter note (in music); and, strange to say, an eccentricity, whim, peculiarity, quirk. It is from this last meaning that we get the adjective *crotchety* (KROCH ih tee): grouchy, crabbed, cranky, irascible, eccentric, capricious, whimsical, erratic. Obviously, its meaning of "hook" or "hooked instrument" is related to *crochet* (kro SHAY) and *crocheting* (kro SHAY ing, the pronunciation having been taken over from the French), needlework done with a hooked needle, and to the shepherd's staff or bishop's crozier, both known as "crooks." There is, of course, the informal use of the word *crook* to mean "dishonest person"—someone not entirely straight, as it were. (Remember "Your President is not a *crook*," the proud statement made on the air by Richard M. Nixon?) It takes some imagination, however, to make the jump from *small hook* to *eccentricity* or *quirk*, except that there is something "out of line" about both hooks and eccentricities. "Faith, thou has some *crotchets* in thy head now," says Mistress Ford to her husband in Shakespeare's *Merry Wives of Windsor* (Act II, Scene 1), signifying that he is acting oddly. The adjective *crotchety* is commoner than the noun, especially in phrases like *crotchety old man*, descriptive of a curmudgeon. *Crotchet* and *crotchety* come from Middle English *crochet* (hook). Speaking of quirks and whims, see also **maggot**.

cryptesthesia (kript es THEE zhee uh, -zhuh) *n*. This is another word for "clairvoyance," perception that is acute beyond normal limits. The word derives from the Greek prefix *krypto-* (hidden, secret), based on *kryptein* (to hide), plus *aisthesis* (perception). We find *crypto-* in such words as *cryptogenic*, describing a disease of unknown origin, *cryptogram*, something written in code, etc. People endowed with *cryptesthesia* are said to be *cryptesthetic* (kript es THET ik); they have the supranormal power of "seeing" things not visible to the generality of mankind, together with special intuitive understanding of people and things.

cuculine, see **accipitrine**

cucullate (KYOOH kuh late) *adj*. *Cucullate* means "hooded" or "cowled," i.e., having or wearing a hood or a cowl, like that worn by monks and members of the Ku Klux Klan. The word comes from Late Latin *cucullatus* (hooded), based on Latin *cucullus* (covering, hood). *Cucullate* sometimes adds a *d* to form *cucullated*, with the same meaning. There is a medieval proverb that goes "Cucullus non facit monachum." ("The cowl does not make a monk.") The Albanians say (in Albanian, naturally): "It takes more than a hood and sad eyes to make a monk." (Didn't somebody say: "Clothes make the man"?) The English poet Richard Lovelace (1618-1656), in *To Althea: From Prison*, wrote: "Stone walls do not a prison make,/Nor iron bars a cage," while his countryman William Wordsworth (1770-1850) disagreed to a degree, in *Humanity*: "Stone walls a prisoner make . . . " The Greek philosopher Aristotle (384-322 B.C.) said: "One swallow does not make a summer," but the American poet Robert Lowell (1917-1977) differed, writing in his poem "Fall": "One swallow makes a summer." We have come a long way from *cucullate*, but a couple of detours do not a journey make—or do they?

cucumiform (kyooh KYOOH muh form) *adj.* This adjective describes anything shaped like a cucumber, which is *cucumis* in Latin. The great English lexicographer and writer Dr. Samuel Johnson (1709-1784) had this to say about that misunderstood vegetable: "A cucumber should be well sliced, and dressed in pepper and vinegar, and then thrown out, as good for nothing." There is no record that he had anything against *cucumiform* objects. Zucchini, a variety of summer squash, are *cucumiform*: likewise most bananas. Or should we say, echoing Johnson's prejudice, that cucumbers are zucchiniform or bananiform—except that there are no such words in the dictionary. There must be lots of things shaped like a cucumber, else *cucumiform* never would have been invented. Make your own list.

culicine, see **accipitrine**

cumbrous (KUM brus) *adj. Cumbrous* is a synonym of *cumbersome* (KUM bur sum); they both mean "burdensome, unwieldy, impeding, getting in the way of," and come, respectively, from Middle English *cumberous* and *cummyrsum*. The verb *cumber* (KUM bur), to hamper, burden, or trouble, is from Middle English *cumbren* (to harass). We are more familiar with *encumber* (en KUM bur), and *encumbrance* (en KUM bruns), a burden and, in law, a lien on property, like a mortgage. All these Middle English sources go back to Late Latin *cumbrus* (heap), from Latin *cumulus* (heap), which came into English intact meaning "heap" and gave its name to a certain type of cloud formation as well. We read in *Luke* 10:44 that "Martha was *cumbered* about with much serving . . . " (According to the New English Bible, she was " . . . distracted by her many tasks . . . " but *burdened* seems closer to the situation; and in the parable about the barren fig-tree, Jesus tells of the man who says to his vineyard-keeper, "Cut it down; why *cumbreth* it the ground?" The New English Bible puts it: "Why should it go on using the soil?") The word *cumber-ground*, for "useless thing," comes from this story. The general idea behind all these *cumber* words is, in a nutshell, that of *burdening*.

cunctator (kungk TAY tur) *n.* A *cunctator* is a procrastinator, a dilatory character, one who postpones, delays, lingers, hesitates, put things off. This word was taken over intact from the Latin, where it was based on *cunctatus*, the past participle of the verb *cunctari* (to delay, to linger). "Never put off to

tomorrow," says a friend of the author, "what you can postpone indefinitely."
Cunctator became a nickname or **agnomen** of Quintus Fabius Maximus
Verrucosus, a Roman general in the second century B.C., who acquired the
epithet for his cautious tactics against Hannibal and the Carthaginians in the
Second Punic War (218-201 B.C.), by avoiding pitched battle while harassing the
enemy along the way. He has gone down in history as *Fabius Cunctator* (Fabius
the Delayer). The title was at first meant to be derogatory, but later acquired a
laudatory aspect in view of the eventual effectiveness of the delaying tactics. The
Roman statesman and orator Cicero (106-43 B.C.), referring to Fabius *Cunctator*,
wrote: "One man, by delaying [*cunctando*, in the original], saved the state for
us." Nowadays, ancient history forgotten (do they teach it anywhere anymore?),
a *cunctator* is simply a procrastinator, a postponer, a wavering, indecisive individual afraid to take decisive action, rather than a cautious wait-and-see type
who finally exhausts the adversary.

cuneal   (KYOOH nee ul), **cuneate** (kyooh nee it, -ate) *adj*. These are alternative forms of the adjective meaning "wedge-shaped," and apply to anything in
that configuration; in botany, to leaves that are triangular and taper to a point.
Cuneiform (kyooh NEE uh form, KYOOH-) also means "wedge-shaped," and is
almost always applied to the written characters found in ancient Assyrian,
Babylonian, Persian, Hittite, etc., clay inscriptions. The term *cuneiform* was the
brain child of the English orientalist Prof. Thomas Hyde (1636-1703) of Oxford.
This form of script dates back to about 3800 B.C. and was still in use for a brief
period after the birth of Christ. It was deciphered in 1802 by the German
archaeologist and philologist Georg Friedrich Grotefend (1775-1853). That was
some decoding job! All these *cune-* terms are based on Latin *cuneus* (wedge).

cusp   (kusp) *n*. A *cusp* is a point; our word is simply the stem of the Latin noun
cuspis. *Cusp* has a number of technical meanings in various branches of science,
the most familiar denoting the points or horns of a new moon. *Cusp* plays a part
in the formation of the familiar names of certain teeth: *cuspid* and *bicuspid*.
Cuspidate (KUS pih date) is the adjective describing anything ending in a point,
like *cuspidated* leaves or teeth. There are no points or *cusps* on *cuspidors*,
however; that word is from the Portuguese, where it means "one who spits,"
based on *cuspir* (to spit), and that, in turn, goes back to the Latin verb *conspuere*
(to spit upon), formed of prefix *con-* (as an intensive) plus *spuere* (to spit),
whose past participle gave us *sputum*. It's a long way from new moons to
sputum, but, to misquote the Greek geometrician Euclid (fl. 300 B.C.) even
further (What he said to Ptolemy I, King of Egypt, c. 367-283 B.C., was: "There is
no royal road to geometry," usually misquoted as "There is no royal road to
learning."), there is no short road between *cusps* and *cuspidors*.

cybernetics   (sye bur NET iks) *n*. *Cybernetics* is the comparative study of
control functions and systems in human bodies and mechanical or electric
systems (e.g., computers) designed to replace them. The word, like *economics*,
politics, etc., is treated as a singular. *Cybernation* (sye bur NAY shun) is control

by machines, and is related to automation, which replaces human thought and manual labor in many phases of manufacturing. The American mathematician Norbet Wiener (1874-1964) is considered the father of *cybernetics*. He had many interesting things to say about the new science. It was in 1948 that he said:

> We have decided to call the entire field of control and communication theory, whether in the machine or in the animal, by the name of *Cybernetics*, which we form from the Greek for steersman. [The Greek noun is *kybernetes*.] . . . This new development [automation] has unbounded possibilities for good and for evil.

In the year of his death, 1964, he wrote (*God and Golem, Inc.*):

> The future offers very little hope for those who expect that our new mechanical slaves will offer us a world in which we may rest from thinking. Help us they may, but at the cost of supreme demand upon our honesty and intelligence. The world of the future will be an ever more demanding struggle against the limitations of our intelligence, not a comfortable hammock in which we can lie down to be waited upon by our robot slaves.

Automate . . . and vegetate?

cyclopean, -ian (sye kluh PEE un, –KLOH pee–) *adj.* A Cyclops was a member of a fabled race of giants living mainly in Sicily, who had only one round eye in the center of the forehead. They forged iron for Vulcan. Their name in Greek was *Kyklops* ("Round-Eye"), based on *kyklos* (circle) plus *ops* (eye). From the name *Cyclops* we get the adjective *cyclopean* (or *-ian*; upper or lower case *c*) meaning "gigantic, vast." In his poem *King's Cross Station* (one of London's railroad terminals), the English essayist, novelist, critic, and occasional poet G.K. Chesterton (1874-1936) wrote:

> Or must Fate act the same grey farce again,
> And wait, till one, amid Time's wrecks and scars,
> Speak to a ruin here, 'What poet-race
> Shot such *Cyclopean* arches at the stars?'

(Note that the poet used the *-ean* spelling, but the *-ian* stress, as required by the meter.) The arches in King's Cross Station are quite vast. Shakespeare was familiar with the Cyclops. In *Titus Andronicus* (Act IV, Scene 3), Titus exclaims:

> Marcus, we are but shrubs, no cedars we;
> No big-bon'd men fram'd of the Cyclops' size;
> But metal, Marcus, steel to the very back . . .

And in *Hamlet* (Act II, Scene 2), the First Player recites:

> And never did the Cyclops' hammer fall
> On Mars's armour, forged for proof eterne,

> With less remorse that Pyrrhus' bleeding sword
> Now falls on Priam.

Cyclopean is a fine adjective to use in indicating vastness, but make sure it is not applied in any ambiguous situation where it may be mistaken to mean "one-eyed."

cygnine, see **accipitrine**

cymotrichous   (sye MOT rih kus) *adj.* If you are *cymotrichous*, you have wavy hair, and that pleasant condition is known as *cymotrichy* (sye MOT rih kee). These terms are formed from two Greeks words, *kyma* (wave) and *thrix* (hair), whose stem is *thrich-*. If you are *leiotrichous*, you have straight, smooth hair, and that state of affairs is designated *leiotrichy*. Those words are from Greek *leios* (smooth) plus, once again, *thrix*. Should you have crisp and woolly hair, you can be described as *ulotrichous*, and said to enjoy—or suffer from—*ulotrichy*, which covers that situation. These last two words are derived from Greek *ulos* (woolly, curly) and our old friend *thrix*. Suggested sign for a beauty parlor out to win over the lexicographical set, especially etymologists with an anthropological bent: TIRED OF YOUR LEIOTRICHOUS OR ULOTRICHOUS CONDITION? COME IN AND LET US MAKE YOU CYMOTRICHOUS! If the sign doesn't appeal to lexicographers or anthropologists, it might pull in the hypochondriacs.

cyprine, see **accipitrine**

dacelonine, see **accipitrine**

daedal(ian), see **icarian**

daltonism   (DAHL tun iz um) *n. Daltonism* is color blindness, especially the congenital inability to distinguish between red and green, so named after the English physicist and chemist John Dalton (1766-1844), who suffered from it and first described it in 1794. The label *daltonism* was introduced by the Scottish physicist Sir David Brewster (1781-1868), the inventor of improved lighthouse illumination and the kaleidoscope. Dalton formulated a law in physics known as "Dalton's Law": The total pressure exerted by a mixture of gases is equal to the sum of the partial pressures of the individual component gases. There are various degrees of *daltonism*, all the way from total (inability to distinguish any colors) to complete partial (confusion of certain bright colors) to incomplete partial (nonrecognition of composite and neutral shades). Sufferers from total color blindness can be guided by traffic lights because the red light is on top, the yellow in the middle, and the green at the bottom, and the position of the brightest itself tells the tale. Gentlemen suffering from *daltonism* don't always prefer blondes.

dap (dap) *n.*, *vb.* To *dap* is to fish by letting the bait bob up and down on the surface of the water. As a noun, *dap* is the name for bait used in that fashion. *Dap* has another meaning: When a ball *daps*, it bounces on the ground, and a *dap*, in this context, is a bounce. The origin of *dap* is obscure, but it is thought to be related to *dab* in the sense of "strike lightly" or "hit feebly" or just "tap." *Dab* is from Middle English, and is considered to be an imitative, if not an onomatopoeic, word.

daysurine, see **accipitrine**

debouch (dih BOOSH, -BOUCH) *n.* As a military term, *debouching* or *debouchment* is used of troops marching out of a narrow passage, like a defile, into open country. In geography, a river or stream is said to *debouch* when it flows out of its confining banks to open country, or out of a narrow valley into a broader one. The general idea behind *debouch* is to emerge, whether referring to troops, a stream, a river, or a road, from a narrow space into an open area. A river can *debouch* into a sea, a street into a square. *Bouche*, derived from Latin *bocca* (cheek, mouth), is French for "mouth," and the French verb *déboucher* gave us *debouch*.

debridement (dih BREED munt) *n.* In surgery, *debridement* is the removal of dead, torn, or contaminated tissue or of any foreign matter from a wound. The word was taken over intact from the French noun *débridement* (literally, unbridling), based on the verb *débrider* (to unbridle a horse—but in surgery, to relieve a constriction by incision). In the imagination of the French, the stripping away of contaminated tissue from the body, often involving the removal of constricting matter, evoked the image of taking the *bridle* off a horse, which, in a sense, is the removal of a constriction; hence *débridement*; thence *debridement*.

decussate (dih KUS ate, DEK uh sate) *vb.*; (dih KUS ate, -it) *adj.* To *decussate* is to cross or intersect in the form of an *X*. As an adjective, *decussate* applies to anything so divided. In botany, *decussate* leaves are pairs running along the stem at right angles to the adjoining pair. *Decussate* road intersections are not common, or safe. The derivation is from Latin *decussatus*, past participle of *decussare* (to divide in the form of an *X*), based on *decussis*, a Roman coin of *decem* (ten) *asses* (an *as* being an ancient monetary unit weighing twelve ounces); the *decussis* was marked with the Roman numeral *X*. Seems a long way from an ancient Roman coin to an uncommon intersection.

defalcation   (dee fal KAY shun, -fol-) *n. Defalcation* is misappropriation of money or property by a person holding it in a fiduciary capacity, like a trustee, guardian, public official, or corporate officer. It comes from Middle Latin *defalcatio* (taking away), based on Latin *defalcatus*, past participle of *defalcare* (to cut off). *Falx* is Latin for "scythe" and its stem, *falc-*, is the source of our word *falcate*, meaning "curved," like a scythe or sickle. Scythes cut things off; so do *defalcators*, in their evil way. It's bad enough to steal a stranger's money; *defalcation* from a trusting soul is worse. A guardian found guilty of *defalcation* would surely be removed and should go to jail. The noun *peculation* (pek yuh LAY shun) covers a wider area, being applicable to any case of embezzlement, though, like *defalcation*, it can be applied to misappropriation of public funds, or, more narrowly, to money or property entrusted to one's care. A mayor's *peculation* of public funds would drive him out of office. Both *defalcation* and *peculation* amount to dipping into the till. *Peculation* and its verb *peculate* (PEK yuh late) are from the Latin noun *peculatus*, based on the past participle of the verb *peculari* (to embezzle), literally to "make public funds private," i.e., make them one's own—a case of illegal "privatisation," as it were, to borrow a British term much in vogue in the Thatcher government, which wants to end state ownership of industries and sell them back into private hands, i.e., to "privatise" them. In this peculiar case, *privatisation* really amounts to what the American market calls "going public." This is another case of British usage in which *public* and *private* confuse Americans. In Britain, a *public* school is a *private* school, and what Americans call a "public school" is a *state* school. In the matter of the state's selling state-owned industries to the public, the British Government calls it "privatisation," while Americans would call it "going public." Incidentally, many words ending in *-ize* in American spelling end in *-ise*, sometimes either *-ise* or *-ize* (why?) in British usage. Hence the *s* in the English *privatisation* mentioned above. Getting back to *peculation* and *peculate*, they are etymologically related to *peculiar*, from Latin *peculiaris* (as one's own), in the sense of "distinctly characteristic of" or "belonging exclusively to" someone or something, as in the *peculiar* (i.e., characteristic) sounds of the music of a certain composer, or the *peculiar* properties or effects of a certain drug. When a person *peculates*, he makes someone else's property *peculiar*, as it were and so to speak, to himself (temporarily, we hope, until the law catches up with the miscreant).

defenestration (dee fen ih STRAY shun) *n. Defenestration* is the act of throwing someone (yes, someone!) or something out of a window. To *defenestrate* (dee FEN ih strate) a person or a thing is to engage in that activity—a strange one indeed, since these words are more commonly applied to situations where what is thrown out of the window is a person, rather than a thing. It is surprising, in view of what must be the infrequency of this type of activity, that there exists a word for it, but then, there exists a word for just about everything. There is a famous incident in history when an act of *defenestration* of people was committed: the *Defenestration* of Prague. It seems that, just before the outbreak of the Thirty Years War in 1618, the two principal Roman Catholic members of the Bohemian National Council were thrown out of a window of the castle at Prague by the Protestant members—one way to settle an argument. They weren't killed. The castle had a moat in which the *defenestrated* twain were lucky enough to land, with only minor injuries. Strangely enough, it is once more to Prague that we have to travel to find a more recent (and this time fatal) instance of what might have been *defenestration*. Jan Masaryk (1886-1948, son of Tomas Garrigue Masaryk, first president of Czechoslovakia) was foreign minister of the Czech government-in-exile in London during World War II. He returned to Prague, retaining that post, when that war ended. A short time after the communist coup in 1948, he fell to his death from a window. Despite the official explanation of suicide, the circumstances have never eliminated the possibility of dastardly *defenestration*. In *A Time of Gifts* (John Murray, London, 1977), the English writer Patrick Leigh Fermor (b. 1915) tells us of the martyrdom of St. Johannes Nepomuk in 1393 by the henchmen of King Wenceslas IV. They hurled Johannes into the River Vltava (also known as the Moldau) from a bridge in Prague. Mr. Fermor adds in a footnote: "There are several instances of *defenestration* in Czech history, and it has continued into modern times [referring, no doubt, to poor Masaryk]. The martyrdom of St [note absence of period, which the British call "full stop," after an abbreviation which ends with the last letter of the word in an unabbreviated word, as in Mr, Dr, etc.] Johannes is the only case of depontication, but it must be part of the same Tarpeian tendency." Mr. Fermor is referring to the Tarpeian Rock—the Mons Tarpeius—on the Capitoline Hill in ancient Rome, from which criminals and traitors were hurled to their death.

dehisce (dih HIS) *vb*. To *dehisce* is to gape, open up, crack, or split. The noun for this activity is *dehiscence* (dih HIS uns), which has a special meaning in biology, denoting the bursting of plant capsules for the scattering of seeds. The derivation is from Latin *dehiscere* (to gape, part) and its noun *dehiscentia* (gaping, splitting open). Writers have used *dehisce* quite outside the field of biology, in describing the splitting of the material in an article of clothing, like the thin silk or voile of a woman's blouse. In such cases, however, we are happy to report that nothing like seeds, or anything else, was scattered.

deicide, see **aborticide**

deictic, **dictic**, see **elenchus**

deipnosophist (dipe NOS uh fist) *n*. This label is applied to a "table-philosopher," a person who converses eruditely at the dinner table. This noun is derived from two Greek words: *deipnon* (dinner) and *sophos* (wise). It was taken from a work entitled *The Deipnosophistae* (Banquet of the Sophists) by Athenaeus, a Greek writer who flourished about the beginning of the third century A.D. The terms *sophist* and *sophistry* have acquired the pejorative implication of speciousness and fallacious reasoning and rhetoric, but in Athenaeus's time, the sophists of ancient Greece were a class of respected itinerant teachers and lecturers. The eminent English lexicographer, poet, critic, and conversationalist Dr. Samuel Johnson (1709-1784) is the foremost example of a *deipnosophist* that leaps to mind. He made of conversation a fine art. More recent *deipnosophists* were H.L. Mencken, the American writer and critic (1880-1956), the American social and literary critic and writer Edmund Wilson (1895-1972), and several members of the Bloomsbury group—the English cultural set that made Bloomsbury Square in London the center of its activities, starting around 1904 and continuing for over three decades. The most famous members were Lytton Strachey, E.M. Forster, Roger Fry, Vita Sackville-West, Virginia Woolf and her husband Leonard, John Maynard Keynes, and Clive Bell. They assembled on Thursday nights for conversations of high literary quality. Any one of these *deipnosophists* would have been an ornament at your dinner table.

delphi(ni)ne, see **accipitrine**

deltiology   (del tee OL uh jee) *n.* This term denotes the collection and study of picture postcards, an activity that engages the attention of a surprisingly large number of persons, and constitutes the business of a number of companies. The subject matter of the postcards is of incredible variety: anything from family groups to ancient bathing beauties to public ceremonies to landscapes to Hollywood stills to salacious Coney Island (New York) and Brighton Beach (England) caricatures to sentimental doggerel. People collect just about everything these days: "Early plastic," like objects made of celluloid, is the vogue at the moment; a short time ago it was old bourbon bottles. *Deltiology* comes from Greek *deltion* (small writing-tablet) plus suffix *-logia*, denoting "study."

démarche (day MARSH) *n.* This is a French loan word meaning "gait," and by extension, "measure, step, course," as in *resort to a* (certain) *measure*, or *take a step*, or *follow a course*. A *démarche* is a plan of action, or a change in a course of action. It is a term often used in the field of diplomacy and denotes a political step or course of action, usually one initiating a fresh policy. At this moment of history (note that we avoided "point in time"), when our foreign policy seems to shift from day to day, *démarche* is a very handy word that one is likely to run across in the columns of the pundits.

demit   (dih MIT) *vb.* This verb is used both transitively and intransitively (see **transitive**), and is found most commonly in Scotland, but used elsewhere as well. To *demit* a position is to resign it, to give it up or relinquish it, and it often refers to public office. Intransitively, to *demit* is simply to resign. It comes from Latin *dimittere* (to send down), based on the prefix *di-*, a variant of *dis-* (away, apart) plus *mittere* (to send). Because of his need for "the woman I love," Edward VIII of England (1894-1972) *demitted* his throne in 1936—i.e., he abdicated.

demiurge   (DEM ee urj) *n. Demiurge* is the name given by the Greek philosopher Plato (427-347 A.D.) to the Creator, the artificer of the world. Gnosticism, a belief of early Christian times, taught that creation was a process of emanation from the original essence or Godhead, and that the *Demiurge*, creator of the material world, was not god, but the Archon, chief of the lowest order of spirits or powers emanating from the supreme Deity. The *Demiurge* endowed mankind with the psyche, the sensuous aspect of the soul, while God himself added the pneuma, the rational aspect. *Demiurge* comes from the Greek *demiourgos* (worker for the people), based on *demos* (people; cf. *democracy*) plus *ergos* (worker; cf. *erg*, unit of work or energy). The *demi-* of *demiurge* has nothing to do with the *demi-* that we took from the French, as in *demigod* or *demitasse*, and they took from the Latin *dimidius* (half).

demography   (dih MOG ruh fee) *n.* This is the study of population, a term derived from two Greek words: *demos* (the people) and *graphein* (to write—the suffix *-graphy* is familiar from *geography*, *stenography*, etc.). *Demography* includes the study of vital and social statistics, such as the birth, marriage, and death rates, migration patterns and population distribution, and, on the basis of the ascertainment of trends, makes predictions as to probable future social changes. *Demographics* (dih muh GRAF iks), treated as a singular noun, is a term for the statistical data of a population, especially those concerning income, education, average age, etc., and as a plural noun, denotes the facts derived from the data. The adjective is *demographic* (dih muh GRAF ik). The *demographic* data of New York City indicate a trend toward the building of high-rental apartment units. A *demographer* (dih MOG ruh fur) is one engaged in *demography*. With the use of polls and computers, *demography* is tending to become an exact science, and is a very useful tool for those advising candidates for public office.

demotic   (dih MOT ik) *adj. Demotic* pertains to anything relating to the common people. In that sense, it can be used as synonymous with "popular." *Demotic* has a narrow, specialized sense as a designation of a simplified form of ancient Egyptian writing in which the priests kept their records. The adjective comes from the Greek *demotikos* (popular, plebeian), based on *demotes* (a plebeian) and *demos* (the common people, the populace). *King Demos* is a facetious term for the electorate, the common people who select the ruler and in that way are "sovereign," as though political machines and chicanery didn't exist. *Demo-*, the Greek prefix from *demos*, is found in words like *democracy* and *demography*. *Demotics*, treated as a singular noun, is sometimes used as a synonym of *sociology*, the study of people, their care and culture.

dendrochronology   (den droh kruh NOL uh jee) *n.* Formed of three Greek nouns, *dendron* (tree), *chronos* (time), and *logos* (word, discourse), *dendrochronology* is the dating of past events through the study of the annual growth rate of tree rings. *Dating*, in a number of sciences, is the determination of the age of objects or events, based on various techniques, including the natural radioactivity of certain minerals, identification of fossils, the carbon-14 method, pollen analysis, and cross-checking with *dendrochronology*, where the age of ancient wood is determined by the ring pattern in its cross section. The pattern of ring widths reflects local climatic phenomena which occurred when the section of wood was part of a living tree. Through the use of overlapping patterns in various samples, *dendrochronological* dating has been carried back over 8,000 years.

depontication, see **defenestration**

derisory (dih RYE suh ree) *adj*. One must be careful about the meaning of this word, especially to avoid identifying or confusing it with *derisive* (dih RY siv). At one time, the dictionaries, both American and English, made no distinction, but those days are—or should be—over: whereas *derisive* means "showing or expressing derision, ridiculing," *derisory* means "inviting or worthy of derision," or, as Fowler puts it, "too insignificant or futile for serious consideration; it is applied to offers, plans, suggestions . . . the word is no longer needed in the sense [i.e., "showing derision"] now nearly monopolised by *derisive* . . . " Both *derisory* and *derisive* stem from the Latin *derisus*, past participle of the verb *deridere* (to mock—from which we get *deride*, *derision*, etc.), formed of the prefix *de-*, used as an intensive, plus *ridere* (to laugh—from whose past participle, *risus*, we get words like *risible* and *risibility*). Remember the distinction: if a silly proposition is offered, one's attitude would be *derisive*; the proposition itself would be *derisory*.

descant (DES kant) *n*.; (des KANT) *vb*. A *descant* in music is an accompaniment above the theme, harmonizing with it or serving as a counterpoint. At times, it is simply the alto voice raised an octave. It is also used as a term in part music for the soprano voice or, in a wider sense, any melody. As a general term outside the music field, a *descant* can be a comment on any subject. As a verb, to *descant* (note different stress) is to sing or, used as a general term outside the field of music, to comment at length on any subject, and there is the variant *discant* (dis KANT). The derivation is from Middle Latin *discanthus*, which goes back to the Latin verb *cantare* (to sing). In *Paradise Lost*, the English poet John Milton (1608-1674) wrote of the "wakeful nightingale":

> She all night long her amorous *descant* sung . . .

Shakespeare liked the word. He used it twice in *Richard III*: once as a verb Act I, Scene 1, by Richard, as Duke of Gloucester, in the soliloquy that opens the play:

> Now is the winter of our discontent
> Made glorious summer by this sun of York . . .
> Have no delight to pass away the time,
> Unless to spy my shadow in the sun
> And *descant* [comment] on mine own deformity . . .

and again as a noun, in Act III, Scene 7, when Buckingham advises Richard to look coy and pious but then to accept the crown:

> Look you get a prayer-book in your hand
> And stand between two churchmen, good my lord;
> For on that ground I'll build a holy *descant* [song, melody] . . .

In his poem *The Passionate Pilgrim*, Shakespeare uses *descant* once more as verb:

> Good night, good rest. Ah! neither be my share:
> She bade good night, that kept my rest away;
> But daff'd me [turned me away] to a cabin hang'd with care,
> To *descant* on the doubts of my decay.

[Two notes: 1. Shakespeare stressed the first syllable in both noun and verb uses of *descant*. 2. Shakespeare innocently libeled Richard, who was neither a rascal nor a hunchback. He gave credence to Henry VII's public relations people—and had to court the Tudor Queen Elizabeth's favor as well. The best authorities prove that Richard was a good guy.]

desiderative   (dih SID uh ray tiv) *n.*, *adj.* This is a grammatical term for a verb derived from another verb, that expresses the desire to do that which is denoted by the underlying or primitive verb. Examples: The Latin verb *micturare* (to desire to urinate; see **micturate**) is the *desiderative* or *desiderative verb* derived from the verb *mingere* (to urinate), whose past participle is *mictus*; the verb *esurire* mentioned under **esurient** means to "hunger," and is the desiderative of *edere* (to eat), whose past participle is *esus*. This grammatical phenomenon is found in Greek as well as Latin.

desideratum   (dih sid uh RAY tum) *n.* A *desideratum* is something desired or needed, the lack of which is a matter of wide concern. It is the neuter form of *desideratus*, the past participle of the Latin verb *desiderare* (to desire). Hamlet (Act III, Scene 1), in his "To be . . ." soliloquy, calls death and the end of all the ills "the flesh is heir to" a "consummation devoutly to be wished," which in itself is a good definition of a *desideratum*. Peace on earth is a *desideratum*; a cancer cure is a *desideratum*; racial harmony is a *desideratum*. The related verb, to *desiderate* (something) is to feel (it) to be lacking, to regret (its) absence. Fowler gives us a warning about this word. He describes it as " . . . a useful word in its place, but . . . so often misplaced that we might be better without it. Readers . . . do not know the meaning of it, taking it for [a] pedantic or facetious form of *desire* . . . Writers . . . are ill-advised in using the word unless they are writing for readers as learned as themselves . . ." What one *desiderates* is a *desideratum*.

desinence   (DES uh nuns) *n. Desinence* is an ending, a termination; *desinent* (DES uh nunt), the adjective, means "terminal, final," describing anything that puts an end to, or constitutes the end of something. Thus, in a sonnet, the 14th line is the *desinence*; in *La Divina Commedia* (*The Divine Comedy*) of the Italian poet Dante Alighieri (1265-1321), the 33rd canto of *Paradiso* (*Paradise*) is the *desinent* one. In a sequential novel like *Strangers and Brothers* (Faber & Faber, London, 1940-1949; Macmillan, London, 1951-1970), the 11-volume series by the English writer C.P. Snow (Baron Snow of Leicester, 1905-1980), the eleventh volume (*Last Things*) is the *desinence*, or the *desinent* installment. *Desinent* and *desinence* can also be applied to a word ending or suffix, like the *-logy* in *geology*, *theology*, etc. *Desinence* is, via the French and Middle Latin *desinentia*, from Latin *desinens*, the present participle of the verb *desinere* (to put down, leave), based on the prefix *de-* (down) plus the verb *sinere* (to allow).

desipient   (dih SIP ee unt) *adj.* This word means "foolish, silly," and its related noun *desipience* denotes that state, with the implication of "folly" or "frivolousness" rather than downright foolishness. The American humorist Artemus Ward (Charles Farrar Browne, 1834-1867) spoke of "occasional *desipience*," echoing the lovely line in Ode 12 of Book IV of the Odes of the Roman poet Horace (65-8 B.C.): "It is pleasant to be frivolous on occasion." (*Dulce est desipere in loco.*) It follows the line: "*Misce stultitiam consiliis brevem*"; in the Wickham translation, the couplet goes: "Mix with your sage counsels some brief folly. In due place to forget one's wisdom is sweet." The English poet Charles Stuart Claverley (1831-1884) in a poem entitled *Beer*, wrote:

> When 'Dulce est desipere in loco'
> Was written, real Falernian winged the pen.

(Falernian wine, made from grapes in Falernus, in the district of Campania in southwest Italy, was Horace's favorite, celebrated by his contemporary Virgil, 70-19 B.C., as well.) *Desipient* and *desipience* are derived from the Latin verb *desipere* (to be silly) and its present participle *desipiens*. *Desipere*, in turn, is formed of the Latin prefix *de-* (away from) and *sapere* (to be wise or sensible), whose present participle *sapiens* gave us our word *sapient*. Horace felt so strongly about the importance of playing the fool and letting oneself go on occasion that he had brought the subject up in an earlier ode as well: Book III, Ode 2, adding yet another laudatory word to the line:

> *Dulce et decorum est desipere in loco.*

Note *et decorum*: it is not only *dulce* (sweet, pleasant) but also *decorum* (proper, becoming) to be a little bit giddy at the right time and place. Good for old Horace!

deus ex machina   (dee us eks MAK uh nuh, day-). This term is a Latin translation of the Greek *theos ek mekhanes*, meaning, literally, "a god from the machine." What machine? The one that was operated in the classical Greek theater, a platform on which the gods rested, from which one or more of them could be let down to the stage, to intervene supernaturally in settling the affairs of mortals. (If the deity in question happened to be female, the *deus* would be a *dea*.) From this theatrical convention of ancient times, the expression has taken on the significance of any contrived providential device to unravel plot difficulties. The *deus ex machina* that solves the problem so abruptly can be a person or an event. It is a favorite device of dramatists and novelists who build up complicated situations that would be almost, if not quite impossible, to resolve without such contrived and often inartistic intervention. The United States Marines were the *deus ex machina* that saved the day in many an old movie. Authors shamelessly resort to the long arm of coincidence as the *deus ex machina* that suddenly makes everything come out just right.

dianoetic   (dye uh noh ET ik) *adj*. This adjective applies to anything pertaining to reasoning, especially that of the digressive or discursive type, or to the intellect in general. It is formed from the Greek prefix *dia-* (through—as found in words like *diagnosis, diameter*) plus the verb *noeein* (to think), so that its literal meaning is "through thought." Conclusions reached *dianoetically* are reasoned, as opposed to those achieved intuitively. *Dianoia* (dye uh NOY uh) is a Greek word for "knowledge through intellect"; formed of *dia-* plus *nous* (mind, intellect), it is a term used by the Greek philosopher Plato (427-347 B.C.). It applies to knowledge of the real world as it exists, which can—according to Plato—only be approximate, as opposed to the ideal world, which exists only in the imagination. *Dianoia* is usually translated, therefore, as "opinion," as distingushed from certainty.

diaphoretic, see **sudorific**

diaskeuast   (dye uh SKOOH ast) *n*. Literally, a reviser or interpolater, from the Greek verb *diaskeuazein* (to make ready), based on prefix *dia-* (through, across, by) plus the noun *skeuos* (tool). A *diaskeuast* is an editor, and it is to be hoped that the *diaskeuast* editing this work will not have to do too much revising or interpolating! The next time this author has a serious disagreement with his editor, it will be pleasant to accuse him or her of being a *diaskeuast* (it does sound like a term of abuse) and silently await the reaction.

diaspora   (dye AS pur uh) *n*. This term, taken over intact from the Greek where it means "dispersion" (based on prefix *dia-*, meaning, inter alia, "through" and "thoroughly," plus the verb *speirein*, "scatter,"), means "scattering, dispersion." With a capital *D*, the *Diaspora* is the name given to the scattering of the Jews after the Babylonian captivity, and is also used collectively for the dispersed Jews. In the age of the Apostles *Diaspora* was the label of the Jews living outside Palestine, and the term is now used to describe those living outside Israel. The *General Letter of James* (1:1) is addressed "to the twelve tribes which are scattered abroad." As a general term, with a lower case *d, diaspora* describes the situation of any group bound by common national origin or creed that is dispersed outside the boundaries of its country. The *diaspora* of the African black peoples as slaves has resulted in minority problems in many parts of the world.

diatribe (DYE uh tribe) *n.* A *diatribe* is a bitter denunciation, a vilifying invective. Cf. **phillipic**. It has an unusual derivation, from Greek *diatribe* (spending of time, pastime, discourse—words hardly related to the present meaning of *diatribe*), related to the verb *diatribein* (to rub away, erode), based on prefix *dia-* (through) plus *tribein* (to rub—a verb that helps to explain **tribadism** as well). Apparently, the effect of a *diatribe* is to wear away or wear down the person at whom it is directed, the way the Roman politician and conspirator Catiline (c. 108-62 B.C.) was worn down by the "Catilinian Orations" aimed at him by the Roman statesman and orator Cicero (106-43 B.C.) which brought about the conspirator's downfall.

didelphine, see **accipitrine**

didine, see **accipitrine**

digitigrade, see **plantigrade**

diglot (DYE glot) *n., adj. Diglot*, as an adjective, means "bilingual"; as a noun, a bilingual book or edition. It is from the Greek adjective *diglottos*, based on the prefix *di-* (two, double) plus *glotta* (tongue). There is a great deal of controversy in the United States on the subject of bilingual, or *diglot*, teaching in our public schools to accommodate the large number of Spanish-speaking Puerto Ricans now living in urban centers. A book in a foreign tongue with the English translation interlined, or on facing pages, like certain "trots" or "ponies," especially in the classics (usually forbidden by the school authorities), is a *diglot*. There are perfectly legitimate *diglots* of some of the classics, like the edition of *La Divina Commedia* (*The Divine Comedy*) of the great Italian Poet Dante Alighieri (1265-1321) with translation on facing pages by Professor Harry Morgan Ayres (1881-1948), with whom the author attended some classes at the University of Rome in 1926/7 while the professor was on sabbatical from Columbia University—a marvelous translation).

digraph (DYE graf) *n.* A *digraph* is a combination of two letters representing a single sound, like the *ai* in *main*, the *ea* in *meat* or *great*, the *sh* in mush, the *ch* in *much*, the *th* in *this* or *thin*, the *ph* in *digraph*. There are *trigraphs* as well: the *tch* in *match*, the *eau* in *beau*, the *ght* in *tight*. *Digraph* comes from the Greek prefix *di-* (two) plus *graphe* (mark), related to the verb *graphein*; *trigraph* from the Greek or Latin prefix *tri-* (three) plus *graphe*. The *digraph* differs from a diphthong in that the latter produces a gliding sound, like the *oi* in *boil* or *toil* or the *oy* in *joy* or *toy*, though some authorities equate the two or at least say that they are "loosely" one and the same. The Greek alphabet uses diphthongs, but single letters where we use consonantal *digraphs*: Θ for *th* as in *thin*; Φ for *ph*: X for *ch* as in German *ach*; Ψ for *ps* as in *psalm*. The Cyrillic alphabets (Russian, Bulgarian, Serbian, etc.) do the same.

dingle   (DING gul) *n.* A *dingle* is a narrow, shady dell or dale, or a small, deep ravine or valley, depending on the context. It is also known in England as a *dimble*, a word now obsolete in the United States, except in some dialects, and where so used, it implies that a stream runs through a little valley. *Dingle* has some wholly unrelated further uses: as a storm door or shed, in some parts of the northern United States, and in others, as the tinkle of a little bell. As a verb, it can mean to "tinkle" or "jingle" like a bell, or to "tingle" in the cold. As a synonym of *dell*, *dingle* is from Middle English *dingle* meaning "deep dell" or "hollow," and is related to Old English *dung* (dungeon) and Old High German *tunc* (cellar).

Dionysian   (dye uh NISH un, -NIS ee un) *adj.* In Greek mythology, *Dionysus* (dye uh NYE sus) was the god of wine, fertility, and drama; Bacchus was his Roman counterpart, with the emphasis on the wine. He was worshipped in drunken, orgiastic festivals called "Dionysia," involving performances from which Greek tragedy and comedy evolved. The adjective *Dionysian* referred to the god, but because of the nature of his worship, it acquired, with a lower case *d*, the sense of "wildly uninhibited, frenzied, orgiastic." Its diametrical opposite was *Apollonian* (ap uh LOH nee un), an adjective applied literally to the cult of Apollo, the classical god of beauty, music, poetry, healing, and prophecy, and with a lower case *a*, as in the case of the extension of *dionysian*, it was broadened to mean "serene, composed, placid, poised." Nowadays, much of rock music and the concomitant dancing it inspires have a *dionysian* atmosphere and beat, often inexplicable and distressing to the folks who were brought up on *apollonian* love songs.

discrete   (dih SKREET) *adj.* This adjective, too often confused with another that is pronounced the same way and is actually an anagram of it—the familiar word *discreet*—means something quite different: "separate, detached, distinct," and in context, "discontinuous," or "abstract," the opposite of *concrete* in the realm of concepts and thinking. They have a common origin, in the Latin *discretus*, the past participle of the verb *discernere* (literally, to separate, set apart; figuratively, to distinguish, discern). Somehow, the Latin participle separated into both *discreet* (circumspect, careful in one's actions, wise in keeping information to oneself) and *discrete*, with the meanings listed above. The noun related to *discrete* is *discreteness*; the noun from *discreet* is *discretion*. *Discretion*, not *discreteness*, is the better part of valor. Fowler says that *discrete* should be accented *DIH skreet*, like *concrete (KONG kreet)* in some of its meanings, with the incidental effect of distinguishing it from *discreet*. Our form of government consists of three *discrete* parts: the executive, the legislative, and the judicial. They don't always act discreetly.

disembogue   (dis em BOHG) *vb*. When something is said to *disembogue*, it is pouring forth and discharging its contents, whatever they may be. This term is used especially of rivers and streams discharging their waters into a lake or ocean. *Disembogue* can also be used transitively in the general sense of "cast out" or "discharge": a stream can *disembogue* its waters into a lake. *Disembogue* is derived from the Spanish verb *desembocar*, based on Spanish prefix *des-*, from Latin *dis* (away) plus *embocar* (to enter the mouth, from Latin prefix *in-*, into, plus Latin *bucca*, cheek or mouth). Used of flowing waters discharging into open waters, as a term in geography, *disembogue* is synonymous with **debouche**.

disjunctive, see **copula**

dithyrambic   (dith uh RAM bik) *adj*. This adjective is based on the noun *dithyramb* (DITH uh ram), from the Greek *dithyrambos*, which was the name given to a wild, vehement ancient Greek choral chant, hymn, or song, and later to any impassioned, sublime prose or poetry, usually irregular in form. *Dithyramb* applies, literally, to that type of composition, but by extension, to any literary form that is rapturous and expressive of wild enthusiams. *Dithyrambic* poetry was originally a wild, rapturous chant to Dionysus (Bacchus, in Roman mythology) and its invention is ascribed to the Greek poet Arion of the seventh century B.C., who must have been a pretty good musician as well as poet, for, according to the Greek historian Herodotus (c. 484-425 B.C.), it was good enough to charm at least one savage beast: Thrown into the sea by pirates, Arion was saved by a dolphin charmed by his song. To carry on *dithyrambically* about something, like a work of art, a performance, an exihibition, a landscape, or the object of one's ardor ("This time it's different!") is to be wildly enthusiastic, nay rapturous on the subject, sometimes stretching the patience of the listener to the breaking point.

diurnal   (dye UR nuhl) *adj*. *Diurnal* means "daily," as in *the milkman's diurnal route*, or "daytime" in its attributive use, "active by day," as in *the diurnal* (as opposed to the nocturnal) *activities* of certain animals and insects. The English poet Swinburne (1837-1909), in *The Garden of Proserpine* (Proserpine was Pluto's wife, and queen of the underworld), used *diurnal* in the second sense:

> Then star nor sun shall waken
>   Nor any change of light:
> Nor sound of waters shaken,
>   Nor any sound or sight:
> Nor wintry leaves nor vernal,
> Nor days nor things *diurnal*;
> Only the sleep eternal
>   In an eternal night.

Earlier, his countryman Wordsworth (1770-1850), in *A Slumber Did My Spirit Seal*, used it in the first sense:

> A slumber did my spirit seal;
>   I had no human fears:
> She seemed a thing that could not feel
>   The touch of earthly years.

> No motion has she now, no force;
>   She neither hears nor sees;
> Rolled round, in earth's *diurnal* course
>   With rocks, and stones, and trees.

and again, in *Influence of Natural Objects*:

> Yet still the solitary cliffs
> Wheeled by me—even as if the earth had rolled
> With visible motion her *diurnal* round!

Shakespeare used it in the same sense, in *All's Well That Ends Well* (Act II, Scene 1), when Helena tells the King of France that she will cure him of his fistula

> Ere twice the horses of the sun shall bring
> Their fiery torcher [torch-bearer] his *diurnal* ring . . .

Diurnal is from Latin *diurnus* (daily—based on *dies*, day). Cf. **quotidian**, which also means "daily," but only in the first sense, and **hebdomedal**.

divagate   (DYE vuh gate, DIH-) *vb.* To *divagate* is to stray, wander, ramble; the word is used in the realm of speech and the realm of the physical world. As to speech, to *divagate* is to digress, to ramble, to be discursive. In the physical world, one reads of a stream *divagating*, and the *divigation* (dye vuh GAY shun) of a country brook is one of the prettiest features of the landscape. *Divagate* comes from the Latin *divagatus*, past participle of the verb *divagari* (to stray, wander off), based on the prefix *di-*, a variant of *dis-* (away, apart) plus *vagari* (to wander), which gave us the noun *vagary* (vuh GAR ee, VAY guh ree), an unpredictable, erratic happening, and the adjective *vagarious* (vuh GAR ee us), erratic, capricious, though it can mean "wandering" or "roving" as well. When a speaker succumbs to excessive *divagation*, his audience often succumbs to sleep. To dispense with *divagation*, at a conference, for example, is to get down to business. Do not confuse *divagate* with *divaricate* (dye VAR uh kate, dih-), which means to "diverge, spread apart, branch off," from Latin *divaricatus*, past participle of *divaricare* (to spread asunder, stretch apart), based on prefix *di-*, a variant of *dis-* (apart, asunder) plus *varicare* (to straddle), and the related adjective *varicus* (with feet apart, straddling).

divaricate, see **divagate**

divination   (div uh NAY shun) *n. Divination* is prophecy, augury, the foretelling of the future. There are all kinds of methods described in history, from the inspired Delphic oracle priestess to the spiritualistic medium in a trance, the fortune-teller gazing into a crystal ball, the use of playing or tarot cards, the reading of palms, and the casting of lots, also known as *cleromancy* (KLER uh man see), from Greek *kleros* (lot) plus *manteia* (divination). *Divination* is from Latin *divinatio*, based on *divinatus*, past participle of *divinare* (to soothsay), from which we get our verb to *divine*, meaning "prophecy." The Latin is related to *divus* (god), a noun connected with *deus* (god), since the art of fortelling was a *divine* or superhuman attribute. The meaning of *divination*, as a literary word, has been extended to include "intuition." And remember that it is through the use of *divining* or dowsing rods, usually forked hazel sticks, that we locate unseen underground things, like water or metal deposits, an occupation that combines augury and intuition and perhaps a bit of godliness? or quackery?

docent   (DOH sent) *n.* A *docent* is a university lecturer. The letterhead on the office stationery of the Austrian neurologist (and founder of psychoanalysis) Sigmund Freud (1856-1939) read:

> Dr. Sigm. Freud
> *Docent* für Nervenkrankheiten
> a. d. Universität

meaning "Lecturer on Neurosis at the University." Sometimes the word is used as a shortened form of *privatdocent*, *-zent* (pree VAT doh tsent), a private lecturer paid by his students, especially in Germany. *Docent* was taken, via German *Dozent*, from *docens*, present participle of *docere* (to teach). *Doctor*, in Latin, means "teacher," and is related to *doctus*, the past participle of *docere*. Thus, it is the title of certain university degrees, as well as the common name for "physician" and in shortened form—*doc*—a common form of address from cabbies to passengers. To get back to *docent*: The American poet David McCord (b. 1897), in a 1945 poem *What Cheer*, wrote:

> The decent *docent* doesn't doze;
> He teaches standing on his toes.
> His student dassn't doze and does.
> And that's what teaching is and was.

dolmen   (DOL mun) *n.* This is the name of a type of prehistoric structure, generally considered to be a tomb, formed of a large flat stone laid across two or more large vertical stones. We got the word from the French, who took it over from *tolmen*—hole of stone, in Cornish, a Celtic language that became extinct c.

1800. (One Dorothy Pentreath of Mousehole, in Cornwall, England [pronounced *Mowzl*, meaning "place in the sun," and having nothing to do with either mice or holes], is said to be the last person who could converse in Cornish.) *Cromlech* (KROM lek), from Welsh *crom*, the feminine form of *crwm* (bent, crooked) plus *llech* (flat stone), is the Welsh equivalent of a Cornish *dolmen*, though *cromlech* applies equally to any circular group of large erect stones lacking a capstone. Welsh is still spoken in Wales; indeed, there is an active and growing movement to enlarge its use in both speech and on radio and television. The Constantine *Dolmen* in Cornwall is one of the largest, 33 feet long, 14 1/2 feet high, and 18 1/2 feet across; it consists of a huge capstone supported by two natural rocks. Another famous large *dolmen* in Cornwall is known as the "Trethevy Quoit." The best-known cromlechs are Wayland Smith's Cave in Berkshire, Kit's Coty House in Kent, both in England, and the Killing-Stone in Louth, Ireland. There are many *dolmens* or *cromlechs* all over Britain. Now, after all this archaeology, do not confuse *dolmen* with *dolman*, a woman's cloak with capelike arm pieces.

doran   (dor AN) *n.* This is an acronym for *Doppler range*, and is the name given to an electronic device used in navigation for computing range. It is based on the principle of the "Doppler effect," named after the Austrian physicist C.J. Doppler (1803-1853) who was the first to note the change in the frequency of sound and light waves that occurred when the distance between source and receiver varied. We have all noted the change in the pitch of a locomotive bell or horn as the train leaves or approaches us: When a train engine rushes by ringing its bell (that doesn't happen much any more) or blowing its horn, the pitch decreases and the sound fades as the train zooms off. The *doran* was developed to measure distance based on the variation of pitch resulting from the Doppler effect, through a correlation best left to physicists.

doxology   (dok SOL uh jee) *n.* A *doxology* is a hymn in praise of God. The *Greater Doxology* is the hymn *Gloria in Excelsis Deo* (Praise to God in the Highest) said or sung as part of the Mass or Eucharist. The *Lesser Doxology* is the *Gloria Patri* (Glory be to the Father, etc.) said or sung at the end of each psalm in the liturgy. The hymn by Bishop Thomas Ken (1637-1711):

> Praise God, from whom all blessings flow,
> Praise Him, all creatures here below,
> Praise Him above, ye heavenly host,
> Praise Father, Son, and Holy Ghost

is also known as the *Doxology*. In using the term, one must specify which *Doxology* is meant. It is derived from Greek *doxologia*, based on *doxa* (honor) plus the suffix *-logia*.

dragoman   (DRAG uh mun) *n.* A *dragoman* is an interpreter, sometimes also a guide. The term is usually applied to persons who professionally interpret Near

Eastern languages, particularly Arabic, Turkish, and Persian, for government offices, tour companies, and the like. The word has traveled all the way from Arabic *targuman* to Medieval Greek *dragomenos* to Old Italian *dragomanno* to Middle French *dragoman*, whence we adopted it: quite a trip! The plural should be *dragomans*, because the final syllable hasn't a thing in the world to do with our word *man*, but English-speaking people, assuming that it did, formed the originally erroneous plural *dragomen*, which has now become a permissible alternative. "Insistence on *-mans*," says Fowler, "is didacticism." *Didacticism*, according to Schur in *1000 Most Important Words* (Ballantine, New York, 1982; Facts On File, New York, 1984), " . . . often covers the situation where communication is overburdened with instructions and explanations."

dragoon (druh GOOHN) *n.*, *vb.* To *dragoon* is to coerce by vigorous, oppressive measures. *Dragoon* was originally the name of a member of certain cavalry regiments or a mounted infantryman armed with a carbine or short musket; modern land tactics have made it an obsolete military term. As a verb, it was used at first to describe the setting of *dragoons*, later, soldiers generally, against opposing forces; then to denote any persecution by armed forces. In current usage, it has come to signify the forcing of any action through oppressive measures, and generally means to "coerce." In recent times, Cambodian town-dwellers were *dragooned* by communist authorities into leaving their urban quarters for the inhospitable open country, where many perished. The term comes from *dragon*, a word at first used by the French for "pistol hammer" because of its resemblance to that legendary creature, and later to the musket and finally to the soldiers so equipped. Other authorities propose a different derivation, directly from the fabulous beast because of the fire-spouting action of the carbine. Except in history books and historical novels, you will not ordinarily run into *dragoon* except as a verb meaning "coerce." The ending *-oon* originates from French words ending in stressed *-on*, especially those whose Italian equivalents end in *-one*, as in *balloon* from French *ballon*, Italian *ballone*, buffoon from French *buffon*, Italian *buffone*, *dragoon* from French *dragon*, Italian *dragone*.

driad, see **oread**

dubiety (dooh BYE ih tee, dyooh-) *n. Dubiety* is doubtfulness. A *dubiety* is a matter of doubt, and is also known as a *dubiosity* (dooh bee OS ih tee, dyooh-). These words, as well as *dubious, dubitable, indubitable*, etc., are of course related to *doubt*, derived from the Latin verb *dubitare* (to waver). *Dubiety* is directly from the related Latin noun *dubietas* (doubt). All the "doubt" words go back via the Latin adjective *dubius* (doubtful) to *duo* (two) *viae* (ways), i.e., fluctuating. An extreme form of *dubiety* is *Pyrrhonism* (PIR uh niz um), a term based on the name of the fourth century Greek philosopher Pyrrho, who founded a school of sceptical philosophy holding that nothing was capable of proof and nothing was real but sensations. Who knows?

dubiosity, see **dubiety**

dyslexia, see **alexia**

dysteleology, see **teleology**

eburnean (ee BUR nee un) *adj.* Anything of ivory or like ivory may be described as *eburnean*; less often, *eburneous* (ee BUR nee us). *Eburnation* (ee bur NAY shun, eb ur-) is a medical term for a pathological condition in which bone or cartilage becomes dense and hard like ivory and is said to be *eburnated* (uh BUR nate ud). All these words stem from the Latin adjective *eburneus* or *eburnus* (made of ivory), based on the noun *ebur* (ivory).

ecdysiast (ek DIZ ee ast) *n.* This word was ingeniously and humorously coined by the American writer, critic, and philologist H.L. Mencken (1880-1956) as a "dignified" synonym for *stripper* or *stripteaser.* Mencken's invention was based on the noun *ecdysis* (EK dih sis), a biological term for the casting off of an outer coat, like the shedding of skins by snakes or of shells by crustaceans, a word taken over from the Greek *ekdysis* (getting out). Apparently, Mr. Mencken felt that Gypsy Rose Lee (Rose Louise Hovick, 1917-1970) contributed enough to our culture to warrant a title superior to "stripper." After all, undertakers are now morticians, hairdressers beauticians, and garbagemen are sanitation engineers. What with the bikini, the monokini (erroneously derived: the *bi-* in *bikini* has nothing to do with the prefix of duality, as in *bicycle, bisexual*, etc., but rather with the atoll Bikini), and finally the spread of the cult of nudism, *ecdysiasm* (invented by the author: cf. *enthusiasm*, or should it be *ecdysiastics*: cf. *gymnastics?*) has become commonplace.

ecliptic, see **solstice**

ecumenical (ek yooh MEN ih kul) *adj.* We are accustomed to meeting this word in connection with movements fostering worldwide Christian unity and the merging of religions in general. The basic thrust of *ecumenicalism* (ek yooh MEN ih kuh liz um), however, is wider: It can pertain to any movement, or for that matter, anything that can be described as "general" or "universal," like an *ecumenical* protest against atomic warfare. *Ecumenical* comes, via Latin *oecumenicus* (belonging to the entire inhabited world), from Greek *oikoumenikos*, based on the verb *oikein* (to inhabit), and sometimes drops the final *-al*, or spells the first syllable *oe*, staying closer to the Greek. *Ecumenicalism* is sometimes shortened to *ecumenism* (ek yooh MEN ih zum) or *ecumenicism* (ek yooh MEN ih siz um). They all denote the beliefs and program of the *ecumenical movement*, whose goal is the unification of all Protestant sects to begin with, and eventually of all Christian doctrines and churches. The World Council of Churches, established in 1948, is the chief instrument of *ecumenicalism*. The Roman Catholic Church has urged *ecumenical* contact with other faiths, especially since the Second Vatican Council in the early 60s. The visit of Pope John Paul II to Canterbury Cathedral in 1984, where he prayed alongside the Archbishop of Canterbury, was a high point. There are international interdenominational organizations all over the world that aim at worldwide religious unity. One God? Why not one Church? God surely is a polyglot.

edacious (ih DAY shus) *adj. Edacious* means "voracious, devouring, gluttonous" and *edacity* (ih DAS ih tee) means "voraciousness, gluttony." *Edacious* is from Latin *edaci-*, the stem of the adjective *edax* (gluttonous, greedy), and *edacity* from Latin *edacitas* (greediness, gluttony). They all go back to the Latin verb *edere* (to eat), which is also the basis of *edible*. The Roman poet Ovid (43 B.C.-c. 18 A.D.), in his *Metamorphoses* (15. 234) wrote of *tempus edax rerum* (time the devourer of [all] things). Though the use of *edacious* is now felt to be on the humorous side—a sort of fancy word for "greedy" or "insatiable"—it has been used by a number of writers in the phrase *edacious time*, referring back to old Ovid, in situations where erosion and destruction resulting from the passage of time is involved, and applied to the crumbling of monuments as well as the fading of fame. In *The Bigelow Papers* (Series II), the American poet and essayist James Russell Lowell (1819-1891), referring to the site of the battle where the minutemen repelled the British on April 19, 1775, wrote: "The Concord bridge has long since yielded to the *edacious* tooth of Time."

effluvium (ih FLOOH vee um). An *effluvium* is an unpleasant or downright noxious exhalation, slight, sometimes invisible, and therefore doubly dangerous, of minute particles; foul and disagreeable vapors from decaying matter, often affecting the lungs, eyes, etc., adversely. *Effluvium* is a Latin word, meaning a "flowing out," related to the verb *effluere* (to flow out). There are other words that come from the same Latin source: *effluence* (EF looh uns), *effluent* (EF looh unt), *efflux* (EF luks), all denoting something that flows out. These are not to be confused with *effluvium*, which involves unpleasant odors or emanations like those coming from garbage dumps or decaying corpses, foul and often harmful. In Bhopal, India, on December 4, 1984, the accidental release of a toxic cloud from a Union Carbide chemical plant killed some 2,500 people and injured—maimed or blinded or both—about 200,000 more, in the worst industrial accident in history. Some *effluvium*!

effuse (ih FYOOHZ) *vb.* **Transitively**, to *effuse* is to disseminate, pour forth; **intransitively**, to flow out. Pronounced differently (ih FYOOS), as an adjective, *effuse* means "spread out loosely" and is used chiefly as a botanical term. We are familiar with the adjective *effusive* in the sense of "excessively demonstrative," as a description, e.g., of a gushing young fan meeting a celebrity, but the verb *to effuse* is rarely encountered and easily mistaken as equivalent to "be *effusive*" or "*act effusively*." This may be an echo of the use of *enthuse* meaning "to show enthusiasm" or "be enthusiastic," a use, incidentally, to be decried as substandard despite its acceptance by many who should know better. (Fowler calls *enthuse* a "back-formation . . . of U.S. origin which in neither country [i.e., Britain or America] has emerged from the stage of slang, or at best colloquial.") *Effuse*, on the other hand, is perfectly legitimate, when used correctly. It is from the Latin *effusus*, past participle of *effundere* (to pour out).

eidetic (eye DET ik) *adj*. This adjective describes persons endowed with the faculty of retaining a vivid and clear image of something previously seen. An *eidetic* person can readily reproduce in his mind, with great accuracy and detail, what he has seen recently or long since. *Eidetic* imagery has been found to be one of the most important elements of chess mastery. *Eidetic* comes from the Greek adjective *eidetikos*, based on *eidos* (something seen, a form; cf. **eidolon**).

eidolon (eye DOH lun) *n*. An *eidolon* is an apparition, image, specter, or an idealized figure, an idol. This is a word taken intact from the Greek, where it means "phantom," based on the Greek noun *eidos* (form—related to the verb *idein*, to see). *Eidos*, too, has been taken over intact, to mean "idea, essence, ideal," and was derived via Late Latin *idealis*. The American poet, essayist, and diplomat James Russell Lowell (1819-1891), in *Among My Papers* (Series II), used the phrase "No real giant, but an *eidolon* of the mind," and another American poet, Edgar Allen Poe (1809-1849), in *Dreamland*, wrote this scary couplet:

> An *Eidolon* named Night
> On a black throne reigns upright.

Ah, those Bostonians, who knew their Greek and so enriched their language!

eldritch (EL drich) *adj*. Anyone or anything described as *eldritch* is weird, eerie, uncanny, spooky, even frightful. There is disagreement about the origin of this word. Some say it is based on Anglo-Saxon *aelf* (elf) and *rice* (powerful, or realm). Elves are mythological creatures in the nature of sprites who can be mischievous and even malicious. Others trace *eldritch* to Old English *el* (strange, uncanny) and *ric* (creature). Still others say that it comes from Old English *elfrice* (fairy realm). Alternative spellings are *eldrich* and *elritch*. However it is spelt or derived, *eldritch* is certainly connected with *elf* and *elfish*. It is not a common word, and more likely to be met with in Scotland than elsewhere. But you don't have to travel to the Highlands of Scotland to meet an *eldritch* creature; the streets of any town are full of them.

eleemosynary   (el ih MOS uh ner ee, -MOZ-, el ee uh-) *adj*. An *eleemosy-nary* institution is one supported by and dispensing charity, like the United Way, the March of Dimes, the American Red Cross and the Salvation Army. The word comes from Middle Latin *eleemosynarius*, based on Latin *eleemosyna* (alms) taken from Greek *eleemosyne* (mercy, compassion), which gave us the much shorter word *alms* as well. A favorite response of a lawyer friend of the author to a client expressing dismay at the size of a bill is: "Sir [or Madame], I do not pretend to be an *eleemosynary* institution!" This does not always serve to calm the client.

elenchus   (ih LENG kus) *n*. An *elenchus* is a logical refutation, any argument that refutes another argument. *Elenctic* (ih LENG tik) is the adjective, and applies to indirect methods of proof, like cross-examination, as opposed to *deictic* (DIKE tik) or *dictic* (DIK tik) which pertains to direct methods of proof, like syllogism. *Elenchus* 'is, via Latin *elenchus*, from Greek *elenchos* or *elegkhos* (refutation), based on *elenchein* (to refute). *Deictic* is from Greek *deiktikos* (serving to show), based on *deiknynai* (to show). The philosophical term *Socratic elenchus* describes a method of eliciting the truth by short questions and answers, and was one phase of the Socratic method, based on question-and-answer procedure, introduced by Socrates, the great Athenian philosopher (c. 470-399 B.C.). The next time your opponent in an argument goes into irrelevancies, hurl at him the lovely phrase: "Ignoratio elenchi!" Those Latin words mean "ignoring the argument," and amount to the fallacy of ignoring the point in question and arguing to the wrong point, refuting a proposition different from what you have set forth. An *ignoratio elenchi* is a ponderous (and, it is hoped, crushing) way of saying, "Irrelevant!"

elenctic, see **elenchus**

elephantine see **accipitrine**

ellipsis   (ih LIP sis) *n*. *Ellipsis* is a term in grammar for the omission from a sentence of a word or words needed to complete the construction or the sense. Intentional *ellipsis* in printing is indicated by a variety of symbols, including a series of periods (...) or of asterisks (***). *Ellipsis* in grammar is demonstrated in the following examples, the omission indicated by a series of plus signs (+ + +): It is a question whether the evils of narcotics is greater than + + + alcohol (+ + + indicates the omission of *those of*); John Gielgud is as good an actor + + +, if not + + + better + + + than Laurence Olivier (omissions: *as, a* and *one*); No other writer has + + + or can hope to attain the heights of Shakespeare (omission: *attained*). This last is a common type of *ellipsis*, where the construction of different parts of the sentence varies because of the difference of the auxiliary verbs required: in this case, *has*, requiring a past participle, and *to*, requiring an infinitive—*has attained, to attain*. Examples of permissible (intentional) ellipses: The torrential rains were unexpected and the workmen + + + forced to quit work. (A second *were* before *forced* can be omitted and makes the sentence smoother.) He is fortunate, and I + + + unfortunate. (An *am* before *unfortunate* would be grammatically correct, but the sentence is more effective without it.) Fowler has an exhaustive article on *ellipsis*. The adjective related to *ellipsis* is *elliptical* (ih LIP tih kul). When it is used as a description of speech or writing, it is pejorative, indicating that the language is excessively economical, tending to be ambiguous, or even cryptic. *Elliptical* happens also to serve a second purpose, in geometry, as descriptive of an object or a figure having the shape of an ellipse, but the uses are so far apart that the context must eliminate any possibility of confusion. Cf. **aposiopesis**, another sort of omission.

embonpoint   (awn bawn PWAN—all *n*'s pronounced nasally as in French) *n., adj.* This is a term taken from the French, and pronounced in the French manner—but see **fin de siècle** as to the limitations when it comes to the pronunciation of French words in an English sentence. *Embonpoint*, as a noun, means "plumpness," and as an adjective, indicates a well-fed appearance. It was formed from the phrase *en bon point*, meaning, literally, "in good form, in good condition." To describe a person in this way is usually meant as a compliment, but sometimes it has a humorously pejorative twist, suggesting that the subject has fed not wisely but too well. Photographs (especially in profile) of such well known "figures" as President William Howard Taft (1857-1930), "Diamond Jim" Brady (1856-1917) and Edward VII of England (1841-1910) display good examples of *embonpoint*.

embosk, see **bosky**

embrangle   (em BRANG gul) *vb.* To *embrangle* is to entangle, enmesh, confuse, muddle, perplex. An employee given contradictory instructions by different superiors becomes *embrangled* in general, and particularly as to what he's supposed to do. Executives who can't delegate are often *embrangled* about conflicting priorities. *Embrangle* is from prefix *em-* (a variant of *en-* before *b* or *p*, as in *embed*, *embody*, *empathy*) plus *brangle*, an obsolete word meaning "brawl" as a noun and "wrangle" as a verb; *brangle* is a fusion of the two.

emolument   (ih MOL yuh munt) *n.* An *emolument* is compensation for services rendered, in the form of a salary or a fee, as opposed to an *honorarium* (on uh RARE ee um), a voluntary payment for services when the situation is such that there is no legal obligation to pay. *Honorarium* is sometimes a more or less euphemistic substitute for *fee*, and is a term derived from the neuter form of the Latin adjective *honorarius* (done or given as an honor). When you see your doctor, you get a bill and pay him an *emolument*. When the Queen of England is visited by hers, if he receives anything, it's an *honorarium*. The author once bought a used Bentley from an English lawyer who had received it from the Queen's obstetrician as an *honorarium*; the latter had received it from Her

Majesty as an *honorarium*; the author paid the lawyer cold cash. *Emolument* is from Latin *emolumentum* (gain, profit—originally a miller's fee, based on prefix *e-*, from, plus *molu-*, a variant of *moli-*, combining form of *molere*, to grind). Do not confuse *emolument* with *emollient* (ih MOL yunt), a softening agent used on skin or tissue; derived from Latin *emolliens*, present participle of *emollire* (to soften), based on the adjective *mollis* (soft).

empennage, see **appanage**

empyrean   (em puh REE un, -pye-; em PIR ee un) *n.*, *adj.* This is the name of the highest of the five heavens in the system codified by the Alexandrian mathematician and astronomer Ptolemy (fl. 127-151). This heaven, in that system, consisted of pure fire, and, in the Christian doctrine, was considered the seat of deity and the angels. The adjective is *empyreal* (em PIR ee ul; em puh REE ul, -pye-), but *empyrean* serves as an adjective as well. Apart from their use in the Ptolemaic system, *empyrean* enjoys the general meaning of "sky, heaven," and the adjective means "heavenly, celestial." Both words come from the Greek *empyrios* (fiery). In *Paradise Lost*, the English poet John Milton (1608-1674) penned these lines:

> Now had the Almighty Father from above,
> From the pure *Empyrean* where he sits
> High-thron'd above all height, bent down his eye.

enate, see **agnate**

encephalon   (en SEF uh lon) *n.* This is a medical term for "brain," taken from the Greek noun *enkephalos*, based on the prefix *en-* (in) plus *kephale* (head). Some of us may be familiar with the terms *encephalogram* (en SEF uh luh gram) and *encephalograph* (en SEF uh luh graf) for an X-ray of the brain, and *encephalitis* (en sef uh LYE tis) for inflammation of the brain, without realizing that the basis of these and other related medical terms is *encephalon*. Some of these other terms are *encephalomalacia* (en sef uh loh muh LAY shuh), degeneration of the brain, *encephalomyelitis* (en sef uh loh mye uh LYE tis), inflammation of the brain and spinal cord, *encephalotomy* (en sef uh LOT uh mee), dissection of the brain, and *encephalitis lethargica* (en sef uh LYE tis luh thar juh kuh), sleeping-sickness, which the British call "sleepy-sickness," commonly associated with Africa and the dreaded tse-tse fly. Suffice it to remember that all these (and other) terms starting with *encephal(o)* come from the Greek word for "brain."

ench(e)iridion   (en kye RID ee un) *n.* An *ench(e)iridion* is a handbook, a manual, a reference book, possibly a short treatise serving as a ready reference source, any of those types of thing small enough to be carried around "in the hand," i.e., handy, conveniently available. It is synonymous with a *vade mecum*

(VAY dee MEE kum, vah-). *Encheiridion* is a Greek word, based on the prefix *en-* (in) plus *cheir* (hand), plus the suffix *-idion*, which has a diminutive effect. *Vade mecum* is a Latin phrase for "Go with me," that acquired the status of a noun applicable generally to something for frequent or regular use that one would carry around with him, like a memorandum book or pocket encyclopedia, a ready reference manual, an instruction booklet with directions for the use of portable tools and that sort of thing. The two rather quaint terms are quite useful, and their synonymity gives the writer his choice between the two classical tongues.

enchorial (en KOR ee ul) *adj. Enchorial* describes something used by the people of a particular country; something domestic. Its common use appears to be as a description of **demotic** writing. It is derived, via Late Latin *enchorius*, from Greek *enchorios*, based on prefix *en-* (in) plus *chora* (place, country). Though *enchorial* is a rare word, there is no reason why one cannot characterize as *enchorial* reggae, the Jamaican music of the people that developed in the 1960s among the poor blacks, especially the Rastafarian religious sect; or raga, the popular Hindu melodic form; or ragtime, the American musical invention that flourished from the 1890s through the 1910s, and produced Scott Joplin (1868-1917) and the immortal *Maple Leaf Rag*. (Reggae, raga, ragtime: Why all these *r*s and *g*s? Sheer coincidence.) *Enchorial* need not be confined to writing or musical forms; it can pertain to dress, diet, marriage, or other customs—anything native to a particular place.

enfilade (EN fuh lade, en fuh LADE) *n.* In French, this word means "suite" (of rooms) or "string" (of words or phases), and is also a military term for a raking fire from the enemy. We use it to denote an open vista, particularly a suite of rooms in a straight line which, with the doors open, expose to view a straight-ahead vista of a continuous passage. The British use *enfilade* as a term for any series of things arranged as though threaded on a string. They and we also use it to denote a raking fire that covers an enemy position from end to end. As a verb, to *enfilade* is to subject a body of troops, a road, a fortification, etc., to raking firepower. The French noun *enfilade* is derived from their verb *enfiler* (to thread, string), based on *fil* (thread).

ennead (EN ee ad) *n.* An *ennead* is a group of nine—persons or things. Whether they know it or not, a baseball team is an **ennead**, a word that comes from the Greek number *ennea* (nine). The combining form of *ennead, ennea-*, is found, e.g., in *enneagon*, a polygon with nine angles and nine sides, synonymous with *nonagon* (NON uh gon), formed from the Latin *nonus* (ninth), based on *novem* (nine), from which we got *November*, from Latin *novembris*, which was the ninth month of the early Roman calendar. An *enneahedron* (en ee uh HEE dron) is a solid figure with nine surfaces. Without going into an entire series, we have *monad* (MO nad, MOH-), meaning, inter alia, "single unit," from Greek *monos* (alone); *dyad* (DYE ad), a group of two, from Greek *dyas* (pair); *triad*

(TRYE ad), a group of three, from Greek *tria* or *treis* (three), and so on. We are more familiar with the Latin series, *solo, duet, trio, quartet*, etc. In any event, when you follow the next World Series (it used to be known as the "World Serious" among the Brooklyn fans in the golden age of Dem Bums—the Brooklyn Dodgers of blessed memory), remember that it is one *ennead* against another, and may the best *ennead* win!

enormity   (ih NOR mih tee) *n.* An *enormity* is an atrocity, something monstrous, outrageous, unforgivably offensive. The Hitler "final solution," with its ensuing genocidal holocaust, was an *enormity* of immeasurable proportions. *Enormities* have been committed throughout history by bloodthirsty conquerors such as Genghis Khan (1162-1227). *Enormity* is derived from the Latin noun *enormitas*, which had the harmless meaning of "irregular shape," and was formed from the prefix *e-* (short form of *ex-* before certain consonants, meaning "away from") plus *norma* (literally, a carpenter's square, and by extension, any rule or standard, from which we get *normal*). *E-* plus *norma* formed the Latin adjective *enormis* (away from the standard, irregular; by extension, enormous). Originally, then, *enormity* meant the same thing as *enormousness* or *immensity*, but over the years it came to be applied only to crimes of *enormous* proportions, i.e., *atrocities*. Its use now to indicate vast size is incorrect. (Fowler is less emphatic; he is content with the warning "inadvisable.") One should not speak of the *enormity* of the Pacific Ocean or the Pyramids or space. There is nothing atrocious about them. One might speak of both the *enormousness* and the *enormity* of the birth rate in India. The Chinese Government considered the *enormousness* of the birth rate there to be such an *enormity* that it formulated a policy of one child to a family. (Incidentally, Fowler says: *"Enormousness* is not a pretty word; the writer [can find] a way out by writing *vastness* or *enormous extent."*

entasis   (EN tuh sis) *n.* This is an architectural term for the slight swelling or convexity given to a shaft or column in order to create the optical illusion that the upright is perfectly straight, and neutralize what would otherwise be the illusion that a column of equal diameter throughout has a slightly concave outline. In the classical Doric column, the swelling begins at the base of the shaft and is at its greatest dimension a bit below its middle point. In the Parthenon (the temple of Athena Parthenos, the virgin Athena, on the Acropolis in Athens), the *entasis* reaches an extent of about 3/8 of an inch from the perpendicular on each side. *Entasis* was taken intact from the Greek, based on the prefix *en-* (in) plus *tasis* (a stretch), related to the verb *enteinein* (to stretch tight).

entelechy   (en TEL uh kee) *n. Entelechy* is actuality, realized existence, as opposed to mere potentiality. In the vitalist school of philosophy advocated by the German biologist and philosopher Hans Driesch (1867-1941), which holds that phenomena are to a certain extent self-determining and only partly controlled by mechanical forces, *entelechy* is the principle that directs processes in an organism toward realization of a certain end. *In Out of My Depths* (Doubleday, Garden City, N.Y., 1983), Paul West defines *entelechy* as "not only something's is-ness, but how its is-ness had evolved and was evolving." The Irish mathematician and astronomer Sir William Rowan Hamilton (1805-1865) tells us: "Aristotle [the Greek philosopher, 384-322 B.C.] defines the soul, the form or *entelechy* of an organized body." The German philosopher Leibniz (1646-1716) wrote: "Give the name of *entelechies* to all simple substances or created monads [in the Leibnitz school, a *monad* is an indivisible entity, the ultimate constituent of the universe] for they have in them a certain perfection." *Entelechy* is from Greek *entelecheia*, based on prefix *en-* (in) plus *telos* (goal) plus *echein* (to have). If all this seems somewhat complicated, suffice it to go back to the first sentence, and then talk it over with the first philosopher you happen to run into.

enteron, see **aliment**

entomology   (en tuh MOL uh jee) *n. Entomology* is the branch of zoology that deals with the study of insects. The word comes from the Greek prefix *entomo-*, based on *entoma* (insects, from *entoma zoa*, literally "notched animals") plus *logos* (discourse), the source of so many English words ending in *-logy* (*biology, geology, philology*, etc.) To *entomologize* (en tuh MOL uh jize) is to engage in the study of insects. *Entomophagous* (en tuh MOF uh gus) is a synonym of *insectivorous,* describing any organism that feeds on insects; formed from *entomo-* plus the Greek suffix *-phagous* (eating, feeding on, based on the verb *phagein*, to eat, devour). *Entomology* is a very broad field, since there are over 675,000 (!) known species of insect. Be careful not to confuse *entomology* with a like-sounding word: *etymology* (et uh MOL uh jee), the study of word derivations, from the Greek noun *etymologia* (studying words). Here's a simple mnemonic: *Etymology* is about woids; *entomology* is about ents.

entrepôt   (AWN truh poh—*n* pronounced nasally, as in French) *n*. An *entrepôt* is a storehouse or bonded warehouse for the transshipment or distribution of merchandise; a commercial center for export-import transactions. This is a French word, based on the verb *entreposer* (to store), which in turn goes back to the Latin preposition *inter* (between) plus *positum*, past participle of *ponere* (to put or place). Entrepôt was modeled on the French noun *dépôt* (depot), but in English the circumflex may be dropped as it has been in *depot*.

eoan   (ee O un) *adj. Eoan* describes things pertaining to dawn or sunrise. It is derived, via Latin, from the Greek noun *eos* (dawn), which, with an upper case *E*, was the name, in Greek mythology, for the goddess of dawn, the mother of the winds and the sister of Helios, the sun god. *Aurora* and *Sol* (later Apollo) were the respective Roman names for these sibling gods, whose parents were the Titans Hyperion and Theia. Eos gave us the lovely adjective *eoan*, and Helios the prefix *helio-*, as in *heliolatry* (hee lee OL uh tree), meaning "sun worship," *heliotrope* (HEE lee uh trope), for any plant that turns towards the sun, etc. An *eoan* sky is the sky at dawn. *Eoan* drowsiness is the sleepy feeling on waking at sunrise. The Russian-born American poet and novelist Vladimir Nabokov (1897-1977) used *eoan* in the sense of "early," as in "the *eoan* stage [i.e., onset] of an attack, in *Look at the Harlequins!* (McGraw-Hill, New York, 1974). Because the sun rises in the east, *eoan* is sometimes used of things pertaining to the east.

epenthesis   (eh PEN thih sis) *n. Epenthesis* is the erroneous insertion of an extra sound in the pronunciation (and sometimes, eventually, the spelling) of a word. The intruding insertion can be a consonant (as in prost*r*ate gland) or a vowel (as in burg*u*lar). *Epenthesis* is generic for both; the insertion of a vowel has a name all to itself: *anaptyxis* (an up TIK sis). *Epenthesis* is intact from the Greek, based on the prefix *ep-*, a variant form of *epi-* before a vowel (on) plus prefix *en-* (into) plus *thesis* (something set down). *Anaptyxis* is also intact from Greek, based on the prefix *ana-* (back) plus the verb *ptyssein* (to unfold). Some examples involving consonants: *condrum* (for *condom*); *reastauranteur*; *scrapegoat*; *asparagrass*. Involving vowels: *mischievious* and *grievious*; *arthuritis*, *athaletic*, *fillum* (for *film*). Involving both: *poison ivory*. For another form of messing about with words, see **metathesis**.

epicedium   (ep ih SEE dee um, -sih DYE um), **epicede** (EP ih seed) *n.* An *epicedium* or *epicede* is a dirge, an elegy, a funeral song or ode. *Epicedium* was taken intact from the Latin, which took it from the Greek *epikedeion*, a noun formed from the neuter of the adjective *epikedeios* (pertaining to a funeral), based on the prefix *epi-* (upon) plus *kedos* (sorrow). The adjectives *epicedial* (ep ih SEE dee ul) and *epicedian* (ep ih SEE dee un) mean "elegiac." *Epicedia* were the stock in trade of paid mourners, trained to produce the atmosphere appropriate to the sad occasion. Funeral parlors nowadays, especially the fancy ones, have piped-in lugubrious electric organ music to keep the tears flowing—a particularly oppressive type of canned art. "Here they come," says a member of the staff, and somebody behind the scenes presses a button. In the old days, they paid their respects with *epicedia*, and the live music seems a more fitting tribute to the dear departed and the grieving survivors. (See also **threnody**.)

epicene   (EP ih seen) *n., adj. Epicene* can be used in a variety of senses. An *epicene*, or *epicene* person, is one having characteristics of both sexes, or one of indeterminate sexual characteristics. *Epicene* can also apply to things; today's fashions in clothes and hair are becoming so *epicene* that it is often difficult to determine the sex of a person even at close range. Another meaning is "effete, weak, ineffectual, feeble." An *epicene* presentation of an advertising campaign, for example, will hardly impress the prospective client. These meanings may seem quite unrelated, but on closer examination, one can imagine a progression from "sharing male and female traits" to "neither one thing nor the other" to "feeble, unimpressive." The word is sometimes applied, in this male-chauvinistic world, to a person who is not adequately macho to the observer, in the sense of "effeminate" as a perjorative. A real he-man ballet dancer who moves with the required grace and delicacy may quite wrongly be labeled *epicene* in the sense of "effeminate" rather than quite correctly in the sense first mentioned above. For those interested in the classical languages, there is a special grammatical use of *epicene*: an *epicene* noun in Latin or Greek is either (1) one that is always of the same gender regardless of the sex of the animal in question (Latin *vulpes* is always feminine, i.e., takes a feminine adjective, whether it means "fox" or "vixen") or (2) one that has a common gender (Latin *bos*, Greek *bous*—bull or cow—will take a masculine or feminine adjective depending on the sex of the animal referred to). Fowler points out that *epicene* "having no real function in English grammar . . . is kept alive chiefly in contemptuous use, implying physical as well as moral sexlessness . . . "

epicrisis (ih PIK rih sis) *n.* As one can see from the stress on the second syllable, this is not a kind of *crisis*, though both words have a common Greek source. An *epicrisis* is an evaluation, a critical study or estimate, usually of a literary work, supplemented by some discussion of the subject matter. *Crisis* (from Greek *krisis*, decision, related to *krinein*, to judge or decide) is a familiar word. The adjective *critical* relates to *criticism*, but goes off in other directions as well, involving uncertainty and danger (a patient in a *critical* condition, a *critical* wound); and *critical* can also mean "decisive" (a *critical* point in an argument). *Epicrisis* is derived from Greek *epikrisis* (determination), related to *epikrinein* (to judge), based upon prefix *epi-* (upon) plus *krinein* (to judge)—this is the common source referred to above. The adjective *epicritic* (ep uh KRIT ik); sometimes *epicritical*, from Greek *epikritikos* (determinative), is a physiological term describing high sensitivity to variations in pain or temperature ("low threshhold") as opposed to *protopathic* (pro tuh PATH ik), describing low sensitivity to such stimuli ("high threshold"). A very versatile source, that little Greek *krisis*.

epideictic (ep ih DIK tik), **epideictical** (ep ih DIK tuh kul), *adj.* These adjectives apply to anything done for show. *Epideictic* is from Greek *epideiktikos*, based on the prefix *epi-* (upon) plus the verb *deiknynai* (to show, display). Show-offs engage in one *epideictic* act after another. The ladies' hats at Royal Ascot are a good example of *epideictic* behavior. The nouveaux riches tend to live in an *epideictic* world, indulging in vulgar display of extravagant apparel, jewelry, objets d'art, cars, and other paraphernalia. Attendance by tone-deaf spectators at the opening night of the opera season, in the old days, was an *epideictic* procedure. So, alack, is often the case with attendance at church. It is likewise to be feared, or at least suspected, that presence at **vernissages** may well be *epideictic* in nature. Can it be that all the French used in the foregoing comment may be an *epideictic* excess?

epigon(e) (EP uh gohn) *n.* An *epigone* is a second-rate imitator of a distinguished predecessor in the arts, philosophy, history, etc., usually one of a previous generation. *Epigonic* (ep uh GON ik) is the adjective, *epigonism* (ih PIG uh niz um) the noun for this sorry practice. These words come, via Latin *epigonus*, from Greek *epigonos* (a person born after—based on the verb *epigignesthai*, to be born after, from prefix *epi-* in the sense of "after" plus *gignesthai*, to be born). The American foreign correspondent and writer Vincent Sheean (1899-1975) wrote of "the obsequious literature of the *epigones*," and the American poet William Rose Benét (1886-1950) said of a minor poet: "Your verse . . . supports a primitive traditionalism and *epigonism*." The American linguists Alexander and Nicholas Humez, in *Alpha to Omega* (David R. Godine, Publisher, Inc., Boston, 1981), quote the definition by the Roman rhetorician Quintilian (c. 35-c. 95) of the Greco-Roman type of humor known as "urbanitas" ("language with a smack of the city in its words, accent and idiom . . . " and insert in brackets their own comment "at which the fledgling *New Yorker* succeeded so well and at which many of its *epigones* so utterly failed"). *Epigonic* poetry, painting, music, and philosophical or historical writing are imitative of the products of an earlier generation. The American use of *epigone* appears to be a special application of the term to inferior imitators in the arts. The British use it in the singular in the general sense of "one of a later generation," without reference to the arts or imitation, and in the plural to denote "undistinguished descendants of the great," like (meaning no offense) the children of Franklin D. Roosevelt and Winston Churchill. In this use, they are alluding to the classical Greek legend of the *Epigoni*, the seven sons of the original seven heroes known as the "Seven against Thebes." The general idea behind the British use of the word, at least in the plural, is expressed in the oft-repeated opinion of just about every generation surveying its own leaders in politics and the arts, and sometimes in sports, that "they don't make them that way any more," referring nostalgically to the heroes of days gone by.

epinosic   (ep ih NOS ik) *adj.* This is a word you won't run into very often. It means both "unhealthy" and "unhealthful." Yes, there is a distinction, as we shall see. *Epinosic* is derived from the Greek prefix *epi-* (upon, over, near, at, after—depending on the context) plus *nosos* (disease). The distinction between *unhealthy* and *unhealthful* is recognized to a certain degree in both American and British dictionaries, in that the first meaning attributed to *healthy* is "in a state of good health," while the first definition of *healthful* is "conducive to good health," i.e., "salutary." However, and in this author's opinion sadly, the two words are also given as mutually synonymous. That really is unfortunate: the nice distinction between *healthy* (in good health) and *healthful* (promoting health) ought to be preserved. The Second Edition of *Webster's Unabridged* condones the blurring, in effect, but has at least the decency to observe that the two words are ". . . interchangeable [only] within certain limits. *Healthy* more frequently applies to that which is in a state of health or vigor; *healthful*, to that which conduces to health . . . a *healthy* (not *healthful*) man; *healthful* (not *healthy*) food . . . " Good old *Webster's Second*! The distinction should not be ignored, in the less than humble opinion of this disinterested but far from uninterested writer. But to get back to our *epinosic*: It appears to cover both *un-healthy* and *unhealthful*, and if you want to preserve the nice distinction recommended above, your definition will have to depend on the context.

epiplexis (ep uh PLEK sis) *n*. This is a rhetorical contrivance whereby a speaker, haranguing a crowd, upbraids them in order to incite them. One of the best known uses of *epiplexis* in all drama is the famous speech of the Tribune Marullus to the crowd at the outset of Shakespeare's *Julius Caesar* (Act I, Scene 1). The commoners have come to " . . . make holiday to see/Caesar, and to rejoice in his triumph . . . " Marullus cries:

> You blocks, you stones, you worse than senseless things!
> O you hard hearts, you cruel men of Rome,
> Knew you not Pompey? . . .
> And do you now put on your best attire?
> And do you now cull out a holiday?
> And do you now strew flowers in his way,
> That comes in triumph over Pompey's blood?
> Be gone!

That was some **epiplexis**! This word, in Late Latin, meant "reproof," from the Greek, based on the prefix *epi-* (upon) plus the verb *epiplessein* (to strike at, reprove).

epiphany (ih PIF uh nee) *n*. An *epiphany* is the appearance or manifestation of a god to a mortal, or any moment of divine revelation, like the appearance of God in the burning bush to Moses in *Exodus* 3:2. The word *epiphany* comes from the Greek noun *epiphaneia* (appearance), based on the prefix *epi-* (near, at, before) plus *phainein* (to show) and the related adjective *epiphanes* (manifest). With an upper case *E*, *Epiphany* is a Christian festival observed on January 6 celebrating the appearance of the Christ-child to the gentiles, the Magi, the three Wise Men from the East. January 6 is the twelfth day after December 25, Christ's birthday, so that Twelfth Night, the eve of the Twelfth Day, used to be a time of feasting and much merrymaking. Shakespeare named his play *Twelfth Night* because it was written to be acted during the Twelfth Night revels.

epistemology (ih pis tuh MOL uh jee) *n*. This is an area of philosophy dealing with human knowledge—its origins, characteristics, methods, and limits. The word is formed of the Greek noun *episteme* (knowledge) plus the suffix *-logy*, used in the names of studies and sciences (e.g., *philology, theology*), from *logos* (discourse). *Epistemology* is a science or discipline distinct from logic, treating the operations of the mind in the knowing process. As to the origins of knowledge, empiricism bases all knowledge on the perceptions of the senses, while rationalism asserts that the mind enlarges knowledge with ideas not derived from empirical experience. Realism and idealism differ in that the former teaches that the object of knowledge is real in itself, while the latter makes the object dependent on the activity of the mind. The foregoing is, obviously, the merest sketch of the various departments of *epistemology*. A full treatment would hardly fit within the confines of this book.

epithalamion, **epithalamium**, see **hymeneal**

epizeuxis (ep ih ZOOHK sis) *n*. *Epizeuxis* is the immediate repetition of a word for the sake of emphasis, taken, via Late Latin, from the Greek, where it means "fastening together, repetition," based on the Greek prefix *epi-* (upon) plus *zeugnynai* (to join). "Hear, hear!" is certainly a more effective comment than "Hear!" "Well, well!" is many times more expressive than "Well!" and "Again and again and again," a favorite expression of Franklin Roosevelt, made a deep impression on his listeners. "Finally, finally!" is a much more powerful demonstration of satisfaction than one "Finally!" All these are examples of *epizeuxis*. And remember those lines from *The Bells* by the American poet Edgar Allan Poe (1809-1849):

> Keeping time, time, time,
>   In a sort of Runic rhyme,
> To the tintinnabulation that so musically wells
>   From the bells, bells, bells, bells,
> Bells, bells, bells.

and those from the *Elegy to the Memory of an Unfortunate Lady* by the English poet Alexander Pope (1688-1744):

> By foreign hands thy dying eyes were closed,
> By foreign hands thy decent limbs composed,
> By foreign hands thy humble grave adorned,
> By strangers honoured, and by strangers mourned!

eponym (EP uh nim) *n*. An *eponym* is a person from whose name something actually or supposedly takes its name, and words derived from *eponyms* are called "eponymous" (eh PON uh mus). Examples: Amelia Bloomer (1818-1894), associated with the women's rights movement of the last century, gave us *bloomers*. Thomas Bowdler (1754-1825) in 1818 published expurgated editions of Shakespeare and Gibbon's *Decline and Fall*; hence, **bowdlerize**. The French inventor Louis Braille (1809-1852) gave us *braille*. E. Clerihew Bentley (1875-1956), the English writer, invented the **clerihew**. J.T. Brudnell, seventh earl of Cardigan, a British cavalryman of Crimean War fame (1797-1868), gave us the *cardigan*. The French doctor Joseph Ignace Guillotine (1738-1814) designed the *guillotine*. Sir Henry Havelock (1795-1857), an English general in India, created the *havelock*, a cap cover with a back flap to protect the neck from rain and sun. The Austrian physician Friedrich Anton Mesmer (1734-1815) was the father of *mesmerism*. The term *Rachmanism*, unfamiliar to American ears but well known in Britain, denotes, according to the definition given in this author's compilation of Briticisms, *English English* (Verbatim, Essex, Connecticut, 1980), "the despicable practice of taking over lower-class residential property and deliberately creating intolerable living conditions in order to force the poor tenants to get out, so that the landlord can then turn the property to more profitable commercial uses. The term is derived from a man named Rachman, who in the 1960s pioneered in this type of manipulation." The British Field Marshall Lord Raglan (1788-1855), commander in the Crimean War, was responsible for the *raglan* sleeve. The Marquis de Sade (1740-1814) gave us *sadism*. The fourth earl of Sandwich (1718-1792) created the *sandwich*. The English General Henry Shrapnel (1761-1842) invented the *shrapnel shell*. The French finance minister Étienne de Silhouette (1709-1767) first concocted the *silhouette*. The English Reverend W.A. Spooner (1844-1930) was responsible for *spoonerism*. And, lest you conclude that *eponyms* are practically the exclusive province of long-departed British generals and miscellaneous Europeans of mostly ancient vintage, how about our very own Shirley Temple and the *Shirley Temple hairdo* and the *Shirley Temple cocktail* (for children—no alcohol)? Finally, there are all those dread diseases named after the doctors who first identified and described them: *Alzheimer's*, *Hodgkin's*, *Parkinson's*, among—sadly enough—many others. Be all that as it may, do not confuse *eponym* with **toponym**. *Eponym* is derived from the Greek prefix *epi-* (upon) plus *onoma* (name).

equine, see **accipitrine**

eristic (eh RIS tik) *n*. Also, as an adjective, *eristical* (eh RIS tuh kul). *Eristic(al)* means "pertaining to controversy." An *eristic* is a quarrelsome, disputatious person, a controversialist, one who enjoys contention and argument for their own sake and loves to "take the other side" to start an argument or keep one going. Such people, often without deep convictions of their own, simply go at it for the enjoyment of the fray. The word is from the Greek *eristikos*, related to the verb *erizein* (to wrangle), based on *eris* (strife, discord). Eris, in Greek mythology, was the goddess of discord, identified in Roman mythology as the goddess Discordia, whose name speaks for itself. What a troublemaker! She and Ate, another Greek goddess, the one who personified recklessness and mischief and vengeance, were responsible for a lot of woe. In Shakespeare's *King John* (Act II, Scene 1) Chatillon, the French ambassador to England, tells King Philip of France of King John's invasion, accompanied by " . . . the mother-queen/An Ate, stirring him to blood and strife . . . " and Antony, in *Julius Caesar* (Act III, Scene 1) soliloquizes:

> And Caesar's spirit ranging for revenge,
> With Ate by his side come hot from hell
> Shall . . .
> Cry 'Havoc,' and let slip the dogs of war . . .

Eris and Ate—quite a pair!

eschatology (es kuh TOL uh jee) *n. Eschatology* is a term in theology, covering any doctrine concerned with final things: death and resurrection, immortality, the second coming of Christ, the last judgment, the future condition of things thereafter. *Eschatology* also denotes the branch of theology that deals with those matters. The word is formed from the Greek adjective for "last," *eschatos*, plus the familiar *-logy* suffix used in the naming of sciences, fields of study, and bodies of knowledge. The adjective is *eschatological* (es kuh tuh LOJ ih kul), and an *eschatologist* (es kuh TOL uh jist) is one devoted to the study of the doctrines defined above.

escheat (es CHEET) *n., vb.* This is a legal term in the field of estate inheritance law. Each of the 50 states has a statute specifying how the property of a deceased person is distributed among his heirs or next of kin if he leaves no will. If there is no will and there are no next of kin, the property reverts to the state, and in that case the estate is said to *escheat.* The author has been involved in one peculiar case where the decedent, who had no heirs whatever, did sign a will dividing what he thought was his entire estate among a number of friends, but the percentages bequeathed, as the result of an arithmetical error on the part of the draftsman, totaled only 95 percent. Result: five percent *escheated* to the state in which the deceased had resided. *Escheat* goes back to English Common Law. The word was derived, via Middle English *eschete* and Late Latin *excadere*, from Latin prefix *ex-* (from) plus the verb *cadere* (to fall).

esculent, see **comestible**

estivate (ES tuh vate) *vb.* Most of us are familiar with the verb *hibernate* (HYE bur nate), which applies to the habit of certain animals, like bears, of spending the winter, usually huddled in close quarters, in a dormant state; also of people, in the sense of "withdraw, remain in seclusion, retire," generally regardless of season. It is from *hibernatus*, past participle of Latin *hibernare* (to spend the winter), based on *hiems* (winter). To *estivate* is the corresponding term applied to the summer season: to spend the summer, and it comes from *aestivatus*, past participle of Latin *aestivare* (to spend the summer), based on *aestas* (summer). Such symmetry, for once, in language which so often is abritrary! Applied to animals, to *estivate* is to spend the summer in a dormant, or at least torpid state, like crabs *estivating* in the sand. The leisured classes often *hibernate* in southern climes and *estivate* at country lodges, in the mountains or by the sea. The English, when India was part of the Empire, *estivated* in their hill stations.

estrus (ES trus) *n.* The *estrus* or *estrum* or *oestrus* is the period when a female animal is in heat or rut, her period of maximum sexual receptivity; via Latin *oestrus*, from Greek *oistros* (gadfly, sting, and by extension, frenzy, as though produced by the sting; and any owner of an unspayed cat will attest to the frenzied sounds emitted by the pet in heat). The *estrone cycle* is the series of physiological changes in the organs of female mammals occurring between rutting periods. *Estrone* (ES trone) is a hormone found in urine during pregnancy, and a commercial form of it, also known as *estrin*, *oestrin*, *oestrone* or *theelin* is used to remedy *estrogen* deficiency, *estrogen* being a female hormone capable of producing *estrus*. More details can be provided by your friendly neighborhood gynecologist.

esurient (ih SOOR ee unt) *adj.* To be *esurient* is to be hungry (in the literal sense, for food) or greedy (for gain or loot), rapacious. *Esurient* is derived from Latin *ensuriens*, present participle of *esurire* (to be hungry; by extension, to long for). The noun is *esurience* (ih SOOR ee uns); the Latin noun is *esuritio*, but we have no such noun as *esurition*. One can never be sure about which part of speech, in the Latin, is going to give us our word. One's *esurience* may be simple gluttony or inordinate rapacity; either way, it is an unlovely quality.

ethnology, see **genethlialogy**

ethology, see **genethlialogy**

ethos (EE thos, ETH os) *n.* The *ethos* of a culture is its basic spirit or character, the fundamental sentiment that pervades its beliefs and practices; the characteristic spirit permeating a nation, an age, or the arts, especially the literature of a social group, whether nation, community, party, or institution. As applied to a nation, according to Fowler, " . . . it is the sum of the intellectual and moral tendencies manifested in what the Germans called the nation's Kultur; like Kultur, it is not in itself a word of praise or blame, any more than *quality*." Applied to drama, *ethos* is the moral constituent that establishes a character's action rather than his thinking or his emotion. *Ethos* was taken intact from the Greek, where it means "custom" or "character."

etiolate, see **etiology**

etiology (ee tee OL uh jee) *n.* In its widest application, *etiology* is the study or the philosophy of causation; more narrowly, the assignment of a cause to a situation. Thus, one might speak of the *etiology* of a custom or ritual. The word comes, via Late Latin, from Greek *aitilogia* (determination of the cause of something), based on the noun *aitia* (cause) plus the suffix *logia* (science, study, body of knowledge). Even more narrowly, in medical science, *etiology* is the study of the cause of diseases, or, more specifically, the actual cause of a disease, e.g., the *etiology* of Legionnaire's Disease. One might be forgiven for the belief that to *etiolate* was to act in the field of *etiology*, but the belief would be quite wrong. To *etiolate* (EE tee uh late) is to bleach or blanch (a plant) by excluding light as done in the cultivation of celery. *Etiolate* is from an entirely different source, the French verb *étioler* (to make or become pale; more specifically, to become stubble, *éteule* being French for *stubble*, from the Latin *stipula*, stalk, straw). *Etiolate*, used **intransitively**, means to "become pale." The process of making something pale, or becoming pale, is known as *etiolation* (ee tee uh LAY shun). Jumping to derivations is as dangerous as jumping to conclusions.

etymon   (ET uh mon) *n*. The *etymon* of a word is its original root or true origin, the form from which the ultimate word is derived. For example: the Greek word *eune* (bed, bedroom, sleeping place) is the *etymon* of *eunuch*. So we see that *eunuch* starts out from the *etymon eune*, to which was added the Greek suffix *-ouchos* (keeping), based on the verb *echein* (to keep, hold). In the same kind of development, *cor* (Latin for "heart") is the *etymon* of our adjective *cordial* (friendly, warm and *hearty*), and *kerd*, a noun in the Indo-European family of languages, is thought to be the *etymon* of *cor* and of Greek *kardia*, from which we get *cardiac* and related words and, indeed, the word *heart* itself. *Etymon* may not be a familiar word, but from it we got the familiar term *etymology* (et uh MOL uh jee), the study of the derivation of words. *Etymon* was taken intact from the Greek; it is the neuter form of the adjective *etymos* (true, real).

eudemonism   (yooh DEE muh niz um) *n*. This is the doctrine or system of ethics that happiness is the test of rectitude or moral virtue; that the basis of moral obligations is found in the likeliness that correct actions will produce happiness. Thus, the related adjective *eudemonic* (yooh dih MON ik) means "conducive to happiness." A *eudemon* (yooh DEE mon) is a good spirit, and *eudemonia* (yooh dih MOH nee uh) is happiness itself. All these words are based on the Greek prefix *eu-* (good: found in words like *euphoria*, *euphemism*, etc.) plus *daimon* (spirit). *Eudemonism* in the system of the English philosopher Thomas Hobbes (1588-1679) is egoistic; in that of the later English philosopher James Mills (1773-1836), the *eudemonism* is altruistic.

euhemerism   (yooh HEE muh riz um, -HEM uh-) *n*. This word, sometimes capitalized in honor of Euhemeris (see below), is the doctrine or theory that explains mythology as legend based upon actual history, and the gods as originating out of the magnification of exceptional human beings; the interpretation of myths by attribution of their origin to real people or historical events. One who subscribes to that theory is a *euhemerist* and to attribute myths to real persons and events is to *euhemerize* (yooh HEE muh rize, -HEM-). This doctrine was originated by Euhemerus, a fourth century B.C. Greek philosopher and mythographer. He was a courtier of King Cassander of Macedonia. In his *Sacred History*, he expounded the theory that the gods were once great kings and exceptional heroes who were revered after death and eventually deified. Euhemerus appears to have been a male chauvinist; apparently, in his system, the goddesses were merely the mates or lady friends of the gods. But how about Aphrodite, Artemis, Athena, Demeter, Diana, Eos, Eris, and all those other girls who seem to have got to Mt. Olympus on their own?

euphuism   (YOOH fyooh iz um) *n*. *Euphuism* (not to be confused with a look-alike word, *euphemism*, with which it has absolutely no connection) is a flowery, affected, precious, high-flown style of language, written or spoken, in imitation of that of the English writer John Lyly (c. 1554-1606), best known for his two-part didactic romance *Euphues, or the Anatomy of Wit* and *Euphues and his England*, a work that advocated a reform of education and manners. Lyly wrote in an affected style, fashionable and much imitated at the end of the 16th century, full of preciosity, strings of alliteration, and antitheses. Lyly named his **protagonist** *Euphues* after the Greek adjective *euphues* (well-grown —descriptive of a man of parts), based on the Greek prefix *eu-* (well) plus *phue* (growth), related to the verb *phuein* (to grow).

ex post facto   (eks post FAK toh) This Latin phrase is the equivalent of "retroactive" or "retroactively" depending on whether the term is used adjectivally or adverbially. Literally, *ex post facto* means "from something done later;" in legal parlance, "on the basis of legislation enacted later." A statute that affects previously completed transactions or previously committed crimes is *ex post facto* legislation, i.e., it seeks to have retroactive effect and thus to change the legal status of an act committed before its enactment. Such legislation, including tax statutes, is occasionally enacted and takes retroactive effect in civil law, but is not effective in criminal law to make illegal what was previously legal, or make punishment more severe than what was on the books when the crime was committed. As to the spelling of the phrase, Fowler says that "the person who knows the Latin words is worse off with it in this disguise than one who does not; it should be *ex postfacto* (*ex* on the footing of, *postfacto* later enactment)." One can only agree (admittedly, it is dangerous not to, with Fowler). As he says, " . . . what is referred to in *facto* is not the 'doing' of the action but the [later] 'enacting' of the law." If in doubt, consult your lawyer.

exanimate   (ig ZAN uh mit, -mate) *adj.* The literal meaning is "lifeless"; *inanimate* is a synonym. But figuratively, *exanimate* is not marked by such fatality: it is used to describe one who is disheartened, depressed, dispirited. It is from Latin *exanimatus*, past participle of *exanimare* (to deprive of breath), based on prefix *ex-* (from) plus (or in this case, minus?) *anima* (breath). The condition is *exanimation*. (Mind your *m*'s and *n*'s!)

exegesis   (-getics), see **hermeneutics**

exiguous   (ig ZIG yooh us, ik SIG-) *adj. Exiguous* describes things that are meager, in small amount, scanty, sparse, piddling, paltry, skimpy. It comes from Latin *exiguus*, based on prefix *ex-* used as an intensive plus the verb *egere* (to be needy, poor, in want). Despite her great influence on the work of the Roman poets Catullus (c. 84-c. 54 B.C.) and Ovid (43 B.C.-A.D. 18) and the English poet Swinburne (1837-1909), all that is left of the writings of the Greek poet Sappho (c. 620-565 B.C.) is an *exiguous* collection of fragments, the longest one consisting of only seven stanzas. Those lean, underweight models who grace our advertisements subsist on an *exiguous* diet. For the noun, one can choose between *exiguity* (eks uh GYOOH ih tee) and *exiguousness* (ig ZIG yooh us nus).

exoteric (ek su TER ik) *adj. Exoteric* is the opposite of *esoteric*, a more familiar word. Anything *exoteric* is suitable for communication to the common people, the multitude, *hoi polloi*; not for the inner circle, the select few. *Exoteric* things are popular, commonplace, marked by simplicity. *Esoteric* matters are the province of the **cognoscenti**. When, in Shakespeare's *Hamlet* (Act II, Scene 2), the **protagonist** says to the First Player: "I heard thee speak me a speech once, but it was never acted, or if it was, not above once; for the play, I remember, pleas'd not the million; 'twas caviare to the general [over the heads of the general public; too refined for their palate] . . . ," he was characterizing the play as *esoteric*. Grade B movies and TV sitcoms are *exoteric*. Does this sound snobbish? It is. *Exoteric* is from Greek *exoterikos*, related to *exoteros* (inclined outward); *esoteric* is from Greek *esoterikos*, related to *esoteros* (inner).

factious, see **factitious**

factitious (fak TISH us) *adj.* Anything described as *factitious* is contrived and artificial, like the prearranged cheering and waving of crowds awaiting a dictator's harangue. It is insincere, produced artificially, not spontaneous, genuine, or natural, and made to order, as it were. *Factitious* is derived from Latin *factitius*, a variant of *facticius* (artificial), based on *factus*, past participle of the verb *facere* (to make). The "hype" surrounding the appearance of rock superstars or spectacular sporting events is a good example of *factitious* enthusiasm. There are several adjectives that one must be careful not to confuse with *factitious*: *factious*, *factitive*, and *fictitious*. *Factious* (FAK shus) describes partisan activities and emotions. Fowler says that "*factious* rancour is the rancour that lets party spirit prevail over patriotism." Political logrolling is a good example of this. *Factitive* (FAK tih tiv) is a grammatical term, describing verbs containing a sense of making, calling, or thinking that take a direct object and an objective complement. Here are some examples: The people *elected* him president. (*Him* is the direct object; *president* is the objective complement.) The group *made* him their leader. An unbiased observer would *call* it a swindle. Sensible people *think* the arms race insane. In these sentences, the verbs are *factitive*. That adjective is from New Latin *factitivus*, based on the verb *factitare* (to do frequently, to declare [something] to be). *Fictitious* is a familiar word, synonymous with *false* or *imaginary*, and is derived from Latin *ficticius* (artificial); it needs no discussion here.

factitive, see **factitious**

faience (fye ANS, fay-) *n.* This is the name given to any type of glazed earthenware, porcelain, or pottery with brightly colored designs, including majolica (also spelt *maiolica*), which is earthenware covered with a tin oxide glaze and very highly decorated. *Faience* is a fine variety of this type of pottery. Its name is derived from the northern Italian city of Faenza, a ceramic center. Majolica is said to be named after the Island of Majorca, where the finest quality of this type of pottery was originally made. Much of it was shipped to Italy. Majolica from Faenza has a deep blue background, and is produced in the form of tiles, jars, bowls, and panels. The clay object is fired, coated with tin enamel, fired again, painted in flashing colors, and finally fired for a third time.

fainéant (FAY nee unt) *n.*, *adj.* The acute accent may be omitted. As both noun and adjective, *fainéant* means "do-nothing." A *fainéant* person, or a *fainéant*, is an idler, and his trait is known as *faineancy* (FAY nee un see), *faineance* (FAY nee uns) or *faineantise* (fay nee un TEEZ). *Fainéant* was taken intact from the French, where it was based on the verb *faire* (to do) plus *néant* (nothing). The term *Roi Fainéant* (Do-Nothing King), meaning "puppet king," was applied to the late Merovingian kings of France, the dynasty founded in the fifth century by Merovius, ruler of the Franks (the Germanic tribe that conquered Gaul after the fall of the Roman Empire, and gave us the name *France*). The Merovingians ruled until their power was usurped by the "Mayors of the Palace" (Royal Stewards), and in 751 Pippin III became King of the Franks and did away with their office. *Fainéant* is a fashionable word for "sluggard." In the next edition of the *New English Bible*, shall we be told: "Go to the ant, you fainéant . . . " (*Proverbs* 6:6)?

falconine, see **accipitrine**

fanfaronade (fan fuh ruh NADE) *n.* This is a lovely word for arrogant bluster, boastful, ostentatious talk or behavior, bragging, bravado. A *fanfaron* (FAN fuh ron) is a braggart, but the word can mean, simply, "fanfare." *Fanfaronade* is from French *fanfaronnade*, taken from Spanish *fanfarronada*. *Fanfaron* was likewise taken from the French, which got it from Spanish *fanfarron* (braggart), and that went all the way back to Arabic *farfar* (garrulous). In Shakespeare's *Merchant of Venice* (Act I, Scene 1), Gratiano describes the kind of man who strives to give an impression of " . . . wisdom, gravity, profound conceit;/As who should say 'I am Sir Oracle,/And when I ope my lips let no dog bark!'" This is a classic example of *fanfaronade*. Cf. **braggadocio, gasconade, rodomontade, thrasonical**.

farouche (fuh ROOHSH) *adj.* *Farouche* was taken over intact from the French, where it has two quite different meanings: "wild, fierce" or "sullen, shy unsociable." When the French describe a woman as "bien *farouche*," they are characterizing her not as *fierce*, but as *very shy*. British dictionaries define *farouche* as "shy, ill at ease, sullen and unsociable, socially inexperienced, unused to company and lacking polish," and although some of them refer to "French: wild," others mention the French origin but refer to Middle Latin *forasticus*, derived from Latin *foras* (out of doors), while American dictionaries refer to "French: 1. fierce; 2. sullenly shy." Fowler says of *farouche*: "The meaning, simply sullen-mannered from shyness (*cheval farouche*, cheval qui craint la présence de l'homme) [*farouche horse, a horse that fears the presence of a man*] . . . is obscured by association with ferocious; according to the OED [*Oxford English Dictionary*] 'the connexion is untenable'; see TRUE AND FALSE ETYMOLOGY." And when we go to that heading, we find in the long list FAROUCHE, not L[atin] *ferox* fierce. So we see that it is Latin *foras* (out of doors; i.e., *wild* in the sense of "untamed," bringing with it the sense of "socially inept," therefore shy and ill at ease, and therefore sullen), rather than Latin *ferox* (fierce) or Latin *ferus* (wild, fierce), that has given us *farouche*.

fascine   (fa SEEN, fuh-) *n*. A *fascine* is a bundle of sticks bound together, used to strengthen ramparts in building up military defenses, or to fill in ditches that impede attack, a use that was revived in World War II. *Fascine* was taken from the French, who got it from Latin *fascina* (bundle of sticks). In ancient Rome, the *fasces* (construed as a singular noun; plural of *fascis*, bundle) was a bundle of rods bound with red thongs, with an axe blade protruding, assigned to the high court judges as a symbol of authority. The *fasces* became the symbol of fascism, introduced by Benito Mussolini in 1919. His charming friend Hitler preferred the swastika.

felicitous   (fih LIS ih tus) *adj. Felicitous* means "befitting, appropriate, strikingly apt, pleasantly ingenious." A *felicitous* expression or act is one exactly suited to the occasion; a *felicitous* comment is one extremely well put, the *mot juste*. A *felicitous* person is one with a particular aptitude for correct or suitable conduct or expression. *Felicitous* is derived from Latin *felicitas* (happiness, good fortune, success), based on the adjective *felix* (favorable, auspicious). The related noun *felicity* (fih LIS ih tee) means "happiness," and to *felicitate* (fih LIS ih tate) is to congratulate; but the special significance of *felicitous* is *appropriateness. Infelicitous* (in fuh LIS ih tus), as one might expect, means "inappropriate" and *infelicitous* remarks are inapt, unsuitable, ill-chosen, gauche, out of place, malapropos, the sort that can cause a bit of squirming by those within earshot. The Irish writer Oscar Wilde (1854-1900) was a master of the *felicitous*. The pompous Mrs. Malaprop, a character in *The Rivals*, a comedy by the Irish dramatist Richard Sheridan (1751-1816), came close to monopolizing the *infelicitous*.

feline, see **accipitrine**

felloe, see **apogee**

feracious   (fih RAY shus) *adj. Feracious* means "fruitful, productive," and comes from Latin *ferax* (fruitful, fertile, prolific), related to the verb *ferre* (to bear, bring forth, produce). We get *fertile* from the related Latin adjective *fertilis. Feracious* can apply to things both tangible and intangible. Thus, it may be said that the spirit of the Renaissance created a *feracious* atmosphere for the development of new approaches to the arts. It is easy to confuse *feracious* with *ferocious*, especially since our rich language includes the adjective *feral* (FEE rul, or FER ul), meaning "wild," and by extension, "ferocious." *Feracious* is far removed from both *feral* and *ferocious*.

feretory (FER ih toh ree) *n.* A *feretory* is an ornate portable bier or shrine for the deposit of saints' relics after they have been carried in a religious procession, or a chapel in which the shrine is deposited. After the procession, the irreplaceable relics are carefully stowed in a *feretory*. The word is from the Latin noun *feretrum* (bier for carrying a body to the grave), which was derived from the Greek *pheretron* (bier), based on the verb *pherein* (to carry). There are relics of all types, all or part of a saint's body, clothing, almost anything connected with the saint. Alas, many are spurious—the tip of Lucifer's tail, for instance, pieces of the cross, vials of Christ's blood. A reliquary is likewise a receptacle for relics, but it is not portable.

feticide, see **aborticide**

fin de siècle (fan duh SYEH kluh—*n* pronounced nasally, second uh almost silent). This French expression means, literally, "end of century"; the century implied is the 19th. The phrase really signifies "toward the end of the 1800s." It refers to the concepts of society, especially the art, characteristic of that period, and broadly means "decadent." That meaning can be understood only as contrasted with the prudery and stuffiness of the greater part of the Victorian age. The expression itself was taken from the title of an 1888 French novel. As to pronunciation, Fowler warns us that "to say a French word in the middle of an English sentence exactly as it would be said by a Frenchman in a French sentence is a feat demanding an acrobatic mouth . . . that should not be attempted . . . All that is necessary is a polite acknowledgement of indebtedness to the French language."

finjan, fingan, see **zarf**

fizgig (FIZ gig), **fisgig** (FIS gig) *n.* This peculiar word is the name for an astonishing assortment of things: a gadabout, giddy, flighty, frivolous, flirtatious, fretful, flustered female (how's that for alliteration?); a damp fireword that goes off with a loud hiss; a gimcrack or flimsy knickknack; a **crotchet**, whine, or quirk; a harpoon (in this meaning, usually spelt *fish gig* and comes from Spanish *fisga*, harpoon); a spinning or whirling toy that makes a loud, whizzing sound as it rotates. A versatile word, with a versatile derivation: *fizz* (hissing or fluttering sound) or late Middle English *fise* (a term of abuse) or Icelandic *fisa* (to fart) plus Middle English *gigge* (girl). God help lexicographers and etymologists!

flagitious (fluh JISH us) *adj.* A *flagitious* person is a villain, capable of the most shameful wickedness. A *flagitious* crime is an unspeakable heinous offense. A *flagitium*, in Latin, is a disgraceful act, a shameful crime; the related adjective is *flagitiosus* (shameful, infamous, disgraceful). *Flagitious* is a strong word; it makes up in force what it lacks in frequency of use. Its synonyms are *nefarious, heinous, atrocious, iniquitous, villainous, vicious, depraved*—not that "synonyms" are exact equivalents, those nuances always creep in—but *flagitious* is pretty terrible no matter how thin you slice it. The Roman poet Horace (65-8 B.C.) in one of his odes (IV.9.45) wrote (Wickham translation):

> The name of the happy man is
> claimed by him who . . .
> dreads disgrace [*flagitium*] as
> something worse than death.

floccillation   (flok suh LAY shun) *n*. This is one of two words denoting the delirious picking at bedclothes by feverish patients. The other is *carphology* (kar FOL uh jee), sometimes defined as delirious *fumbling* with bedclothes, but there cannot be any real distinction between delirious picking and delirious fumbling, so the words may, for practical purposes, be treated as synonymous. *Floccillation* is derived from Late Latin *floccillus*, a diminutive of Latin *floccus* (flock of wool), a word that has been taken into English as is. *Carphology* comes from New Latin and Late Latin *carphologia* (fumbling with or picking at blankets), derived in turn from Greek *karphologia*, indicating that this picking and fumbling has been going on for a long time. Since the medical profession seems to need two words to describe this pathological activity, more of this fumbling and picking must happen than meets the layman's eye. But be careful not to confuse *carphology* with *carpology* (kar POL uh jee), a branch of botany concerned with fruits, a word based on Greek *karpos* (fruit). The omission or addition of a single little *h* can make a world of difference—the gulf between delirious fumbling and rational study. See also the last sentence of **apothegm**.

floccinaucinihilipilification   (floks ee nos ee nih hil ee pil ih fih KAY shun) *n*. Yes, Virginia, there is a *flocci* . . . etc., albeit it is unlikely that you will run into it or it into you. It exists, a solemn entry in British English dictionaries, a jocular concoction of Latin nouns in the genitive (possessive) case to form a jawbreaker denoting the act of belittling someone or something, expressing the opinion that he, she, or it is of little or no value. The four genitives all mean "trifle" or "nothing" and are: *flocci*, from *floccus* (literally, tuft of wool—from which we get *flock*—but figuratively, trifle); *nauci*, from *naucum* (trifle); *nihili*, from *nihilm* (nothing—from which we get *nihilism, annihilate*, etc.); and *pili*, from *pilus* (literally, a single hair—from which we get *pilose, pilous, pilosity*, etc.—but figuratively, trifle); plus *-fication*, a suffix of action nouns from Latin *-ficatio*, normally related to verbs ending in *-fy*, e.g., *deify/ deification, intensify/intensification*, etc. *Floccinaucinihilipilification* is said to have been invented by a group of boys at Eton College in Berkshire, England, founded in 1440 by Henry VI, who would never have anticipated this development. But the Scottish novelist Sir Walter Scott (1771-1852) differs, attributing the invention to the English poet William Shenstone (1714-1763), who, in a 1777 letter, wrote: "I love him for nothing so much as his *f-p-n-p-fication* of money." (See **pelf**.) Shenstone's use of only the initals of the constituent Latin genitives would seem to indicate that the word was known to him, rather than invented by him, supporting the Eton College attribution.

floccus   (FLOK us) *n. Floccus*, which is Latin for "tuft of wool," is English for "tuft of woolly hairs." See **floccillation** and **floccinaucinihilipilification**. *Floccus* gives us lots of words besides those two: *floccose* (FLOK ose, flok OSE), *floccular* (FLOK yuh lur), and *flocculent* (FLOK yuh lunt), all meaning "woolly"; flocculate (FLOK yuh late), to form into wooly tufts; *floccule* (FLOK yoohl) and *flocculus* (FLOK yuh luhs), a small tuft of wool or anything resembling one; *flocculence* (FLOK yuh luns), the state of being woolly. There are others, but by now you've got the general idea. Sheep are woolly, but *flock*, the collective noun for *sheep* (and other animals, including parishioners), has nothing to do with *floccus*; we get that kind of *flock* from Old English *flocce* (*flock*, in the sense of "company," "group," or "gathering"). Under the **rubric** COLLECTIVES, Fowler tells us that *flock*, or its plural, *flocks*, can be used to mean "woollen waste"; thus, we are told, "a mattress of *flock* or *flocks*; the *flock* has, the *flocks* have, not been disinfected." In any event, *floccus* (the Latin one) has certainly supplied us with a flock of words!

floruit   (FLOR yooh it) *vb*. In reference books, usually abbreviated to *fl.*, less often *flor*. This is a Latin word, meaning "he (or she) flourished"; the third person singular perfect of *florere* (to bloom, flower; by extension, to be in one's prime, to flourish). In abbreviated form, it is put after the name of a person to indicate when he or she "flourished," i.e., was active, in cases where the dates of birth and death are unknown. If an approximate or questionable date is known, it can be preceded or followed by the letter *c* or *c*., an abbreviation of the Latin preposition *circa* (about): thus, Archimedes (c. 287-212 B.C.); or a question mark: thus Canalizo [a Mexican general] (1797?-?1847). But if even the approximate dates are unknown, the name is usually followed by *fl.* and a date or an era: thus, Euclid (*fl.* 300 B.C.); Galen (*fl.* 2nd century A.D.); St. Thomas Malory (*fl.* 1470). As time goes on, with more and more data being stored in computers, the famous of our age—Einstein, Marilyn Monroe, et al.—will need no *fl.*s, *flor.*s, *c*.s, or *?*s after their names.

flummery   (FLUM uh ree) *n*. Used in its literal sense, the name *flummery* covers any one of a number of concoctions made of flour, milk, eggs, and sugar or honey and miscellaneous added ingredients. The term can also cover blancmange, or what the Scots call "sowens" or "sowans," a dish made from the mealy powder remaining with the husks of oats. But if you come across *flummery*, you will find that it will more likely have been used in its figurative, and quite different sense: anything insipid, or false and empty compliments, the kind emanating from sycophants. The literal and figurative senses may be quite distinct, yet there may be a logical connection, for the various drinks listed above seem rather insipid. In any event, *flummery* is from Welsh *llyru*, based on the adjectives *llymrig* (harsh, raw) and *llym* (sharp, severe). So say the dictionaries, but it all seems rather mysterious and flummoxing (no etymological connection) and it would appear more hospitable and kinder to offer someone the literal dish than to dish out the figurative stuff.

foofaraw   (FOOH fuh raw) *n*. This bit of informal American, as well as its variant *fofarraw* (FOH fuh raw), has two distinct meanings: a big fuss about very little, i.e., much ado about nothing; or flashy finery, too many frills. Literary policeman's question: "What's going on here? What's all this *foofaraw* about?" Or, in the second sense, from a lady wearing a lorgnette (if you can find one): "She could certainly dispense with all that *foofaraw*!" A lovely-sounding word and, say the authorities, origin unknown; but in the first sense, could it be a corruption of *free-for-all* (in baby-talk)? The British appear not to use this word, but, in the *to-do* sense, have a nice equivalent: *gefuffle*, also spelt *kerfuffle* and *cufuffle*, all loosely used as synonyms for their word *shemozzle*, which is also spelt *shemozzl*, *chimozzle*, and at least half-a-dozen other ways—you takes your choice.

formication   (for muh KAY shun) *n*. *Formication* is a tingling sensation, the feeling that ants or other insects are crawling all over you. One might experience *formication* at the sight of something horrifying or terribly frightening. Horror movies are especially aimed at producing *formication* in the audience. *Formica* is Latin for *ant*, and gives us the adjective *formic* (pertaining to ants), the noun *formicary* (ant nest), and *formic acid* (a substance exuded by ants). One must be careful in the pronunciation of this word, the *m* being so close to *n* in the alphabet. See also the last sentence of **apothegm**.

formicine, see **accipitrine**

fortis   (FOR tis) *n*., *adj*. The plural of the noun is *fortes* (FOR teez). *Fortis* is a term in phonetics that applies to the sound of letters (or combinations of letters) of the alphabet pronounced strongly, with relatively great muscular force and breath pressure, producing a strong, rather explosive sound. These are *f, k, p, t, s*, sometimes *h* and the combinations *sh* and *th* as in *thin*. The term *fortis* was taken over intact from Latin, where it means "strong, powerful." *Lenis* (LEE nis, LAY-), *n*. and *adj*. (plural of the noun is *lenes*, LEE neez, LAY-), is the term in phonetics that applies to letters (or combinations of letters) of the alphabet pronounced with relatively weak muscular force and breath pressure, producing a mild, weak sound. These are *b, d, g, j, v, z* and the combinations *th* as in *this* and *zh*. *Lenis* was taken as is from Latin where it means "smooth, soft, gentle." [Incidentally, *phonetics* (fuh NET iks, foh-), treated as a singular noun despite its plural form (cf. *economics, physics*, etc.), is the science of speech sounds.]

foudroyant (fooh DROY unt) *adj. Foudroyant* describes things that are striking, stunning, sudden and overwhelming, dazzling. *Foudroyant* is taken from the French, where it is the present participle of *foudroyer* (strike with lightning), based on *foudre* (lightning), derived from Latin *fulgur* (lightning). There is a special use of *foudroyant* in medicine, where it describes a disease that begins suddenly and in a severe form, like a serious heart attack suffered by a patient who has had no previous history of the illness—an affliction out of the blue. Getting back to the word's general use: One turns a corner and gets one's first sight of the Taj Mahal—the effect is *foudroyant.* The same goes for the immense statuary at Abu Simbel, rescued, in a stupendous engineering feat, from the rising waters of the Nile. But it's not all architecture: Love at first sight is *foudroyant* in the extreme, complete with a rush of blood and palpitations.

freebooter (FREE booh tur) *n.* A *freebooter* is a pirate or buccaneer, one who roves about *freely* in search of *booty*; an anglicization of the Dutch noun *vrijbuiter,* based on *vrij* (free) plus *buit* (booty). *Vrijbuiter* gave rise to another word, *filibuster,* first applied to the pirates of the West Indies in the 17th century, and later to the unlawful groups organized from the United States to invade and foment revolution in some Spanish-American regions, e.g., those of Cuba in 1850-1851, Sonora in 1853-1854, and Lower California in 1855. Shades of Nicaragua in 1986? *Filibuster* was metamorphosed into a term for obstructive tactics in legislative proceedings through endless speeches.

frequentative (frih KWEN tuh tiv) *n., adj.* A verb, as everyone knows, expresses an action. A *frequentative* verb, or a *frequentative* (used as a noun) serves to express the frequent repetition of that action. This is common in Latin. See, for example, **mussitation**; another case in Latin is *haerere* (to stick)/ *haesitare* (to keep sticking), from whose past participle, *haesitatus,* we get *hesitate*—to "keep sticking" without making a decision. *Frequentatives* occur in English as well. Examples: *chat/chatter, twink/twinkle, spark/sparkle, drip/ dribble*. In each case, the *frequentative* expresses the continual repetition of the action of the original verb. If you keep *dripping*, you *dribble*; if you keep *twinking*, you *twinkle*; if you go on *sparking*, you *sparkle*, and if this author keeps on *chatting*, he'll be accused of *chattering*.

friable (FRYE uh bul) *adj.* One might be forgiven for thinking that something *friable* was something that could be fried, i.e., fryable, like a fryer, a young chicken; but like *ply* and *pliable, fry* and *friable* are unrelated. *Friable* describes anything easily crumbled or broken, like *friable* rock, or a *friable* growth or tumor that breaks and bleeds. *Fry* and *friable* come from different roots: *fry* is from Latin *frigere* (to roast, parch) while *friable* is from Latin *friabilis,* based on *friare* (to crumble). Sandstone is easy to work because it is *friable*. Blood in the urine is sometimes the result of the breaking of a *friable* polyp on the inner wall of the bladder. Col. Sanders should not come to mind when you see the word *friable*.

fribble (FRIB ul) *n., vb., adj.* To *fribble* is to trifle, to act in a silly, frivolous way. To *fribble* or *fribble away* one's time is to fritter it away. A *fribbler* is a trifler, but *fribble*, as a noun, can also denote anything trifling or frivolous. As an adjective, *fribble* describes anything that is trifling or frivolous, trivial, inane, vacuous. *Fribble* is thought to be a variation of the rarely seen colloquial verb *frivol*, a back formation from *frivolous*. To *frivol* is to act frivolously, to trifle, and to *frivol away* one's time is to waste it. *Frivolous* itself is from the Latin *frivolus* (inane, trifling, worthless) which can thus be considered the ancestor of *fribble*. There may be an echo of *dribble* here, for *dribble* means, inter alia, to "drivel," and that, in turn, can mean to "prattle childishly" or even idiotically and, in that sense, to behave in a *fribbling* manner. Whether you *fribble*, *frivol*, *dribble*, or *drivel*, you are frittering away your precious time and ought to stop it and get down to business.

fringilline, see **accipitrine**

frottage (fraw TAHZH) *n.* *Frottage* is a word taken over intact from the French, where, based on the verb *frotter* (to rub), it means "rubbing" or "polishing." *Frottage* in English, however, has two very distinct meanings. In the field of arts and crafts, *frottage* is the technique of taking a "rubbing" from an uneven surface, by rubbing graphite over paper laid on top of the rough texture. A common practice in England is to lay a piece of paper on top of a plaque containing an inlaid brass figure embedded in a church floor over a tomb, and to rub a crayon or pencil over the paper in order to obtain a representation of the figure of the entombed personage. In a quite different field, *frottage* is the practice of obtaining sexual gratification by rubbing against someone, both parties usually being clothed. This happens occasionally in crowded subway cars and other confined spaces without the consent of the passive party, who often responds by slapping the naughty one in the face. The active participant is known as a "frotteur" (fraw TUR).

fructiferous (fruk TIF uh rus, frook-) *adj.* Whereas *fruitful* (meaning literally "bearing fruit abundantly") is used in the main in its figurative sense of "profitable, productive," *fructiferous* is used only in the literal sense of "fruit-producing," referring to the kind of fruit we eat, not the "fruit" of one's labors. *Fructiferous* is from Latin *fructiferus*, based on *fructus* (fruit) plus the suffix *-fer* (producing), from the verb *ferre* (to bear). To *fructify* (FRUK tuh fye, FROOK-) is to bear fruit or to cause to bear fruit, i.e., to fertilize, while *fructuous* (FRUK chooh us) means "productive." A *fruct-* word rarely seen nowadays is *Fructidor*, the name of the twelfth month in the French revolutionary calendar (August 18 to September 16), that being the month when most fruit (*fructus*) is given (*doron* is Greek for "gift"). *Fructidor* is an example of a hybrid word, one composed of parts taken from different languages (Latin *fructus* and Greek *doron*), like *television*, composed of Greek prefix *tele-* (far) plus *vision*, from Latin *visio* (view).

fructify, see **fructiferous**

fructuous, see **fructiferous**

fugacious   (fyooh GAY shus) *adj.* Anything described as *fugacious* is fleeting, short-lived, ephemeral, soon over and done with, the opposite of persistent or lasting. We are familiar with the Latin expression *Tempus fugit* (often inscribed on clocks and sundials). *Fugit* is a form of the Latin verb *fugere* (to flee), but the common translation is *Time flies*, probably because of the alliterative vowel sounds. A related Latin adjective is *fugax* (fleeing, fleeting), the stem of which is *fugac-*. There is another related Latin adjective, *fugitivus*, which gave us *fugitive*. The Roman poet Horace (65-8 B.C.) wrote of "fleeting years (that) slip by" in his lament to his friend Postumus:

> Eheu *fugaces*, Postume, Postume
> Labantur anni.

Infatuations tend to be *fugacious*, as is human physical beauty, all too soon. A politician's strength is based on that most *fugacious* of emotions, public favor. There are two nouns related to *fugacious*: *fugacity* (fyooh GAS ih tee) and *fugaciousness*. *Fugacity* is much easier to pronounce than *fugaciousness*. (Incidentally, *eheu* in Horace's ode means "alas, ah me, woe is me" and that sort of thing, and is pronounced *eh HYOOH.*)

fugle   (FYOOH gul) *vb.* To *fugle* is to act as a model or guide, a semantic change from its basic meaning of to "signal." It is a colloquial word, a back formation from *fugleman*, a political party leader or more generally, the manager, organizer, or spokesman of any type of group. *Fugleman* came to us as a variation of the German noun *Flügelmann* (literally, flank man) based on *Flügel* (wing) plus *Mann* (man), originally a soldier who used to be placed in front of a regiment or company being drilled, to demonstrate the routine, the way airline stewardesses go through the motions while passengers are being instructed in how to behave if . . . The American novelist Jack Kerouac (1922-1962)—whose work was characterized by the American writer Truman Capote (1924-1984) in these unkind words: "It really isn't writing, is it? It's . . . er . . . typing."—*fugled* for the entire Beat Generation, those who grew up after World War II and in the late 1950s, defied the conventions, advocated detachment from society, promoted relaxation of the inhibitions it imposed, and supported the ideals of the flower children.

fulciline, see **accipitrine**

fuliginous   (fyooh LIJ uh nus) *adj. Fuliginous* describes things that are smoky, sooty, of the color of soot, dusky, dark, dingy, dark gray, dull brown, or black. *Fuliginous* is from Latin *fuliginosus*, based on the noun *fuligo* (soot).

Apart from its literal use as a color, *fuliginous* has been used metaphorically, as in the description of an ironical sense of humor, and in such a use, it means "darkly mysterious." Fowler criticizes the use of *fuliginous* in his article on "polysyllabic humor," in which he writes of the "impulse that suggests long . . . words as a means of entertaining the reader or hearer," and gives *terminological inexactitude* for *lie* or *falsehood* as an example "much less amusing at the hundredth than at the first time of hearing." He gives examples other than *fuliginous*, some of which can be found in this very book: **esurient**, **fugacious**, **matutinal**, **minacious**, and in his article on "pedantic humour," he says that "the incongruity between simple things to be said and out-of-the-way words to write them . . . [may have charm] for the reader who never outgrows **hobbledehoy**hood; but for the rest of us it is dreary indeed." (Yet note Fowler's use of **hobbledehoy**hood, based on yet another "challenging word" found in this book.) Under his headword *fuliginous*, he says "Chiefly in POLYSYLLABIC HUMOUR," and then goes on to give as an example: "At present it is a *fuliginous*, not to say mysterious matter." Be all the above as it may, remember that this book is a glossary of "challenging words" explained—not necessarily recommended!

fuliguline, see **accipitrine**

fulvous   (FUL vus) *adj. Fulvous* covers a broad range of the spectrum in the tawny department: dull to medium brilliant yellowish brown, gray, or red. It comes from Latin *fulvus* (deep yellow, reddish yellow, tawny), where the poets used it to describe anything from lions and wolves to sand and gold. There is a species of tropical long-legged duck, the *dendrocygna bicolor*, known as the "*fulvous* tree duck" to those interested in ornithology. *Tawny*, incidentally, comes from Middle French *tané*, past participle of *taner* (to tan).

funambulist   (fyooh NAM byuh list) *n.* A *funambulist* is a tightrope artist; *funambulism* (fyooh NAM byuh liz um) is the art. To *funambulate* (fyooh NAM byuh late) is to practice the art; *funambulation* (fyooh nam byuh LAY shun) is the act of tightrope walking or dancing; *funambulator* (fyooh NAM byuh lay tur) is synonymous with *funambulist*; and *funambulatory* (fyooh NAM byuh luh tor ee) describes the art or activity. In each case, the first syllable is pronounced like our word *few*. All these words stem from the Latin *funambulus* (ropedancer), based on *funis* (rope) and *ambulare* (to walk).

fundament   (FUN duh munt) *n.* We are familiar with the adjective *fundamental*, a synonym of *basic*, *underlying*, which describes anything that goes to the root of the matter and is an essential part of whatever may be involved. We speak of *fundamental* rules, *fundamental* principles, a *fundamental* change or revision, a *fundamental* concept or idea. And *fundamentalism* denotes strict observance of traditional orthodox religious beliefs, the infallibility of the Bible as history and the literal acceptance of the creeds as the basic principles of Protestant Christianity. A far cry from *fundament* itself, meaning "buttocks," a.k.a. the *arse*, *behind*, *derrière*, and *nates*, with the additional meaning, according to some dictionaries of "anus," a.k.a. the *ass-hole*, *bung-hole*, and lots of other disagreeable nicknames. The *fundament*, then, refers to the lower part of the torso in general. (*Fundament* is also used occasionally to denote the physical features of a given geographical area: climate, soil, drainage, etc.) It is derived, via Middle English and Old French *fondemont*, from Latin *fundamentum* (foundation), related to the verb *fondare* (to found, lay the foundation of).

fungible (FUN juh bul) *n., adj.* A *fungible* article is one that is interchangeable, i.e., it can be exchanged for or replaced by another of similar nature. It is thus differentiated from something that is one-of-a-kind, a unique individual specimen. As a noun, a *fungible* is anything that fits that description, like money, grain, a standard **artifact** like an automobile, umbrella, pen, or article of furniture—things off the assembly line—as opposed to an original work of art. The term *fungible*, in legal parlance, applies to things that are generally classified by number, weight, or measure. *Fungible* is derived from Middle Latin *fungibilis*, based on the Latin verb *fungi* (to serve as or in place of). A pound of mushrooms is *fungible*, but that is because they are replaceable, not because they are *fungi*. To pun is human, to forgive superhuman.

fustian (FUS chun) *n., adj.* A strange word, *fustian*, in the diversity and apparent dissociation of its several meanings. First of all, *fustian* is the name of a thick twilled cotton fabric, or a blend of cotton and flax or low grade wool with a short nap, usually dyed a dark color; and as an adjective, *fustian* describes cloth so made. But *fustian* is now used chiefly in a wholly different sense, miles from cloth or fabric: It means "bombast," written or spoken, "turgid, inflated language, purple prose," and finally, "claptrap, rant, hogwash, palaver, prattle, drivel"; and as an adjective, "pompous, bombastic, nonsensical, worthless." *Fustian* is a Middle English word, from Old French *fustaigne*, derived from Middle Latin *fustaneus*, referring to cloth made in El-Fustat, a suburb of Cairo. This peculiar dichotomy of meanings suggests that the material from El-Fustat was of pretty poor value. Shall we complicate matters further? *Fustian* is also the name of a drink made of white wine, egg yolk, lemon, spices, and other miscellaneous ingredients—a concoction with possibilities. To *fustianize* (FUS chun ize) is to write in a bombastic manner, and a writer who descends to that level is a *fustianist* (FUS chun ist). From the pen of the English poet Alexander Pope (1688-1744), in the *Epistle to Dr. Arbuthnot*, out of his *Prologue to Imitations of Horace*, flow these words:

> Means not, but blunders round about a meaning;
> And he whose *fustian*'s so sublimely bad,
> It is not poetry, but prose run mad.

Shakespeare used *fustian* in *Othello* (Act II, Scene 3), when Cassio, in despair after Othello cashiers him, cries: "I will rather sue to be despised than to deceive so good a commander ... Drunk! ... and squabble, swagger, swear, and discourse *fustian* with one's own shadow!" In *Henry IV, Part 2* (Act II, Scene 4), Doll Tearsheet tells Bardolph: "For God's sake, thrust him [Pistol] down stairs! I cannot endure such a *fustian* rascal." And in *Twelfth Night* (Act II, Scene 5), after hearing Malvolio's doggerel:

> I may command where I adore;
>   But silence, like a Lucrece knife,
> With bloodless stroke my heart doth gore:
>   M, O, A, I, doth sway my life,

Fabian exclaims: "A *fustian* riddle!" All these uses refer to bombast, prattle, and drivel. But Shakespeare used *fustian* also in its material sense. In *Taming of the Shrew* (Act IV, Scene 1), Curtis asks Grumio: "Where's the cook? is supper ready, the house trimmed, rushes strewed, cobwebs swept, the serving-men in their new *fustian* ... ?" The English dramatist John Heywood (c. 1497-c. 1580), in his play *Faire Maide of the Exchange* (Act II, Scene 2), used *fustian* in the figurative sense: " . . . Some scurvy quaint collection of *fustian* phrases and uplandish words." A strange and versatile word, *fustian*.

gabion   (GAY bee un) *n.* A *gabion* is a wickerwork cylinder or bottomless basket filled with earth, formerly used in fortification as a military defense. The same type of wicker container filled with stones and sunk in water was used in laying foundations of dams or jetties. A defense wall formed of *gabions* was known as a *gabionade* (GAY bee un ade); *gabionage* (gay bee un AJE) is the name given to a series of *gabions*; a fortification using *gabions* is said to be *gabioned* (GAY bee und). *Gabion* is a French word, taken from the Italian *gabbione* (large cage), based on *gabbia* (cage; the ending *-one* is an augmentative), derived from Latin *cavea* (cavity, cage). With the availability of poured cement, the *gabion* became outmoded.

galimatias   (gal uh MAY shee us, -MAT ee us) *n.* This word, taken intact from the French (who pronounce it: gahl ih MAH tee ah) means "nonsensical talk, gibberish, twaddle, confused and meaningless babble, unintelligible jargon and mishmash," sometimes with the implication that the balderdash is not only senseless but somewhat pompous. The English writer Horace Walpole (1717-1797) used this curious word in describing a certain lady in these terms: "Her talk is a *galamatias* of several countries." It seems likely that *galamatias* is somehow etymylogically related to **gallimaufry**, but where the *-atias* came from is a matter of doubt. One possibility is that it was suggested by the Greek noun *amathia* (ignorance), resulting in a "galamatian" word for "ignorant twaddle."

gallimaufry   (gal uh MAW free) *n.* A *gallimaufry* is a jumble, a hodge-podge, a mishmash, a farrago, a salmagundi, a miscellany, a potpourri, an olio, a confused medley. This word has a very *gallimaufry* of synonyms, perhaps because life presents such a *gallumaufry* of *gallimaufries*. It comes from Middle French *galimafrée*, meaning "ragout," and that seems to have come out of the blue. In cooking, a *gallimaufry*, as one might have guessed, is a stew or ragout or hash. The *Times Literary Supplement* spoke of a work "written in a remarkable *gallimaufry* of languages: and *Time* characterized a play as "a *gallimaufry* of didactic speeches, romantic flourishes and characters for several unrelated kinds of plays." The languages of India are a *gallimaufry* of tongues. The English poet Edmund Spenser (c. 1552-1599) called " . . . our English tongue a *gallimaufry* or hodgepodge of all other speeches." Where there is unplanned municipal building, the result is often an unpleasant *gallimaufry* of styles.

gallinaceous   (gal uh NAY shus) *adj.* This adjective is applied to anything having to do with domestic fowls. It is from Latin *gallainaceus* (pertaining to poultry), based on *gallus* (cock), *gallina* (hen). Most people like to eat chicken, but never give a thought to the fact that, at one time, chickens were not domestic, but wild. Darius I (the Great, c. 549-c. 485 B.C.), king of Persia from 521 B.C. to 486 B.C., accomplished many things: put down revolts, set up a vast administrative system, succeeded in lengthy military campaigns (though he lost at Marathon in 490 B.C.). But one of his greatest accomplishments was the domestication of the chicken, a *gallinaceous* feat, and from there it was a straight line to Col. Sanders.

galline, see **accipitrine**

gambado   (gam BAY doh) *n.* This word has several meanings. A *gambado* is one of a pair of large boots or leather gaiters attached to a saddle in place of stirrups, but the term can apply more generally to any long legging or gaiter. In this meaning, *gambado* is based upon the Italian noun *gamba* (leg), which gave us as well the slang for girls' legs, *gams*. *Gambado* (sometimes *gambade*—gahm BADE or gam BAHD) is also used of a leap, bound, or spring of a horse, and more generally, to any fantastic movement, antic, caper, or escapade. In this use, *gambado* is a modification of the French *gambade* (antic, skip, romp, gambol), and we got *gambol* as well from Middle French *gambade*. The context will make it clear which *gambado* one is dealing with, and in any event, boots and gaiters are hardly attached to saddles these days.

gargantuan (gar GAN choo un) *adj.* Anyone or anything described as *gargantuan* is huge, gigantic, vast, of enormous proportions. The adjective, often capitalized, is derived from *Gargantua*, the amiable giant king whose exploits are recorded in the novel of that name, one of the two great satirical works by François Rabelais (1494-1553). His books, full of coarse, broad, boisterous wit and humor, are characterized by the type of licentious language associated with the adjective **Rabelaisian**. Gargantua was noted for his incredibly voracious appetite (*garganta* is Spanish for "gullet"; cf. French *gargouille*, throat, and English derivatives *gargle* and *gargoyle*), so great that on one occasion the insatiable guzzler swallowed whole five pilgrims—with their staves!—mixed in a salad. In Shakespeare's *As You Like It* (Act III, Scene 2), Rosalind asks Celia a torrent of questions about Orlando and winds up: "Answer me in one word." Celia replies: "You must borrow me Gargantua's mouth first: 'tis a word too great for any mouth of this age's size . . . " One can speak of the *gargantuan* appetite of a **trencherman**, the *gargantuan* length of one of those endless historical novels, or the *gargantuan* task of cleaning up after a hurricane. Gargantua fathered the giant Pantagruel, the hero of the other great novel by Rabelais. The giant son lent his name to the adjective **pantagruelian**. For a synonym of *gargantuan* derived from another famous satirical novel, see **brobdingnagian**.

garruline, see **accipitrine**

gasconade (gas kuh NADE) *n., vb. Gasconade* is inordinate boasting, extravagant bragging. To *gasconade* is to indulge in *gasconade*. The word comes from *Gascony* (in French, Gascogne), once a province in southwestern France, whose natives, the *Gascons*, were famous for their boastful ways. A *gascon* (lower case *g*) is a braggart. There are legends about Gascons. "What's your opinion of the Louvre?" someone asks a Gascon, who replies: "Not so bad; it reminds me of the rear of my father's stables." This was extreme braggadocio since the Gascons were proverbially poor. Cf. **braggadocio, fanfaronade, rodomontade, thrasonical**.

gastronome (GAS truh nome) *n.* A *gastronome* is an epicure or gourmet. (Please, despite those permissive dictionaries, do your best to preserve the proper distinction between *gourmet* and *gourmand*.) *Gastronome* is a back formation from *gastronomy* (ga STRON uh mee), the art, lore and science of the true gourmet. Cf. **aristology** and **Lucullan**. *Gastronomy* is derived from the Greek prefix *gastro-* (*gastr-* before a vowel), the combining forms of *gaster* (stomach), as in *gastric, gastritis, gastrointestinal*, etc., plus the Greek suffix *-normia*, based on *nomos* (law) from which we get *-nomy*, as in *astronomy, economy, bionomy*, etc. *Gastr-* and *gastro-* words have nothing to do with *gas*, the kind that hurts your tummy and gives us, in addition, the pain of all those television commercials. That word *gas* was coined by the Flemish chemist J.B. van Helmont (1577-1644), suggested by the Greek noun *chaos* (atmosphere; the vast, unfathomable space out of which the universe arose). (In Flemish, the letter *g* is pronounced like the Greek *chi*, or the Yiddish *ch* as in *chutzpa*, so that to van Helmont, *gas*, with *a* as in *art*, wasn't very far from properly pronounced *chaos* in Greek.

gazelline, see **accipitrine**

genethlialogy   (jih neth lee AL uh jee) *n*. This is a term in the "science" of astrology denoting the art of making astrological calculations, also known as "casting nativities," based on the plotting of heavenly bodies at the time of the subject's (victim's?) birth. The Greek noun *genethlialogia* is based on *genethlia* (births) plus the Greek suffix *-logia*, from which we get our familiar *-logy*, as in *astrology, geology, theology*, and some less familiar *-logies*, like *ethnology* (the study of cultures), *ethology* (animal behavior, habitat), *limnology* (lakes and ponds), *malacology* (mollusks), *pedology* (children), *soteriology* (salvation), *storiology* (folklore), *thremmatology* (propagation under domestication), *threpsology* (nutrition), *uranology* (astronomy); and there are many more. But getting back to *genethlialogy*, the related adjective *genethliac* (jih NETH lee ak) is used to describe anything pertaining to birthdays, especially the position of the stars at one's birth, said to be a basic consideration in astrology. *Genethlialogy* is not only an alleged science; it is big business, as evidenced by book and periodical sales, syndicated newspaper columns, correspondence courses and heaven (?) knows what else. There are those who won't make a move without a *genethlialogical* consultation. Heaven (what, again?) help them.

gerontology   (jer un TOL u jee) *n*. *Geront-* is the stem of the Greek noun *geron* (old man), and gives us the prefix *geronto-*. Add the Greek suffix *-logia* to get our *-logy*, used in the names of studies, sciences, or bodies of knowledge, and we wind up with *gerontology*, the scientific study of old age, the process of aging, and the problems of the elderly. There are government bodies and committees, local, state, and federal, that deal with the special problems and needs of the aging. Ah me . . . !

> Gaudeamus igitur
> Juvenes dum sumus.
> Post jucundam juventutem
> Post molestam senectutem
> Nos habebit humus.
>
> Let us live then and be glad
> While young life's before us.
> After youthful pastime had,
> After old age hard and sad,
> Earth will slumber o'er us.

This is a medieval student's song, traced back to 1626. So much, then, for *gerontology*!

gerrymander   (JER ih man dur, GER-) *n., vb.* A *gerrymander* is the redrawing of the boundaries of electoral districts within a certain area in such a way as to give a political party an undue advantage in election results. The favored party acquires a majority in a large number of districts, the opposing party in fewer districts than before the *gerrymandering*. As a verb, to *gerrymander* is to engage in such shenanigans. The peculiar word came about in an amusing way, from the name of a Massachusetts governor, Elbridge Gerry (1744-1814), whose party so redistricted that state in 1812. (One might have supposed that they had their hands full with the War of 1812, but there's always a little time left over for political skulduggery.) The artist Gilbert Stuart (1755-1828), seeing the map of the redistricting, noted the resemblance of one of the new districts to the outline of a salamander and did a bit of converting of the map to that shape, by adding wings, a head, and a tail. He showed the result to a Boston newspaperman named Russell who coined the word *gerrymander*. Gerry pronounced his name with a hard *g*, but the erroneous *j-* pronunciation so caught on that the word is still occasionally spelt with an initial *j*, possibly (according to Fowler) by association with *jerrybuilt*.

gibbous   (GIB us, JIB-) *adj.* This is the description used in astronomy for the moon (or any heavenly body that waxes and wanes like the moon—to our view) when it is more than half "full," so that it appears convex at both edges. *Gibbous* comes from the Latin adjective *gibbosus* (humped), based on *gibba* or *gibbus* (hump), and is also spelt *gibbose* (GIB ose, JIB-). *Gibbosity* (gih BOS ih tee, jih-) is the noun for the quality of being *gibbous*, but in its more general sense applies to any swelling, bump, or protuberance. The monstrosity on the face of Cyrano de Bergerac, or Pinocchio when he lied, was an extreme case of *gibbosity* of the proboscis.

giraffine, see **accipitrine**

glabrous   (GLAY brus) *adj. Glabrous*, a term used in anatomy, zoology, and botany, describes the condition of any organism that is smooth-skinned, without hair or down, i.e., bald. The Latin adjective *glaber* (hairless) is the source of this adjective. It was because of the *glabrous* condition of Aeschylus's pate (Aeschylus, the father of classical Greek drama, 525-456 B.C.) that an eagle dropped a tortoise on it, in order to break the shell, in the mistaken belief that the *glabrous* dome was a stone. Thus died Aeschylus, or so says the legend. If you have a *glabrous* skull, stay away from places where eagles abound, or wear a wig.

glacis   (GLAY sis, GLAS is) *n.* In days of yore, soldiers would build a bank sloping down from their fort, so that an attacking foe would be an easier target for the defenders' missiles. This word is from the French, who got it, via the Old French verb *glacier* (to slide, slip) from Latin *glacies* (ice). Nowadays *glacis* denotes any gentle slope. Forts are obsolete as defenses, and a *glacis* in the old sense wouldn't be much help anyway in the face of rockets and similar contrivances.

glaucous   (GLAW kus) *adj. Glaucous* describes anything pale bluish green or greenish blue, and in botany, things like plums covered with a fine, powdery whitish, greenish, or bluish bloom. *Glaucescence* (glaw SES uns) is the noun for this quality, and *glaucescent* (glaw SES unt) is the description of anything in nature that is somewhat *glaucous. Glaucous* is from the Latin adjective *glaucus* (the *-us* ending of the masculine form of Latin adjectives usually becomes *-ous* in English) meaning "bluish or greenish gray."

gloss   (glos) *n., vb.* This word has two entirely distinct meanings, each with its own derivation. We need not dwell on the noun *gloss* meaning "luster" or "shine," sometimes with the implication of a superficial, deceptive appearance, or the verb *gloss* (usually *gloss over*) meaning to "make [something] look good" when it isn't, as when one *glosses over* the flaws in something—whether tangible, like a paint job, or intangible, like a brief or an argument—giving it a specious appearance of soundness. This *gloss* is of Scandinavian origin, from Danish *gloos* (glowing) via Middle High German *glozen* (to shine), and is akin to our word *glow*, from Middle English *glowen*. The other *gloss* is the less familiar one and an entirely different and often confusing matter: *gloss*, meaning "explanation" or "interpretaion," usually by means of a note, marginal or interlinear, of a difficult term or obscure expression in a text. The related verb to *gloss* means to "annotate" by the insertion of *glosses*. But—caution here—through confusion with the other gloss, this *gloss* has acquired the meaning of "give a false or specious interpretation of [something]"; and here, too, we see *gloss over*, as in *glossing over* a difficult situation with a pat solution that doesn't solve the problem. This *gloss* is via Middle English *gloze* and Late Latin *glos(s)a* (difficult word, and by extension, a word needing explanation, annotation, comment) from Ionic Greek *glossa* (tongue, language). To *gloze* is a derived verb, also with two different meanings: to "*gloss* over, explain away," and to "shine or brighten." Fowler has something to say about the confusion between the two *glosses*: "The development of a word meaning explanation into one meaning misrepresentation . . . has meant that in popular as opposed to learned speech . . . *gloss* [meaning "comment"] is seldom without the suggestion of something sophistical. The two verbs, *gloss* (or *gloze*), to comment, and *gloss*, to put a luster on, have been even more closely assimilated into the meaning of extenuate in a specious way, especially the phrasal verb *gloss* or *gloze over*. As stated earlier—caution!

gloze, see **gloss**

glyptic, see **glyptography**

glyptography   (glip TOG ru fee) *n. Glyptography* is the art of engraving stones and gems. The related word *glyptic* (GLIP tik) describes anything pertaining to carving on gems or stones. *Glyptics* (treated as a singular noun) is the art of gem engraving. *Glyptikos* is the Greek adjective describing that type of engraving or stone carving; *glyptos* means "carved," from *glyphein* (to engrave). *Glyptography* is built of *glyptos* plus *graphein* (to write, draw, engrave).

gnathonic   (na THON ik) *adj.* A *gnathonic* person is a parasite, a fawning toady, a sycophant. *Gnatho* is the name of such a character in *Eunuchus* (*The Eunuch*), a comedy by the Roman playwright Terence (c. 190-c. 159 B.C.), and *gnatho* means "parasite" generally in Latin. *Gnathonic* is from Latin *gnathonicus*, an adjective based on the character of *Gnatho* in the play. For another adjective based on another character in the same play, see **thrasonical**. *Gnathos* is a Greek noun meaning "jaw," from which we get *gnathic* (NATH ik) and *gnathous* (NATH us), both meaning "pertaining to the jaw," as well as the suffix *-gnathous*, referring to the jaw, as in *prognathous* (PROG nu thus, prog NA-), describing a person having protruding jaws. It is difficult to see the connection between *Gnatho*, the character in *Eunuchus*, and *gnathos* (jaw), unless the parasitic sycophant happened to be acted by a *prognathous* actor.

gnome   (nome, NOH mee)   *n.* There are two kinds of *gnomes*: (1) the legendary shriveled old men who live in the interior of the earth and are also known as *trolls* (these are *chthonic* or *chthonian* characters, that adjective meaning "relating to beings dwelling under the earth" in classical mythology, and based on the Greek noun *chthon, earth*) and (2) terse expressions of general truth, also known as *aphorisms*. The first type is quite familiar from childhood literature and cartoons, the second kind less so. The two come from different sources: the little old men from New Latin *gnomus*, the pithy sayings from Greek *gnome* (opinion, judgment). *Gnome*, in the second sense, has a related adjective, *gnomic* (NOHM ik, NOM ik, take your choice), describing writing full of *gnomes* or maxims or pithy statements of general truth, and a *gnomist* (NOH mist) is a writer of aphorisms, while *gnomology* (noh MOL uh jee) is an anthology of aphorisms. Fowler points out that there is a *gnomic* past tense, to state a fact true of all times, including the present, thus: "Men were deceivers ever." Certain Greek poets of the seventh and sixth centuries B.C. are known as the *gnomic* poets, because their poetry is *gromic*, packed with aphoristic statements. There is a series of *gno-* words, all taken from the Greek, and related to the verb *gignoskein* (to know): *gnosis* (NOH sis; knowledge of spiritual mysteries); *gnostic* (NOS tik—knowing, especially with respect to mystical and esoteric matters); and the more familiar *agnostic* (ag NOS tik, from the Greek *agnostos*, describing one who asserts that the essential nature of all things, including God, is unknown and unknowable, and that one can know only what one experiences and can believe only in material phenomena). *Gnostic* means "knowing"; *agnostic* is simply *gnostic* with the Greek prefix *a-*, the so-called alpha privative, meaning "not," stuck in front: "not knowing." Another *gno-* word, having nothing whatever to do with trolls, aphorisms, or theology, is *gnomon* (NOH mon), which is the name of the upright part of a sundial that casts the shadow that tells the time. *Gnomon* was taken as is from the Greek, where it means "one that knows" or "indicator," in this case the indicator of the time of day (if the sun is out). Incidentally, why the *k-* in know? Via Middle English, Old English, and Latin, it simply goes back to the second *g-* (via Latin *gnovi*, I know), in *gignuskein*.

gnomon, see **gnome**. It's a long entry and you'll have to read all the way through.

gnosis, **gnostic**, see **gnome**

goliard (GOLE yurd) *n*. *Goliards* were itinerant scholars and poets of the 12th and 13th centuries who wrote ribald and satirical Latin verse. They were erudite buffoons and jesters, given to drunken riotous behavior. The word is Middle English, and comes from Old French *goliart* or *goliard* (drunkard or glutton), which was derived, via French *gueule* (throat), from Latin *gula* (throat; by extension, gluttony). The *goliards* begged their way as they wandered about the country, and eventually increased their numbers until they developed into a horde of riotous vagabonds who came to be known as *ordo vagorum* (order of vagabonds; *vagorum* is the genitive plural of the latin adjective *vagus*, wandering, here used as a noun). Their legendary leader, named Bishop Golias (Goliath), is now thought to be a literary figment, invented **ex post facto** from the name *Goliard*. They were a scandalous bunch, but their Latin verse and songs, modeled after medieval hymns, had literary merit. They were in praise of wine, women, and the open road, often in satirical attack on the immoral side of official church life and its practitioners. Their songs are known as *carmina burana*, after the collection found in the Abbey of Benediktbeuren. A number of them were set to music in 1937 by the German composer Carl Orff (1895-1982) and are often performed as a secular cantata under the title *Carmina Burana*.

goluptious (gol UP shus) *adj*. This is slang for "delicious, delightful, splendid." The *Dictionary of Slang and Unconventional English* of the British lexicographer Eric Partridge (1894-1979) lists a great many spellings of this scrumptious word: *galoptious*, *galuptious*, *goloptious*, plus all of those with the ending *-shus* instead of *-tious*, but states: "The best form is *goluptious*, for the term is a 'facetious perversion . . . of *voluptuous* . . .' according to the English etymologist and lexicographer Ernest Weekley (1865-1954)." Partridge calls it "a fanciful adjective of the *catawampus*, *scrumptious* type . . ." *Catawampus* (also *-pous*, *-ptious*) is slang for "avid, fierce, eager," suggested by *catamount*, a synonym of *cougar. Scrumptious* is colloquial for "delectable," suggested by *sumptuous.*

grammalogue   (GRAM uh log) *n.* A *grammalogue* is a word represented by a symbol or letter. *And* is a *grammalogue* represented by the **ampersand** &; *dollar* by *$; cent* by ¢; *pound sterling* by £; *plus* by +; *minus* by −; *divided* by ÷; times by ×; in etymology, *derived from* by ‹; *and so forth* by &c. (as well as by *etc.*). Conversely, a *logogram* or *logograph* (LAWG uh gram, LOG-; LAWG uh graph, LOG-) is a symbol representing a word or phrase. & is the *logogram* of *and*; $ of *dollar*; etc. Both words are constructed, in inverse order, of the Greek nouns *gramma* (letter) and *logos* (word).

grammaticaster, see **poetaster**

graphology   (gra FOL uh jee) *n. Graphology* is the study of handwriting, especially as an indication of the personality, character, disposition, and aptitudes of the writer; the art of inferring those aspects from one's handwriting. A practitioner of this study or art is a *graphologist* (gra FOL uh jist). These words are derived from the Greek noun *graphe* (writing) plus the suffix *logia*, from which we get our suffix *-logy*, indicating a science or study or body of knowledge pertaining to a particular subject, as in *biology, theology, zoology,* etc. *Graphologists* are not "handwriting experts." That is another field entirely: the identification and authentication of signatures or other writings as those of a particular person by close examination of the peculiarities of the script.

grisaille   (grih ZYE, -ALE) *n.* This word was taken over intact from the French, where *gris*, pronounced *gree*, is the word for "gray" and a *grisaille* is the name for any sketch or painting executed wholly in tones of gray. A *grisaille*, then, is a monochromatic work of art in shades of gray, and the term applies to stained glass windows as well as paintings and sketches. There is a related word in French, *camaïeu* (pronounced kah MAH yoo) meaning "cameo" but also applied to a monochrome painting in any shade as well as gray. *Grisaille* was a Renaissance technique of painting that simulated sculpture. One of the foremost examples is the 1436 equestrian portrait in the Cathedral of Florence by the Florentine painter Paolo Uccello (c. 1396-1475) of Sir John de Hawkwood (d. 1394), an English soldier who went to Italy in 1362 and became a *condottiere* (kon duh TYAIR ay), a word taken from the Italian designating a leader of a private army or band of mercenaries in Italy, a type active in the 14th and 15th centuries. *Condottiere* is also applied to any soldier of fortune or mercenary. The Italian word is derived from Latin *conductus* (mercenary soldier; literally, one led), from the past participle of *conducere* (to bring together).

groin, groyne   (groyn) *n.* A *groin* or *groyne* is a small jetty or breakwater extending from a shore to check beach erosion and sand-drifting. The origin of this word is uncertain; it is probably from Old French *groign* (snout) or Latin *grunnire* (to grunt).

groomsman, see **paranymph**

grumous (GROOH mus) *adj. Grume* is a viscous fluid, especially clotted blood, and from it we get *grumous*, which means "clotted" and applies to things that resemble a clot of blood. Both noun and adjective are from Latin *grumus* (hillock or small heap), which figures as well in the derivation of our word *crumb. Grumous* sounds like an adjective invented by Lewis Carroll for Alice, but no, it's a real word.

gulosity (gyooh LOS ih tee) *n. Gulosity* is gluttony or greediness. It is a literary word, stemming from Late Latin *gulositas*, derived from Latin *gulosus* (gluttonous), based on *gula* and *gulo* (glutton). One of the most famous practitioners of *gulosity* in literature is Gargantua, a legendary giant renowned for his incredible appetite. His name is based on the Spanish noun *garganta* (gullet). The French satirist François Rabelais (c. 1490-1553) made Gargantua the hero of his novel of that name. He was the father of Pantagruel, whose name is the title of Rabelais's other great novel. Gargantua's great exploits in *gulosity* included that in which he swallowed, in a salad, five pilgrims together with their staves. Our Victorian forebears, with their ten-course meals and vast bellies, were obviously addicted to *gulosity.*

gyre (jire) *n.* A *gyre* is a ring, a circle, or a circular or spiral turn or movement. *Gyre* is, via Latin *gyrus*, from Greek *gyros* (ring, circle), which gave us the prefix *gyro-*, as in *gyrocompass, gyroscope*, etc., and is related to our *gyrate* (whirl, move in a circle), from Latin *gyratus*, past participle of *gyrare* (to wheel around). The English mathematician and writer Lewis Caroll (Charles Lutwidge Dodgson, 1832-1892), in *Through the Looking-Glass*, used *gyre* as a verb (with a hard *g* as in *go*) meaning "spin around" or "gyrate" when

> . . . the slithy tove
> Did *gyre* and gimble in the wabe . . .

Gyring, whether with a soft or a hard *g*, and whether in or out of the wabe, makes a person dizzy.

gyve (jive) *n., vb.* The noun is usually in the plural: *gyves*, which are shackles or fetters, mostly, but not always to bind the legs. To *gyve* is to shackle, bind. It is from Middle English *give* (jive). In Shakespeare's *Romeo and Juliet* (Act II, Scene 2), Juliet says to Romeo:

> 'Tis almost morning; I would have thee gone;
> And yet no further than a wanton's bird,

> Who lets it hop a little from her hand,
> Like a poor prisoner in his twisted *gyves*,
> And with a silk thread plucks it back again . . .

The English poet Thomas Hood (1799-1845) wrote of *gyves*, but for wrists rather than legs, in *The Dream of Eugene Aram*:

> Two stern-faced men set out from Lynn,
>   Through the cold and heavy mist;
> And Eugene Aram walked between,
>   With *gyves* upon his wrists.

So much for *gyves*; *stern-faced* is a **bahuvrihi**.

haecceity, *see* **quiddity**

hagiology   (hag ee OL uh jee) *n. Hagiology* is the field of literature treating the lives and legends of the saints. *Hagiography* (hag ee OG ruh fee) is writing in that field. A *hagiographer* or *hagiographist* or *hagiologist* is one who writes about saints. A *hagioscope* (HAG ee uh skope) has nothing to do with writing or saints, but is rather a *squint*, i.e., a small, oblique opening in a church wall affording a view of the high altar. In all these words, an alternative pronunciation of the first two syllables is *hay jee*. Incidentally, a saint, in the technical sense, is a person who is canonized, i.e., officially recognized by the Christian Church as having won a high place in heaven as a result of exceptional holiness, and entitled to veneration on earth. Sainthood, in effect, is a sort of celestial knighthood, bestowed by ecclesiastical authorities; recorded miracles help a lot. The prefix *hagio-* in all the words mentioned above is derived from Greek *hagios* (holy). The following is the opening paragraph of a review by Clare Stancliffe of two books on the subject in the August 14, 1984, issue of the (London) *Times Literary Review* headed "*Hagiographical* Deductions: *Saints and their Cults*, by Stephen Wilson, Editor (Cambridge University Press, 1984) and *Saints and Society*, by Donald Weinstein and Rudolph M. Bell (University of Chicago Press, 1984)":

> Saints, their cults and their lives, are a Cinderella subject. After years of relative neglect, historians and sociologists are now blowing the dust off those innumerable volumes of saints' lives and miracle stories and discovering ways of tapping their contents. Instead of sticking on the question of who St Nicholas was and what he did, scholars are now asking, what function did he perform in society, and what can we learn from the practice of

his cult? As Stephen Wilson succinctly puts it, "saints belong to and reflect the societies which produce and honour them". A perceptive study of saints' cults therefore yields insights into those societies—insights which are all the more valuable, in relation to societies with restricted literacy, for being based on what people do, not what they say.

hagioscope, see **hagiology**

haha (HAH hah) *n.* A *haha* is a sunk fence, consisting of a ditch that is not visible until one is close upon it; a hidden obstacle, acting as the boundary of a garden or a park. If one is standing on a lawn, for instance, gazing at a bordering field where cattle graze, one might see a herd staring back, but politely stopped at the invisible boundary. The whole landscape seems level and unbroken, with no separation between field and garden, and one wonders at the tact, restraint, and good manners of the animals, but on closer inspection, as one approaches the boundary, a fairly deep ditch with its wall on the lawn side consisting of brick or stone will be discovered and the riddle solved: The cattle simply can't get across the ditch and onto the lawn. *Haha* is taken from the French, and, pronounced *ah-ah*, is believed to owe its origin to the supposed cry of surprise at the discovery of the ingeniously hidden obstacle to the animals' progress, with no hedge or fence to mar the unbroken landscape. The *haha* is no laughing matter. This was the experience of the author very late one moonlit night on his first visit to Glyndebourne, the lovely opera center in the middle of the Sussex (England) countryside, where he was being shown around by a friend connected with that establishment, long after the performance was ended and the audience had departed. As he looked across the beautiful lawn, his gaze was returned by a line of cattle silently and mysteriously standing at attention a short distance away. Only on closer inspection, with the discovery of a *haha*, was the mystery of the respectful herd cleared up. "Aha!" rather than "Haha!" was the visitor's reaction.

halidom (HAL ih dum) *n.* A *halidom* is any holy or sacred place, like a church, a shrine, or a sanctuary. The word comes from Old English *haligdom*, based on *halig* (holy) plus *-dom*, a suffix denoting dominion, state, or power, as in *kingdom*, *Christendom*, etc., from Old English *dom* (judgment). *Halidom*, with variant spellings, was used in oaths, particularly in Shakespeare. In *Two Gentlemen of Verona* (Act IV, Scene 2), when Julia asks Host a question, he answers: "By my *halidom*, I was fast asleep." In *The Taming of the Shrew* (Act V, Scene 2) when Katharina, after refusing to come to Petruchio, finally does show up, Baptista exclaims: "Now, by my *holidam*, here comes Katharina!" and Nurse uses the same oath in *Romeo and Juliet* (Act I, Scene 3). Another variant occurs in *Henry VIII* (Act V, Scene 1), when the king asks Cranmer: "Now, by my *holidame,*/What manner of man are you?" These oaths are roughly the equivalent of today's somewhat weaker sounding "For heaven's sake!"

halieutic   (hal ee OOH tik) *adj.*; in the plural, *n. Halieutic* applies to things having to do with fishing. *Halieutics*, plural in form but treated as a singular noun (like *economics, physics*, etc.), is the art and science of fishing, or a treatise on fishing. *Halieutic* comes from the Greek adjective *halieutikos*, based on *halieus* (fisherman), in turn based on *hals* (the sea). The best known treatise on *halieutics* is, of course, *The Compleat Angler; or, The Contemplative Man's Recreation*, of the English writer Izaak Walton (1593-1683), which is not confined to the technique of fishing, but dwells as well on peace and virtue.

hamadryad, see **oread**

hamartia   (hah mar TEE uh) *n.* The Greeks, who had a word for just about everything (except H-bomb and that sort of thing), concocted *hamartia*, a term for the tragic flaw or defect in the protagonist of a drama that causes an error in judgment and precipitates his downfall. Its general meaning is "fault, failure, error of judgment, sin," and it is related to the verb *hamartanein* (to err). The term was applied originally to Greek tragedy, and the concept was developed in the *Poetics* of the Greek philosopher Aristotle (384-322 B.C.), who wrote that tragedy was an "imitation of a painful action" (usually resulting in death) which by pity and fear purged the soul of those emotions. *Hamartiology* (hah mar tee OL uh jee) is the area of theology that deals with sin—a pretty wide area. It might be said that the *hamartia* of President Nixon and his associates was the failure to recognize the enormity and consequences of the obstruction of justice that led to their downfall. Other examples of *hamartia* are the "pride [that] goeth before destruction and an haughty spirit before a fall" (Proverbs 16:18). The Greek playwright Sophocles (c. 495-406 B.C.), in *Oedipus Rex*, gave examples of *hamartia* in these lines:

> The tyrant is a child of Pride
> Who drinks from his great sickening cup
> Recklessness and vanity,
> Until from his high crest headlong
> He plummets to the dust of hope.

Il Duce and Der Führer should have studied their Sophocles, who further said, in his *Trachiniae*: "A prudent mind can see room for misgivings, lest he who prospers should one day suffer reverse." Reverse indeed: Il Duce was hanged upside down. There is an anonymous Greek proverb, written in the temple at Delphi: "Gnothe teauton" ("Know thyself"), quoted by the Roman poet Juvenal (c. 60-140) in his *Satires*: "From the gods comes the saying 'Know thyself,'" and centuries later by the English poet Alexander Pope (1688-1744) in *An Essay on Man*: "Know thyself ... " It is only by knowing thyself that thou wilt rid thyself of thy *hamartia*.

haplology   (hap LOL uh jee) *n. Haplology* is the **syncope** of a syllable (see **syncope** under **aph(a)eresis**: the omission of one or more letters from the middle of a word). Some examples of *haplology*: *conservatism* reduced from *conservativism*; *idolatry* from *idololatry*; *syllabication* from *syllabification*; Englishmen say "lit'ry" for *literary* (a double *haplology*: two syllables missing) and children say "lib'ry" for *library*. *Haplology* is formed from the Greek prefix *haplo-*, combining form of *haploos* (single) plus *logos* (word). **Syncope** involves the loss of a medial letter in poetry: *ever* become *e'er*, *never* *ne'er*, while *haplology* involves the loss of a whole syllable. (See also **aph(a)eresis.**)

haptic (HAP tik) *adj.* *Haptic* applies to things pertaining to the sense of touch. *Haptics* (treated as a singular) is the science of interpreting data obtained through touch. *Haptotropic* (hap tuh TROP ik) describes things like plant tendrils (leaves or shoots) that curve in response to touch. *Haptotropism* (hap tuh TROP iz um) is the same as *thigmatropism* (thig MOT ruh piz um) or *stereotropism* (ster ee OH truh piz um, steer-), response to the stimulus of touch. The prefix *hapto-* or *hapt-* is based on the Greek verb *haptein* (to touch, fasten); the suffixes *-tropic* and *-tropism* are from the verb *tropein* (to turn); the prefix *thigma-* is from the noun *thigma* (touch) and the prefix *stereo-* is from the adjective *stereos* (solid). These Greek-derived words aren't used about people, but it isn't only tendrils and such that respond to touch. How about lovers, and erogenous zones?

haptotropism, see **haptic**

hardscrabble (HARD skrab ul) *adj.* A *hardscrabble* job is one that pays a paltry reward for hard work, a niggardly return for the effort involved, like the *hardscrabble* life of farmers on the dry and stony land of southern Italy. To *scrabble* is to scratch at something, to scramble and grab for something in a disorganized way; a *scrabble* is a disorderly struggle to get hold of something. *Scrabble* is from Dutch *schrabellen* (to scratch), a variant of *schrafen* (to scrape). The *hard-* part is self-explanatory. *Hard-scrabble* (the British favor hyphens) is an adjective, in British usage, meaning "yielding subsistence only with great difficulty," and as a noun, "land difficult to work." The concept of *hardscrabble* enters into the frequent jocular (?) response to "How are you?"—"Overworked and underpaid"—sometimes uttered by advertising executives earning not a penny over $250,000 a year.

haruspex (huh RUS peks, HAIR uh speks) *n.* This was the title, in ancient Rome, of a lower order of priests who prophesied by examining the entrails of animals killed in sacrifice. The custom was handed down by the Etruscans. The practice is known as *haruspication* (hair us puh KAY shun) or *haruspicy* (huh RUS puh see). The verb is *haruspicate* (huh RUS puh kate). *Haruspex* is a Latin word, based on Etruscan *haru*, Latin *hira* (entrail) plus *specere* (to look at: *spexi* means "I have inspected"). The Roman Censor (a government official) Cato (234-149 B.C.) was not impressed by this type of divination. He said: "I wonder how one *haruspex* can keep from laughing when he sees another." This made him very unpopular with *haruspices*.

hebdomedal   (heb DOM uh dul) *adj*. An alternative form is *hebdomedary* (heb DOM uh der ee). In either form, this adjective means "weekly." A *hebdomedal* newspaper comes out once a week. *Hebdomedal* is from Late Latin *hebdomedalis*, *hebdomedary* from Church Latin *hebdomedarius*. Cf. **diurnal** and **quotidian**, both meaning "daily," and *mensal* (monthly). In *The Wrecker*, by the Scottish novelist Robert Louis Stevenson (1850-1894) and his stepson, Lloyd Osbourne, Pinkerton conceives an idea for a new business: "PINKERTON'S HEBDOMEDARY PICNICS! (That's a good, catching phrase, '*hebdomedary*,' though it's hard to say. I made a note of it when I was looking in the dictionary how to spell *hectagonal*. 'Well, you're a boss word,' I said. 'Before you're very much older, I'll have you in type as long as yourself.' . . .) . . . Pinkerton's *Hebdomedary* Picnics was soon shortened, by popular consent, to the Dromedary."

hebephrenia, see **hebetic**

hebetate   (HEB ih tate) *vb*. To *hebetate* is to dull or blunt. The term is applied usually where the *hebetation* (heb ih TAY shun) acts upon a person's sensitivity or a faculty. The political life often tends to *hebetate* one's ethical sensibilities, alas. The verb is derived from Latin *hebetatus*, past participle of *hebetare* (to make dull, to deaden), based on the adjective *hebes* (dull, blunt, sluggish). The expression *sensus hebes* (literally, dull sense; figuratively, dullness of the senses, i.e., insensitivity) appears in the Prologue to the *Polycraticus*, a treatise on government by the English scholar and prelate John of Salisbury (c. 1115-1180). The related noun *hebetude* (HEB ih toohd, -tyoohd) denotes listlessness, lethargy, and the adjective is *hebetudinous* (heb ih TOOHD ih nus, -TYOOHD). Both words are from Late Latin *hebetudo* (dullness). These *hebe-* words are in no way related to **hebetic** and **hebephrenia**, which involve entirely different derivations.

hebetic   (hih BET ik) *adj*. *Hebetic* applies to anything pertaining to puberty, or happening during puberty. It is derived from Greek *hebetikos* (youthful), based on the noun *hebe* (youth), and it is to be remembered that *Hebe* was the Greek goddess of youth, born of Zeus and Hera (a legitimate birth on Olympus, for a change!) and cup-bearer to the gods, with the power of restoring youth and strength to both gods and mortals. Hebe was succeeded by the god Ganymede, Zeus's cup-bearer, in a bit of political manipulation. On a sadder note: *hebephrenia* is a form of insanity that occurs in late childhood, involving incoherence and delusions, and ending in complete dementia. This term is based on *hebe* (youth) plus the Greek noun *phren* (mind). The *hebe-* in these words has naught to do with the *hebe-* based on Latin *hebes* (dull, blunt) in **hebetate** and **hebetude**.

hebetude, see **hebetate**

helot   (HEL ut, HEE lut) *n.* A *helot* is a serf, or more generally, a slave. With an upper case *H, Helot* was the label given to a member of a class of society owned by the state in ancient Sparta, *helotes* in Latin, *heilotes* in Greek. *Helots* were bound to the land, farmed it, and paid part of the produce to the ruling class, the Spartiates. They could not be sold, and remained for their lives tied to the land, without civil rights of any sort. The story goes that the Spartiates would on occasion make a *Helot* drunk and exhibit him to the youth to demonstrate the evils of drink. The Scottish biographer James Boswell (1740-1795) quotes the English lexicographer and writer Dr. Samuel Johnson (1709-1784) as having said of an acquaintance: "He is a man of good principles; and there would be no danger that a young gentleman should catch his manner; for it is so very bad, that it must be avoided. In that respect, he would be like the drunken *Helot.*" *Helot* is used as a biological term applied to a plant or animal living symbiotically with another to which it is subject—a special usage. *Helotism* (HEL uh tiz um, HEE luh-) or *helotry* (HEL uh tree, HEE luh-) is serfdom.

hendiadys   (hen DYE uh dis) *n.* The *hendiadys* principle or construction, chiefly a convention of classical Greek and Latin, is one in which two nouns connected by *and,* as though they were independent components, are used to express an idea that would normally be covered by a noun and an adjective. Example: to eat from *dishes and silver* for eat from *silver dishes;* her eyes were like *pools and crystal,* for *crystal pools.* This construction is poetic and infrequently found in English; when used, it is in expressions like *nice and warm* for *nicely warm; try and convince him* for *try to convince him; grace and favor* for *gracious favor.* These illustrations in English are combinations of two adjectives, or two verbs, or two nouns; it is in the classical languages that the construction is normally composed of two nouns, where the second noun serves as an adjective modifying the first. There are expressions mistakenly considered to be *hendiadys,* where the two components connected by *and* are independent, rather than the second noun's being in the subordinate position. Examples: *assault and battery; might and main; toil and moil* (*moil* means "drudgery"); *hue and cry; leaps and bounds.* These are merely bits of tautology used for emphasis, usually a fruitful source of clichés. *Hendiadys* is, via Middle Latin, from Greek: *hen dia dyoin* (one by two).

henotheism, see **henotic**

henotic   (hen OT ik) *adj. Heno-* is a Greek prefix meaning "one," from *hen,* the neuter form of *heis* (one), and from *heno-* came the Greek adjective *henotikos,* and our word *henotic,* describing anything that tends to unify or reconcile. The blitzkrieg had a *henotic* effect upon the people of London, bringing them together in a way that transcended class distinctions. The *henotic* efforts of Abraham Lincoln helped heal the wounds of the Civil War (though some folks down there seem still to be fighting it, at least verbally). *Heno-* also appears in the noun *henotheism* (HEN uh thee iz um), the worship of one god in

particular, one believed supreme or worthy of special veneration, without denying the existence of other gods, representing a stage between polytheism and
monotheism. You pays your money and you takes your choice. *Heno-*, plus
English *theism*, from the Greek noun *theos* (god), akin to Latin *deus*, gave us
henotheism.

herculean   (hur kyooh LEE un) *adj.* A *herculean* task is one extremely
difficult to perform. A *herculean* person is one of great strength and courage, or
one of enormous size. Hercules, a great hero of classical mythology, a figure of
superhuman strength and valor, was a son of Zeus himself. As penance for killing
his wife and children in a fit of madness, Hercules had to perform 12 almost
impossible tasks—the 12 labors of Hercules, listed in most unabridged
dictionaries—whose accomplishment gained him immortality. (One of the 12
was to cleanse the Augean stables, which housed the herd of 3,000 oxen belonging to King Augeas of Elis in Greece and had not been cleaned for 30 years.
Hercules got through that one by diverting the course of a river through the
stables. To *cleanse the Augean stables* means, figuratively, to "clear away an
accumulation of corruption," and the word *Augean* itself has come to mean, in
the figurative sense, "wearisome and distasteful, laborious and unpleasant," as
applied to a task or an assignment.) Getting back to old Hercules: Any exceedingly difficult, backbreaking task may be described as *herculean*—one, so to
speak, requiring the strength and patience of a Hercules. The English poet John
Milton (1608-1674) used *Herculean* (with the alternative pronunciation hur
KYOOH lee un; not much heard any more) in the sense of "extremely strong,
powerful," when he wrote:

> So rose the Danite strong
> *Herculean* Samson, from the harlot lap
> Of Philistean Dalilah.

But the common use of *herculean* is to describe a particularly onerous task.
D-Day has often been described as a "*herculean* effort."

hermeneutics   (hur muh NOOH tiks, -NYOOH-) *n. Hermeneutics*, treated
as a singular noun (like *economics, politics*, etc.), is the science of interpretation, especially of the Bible. The adjective *hermeneutic* or *hermeneutical*
means "explanatory," i.e., concerned with interpretation. The word comes from
Greek *hermeneutikos* (skilled in interpretation), related to the verb
hermeneuein (to explain, make clear, interpret), all based on the god Hermes,
the herald and messenger of the Greek gods, patron of the arts and eloquence
(and, incidentally, of herdsmen, roads, commerce, invention, cunning, and
thievery—he covered a lot of ground! After all, he did have wings on his ankles,
like his Roman counterpart, Mercury, a mercurial sort of chap.). Any commentary or series of annotations to a text can be described as *hermeneutic*.
Hermeneutic(s) is to be distinguished from an *exegesis* (ek sih JEE sis), which is

the concrete interpretation (also primarily of the Bible) itself; but the adjective *exegetic* (ek sih JET ik) and the noun *exegetics* are synonymous with *hermeneutic* and *hermeneutics* respectively. *Exegesis* and its related words are from Greek *exegesis* (interpretation), based on prefix *ex-* (out of) plus the verb *hegeesthai* (to guide). Irrelevant Note: In a characteristically hilarious piece entitled *The UFO Menace*, in *Side Effects* (Random House, New York, 1981), the American humorist, actor, film director, and producer Woody Allen (b. 1935) narrates an encounter by "two Louisiana factory workers" that starts: "Roy and I was catfishing in the bog" and goes on about several creatures who emerge from a bright-yellow sphere, speaking in a strange tongue. After a while " . . . they had mastered my own language, but they still made simple mistakes like using '*hermeneutics*' when they meant 'heuristics.'" It happens that in *1000 Most Important Words* by this author (Ballantine Books, New York, 1982; Facts On File, New York, 1985), *heuristic* is defined as a term applied to teaching methods, meaning "helping to learn, encouraging students to find out for themselves . . . akin to the Socratic method," and the derivation is given as "from New Latin *heuristicus*, based on Greek *heuriskein* (to find out)." There isn't the slightest connection between the two words, as every extraterrestrial person should know, and those creatures should be ashamed of theirselves.

herpestine, see **accipitrine**

herpetology   (hur pih TOL uh jee) *n*. *Herpetology* is the branch of zoology that deals with reptiles and amphibians. It comes from the Greek noun *herpeton* (creeping thing, reptile) based on the verb *herpein* (to creep) plus the familiar suffix *-logia*, used in the names of sciences and fields of knowledge, from which we get our common suffix *-logy*. (The all-too-familiar disease *herpes* is a Greek word meaning "creeping," also related to the verb *herpein*.) A *herpetologist* (hur pih TOL uh jist) is a specialist in *herpetology*. *Ophiology* (of ee OL uh jee, ohf-), derived from Greek *ophis* (snake) and *-logia*, is the branch of *herpetology* that deals with snakes, and *ophidian* (oh FID ee un) is both an adjective describing anything pertaining to snakes and a noun meaning "snake," derived from Greek *ophidion*, diminutive of *ophis* (serpent). *Ophiolatry* (of ee OL uh tree, ohf-) is snake worship, formed from same *ophis* plus the suffix *-latry*, based on *latria* (worship), found in words like *idolatry*.

heterochthonous, see **autochthon**

heteroclite   (HET uh ruh klite) *n*., *adj*. *Heteroclite* means "abnormal, anomalous, off the beaten path," and as a noun, anyone or anything that fits that description—in man, a maverick, someone who doesn't fit the usual pattern, the conventions. Most great men and women were heteroclites—Caesar, Churchill, Shakespeare, Mme. Curie, Einstein. The word is from Greek *heteroklitos*, built on the prefix *hetero-* (other, different; as in *heterogeneous, heterodox*, etc.) plus *klitos* (past participle of *klinein* (to bend)—in other words, "bent the other way." *Klinein* also means to "inflect," and that gives *heteroclite* a special usage in grammar, both as noun and adjective. To *inflect* is simply to vary the ending of a word, depending on its function in a sentence: The *boy* is here; the *boys* are here; the *boy's* eyes are blue; the *boys'* eyes are of different colors. (Inflecton applies to adjectives and verbs as well and isn't all that simple, but let's leave it at that.) In Latin, nouns are classified into five "declensions" depending on the way in which they are inflected. If a noun has endings in more than one declension, it is *heteroclite*, or *a heteroclite*. For those who are interested, look up the declensions of *domus* (home) and *pecus* (cattle, or a single head of cattle). That will do for the moment, except for the very *heteroclite heteroclites* who want to keep delving.

heterodox   (HET ur uh doks) *adj.* A *heterodox* belief is one not in accord with orthodox doctrines. We are familiar with *orthodox*, from Greek *orthodoxos* (correct in opinion), based on the prefix *ortho-*, from the adjective *orthos* (straight, correct) plus *doxa* (opinion), related to the verb *dokein* (to think); but less so with *hererodox*, from Greek *heterodoxos* (holding another opinion), based on the Greek prefix *hetero-*, from the adjective *heteros* (other, different) plus the same *doxa*. *Heterodoxy* (HET ur uh doks ee) is the word for a *heterodox* view. *Orthodox* and *heterodox* depend on the individual's point of view. According to the *Memoirs* of the English chemist, writer, and clergyman Joseph Priestly (1733-1804), Bishop William Warburton (1698-1779) remarked to Lord Sandwich (1718-1792; the fourth earl of Sandwich, the **eponym** of the sandwich, which he invented by ordering a waiter to bring him a slice of ham between two slices of bread so that he could continue gambling all day, as was his wont, without having to stop to use a knife and fork): "Orthodoxy is my doxy; *heterodoxy* is another man's doxy." The English historian Thomas Carlyle (1795-1881), in his *History of the French Revolution*, created the sardonic phrase: "the difference between Orthodoxy or My-doxy and *Heterodoxy* or Thy-doxy." *Doxy* is an archaic jocular word meaning "opinion, doctrine, religious views," back-formed from *orthodoxy* and *heterodoxy*. The other meanings of *doxy* ("paramour" or "prostitute") have nothing to do with the case.

hexaëmeron   (hek suh EM uh ron) *n.* The *hexaëmeron* is the six-day period of the creation of the world, or a written report of them, especially *Genesis*. *Hexaëmeron* is formed of the Greek prefix *hexa-*, from *hex* (six) plus *hemera* (day). "And on the seventh day God ended his work which he had made; and he rested on the seventh day from all his work which he had made." (*Genesis* 2:2.) One might be surprised to read, in the *New English Bible* (2:2): "On the *sixth* day God completed all the work he had been doing . . . " Choose your Bible: It took six days; hence *hexa*ëmeron. The word is sometimes written without the *ë*: *hexameron*, and in this form is easy to confuse with the *Heptameron* (*hepta*, Greek for *seven*), quite a different bit of literature—a collection of medieval stories written by or ascribed to Marguerite of Angoulême, queen of Navarre

(1492-1549), supposed to have been told in seven days—or even with the *Decameron* (*deka*, Greek for *ten*) of the Italian poet and writer Boccaccio (1313-1375), a series of 100 tales to be related among a group of friends within a period of ten days, and much naughtier than the *hexaëmeron*.

hibernal, see **hiemal**

hidrosis, see **sudorific**

hiemal   (HYE uh mul) *adj.* Hiemal means "wintry," and is descriptive of anything pertaining to winter. *Hiemal* comes from Latin *hiemalis* (wintry), based on the noun *hiems* (winter). *Hibernal* (hye BUR nul) is synonymous with *hiemal*, and is derived from Latin *hibernalis* or *hibernus*, related to the verb *hibernare* (to pass the winter), whose past participle, *hibernatus*, gave us the verb *hibernate*. What is cozier than to sit by the blazing fire on a raw *hiemal* (or *hibernal*) night?

hieratic   (hye uh RAT ik, hye RAT-) *adj. Hieratic* and *hieratical* describe things pertaining to the priesthood. In a narrower use, *hieratic* applies to a special form of ancient Egyptian writing based on a simplified, abridged form of hieroglyphs used by priests in record keeping. *Hieratic* is derived, via Latin *hieraticus*, from Greek *hieratikos* (priestly), based on the prefix *hiero-*, from *hieros* (sacred), from which we got such words as *hierarchy*, *hieroglyphic*, etc. The *-glyph* part comes from Greek *glyphe* (carving), based on the verb *glyphein* (to hollow out). We must remember that the "writing" was originally engraved on clay or stone.

hinny   (HIN ee) *n., vb.* A *hinny* is the progeny of a female donkey (or she-ass) and a stallion, the converse of a *mule*, which is the result of a union between a male donkey (or he-ass) and a mare, although *mule* is used generically as well to denote any offspring of a donkey and a horse, regardless of the sexes of the cooperating couple. *Mule* is used even more widely in biology to designate any hybrid, and strangely enough, particularly that between canaries and other types of finch. The mule is also a symbol of stubbornness, but the *hinny* has escaped that calumny. *Hinny* is from Latin *hinnus*, derived from Greek *ginnos* or *hinnos* (mule). *Hinny* is also used as a verb meaning to "whinny" or "neigh," coming, via the French verb *hinnir*, from Latin *hinnire*.

hippopotamine, see **accipitrine**

hippotigrine, see **accipitrine**

hirudine, see **accipitrine**

hirundine, see **accipitrine**

historicism, see **historicity**

historicity   (his tuh RIS ih tee) *n*. "This ugly word," says Fowler, "has . . . a real use as a single word for the phrase *historical existence*, i.e., the having really existed or taken place in history as opposed to mere legend or literature." In other words, *historicity* is historical authenticity. Did the Red Sea really open at Moses's command? Did the walls of Jericho actually crumble at Joshua's blast? Did the miracle at Cana really occur? There are schools of thought that question the authenticity of these events. This has nothing to do with *historicism* (his TOR ih siz um), which has several distinct meanings: the belief that history is the result of unvarying principles rather than the work of man; excessive respect for historical institutions, such as traditions and laws; a search for principles of historical evolution that explain, and would help to foretell historical happenings or phenomena. (As to *historicity*, see also *mythicize*, discussed under **mythopoeia**.)

hobbledehoy   (HOB ul dee hoy) *n*. A *hobbledehoy* is a clumsy, awkward stripling in the age between boyhood and manhood. (Fowler uses the term *hobbledehoyhood* to denote the condition; see the Fowler quotation in the discussion under **fuliginous**.) *Hobbledehoyish* is the adjective. Most dictionaries give up on the derivation: "origin unknown" or "uncertain." The *Random House College Dictionary* theorizes: "[var. of *hoberdyhoy*, alliterative compound = *hoberd* (var. of *Roberd* Robert) + -Y^2 + *hoy* for BOY (*b* whence *h* for alliteration's sake)]." (The -Y^2 referred to is a **hypocoristic** suffix.) This etymological exercise sounds somewhat labored. To quote poor Mercutio in Shakespeare's *Romeo and Juliet* (Act III, Scene 1): "not so deep as a well, nor so wide as a church door . . . 'tis enough, 'twill serve."

hologram, see **holograph**

holograph   (HOHL uh graf, hol-) *n.*, *adj*. As an adjective, *holograph*, also *holographic* (hohl uh GRAF ik, hol-), *holographical* (hohl uh GRAF ih kul, hol-), describes a document entirely in the handwriting of its author. As a noun, a *holograph* is the document itself. The word is derived, via Late Latin *holographus*, from Greek *holographos*, based on the Greek prifix *holo-*, the combined form of *holos* (whole, entire) plus *graphos* (written). An authenticated *holograph* letter signed by a famous literary or historical character can become very valuable in the autograph market. *Autograph* can mean anything from a mere signature to anything handwritten, and speaking of autographs brings to mind the caustic comment of the English essayist Charles Lamb (1775-1834) in his "Popular Fallacy XI, That We Must Not Look a Gift Horse in the Mouth":

> A presentation copy . . . is a copy of a book which does not sell, sent you by the author, with his foolish autograph at the beginning of it; for which, if a

stranger, he only demands your friendship; if a brother author, he expects from you a book of yours, which does not sell, in return.

(How true, from mine own experience, dear Charles!) Do not confuse *holograph* with *hologram* (HOH luh gram; HOL uh-), formed of the same *holo-* plus *-gram*, from the Greek suffix *-gramma*, combining form of *gramma* (a writing or drawing). A *hologram* is a 3-D image (three-dimensional photograph) made by a process involving lasers.

holus bolus   (HOH lus BOH lus) *adverbial phrase.* This colloquial expression means "all in a lump, all at one gulp, all at once, altogether," It is a bit of sham Latin based either on *whole bolus* (a *bolus* being a *lump*, in veterinary medicine a *round mass* larger than the usual size of a pill; more generally, any soft lump, usually of chewed food), or on two Greek words, *holos* (whole) and *bolos* (lump). It can be used where one might have said *in* or *at* or *with one fell swoop* (*fell* meaning "fierce, dire, deadly," and *swoop* meaning "sudden onslaught"), i.e., by one terrible blow, by one decisive act, suddenly. In Shakespeare's *Macbeth* (Act IV, Scene 3), Macduff, on learning from Ross that his "wife and babes" had been "savagely slaughtered," cries, "At one fell swoop?" This terrible "fell swoop" has sometimes been thoughtlessly and jocularly distorted, by those ignorant of its origin, into "swell foop." Blasphemy! Another bit of joke-Latin, *omnium gatherum* (motley collection) formed of Latin *omnium* (of all) and *gatherum* (sham Latin for "gathering") is amusing, and without blame.

homarine, see **accipitrine**

Homeric   (hoh MER ik) *adj.* Literally, *Homeric* describes anything pertaining to Homer, or resembling him or his works, or worthy of him—Homer, the great Greek poet (c. 850 B.C.) to whom the authorship of *The Iliad* and *The Odyssey* is attributed. In the 19th century, the "Homeric question" was that of the verifiability of that attribution: the question whether the two great epic poems were simply collections of old narrative poems. That dispute of scholars has been ended, and there is general agreement that Homer wrote the poems, based on old legends. *Homeric laughter* is loud and hearty, like the laughter of the gods when they saw the lame Hephaestus (Vulcan, in the Roman Olympian hierarchy) hobble. He took Juno's side in her struggle with Jupiter, who threw him out of heaven. He took nine days to fall and broke a leg when he finally crashed to earth—hence the lameness. Apart from all references to Homer himself, *Homeric* is used figuratively for *heroic, titanic, epic,* as in the *Homeric* conflict of our World Wars. *Homeric* is from the Greek *Homerikos*, based on *Homeros*, the Greek name for *Homer*. The American poet and writer Walt Whitman (1819-1892) wrote: " . . . really great poetry is always (like the *Homeric* or Biblical canticles) the result of a national spirit, and not the privilege of a polished and select few . . . "

hominine, see **accipitrine**

homonym   (HOM uh nim) *n.*, **homophone** (HOM uh fone, HOH muh-) *n.*
These words are too often used interchangeably. Strictly speaking (the right way
to speak), *homophone* is the more inclusive term: a word pronounced the same
as another but differing in meaning, whether spelled the same way or not;
whereas a *homonym* is a word pronounced *and* spelled the same way as
another, but differing in meaning. Examples of *homophones* that are spelle'
differently: *heir, air, ere, e'er; two, too, to; straight, strait; stake, steak; freeze,
frieze; guilt, gilt; sign, sine*. Examples of *homophones* that are spelled the same
way and are therefore *homonyms* as defined above: *till* (until), *till* (cash box),
till (work the soil); *chase* (pursue), *chase* (work metal); *rock* (sway to and fro),
rock (stone), *rock* (slang: diamond), *rock* (type of music). *Homophone* is a back
formation from *homophonous*, meaning "pronounced the same," from the
Greek *homophonos*, based on *homo-* (same) and *phone* (sound). *Homonym* is
from the Greek *homonymon*, neuter form of *homonymos*, based on *homo-*
(same) and *-onymos*, from *onoma* (name, word). Because of the peculiarites of
both spelling and pronunciation in English, there are many sets of *homophones*
in our language. It must be hell for foreigners.

homophone, see **homonym**

honeyfuggle, see **sockdol(l)ager**

hornbook, see **ampersand**

horripilation   (ho rip uh LAY shun) *n. Horripilation* is gooseflesh, the bristling of one's skin produced by fright or horror, or just extreme cold. This
dramatic word comes from Late Latin *horripilatio*, based on Latin *horripilatus*,
past participle of *horripilare* (to bristle), which is based in turn on *horrere* (to
bristle) fortified by *pilus* (hair). To *horripilate* (ho RIP uh late) someone is to
produce *horripilation* in him, i.e., to cause him to suffer gooseflesh, to make his
hair stand on end. *Bristling* is what happens when one gets the *feeling* that his or
her hairs are standing on end—a phenomenon that is clearly visible when it
happens to cats, dogs, and certain other animals, but not to man, for whom it is
just a sensation. See **formication** for a somewhat related experience. The
English film director Alfred Hitchcock (1899-1980) was a master at directing
spine-chilling films that *horripilated* his audience. Ghost stories around a
campfire are a good source of *horripilation*, to say nothing of strange sounds
downstairs in the middle of the night.

hortatory   (HOR tuh tor ee) *adj.* Also **hortative** (HOR tuh tiv). A *hortatory*
or *hortative* message or speech is one that urges or encourages a certain course
of action. *Hortative* is from Latin *hortativus* (encouraging), based on *hortatus*
(encouragement). *Hortatory* is from Late Latin *hortatorius* (encouraging). All
these words go back to *hortatus*, past participle of the Latin verb *hortari* (to
urge or encourage). We are familiar with our verb to *exhort*, from Latin *ex-
hortari* (to exhort, encourage), which has a somewhat more cogent tone than

the adjectives, in that it contains a note of urgency rather than mere encouragement.

houghmagandy (hok muh GAN dee) *n. Houghmagandy* is fornication, a word found mostly in Scotland, denoting a practice that knows no boundaries. And that's the long and short of it.

Hudibrastic, see **ratiocinate**

hugger-mugger (HUG ur MUG ur) *n., vb., adj., adv.* Through all its uses as these various parts of speech, *hugger-mugger* involves two basic concepts, secrecy and disorder. True, these are distinct concepts—except that acts committed clandestinely are apt to be done in haste, and consequently in disorder. In any case, as a noun, *hugger-mugger* means "secrecy, concealment" or "confusion, muddle"; as a transitive verb, " to conceal, hush up"; as an intransitve verb, "to act secretly," sometimes "to seek secret counsel"; as an adjective, "secret" or "confused"; as an adverb, "secretly" or "in confusion." It was spelt *hucker-mucker* in the 16th century; there was a Middle English verb *mokere* (to conceal, hoard) and a Middle English verb *hoder* (to muddle). Lots of possible derivations; something of a muddle in itself. In Shakespeare's *Hamlet* (Act IV, Scene 5), King Claudius, concerned about "the people muddled" as to the killing of Polonius, tells Queen Gertrude:

> . . . and we have done but greenly [foolishly]
> In *hugger-mugger* to intern him . . .

Here, Shakespeare uses *hugger-mugger* to mean "in secrecy and haste," in a manner that would arouse suspicion of dirty work at the crossroads. *Hugger-muggery* means "secret doings," suggesting haste, concealment and confusion—a word almost onomatopoeic, especially if pronounced in a stage whisper. The American writer Elliot Paul (1891-1958) wrote a detective thriller and dubbed it *Hugger-mugger in the Louvre* (Random House, New York, 1940).

humanist (HYOOH muh nist, YOOH-) *n.* Although the term *humanist* can be applied literally to a student of human nature, the main use of this word is to denote one having deep concern for the welfare of the human race—a matter of no little regard since the invention of the delightful H-bomb. There is also a specialized use of *Humanist* (note upper case *H*) as a label for a member of a contemporary cult substituting faith in man for faith in God; faith in the supreme value and self-perfectibility of the human character. Wrote the American journalist and writer Walter Lippmann (1889-1974), explaining the central doctrine of *Humanism* as involved with distinctively human ideals and interests as opposed to religious concerns:

> To replace the conception of man as the subject of a heavenly king . . .
> *humanisn* takes as its dominant pattern the progress of the individual from
> infancy to self-governing maturity.

But *humanist* has also the entirely dissociated meaning of "classical scholar," one versed in the study of the "humanities," either classical Greek and Latin language and literature, or the liberal arts generally (philosophy, art, literature, etc.) as opposed to the sciences. *Humanist* is not to be confused with *humanitarian*, one engaged in the promotion of human welfare, either through service or as a philanthropist. The Latin basis of both words is *humanus* (human), but *humanist* itself is from the Italian noun *unamista*.

hundredweight   (HUN drid wate) *n.* It depends upon where you're doing the weighing. A *hundredweight* in the U.S. = 100 lbs., or 1/20 of a U.S. ton, which = 2,000 lbs. A *hundredweight* in the U.K. is 112 lbs., because in the U.K. a ton = 2,240 lbs., and 1/20 of that is 112. The U.S. ton is known as the "short ton," the U.K. ton as the "long ton." So, when you hear or read *hundredweight*, pay attention to the geography. Incidentally, in the U.K., despite the introduction of the metric system, the custom still persists in expressing people's weights in "stones," a stone being 14 lbs. ("I'm thinning, dear; my doctor insists I lose at least a stone!") For an extended study of British weights and measures, see this author's *British English, A to Zed* (Facts On File, 1987), particularly Appendix II.C.1.

hyalography   (hye uh LOG ruh fee) *n.* This is the art or technique of lettering or drawing on glass by etching or engraving. *Hyalos* is *glass* in Greek, and gave rise to the adjective *hyaline*, glasslike or vitreous, which is also used as a literary noun for "smooth sea" or "clear sky." *Hyaloid* is a term used in anatomy for "glassy" in the sense of "thin and transparent," like the membrane covering the jelly-like tissue filling the eyeball. But away from anatomy and back to glass and etching: *hyalo-* is the prefix from *hyalos*, and that prefix, plus the suffix *-graphy*, from Greek *graphia*, based on *graphein* (to draw or write) add up to *hyalography*, the technique first mentioned above, now a vanishing art, practiced only here and there, especially in Venice, Italy, where one can still see beautiful designs and lettering engraved on glass vases, goblets, and pitchers.

hydromel   (HYE druh mel) *n.* Just as the word is a combination of the Greek words *hydro* (water; in combining form, *hydro-*, as in *hydrogen, hydroplane, hydroelectric*, etc.) and *meli* (honey), *hydromel* is a mixture of water and honey, a word taken from the Greek noun *hydromeli*. This liquor, left to ferment, turns into mead, an alcoholic beverage popular in olden times and still found in some English pubs. *Mead* was *mede* in Middle English, *me(o)du* in Old English, and is related to the Greek noun *methy* (wine). Mead, made from *hydromel* (with the addition of yeast, malt, etc.), was a favorite breakfast drink in Merrie Olde long before the introduction of tea or coffee, and that may account for some of the strange happenings and goings-on there in days of yore.

hyenine, see **accipitrine**

hylobatine, see **accipitrine**

hymeneal (hye muh NEE ul) *n., adj.* As an adjective, *hymeneal* describes anything relating to marriage. As a noun, a *hymeneal* is a marriage song. This word is derived, via Latin *hymenaeus*, from Greek *hymenaios*, based on *Hymen*, in classical mythology the god of marriage, shown as a beautiful youth bearing a torch and a veil, said to be a more mature Eros or Amor or Cupid. With a lower case *h*, the *hymen* is the anatomical term for the membrane that partially closes the mouth of the vagina, a word taken intact from the Greek, a symbol of virginity and obviously related to the concept of the very marriage which deprives the bride of it (at least in the old days). A word related to *hymeneal* is *epithalamion* (ep uh thuh LAY mee un), also *epithalamium* (ep uh thuh LAY mee um), a song or poem honoring the bride and bridegroom. The origin of this word is the Greek *epithalamion*, the neuter form of the adjective *epithalamios* (nuptial), based on *thalamos* (bedroom). Apparently, with *hymeneals* and *epithalamia*, there was a great deal of singing at ancient Greek and Latin weddings. Nowadays it seems to be limited to a wedding march and the rather insipid *Oh Promise Me* . . .

hyperbaton (hy PUR buh ton) *n.* Based on the Greek prefix *hyper-* (excessive) plus *baton*, the root of *bainein* (to go), *hyperbaton* is a figure of speech in which natural word order is changed, usually for emphasis or effect. Example: "That I have to see!" The English poet Robert Browning (1812-1889) wrote a poem entitled "Wanting—is What?"

> Wanting—is what?
> Summer redundant,
> Blueness abundant,
> —Where is the blot?

This poem was satirized by an anonymous poet in the English comic weekly *Punch*, issue of April 21, 1883, raising the ante from three to four:

> Browning is—what?
> Riddle redundant,
> Baldness abundant
> Sense, who can spot?

Fowler gives the example: "That whiter skin of hers than now." This poetic kind of word order invasion leads to—what? Mainly confusion.

hypocoristic (hye puh kuh RIS tik, hip uh-) *adj. Hypocorism* (hye POK uh riz um, hih-) is the use of a pet name, or of baby talk by a grown-up; a *hypocorism* is a pet name or a diminutive, an endearment, from Greek *hypokorisma* (pet name), related to the verb *hypokorizesthai* (to use baby talk or pet or endearing names, or to play the child), based on the Greek prefix *hypo-* (under) plus *koros* (boy) and *kore* (girl). *Hypocoristic*, from Greek *hypokoristikos* (diminutive) is the adjective, meaning "endearing," and applicable to pet names, diminutives, and euphemisms in general. The letter *-y* used as a suffix has several functions, one of which is *hypocoristic*: *Bill* becomes *Billy, John Johnny, Fred Freddy*, etc.; *kitty, pussy*, and *doggy* ḇecome important members of the family; *-ie* often takes the place of the *hypocoristic -y*, as in *birdie, horsie, lassie, laddie*, etc.

hysteron proteron   (HIS tuh ron PROT uh ron). These Greek words, the neuter forms of the adjectives *hysteros* (latter) and *proteros* (former), form a phrase that means, literally, "latter, former" or "later, earlier" and has two uses in our language. Both, to quote Fowler, put the cart before the horse. In rhetoric, *hysteron proteron* is a figure of speech in which the rational or logical order of two or more elements is reversed, as in *bred and born*; (an economist's description of the British coal industry) *a prosperous and viable industry*; (from *The Indian Serenade*, by the English poet Shelley, 1792-1822) *I die! I faint! I fail!; then came the thunder and the lightning*. In the branch of philosophy known as logic, *hysteron proteron* is the label of a defective argument or logical fallacy that begs the question by assuming as a premise the very conclusion that is to be proved. Thus, in Shakespeare's *Much Ado About Nothing* (Act IV, Scene 2), Dogberry, the constable of great dignity but no sense, addresses the prisoners Boarachio and Conrade in these terms: "Masters, it is proved already that you are little better than false knaves; and it will go near to be thought so shortly . . . I say to you, it is thought you are false knaves."

hystricine, see **accipitrine**

iatric   (eye A trik, ee-) *adj. Iatric* applies to anything relating to a physican, or medicine in general. *Iatros* is *physician* in Greek; *iatrikos* is the adjective. *Iatrogenic* (eye a truh JEN ik) applies to an illness or neurosis caused by a doctor's examination, treatment for the wrong illness, or mistaken diagnosis; from prefix *iatro-*, based on *iatros*, plus suffix *-genic*, producing. *Iatrogenic* ailments are often the subject of medical malpractice suits, which have become so common that medical malpractice insurance rates have gone sky high and, proportionately, doctors' fees. *Iatrogenic* ailments are often the basis for the cliché about the "cure" being worse than the illness.

iatrogenic, see **iatric**

ibidine, see **accipitrine**

icarian   (ih KAR ee un) *adj.* As we shall see, *icarian* means "inadequate," in certain contexts. Icarus, in Greek mythology, was the son of Daedalus, the Athenian architect who built the labyrinth for King Minos of Crete. His name in

Greek was Daidalos, which, with a lower case *d*, means "skillful." Minos imprisoned both father and son. For their escape, the ingenious Daedalus fashioned a pair of wings for each of them, from bird feathers and wax. Daedalus was successful, but, though warned by his father, Icarus flew too close to the sun, which melted his wings, and he plunged into the sea and drowned. According to the Humez brothers, American authors of *Alpha to Omega* (David R. Godine, Publisher, Inc., Boston, 1981), Icarus's fate was "a lesson to subsequent centuries of children who might otherwise have seriously considered disobeying their wise and prudent parents." The brothers Humez point out the parallel with the tale of Phaeton, son of Apollo, the god who drove his chariot daily across the sky. Phaeton pestered Apollo to let him do the driving for a day ("Pop, can I have the car tonight?"), got his way, lost control, swooped too close to earth, fell out, and was killed—another case history of children who aren't ready to assume control of daddy's business. Shakespeare mentions Phaeton in *King Richard II* (Act III, Scene 3), where Richard, sensing the approach of doom, cries:

> Down, down I come, like glistering Phaeton
> Wanting the manage of unruly jades.

(Like glistening Phaeton, unable to control the wild horses). After all this, we finally come to the adjective *icarian*, as in *an icarian method*, one inadequate for the accomplishment of an ambitious goal. Then what about Daedalus? He gave us the adjective *daedal* (DEE dul) or *daedalian* (dee DAY lee un, -lyun), a description of anything displaying artistic or inventive skill, particularly if it is of an ingenious or intricate nature. In *Prometheus Unbound*, the English poet Shelley (1792-1822) wrote these lines:

> Language is a perpetual Orphic song,
> Which rules with *Daedal* harmony a throng
> Of thoughts and forms, which else senseless and shapeless were.

As to *Orphic* (OR fik): it comes from *Orpheus*, also of Greek mythology, who, with his music, charmed Hades, King of the Underworld, into letting him lead his dead wife Eurydice away, but broke his promise not to look back at her until they got to earth and thus lost her forever. *Orphic* music is music that casts a spell. We've delved quite deeply into Greek mythology, but just remember: *icarian* is over-ambitious and inadequate and *daedal* is ingenious and inventive.

iconodule (eye KON uh doohl, -dyoohl) *n.* An *iconodule*, literally, is one who venerates *icons* (in the Eastern Church, images of sacred persons), and the practice is known as *iconoduly* (eye KON uh dooh lee, -dyooh-). We are more familiar with the words that denote their antithesis: *iconoclast* (eye KON uh klast) and *iconoclasm* (eye KON uh klas um). Literally, an *iconoclast* is a destroyer of icons and *iconoclasm* is the practice. In the eighth century, reformers in the Eastern Church led a movement against the veneration of icons which was opposed by monks and popes. The struggle took a political turn, and was finally resolved in 843 by the Empress Theodora in favor of the icons. The opposing parties were known as *Iconoclasts* and *Iconodules*. All that is fairly ancient stuff, and, except in history books, *iconoclast* denotes one who attacks traditional beliefs and *iconodule* (a far less common word) one who clings to them. An *iconodule* is, so to speak, a fundamentalist. The *iconolast-iconodule*, or modernist-fundamentalist, controversy broke into the limelight with the 1925 Scopes evolution trial. That year, Tennessee enacted a statute making un- lawful the teaching in public schools of any theory that ran counter to belief in the divine creation of man according to *Genesis*. John T. Scopes, a biology teacher, was tried for teaching Darwinian evolution in a Tennessee school. The American political leader William Jennings Bryan (1860-1925) appeared for the prosecution, the famous American lawyer Clarence Darrow (1857-1938) for the defense. Bryan won his case (later reversed on a technicality) but Darrow's examination of him went far to discredit fundamentalist interpretation of the Bible and no other state followed Tennessee's example. Darrow was an *iconoclast*, Bryan an *iconodule*. Iconoclast is from Greek *icon* (image) and *klastes* (breaker); the suffix in *iconodule* is from Greek *loudos* (slave, servant).

ideate (EYE dee ate, eye DEE ate) *vb*. *Ideate* can be used **transitively** or **in- transitively**. One can simply *ideate*, i.e., think, like the *Thinker*, the masterpiece by the French sculptor Rodin (1840-1917); or one can *ideate* something, form or have an *idea* of it, imagine it, preconceive it. *Idea* comes, via Late Latin, from the Greek noun *idea* (pattern), related to the verb *idein* (to see); *ideate* is from Late Latin *ideatus*, past participle of *ideare* (to form an idea). Inventors are *ideaters*. The English inventor Thomas Newcomen (1663-1724) *ideated* the steam engine. The legend that the Scotsman James Watt (1736-1819) *ideated* the steam engine while watching the lid of his mother's kettle rattle up and down on the kitchen stove is apocryphal. While repairing a model of Newcomen's engine at the University of Glasgow, Watt *ideated* a new and better type. Edison (1847-1931) was a prolific *ideater* of practical instruments, while Einstein (1879-1955) *ideated* in the abstract.

idiographic, see **nomology**

idiopathic (id ee oh PATH ik) *adj*. This is a medical term applicable to a disease of an unknown cause, a state peculiar to the individual patient, a pathological condition the physician cannot diagnose. He looks you over, asks you a lot of questions, says it might be this or might be that, and winds up baffled and leaving you unsolaced. It's one of those terms like "essential," as used in *essential hypertension*, where *essential* doesn't mean "necessary" or "indis- pensable" or anything like that, but merely "what it is by its very nature," i.e., it's there because it's there, going right to the root of *essential*, the first four letters: *esse*, latin for "to be." *Idiopathy* (id ee OP uh thee), denoting a disease existing all on its own, a primary ailment not the result of an identifiable previous condition, is from Greek *idiopatheia* (a subjective feeling, peculiar to oneself), based on *idios* (own, private) plus *pathos* (suffering).

ilk (ilk) *n.* The common use of *ilk* is in the phrase *of that ilk,* and, correctly employed, has a distinctly limited use. It applies properly only when the surname of a person is the same as the name of his estate or the place he's from. In a series of letters to *The Times* (London), Sir Iain Moncreiffe, of Easter Moncreiffe, Perthshire, signed himself "Iain Moncreiffe, Of That Ilk," meaning "Iain Moncreiffe of Moncreiffe." Quoting from *British English, A to Zed* (Facts On File, 1987) by this author: "A friend of the author named Hector Cameron was a Cameron of Cameron, and once announced himself over the telephone as 'Cameron of that ilk.' The uneducated (at that time) author, to his shame, ascribed it to drink. There are MacDonalds *of that ilk* (MacDonalds of MacDonald), Guthries *of that ilk* (Guthries of Guthrie) and so on. From a Sassenach misunderstanding of usage, *ilk* has acquired the meaning 'sort' or 'kind'; used generally in a pejorative sense: *Al Capone, and people of that ilk,* or even (heaven forfend!) *Freudians* (or *communists,* etc.) *and their ilk.*" The use of *ilk* is now expanded to include "family," "class," or "set" as well as "kind." Fowler says of *ilk*: "This SLIPSHOD EXTENSION has become so common that the OED [Oxford English Dictionary] Supp [lement] was constrained to add to its definitions 'also by further extension, often in trivial use, —kind, sort'. The COD [Concise Oxford Dictionary] calls it vulgar." *Ilk* is, via Middle English *ilke*, from Old English *ilca*. Incidentally, the adjective *Sassenach* mentioned above is defined in *British English, A to Zed* as follows: "From the Gaelic for *Saxon*, an opprobrious term used by Scots, and sometimes by the Irish as well, to designate and derogate the English."

illation (ih LAY shun) *n. Illation* is the act of inferring from data or the resulting inference or conclusion drawn. The adjective, *illative* (IL u tiv, ih LAY tiv), applies to anything that pertains to or introduces or expresses an inference. The word *therefore* is an *illative* word: It introduces a conclusion drawn from what has gone before. *Illation* is from Late Latin *illatio* (a carrying in), related to *illatus,* past participle of *inferre* (to infer), based on the prefix *il-* (in; a variant of *in-* before *l*) plus *latus* (carried). One must not jump to *illations,* though some people say it's the only exercise they get.

illative, see **illation**

illuminati (ih looh mu NAY tye, -NA tee) *n. pl.* The *illuminati* are those endowed with superior knowledge, information, or enlightenment, or who claim to possess it. Historically, the term was applied to a sect of Spanish heretics of the 16th century and later to the members of a German secret society, established in 1776 along the lines of Freemasonry. But *illuminati* is used today as a somewhat pejorative term applied to those whose claim to superior enlightenment may be far from justified. *Illuminati* is the masculine plural of Latin *illuminatus*, past participle of *illuminare* (to light up), used as a noun.

imbroglio   (im BROHL yoh) *n.*; **intaglio** (in TAL yoh) *n.*; **seraglio** (sih RAL yoh) *n.* If you should happen to come across an *intaglio* of an *imbroglio* occurring in a *seraglio*, you would be looking at an incised carving of a bitter row arising in a harem; and if you wanted to announce your discovery with the correct pronunciation, you would be careful to keep all the *g*'s mute (like the one in Modigliani, the Italian painter, 1884-1920, who was also a sculptor but never incised a row in a harem). One justification for lumping these three words in one entry is that they are all taken from the Italian and therefore follow the pronunciation rule given above. Another is that, however unlikely the event, an *intaglio* of an *imbroglio* in a *seraglio* makes a nice sound. *Imbroglio*, in Italian, is associated with the verb *imbrogliare* (to embroil). In English, an *imbroglio* is a difficult situation, a complicated disagreement or misunderstanding, leading to a bitter dispute. *Intaglio*, in Italian, is associated with the verb *intagliare* (to cut in, engrave). An *intaglio* is an incised carving, one on which the design or figure is below the surface of the material, thus the antithesis of a relief. In both cases, the English word has the same meaning as its Italian forebear. *Seraglio* presents a somewhat different story. Its common meaning in English is "harem," and one of its meanings in Italian is the same, but there are two *r*s in the Italian *serraglio*, and its primary meaning ("harem" came later) is "menagerie, cage for wild beasts." Draw your own conclusions.

imbrue   (im BROOH) *vb.* To *imbrue* something is to soak or drench it, especially with blood. It is not to be confused with *imbue* (im BYOOH), used in connection with inspiring a person with opinions or sentiments (e.g., to *imbue* someone with patriotism). According to the dictionaries, it, too, can mean to "drench with blood," but this must be a rare use indeed. The English poet John Milton (1608-1674) wrote of "Derwen stream [the River Derwen] in Lancashire with blood of Scots *imbrued*." The hands of both Macbeth and his Lady were *imbrued* after the slaughter of King Duncan (Shakespeare's *Macbeth*, Act II, Scene 3). In *Pyramus and Thisbe*, the play within a play in *Midsummer-Night's Dream* (Act V, Scene 1), Thisbe, finding Pyramus dead, moans:

> Asleep, my love?
>   What, dead, my dove?
> O Pyramus, arise!
>   Speak, speak! Quite dumb?
>   Dead, dead! A tomb
> Must cover thy sweet eyes . . . .
>   Come, trusty sword:
> Come, blade, my breast *imbrue* . . .

and, true to the stage directions, stabs herself. In Shakespeare's *Henry IV, Part 2* (Act II, Scene 4), in a brawl scene, Falstaff tells Bardolph to quoit [throw] Pistol downstairs, and Pistol snatching up his sword, cries: "What! Shall we have inci-sion? Shall we *imbrue?*" *Imbrue* is, via Old French *embreuver*, from Late Latin *imbiberare*, based on Latin *imbibere* (to drink in), whereas *imbue* is from Latin *imbuere* (to steep, soak).

imprimatur   (im prih MA tur, -MAY-, -prye-) *n.* An *imprimatur* is an official license to print and publish a book or tract, especially as issued by the Roman Catholic Church in the case of a religious work; often followed by the Latin phrase *nihil obstat* (there is no objection) issued by the religious censor, negat-ing any unorthodox pronouncement. *Imprimatur* is Latin for "Let it be printed," and can be used in the more general figurative sense of any sanction, license, or authoritative approval. Do not confuse it with *imprint*, the name of the publisher or printer or place of publication or printing appearing at the front or end of a book, or with *imprimatura* (im pree muh TOOR uh), a term in painting taken from the Italian for a colored wash or underpainting made in connection with the preliminary drawing.

incunabula   (in kyooh NAB yuh luh) *n. pl. Incunabula*, in the commonest use of the word, are extant copies of books printed before 1500, during the early stages of the use of movable type. The word is rarely found in the singular: *in-cunabulum* (-um). The Gutenberg Bible, printed at Mainz, Germany, about 1455 (so called because it is ascribed to Johannes Gutenberg, 1397-1468, said to be the inventor of printing with movable type) is the most famous example of an *incunabulum*. The word is used, but rarely, in the literal sense of the "first stages" or "infancy" of anything. Thus, cylindrical phonograph records or old one-sided 78s might be described as the *incunabula* of the recording industry. *Incunabula* has a complex and interesting derivation. *Cunae* is a Latin noun, plural in form but singular in meaning, for "cradle"; *-bula* is a neuter plural diminutive suffix, so that *cuna-* (stem of *cunae*) plus *-bula* produced *cunabula*, another word for "cradle," and by prefixing *in-* (in), the Romans created *in-cunabula*, meaning literally "swaddling clothes," and figuratively "infancy." Thus, books produced in the *infancy* of printing from movable type are called *incunabula*. The term was first applied to printing by one Bernard von Mallinckrodt in a 1630 tract on printing. He characterized the era from Gutenberg to 1500 as "prima typographiae *incunabula*," the period when typography was in its "swaddling clothes." *Incunabula* are rare and valuable. Don't waste time looking for them in secondhand bookstores.

indefectible   (in dih FEK tuh bul) *adj.* What is *indefectible* is unfailing, not subject to defect, failure, or imperfection; faultless; the negative form of *defectible* (liable to defect, failure, or error). Both stem from *defect*, derived from Latin *defectus*, past participle of *deficere* (to fail, be wanting), whose present participle *deficiens* gave us *deficient*. To the true Catholic believer, God is *indefectible*, whereas the Pope is merely infallible.

inexpugnable (in ik SPUG nuh bul) *adj. Inexpugnable* means "impregnable, unassailable, invincible," and can be used both literally and figuratively. It is from Latin prefix *in-* (not, un-) plus *expugnabilis* (capable of being taken by storm), based on *expugnare* (to capture, take by storm), and it all goes back to *pugna* (fight, battle), which eventually gave us *pugnacious, pugilist*, etc. *Inexpugnable* is not to be confused with the look-alike *inexpungible* (in ik SPUN juh bul), meaning "ineffaceable, indestructible," from Latin *in-* plus *expungere* (to cancel, obliterate). The American psychologist and philosopher William James (1842-1910), in *The Will to Believe—Reflex Action and Theism*, wrote:

> Man's chief difference from the brute lies in the exuberant excess of his subjective propensities—his preeminence over them simply and solely in the number and in the fantastic and unnecessary character of his wants, physical, moral, aesthetic, and intellectual. Had his whole life not been a quest for the superfluous, he would never have established himself as *inexpugnably* as he has done in the necessary.

"*Inexpugnably*," says James; i.e., unassailably, invincibly, impregnably. (But that was before the H-Bomb.) *Inexpungible*, on the other hand, might well describe an ineffaceable memory of a never-to-be-forgotten sight, or experience, like one's first view of the Piazza San Marco in Venice or of the Grand Canyon, or better still, of one's sensation of love at first sight.

inexpungible, see **inexpugnable**

infelicitous, see **felicitous**

inspissate (in SPIS ate) *vb.* To *inspissate* is to thicken; to make or become thicker or denser, as by evaporation. It is from Latin *inspissatus*, past participle of *inspissare*, based on *spissare* (to thicken), related to *spissus* (thick). The English lexicographer, poet, and critic Samuel Johnson ("Dr. Johnson," 1709-1784) used the evocative expression "*inspissated* gloom," much more moving than *inspissated oatmeal*, for instance, thickened by being allowed to stand too long on top of a cold stove.

instate (in STATE) *vb.* It is strange how much more familiar the verb *reinstate* is than *instate*, for persons and things can't be *reinstated* without first having been *instated*. True it is that things get *repeated* without first having been "peated," and there may well be other such cases, but somehow *instate* is a perfectly good verb: to put or place someone or something into a certain state, condition, or position. Yet *instate* has just about completely given way to *install*. A new official is *installed*, his assistants are *installed*, something goes wrong, out they go, things clear up, and they are *reinstated* rather than *reinstalled*. Strange are the ways of language. It's like what the Roman poet Virgil (70-19 B.C.) said about woman: "Varium et mutabile semper/Femina" ("A fickle thing and changeful is woman always!"). Just substitute *lingua* (language) for *femina*, though the sentence becomes a thousand times less dramatic. Or sexist.

intaglio, see **imbroglio**

intercalary, see **intercalate**

intercalate (in TUR kuh late) *vb*. To *intercalate* is to interpolate, and is a term used in the insertion of an extra day or month in a calendar, in the way February 29 is *intercalated* each leap year in our calendar, or five extra days were added to the French Revolutionary calendar (see **pluvious**) or an additional month to the Jewish calendar in certain years. Such complementary days or months are labeled "intercalary." *Intercalate* is from Latin *intercalatus*, past participle of *intercalare* (to insert, especially a day or month in the calendar); *intercalary* is from Latin *intercalaris* (inserted) or *intercalarius* (intercalary).

internecine (in tur NEE seen, -sine; -NES een, -ine) *adj. Internecine* has had a curious history, in having come to mean "mutually destructive," applicable to conflicts arising within families, political parties or other groups. It is from Latin *internecinus* (murderous, deadly—nothing "mutual" involved here), based on the prefix *inter*, which, to be sure, usually means "between" and connotes mutuality, exchange, etc., plus *necare* (to kill). But in certain Latin words, the *inter-* prefix has nothing to do with "betweenness" and has instead the force of "to extermination." Examples: *interire* (to perish), *intercidere* (to demolish), *interimere* (to annihilate), *interscindere* (to tear asunder). In no one of these Latin verbs does *inter-* have the force of mutuality, but only that of utter destruction. Be that as it may, since *inter-* implies exchange and mutuality in English (and usually in Latin), the true force of our *inter-* and its Latin forebear has been in this case misinterpreted; hence the current meaning of *internecine*.

intransitive, see **transitive**

invaginate (in VAJ uh nate) *vb. Invaginate* has three distinct meanings, none of them sexual. **Transitively**, to *invaginate* an object is to ensheath it, to push it into a close-fitting cover, such as one made to receive a tool or a sword. **Intransitively**, to *invaginate* is to *become invaginated*, i.e., to receive something *invaginated*. To *invaginate* a tube is to turn it inside out. *Invaginate* is from Latin prefix *in-* (in, into) plus *vagina* (sheath, scabbard); *vagina* in Latin, like *invaginate* in English, has no sexual meaning or connotation. That came from our imaginative English linguists. When you watch those duelling scenes in adventure films and Shakespearean stage productions, there's a great deal of the drawing and *invaginating* of swords, with nary a female in sight.

iota, see **alpha and omega**

irenic (eye REN ik, -REE-) *adj.* At first glance, one might assume that *irenic* was part of the *ire, ireful, irate, irascible* family based on the Latin noun *ira* (wrath), but the assumption would be wrong. Quite the contrary: We are dealing with an adjective derived from *Irene*, the classical goddess of peace and wealth (Eirene in the original transliteration), usually represented as a beautiful young woman carrying on one arm the infant Plutus, the god of wealth (who lent his name to our word *plutocrat*). This representation is in accordance with the statue by Cephisodotus the Elder (fl. fourth century B.C., believed to be either the father or the brother of the greatest of Greek sculptors, Praxiteles, fl. c. 370-333 B.C.) erected in Athens c. 370 B.C. on the occasion of the peace with Sparta. The alliterative phrase *peace and plenty* arose from that combination of Eirene and Plutus—an abundance of goods and luxuries in a time of peace.

irrefragable   (ih REF ruh guh bul) *adj*. Not to be confused with **irrefrangible**, this adjective applies to whatever cannot be refuted or denied. It is from Latin *irrefragabilis*, based on the prefix *ir-* (not; a variant of *in-* before *r*) plus *refragari* (to oppose, resist); or possibly based on *ir-* plus the prefix *re-* (backwards) plus *frangere* (to break). *The Irrefragable Doctor* was an epithet given to Alexander of Hales (died 1245; also known as "The Unanswerable Doctor"), a Franciscan, a lecturer at the University of Paris, the author of the first exposition of Christian doctrine introducing the teachings of the Greek philosopher Aristotle (384-322 B.C.) as a prime authority, and an important influence on St. Thomas Aquinas (1225-1274). Persons who believe their opinions or arguments are *irrefragable* are extremely hard to deal with.

irrefrangible   (ir ih FRAN juh bul) *adj*. Not to be confused with **irrefragable**, *irrefrangible* means "inviolable," applying to anything that should never be broken or violated. The positive form, *refrangible* (rih FRAN juh bul), means "refractable," as rays of light, i.e., deflectible at certain angles when entering obliquely from another medium of different density, e.g., from air into water. Thus, *irrefrangible* has the special meaning in optics of "incapable of being refracted," but the common meaning "inviolable" would apply to a vow or an oath or a secret that must be kept. *Irrefrangible* comes from the Latin prefix *ir-* (not; a variant of *in-* before *r*) plus *refrangibilis*, based on *refringere* (to break), whose past participle *refractus* gave us *refract*; and that goes back to *frangere* (to break), whose past participle *fractus* produced *fractio* (a breaking in pieces), and that gave us *fraction*.

ithyphallic   (ith uh FAL ik) *n., adj*. In the Bacchanalia, ancient festivals of Bacchus (god of wine in classical mythology), where drunkenness and licentiousness were rampant, a large statue of an erect penis was carried in the line of the procession. In its original and literal use, *ithyphallic* pertained to that artifact, but it came to mean "lewd, obscene, grossly indecent, shameless" in general usage. As a noun, *ithyphallic* was the name for a licentious poem. The noun *ithyphallus* (ith uh FAL us) means "erect penis" (in the flesh, not a statue). *Ithyphallic* is from Greek *ithyphallikos*, based on *ithys* (straight) plus *phallos* (phallus). *Ithyphallic* jokes should not be told at the dinner table in the presence of ladies.

izzat (IZ ut) *n. Izzat* is personal dignity, honor, self-respect, prestige, credit, reputation. It comes, via Hindi and Persian *'izzat*, from Arabic *'izzah* (glory). Who can forget the *izzat* maintained by Jacqueline, widow of the slain President Kennedy, during the ordeal of the swearing-in of Johnson in Dallas and throughout the ordeal of the funeral in Washington? *Izzat* is a virtue much to be commended, showing man at his best under the most painful of circumstances. *Man?* Mankind! No sexual distinctions here! *Izzat* has nothing to do with *izard*, the ibex that lives in the Pyrenees, or *izzard*, a British dialectical name for the letter *z*, called *zed* in standard British English.

jactation (jak TAY shun) *n. Jactation* has two totally distinct meanings. It is bragging, boasting, like **braggadocio, fanfaronade, gasconade, rodomontade**, and **thrasonical** behavior in general. There would seem to be no end of words for this human weakness. *Jactation* comes from Latin *jactatio* (boasting, ostentation), related to *jactatus*, past participle of *jactare* (to boast). But *jactate* and its Latin sources all wear another hat: In pathology, *jactation* is nervous, restless tossing about, convulsive body movements, because Latin *jactare* also means to "fling about, toss," and only by transference to "broadcast" words, to fling them about, and thus, to "boast." To complicate matters, there is a confusingly similar term, *jactitation* (jak tih TAY shun), which is a legal term for a false boast or claim that causes harm to another and can lead to a lawsuit; and this word, too, has a distinct meaning identical with that second meaning of *jactation*: "tossing about." Here the source is Middle Latin *jactitatio* (tossing), related to *jactitatus*, past participle of *jactitare* (to keep tossing about). To sum up: *jactation* and *jactitation* are identical in the terminology of pathology: to "toss about"; otherwise, *jactation* is boasting, pure and simple, while *jactitation* is the false and harmful variety. Apart from the medical symptoms, *jactate* all you want, if you're silly enough to brag: but stop short of *jactitating* or you may land in court.

jactitation, see **jactation**

jehu (JEE hyooh) *n.* A *jehu* is a fast driver, with the implication of recklessness and disregard of danger to others. *Jehu* was a king of Israel, a bloodthirsty warrior noted for his wild chariot attacks. We read in *II Kings* 9:20,

> " . . . he driveth furiously."

There were no traffic rules or constraints in those days; there are many now who drive as though that were still the case.

jeremiad (jer uh MYE ud) *n.* A *jeremiad* is a tale of woe, a lamentation, a doleful complaint, a plea for compassion, deriving its name from the *Lamentations of Jeremiah*, the Old Testament prophet of the sixth and seventh centuries B.C. A book of the Bible attributed to him bears his name. He called for moral reform, threatening doom if his message went unheeded. It is the prediction of doom and disaster that we associate with his name. "How doth the city sit solitary, that was full of people! how is she become as a widow! ... She weepeth sore in the night ... all her friends ... are become her enemies ... Jerusalem hath grievously sinned ... The joy of our heart is ceased ... O Lord ... wherfore dost thou ... forsake us ... thou art very wroth against us." Thus spake Jeremiah; but how very boring it can be to be forced to listen to the *jeremiads* of one's trouble-prone acquaintances! *Jeremiah* is a name given to any person who takes a gloomy view of his times and denounces what is going on in the world.

jorum (JOR um) *n.* A *jorum* is a large drinking-bowl, the kind generally used for serving punch. (*Punch*, incidentally, is said to be derived from *puncheon*, a large cask—an instance of **metonymy**?) *Jorum* can be used as well to denote the contents of that type of bowl or any great amount of drink, as in *We drank a jorum of wine*. Figuratively, *jorum* may be used to describe a great lot of anything: *With that second Rolls, those people must have a jorum of money*, and *Lot had a jorum of woes*. The word came from the name of Joram, son of King Toi of Hamath, who, according to *II Samuel* 8:10, "sent Joram his son unto King David ... And Joram brought with him vessels of silver, and vessels of gold, and vessels of brass ... "

jugulate (JOOH gyuh late) *vb.* To *jugulate* someone is to cut his throat or strangle him, both rather unpleasant procedures and obviously related (etymologically, not sociologically) to the jugular vein. But the word has a figurative and much more merciful use: to check or suppress by drastic measures, usually applied in medical parlance to the treatment of diseases. One case might be the amputation of an affected part, often the leg. Putting a gag into the mouth of a logorrhea sufferer would be less drastic, but might do the trick. *Jugulate* comes from Latin *jugulatus*, past participle of *jugulare* (to cut the throat of), based on *jugulum* (throat).

jussive (JUS iv) *n., adj. Jussive* describes a word or phrase expressing a command, usually a mild one, or having the effect of a command. As a noun, *jussive* is a grammatical term for a word, form, or mood expressing a command. "May I come in?" "Do!" The *Do!* is a mild command. "Halt! Who goes there?" *Halt!* is much less mild (the man uttering it has a gun on him) but both are *jussives*. Any verb in the imperative mood (used in commands, requests, etc.) is *jussive. Stay*, in "Stay a while," is *jussive*. Polite people introduce *jussives* with *Please* ... *Jussive* is from Latin *jussus*, past participle of the verb *jubere* (to command). The neuter form, *jussum*, means "command." It comes as a surprise to a Latinist that the first syllable is pronounced *jus-* rather than *joohs*, the Latin pronunciation (as far as we know—no recordings or tapes in those days).

justiciable   (ju STISH ee uh bul) *adj.* A *justiciable* issue or controversy is one within the jurisdiction of a court; one that can be resolved or settled pursuant to law, or in judicial proceedings. The adjective is from Middle Latin *justitiabilis*, based on Latin *justitia* (justice). What would an *unjusticiable* or *nonjusticiable* issue be? In disputes between governments and trade unions, particularly in Britain, the unions sometimes claim that resort by the government to the courts can have no effect because the dispute is not *justiciable*, i.e., that there are aspects of the controversy that must be resolved by negotiation, basic issues lying outside the jurisdiction of the courts, so that a court ruling would be of no effect and could be disregarded by the union.

juvenescence   (jooh vuh NES uns) *n. Juvenescence* is the transition from infancy or early childhood to youth. It comes from Latin *juvenescens*, present participle of *juvenescere* (to attain youth—in the sense of "growing up" or "regaining youth"). *Juvenescence*, as well as the common word *juvenile*, and **juvenilia**, all go back to the Latin adjective *juvenis* (young), which may be familiar from the medieval students' song, "Gaudeamus igitur./*Juvenes* dum sumus ... " (Let us rejoice, then, while we are young ...)—*juvenes* is the plural of *juvenis*. There is a story about the United States Supreme Court Justices Oliver Wendell Holmes (1841-1935) and Louis D. Brandeis (1856-1941) tarrying on the warm summer day the session ended for the seasonal break. Brandeis, trying to interest Holmes in the details of a complicated case he was going to work on during the vacation, noticed that Holmes's attention was wandering: He was watching the girls go by in their summer dresses. "Ollie!" cried Louis, "you're not listening!" "Oh to be seventy again!" sighed the octogenarian Ollie. He wanted to *juvenesce* in the second sense—to regain youth, à la Ponce de León (c. 1460-1521), the Spanish explorer who searched for the Fountain of Youth. A good story, even if it didn't happen. *Juvenescence* is one of a series of nouns formed from present participles of Latin verbs having to do with the ages of man: *pubescence*, the attaining of puberty, from *pubescens*, present participle of *pubescere* (to attain puberty), and *senescence*, present participle of *senescere* (to grow old), both, like *juvenescence*, accented on the penultimate syllable. Each of these three words has a corresponding adjective ending in *-ent*: *juvenescent*, *pubescent*, *senescent*. If this is beginning to remind you of the *Seven Ages of Man* speech of Jacques in Shakespeare's *As You Like It* (Act II, Scene 7), so much the better.

juvenilia   (jooh vuh NIL ee uh) *n. pl. Juvenile*, from Latin *juvenilis* (youthful), is a familiar word. *Juvenilia* is the neuter plural of that Latin adjective and means, literally, "youthful things." It is a term for either artistic works produced in youth or those suitable for the young, applied primarily to literary output but applicable to the other arts as well. The youthful music of Purcell (c.

1658-1695), Mozart (1756-1791), and Mendelssohn (1809-1847), and the poetry of Keats (1795-1821) and Shelley (1792-1822), as well as the youthful novels ("The Italian Girl," "A Room with a View") of E.M. Forster (1879-1970), written in his early twenties, qualify as *juvenilia* in the sense of youthful production. *Alice in Wonderland* and *Through the Looking-Glass*, by Lewis Carroll (Charles Lutwidge Dodgson, 1832-1898), *Stuart Little* and *Charlotte's Web*, by E.B. White, the American humorist and poet (1899-1985), as well as the countless "children's books" that flood the market year after year, qualify as *juvenilia* in the second sense.

kame, see **quarrel**

katabasis (**catabasis**), see **anabasis**

kedgeree   (KEJ uh ree) *n*. *Kedgeree* is a delicious concoction of Indian origin: rice, cooked with butter and dal (a puree of beans, peas, lentils, known collectively as *pulse*), flavored with spices, shredded onions, and other **ad hoc** ingredients. Imported into England and Europe, the dish was enhanced with flakes of fish and hard-boiled eggs, as well as other ingredients to taste—a very useful employment of fish left over from a previous meal. The word (like the dish) comes from India: *khichri*, based on Sanskrit *k'rsara* (dish of rice and sesame). Under the entry *haggis* in this author's *British English, A to Zed* (Facts On File, 1987), we read: "In one dictionary after another the definitions are strewn with *etc.*'s: *hearts, liver, etc., stomach of a sheep, etc.*, etc. This sort of thing tends to make one suspicious. There are fierce partisans on both sides of this *de gustibus* specialty." The dictionaries (and cookbooks) give the same treatment to *kedgeree*, but should not arouse your suspicions; it's delicious.

kern (kurn) *n*. In printing, a *kern* is the part of the face of a letter that projects beyond its body, like the part that makes a *Q* out of an *O*, or a *y* out of a *v*. In italics, the projecting parts of *f* and *j*, for example, are *kerns*. The word is derived, via French *carne* (corner), from Latin *cardo* (hinge).

kickshaw   (KIK shaw) *n*. *Kickshaw* has a number of distinct meanings: tidbit, delicacy, fancy dish (the last usually derogatory); or toy, trifle, trinket, something showy but worthless. It is a corruption of the French *quelque chose* (something) as the result of popular etymological development. It happened a long time ago, but in more recent times, we have seen the *blanc* of *vin blanc* (white wine) brought back by the British soldiers from France as *plonk*, which has now become British slang for any cheap wine, regardless of color, so the corruption continues. Originally, there was an *s* at the end of *kickshaw*, making the second syllable closer to *chose*, but it became "singular" by back formation. In Shakespeare's *Henry IV, Part 2* (Act V, Scene 1), Justice Shallow is telling his servant Davy what compensation he demands from William the cook for some lost sack (wine: another corruption from the French *sec*, dry): "Some pigeons, Davy, a couple of short-legged hens, a joint of mutton, and any pretty little *kickshaws* . . ." That was in the sense of "fancy dish" or "delicacy." Shakespeare used it in the other sense ("trifle") in *Twelfth Night* (Act I, Scene 3), when Sir Andrew Aguecheek tells Sir Toby Belch: "I delight in masques and revels . . . ," and Sir Toby asks, "Art thou good at these *kickshawses* . . . ?" and Sir Andrew answers. "As any man in Illyria . . . " and relates how well he dances the galliard and back-trick (contemporary dances).

kinesics   (kih NEE siks) *n.* Treated as a singular noun (like *economics*, etc.), *kinesics* is the study of body language, body movements and gestures as a method of communication without speech. It is derived from Greek *kinesis* (movement), related to the verb *kineein* (to move), and *kinesics* can mean "body movement" itself, as well as its study. Nodding to indicate the affirmative and turning the head from side to side to indicate the opposite are examples of *kinesics*. Waving as a gesture of greeting or farewell, raising a clenched fist as one of defiance or solidarity with a group, the rude gestures of thumbing or holding one's nose, the V-for-victory sign—these are all examples and there are many more. In cricket the umpire never speaks; he has gestures for "no-ball" (the bowler overstepping the crease, like a foot-fault in tennis) and "wide" (roughly the equivalent of a "ball" in baseball), and by pointing, indicates to a batsman that he is "out" for protecting his wicket by putting "leg before wicket." The umpire in baseball likewise uses *kinesics* to indicate whether a runner is safe or out at base. The fluttering eyes of a maiden send her gentleman friend a message of consuming interest: *kinesics* indeed.

koniology   (koh nee OL uh gee) *n.* This is the study of dust, germs, pollen, and other allergenic impurities suspended in the atmosphere. A *konimeter* (kon IM ih tur) is an instrument for measuring the dust in the air. A *koniscope* (KON ih skope) estimates the amount of suspended dust. *Koniology* is a field explored by allergists. The source of all these words is Greek *konis* (dust).

lacertine, see **accipitrine**

laches   (LACH iz) *n. Laches*, which looks like a plural noun but is singular, is a term used in law to denote such a degree of delay in the assertion of a claim or the bringing of a lawsuit as will bar the claimant or plaintiff from further proceeding. This is a concept in "equity," that area of the law dealing with the application of principles of natural justice in the determination of the rights of the parties and the disposition of controversies. *Laches* is a general defense, as opposed to specific and rigid statutes of limitation that vary from state to state and as to varying types of lawsuit (e.g., torts as opposed to breach of contract) and in express terms bar the bringing of a legal action after the lapse of a specific period, for example, six years for the institution of suit based on a promissory note, which becomes "outlawed" after that lapse of time beyond the maturity date. *Laches* was derived from Anglo-French *lachesse*, which came from Latin *laxus* (lax, loose, relaxed, postponed).

laconism (LAK uh niz um) *n.* Or **laconicism** (luh KON uh siz um). *Laconism* may be considered an example of **haplology**; see also **aph(a)eresis**. We are more familiar with the adjective *laconic* (luh KON ik) than the noun *laconism*, a concise style of language, brevity; also applied to a short, pithy statement. Laconia was long ago a country in the southern part of Greece, with Sparta as its capital. The Spartans were concise, brusque, and pithy in their speech, hence *laconic*, under which entry in this author's *1000 Most Important Words* (Ballantine, New York, 1982; Facts On File, New York, 1985) we read: "Philip of Macedonia wrote to the Spartan officials: 'If I enter Laconia, I will level Sparta to the ground.' Their answer: 'If.' Caesar's famous 'Veni, vidi, vici' ('I came, I saw, I conquered') is a famous example of *laconic* speech—not a word wasted." When General Sir Charles Napier (1782-1855) finally completed the conquest of Sind, a province of India, the story goes, he cabled the War Office one word: "Peccavi" (Latin for "I have sinned"). Quite a *laconism*, and quite a **paronomasia** in the bargain, even though the cable is generally believed to be apocryphal. And finally, the message radioed by an American pilot in World War II: "Sighted sub, sank same," an alliterative *laconism*.

lacustrine (luh KUS trin) *adj. Lacustrine* applies to things having to do with lakes; animals, fish, and plants living and growing in lakes, and geological strata formed at the bottom or along the shores of lakes. *Lacustrine* ecology has suffered enormously as a result of pollution from the disposal of chemical waste matter into lakes by nearby factories devoid of conscience in such matters. The *Lacustrian* Age was the age of lake-dwellings built on piles driven into the beds or shores of lakes. Remains of them have been found in Africa and Asia, but the most renowned are those of the Neolithic (Stone Age) peoples of the Alpine areas of Europe, especially Switzerland, who developed a high degree of skill in agriculture and the arts. Discoveries have been made of numerous village clusters, up to as many as 50, on a single lake where *lacustrine* people dwelt from c. 2500 B.C. until the seventh century B.C., when their territory was invaded by the Celts. The *lacustrine* way of life provided a ready supply of fish, marsh fowl, and fertile open crop land. The adjective comes, via Italian *lacustre*, from Latin *lacus* (lake).

lamia (LAY mee uh) *n*. The *lamiae* (LAY mee eye), in classical mythology, were a race of monsters with female heads and breasts and the bodies of serpents, who enticed young people and little children in order to devour them. The story went that the original *lamia* was a Queen of Libya with whom Jupiter fell in love. Juno became furiously jealous and stole the children of the queen, who went mad and vowed vengeance on all children. *Lamia* became a term for any vampire or she-demon. The literal meaning of *lamia* in Greek is "female man-eater." In medieval times, witches were sometimes called *lamiae*. The English poet John Keats (1795-1821) wrote a poem entitled *Lamia* a short time before his untimely death. In it, a bride, recognized as a *lamia* by the philosopher Apollonius of Tyana (born shortly before the birth of Christ), vanishes instantaneously. Keats based his theme on an incident related in *The Anatomy of Melancholy* of the English churchman and writer Robert Burton (1577-1640), who took it from *The Life of Apollonius* by the Greek philosopher Flavius Philostratus (born c. 170). The enticement or devouring of the young has long been a theme in legend, all the way from the Minotaur of Crete to the Pied Piper of Hamelin. There were no Missing Persons Bureaus in those days to trace the Hamelin kiddies.

Laodicean (lay od ih SEE un) *n*., *adj*. As an adjective, this word describes anyone who is generally indifferent, uninterested, and lackadaisical, and especially so in matters of religion. As a noun, *Laodicean* is a label for such a person. *Laodicea* is the ancient name of Latakia, a seaport in northwestern Syria. In *Revelation* 1:11, John was told: "What thou seest, write in a book and send it unto the seven churches which are in Asia . . ." of which the church of Laodicea was one. In 3:14-16, John was directed: " . . . Unto the angel of the church of the Laodiceans, write . . . 'Thou art neither cold nor hot . . . So then because thou art lukewarm . . . I will spue thee out of my mouth . . . '" It is from those words that *Laodicean* acquired the meaning given above.

lapidary (LAP ih der ee), also **lapidist** (LAP ih dist) *n*. Both forms of this noun denote a cutter and polisher of gemstones. *Lapidary* is also the name of the art itself, as well as that of engraving inscriptions on stone monuments. A *lapidarist* (luh PID uh rist: note change of stress) is a gem expert, a connoisseur of precious stones, also known as a *gem(m)ologist* (je MOL uh jist); and *gem(m)ology* (je MOL uh jee) is the study and science of gemstones. The *gem*-words come from Latin *gemma* (bud, jewel); the *lapid*- words from *lapid*-, the stem of Latin *lapis* (stone), and none of the latter should ever be confused or associated with **lapidate**.

lapidate (LAP ih date) *vb*. To *lapidate* is to stone to death, an old Biblical penalty first suggested by the Lord to Moses, as set forth in *Leviticus*, for various crimes including adultery, incest, homosexuality, and other such naughty practices, and latterly instituted by the Ayatollah Khomeini of Iran for similar offenses. Jesus was gentler: "He that is without sin among you, let him first cast a stone at her." (*John* 8:7.) Whatever one's views may be on the question of capital punishment, *lapidation* (lap ih DAY shun) is beyond the pale; and never, never associate it with those honest gem cutters and stone engravers discussed under **lapidary**, even though it comes from the same source, *lapid-*, the stem of the Latin noun *lapis* (stone). Further, *lapidate* has nothing to do with *dilapidate* or its more familiar form *dilapidated*, which comes from Latin *dilapidatus*, past participle of *dilapidare* (to demolish), based on the prefix *di-* (asunder; variant of *dis-* before certain consonants) plus the same old *lapid-*. From "dismantled, stone by stone," *dilapidated* has come to mean "fallen into decay," through neglect or abuse, and can apply to things having no connection with stones, from wooden houses to clothing in rags to moldy furniture and books, to say nothing of ravaged bodies.

lapine, see **accipitrine**

lari(di)ne, see **accipitrine**

latitudinarian   (lat ih toohd uh NAR ee un, -tyoohd-) *n.*, *adj. Latitude*, apart from its use in geography, used figuratively denotes tolerance of freedom of belief or action, freedom from dogma or narrow restrictions of any sort. It is from Latin *latitudo* (breadth), based on *latus* (wide). *Latitudinarian*, as an adjective, applies to those permitting or characterized by such an attitude, in opinion or behavior, and as a noun, to persons of *latitudinarian* persuasion. It has a special significance in matters of religion, describing a person allowing latitude in that field, indifferent as to creed, dogma, and ritual. In the Church of England, the label *latitudinarian* was first applied in the middle of the 17th century as a term of opprobrium to members of the clergy who underrated dogma and practice and came to favor and encourage laxity in that area. *Latitudianarianism* in religion was opposed and eventually checked by the emergence of the Evangelicals, who emphasized the Gospel and the importance of scriptural authority. The term is now applied generally to people who attach little importance to dogma and orthodoxy, like David Jenkins, the current bishop of Durham, who was installed, over wide protest, by the archbishop of York despite the bishop's previous statements disavowing belief in the Virgin Birth or the Resurrection. (Lightning struck the roof of Yorkminster, the Cathedral of York, a few days later. Form your own conclusions.)

lazar, see **lazaretto**

lazaretto   (laz uh RET o) *n.* A *lazaretto* is a hospital for patients suffering from contagious diseases, especially leprosy. The term is applied as well to any building or ship maintained for those detained in quarantine. It is also a nautical term for a small storeroom in the hull of a ship, especially one at the very stern. Context should make it clear which kind of *lazaretto* one is dealing with. It is from an Italian word in the Venetian dialect, *lazareto*, formed from *lazar* (LAZ ur), a leper or anyone suffering from a loathsome disease, plus *(N)azareto*, a hospital in Venice maintained by the Church of Santa Maria di Nazaret (St. Mary of Nazareth). *Lazar* comes from the name of Lazarus, the diseased beggar in the Bible parable of the rich man and the beggar in *Luke* 16:19-31.

legerdemain   (lej ur duh MANE) *n. Legerdemain* (which used to be written as three words, *léger de main*, meaning "light of hand" in Middle French) is sleight of hand, prestidigitation, the practice of magic tricks like pulling rabbits out of hats, jugglery, etc., all very fine things; but by extension, trickery, deceit, duplicity, chicanery, all very bad things. The Americn magician Harry Houdini (Erich Weiss, 1874-1926) was a world-famous practitioner of the art of *legerdemain* in its literal, good sense. Politicians, especially diplomats, are experts in verbal *legerdemain*, also known as word twisting, double talk and gobbledegook. Lawyers who put excessive strains on the King's English out of extreme zeal in the practice of advocacy have been known to practice this type of linguistic *legerdemain*, more's the pity, doing violence not only to language, but, on occasion, to justice.

leiotrichous, see **cymotrichous**

leitmotif, **-tiv** (LITE moh teef) *n.* This noun is taken from the German noun *leitmotiv*; the prefix *leit-* is based on the verb *leiten* (to lead); *motiv* is German for *motif*. First applied to the music drama of Wagner, the term denoted a melodic passage accompanying and associated with each appearance of a particular character or each occurrence of a particular situation. Thus, the same musical theme was heard with each appearance of Siegfried, Sieglinde, et al., or with each approach of danger or climactic violence, or a love scene. The term was later extended to music generally, and finally to any life experience, to signify a dominant motive, a controlling emotion, any driving force. In this extended usage, the *leitmotif* of one person's career may be the accumulation of great wealth, while in the case of another it may be the attainment of fame or power, and in the life of still another, the creation of lasting art. People do not always accomplish their *leitmotifs*. The *leitmotif* of Hitler's career was to build a Reich that would last 1,000 years. He failed by about 988. Columbus's *leitmotif* was to find a western passage to Asia. He missed by a good many thousand miles. Napoleon . . . Shall we go on?

lemma   (LEM uh) *n.* We are all too often faced with—or on the horns of—a *dilemma* (dih LEM uh, dye-), a quandary or predicament involving a choice between two unsatisfactory courses of action. *Dilemma* was taken intact from the Greek, based on the prefix *di-* (from *dis*, twice) plus *lemma* in the sense of "assumption." The literal meaning of *lemma* in Greek is "anything received, an assumption, a premise taken for granted," based on the verb *lambanein* (to take, assume). If you are faced with two *lemmas*, you are in a *dilemma*: If I go out in this weather, I'll get soaked; if I don't, I'll miss the concert. Two *lemmas* = one *dilemma*. If there is a third possible choice (if I stay in and get it on the radio, I'll hear it but the sound won't be as good and I won't see Maestro X conduct), you are in a *trilemma*, where there is the choice among three unsatisfactory alternatives. Three *lemmas* = one *trilemma*. What about four? Yes, *tetralemmas* exist, in both life and dictionary (Greek prefix *tetra-*, four, plus old friend *lemma*) and wouldn't it be hell to be on the horns of one of those? But there it stops. You may have five unacceptable choices (one of those confusing restaurant menus), but *pentalemma* (*penta-* is a combining form of *pente*, Greek for "five") still remains to be concocted.

lemurine, see **accipitrine**

lenis, see **fortis**

leonine, see **accipitrine**

leporine, see **accipitrine**

leptocephalic   (lep tuh suh FAL ik) *adj*. This adjective describes persons with narrow skulls. It is formed from the Greek prefix *lepto-*, based on the adjective *leptos* (narrow) plus the noun *kephale* (head). There are other *lepto-* adjectives: *leptocercal* (lep tuh SERK ul), describing animals with slender tails (*kerkos*, tail); *leptodactylous* (lep tuh DAK tuh lus), for those with slender toes (*daktylos*, finger, toe); *leptorrhine* (LEP tuh reen), for narrow-nosed beings (*rhis*, nose); *leptosome* (LEP tuh some), for those of slender build (*soma*, body), cf. **asthenic**. Quite a family, these *lepto-* adjectives. There appears to be no *lepto-* word for *thin-skinned*, i.e., *sensitive*, such as *leptodermatous*, using *derma* (skin), as an antonym of **pachydermatous** in the figurative sense. Well, you can't have everything.

leptocercal, see **leptocephalic**

leptodactylous, see **leptocephalic**

leptorrhine, see **leptocephalic**

leptosome, see **leptocephalic**

lethe   (LEE thee) *n*. *Lethe* is oblivion, forgetfulness of the past; a word arising from *Lethe*, a river of the underworld in classical mythology, of whose waters the souls of all the dead had to drink, in order for them to forget the past. The River Lethe gave rise to another word, *lethargy*, from Greek *lethargia* (drowsy forgetfulness), based on *lethargos* (drowsy), from *lethe* plus *argos* (idle). *Lethe* and oblivion were on the minds of many poets and writers. In *The Dunciad*, the English poet Alexander Pope (1688-1744) wrote:

> Here, in a dusky vale where *Lethe* rolls . . .
> Old Bavius sits, to dip poetic souls,
> And blunt the senses.

Bavius was a first century **poetaster**, rescued from oblivion by the contempt of the greatest of Roman poets, Virgil (70-19 B.C.). The English poet John Keats (1795-1821), in his *Ode to Melancholy*, warned:

> No, no, go not to *Lethe*, neither twist
> Wolf's-bane, tight-rooted, for its poisonous wine.

Wolfsbane is aconite, a poisonous plant. Keats again, in his *Ode to a Nightingale*:

> My heart aches, and a drowsy numbness pains
> My sense, as though of hemlock I had drunk,
> Or emptied some dull opiate to the drains
> One minute past, and *Lethe*-wards had sunk.

When, in Shakespeare's *Hamlet* (Act I, Scene 5), Hamlet assures the ghost of his father that he will seek revenge, the Ghost answers:

> I find thee apt;
> And duller shouldst thou be than the fat weed
> That rots itself in ease on *Lethe* wharf,
> Wouldst thou not stir in this.

The English poet Thomas Campbell (1777-1844), in the poem *Absence*, wrote:

> 'Tis *Lethe*'s gloom, but not its quiet,—
> The pain without the peace of death.

The Roman poet Horace (65-8 B.C.), in an epode, wrote of " . . . a deep oblivion, as though with thirsty throat I'd drained the cup that brings the sleep of *Lethe*." John Milton (1608-1674), in *Paradise Lost*, speaks of " . . . a slow and silent stream,/*Lethe* the river of oblivion . . . " and more recently, the German novelist Thomas Mann (1875-1955), in *The Magic Mountain*, says: "Time, we say, is *Lethe* . . . "

licentiate   (lye SEN shee it, -ate) *n. Licentiate* is the title conferred upon one who has been granted a *license* from an institution, especially a university, to practice a profession or art. Some European universities give degrees somewhere between those of bachelor and doctor. Graduates holding such degrees are known as *licentiates. Licentiate* is from Middle Latin *licentiatus*, past participle of *licentiare* (to license), derived from Latin *licentia* (freedom, leave). Being a *licentiate* has nothing to do with being *licentious* (from Latin *licentiosus*, arbitrary), though one can, of course, be both, and both words go back ultimately to *licentia*, which is related to Latin *licet* (it is allowed), a form of the verb *licere*, whose present participle is *licens* (unrestrained).

lilliputian (lil ih PYOOH shun) *n., adj.*: **brobdingnagian** (brob ding NAG ee un) *adj.* Both these words, often capitalized, come from *Gulliver's Travels*, the 1726 satirical masterpiece of the English author Jonathan Swift (1667-1745), which describes the visits of his hero Lemuel Gulliver to the imaginary countries of Lilliput, Brobdingnag, and other places whose names have not given rise to adjectives in common use. Lilliput was inhabited by tiny people, the Lilliputians. Hence *lilliputian*, as an adjective, means "extremely small," and by extension, "petty, small-minded, narrow, insignificant, picayune." Dinky toys are *lilliputian* models of the original cars, trucks, etc., and a friend of the author quite appropriately (if somewhat obviously) named his chihuahua "Lilliput." The American journalist William Allen White (1868-1944, the "sage of Emporia"), wrote of the "lilliputian senators," referring to their pettifogging ways. The imaginary land of Brobdingnag was peopled by giants; hence the adjective *brobdingnagian* means "huge, vast, tremendous, mammoth, gigantic." It is sometimes said that Italy, on the map, resembles a *brobdingnagian* boot. A hummingbird is *lilliputian*; a whale is *brobdingnagian*.

limen, see **algesia**

limnology, see **genethlialogy**

lingua franca, see **pidgin**

literati (lit uh RAH tee, -RAY-) *n. pl.* The *literati* are the intelligentsia, the intellectuals, men of letters, the learned, the scholars. *Litterati*, in Latin, is the plural of *litteratus* (lettered, learned, educated). The *literati* are miles above the merely *literate*, though that word comes from the same Latin source. There are many other *liter-* words: *literacy, literal(ly), literature*; they all go back to Latin *lit(t)era* (letter of the alphabet) and prefer the single *l*, while *letter* kept both.

logogram, see **grammalogue**

logogriph (LO guh grif) *n.* A *logogriph* is a word puzzle, sometimes an anagram, at other times a riddle in which one is supposed to discover a word from other words made up of its letters (example supplied by *Webster's Unabridged*, Second Edition: *chatter*, from *cat, hat, rat, hate, rate*, etc.—they could have given *chatterer*), or (what's worse) from synonyms of other words, or (what's even worse than that) verses containing such synonyms. Whatever the riddle, *logogriph* comes from Greek *logos* (word) plus *griphos* (net, fishing basket, riddle—the connection among these meanings being, one supposes, that the riddle is made up of a basket of other words). Submitted, in category 3: "This is the forest primeval," (opening line of *Evangeline*, by the American poet Henry Wadsworth Longfellow, 1807-1882). *Forest = grove; primeval = earliest*; from *grove* and *earliest* select the letters that make up the answer: *overeager*. There must be easier ways to make a living.

logomachy   (lo GOM uh kee) *n*. *Logomachy* is a controversy (usually literary) about words (the kind readers of this book may engage in with the author), or a dispute marked by the incorrect use of words (the kind readers and the author will never engage in); and *logomachy* is also the name of a game played with a set of cards each bearing one letter of the alphabet, for the formation of words. It comes from Greek *logomachia*, based on *logos* (word) plus suffix *-machia* (-fighting), from *mache* (fight). Imagine a hot dispute about the connection between the words *sorrow* and *sorry*. Jones maintains that they come from the same root. Smith says nay. They put it to Green, a philologist, who points out that *sorrow* is from Old English *sorg*, cognate with German *Sorge* (grief, sorrow, worry), while *sorry* is from Old English *sarig*, cognate with Low German *serig* and Old High German *serag*. Smith wins, whereupon Jones gets sore (which comes from Old English *sar*, cognate with Dutch *zeer*, if you must know) and indulges in a dispute with both Smith and Green in which he recklessly uses incorrect expressions like "the both of you" and "equally as illiterate." Then they all calm down and play a game with a set of those one-letter cards. Three *logomachies* for the price of one.

louche   (loohsh) *adj*. A *louche* person, or *louche* conduct, is devious, perverse, untrustworthy, sinister. *Louche* was taken over from the French as is. In French, its literal meaning is "squint-eyed," but the French use it in a figurative sense to describe persons or behavior of dubious character, equivocal, disreputable, shifty, shady, or more informally, fishy. They got *louche* from the Latin *luscus*, which means "one-eyed," and the figurative use of *louche* to mean "shifty" or "fishy" seems quite unfair to perfectly honorable people who happen to have lost an eye somewhere along the line. Like Caesar's wife, who "must be above suspicion" (a traditional saying, based on an alleged remark by Caesar according to the Roman historian Plutarch, 46-120)—Caesar divorced Pompeia not because he believed her guilty, but on mere suspicion of guilt, when her name came up in an accusation against a public figure named Publius Clodius, according to another Roman historian, Suetonius, 75-150—we should all be careful not even to appear *louche*. If you think it discursive to drag in a bit of possibly apocryphal Roman history or gossip in a discussion of *louche*, you're right.

lubricious (looh BRISH us), also **lubricous** (LOOH brih kus) *adj. Lubricious*, describing a surface, means "oily, slippery"; applied to a person, "unstable, shifty," or more commonly, "lewd, lascivious, lecherous." The source is Latin *lubricus* (slippery), which in Middle Latin came to mean "unstable." The noun *lubricitas* in Middle Latin means "lechery." *Lubricious* well describes the smooth, oily, slippery, lewd, lascivious, and lecherous old-time movie villain who hissed at the terrified young slip of a girl, "Aha, my proud beauty!" and strove with might and main to take unfair advantage of the poor thing. Next week *East Lynne*.

lucubrate (LOOH kyoo brate) *vb*. To *lucubrate* (not to be confused with *lubricate*) is to toil, study, or write painstakingly, laboriously, especially at night; to burn the midnight oil, as it were. If the word is used in the context of writing, the implication is one of erudition and scholarship. In the writing of this book, the author has indeed *lucubrated*. The noun is *lucubration* (looh kyoo BRAY shun), signifying toil, study, or writing, especially at night. *Lucubrate* comes from Latin *lucubratus*, past participle of *lucubrare* (to work by night) and the noun is from *lucubratio* (nocturnal study, working by night, or by lamplight). These Latin words are based upon *lux* (light), whose stem is *luc-*. A related word is *luculent* (LOOH kyoo lunt), an adjective meaning "clear, lucid," that comes from Latin *luculentus* (bright, full of light). A good teacher will be able to furnish *luculent* explanations and interpretations to his students, who can then go on to praiseworthy *lucubration* and lots of A's. *Luculent* sometimes has the force of "convincing." A *luculent* explanation would normally be convincing and cogent.

luculent, see **lucubrate**

Lucullan (looh KUL un), **Lucullean** (looh ku LEE un), **Lucullic** (looh KUL ik) *adj*. The usual form is *Lucullan*. A *Lucullan* meal is profusely lavish and luxurious, elegant enough for any epicure, a meal, in fact, fit for the gods. The adjective derives from Lucius Licinius Lucullus (c. 110-57 B.C.), a Roman general and politician who devoted his later years to a rich, elegant way of life, with the emphasis on gourmet food and drink of the highest standard of elegance. He was famed for his banquets, but once, while a lavish supper was in preparation, a friend inquiring who were to be his guests that evening received the answer: "Lucullus will sup tonight with Lucullus." This has come to be quoted of any gourmet who, though dining alone, is as fussy about the meal as though royalty were expected. The sentence, rightly or wrongly, is sometimes applied to gluttonous feeding, though Lucullus himself was a gourmet rather than a gourmand. The highest praise you can give your hostess after a superb meal is to extol it as *Lucullan*. If she doesn't understand, send her a copy of this book with an inscription calling attention to page 198 together with your thanks for a *Lucullan* feast.

Luddite   (LUD ite) *n.* Under the leadership of Ned Ludd, a semi-mythical 18th-century worker also known as "King Ludd" from Leicestershire, a county in the north of England, bands of English textile workers, during the years 1811-1816, rioted and smashed new industrial machinery in the manufacturing districts of the northern counties of Nottinghamshire, Lancashire, Cheshire, and Yorkshire. They blamed the machinery for their unemployment and distress. Ned Ludd was said to have originated the idea and his followers were called *Luddites*. Their doctrine was given the name of *Luddism* or *Ludditism*. The *Luddites* were right in their belief that the introduction of the machinery eliminated jobs and caused unemployment, but their methods of combating the evil were on the crude side. A similar situation arose in the southern counties in the period 1830-1833, when the "Swing Riots" of the agricultural laborers were touched off by the introduction of new threshing machinery, causing unemployment and distress. Machines were smashed and hay and grain ricks set afire. A "Captain Swing" was held to be the leader of the movement, but unlike the semi-mythical Ned Ludd he appears to have been a wholly imaginary character. The English humorist Richard Harris Barham (1788-1845), in *The Ingoldsby Legends*, wrote about the legendary captain:

> The neighbors thought all was not right,
> Scarcely one with him ventured to parley,
> And Captain Swing came in the night,
> And burnt all his beans and his barley.

Many an unemployed worker today believes Ludd and Swing were right, and blames his condition on "progress."

lumbricine, see **accipitrine**

lupine, see **accipitrine**

lustral, lustrate, lustration, see **lustrum**

lustrum   (LUS trum) *n.*, also **luster** (LUS tur). A *lustrum* is a period of five years. In ancient Rome, the census was taken every five years, after which the authorities performed a *lustrum* (lustration), a ceremonial purification, a purificatory sacrifice conducted by the censors for the population. To *lustrate* (LUS trate) is to purify ceremonially, and *lustral* (LUS trul), literally "pertaining to the *lustrum* ceremony," acquired the meaning "occurring every five years," synonymous with *quinquennial* (kwin KWEN ee ul), based on Latin *quinque* (five) plus *annus* (year). Lustrum is a Latin word, based on the verb *lustrare* (to purify). The president of the United States is elected for a *quadrennium*, a period of four years (from a New Latin alteration of the Latin *quadriennium*); the prime minister of Britain serves for a *lustrum*, or *quinquennium*, i.e., five years—unless something happens to cause the Government to fall, or the

Government, to test public opinion in a crisis, thinks the time is ripe to hold a general election (called a "snap election") before the *lustrum* expires. The British don't call it a *lustrum*, though there's no reason why they shouldn't, except that nobody gets purified at its conclusion.

lutrine, see **accipitrine**

lycanthropy   (lye KAN thruh pee) *n.* This is a type of madness in which a human being imagines himself to be a wolf (at times, another animal) and acts and sounds like one. *Lycanthropy* also applies to the case of a person's assuming the form of a wolf—in old legend. One affected with this form of insanity is a *lycanthrope* (LYE kun thrope, lye KAN thrope) or a werewolf in folklore. The words come from Greek *lykanthropia* and *lykanthropos*, based on *lykos* (wolf) plus *anthropos* (man), adding up to *wolf-man*. The *were-* in *werewolf* comes from Old English *wer* (man), cognate with Latin *vir*, from which we get *virile*, *virility*, etc., so that *werewolf* changes the order of the components to *man-wolf*. *Wolf-man* or *man-wolf*, this has nothing to do with the unpleasant kind of wolf that some men turn into in the presence of an attractive woman.

lyncine, see **accipitrine**

macaronic   (mak uh RON ik) *adj.* This peculiar word, a jocular concoction from *macaroni*, is applied, in a narrow sense, to language characterized by a mixture of Latin and non-Latin words, or by non-Latin words given phony Latin endings; in a broader sense, to prose or verse composed of any mixture of languages; in its broadest sense, to anything mixed or jumbled. As a noun, *macaronics* (plural in form, singular in meaning, like *economics*) means "*macaronic* language," particularly in verse form. *Omnium gatherum*, a bit of British mock Latin meaning "mixture," any motley collection of persons or things, or sometimes "open house," a party open to all comers, is a sample of *macaronic* language (*omnium* is the genetive plural of *omnis*, Latin for "all"; *gatherum* is a phony Latinization of *gather*). Merlinus Coccaius (1491-1544), a monk of Mantua, Italy, wrote a poetical rhapsody using words of various languages, entitled *Liber Macaronicorum* (Book of Macaronics). An example of *macaronic* verse of mixed Latin and English, from *The Elderly Gentleman* by J.A. Morgan:

> Prope ripam fluvii solus [By the bank of the river alone]
> A senex [old man] silently sat,
> Super capitum ecce [on his head behold] his wig
> Et wig super, ecce [And on top of his wig, behold] his hat.

Eventually, Zephyrus . . . in rivum projecit (the wind blew into the stream) his hat! In the third line, *capitum* is an incorrect form; the *-um* should be *-e*, though it serves the meter. In his lecture on Pepys's diaries (Samuel Pepys, English diarist, 1633-1703), at the Royal Society of Arts, recorded in its *Journal* of May 1984, Robert Latham, a fellow of Magdalene College, Cambridge, and editor of the most recent edition of the diaries, described the "amorous passages" as "written in a *macaronic* mixture of language—English, French and Spanish for the most part."

machicolation (muh chik uh LAY shun) *n.* This is an architectural term for an opening in a castle parapet (defensive wall) or balcony floor through which molten lead, boiling oil, miscellaneous missiles, and other charming weapons could be cast down upon the heads of the hapless attackers. The term was also applied to a balcony or parapet provided with such openings. To *machicolate* (muh CHIK uh late) a parapet or projecting gallery floor is to provide it with *machicolations.* These words are, via French *mâ chicoulis*, from Middle Latin *machicol(l)atus*, past participle of *machicol(l)are*, a Latinization of Old French *machecoller*, derived from the *mache-* of Old French *macher* (to mash, crush) plus *coller* (to flow) or *col* (neck). Whatever the derivation, and however quaint these military devices and tactics may seem in the atomic age, *machicolations* were very effective in their day, and novelists like the Scottish Sir Walter Scott (1771-1832) and France's Victor Hugo (1802-1885), with their castles and cathedrals and rousing battle scenes, could hardly have done without them.

macropine, see **accipitrine**

macropodine, see **accipitrine**

maggot (MAG ut) *n.* Those nasty little squirmy creepy-crawly things are leg-less grubs, the larvae of certain insects of the order Diptera, the common members of which are the housefly, mosquito, and gnat. They are used for bait in England, where they are called "gentles." But *maggot* has another quite distinct meaning, possibly archaic in America, but not in Britain: "whimsical fancy, odd fad, **crotchet**." It comes from Old English *magot*, an unexplained variant of *maddock*. There would seem to be no possible connection between the two disparate meanings, but there is one: The strange notion in olden times that odd or whimsical people had *maggots* (the creepy-crawly variety) in their brains. In *Women Pleased*, a play by the English dramatist John Fletcher (1579-1625; he was the collaborator of Francis Beaumont, 1584-1616; *Beaumont and Fletcher* is a linkage as established as *Gilbert and Sullivan*), we find this bit of dialogue:

> Are you not mad, my friend? What time o' th' moon is't?
> Have you not *maggots* in your brain?

Maggots in the brain has the ring of *bats in the belfry* or *rats in the garret*, and *Brewer's Phrase & Fable* mentions the Scottish *head full of bees*, the French *rats in the head*, and the Dutch *mouse's nest in the head*. So, going back to old Fletcher, we do come up with a logical connection between *maggots* and whimsies. The English novelist and poet Sylvia Townsend Warner (1893-1978), a constant contributor to *The New Yorker* magazine (and, incidentally, a good friend of this author), wrote a wonderful short novel published by Viking Press in 1927 entitled *Mr. Fortune's Maggot*. But Miss Warner and the special quaint meaning of *maggot* were unknown to the author at that time. Idle curiosity in a bookshop quickly established that the slim volume was neither a work on **entomology** nor a follow-up on *The Compleat Angler* of Izaak Walton (1593-1683). Right under the title, on a flyleaf, there is printed:

> "MAGGOT 2. A nonsensical or perverse fancy;
>   a **crotchet**."

magisterial   (maj ih STEER ee ul) *adj*. What is *magisterial* is authoritative, important, weighty, a matter of consequence, or, in a different context, domineering, overbearing, high-handed. The first meaning is laudatory; the second, far less flattering and in fact pejorative, and one must be careful to distinguish. We get the word from Middle Latin *magisterialis*, based on Latin *magister* (master), which goes back to the Latin comparative adverb *magis* (more, more so, to a greater extent). In *Law and Literature*, a lecture given in 1931, the great jurist and Supreme Court Justice Benjamin Cardozo (1870-1938) described six types of judicial writing. The first was " . . . the type *magisterial* or imperative . . . ," and it is difficult to know just how he was using the word. But it is clear that the word expresses praise in a passage about Winston Churchill (1874-1965) by the English writer, editor, and columnist Godfrey Smith (b. 1926) in *The English Companion* (Pavilion Books, London, 1984): "He not only led his nation to a triumphant victory in the Second World War; he wrote a *magisterial* six-volume history of it."

maieutic   (may YOOH tik) *adj*. This word has an interesting meaning and an amusing derivation. It comes from Greek *maieutikos* (pertaining to midwifery), related to the verb *maieuesthai* (to act as midwife), based on the noun *maia* (midwife). It applies, however, to the performance of a "midwife's" services in the realm of thoughts or ideas, especially the method employed by the Greek philosopher Socrates (c. 469-399 B.C.) in creating knowledge by questioning, a procedure known as the "Socratic method." Socrates considered himself a "midwife" in bringing to birth the ideas and thoughts of others by means of his questions. Fowler says that *educative* (ED oo kay tiv, ED yoo-), "contains the same notion, but much overlaid with different ones, and the literary critic and the pedagogue consequently find *maieutic* useful enough to pass in spite of its touch of pedantry." Don't automatically scoff at pedantry, or for that matter, snobbery, both of which can serve a useful purpose in small doses.

malacology   (mal uh KOL uh jee) *n*. This is the study of mollusks and the science dealing with them. The term *mollusk* covers snails, oysters, clams, and mussels, which are hard on the outside but soft inside, as well as octopuses and squids, which are soft all over. It is this softness that explains the derivation of *mollusk* from Latin *molluscus* (softish—from *mollis*, soft). The *malaco-* is from Greek *malakos* (soft), plus *logos* (study, discourse). Thus we see the etymological connection between *malacology* and *mollusks*. (See also **genethlialogy**.)

mallecho   (MAL ih choh) *n*. As the play within the play begins in Shakespeare's *Hamlet* (Act III, Scene 2) and the players act out the poisoning of the king and the wooing and winning of the queen by the poisoner, Ophelia enters and cries, "What means this, my lord?" and Hamlet answers, "Marry, this is miching *mallecho*; it means mischief." Thus Shakespeare himself supplies the definition: mischief. *Mallecho* was derived from the Spanish noun *malhecho* (evil deed), based on the prefix *mal-* (evil) plus *hecho* (deed). *Miching* (MICH ing) is an adjective made of the present participle of the verb *miche*, meaning to "skulk" or "slink," thought to be a variant of *mooch* (British slang for "slouch about" or "skulk," differing from the American slang usage, to "scrounge," both, however, coming from the same source, Middle English *michen*, to skulk or hide). The English poet Robert Herrick (1591-1674), in a lovely poem about his domestic animals, included:

> A cat
> I keep, that plays about the house
> Grown fat
> With eating many a *miching* mouse.

Micher appears in Shakespeare in the sense of "thief" or "truant." In *Henry IV, Part I* (Act II, Scene 4), Falstaff asks Prince Henry,

> Shall the blessed son of heaven prove a *micher* and eat blackberries? a question not to be asked. Shall the son of England prove a thief and take purses? a question not to be asked.

Thus, *miching mallecho* means "sneaky mischief." You may never run into this eloquent phrase in contemporary literature, unless you happen to read *An Awkward Lie* by the English whodunitist Michael Innes (b. 1906-), where his detective Sir John Appleby, considering the mysterious disappearance of a corpse from a golf bunker, wonders about this "elaborate piece of *miching malicho*." *Malicho* is a variant of *mallecho*, or vice versa. Some authorities say that it is vice versa, *mallecho*, influenced by the Spanish, being a learned emendation of *malicho*, the form favored by Michael Innes.

manatine, see **accipitrine**

manes (MAY neez) *n. Manes* can be treated as a plural noun for the shades of the departed, the spirits of the dead, or as a singular noun for the shade or spirit of an individual. It is a Latin word whose literal meaning is "the good ones" (from Old Latin *manus*, good), and was applied figuratively, as now in English, to the spirits of the dead or the spirit of a single departed one. In Latin it was always treated as a plural grammatically. To appease a person's *manes* is to do what would have pleased him or what was his due in his lifetime. The *manes* of a deceased could not sleep quietly, it used to be believed, until his survivors fulfilled his wishes. On February 19 of each year, the Romans made sacrifices to the shades of their family and friends, in the same way that Roman Catholics are supposed to devote November 2 to prayer and the giving of alms to honor the departed faithful.

mangonel (MANG guh nel) *n.* A *mangonel* was a huge military apparatus for hurling stones, darts, javelins, etc., operated by a large crew and involving huge wheels, pulleys, etc. The name of the machine is, via Latin *manganum*, from Greek *manganon* (engine of war). However naive and quaint the *mangonel* appears to us in this day of rocket artillery (cf. **machicolation** and the military tactics discussed thereunder), it did a respectable amount of damage to walls, fortifications, and personnel in its day.

mansuetude (MAN swih toohd, -tyoohd) *n. Mansuetude* is meekness, gentleness, mildness, docility. The word comes from Latin *mansuetudo* (tameness), related to *mansuetus* (tamed), based on *manus* (hand) plus *suetus* (tame), past participle of *suescere* (to grow accustomed). An animal *accustomed* to the *hand* is tame, gentle, docile. In *John* 13:34 we read: "A new commandment I give unto you, That ye love one another," and in *Romans* 13:8, "Owe no man anything, but to love one another." This is the doctrine of the *mansuetude* of Christian love. What a world it would be if . . .

mantic (MAN tik) *n., adj. Mantic* applies to things relating to augury and prophesy. A *mantic* person has the gift of **divination**, of foretelling the future. ("Beware the Ides of March!" etc.) The word comes from Greek *mantikos* (prophetic), an adjective from *manteia* (divination), which gave us our suffix *-mancy*, as in **myomancy**, **rhabdomancy**, etc. Used as a noun, a *mantic* is one possessed of prophetic powers, a seer. There have been many *mantics* in folklore and history, like **Cassandra**, Nostradamus (the French astrologer Michel de Nostredame, 1503-1566), to say nothing of our very own Jeanne Dixon, whose stuff (and nonsense?) is taken seriously by millions.

mariticide, see **aborticide**

matrilocal   (MA truh loh kul) *adj*. In the science of anthropology (the study of man, including his social customs), the term *matrilocal* applies to the custom of the newlyweds' going to live with the wife's family. *Uxorilocal* (uk SOR uh loh kul, ug ZOR-) means the same thing. *Patrilocal* (PA truh loh kul, pay-) covers the converse arrangement of the new couple's residing with the husband's family. In primitive cultures, one can substitute *tribe* for *family* in these definitions. All three words are based on combinations of the Latin prefixes *matri-*, from *mater* (mother), *uxori-*, from *uxor* (wife), and *patri-*, from *pater* (father), with *-local*, from *locus* (place). Apparently, the in-law problem and attendant bad jokes were not a part of earlier cultures.

matutinal   (muh TOOHT un ul, -TYOOHT-) *adj*. A *matutinal* event is one occurring in the morning, early in the day. *Matutinal* describes anything relating to the morning, or happening in the morning. It comes from Late Latin *matutinalis* (early), derived from Latin *matutinus* (of the morning), based on Matuta (muh TOOH tuh, -TYOOH-), in Roman mythology the goddess of the dawn, as well as childbirth, and the oceans and harbors (a busy goddess!), sometimes known as *Mater* (Mother) *Matuta*. After performing his *matutinal* **ablutions** and perhaps saying his *matutinal* **orisons**, eating his *matutinal* **refection**, and, if he has a job, *matutinally* departing for work, interrupted only by his **meridional** repast, our polysyllabic *protagonist* (unless it's one of those late nights at the office) **crepuscularly** returns home to the wife and kiddies. Changing the subject: The lark is a *matutinal* bird. Shakespeare gives us the saddest parting of lovers in *Romeo and Juliet* (Act III, Scene 5), when morning is heralded by the singing of a bird. "It was the nightingale, and not the lark," says Juliet, though she knows better, and Romeo faces reality and says, "It was the lark, the herald of the morn . . . "

maudit   (moh DEE) *n., adj. Maudit* applies to a lost soul, a loser, a person beyond redemption, beset by unearned bad luck. The French poet Paul Verlaine (1844-1896) wrote a prose work entitled *Les Poètes Maudits* (literally, The Cursed Poets), consisting of sketches of six fellow poets, including Stéphane Mallarmé (1842-1898) and Arthur Rimbaud (1854-1891) among the six whose art went neglected and unappreciated in their day. They were symbolists, influenced greatly by Charles Pierre Baudelaire (1821-1867), conveying impressions by suggestion rather than literal statement, experimenting with form, particularly free verse. Verlaine and his contemporaries led wretched lives; hence the epithet *maudit*. The term could well be applied to the hopeless drug addicts and other derelicts who live on the streets. *Maudit* is the past participle of the French verb *maudire* (to curse).

maunder (MAWN dur) *vb*. To *maunder* is to drivel, to talk aimlessly, in a silly, dreamy, meaningless way, or to move or act in a confused, listless, rambling way. Most directions give its etymology as "unknown," but the *Concise Oxford* takes a "perhaps" shot at the obsolete *maunder* (beggar, beg). Fowler says that the etymology is uncertain, but " . . . it is clear that it is not a corruption of *meander* . . . But it is also clear from the way some people use *meander* that they take the two words to be merely variant pronunciations. *Meander* means to follow a winding course, was originally used of rivers, is still often so used, describes frequent but not violent change of direction rather than aimlessness, and is applied more often to actual locomotion than to vagaries of the tongue. *Maunder* is best confined to speech, and suggests futility rather than digression, dull discontent rather than quiet enjoyment, and failure to reach an end rather than loitering on the way to it." *Meander* does have a well-known etymology, and an interesting one: via Latin *maeander*, from Greek *maiandros* (a winding), from *Maiandros*, the Greek name for the Menderes River, famous for its tortuous course.

mediatize (MEE dee uh tize) *vb*. To *mediatize* a state is to annex it. The *mediatized* state is usually a smaller one than the annexing power. The former government is permitted to keep certain local governing powers. When Great Britain was expanding its empire, most of the provinces of India were *mediatized*, and the former sovereigns were allowed to retain some governing rights; they became "*mediatized* princes." The word was formed after the model of the German verb *mediatisieren*. The annexed state held its powers *mediately*, i.e., subject to the annexing power, rather than *immediately*, i.e., on its own, independently; in other words, indirectly rather than directly. Great Britain's imperial expansion involved many parts of the world other than India, and in more recent times, the USSR and Hitler's Germany did a fair amount of *mediatizing*, which would appear to be a euphemism for . . . shall we say, *grabbing*?

medicaster, see **poetaster**

megapterine, see **accipitrine**

megillah (muh GIL uh) *n*. *Megillah*, in Hebrew, means "scroll," in particular one that contains the *Book of Esther*, *Ecclesiastes*, the *Song of Solomon*, the *Book of Ruth*, or the *Book of Lamentations*. *Megillah* became Yiddish, later American slang for any long-winded acount. In Yiddish, it was often preceded by *ganze* (GAHN tse), from German *ganz* (whole, complete). A *ganze megillah* is an exhaustive (and usually exhausting) account, the implication being that the long and elaborately detailed narrative concerned a minor matter worthy of only a much more condensed report. *Megillah* is one of a number of Yiddish words that have been naturalized into the American slang vocabulary: *meshugah* (muh SHOO guh) for "crazy, nuts"; *nosh* for "snack"; *chutspah*

(CHOOT spuh—*ch* as in German *ach*) for "brazen cheek, unmitigated gall"; *shlepp* (shlep) for "carry," to name a few that have emigrated far and wide from Brooklyn and the Bronx.

meleagrine, see **accipitrine**

melioration, see **meliorism**

meliorism   (MEEL yuh riz um, MEE lee uh-) *n. Meliorism* is the belief that everything tends to get better and better. One who lives by this doctrine is a *meliorist* (MEEL yuh rist, MEE lee uh-). These words are derived from Latin *melior* (better), the comparative of *bonus* (good). The superlative is *optimus* (best), which gave us *optimism* and *optimist*. It may be hard to find much difference between the attitudes of *meliorists* and *optimists*, but the English novelist George Eliot (1859-1890) did find a shade of difference: The English poet A.E. Houseman (1859-1936) wrote, in an autobiographical note: "I am not a pessimist but a pejorist (as George Eliot said she was not an optimist but a meliorist) . . . " In Latin, *pejor* means "worse" and *pessimus* means "worst." A pejorist (whose doctrine is known as *pejorism*) believes that everything is getting worse; a pessimist thinks that it's all going to be as bad as possible: superlatively bad, shall we say, in this atomic age? In any event, George Eliot thought that the world was going to get better—but not as good as possible; and that is the fine difference between *meliorism* and *optimism*. Other words from *melior* are *ameliorate* (uh MEEL yuh rate, -ee uh-), to improve; *amelioration* (uh meel yuh RAY shun), improvement generally, but with a special use in linguistics: semantic change to a better, i.e., more favorable meaning, the way *Okie*, once a pejorative term for a migrant farm worker, usually from Oklahoma, became merely a colloquial nickname for any Oklahoman, and exactly opposite to the way *egregious* (from Latin *egregius*, extraordinary, preeminent, based on prefix *e-*, out of, plus *grege*, a form of *grex*, herd, i.e., out of the herd) changed from *preeminent* to *glaring, flagrant, notorious*, as in *an egregious blunder*. But caution: *meliority* (meel YOR ih tee, mee lee OR-) has nothing to do with attitudes about which way the world is moving; it is only an uncommon synonym for *superiority*.

meliority, see **meliorism**

menology   (mih NOL uh jee) *n.* A *menology* is a calendar or register of saints' days, especially of the Greek Church; from Late Greek *menologion*, based on *men* (month) plus *logos* (discourse, account). We are familiar with the use of the prefix *meno-*, in such words as *menopause*, for instance. A *menology* shows all the festivals celebrated during the year honoring saints and martyrs, with brief biographical notes of each.

mensal, see **hebdomedal**

mephitine, see **accipitrine**

mephitis   (muh FYE tis) *n*. This is the term for a noxious emanation from the earth, such as a poison gas, but the word is also applied to something less deadly, like any foul, noisome stench, even if not actually poisonous. The adjective is *mephitic* (muh FIT ik), describing any offensive odor, noxious or not. Exposure to *mephitic* exhalations are to be avoided; they may or may not be poisonous, but they certainly are exceedingly offensive. Swamps give off *mephitic* odors. Living within smelling range of the *mephitic* emanations from certain industrial operations, like oil refineries, can be unhealthful, and is undoubtedly unpleasant. It is often not worthwhile putting up with the *mephitic* odors of a compost pile, despite its value as fertilizer. *Mephitis* was taken over as is from Latin; *mephitic* from Late Latin *mephiticus*. Appropriately enough, *mephitine* (see **accipitrine** and list of *-ine* adjectives attached) means "pertaining to skunks."

merkin   (MUR kun) *n*. A *merkin* is a sort of pubic wig consisting of false hair for the female pudenda. Some authorities say that *merkin* is a variant of *malkin*, a noun with several meanings, including "mop" (especially the kind used by bakers for cleaning out ovens) and "cat." Other authorities are content with "origin unknown." Whether or not there is a connection between *merkin* and *malkin* meaning "cat" (there is a close connection between *cat* and *pussy*), and however unlikely it is that you will run across this word in your reading, the burning question remains: What is or ever was the occasion for the use of this commodity? The early stages of retirement from the profession of modeling bikinis? On this, the dictionaries are silent.

metalinguistics   (met uh ling GWIS tiks) *n*. As with other *-ics* words (*economics, politics*, etc.) *metalinguistics* is construed as a singular noun. It is the study of the relationship between a language and other aspects of a particular culture, of language in relation to meaning, of "body-language," i.e., expression or gesture accompanying speech, etc. It is a hybrid (derived in part from Greek, in part from Latin), based on the Greek prefix *meta-* (along with, beyond) plus the Latin noun *lingua* (tongue, language). Fowler defines *hybrids* (in the context of language) as "words formed from a stem or word belonging to one language by applying to it a suffix or prefix belonging to another." *Television* is a good example: *tele-* (a Greek prefix meaning "distant," especially "transmitting over a distance") plus *vision*, from Latin *visio*, meaning "a seeing" or "view," based on *visus*, past participle of *videre* (to see).

metathesis   (muh TATH ih sis) *n*. This is the name applied to the transposition of letters or sounds in words. It was taken over intact from the Greek, where it means "transposition," based on prefix *meta-* (beyond) plus *thesis* (something set down). Examples: *aks* for *ask*; chaise *lounge* for chaise *longue*. In Old English, *bird* was *bridd* and third was *thrid*. The modern forms were the result of *metathesis.* Similar transposition turned Spanish *tronada* (thunderstorm) into *tornado.* Spoonerism is a type of *metathesis,* in that the initial sounds of two words are transposed. *Spoiled brat* becomes *broiled sprat; half-formed wish* comes out as *half-warmed fish; loving shepherd* turns up as *shoving leopard.* Spoonerisms were named after the absentminded Rev. Canon W.A. Spooner (1844-1930), warden of New College, Oxford. *Kinkering Kongs* was his *metathesis* of *Conquering Kings.* Other kinds of tampering with words are discussed under **epenthesis** and **paragoge**.

metempsychosis   (muh tem suh KOH sis, -temp-, met um sye-) *n.* This word has nothing to do with *psychosis,* despite its last three syllables. *Metempsychosis* is transmigration of a soul, its passage after the death of a human being or an animal into the body of another human being or animal. It is taken intact, via Late latin, from the Greek, based on the verb *metempsychousthai* (to pass from one body into another), constructed of the prefix *meta-* (indicating change) plus *en-,* which becomes *em-* before *p* and other consonants (in) plus *psyche* (soul). *Methempsychosis* is an ancient belief in the transition of the soul into another body. The Brahmins of India, worshipers of Brahma (the Absolute, God conceived as wholly impersonal, later as the Creator of the universe), and Buddhists expanded the belief to include *metempsychosis* into plants as well as animals. In the play *Faustus* by the English dramatist Christopher Marlowe (1564-1593) we read the lines:

> Ah, Pythagoras' *metempsychosis* . . .
> O soul, be changed into little water drops
> And fall into the ocean, ne'er be found . . .

It is to Pythagoras, the Greek philosopher and mathematician (c. 582-c.500 B.C.) century) that the doctrine of *metempsychosis* is attributed.

metonymy   (mih TON uh mee) *n. Metonymy* is a figure of speech, a rhetorical device, in which a suggestive word is substituted for the name of a related person or thing, like *the Crown* or *the Scepter* for the sovereign, *wealth* for people of means, *the bottle* for alcoholic spirits, strong drink, *a good table* for lavish food, *the ring* for boxing, *Virgil* or *Homer* for their works. *Metonymy,* like the names of most figures of speech, has a Greek origin, in this case *metonymia* (change of name), based on *met-* (shortened form of *meta-,* a prefix usually signifying change) plus *onyma* (name). *Metonymy* is a rhetorical term, but it is not reserved for rhetoricians; we use it all the time in common speech: "He hits *the bottle*"; "We counted noses" or "*heads*"; "We went to *the track.*" In an article entitled "On the Stump," in the June 1, 1983 issue of the English magazine *Punch,* Roy Hattersley, of the British Labour Party, writes about cricket periodicals, including the *Wisden Cricket Monthly,* " . . . the real voice of the cricket establishment . . . Indeed, the very name of *Wisden* is indivisible from cricket. [Note: John Wisden was a great cricketer of the 1850s. In 1864 he

produced the first issue of the *Wisden Cricketers' Almanack*, still published
annually and the Bible of English and international cricket.] It is—together with
Hansard [the official report of British parliamentary proceedings—their equivalent of the U. S. *Congressional Record*—initiated by Luke Hansard in 1774],
Debrett [*Debrett's Peerage, Baronetage, Knightage, and Companionage*, first
compiled by John Debrett in 1802 and published continually ever since] and
Burke [*Burke's Peerage, Baronetage and Knightage*, first compiled by John
Burke in 1826 and published continuously to date]—one of those words which
stand *metonymy* on its head. The name of a person has turned into the name of
an institution . . . " One must admire Mr. Hattersley's insight into *metonymy*. In
the field of etymology, there is a phenomenon known as "*metonymic* transference," the process by which a word changes its meaning in a "metonymic"
way. In Latin, *arena* (usually in the form *harena*) means "sand." The sports field
in the amphitheater was covered with sand, and eventually, *(h)arena* came to
mean what it means in English today: a sports center or, more widely, the scene
of any contest or struggle (e.g., the "political arena"). By *metonymy*, the suggestive word was substituted for a related thing in the original language, and by the
time it got to us, the original meaning was lost through *metonymic* transference.

miching, see **mallecho**

micturate   (MIK chuh rate) *vb. Micturate* is another word for *urinate*, from
the Latin *micturire* (to want to urinate), a **desiderative** verb based on *mictus*,
past participle of *mingere* (to urinate). *Micturition* (mik chuh RIH shun) is
urination. There are several euphemisms for this bodily function: *pass water*,
make water, use the powder room or *boys'* or *gents'* or *girls' room, wash one's
hands, go to the bathroom* ("Look daddy, Fido went to the bathroom on the
petunias!"), etc., and in British English *spend a penny*—a reference to the insertion of a coin (it once was a penny) to unlock those little cabinets in ladies'
rooms. *Micturate* is not a euphemism, just a synonym.

millenarian   (mil uh NAR ee un) *n.* A *millennium* (note double *n*) is a
thousand years (Latin *mille*, one thousand, plus combining form of *annus*,
year). In *Revelations* 20:1-7, the *millennium* is the period of a thousand years
during which Jesus will return to earth and live with His saints and then take
them up to heaven. A *millenarian* is a believer in that *millennium*, and this
belief of early Christians is now held by Mormons and Adventists. The spelling of
millenarian with a single *n* shows that it is not directly based on *millennium*,
but is a word in its own right, formed independently of *annus*. A synonym of
millenarian is *chiliast*, based on the Greek equivalent of *mille, chilioi*.

milvine, see **accipitrine**

mimesis   (mih MEE sis, mye-) *n.* In rhetoric, *mimesis* is the reproduction of a
person's supposed or imaginable words, a device much resorted to by the

writers of "historical" novels, in the reconstruction of events and the thoughts and sayings of personages. (Then Abe turned to his mother and said: "Some day, I'm goin' to live in that big white house . . . ") It happens all the time in historical plays. ("I am dying, Egypt, dying . . . ") In zoology, *mimesis* is quite a different story, the mimicry by one animal of the appearance of another that is distasteful to the predators of the imitator, or the imitation of a natural object like a leaf, or bark, that would be ignored by a predator. *Mimesis* is intact from the Greek, where it is related to the verb *mimeesthai* (to copy). Related words are *mime* (from Greek *mimos*, imitator); *mimetic* (from Greek *mimetikos*, imitative); *mimic* (from Greek *mimikos*, mime-like); *mimicry*; and *mimeograph*, tacking on the Greek suffix *-graph*, based on the verb *graphein* (to write).

mimetic, see **mimesis**

minacious (min AY shus) *adj.*; **minatory** (MIN uh tor ee) *adj.* Both these words mean "threatening," and both are of Latin ancestry: *minacious* from *minax* (menacing, threatening), *minatory* from *minatus*, past participle of *minari* (to threaten). Of the two, *minatory* is the more common. The primary meaning in Latin of *minax* is "projecting, jutting out," and of *minari* is to "project, jut out," and the concepts of *jutting out* and *threatening* must have merged in the past from the threat posed by an overhanging cliff or balcony that might collapse or from which rocks and other projectiles might be cast down. Projection and threat certainly merged in the position of Mussolini's chin when he was riding high and making those speeches from the balcony of the Palazzo Chigi in Rome, witnessed by this author when he was a graduate student at the University of Rome.

minatory, see **minacious**

misocapnic, see **philogyny**

misoclere, see **philogyny**

misogamy, see **philogyny**

misogyny, misogynous, misogynic, misogynistic, see **philogyny**

misology, see **philogyny**

misoneism, see **philogyny**

misprision (mis PRIZH un) **n.** This is a legal term that has a number of technical meanings, but its principal use is to denote failure to notify the authorities of another person's felony. *Misprision* is in itself a crime. It comes, via Old French *mesprision*, from the prefix *mis-* (in the sense of *non-*) plus Latin *prensio*, a variant of *prehensio* (seizure, arrest). This noun has nothing to do with *misprize* (mis PRIZE), to scorn or undervalue, which has a different derivation: via Middle English from Middle French *mépriser* (to scorn).

misprize, see **misprision**

monolithic   (MON uh LITH ik) *adj*. A *monolith* (MON uh lith), literally, is a large single block of solidly uniform stone, usually a pillar or column constructed of one piece. Figuratively, the term is applied to anything suggestive of a *monolith* because of its massiveness and uniform solidity, top to bottom, and hence of its intractability. The adjective *monolithic* is often applied to nations, particularly of the communistic persuasion, that are massive and uniform throughout in their political structure, and therefore tend to be intractable in their international dealings. Senator James W. Fulbright (b.1905), in a memorable speech in the Senate in 1964, dared to differ from the prevailing view when he said, "The master myth of the cold war is that the communist bloc is a *monolith* . . . " The intervening history of Sino-Russian relations appear to have borne him out. One speaks also of a *monolithic* company or organization that is self-sufficient, in that it commands the source of its raw materials, its labor supply, its manufacturing facilities and sales outlets. The United States Government often uses legal means to break up *monolithic* organizations. The derivation from the Greek *monos* (alone) and *lithos* (stone) speaks for itself. We find *monos* in many words: *monogamy, monopoly, monotony*; likewise *lithos*: *lithography, lithoid, lithosphere*.

morphology   (mor FOL uh jee) *n*. *Morphology* has several meanings, all dealing with *form*, and in its broadest use, applies to the study of the form and structure of anything. The prefix *morpho-* is the combining form of the Greek noun *morphe* (form). In biology, *morphology* is the aspect dealing with the forms of animals and plants. In geology, it is the study of the features, origin, and development of land forms, and is known as *geomorphology* (jee oh mor FOL uh jee), *geo-* being the combining form of Greek *ge* (earth). In grammar, *morphology* is the study of word formations, their makeup, etymology, and inflection (changes in their endings or form depending on syntactic function, as in *boy, boys, boy's boys'* or *go, goes, going, gone, went*; much more complex in other languages).

mortmain   (MORT mane) *n*. From Middle English *morte mayne*, based on Middle Latin *mortua manus* (dead hand), this term in law applies to the perpetual holding of title to land by a corporation or charitable trust, such as a church. The term originally described the holding of land by a religous body, but today it covers such holding by any charitable or business corporation. In medieval times, the church and monasteries acquired vast amounts of land, which were exempt from taxation and other feudal dues, a fact which laid an enormous burden on secular property. Beginning as far back as the reign of

Edward I (1272-1307) and continuing right up to the 1800s, laws were enacted in England and other countries to restrict *mortmain* holdings by religious bodies, limiting that type of ownership to what was absolutely necessary. This has never been a serious problem in the United States.

moschine, see **accipitrine**

mote   (mote) *n*. A *mote* is a speck or tiny particle, usually in the context of dust. Geoffrey Chaucer, one of England's earliest poets (c. 1340-1400), wrote, in the *Tale of the Wyf of Bathe* [Wife of Bath], of "hooly freres . . . /As thikke as *motes* in the sonne-beem . . . " [as thick as *motes* in the sunbeam]. "Sudden in a shaft of sunlight/ Even when the dust moves/ There arises the hidden laughter/ of children in the foliage. . . ," from the poem *Burnt Norton*, by the American-born British poet T.S. Eliot (1888-1965) is a modern reference to Chaucer's lovely simile. In Shakespeare's *King John* (Act IV, Scene 2), Hubert de Burgh goes through the motions of preparing to put out, with hot irons, the eyes of young Arthur, at the command of Arthur's uncle, King John, and says:

> Come, boy, prepare yourself.
> *Arthur*. Is there no remedy?
> *Hubert*. None, but to lose your eyes.
> *Arthur*. O heaven! that there were but a *mote* in yours.
> A grain, a dust, a gnat, a wandering hair,
> Any annoyance in that precious sense;
> Then feeling what small things are boisterous
> [rough, massive] there,
> Your vile intent must needs seem horrible.

The best known use of *mote* appears in the Bible, at *Matthew* 7:1-4:

> Judge not, that ye be not judged . . . And why beholdest thou the *mote* that is in thy brother's eye, but considerest not the beam that is in thine own eye? . . . Or how wilt thou say to thy brother, Let me pull out the *mote* out of thine eye; and, behold, a beam is in thine own eye? Thou hypocrite, first cast out the beam out of thine own eye; and then shalt thou see clearly to cast out the *mote* out of thy brother's eye.

This excellent advice is couched in quite different terms in the *New English Bible*:

> Pass no judgment, and you will not be judged . . . Why do you look at the speck of sawdust in your brother's eye, with never a thought of the great plank in your own? Etc., etc.

This new version may be far less poetic than the old familiar language, but since *beam* in the King James must mean "plank," *mote* would logically refer to a speck of sawdust. In either case—plain dust or sawdust—a *mote in the eye* is a trifling fault one finds in someone else, while blind to a much greater fault in oneself. *Mote* is from Old and Middle English *mot* (speck).

muliebrity   (myooh lee EB rih tee) *n. Muliebrity* is womanhood, the female nature, the characteristics of a woman; more abstractly, effeminacy, softness. The word is, via Late Latin *muliebritas*, from Latin *muliebris* (womanly), based on *mulier* (woman). Its counterpart is *virility*, from Latin *virilis* (male), based on *vir* (man), but whereas *muliebrity* is most often used in the literal sense of "womanhood," *virility* is commonly understood to indicate the abstract qualities of vigor, strength, and ruggedness associated with "the stronger sex." 'Twas ever thus: the sexual chauvinism of language. *Man* and *mankind* embrace the whole human race, including *woman* and *womankind*. We hear about *homo sapiens*; how about *mulier sapiens*? In chess, even the queen is a *man*. And even an all-female crew of a lifeboat would *man* it! Up the E.R.A.!

murine, see **accipitrine**

mussitation   (mus ih TAY shun) *n. Mussitation* is muttering to oneself, in a very low voice, if any, soundlessly making speaking movements. Lots of people *mussitate* while thinking things over, solving problems, planning the next move or the day's activities, cooking with exact measures of numerous components, rehearsing excuses. *Mussitation* is the converse of ventriloquism, where one speaks without making any speaking movements. The word is from Latin *mussitatus*, past participle of *mussitare* (to grumble inaudibly, keep muttering to oneself). *Mussitare* is what the grammarians call a **frequentative** of *mussare* (to murmer, mutter).

musteline, see **accipitrine**

myocardium, see **myomancy**

mygenic, see **myomancy**

myology, see **myomancy**

myomancy   (MYE o man see) *n.* The Greek prefix *myo-* appears in a number of words pertaining to *muscle*, since *myo-* is the combining form of the noun *mys* (muscle). Thus we have *myocardium* (heart muscle), *myogenic* (originating in a muscle, said of a physical sensation), *myology* (the study of muscles), and other *myo-* words having to do with muscles. What about *myomancy*, then? Well, we said *myo-* was based on the noun *mys*—but *mys* has a second and entirely distinct meaning: it means "mouse" as well as "muscle." And *-mancy* is a suffix based on the Greek noun *manteia* (**divination**, prophesy). All this, with the result that *myomancy*—surprise!—is divination or prophecy based on watching the movements of mice. With all due respect to palmists, astrologers, and the readers of tea leaves and tarot cards—why not?

myrmidon   (MUR mih don, -dun) *n.* A *myrmidon* is any follower or servant or underling who carries out his superior's orders remorselessly, blindly, without pity or fear or merest thought of contradiction. The word was taken from the *Myrmidons*, in classical mythology a fierce, warlike people of ancient Thessaly, in northern Greece, whose king was Achilles. They accompanied him to the siege of Troy. Shakespeare makes much of Achilles's *Myrmidons* in *Troilus and Cressida.* In Act V, Scene 5, Ulysses says:

> . . .great Achilles
> Is arming, weeping, cursing, vowing vengeance . . .
> Together with his mangled *Myrmidons.*

In Scene 7, Achilles commands:

> Come here about me, you my *Myrmidons* . . .

and gives them orders to slay Hector where they find him. Again, in Scene 7, he cries:

> Strike, fellows, strike! . . .
> On! *Myrmidons*, and cry you all amain
> 'Achilles hath the mighty Hector slain.'

A chief characteristic of the *Myrmidons* was their fierce, unflinching devotion to their leader, whom they obeyed without scruple. Hence *myrmidon*, with a lower case *m.* The prime example in modern times is Adolf Eichmann, who was executed by the Israelis as a war criminal despite his defense that he was "simply" carrying out his masters' orders—the common defense of war criminals on trial. The British use *myrmidon* in a somewhat wider sense; to denote any hired ruffian or thug, and *myrmidon of the law* as a pejorative to signify "policeman" or other officers of the law employed to execute writs of attachment and the like.

mythicize, see **mythopoeic**

mythomania, see **mythopoeic**

mythopoeic   (mith uh PEE ik) *adj. Mythopoeic* describes anything related to myth-making, or giving rise to a myth. *Myth* comes from Greek *mythos* (story), and *mythopoeic* from Greek *mythopoios* (making stories), based on *mytho-*, the combining form of *mythos*, plus the suffix *-poios* (making), from the verb *poiein* (to make). We are familiar with the noun *mythology*, but not with *mythomania* (mith uh MAY nee uh), which is not a craze for reading or hearing myths, but a psychiatric term for excessive exaggeration or lying to an abnormal degree. To *mythicize* (MITH ih size) an event is to treat or explain it as a myth, and this practice is known as *mythicization* (mith uh sye ZAY shun). The controversial Bishop Jenkins of Durham, England, scandalized adherents to the Anglican faith by *mythicizing* the Virgin Birth and the Resurrection. See also **historicity**.

naiad, see **nereid**

neologism   (nee OL uh jiz um), **neology** (nee OL uh jee) *n.* A *neologism* or *neology* is a new-coined word or phrase, or a new usage. The term can also be applied to the introduction or use of a new word or a new meaning of a word or phrase. One who indulges in that practice is a *neologist* (nee OL uh jist); the practice can be described as *neologistic* (nee ol uh JIS tik) or *neologistical* (nee ol uh JIST uh kul). *Neologism* comes from the French *néologisme*, derived from the Greek prefix *neo-* (new) plus the Greek noun *logos* (word). The Irish writer James Joyce (1882-1941) made masterful uses of *neologisms* in the linguistic inventions introduced in his great novel *Ulysses*, published in 1921, and went even further in his extremely difficult last major work *Finnegans Wake*, published in 1939. A friend of the author, Henry Morton Robinson (1898-1961), a writer himself, coauthored with Joseph Campbell a *Skeleton Key to Finnegan's Wake*, and was somewhat miffed when this author suggested he then write a *Key to the Key.* Both Joyce's novels are rich in their play with words and are the quintessence of *neologism*. Another use of the terms *neologism* and *neology* is to denote the adoption of new or rationalistic religious views or doctrines, or new interpretations of holy writings. Some examples of contemporary *neologisms:* guesstimate; cheesecake (photographs of female shapeliness); *snafu* (acronym for "situation normal: all fucked up"); *corny; wolf* (male who makes amorous advances to lots of women); *soap opera; baloney, applesauce, eyewash* and *banana oil* (nonsense); *grapevine* (unofficial communication system or rumor); *piece of cake* (task easily accomplished); *chicken* (young girl, or scared); *sexpertease*, from a 1950 short short story entitled *Great in the Hay* by the American writer Norman Mailer (b. 1923).

neoteric   (nee uh TER ik) *n., adj.* The adjective means "modern, of recent origin, new." A *neoteric* is a modernist, one who admires modern ideas, ways, art forms; a modern writer, thinker, etc. *Neoteric* comes, via Late Latin *neotericus*, from Greek *neoterikos* (youthful), equivalent to *neoteros* (newer, younger), the comparative of *neos* (new), which gave us the familiar prefix *neo-* (new, recent), as found in words like **neologism**, *neophyte, neoclassic*, etc. *Neon*, the neuter form of *neos*, was the name given to the inert gas discovered by Sir William Ramsey and M.W. Travers in 1898, and is Greek for "something new." Apparently, they didn't know what else to call it. "Nuisance," they should have called it, when you consider the look of our urban streets at night.

nepenthe   (nih PEN thee) *n*. This is the name of an Egyptian drug taken by the ancients to banish sorrow or care and make people forget their woes. *Nepenthe* has now been applied to anything that has that effect. The name comes from Greek *nepenthes* (soothing herb), noun use of the adjective meaning "without sorrow," based on prefix *ne-* (not) plus *penthos* (grief). It is mentioned in the *Odyssey*—a drug given by Polydamna, wife of King Thonis of Egypt, to Helen (daughter of Jupiter, in the guise of a swan, and Leda), wife of Menelaus, King of Sparta. Her elopement with Paris, Prince of Troy, resulted in its siege and destruction by the Greeks. The English poet John Milton (1608-1674) mentions this incident in *Comus*:

> That *nepenthes* which the wife of Thone
> In Egypt gave to Jove-born Helena . . .

Fowler says: "The *-s* is part of the Greek word and should have been retained in English; but it has very commonly been dropped, probably from being mistaken for the plural sign, cf. *pea* for *pease* etc. . . . But in ordinary use the word has been superseded by *tranquilliser*." (Note double *l*, and *s* for *z*, in British English spelling, though *-ize* has taken over in some words in Britain. And our *inning* for their *innings* is another example of the dropping of an *-s* mistakenly taken as the sign of a plural.)

nephalism   (NEF uh liz um) *n*. *Nephalism* is the creed of the teetotaler, the complete abstinence from alcohol. It is from Greek *nephalios* (sober), related to the verb *nephein* (to be sober). A teetotaler is a *nephalist* (NEF uh list). An alcoholic friend of the author, trained in the classics and redeemed by Alcoholics Anonymous, now refers to *nephalism* as *neverlism*, and who can begrudge him his little pun?

nereid   (NEER ee id) *n*. A *nereid*, in classical mythology, is a sea nymph, one of the 50 or 100 daughters, by the Oceanid (see **oread**) Doris, of Nereus, an old sea god who lived with his *nereids* in the depths of the sea, particularly the Aegean. Do not confuse the saltwater *nereids*, who live in the ocean, with the freshwater *naiads*, who inhabit lakes and streams, or you may be in trouble with Nereus, who not only can transform himself into fire, water, and many other shapes, but is strong enough to wrestle with Hercules. One must be careful about these things.

nescience   (NESH uns, -ee uns) *n*. *Nescience* is ignorance, lack of knowledge. It comes from Late Latin *nescientia*, based on the prefix *ne-* (not) plus Latin *scienta* (knowledge), which gave us our noun *science*. *Nescience* is one of a group of words composed of a prefix plus *-science*: *omniscience* (om NISH uns—universal knowledge); *prescience* (PREE shee uns, -shuns, PRESH ee uns, PRESH uns—foreknowledge). All these words have related adjectives: *nescient* (ignorant), *omniscient* (all-knowing), *prescient* (clairvoyant, prophetic). It is the *nescience* of the masses that permits the rise of demagogues. In Shakespeare's *Julius Caesar* (Act I, Scene 1), the Tribune Marcellus, disgusted with the *nescient* common throng, calls them "You blocks, you stones, you worse than senseless things . . . " In these days when reading has so much given way to sitting in front of the boob tube (awake or asleep), *nescience* is fast becoming epidemic.

nestorine, see **accipitrine**

nictitate   (NIK tih tate), also **nictate** (NIK tate) *vb*. To *nictitate* (or *nictate*) is to close and open one's eyes, i.e, to wink. It is from Middle Latin *nictitatus*, past participle of *nictitare*, the **frequentative** of Latin *nictare* (to wink), itself the frequentative of *nicere* (to beckon). *Nictitation* (nik tih TAY shun) is winking, a time-honored method of flirting (old-fashioned), or showing one is wise to what's happening, or simply beckoning, as indicated by the connection between the Latin verbs *nicere* (beckon) and *nictare* (wink). For some reason, *nictitation*, with a little shake of the head, evokes the image of Mae West and "Why doncha c'm up an' see me some time?"

nimiety   (nih MYE ih tee) *n*. A *nimiety* of something is too much of it, an overabundance, the opposite of a *paucity*. *Nimiety* is from Late Latin *nimietas*, based on the Latin adjective *nimius* and adverb *nimis* (very much, too much). *Paucity* is from Latin *paucitas* (scarcity), based on the adjective *pauci* (few; plural of *paucus*). The Roman playwright Terence (c. 190-159 B.C.), in his comedy *Andria*, expressed the view that " . . . the most important thing in life was never to have too much (*nimis*) of anything," while the English lexicographer and writer Samuel Johnson (1709-1784) wrote: "It is very strange, and very melancholy, that the *paucity* of human pleasures should persuade us ever to call hunting one of them," which brings to mind the words of the Irish playwright and poet Oscar Wilde (1854-1900): "The English country gentleman galloping after a fox—the unspeakable in full pursuit of the uneatable." The next time your host asks how much vermouth you want in your martini, reply: "Neither a *nimiety* nor a *paucity*," and see what happens. You may never be invited there again.

noctambulism   (nok TAM byuh liz um) *n*. *Noctambulism*, like its more familiar synonym *somnabulism*, is another word for "sleepwalking." *Noctambulation* (nok tam byuh LAY shun), like *somnabulation*, means the same thing, and a *noctambulist* (nok TAM byuh list), like a *somnabulist*, is a sleepwalker. All the *noct-* words are based on Latin *nox* (night) plus *ambulare* (to walk), while *somnabulism* and its associated words are built on Latin *somnus* (sleep) and *ambulare*. Another *noct-* word is *noctivagant* (nok TIV uh gunt), night-wandering, involving Latin *vagari* (to wander). *Noctuary* (NOK tooh uh ree), a record of night happenings or thoughts, is built on the model of *diary*, the *u* being borrowed from Latin *nocturnus* (by night), and where would Chopin have been without that word? Freudian psychoanalysts set great store by dreams, and often advise patients to enter them in a *noctuary* on awakening, though they never seem to use that word.

noctilionine, see **accipitrine**

noctivagant, see **noctambulism**

noctuary, see **noctambulism**

nodus   (NO dus) *n.* A *nodus* is a knotty point, a difficult situation, a complication in the plot of a play or story. In *De Arte Poetica* (on the Art of Poetry), the Roman poet Horace (65-8 B.C.) warns against those convenient coincidences that writers sometimes grasp at: "A god should not intervene unless a *nodus* develops worthy of his interference."

noesis   (noh EE sis) *n. Noesis* is intellectual activity, the exercise of reason. It was taken intact from the Greek, where it means "intelligence" or "thought," based on the verb *noein* (to think). The adjective *noetic* (noh ET ik) describes things pertaining to the intellect, as does the Greek source, *noetikos*, and is used as well to mean "purely intellectual" (as opposed to emotional or intuitive) or "abstract." *Noetics*, treated as a singular noun, is the science of the mind or intellect. Scientists must put aside bias, preference, or emotion, and determine results purely *noetically*.

nomology   (no MOL uh jee) *n. Nomology* is the science of law. The word comes from the Greek prefix *nomo-*, the combining form of *nomos* (law), related to the verb *nemein* (to control, manage). *Nomothetic* (nom uh THET ik) means "legislative, lawgiving" or "based on law," or applies to the study or formulation of universal laws, as opposed to *idiographic*, which relates to the study of individual case. *Nomothetic* is from Greek *nomothetikos*: *nomo-* plus *-thetikos*, from *thetos* (set), past participle of *tithenai* (to lay down), while *idiographic* involves the Greek prefix *idio-* (peculiar, individual), plus *-graphikos*, related to *graphein* (to write). Our word *thetic* (THET ik), meaning "positive," also comes from *thetikos*.

nomothetic, see **nomology**

notchel   (NOCH ul) *n., vb.* To cry someone *notchel* is to give notice, usually by advertisement, of refusal of responsibility for that person's debts. To *notchel*

someone means the same thing. These are dialectical colloquial terms of unknown origin. The person whose debts are involved is generally the wife who
has left the bed and board of the *notcheler* (serves her right). Occasionally, the
notchelee is an ex-business partner.

noumenon   (NOOH muh non, NOU-) *n.* A *noumenon* is a thing whose existence can be assumed only by purely intellectual nonphysical intuition, conceived by reason as opposed to perception by any of the physical senses. A
noumenon is an unknowable object whose actual existence is theoretically
problematic, especially God and the soul. The concept of the *noumenon* is part
and parcel of the philosophical system of the German philosopher Immanuel
Kant (1724-1804), the antithesis of a *phenomenon*, a thing as it appears in actual
experience. *Noumenon* is from Greek *nooumenon* (thing being perceived), a
noun use of the neuter form of the present participle passive of *noein* (to think).
See also **noesis**, **nous**.

noun of assembly, see **collective noun**

noun of multitude, see **collective noun**

nous   (noohs, nous) *n.* In Greek philosophy, *nous* was the Platonic term for
mind, intellect, intelligence; now, in upper-class colloquial usage, *nous* is
common sense, horse-sense, understanding; in slang, *savvy*; sometimes it is
used for "gumption." It is a Greek word, (related to **noesis**) taken into English.
In *The Dunciad*, a bitter satire on dunces and literary hacks aimed principally at
the English poet and critic Lewis Theobald (1688-1744) who in his *Shakespeare
Restored* pointed out errors in the edition of Shakespeare by the English poet
Alexander Pope (1688-1744), Pope wrote a couplet demonstrating *his*
pronunciation of *nous*:

> Thine is the genuine head of many a house,
> And much divinity without a *NOUS*.

According to *Brewer's Phrase & Fable*, " . . . the system of divinity referred to . . .
is that which springs from blind nature," i.e., "without a *NOUS*."

novercal   (noh VUR kul) *adj.* Legend has it that stepmothers are harsh and
cruel to their stepchildren: Snow White and Cinderella and that crowd had very
tough going. That was because of the *novercal* aspect of the relationship with
daddy's new wife. *Noverca* is "step mother" in Latin, and *novercalis* describes
anything pertaining to stepmothers. There must, of course, be good, kind, loving
stepmothers, who don't exhibit the fearful *novercal* qualities celebrated by the
Brothers Grimm and Hans Christian Andersen. *Vitricus* is Latin for "stepfather,"
but the expectable "vitrical" never made it into the English language.

numen, see **numinous**

numinous   (NOOH muh nus, NYOOH-) *n. adj.* Anything described as *numinous* is spiritual, has a sacred quality, is mysterious and awe-inspiring. *Numen* (NOOH mun) is literally "nod" in Latin, related to the verb *nutare* (to nod, or keep nodding), and by extension came to mean "divine will" (as indicated by the *nod* of a god). *Numen* was taken over intact, to mean "divine power" or "spirit," and gave rise to the adjective *numinous*, which denotes a quality that is divine, especially in the sense that it is beyond human understanding. There is something *numinous* in the late quartets of Beethoven. Dark forests have a *numinous* quality that inspires reverence and awe. The Roman satirist Juvenal (60-c.130) wrote that if people had foresight, Fortuna wouldn't be a goddess—she would have no *numen*.

nuncupative   (NUNG kyuh pay tiv, nung KYOOH puh tiv) *adj.* This adjective means "oral" and is more or less confined to the term *nuncupative will*, denoting a last will and testament spoken aloud to a witness or witnesses, rather than one in written form executed with the usual formalities. The word comes from Late Latin *nuncupativus*, derived from Latin *nuncupatus*, past participle of the verb *nuncupare* (to name, call by name; in connection with wills, to nominate as heir or legatee), probably based on the phrase *nomen capere* (literally, to take a name; figuratively, to utter a name publicly). *Nuncupative* wills are usually recognized if made by a person in extremis, i.e., in anticipation of imminent death, or by soldiers on the battlefield or sailors engaged in battle—those unable to get to lawyer Jone's office, talk things over, and come back to sign a document in the presence of witnesses with the customary rigmarole—but statutory rules differ in various jurisdictions. *Nuncupative* wills are rare. Even if you are young and healthy, find a lawyer to prepare a will, execute it at his or her office, put it in a safe place, preferably with your lawyer, but not in your safe deposit box, because that might necessitate getting a court order to open the box in order to get the will for probate. Incidentally, *nuncupative* is all too often misspelt *noncupative*, the *nun-* degenerating into *non-* under the influence of the *un-* in *unwritten*.

nympholepsy   (NIM fuh lep see) *n.* The ancients believed that a kind of ecstasy or frenzy took hold of a person who had caught sight of a nymph. Such a person was known as a *nympholept* (NIM fuh lept), in Greek, *nympholeptos* (one caught by nymphs), based on *nymphe* (nymph) and *leptos* (seized). *Nympholepsy* was formed of a blend of *nympholept* and *epilepsy* in the sense of "seizure." Apart from the delightful world of nymphs, *nympholepsy* denotes any frenzied yearning for the unattainable, and a *nympholept* is a person with such a yearning, someone inspired by violent enthusiasm for an unattainable ideal.

obeah (O bee uh), **obi** (O bee) *n*. This is a West African word for a type of voodoo, sorcery, or witchcraft engaged in among black persons mainly in Africa and the West Indies, particularly Haiti. The words are also applied to any charm or fetish employed in the ceremony. The original West African meaning of these words was an object buried in the ground to cause illness, death, or other grave misfortune.

obi, see **obeah**

obiter dictum (OB ih tur DIK tum). This expression applies generally to any incidental or cursory remark not necessarily germane to the subject under discussion, but its use is practically confined to the law, to describe a judge's incidental expression of opinion, not essential to his decision in giving judgment, and therefore not binding as setting a precedent. In Latin, *obiter* is an adverb meaning "in passing, by the way, incidentally," and *dictum*, the neuter form of *dictus*, the past participle of *dicere* (to say), means, literally, "a thing said," so that an *obiter dictum* is a thing said incidentally, not constituting a point essential to the decision reached. The English politician and writer Augustine Birrel (1850-1933), professor of law at University College, London, wrote a series of witty and polished essays published in 1884 under the title *Obiter Dicta*. His name gave rise to the term *birrellism*, a name for a good-humored but thoughtful comment tinged with irony. *Obiter* is formed from the Latin prefix *ob-* (toward) plus *iter* (way): *toward the way*, as it were, but not *to the point.*

objurgate (OB jur gate) *vb*. To *objurgate* is to denounce harshly, to upbraid vigorously, to berate sharply, to reproach in no uncertain terms, to give 'em hell. *Objurgate* is from Latin *objurgatus*, past participle of *objurgare* (to scold, chide, reprove), based on prefix *ob-* (against) plus *jurgare* (to rebuke), based in turn on *jur-*, stem of *jus* (law, right) plus *agere* (to drive). *Objurgation* (ob jur GAY shun) is the noun, and a great deal of it is heard at the United Nations (which is given as an example of **oxymoron** in another part of this book).

oblate (OB late, ob LATE) *n*. An *oblate* is a layman residing and serving in a monastery, not under monastic vows or regulations. There are various Roman Catholic organizations to which laymen, known as *oblates*, devote their services in special religious or charitable work. The term is from Latin *oblatus*, past participle of *offerre* (to offer). *Oblation* (o BLAY shun), as a general term, applies to any offering for charitable or religious purposes; specifically, in the Eucharist, it denotes the offering of bread and wine. One of the novels of the French writer Joris Karl Huysmans (1848-1907) is entitled "The Oblate."

Occam's razor (OK umz RAY zur). This is the popular name of a maxim originated by Willian of Ockham (d. 1349), the Franciscan scholastic philosopher, born, it is believed, at Ockham, Surrey, England. He was known as the *Doctor Singularis et Invincibilis* (Singular and Invincible Doctor) because of his remarkable intellectual prowess. His maxim: All superfluous assumptions raised in the discussion of a subject under analysis should be eliminated, i.e., the fewest possible assumptions are to be made in explaining a thing. William "dissected" all questions as with a razor; hence the expression *Occam's razor*. He argued that many questions previously considered accessible to human knowledge (immortality, God's existence, the soul) were objects exclusively of faith and must be excluded from the fund of man's intellectual knowledge. William was of Ockham, and from Missouri as well.

oceanid, see **oread**

octopine, see **accipitrine**

odyssey (OD ih see) *n*. An *odyssey* is a long, adventurous journey, a wandering full of hardships and notable experiences. The word comes from the epic poem *The Odyssey*, attributed to the eighth century B.C. Greek poet Homer, also the reputed author of *The Iliad*, the epic poem about the siege of Troy, whose Latin name was *Ilium*. Odysseus, the hero of *The Odyssey*, was King of Ithaca and the greatest, most valorous, and wisest of the Greek leaders in the Trojan war. His Latin name was *Ulysses*. *The Odyssey* celebrated the trials and tribulations of Odysseus during his ten years' journey (*odyssey*) to return to Ithaca at the conclusion of the Trojan war, and eventually lent its name to any long, trying journey marked by memorable experiences.

oeillade (u(r)-ee AD) *n*. This is a French word taken into English, whose meaning depends on the circumstances. It can denote an innocent glance, or a less than innocent ogle or leer with amorous implications. *Oeil* (u(r)-EE, pronounced as one syllable) is French for "eye" and the *-ade* suffix is common in both French and English nouns denoting action (*blockade, renegade, tirade,* etc.). In Shakespeare's *King Lear* (Act IV, Scene 5), Regan says to Oswald, her sister Goneril's steward:

> I know your lady does not love her husband;
> I am sure of that: and at her late being here
> She gave strange *oeillades* and most speaking looks
> To noble Edmund . . .

And in *Merry Wives of Windsor* (Act I, Scene 3), Falstaff, speaking to Pistol of Mistress Page, says: " . . . who even now gave me good eyes too, examined my parts with most judicious *oeillades*; sometimes the beam of her view gilded my foot, sometimes my portly belly . . . " In *Lear*, *oeillades* takes the form *eliads*, in *Merry Wives*, *iliads*; *oeillades* is the form in modern editions. Elizabethan spelling leeves mutch to bee deezyr'd.

oenologist, see **oenology**

oenology (ee NOL uh jee) *n. Oenology* is the science of viniculture, the knowledge and study of wines. An *oenologist* (ee NOL uh jist), as you might expect, is one engaged in that field. There are a great many would-be *oenologists*, amateurs in the field, who on the slightest provocation, or none at all, will gladly tell you rather more than you care to know about wines, châteaux, regions, which slope, etc. There is a whole series of *oeno-* words, based on the Latin prefix *oeno-*, from the Greek *oino-*, based on *oinos* (wine). Thus, in addition to *oenologist*, we have *oenophilist* (ee NOF uh list), combining *oeno-* and the suffix *-phil*, from Greek *philos* (dear, loving)—a lover of wine; *oenophobist* (ee NOF uh bist), *oeno-* plus—*phob*, from the Greek *phobos* (fearing)—a hater of wine; *oenopoetic* (ee nuh poh ET ik), *oeno-* plus *poetic*, from Greek *poetikos* (productive)—describing anything relating to the making of wine; and *oenomel* (EE nuh mel), *oeno-* plus *mel*, from Greek *meli* (honey)—a mixture of wine and honey, a word which has as well the meaning of "something combining strength and sweetness," used in a figurative sense, especially in the field of language or thought. Perhaps, as in the case of the quasi-*oenologist* mentioned above, you have been told more than you cared to know about *oeno-*; it is to be hoped that it is not so. But we must say something about the word *wine* itself, which presents an interesting etymological problem: Is it related to German *Wein* or to Latin *vinum* and Greek *oinos*? Probably all of them. Incidentally, Oeno, the daughter of Anius, a son of Apollo and the king of Delos, was empowered by Dionysus to change *anything* into wine. This has nothing to do with the miracle at Cana (John 2:1-11).

oenomel, see **oenology**

oenophilist, see **oenology**

oenophobist, see **oenology**

oenopoetic, see **oenology**

oligopoly (ol uh GOP uh lee) *n.*; **oligopsony** (ol uh GOP suh nee) *n.* These words that sound confusingly alike are taken together for that reason, and because they are the converse of each other and both relate to market conditions. An *oligopoly* is a sellers' market, the condition that obtains when there is a dearth of sellers and a small group of firms control the market, producing a state of limited competition. Prices go up. An *oligopsony* is a buyers' market, when there are few buyers and each competitive buyer influences the market. Prices go down. *Oligopoly* comes from the Greek prefix *oligo-*, a combining form of *oligos* (little, few) plus the Greek verb *polein* (to sell). *Oligopsony* is derived from the Greek prefix *olig-*, combining form of *oligos* before a vowel, and the Greek noun *opsonia* (purchase of food).

oligopsony, see **oligopoly**

olio (OH lee oh) *n*. An *olio*, literally, is a stew made up of a large number of ingredients. Figuratively, *olio* is used for a medley, whether of musical pieces or literary passages. *Olio*, going further, can cover any miscellany, whether of styles, colors, ideas, or whatever. See **gallimaufry**. *Olio* comes from the Spanish noun *olla* (pot, stew), which is derived from Late Latin, where it means "jar" or "pot."

omphalos (OM fuh lus) *n*. The literal meaning of this word, taken intact from the Greek, is "navel." It is used figuratively to mean "central point" or "hub." *Omphalos* was the name originally applied to a conical stone in the temple of Apollo at Delphi that was reputed among the ancients to mark the exact center of the earth (then thought to be flat). Legend had it that when Zeus, in his quest for the earth's center, started two eagles of equal speed simultaneously, one from the eastern rim of the earth, the other from the western, they met at Delphi. Any centrally located place came to be called the *omphalos* of its region. In addition to denoting the geographical center, *omphalos* can be understood in the sense of a spiritual hub, so that Rome or the Vatican is the *omphalos* of Roman Catholicism, while Jerusalem is the *omphalos* of Judaism.

onager (ON uh jur) *n*. This word has two distinct meanings, which appear at first to have nothing whatever to do with each other, and indeed, the connection is tenuous. An *onager* is a wild ass, habitat central and southwestern Asia. It is from Greek *onagros*, based on *onos* (ass) plus *agrios* (wild), related to *agros* (field). *Onager* is also the name of an ancient and medieval war machine in the nature of a great catapult operated as a sling for throwing large stones loaded into a bag or wooden bucket. *Onager* was a colloquial term in Late Latin for *scorpion*, a Biblical name (I *Kings* 12:11) for a *whip* or *scourge*, figurative for that military device with a "tail" that "stung." A wholly different word, *trebuchet* (TREB yoo shet) was also the name of a medieval engine of war for launching heavy missiles. *Trebuchet* was derived from Old French *trebucher* (to overturn). Both *onagers* and *trebuchets* served to make breaches in defense walls, with sorry results for the defenders.

oneiric (oh NYE rik) *adj*. *Oneiric* describes anything relating to dreams. There is a group of *oneiro-* words based on the Greek noun *oneiros* (dream) and the ancient Greek god of dreams *On(e)iros*. The *e* in *oneiro-* is optional. An *oneirocritic* is an interpreter of dreams and *oneirocriticism* is the interpretation of dreams, from *oneirokritikos* (pertaining to dream interpretation), based on *oneiro-* plus *kritikos* (judging, skilled in judgment). *Oneiromancy* is prophecy based on dreams, *oneiro-* plus *manteia* (**divination**). *Oneirodynia* is troubled sleep, nightmare, *oneiro-* plus *odyne* (pain). *Oneirology* is the study of dreams, *oneiro-* plus *logos* (word, discourse). An *oneiroscopist*, like an *oneirocritic*, is an interpreter of dreams, *oneiro-* plus *skopia* (watching). Altogether, a very dreamy subject, and an oneirodynia-free night's sleep to you.

oneirocritic, see **oneiric**

oneirodynia, see **oneiric**

oneirology, see **oneiric**

oneiromancy, see **oneiric**

oneiroscopist, see **oneiric**

oniomania   (oh nee uh MAY nee uh) *n*. A *mania*, we know, is a craze; from the Greek, via Latin, *mania* (madness). *Onios* is Greek for "for sale," hence *oniomania*, a mania or craze for buying things, abnormal acquisitiveness, and one afflicted with it is an *oniomaniac* (oh nee uh MAY nee ak). One of the most renowned *oniomaniacs* of modern times was the American newspaper publisher William Randolph Hearst (1863-1951), whose ranch and castle in San Simeon, California, were famous as a depository of art, antiques, objets d'art, and miscellanea of every description. A more recent *oniomaniac* was the subject of a BBC (London) documentary shown on July 14, 1985 on the *Great Collections* series, described in the previous day's (London) *Times* program notes as follows: "Henry P. McHenny . . . admits that he cannot resist buying things and has the money to indulge his passion . . . bolstered by funds provided by his mother, he began a lifetime's buying spree . . . " The film showed him "surrounded by one of the finest collections of 19th century French paintings." *That's* real *oniomania*!

onomastic   (on uh MAS tik) *adj*. *Onomastic* applies to anything pertaining to proper names. *Onomastics*, as a noun construed as singular (cf. *economics*, *politics*, etc.), is the study of proper names, their origin and history. *Onomatology* (on uh muh TOL uh jee) is synonymous with *onomastics*. An *onomasticon* (on uh MAS tuh kon) is a dictionary of proper names. All these words are based on the Greek adjective *onomastikos*, equivalent to *onomastos* (named), past participle of *onomazein* (to name), stemming from *onoma* (name). *Onomastic* has a special use in law, describing a signature to a handwritten document written in handwriting different from that in which the document itself is written.

onomasticon, see **onomastic**

onomatology, see **onomastic**

ophidian, see **herpetology**

ophiolatry, see **herpetology**

ophiology, see **herpetology**

oread (OR ee ad) *n*. An *oread*, in classical mythology, is a mountain nymph. The *oreads* were the companions of the Greek goddess Artemis, whose Roman name was Diana, goddess of the hunt and the woodlands, and considered sacred to the moon. The name *oread* is derived from the Greek noun *oros* (mountain); in *oread*, *naiad*, etc., *-ad* is a Greek suffix with the effect of "related to." The *oreads* are mentioned by the English poet Shelley (1792-1822; alas, so young!) in the *Witch of Atlas*, along with other nymphs:

> The Ocean-nymphs and Hamadryades,
> *Oreads* and Naiads, with long weedy locks . . .

The naiads were water-nymphs who populated lakes and streams. The dryads or hamadryads were tree-nymphs. The ocean-nymphs Shelly mentions were the oceanids. Lots of nymphs, lots of romance; what innocence! See also **nereid**.

orison (OR i zun) *n*. An *orison* is a prayer. Rarely met with nowadays, it was much favored by Shakespeare. Perhaps the most familiar use of it by anyone is from Hamlet's speech to Ophelia in Act III, Scene 1, as she enters at the end of the "To be, or not to be . . . " soliloquy:

> Soft you now!
> The fair Ophelia! Nymph, in thy *orisons*
> Be all my sins remember'd . . .

In *Romeo and Juliet* (Act IV, Scene 3), Juliet says to her nurse:

> I pray thee, leave me to myself tonight;
> For I have need of many *orisons*
> To move the heavens to smile upon my state,
> Which, well thou know'st, is cross and full of sin.

In Act I, Scene 4 of *Henry VI, Part 3*, as Lord Clifford is about to carry out Queen Margaret's command to kill the Duke of York, she says:

> Nay, stay; let's hear the *orisons* he makes.

Orison is from French *oraison* (oration, prayer), derived from Latin *oratio*, based on *orare* (to speak, pray).

orogeny, see **orography**

orography (oh ROG ruh fee) *n*. *Oro-* is a Greek prefix, the combining form of *oros* (mountain), and our suffix *-graphy* is from *-graphia*, a Greek suffix based on the verb *graphein* (to write), denoting drawing, writing, and describing, as well as an art or science, as in *geography*, *photography*, etc. Together, *oro-* and *-graphy* make *orography*, the earth science dealing with mountains. The related word, *orogeny* (oh ROJ uh nee, or-) covers the study of the origin and formation of mountains; from the same *oro-*, plus the suffix *-geny*, from the Greek suffix *-genia*, based on *genes* (born, produced). Logically enough, an *orometer* (oh ROM ih tur) is a barometer showing elevation above sea level, used in the measurement of the heights of mountains and volcanoes.

orometer, see **orography**

orotund   (OR uh tund) *adj.* This is an adjective descriptive of a full, rich, articulate voice or speech, but it has acquired as well the pejorative meaning of "pompous" when applied to a style of speaking. It comes from the Latin phrase *ore rotundo* (with a round mouth; figuratively, well-turned speech). That quality of voice or speech is known as *orotundity* (or uh TUN dih tee). The Roman poet Horace (65-8 B.C.) in *Ars Poetica* (*The Art of Poetry*, Wickham translation), wrote: "It was the Greeks who had at the Muse's hand the native gift, the Greeks who had the utterance of finished grace." The Latin for the last four words is "ore rotundo . . . loqui," literally "to speak with a round mouth." *Ars Poetica* brings to mind the couplet from *Prologue to the University of Oxford* by the English poet John Dryden (1631-1700):

> So poetry, which is in Oxford made
> An art, in London only is a trade.

orphic see **icarian**

orthoepy, see **cacoepy**

orthography   (or THOG ruh fee) *n. Orthography* is correct conventional spelling, and is also the name of that section of grammar dealing with letters generally and spelling. *Orthography* comes, via Latin, from Greek *orthographia* (correct writing), based on the prefix *ortho-*, from the adjective *orthos* (straight, correct) and the verb *graphein* (to write). *Orthography* has a special meaning in drafting, for a technique of perspective projection used in maps and elevations in which the viewer is in theory infinitely far away so that the projection lines are parallel and a scale drawing results. In this technical sense, *orthography* is also called *orthogonal* (or THOG uh nul) *projection.*

oscine, see **accipitrine**

oscitance, oscitancy, oscitation, see **oscitant**

oscitant   (OS ih tuhnt) *adj. Oscitant*, literally, describes a person yawning with drowsiness, but figuratively, it is used to mean "drowsy," or "inattentive, dreamy, off in a world of one's own, oblivious, wool-gathering," and that sort of thing. Its use has been expanded to include "dull, lazy, unmindful, neglectful." The daydreaming youngster who forgets his chores may well be described as *oscitant*. The word is from Latin *oscitans* (yawning), the present participle of *oscitare* (to yawn, gape), based on *os* (mouth) plus *citare* (to put into violent motion). To be in an *oscitant* state is *oscitance* (OS ih tuhns) or *oscitancy* (OS ih tuhn see); *oscitancy* means "yawning" or "sleepiness," but its use has been extended to include "stupidity." *Oscitation* (os ih TAY shuhn) means "yawning" or "sleepiness," depending on the context. If the context includes a political speech, it could mean either or both.

osseous   (OS ee uhs) *adj. Osseous* describes things consisting of bones, containing bones, or bonelike. Anything bony can be described as *osseous*, or *osteal* (OS tee uhl). *Osseous* comes from the Latin *osseus* (bony), based on the noun *os* (bone), the basis of many medical terms starting with the prefix *osteo-*. *Ossiferous* (o SIF uhr uhs) applies to anything containing bones, and often refers to fossil bones. An *ossuary* (OSH ooh air ee) also known as a *charnel house* (a repository for corpses, from Late Latin *carnale*, noun formed from the neuter of Latin *carnalis*, based on *carn-*, stem of *caro*, flesh) is a receptacle for the bones of the dead, from Late Latin *ossuarium*; also a bone-urn, or a cave in which ancient bones are discovered.

ossiferous, see **osseous**

ossuary, see **osseous**

osteal, see **osseous**

ostracine, see **accipitrine**

oubliette   (ooh blee ET) *n*. This rather pleasant-sounding word, taken from the French, suggests a fragile piece of Louis XV furniture or a lovely old-fashioned flower out of a cottage garden—but not so! It is, in fact, the name of something quite dreadful: a secret pit in the floor of a dungeon, enclosed by four thick walls, accessible only through a trap door at the top, through which the wretched prisoner would be flung—and forgotten. Hence the name: *oubliette* comes from the French verb *oublier* (forget). Horrid thought! The French use *oubliette* methaphorically in the expression *mettre aux oubliettes*, meaning "assign to oblivion."

ovibovine, see **accipitrine**

ovine, see **accipitrine**

oviparous, see **viviparous**

ovoviviparous, see **viviparous**

oxymoron   (ok sih MOR on) *n*. An *oxymoron* is a figure of speech utilizing the joining of seemingly self-contradictory terms to produce the effect of irony through paradox. The word was taken intact from the Greek neuter form of the adjective *oxymoros* (pointedly foolish), based on the adjectives *oxys* (sharp) plus *moros* (foolish—from which we get *moron*). Examples: to *make haste slowly*, to *kill with kindness, benign neglect, interesting bore*; and the famous lines from *Lancelot and Elaine*, by the English poet Alfred Lord Tennyson (1809-1892):

> The shackles of an old love straiten'd him,
> His honour rooted in dishonour stood,
> And faith unfaithful kept him falsely true.

Honour rooted in dishonour—faith unfaithful—falsely true! Now, there's a collection of *oxymora* if there ever was one. A waggish friend of this author, disillusioned by the news of the day, has suggested, as *oxymora, United Nations* and *peace-keeping force*. A few additional suggestions: *civil service; military intelligence; jumbo shrimp*.

pachydermatous   (pak ih DUR muh tuhs) *adj. Pachyderm* (PAK ih durm) is a familiar term for *elephant* and certain other thick-skinned animals that are hoofed and do not chew their cud. The derivation is from Greek *pachys* (thick) and *derma* (skin). *Pachydermatous* is the adjective. The word *pachyderm* is applied figuratively to a person who is "thick-skinned," i.e., insensitive, especially to criticism, insults, or ridicule, or to his surroundings, and *pachydermatous* describes a person or a personality of that sort. There are ham actors who have somehow developed a *pachydermatous* indifference to boos, jeers, and ridicule. *Pachydermatous* people are more than uncouth or boorish; they are simply impervious to the reactions they produce.

palimpsest   (PAL imp sest) *n*. This is the name for a piece of parchment, vellum, or other writing surface from which the original writing has been completely or partially erased to provide room for another writing—a common practice in ancient times because of the scarcity of material. We owe the discovery of certain ancient texts, notably the *De Republica* of the Roman statesman and writer Cicero (106-43 B.C.), to *palimpsests* on which enough of the original writing has remained to make possible the restoration of the entire text. In the case of the Ciceronian work, the partial erasure had been made to provide room for a discourse by St. Augustine on the Psalms. There exist interpolated *palimpsests*, where the new text is inserted between the lines of the original writing. *Palimpsest* comes via Latin *palimpsestus* from Greek *palimpsestos* (rubbed again), based on *palin* (again) plus *psestos*, past participle of *psen* (to rub off, scrape.)

palindrome   (PAL in drome) *n.* A *palindrome* is a word or a series of words that reads the same way backward or forward. It is from Greek *palindromos* (running back, recurring), based on *palin* (again) plus *dromos* (running, course). Here are some examples: *rotator*; *nurses run*; (what Adam said to Eve—herself a *palindrome*—when he first made her acquaintance): "Madam, I'm Adam"; (what Napoleon said when his luck ran out): "Able was I ere I saw Elba"; (a campaign slogan apocryphally credited to Teddy Roosevelt's speechwriters): "A man, a plan, a canal, Panama"; *deified*, and a couplet in which it appears: "Dog as a devil deified/Deified lived as a god." The first recorded *palindrome* in the English language is ascribed to the poet John Taylor (1580-1653) and goes: "Lewd did I live & evil did I dwel," but he, with characteristic Elizabethan scope in spelling, chose to spell *dwell* with one *l* and used an **ampersand**. *Palindromes* exist in other languages. For example, the French give us: "Léon n'osa rêver à son Noël" (Leon didn't dare dream about his Christmas), but you have to ignore the diacritics. One who dreams up these things is a *palindromist* (pal IN dro mist). The adjective is *palindromic* (pal in DROM ik, -DRO mik). *Palindrome* applies to numbers, too: e.g., 2270722. *'Nuf fun* with *palindromes?*

palinode   (PAL uh node) *n.* A *palinode*, literally, is a poem in which the poet retracts something expressed in an earlier poem, but *palinode* has come to denote any retraction or recantation or disavowal. This noun comes, via Late Latin *palinodia*, from Greek *palinoidia* (singing anew, recanting), based on *palin* (again, back) plus *oide* (song). There are *palinodes* famed in history. The Greek lyric poet Stesichorus (fl. c. 600 B.C.), of whose works only fragments survive, wrote a *palinode* to Helen of Troy recanting a previous poem describing her as evil, for which he had been struck blind by the gods. The Roman poet Horace (65-8 B.C.) wrote an ode (Book I, Ode 16) in which he apologizes for an earlier scurrilous poem, ending his *palinode*: "Now I am anxious to replace bitter taunts with soothing strains, if only, after I recant my taunts, you become my friend and restore my peace of mind." The English poet Isaac Watts (1674-1748) wrote a *palinode* retracting earlier praise for Queen Anne and expressing his disillusionment because of her acts in the later part of her reign. More latterly, Patrick Leigh Fermor, the English writer (b. 1915), in his travel-memoir *A Time of Gifts* (Harper & Row, New York, 1977), speaks of the "disillusioned *palinodes* that lay in wait for most of [his] . . . friends" who had earlier succumbed to left-wing opinions. Here, *palinode* was used in its general sense of "retraction" or "disavowal."

pallium   (PAL ee um) *n. Pallium* (a Latin word) is the name of the large rectangular cloak worn as an outer garment in classical times by Greek men, and in imitation, by learned Roman men. In matters of church dress, the *pallium* is the woolen garment worn by the pope and conferred by him upon bishops, as a symbol of office. It consists of a narrow band resting on the shoulders, with loosely hanging flaps in front and behind. The verb to *palliate* and the noun *palliative* come from Late Latin *palliatus* (cloaked, covered), related to the *pallium* that cloaked the body.

palmary   (PAL muh ree) *adj.* The leaf of the palm tree has long been considered a symbol of victory, excellence, preeminence. The motto of Admiral Nelson (1785-1805) was "Palman qui meruit, ferat" (Let him bear the palm who merits it). From this symbolism came the word *palmary*, meaning "praiseworthy, preeminent," derived from Latin *palmaris* (deserving the palm; excellent, admirable), based on *palmarius* (pertaining to the palm tree, *palma* in Latin). A *palmary* achievement, like the landing of the men on the moon, or the winning of a Nobel Prize, is a notable one, deserving reward and acclaim.

paludal   (puh LOOHD ul) *adj. Paludal* applies to anything having to do with swamps or marshes, or produced by marshes, like diseases, especially malaria, or miasma, noxious atmosphere arising from rotting organic matter. *Paludal* comes from Latin *palud-*, the stem of *palus* (swamp). *Paludism* (PAL yuh diz um) is a medical term for malaria. The *paludal* countryside was one of the main problems encountered in the digging of the Panama Canal, producing malarial conditions that had to be overcome so that construction could continue.

paludism, see **paludal**

pandemic   (pan DEM ik) *adj. Pandemic* means "universal" or "general." Applied to a disease, it describes a condition prevalent throughout a country, a continent, or the entire world, like smallpox in the old days. There is now a *pandemic* dread of an atomic war. Starvation is *pandemic* in some African countries. *Pandemic* is from Greek *pandemos* (common), based on the prefix *pan-* (all) plus *demos* (people). It is a long step further than *epidemic* (from Greek *epidemia*, among the people, based on the prefix *epi-*, upon, plus *demos*), which describes unhappy conditions prevalent in a community, rather than the entire world or a very large part of it.

panjandrum   (pan JAN drum) *n.* This is a mock title used of a self-important, pompous, pretentious person, a burlesque of a self-imagined potentate. The word is a piece of pseudo-classical nonsense consisting of the Greek prefix *pan-* (all) plus the humbug-Latin *-jandrum*, so that the word is not only nonsense but hybrid in the bargain. *Panjandrum* was concocted by the English playwright and actor Samuel Foote (1720-1777) in a bit of gibberish composed to test the memory of the old actor Charles Macklin (c. 1697-1797) who had boasted that he could remember anything after reading it once. He was so angry when he saw the passage that he refused to have anything to do with it. Here is the passage, with certain variations in spelling indicated in parentheses:

> So she went into the garden to cut a cabbage leaf (cabbage-leaf) to make an apple pie (apple-pie), (;) and at the same time a great she-bear, coming up the street, pops its head into the shop (came running up the street and popped its head into the shop). "What! No soap?" So he died, and she (—) very imprudently—married the barber. (;) And (and) there were present the Picninnies, (and the) Joblillies, (and) the Garyalies (Garyulies), and the grand (Grand) *Panjandrum* himself, with the little round (red) button at top (a-top), and they all fell to playing the game of catch as catch can (catch-as-catch-can) (,) till the gunpowder ran out at the heels of their boots.

Panjandrum is now used as a jocular pejorative to signify a person in high position who takes himself too seriously.

panoptic (pan OP tik) *adj.* Literally, *panoptic* applies to anything that makes it possible to view all parts of something, the way a *panoptic* aerial view of enemy emplacements reveals all the elements. Figuratively, *panoptic* can be used in the sense of "exhaustive all-inclusive," describing something that considers all the aspects of a given subject, like a *panoptic* treatment of a particular era, or a *panoptic* view of the contemporary novel. The name *panopticon* (pan OP tuh kon) was applied by one Jeremy Bentham to a prison of his design, circular in form, with a warden's room in the center permitting him to oversee all inmates' cells from a single vantage point. *Panoptic* is from the Greek adjective *panoptes* (all-seeing); *panopticon* is from Greek prefix *pan-* (all) plus *optikon* (sight).

panopticon, see **panoptic**

pantagruelian (pan tag rooh EL ee un) *adj.* This term may be applied to the conduct of any jolly, drunken, coarse, boisterous boon companion of the nature of Pantagruel, the son of Gargantua (see **gargantuan**) and the hero of the satirical novel bearing his name by the French novelist François Rabelais (1495-1553). Like his father, Pantagruel was a giant of incredible proportions, under whose tongue there was room enough to shelter a whole army from the rain, and in whose mouth and throat there was space enough for entire cities. Pantagruel's name came from the Greek *pan* (all—cf. the *pan-* in *panorama*, *pantheism*, etc.) plus Arabian *gruel* (thirsty), based on the fact that he was born during a drought that lasted more than three years. *Pantagruelism* is coarse, lusty, boisterous humor and clowning, but in reality (as the novel shows), behavior of serious purpose.

pantherine, see **accipitrine**

parachronism   (pa RAK ruh niz um) *n.*; **prochronism** (PROH kruh niz um, PROK ruh -) *n.* These words are taken together because they are both types of *anachronism* in the sense of "error in chronology." A *parachronism* is the assignment of a date that is too late; a *prochronism* the assignment of a date that is too early, and this word is a synonym of **prolepsis** used in that sense. *Parachronism* is derived from the Greek prefix *para-* (beyond) plus *chronos* (time); *prochronism* is from the Greek prefix *pro-* (before) plus *chronos*. Both are incorrect time references, or *anachronisms* (from Greek *anachronismos*, formed of prefix *ana-*, backwards, plus our old friend *chronos*). *A Connecticut Yankee in King Arthur's Court*, by the American humorist Mark Twain (Samuel Langhorne Clemens, 1835-1910), is an example of a *prochronistic* spoof. Shakespearean plays done in modern dress are *parachronistically* disturbing. *The Time Machine* of the English novelist H.G. Wells (1866-1946) worked both ways.

paraclete   (PAR uh kleet) *n.* A *paraclete* is a person called upon for aid or support in time of need; an advocate or intercessor. With an upper case *P*, *Paraclete* is used as a title of the Holy Ghost, the Comforter, in *John* 14:26, when Jesus, comforting his disciples, says: " . . . The Comforter, which is the Holy Ghost, whom the Father will send in my name, he shall teach you all things . . . " (In the *New English Bible*, the Holy Ghost is called "your Advocate, the Holy Spirit.") *Paraclete* is from the Late Greek *parakletos* (comforter: literally, one called in to aid), related to the verb *parakaleein* (to call in), based on the prefix *para-* (beside) plus *kaleein* (to call). In the poem *Veni, Creator Spiritus* of the English poet John Dryden (1631-1700), we read the lines:

> O source of uncreated light
> The Father's promised *Paraclete*!

The French scholar, philosopher, and theologian Peter Abelard (1079-1142), of Abelard and Héloïse fame, founded a school called *Paraclete*, where he and Héloïse were buried until their remains were removed to Père-Lachaise cemetery, Paris, in 1817.

paradigm   (PAIR uh dim, -dime) *n.* In grammar, a *paradigm* is a complete set of the inflected forms that can be built on a single stem, e.g.: *girl, girl's, girls, girls'; love, loves, loving, loved*. In highly inflected languages, the list would be many, many times longer: in nouns, all the cases, singular and plural, sometimes also dual; in verbs, all the persons, tenses, voices, moods, participles, and their inflections. As a general term apart from grammar, *paradigm* can mean "example, pattern, model." It is from Greek *paradigma* (pattern), related to the verb *paradeiknynai* (to show side by side), based on the prefix *para-* (beside) plus *deiknynai* (to show—also discussed under **elenchus** with respect to *deictic*).

paragoge   (pair uh GOH jee) *n.* A *paragoge* is the addition of one or more letters, or a sound, to the end of a word, whether as language develops (among*st*, amid*st*, again*st*; peasan*t*—cf. French *paysan*), or as a result of illiteracy (drown*d*, acros*t*, heigh*tth*, chance*t*—pronounced *chanst*). *Paragoge* was taken intact, via Late Latin, meaning "lengthening of a word," from the same word in Greek, meaning "leading by" or "change," based on *paragein* (to lead past), formed of prefix *para-*, *par-* before a vowel, plus *agein* (to lead). See also **epenthesis** and **metathesis**.

paralipsis, see **apophasis**

paranymph   (PAIR uh nimf) *n.* A *paranymph* is a bridesmaid, or (surprisingly enough!) a best man, also known as a *groomsman*, at a wedding. The one word can apply to either sex. The Greek source of this word, *paranymphos*, could do for either the friend of the groom who accompanied him when he went forth to fetch the bride, or the bridesmaid who escorted the bride on her way to the groom, in accordance with the customs of ancient Greece. This is strange in view of the etymological basis of the word: *para-* (beside) plus *nymphe* (bride), but it can be supposed that the context would eliminate any ambiguity. All the English news reports of the marriage of England's Prince Andrew (now Duke of York) to Sarah Ferguson referred to Andrew's younger brother Prince Edward as Andrew's *supporter*, the term replacing *best man* in the case of a royal wedding.

paraph   (PAIR uf) *n.* A *paraph* is a flourish after a signature to a document, originally to prevent forgery, later merely for decorative purposes and sometimes to lend importance. *Paraph* was taken from the French *paraphe*, based on Middle Latin *paragraphus* (the paragraph symbol:), *shortened* from *paragraph* to *paraph* by **syncope**. Never confuse paraph with **paraphilia**! People who indulge in fancy flourishes after their signatures may have quite normal sexual appetites.

paraphilia   (pair uh FIL ee uh) *n.* *Paraphilia* is sexual perversion, and a *paraphiliac* is a person who indulges in abnormal sexual practices. (Just what is "normal" and what isn't is another matter; some would understand *paraphilia* to signify any sexual activity other than the missionary position, but one man's meat . . . This subject is for a quite different book.) *Paraphilia* comes from the Greek prefix *para-* (beside, amiss, abnormal) plus *philia* (liking for).

parapraxis, **parapraxia**, **parapraxic**, see **praxis**

pararhotacism, see **rhotacism**

parataxis   (pair uh TAK sis) *n.* This is a grammatical term for putting together clauses or sentences without a connective. Examples: Don't worry, I'll see to everything. You're so kind, I don't know what I'd have done without you. Come along, dear, we'll be late. *Parataxis* is from the Greek prefix *para-* (beyond) plus *taxis* (arrangement).

pardine, see **accipitrine**

parietal   (puh RYE ih tul) *adj*. If you said *parietal* to a doctor, he would think of a medical problem having to do with the skull, and *parietal* has other meanings in biology and botany too technical to go into here. The sense of *parietal* you are apt to come across pertains to the rules and regulations of a college with respect to what goes on within its walls, *parietal* being from Late Latin *parietalis* (pertaining to walls) based on Latin *paries* (wall). When this author was at college (then an all-male institution, whose *parietal* adornment was ivy), it was a *parietal* rule that no one appeared in class or dining-hall without jacket and tie. ("This rule is not negotiable," the rule book stated.) A very serious *parietal* mandate pertained to the presence of a female in a dormitory room outside of closely restricted occasions (even at those the door had to remain open): penalty, nothing less than expulsion. Nowadays, with most institutions coeducational and dormitories unisex, anything goes. (Are there any surviving parietal rules?)

paronomasia   (pair uh noh MAY zhuh, -zhee uh) *n. Paronomasia* covers puns and other types of plays on words, like jokes based on **homophones** and **homonyms**, etc. Fowler points out the "best known of all (though concealed in English)," in *Matthew* 16:18: "*Thou art Peter* (Greek *Petros*), *and upon this rock* (Greek *petra*) I will build my church." Another pun "concealed in English" was uttered by the English classical scholar Richard Porson (1759-1805), who, returning home at night somewhat in his cups, seeking both whiskey and a candle, muttered: "Oude tode oude tallo" ("Neither one nor the other," in Greek), *tode* being a pun on *toddy* and *tallo* one on *tallow*. Complicated, but ingenious. Porson, incidentally, drank too much and there is a tale about the start of an after-dinner speech made by the English poet A.E. Housman (1859-1936) at Trinity, Cambridge, where Porson taught: "Cambridge has seen strange sights. It has seen Wordsworth [the English poet, 1770-1850] drunk and Porson sober. Tonight, gentlemen, you see a better scholar than Wordsworth and a better poet than Porson, neither drunk nor sober, just betwixt and between." What Housman really meant was that he was a better poet than Wordsworth and a better scholar than Porson! And how's this for a concealed pun? After two years of fighting in India, the British General Sir Charles Napier (1782-1853), in 1843, sent home a dispatch announcing his conquest of the elusive province of *Sind*—in a single word: "Peccavi." This is Latin for "I have *sinned*." Fun, even if apocryphal; and it is to be presumed that the boys at the War Office had worked hard at their classics at Eton and Harrow. *Paronomasia* is from Greek, where it means "slight name-change," based on prefix *para-* before a vowel (beside) plus *onoma* (name). Shakespeare did not hesitate to use puns, even under horrendous circumstances. In *Romeo and Juliet* (Act III, Scene 1), after Mercutio is hurt in the duel with Tybalt, dying, he jests: " . . . ask for me tomorrow, and you shall find me a *grave* man . . . " And in *Macbeth* (Act II, Scene 2), Lady Macbeth tells Macbeth to "smear/The sleepy grooms with blood," and when he refuses, she says, "If he [Duncan] do bleed,/I'll *gild* the faces of the grooms withal;/For it must seem their guilt." Under lighter circumstances, in *Merry Wives of Windsor* (Act I, Scene 3), the fat, boastful Falstaff says to his cronies Pistol et al.: "My honest lads, I will tell you what I am *about*," and Pistol puns: "Two yards, and more." Falstaff responds: "No quips, now, Pistol. Indeed, I am in the *waist* two yards *about*, but I am now *about* no *waste*; I am *about* thrift." See, too, Shakespeare's puns in *Henry IV, Part 1*, discussed under *termagant*. The Austrian pianist Artur Schnabel (1882-1951) invented a spoonerism in German that (like the Lord's pun to Matthew and Porson's in Greek) is "concealed" in English:

Vor vierzig Jahr' war *Schnabel nur*
Am Ende einer *Nabelschnur*.

(Forty years ago Schnabel was only—*war Schnabel nur*—at the end of an umbilical cord—*Nabelschnur*.) The English writer Laurence Sterne came up with a "concealed" pun in French. Having dined in a French inn with a fair French companion, he was asked for payment after he had already paid, and had to pay again. He said, "Sur mon *foie*, j'ai *déchargé* deux fois." This was bad French for "Sur ma *foi*, j'ai *payé* deux fois." What he meant to say, in English, was "Upon my faith (*ma foi*), I've paid (payé) twice." Instead, in his bad French, he said: "Upon my liver (*mon foie*) I've *discharged* twice." The witty lady came back with a pun: "Mieux que sur mon *con*." She said *con* (cunt) instead of *compte* (account). In other words, "Good thing you didn't discharge twice upon my cunt." Naughty lady. Can we say that Sterne con-cock-ted that one? Writing in *The Listener*, the BBC weekly program magazine, of August 8, 1985, Fritz Spiegel discusses word-plays, intentional and accidental, involving dat ole debbil sex. "With 'organ'," he writes, "you never know whether the user is being innocent . . . But surely Dickens cannot have been so innocent when he wrote (in *Martin Chuzzlewit*): 'She touched his organ, and from that bright epoch, even it, the old champion of his happiest days, incapable as he had thought of elevation, began a new and deified existence.'" And "E.M. Forster apparently had no misgivings about writing (in *A Room with a View*): ' . . . I do detest conventional intercourse. Nasty! . . . Oh, the Britisher abroad!'" We could continue in this vein, but space does not permit futher intercourse. However, see also **collective noun**.

paronym   (PAR uh nim) *n.* A *paronym* is a word based upon the same root, i.e., having the same derivation, as another. It is from Greek *paronymon*, the neuter form of *paronymos*, based on *para-* (*para-* before a vowel) plus *onoma* (name). The adjective is *paronymic* (par uh NIM ik) or *paronymous* (puh RON uh mus). Examples of *paronymous* pairs or groups: *wise, wisdom*; *dote, dotage, dotard*; *will* (noun), *willing* (adjective); *free, freedom*; **paronomasia**, *paronym*. One must not assume that words that sound alike and are somewhat related in meaning are *paronyms*. *Sorrow* and *sorry* may appear to be *paronymous*, but *sorry* is from Old English *sarig*, Low German *serig*, while *sorrow* is from Old English *sorg*, German *Sorge*.

parrhesia   (pa REE syuh, -zyuh) *n. Parrhesia* is boldness of speech. In oratorical rhetoric, i.e., the art of influencing an audience, *parrhesia*, in the words of William Safire (*On Language*, in *The New York Times Magazine* of October 21, 1984), "has a specialized meaning: 'warning of potential offense, and asking pardon in advance.'" The expression *with all due respect* (in Britain, they shorten it to *with respect*) is an example of *parrhesia*: What it really means is, "I haven't the slightest respect for you and certainly not for what you just said, and I'm going to show you up before this prestigious audience for the blithering idiot you are . . . !" In *Words Fail Me* (Hamish Hamilton, London, 1980), the English linguist and columnist Philip Howard calls *with (all) respect* a "Benedict Arnold phrase," and goes on: "In academic circles, the man who begins his remarks *with respect* means 'I am about to demolish your argument and if possible you with a buzz-saw of disrespect.'" Mr. Howard then quotes Alfred Friendly, the witty *Washington Post* journalist: "When, in argument, an Englishman says to me, 'With all respect . . . ,' I know he means that he has no respect at all for what I have said . . . I rather like it. In telegraphing the punch, it gives me a moment to prepare myself for the fact that he is about to knock the neck off a bottle and ream me a new arse-hole with what remains." Mr. Safire quotes President Reagan's frequent oratorical use of "Forgive me, but . . . " as an example of *parrhesia*, which amounts to a warning that he is about to follow up his plea for forgiveness with a withering blast at his political adversary. The word comes from the Greek prefix *para-* (beside, beyond—as in, e.g., *parapsychology*) plus *rhesis* (speech). Forgive me, but you ought to pay more attention to the derivation of our wonderful English words.

parricide, see **aborticide**

parturient, see **parturition**

parturition   (par too RISH un, -tyoo-, -choo-) *n. Parturition* is childbirth, the act of producing offspring. It is from Late Latin *parturitio* (labor in childbirth), from Latin *parturitus*, past participle of *parturire* (to have labor pains), related to *parere* (to give birth to, to bring forth). *Parturient* (par TOOR ee unt, -TYOOR-) describes the state of being in labor, about to give birth; figuratively, it can apply to producing ideas (offspring of the mind), concepts, inventions. *Parturient* is from the present participle of *parturire, parturiens*. Related words are *postpartum* (post PAR tum) and *antepartum* (AN tee par tum). *Postpartum* pertains to the period after childbirth, derived from Latin *post* (after) plus *partum*, accusative form of *partus* (birth); *antepartum* to the period preceding childbirth, derived from Latin *ante* (before) plus *partum*. *Postpartum* (or its more familiar synonym *postnatal*) depression is a condition sometimes experienced by women after childbirth, resulting from a sudden drop in the hormone progesterone.

pasquinade (pas kwuh NADE) *n., vb.* This word has an amusing history. A *pasquinade* is an anonymous satirical and sometimes scurrilous attack or lampoon posted in a public place. To *pasquinade* a person is to attack him in that way. The attack is most often political in nature. The story runs that in the 15th century there lived in Rome a tailor (some say barber) named Pasquino, who was famous for his stinging, sharp-tongued wit. After his death, a mutilated ancient Roman statue was unearthed and put up in the vicinity of the Piazza Navona, opposite Pasquino's house. Nobody knew whom the statue represented, so the people called it *Pasquino*, and thereafter annually affixed political, religious, and personal satires to it which were given the name *pasquinata* in Italian, and from that came *pasquinade*. The story goes on to tell us that in another part of Rome there stood a statue of Mars called *Marforio*, to which those attacked in *pasquinades* affixed their replies if so inclined. Both the *pasquinades* and the replies were in verse, mostly doggerel.

passel (PAS ul) *n.* A *passel* is a group, of indeterminate number but with the implication that the number is somewhat large. The funeral of John F. Kennedy was attended by a *passel* of heads of state. Summit meetings usually involve a *passel* of expert advisers. A *passel* is not necessarily a *swarm*, a term that would more aptly apply to the clique or claque that surrounds professional boxers and rock stars when they appear out of the ring or off the stage. *Passel* is simply a modification of *parcel*, which comes, via French *parcelle* (portion, particle) from Latin *particula* (particle; diminutive of *pars*, part). Strange, that a word whose ancestor meant "small part" should come to have the implication of a large mass.

passerine, see **accipitrine**

passim, see **sic**

pathetic fallacy (puh THET ik FAL uh see). We are familiar with both words, but in this phrase, their individual meanings go off in unusual directions: *Pathetic* means "produced by one's feelings" and *fallacy* means "figure of speech" or "literary license." The phrase was coined by the English writer and art critic John Ruskin (1819-1900) in his work *Modern Painters* and denotes the tendency to ascribe human emotions to nature, to anthropomorphize, to endow animals and inanimate objects with human characteristics. (*Anthropomorphize*, from Greek *anthropos*, man plus *morphe*, form.) Examples: The American marine biologist and writer Rachel Carson (1907-1964) wrote *The*

Cruel Sea. The Scottish poet Robert Burns (1759-1796) wrote: "How can ye chant, ye little birds,/And I sae weary fu' o' care!" The "friendly skies" of a certain airline was dreamt up by an advertising agency. In *pathetic fallacies*, flames devour, tempests are pitiless, and mountains challenge. There is nothing "pathetic" or "fallacious," in the ordinary sense, about *pathetic fallacies.*

patrilocal, see **matrilocal**

paucity, see **nimiety**

pavonine, see **accipitrine**

pecksniffian   (pek SNIF ee un) *adj.* This wonderfully expressive word is applicable to any hypocrite endeavoring to impress upon his fellows that he is a person of great benevolence or high moral standards. It comes from a character named Seth Pecksniff, in *Martin Chuzzlewit* (another great name) by the English novelist Charles Dickens (1812-1870), who described Pecksniff as having " . . . affection beaming in one eye, and calculation shining out of other." The American writer and critic H.L. Mencken (1880-1956), in *The American Language*, called Philadelphia "the most *pecksniffian* of cities." He was quite an inventor of words; for example, *bibliobibulus*, meaning "one who gets drunk on books" (*biblio-*, as in *bibliophile*, plus *bibulous*, addicted to drink): "There are some people who read too much: the bibliobibuli. I know some who are constantly drunk on books, as other men who are drunk on whiskey or religion." This passage is from his *Mencken Chrestomathy* (see **chrestomathy**).

peculate   (PEK yuh late) *vb.* To *peculate*, or engage in *peculation* (pek yuh LAY shun), is to embezzle, i.e., to appropriate someone else's money or other asset entrusted to one's care. *Peculate* is from Latin *peculatus*, past participle of *peculari* (to embezzle: literally, to make public property "private"). *Peculate* is etymologically related to *peculiar*, from Latin *peculiaris* (as one's own), in the sense of "distinctly characteristic of" or "belonging exclusively to" someone or something, as in the *peculiar* (characteristic) sounds of the music of a certain composer, or the *peculiar* properties or effects of a certain drug. When a person *peculates*, he makes someone else's property *peculiar*, so to speak, to himself (temporarily, we hope—until the cops catch up with him).

peculation, see **defalcation**

pedicular, see **pediculosis**

pediculicide , see **aborticide**

pediculosis   (puh dik yuh LOH sis) *n.* This word denotes the unhappy state of being infested with lice. The adjective is *pediculous* (peh DIK yuh lus).

Pedicular (puh DIK yuh lur) describes anything pertaining to lice. All these words are from Latin *pediculus*, deminutive of *pedis* (louse).

pedology, see **genethlialogy**

pedophile, **pedophilia**, see **catamite**

pejorism, see **meliorism**

pelagic (puh LAJ ik) *adj. Pelagic* means "pertaining to the ocean." In biology, *pelagic* is the term applied to plants and animals inhabiting the surface of the sea, far from land. The word comes, via Latin *pelagicus*, from Greek *pelagikos*, based on the noun *pelagos* (sea). Pelagic is synonymous with *thalassic* (thuh LAS ik), which too means "pertaining to the ocean," although it is sometimes distinguished from *pelagic* (or *oceanic*) as applying to seas, gulfs, etc., rather than oceans—a rather thin distinction. *Thalassic* is somewhat wider than *pelagic* as a biological term, meaning "marine" generally, so that it applies to plants and animals growing and living in the sea, whether or not at or near the surface. The Greek noun *thalassa* (ocean) is the source here. In *The Anabasis* of the Greek historian Xenophon (c. 430-c. 355 B.C.), he reports that when the ten thousand Greeks, in their retreat (*katabasis*: see **anabasis**) from the interior of Babylonia first caught sight of the sea, they cried out, in their relief, "Thalatta! Thalatta!" (The sea! The sea!), *thalatta* being an Attic form of *thalassa*. The German poet Heinrich Heine (1797-1856) wrote a poem entitled "Thalatta! Thalatta!," with the lines "Thalatta! Thalatta! Hail to thee O Sea, ageless and eternal." The English poet Barry Cornwall (1787-1874) in his poem *The Sea* wrote the lines:

> The sea! the sea! the open sea!
> The blue, the fresh, the ever free!

And the English novelist Iris Murdoch (b. 1919 and still going strong, God bless her!) wrote a novel entitled *The Sea! The Sea!* in which her hero lives in a house by the edge of the sea, which plays an important role in the story.

pelf (pelf) *n.* This is a contemptuous pejorative for "money, riches," or "filthy lucre," from *lucrum*, Latin for "profit"; in slang—"loot," and appropriately so, for *pelf* is from Middle English and Old French *pelfre* (booty) and is probably connected with *pilfer* (to steal in small quantities, acquire through petty theft). Money is often regarded contemptuously: "It's only money"; or "Who steals my purse steals trash," says Iago (Shakespeare's *Othello*, Act III, Scene 3) to Othello, "'tis nothing . . . "; and from the *First Epistle of Paul to Timothy*: "The love of money is the root of all evil." "I have arrived at a **flocci-nauci-nihili-pili-fication** of money," wrote the Scottish novelist Sir Walter Scott (1771-1832) in his *Journal*, "and I thank Shenstone [the English poet William Shenstone (1714-1763) in a 1777 letter] for inventing that long word." (But see

floccinaucinihilipilification for the true authorship and spelling of that word.) Scott harps again on the belittling of money in *The Lay of the Last Minstrel* ("Breathes there a man with soul so dead" etc.): "High though his titles, proud his name,/Boundless his wealth as wish can claim;/Despite those titles, power and *pelf*,/The wretch concentered all in self,/Living shall forfeit fair renown,/And doubly dying shall go down/... Unwept, unhonour'd, and unsung." So much for *pelf!* In *Timon of Athens*, Shakespeare uses *pelf* when, in Act I, Scene 2, the "churlish philosopher" Apemantus, spurning Timon's food and drink, poetizes: "Immortal god, I crave no *pelf*,/I pray for no man but myself..." So much for *pelf* again!

pellucid   (puh LOOH sid) *adj. Pellucid* means "clear," both physically, as in a *pellucid stream* or *lake*, and figuratively, as in *pellucid prose*, i.e., writing that is explicit in meaning. *Pellucid* is from Latin *pellucidus*, a variant of *perlucidus*, based on the prefix *per-* (thoroughly, utterly) plus the adjective *lucidus* (light, clear, lucid). The waters off Carribean shores all are usually beautiful in color and *pellucid*. The writings of the American novelist Henry James (1843-1916) and those of the English poet and novelist Thomas Hardy (1840-1928) are notable for their *pellucid* quality. American author Edgar Rice Burroughs (1875-1950), the creator of Tarzan, wrote a screwball fantasy, called *Pellucidar*, about a hollow inner earth with a small, perpetually shining (naturally) sun at its center—all accessible through a polar opening.

Pelmanism   (PEL muh niz um) *n.* This is the name quite arbitrarily given to a memory-training system known as the Pelman Institute, established about 1900 by its founder, W.J. Ennever. He chose that name because he thought it easy to remember. The wide advertising of the course led to the coining of the verb to *pelmanize*, to get good results through memory training. A similar system instituted by a man named Cody swept the United States not long thereafter. His ubiquitous advertisements showed a salesman making a terribly good impression on a potential customer by greeting him (he had only met him once, and some time previously) with: "Mr. Addison Sims of Seattle!" This became a jocular greeting among the enlightened, along with "Dr. Livingstone, I believe?" *Pelmanism* became as well the name of a children's card game that depended largely on mental concentration and memory.

penelopize   (pih NEL uh pyze) *vb.* To *penelopize* is to act like Penelope (pih NEL uh pee), the wife of Ulysses (Odysseus, in Greek mythology) and the model of all domestic virtues. According to Homer, she was beset by suitors at Ithaca, where her husband was king, while he was away at the siege of Troy. To get rid of them and their pestering, she promised to choose one of them as soon as she had finished making a shroud for her father-in-law, Laertes. Each night she unraveled what she had produced the previous day, and thus succeeded in postponing her choice until Ulysses came home, whereupon he slew all the suitors. The "Web of Penelope" is a piece of work never-ending, but always in process. Cf. **sisyphean**, but Penelope's never-ending task was self-imposed.

pentimento (pen tuh MEN to) *n*. A *pentimento* is the emergence or reappearance of earlier underlying painting (part of a "first draft," as it were) which eventually shows through the finished painting because of the increasing translucence, through aging, of the superimposed layer. *Pentimento* means "repentence" or "regret" in Italian, related to the reflexive verb *pentirsi* (to repent), from Latin *paenitere* (to regret). The artist "repents" or "regrets" what he first painted, changes his mind, and corrects it by painting over it, but the original brush strokes show through in the course of time. The American dramatist Lillian Hellman (1905-1984) wrote an autobiographical work entitled *Pentimento*, subtitled "A Book of Portraits" (Little, Brown & Co., Boston, 1973) which explains the titles in these moving words:

> Old paint on canvas, as it ages, sometimes becomes transparent. When that happens it is possible, in some pictures, to see the original lines: a tree will show through a woman's dress, a child makes way for a dog, a large boat is no longer on an open sea. That is called pentimento because the painter "repented," changed his mind. Perhaps it would be as well to say that the old conception, replaced by a later choice, is a way of seeing and then seeing again.
>
> That is all I mean about the people in this book. The paint has aged now and I wanted to see what was there for me once, what is there for me now.

perigee, see **apogee**

periphrase, see **periphrasis**

periphrasis (puh RIF ruh sis), also **periphrase** (PER uh fraze) *n*. Either of these words means "circumlocution," a roundabout way of expressing oneself, or a phrase so expressed. The adjective is *periphrastic* (per uh FRAS tik). *Periphrasis* was taken as is from the Greek, based on the prefix *peri-* (around) plus *phrasis* (speech), related to *phrazein* (to speak). In a *periphrasis*, one uses a longer expression when a shorter and plainer one would do, introducing double negatives, passives, superfluous descriptive epithets, abstract generalities, and the like. The young mother was pushing her baby along in a *little four-wheeled carriage fitted with a mattress, pillows and a coverlet*. All that is *periphrasis* for *baby carriage*, and the British make it even shorter with "pram," an abbreviation for *perambulator*. In his *Les Précieuses ridicules* (The Ridiculous Precious Ladies), a comedy by the French dramatist Molière (1622-1673) satirizing the affected intellectualism and preciosity of the ladies of fashion, he has them using ridiculous *periphrases* for common objects too "vulgar" to mention by name, e.g., "conveniences for sitting" for *chairs*. The manuscript for this book was first written with a writing instrument using a built-in resevoir of ink, and then copied on a machine in which keys are pressed to transfer letters and words and punctuation marks to paper.

perlustration (pur lus TRAY shun) *n*. A *perlustration* is a thorough survey or inspection, whether of a document or collection of documents, or an institution such as a museum or an installation. The verb is *perlustrate* (to traverse, wander through, survey, examine), based on Latin prefix *per-* (through, thoroughly) plus *lustrare* (review, observe, examine). In the foreword to *The Birds Fall Down*, a novel by the English writer Rebecca West (1892-1983), we read of the Tsarist Government's "... astounding interference with liberty such as the violation of the mails, known as *perlustration*."

perspicuous (pur SPIK yooh us) *adj.* A *perspicuous* person, *perspicuous* language, or a *perspicuous* arugment is clear, lucid, readily understandable, unambiguous. The noun is *perspicuity* (pur spuh KYOOH ih tee), meaning "clarity, intelligibility." Do not confuse this pair with *perspicacious* and *perspicacity*, which express sharp mental perception and discernment. *Perspicacity* has to do with seeing clearly, *perspicuity* with clarity of style, freedom from obscurity. A look at their Latin ancestors will make the distinction clear. *Perspicuous* is from *perspicuus* (transparent), related to the verb *perspicere* (to look through), based on prefix *per-* (through) plus *specere* (to look), while *perspicacious* is from *perspicax* (sharp-sighted), based on the same two elements but *perspicuous* is passive, as it were (look-through-able) while *perspicacious* is active (look-through-ing). Fowler has this to say: "*Perspicacious, -acity*, mean having or showing insight; *perspicuous, -uity*, mean being easy to get a clear idea of. *Shrewd* and *shrewdness*, *clear* and *clearness*, or other short words, are used in preference by those neither learned nor pretentious. The learned can safely venture on the *perspic-* pair ... The usual mistake is to write *-uity* for *acity* ..." and examples follow. From the pen of the Arabian writer Hariri (1054-1122), in *Makamet*, about the adventures of the old rogue Abu Zaid who lives by his wits through clever talk, we find this prayer:

> We praise Thee, O God,
> For whatever *perspicuity* of language Thou has taught us
> And whatever eloquence Thou hast inspired us with.

petard (pi TARD) *n.* A *petard* was a heavy explosive engine of war, filled with gunpowder and fastened to gates to blow them in or to walls, barricades, etc., to smash them and form a breach. The soldier whose job it was to fire the device was always in danger of blowing himself up as well, in which case he would wind up *hoist with his own petard*. In Shakespeare's *Hamlet* (Act III, Scene 4), the prince says to the queen.

> ... 'tis the sport to have the engineer
> Hoist with his own *petar* ...
> But I will delve one yard below their mines,
> And blow them at the moon.

(Shakespeare spelt it *petar*, possibly influenced by the French pronunciation of *petard*, in which the *-d* is silent.) Hamlet was speaking of Rosencrantz and Guildenstern, commissioned by King Claudius to escort him to England and see to his death; but as the play develops, it is they who will be done in, and thus *hoist with their own petard*. To be thus hoist is to be caught in the trap laid for someone else. This was indeed the fate of certain inventors of torture devices and dreadful places of imprisonment, like the Bastille built by Hugh Aubriot, Provost of Paris c. 1360, where he was the first to be imprisoned. In the Book of Esther 7:9, Haman was hanged on the high gallows he had devised for the hanging of Mordecai, and the witch-hunter Matthew Hopkins, tried for witchcraft under the rules he had set up, was himself executed as a wizard in 1647. *Petard* has an amusing derivation: via Middle French *petard*, related to *peter* (to fart), from the Latin *peditum* (breaking wind), neuter form of *peditus*, past participle of *pedere* (to fart). In this age of jet propulsion, doesn't that derivation give *hoist with one's own petard* a new twist?

peteman (PEET mun) *n*. A *peteman* is a safecracker, in American thieves' slang. *Peterman* is the British form, based on British slang for safe: *peter*. Eric Partridge (1894-1978), the British lexicographer who specialized in slang, in his *Dictionary of Slang and Unconventional English*, quotes from *Limey Breaks In* by one James Spenser, published in 1934, as follows: "A 'peter' is a safe made from tool-proof steel and usually has safety linings made from a special sort of cement." Partridge goes on to say: "? origin: perhaps because 'netted' by thieves: in allusion to Simon Peter's occupation." Partridge was ingenious in matters of troublesome derivation. This one seems far-fetched.

pharisee (FAR ih see) *n*. A *pharisee* (with a lower case *p*) is a sanctimonious hypocrite, narrow-minded and self-righteous. The word derives from the *Pharisees*, a Hebrew sect which flourished during the first century B.C. and the first century A.D. in Judea. They sought to ensure that the nation was governed in strict conformity to religious law. Jesus denounced them for their fundamentalist hypocrisy. Their name came from the Hebrew word *perusim* (the separate ones—based on the verb *perash*, to separate or set apart); it became *pharisaios* in Greek, and came to be applied to any self-righteous person. The adjective is *pharisaic* (far ih SAY ik) or *pharisaical* (far ih SAY ih kul), and characterizes anyone who insists on strict observance of religious law without regard to the spirit behind it, or any self-righteous hypocrite. There are unbearable people with narrow, *pharisaical* views, who think they are the sole possessors of virtue. In *The Acts of the Apostles* 26:5, Paul, defending himself before King Agrippa, says: " . . . After the most straitest sect of our religion I lived a *Pharisee*." The American poet James Russell Lowell (1819-1891), in *The Pious Editor's Creed* (*The Bigelow Papers*, First Series), has this to say:

> I do believe in Freedom's cause,
>   Ez fur away ez Payris is;
> I love to see her stick her claws
>   In them infarnal *Phayrisees* . . .

The Russian poet and novelist Boris Pasternak (1890-1960) wrote in his poem *Hamlet*:

> I am alone; all drowns in the *Pharisees'* hypocrisy.
> To live your life is not as simple as to cross a field.

(The second line is from an anonymous Russian proverb: To live a life through is not like crossing a field.)

pharos   (FAR os) *n.* A *pharos* is a lighthouse, or any beacon for the guidance of mariners. The word comes from the Greek name of the island off Alexandria, Egypt, where Ptolemy Philadelphus (Ptolemy II, c. 309 -c. 247 B.C., king of Egypt 285-c. 247 B.C.) built a lighthouse 450 feet high and visible at a distance of 42 miles. Some of it fell in 793 and the rest was destroyed by an earthquake in 1375. Ptolemy's *pharos* was one of the Seven Wonders of the (ancient) World.

phasianine, see **accipitrine**

phatic   (FAT ik) *adj.* A *phatic* communication is one that uses speech to express feelings and sociability rather than information, ideas, or specific meaning. The adverb is *phatically* (FAT ik ul ee), the noun *phasis* (FAY sis). The adjective appears mostly in the expression *phatic communion*. Friends who meet on the street often wind up their conversations with a bit of *phatic* communion: "Well, take care of yourself." "Have a nice day!" has become a bit of automatic *phasis* that has replaced "So long!" or "'Bye now!" In the novel *Rates of Exchange* (Secker & Warburg, London, 1983), the English writer Malcolm Bradbury (b. 1932) places his protagonist, Prof. Petworth, in an imaginary Iron Curtain country whose language Petworth, though a linguist, doesn't understand. He is having difficulty communicating with the unattractive stewardess in a dingy plane, and thinks about the delights of air travel back home where " . . . stewardesses . . . offer smiles and adulterous glances, promises of intimate excess, display made-up faces and nice legs, utter cries of 'Enjoy your flight' and 'Fly us again' and 'Have a nice day.' Indeed, they transmit what a linguist . . . calls *phatic* communion, which is to say, non-verbal intercourse, speechless communication, the kind of thing babies and lovers . . . constantly use." Speechless, yes, in the special sense of non-communication. *Phatic* comes from Greek *phatos* (spoken), past participle of *phanai* (to speak). *Phasis* (utterance) was taken intact from the Greek. Anyway, have a nice day.

philanderer   (fih LAN dur ur) *n.* Sometimes too great familiarity with classical roots may be misleading, strange as it seems. *Phil-*, a variant of *philo-* used before vowels, is a common Greek prefix, the combining form of the adjective *philos* (loving), as found in many English words derived from Greek: *philanthropy* (*anthropos*, man), *philology* (*logos*, word), *philosophy* (*sophia*, wisdom). So it would seem that *philanderer*, composed of *phil-* plus *andros*, another Greek noun for "man" or "husband," should mean "one who loves men," but it doesn't, for it has been altered from its original Greek meaning—a term of praise for a loving wife, who, like Frankie of Frankie and Johnnie, loved her man—and misapplied as a pejorative for a "faithless husband," or at least a woman-chaser who makes love without serious or honorable intentions. This inversion may have come about as a result of the use of *Philander* by the Italian poet Ariosto (1474-1533) as the name of a lover in his poem *Orlando Furioso*, the epic treatment of the *Roland* legend, and later by the collaborating English playwrights Beaumont (1584-1616) and Fletcher (1579-1625) in their play *The Laws of Candy*. To *philander*, as a verb, is to act the *philanderer*, the rake, womanizer, Don Juan, Lothario, Casanova—there is no end of them in literature in this naughty world.

philately, see **philogyny**

phillipic   (fih LIP ik) *n*. A *phillipic* is a **diatribe**, a speech or writing of extremely bitter denunciation and vilification, a tirade, a tongue-lashing loaded with invective. The word arose from the general application of the term originally applied to the orations of the Greek stateman and orator Demosthenes (c. 384-322 B.C.) to rouse the Athenians against the encroachments of Philip II of Macedon (382-336 B.C.), the father of Alexander the Great (356-323 B.C.). Other examples of *phillipics* are the orations of the Roman philosopher, stateman, and orator Cicero (106-43 B.C.) against the Roman politician and conspirator Catiline (c. 108-62 B.C.)—the four *Catalinian Orations* familiar to high school students of Latin. More recently, Senator Joseph McCarthy (1908-1957) was on the receiving end of a *phillipic* delivered during the "Army Trials" by defense counsel Joseph N. Welch (1890-1960), of Boston, Massachusetts, which did much to condemn McCarthy as a dangerous and irresponsible demagogue and witch-hunter and to damage his career. ("Senator, have you no shame . . . ?" etc., etc.)

phillumeny, see **philomath**

philogyny   (fih LOJ uh nee) *n*. *Philogyny* is love of women. The adjective is *philogynous* (fih LOJ uh nus). One who loves women is a *philogynist* (fih LOJ uh nist). *Philogynia* is Greek for "love of women," based on the prefix *philo-* (loving), *phil-* before a vowel, from the Greek adjective *philos* (loving) plus *gyne* (woman). The opposite of *philogyny* is *misogyny* (mih SOJ uh nee, mye-), hatred of women, from Greek *misogynia*, based on the prefix *miso-* (referring to hate), *mis-* before a vowel, the combining form of *misein* (to hate) or *misos* (hatred), plus the same *gyne*. The adjectives are *misogynous* (mih SOJ uh nus), or *misogynic* (mih SOJ uh nik), or *misogynistic* (mih soj uh NIS tik), with *my-* as an alternative first syllable in all three. (Woman-hating was and is widespread enough for the adjective to take three forms.) There are a good many Greek-based *philo-* and *miso* (sometimes *phil-* and *mis-*) words. To name a few: *philol-*

ogy (*logos*, word); *philosophy* (*sophia*, wisdom); *philanthropy* (*anthropos*, man); *philately* (*ateleia*, freedom from delivery charges); *misanthropy* (*anthropos*, man); *misocapnic* (mih so KAP nik), smoke-hating, particularly tobacco smoke—a burning (?) issue today (*kapnos*, smoke); *misoclere* (MIS o kleer), clergy-hating (*kleros*, clergy); *misogamy* (mih SOG uh mee), hatred of marriage (*gamos*, marriage); *misology* (mih SOL uh jee), hatred of reason or knowledge (*logos*, reason); *misoneism* (mih so NEE iz um), hatred of novelty (*neos*, new). *My-* is an alternative first syllable in all those. There appear to be more things to hate than to love in this world. Getting back to a *phil*-word, Fowler has this to say about *philately* and *philatelist*: "The derivation is, through French, from Greek *ateliea*, exemption from tax; the word thus means fondness for the symbols that vouch for no charge being payable, namely stamps. It is a pity that for one of the most popular scientific pursuits one of the least popularly intelligible names should have been found. The best remedy now is to avoid the official titles whenever *stamp-collecting* and *-collector* will do." " . . . least popularly intelligible . . . " indeed: That is why *philately* and 999 other words have been included in this book!

philomath   (FIL uh math) *n*. A *philomath* is a lover of learning, an enthusiast for study and knowledge; not especially concerned with *math*, short for *mathematics*, though that comes from Greek *mathematike* (scientific), related to *math-*, the root of *mathanein* (to learn), the same *-math* as that in *philomath*. *Philomathes* is Greek for "fond of learning." *Philo-* (*phil-* before a vowel) is a common prefix consisting of the combining form of *philos* (loving), related to the verb *phileein* (to love), while *-phile* is a common suffix from the same source (*philanthropy*, *philology*, *philosophy*; **ailurophile**, *bibliophile*, *Francophile*). In the *philo-* department, we also have *philately* (fih LAT uh lee), stamp-collecting (literally, love of postage stamps), the *-ately* being from *ateleia* (literally, freedom from taxation, i.e., cost-free, showing the addressee's freedom from delivery charges by affixing a stamp) and *phillumeny* (fih LOOH muh nee), the collection of matchbox labels (what will they think of next?), a hybrid word, with a Greek prefix tacked onto a Latin noun (*lumen*, light), formed, e.g, like *television* (Greek *tele-*, far, as in *telegraph*, *telephone*, etc.) plus Latin *visio* (view).

philosophaster, see **poetaster**

phocaenine, see **accipitrine**

phocine, see **accipitrine**

phylactery   (fuh LAK tuh ree) *n*. During daily morning prayers (except on Saturday—the sabbath—and religious holidays), orthodox Jewish males past the age of 13 wear *phylacteries*, small black leather cubes containing verses of the Old Testament inscribed on parchment. One is strapped to the left arm, the other to the forehead, in a manner prescribed by religious law. One cube contains a square of parchment with passages from *Exodus* 13:1-10 (Moses said to the people: "And it shall be for a sign unto thee upon thine hand, and for frontlets between thine eyes . . . "). The other contains passages from *Deuteronomy* 6:4-9 ("And thou shalt bind them for a sign upon thine hand, and they shall be frontlets between thine eyes.") and 11:13-21 ("Therefore shall ye lay up these my words in your heart and in your soul, and bind them for a sign upon your hand, that they may be as frontlets between your eyes.") *Phylactery* is from Greek *phylakterion* (safeguard, amulet), related to the verb *phylassein* (to watch). The term for *phylacteries* in Yiddish is *t'fillin*, from Hebrew *tefilla* (prayer).

picaresque   (pik uh RESK) *adj.* This adjective generally applies to a certain type of novel dealing sympathetically with attractive rogues and adventurers; full of entertaining, sometimes satirical episodes, often involving vagabonds and other social parasites, and incidentally painting a picture of the everyday life of the common people. The *picaresque* novel was first developed in Spain; *picaresque* was taken, via French, from Spanish *picaresco* (roguish, knavish), based on *picaro* (not only roguish and knavish but low and vile as well, malicious, mendacious, mischievous, crafty, and sly), which as a noun means "rascal, rogue, knave." The earliest example of this type of Spanish novel is *Lazarillo de Tormes*, anonymously issued in Spain c. 1553, the prototype of *picaresque* fiction. *Gil Blas*, from the pen of the French novelist Alain René Le Sage (1668-1747), followed in 1715 and *Moll Flanders*, by the English writer Daniel Defoe (1660-1731), appeared in 1772. The *picaresque* novel still flourishes, for example, in works like *Fanny* (New American Library, New York, 1980) by the American poet and writer Erica Jong (b. 1942), who is a neighbor of the author and had photographs taken of her in costume in his 1710 house as part of *Fanny*'s advance publicity campaign.

picine, see **accipitrine**

pidgin   (PIJ un) *n., adj. Pidgin* is a *lingua franca* (see definition below), a supplementary language, developed by peoples speaking different languages, usually a simplified form of one of the languages, corrupted as to pronunciation, with its syntax a combination of grammatical features common to the languages involved. *Pidgin* sometimes takes the form *pigeon*. The word *pidgin* is the best the Chinese could do with the word *business*, and is usually found in the expression *pidgin* (or *pigeon*) *English*, a jargon consisting for the most part of a combination of mispronounced English words and elements of Chinese syntax, used primarily in commercial circles in Chinese ports but also in other parts of the Far Eastern world. The *pidgin English* word most familiar to Western ears is *chop-chop*, meaning "quick(ly)." This familiarity is based chiefly on grade-B movies set in allegedly exotic parts of the Far East. The Chinese have a hard time with the sound of the letter *r*, usually converting it into the sound of *l*, so that *sorry* becomes *solly*, *marry mally*, *tree te-lee*, etc. Also, the sound *-ee* is often added to an English word, as in *nye-fee* for *knife*. In Chinese grammar, a word (called "classifier") is inserted between a number and the noun it modifies. This becomes *piece* in *pidgin English*: *one piece* means "one," *two piece* "two," etc. *Pidgin*, by itself as a noun, covers any combination and distortion of two languages with elements of both in a simplified grammar. English-speaking people confused the (to them) nonsensical word *pidgin* with the familiar *pigeon*, so that one runs across the term *pigeon* (or *Pigeon*) *English* occasionally. This explains the expression "That's not my pigeon" or "This isn't my pigeon," meaning "This is not my business, not my affair, not my responsibility; this has nothing to do with me." *Pidgin* can be classified as a *lingua franca* (literally, Italian for "Frankish language"): originally a jargon or mixed language consisting of simplified Italian combined with elements of Provençal, French, Spanish, and a bit of Greek and Arabic, spoken in ports of the Mediterranean; but the expression came to be applied to any hybrid language used over a wide area as a common means of communication, especially in commercial circles, among peoples who speak different languages. In the novel *Rates of Exchange* by the English novelist Malcolm Bradbury (b.1932; Secker & Warburg, London, 1983), the wife of a British Embassy official in an obscure Iron Curtain country is giving a party. She doesn't speak the very difficult native tongue, and Magda, the native cook, doesn't speak a word of English. Magda approaches, and the hostess has to give her some instructions. She excuses herself to a guest, saying, " . . . I'm afraid I must try my *pidgin*." It works: the soup gets to the table on time. Prince Charles of England is known in Fiji as "Number 1 pickaninny him belong Mrs. Queen." The noun *pickaninny* is itself taken from *pidgin*, which got it from Portuguese *pequenino* (very small). *Brush Up Your Pidgin*, a slim volume by Dorgan Rushton (Willow Books, Collins, London, 1983), is informative on this subject and amusing as well. (Note: *brush up* is British English for *brush up on*.)

pilgarlic   (pil GAR lik) *n*. This curious old word, now no longer current, comes from *peeled garlic*, an old metaphor for a baldheaded person, whose pate looks like a peeled garlic bulb. In addition, an obsolete verb *pill* meant, among other things, "make or become hairless." The English chronicler John Snow (c. 1525-1605) said of an acquaintance who was losing his hair: "He will soon be peeled garlic like myself." *Pilgarlic* is also used as a facetious term of contempt or pity, to describe a person as a poor wretch or a sad sack, especially one abandoned by his friends, and was used of oneself as a term of self-pity. We find it so used in a passage from *Pantagruel*, from the pen of the French satirist Rabelais (c. 1490-1553): " . . . we jogged off to bed for the night; but never a bit could poor *pilgarlic* sleep one wink, for the everlasting jingle of bells."

piscifauna, see **avifauna**

piscine, see **accipitrine**

pismire (PIS mire, PIZ-) *n.* A *pismire* is an ant, but the term has been applied contemptuously to a despicable individual. Robert Penn Warren, the American poet and novelist (b. 1905), used it that way. "What do you think I'd do with a young *pismire* like you?" Shakespeare knew the word. In *Henry IV, Part I* (Act I, Scene 3), the impetuous young Harry Percy, known as Hotspur, cannot bear to hear the name of Bolingbroke:

> Why, look you, I am whipped and scourged with rods,
> Nettled and stung with *pismires*, when I hear
> Of this vile politician, Bolingbroke.

In the same play (Act III, Scene 1) the same Hotspur uses the word *ant*. In reviling Mortimer's father, he says:

> . . . sometimes he angers me
> With telling me of the moldwarp [mole] and the *ant* . . .

In the earlier speech, the Bard obviously needed a two-syllable synonym for *ant*. *Pismire* is derived from Middle English *pissemyre* (a urinating ant, based on Middle English *pisse*, urinate, plus obsolete *mire*, ant). A *pismire*, then, is a urinating ant, i.e., an ant exuding formic acid. See **formication**.

plantigrade (PLAN tih grade) *n. adj. Plantigrade* applies to animals that walk on the whole sole of the foot, as opposed to *digitigrade* (DIJ ih tuh grade), describing animals that walk on toes. *Plantigrade* is from New Latin *plantigradus*, based on Latin *planta* (sole) plus *gradus* (step) or *gradi* (to walk). *Digitigrade* is from Latin *digitus* (finger, toe) plus *gradus* or *gradi*. The human race and bears are *plantigrade*, while most mammals are *digitigrade*, especially horses and cattle, which walk on the tips of one or two digits of each foot. Ballerinas walk *plantigradely* and dance *digitigradely*.

pleonasm (PLEE uh naz um) *n. Pleonasm* is the use of more words than are required to give sense; in short, redundancy. Examples: *free gift*; *hear with one's own ears, see with one's own eyes*; *save and except*; *of any sort or kind*; *in any way or manner*; *equanimity of mind*; *alas and alack*; *rags and tatters*; *shape or form*; *obviate the necessity of. Alas and alack*, like *lo and behold*, if not overdone, may be permissible for emphasis; perhaps the same may be said for *rags and tatters*. When Mr. Jones *makes, publishes and declares* this to be his *Last Will and Testament*, his lawyer is guilty of two *pleonasms* (or should we say *not one but two*?), and legal *verbiage* (defined as "overabundance or superfluity of words," also known as "verbosity") is notorious. This is not so much a case of the *care, concern and solicitude* of the lawyer as it is a result of tradition and the ancient practice of hiring scribes who were paid by the word. Lord *save me and preserve me* from that *practice, custom and convention*! And from all *redundancies, tautologies and pleonasms*! The adjective is *pleonastic* (plee uh NAS tik). *Pleonasm* comes, via Late Latin *pleonasmus*, from Greek *pleonasmos* (redundancy), **verbid** of *pleonazein* (to be, or have, more than enough), based on prefix *pleo-*, a variant of *plio-* (more), combining form of *pleion* (more), comparative of *polys* (much), from which we get our many *poly-* words.

plethoric (ple THOR ik, PLETH uh rik) *adj. Plethoric* is based upon the fairly familiar word *plethora* (PLETH uh ruh), meaning "superabundance," taken intact from the Greek, where it means "fullness." *Plethoric* is its adjective, meaning "excessive, overfull, turgid." When pompous, garrulous Polonius, in Shakespeare's *Hamlet* (Act I, Scene 3), utters his long string of moral maxims to his son Laertes who is leaving for France ("Give thy thoughts no tongue ... " etc., etc., etc., he gives him a *plethora* of paternal advice; it is, to say the least, a *plethoric* speech. Some of the discussions in this here book may seem *plethoric* to some readers, but too much, let us hope, is preferable to too little.

Plutonian (plooh TOH nee un) *adj.*; also **Plutonic** (plooh TON ik). *Pluto*, in classical mythology, was the god of the underworld (Hades, not cosa nostra). *Plutonian* describes anything relating to Pluto or his underworld, and can be used as a synonym of *infernal*. Pluto is also the name of the planet ninth in order from the sun, the outermost in the solar system. It is next beyond the planet Neptune, which gave its name to the element neptunium, atomic number 93; and so Pluto gave its name to the element plutonium, that substance of horrendous overtones. *Plutonian*, with either upper or lower case *p*, is the name of the geological theory that the condition of the earth's crust today is the result of subterranean heat (the fires of hell?). In any case, plutonium is one helluvan element. The American poet Edgar Allan Poe (1809-1849) used *Plutonian* in his famous poem *The Raven*:

> "Ghastly grim and ancient Raven wandering
>   from the nightly shore—
> Tell me what thy lordly name is on the
>   Night's *Plutonian* shore!"
> Quoth the Raven, "Nevermore."

His countryman James Russell Lowell (1819-1891), in *A Fable for Critics*, published in 1848 while poor Poe was still alive, expressed mixed feelings about him:

> There comes Poe, with his raven, like Barnaby Rudge,
> Three fifths of him genius and two fifths sheer fudge.

pluvious (PLOOH vee us) *adj. Pluvious* means "rainy" and can be applied to anything pertaining to rain, like *pluvious conditions* or *pluvious areas*. The related adjective *pluvial* (PLOOH vee ul) is synonymous, often with the implication of a very rainy condition, and in geology is used to describe conditions caused by rain, such as *pluvial erosion* or *pluvial flooding*. *Pluvia* is Latin for "rain," coming by back formation from the adjective *pluvius* (rainy)—*pluvia* being the feminine form modifying *aqua* (water) understood. A related Latin adjective, *pluvialis* (pertaining to rain), gave us *pluvial*. The Roman god Jupiter was described by the Roman poet Tibullus (c. 54-c. 18 B.C.) as "Jupiter pluvius" (Jupiter the rain-bringer.) That Jupiter certainly got around and had a finger in lots of pies. *Pluviôse* was the name assigned to the fifth month (January 20 to February 18) in the French Revolutionary calendar, adopted on October 5, 1793, as of September 22, 1792, by the National Convention. It remained in force until January 1, 1806, when Napoleon restored the Gregorian calendar. The Revolutionary calendar (designed by one Gilbert Romme, 1750-1795) was composed of 12 30-day months plus five intercalary (see **intercalate** and **bissextile**) or complementary days called "sansculottides," so named in honor of the "sans culottes" (French for "without breeches"), the French revolutionary name for the extremists of the working class. These extra days were non-working holidays. Every fourth year a sixth extra day was added. It was the French poet Fabre d'Eglantine (1755-1794) who gave the months their names, including *Pluviôse*.

pococurante (poh koh kooh RAN tee) *n., adj.* A *pococurante* is an easy-going, nonchalant, indifferent person, who exhibits a minimum of interest in anything. As an adjective, it describes that type of individual, for whom the popular slang of the moment is "laid back." *Pococuranti* are relaxed and un-harried, enjoy a carefree life-style, aren't bothered by social pressures or responsibilities. *Poco curante* is Italian for "caring little." The term for this attitude is *pococurantism* (poh koh koo RAN tiz um). The Italians have an enviable flair for the *mot juste* in this department. It is to them we owe the *dolce far niente*, literally, the *sweet-do-nothing*—pleasant idleness, complete relaxa-tion—untroubled by the so-called Judeo-Protestant work ethic; and they presented us with the expression *la dolce vita*, the sweet life—devoted to luxurious sensuality. The Spanish gave us *mañana*, tomorrow—never do today what you can put off to tomorrow—or indefinitely—or forever!

poetaster (POH it as tur) *n.* This is the label bestowed upon a second rate poet, a writer of inferior verse. A great deal of doggerel issues from the pens of *poetasters*, who are also called "rhymesters" or "versifiers." The suffix *-aster*, taken from Latin, is used to form nouns that denote inferior versions of the real thing. Thus, a *criticaster* (KRIT ih kas tur) is an incompetent, inferior critic, in whatever field he covers; a *grammaticaster* is a grammatical pedant, a petty grammarian; a *medicaster* is a quack; a *philosophaster* is a superficial philosopher, one who poses as a philosopher; the *oleaster* is the wild olive tree which bears inedible bitter fruit—olive-shaped, but of no use (*olea* is Latin for "olive tree"). There is also an *oleaster* which resembles it bearing yellow flowers but no fruit. You are welcome to make your own *-aster* words (acrobaster? educaster? artistaster?), but a *disaster* is not an inferior *dis*. In the long (1,070 lines) poem *English Bards and Scotch Reviewers* (1809) in which the English poet Lord Byron (1788-1824) reviled a long list of English poets and Scottish critics, we read, as just one sample, this couplet:

> Let simple Wordsworth chime his childish verse,
> And brother Coleridge lull the babe at nurse . . .

and later on, toward the end:

> Nay more, though all my rival rhymesters frown,
> I too can hunt a *poetaster* down . . .

And the English novelist Thackeray (1811-1863) exclaimed: "Away with *poetastering* at dinner parties!"

pogonology (poh goh NOL uh jee) *n. Pogonology* has nothing whatever to do with the art of using the pogo stick, a long upright stick with a crossbar on a strong spring; one stands on the crossbar and propels himself along the ground in a series of leaps. But to get back (without leaping) to *pogonology*: it is the study of beards, from Greek *pogon*, (beard) and the common suffix *-ology* to indicate science or study, as in *geology, theology,* etc. *Pogonotomy* (poh goh NOT uh mee) is shaving, from *pogon* plus *tome* (cutting). *Pogonotrophy* (poh goh NO truh fee) is beard-growing, from *pogon* plus suffix *-trophia* (growth, nourishment), related to *trophe* (food). Beards are back in fashion, so that all these *pogo-* words have become quite important.

pogonotomy, see **pogonology**

pogonotrophy, see **pogonology**

polder (POHL dur) *n., vb.* A *polder* is a tract of low-lying land reclaimed from the sea and thereafter protected against flooding by a system of dikes, an operation that occurs quite frequently in the Netherlands, where so much of the land is nether. *Polder* is a Dutch word, taken over intact, and is also a verb denoting this operation.

polity (POL ih tee) *n. Polity* has nothing to do with *policy* or *politics* or *politeness. Polity* is a form or system of civil government, for example, a democratic *polity*, a communist *polity. Polity* has another meaning as well: "state," or any other organized community or body of people living under a system of government, unlike an **ad hoc** group. *Polity* comes, via Latin *politia*, from Greek *politeia* (citizenship, form of government), related to *polites* (citizen). In *The Republic* of the Greek philosopher Plato (c. 428-348 B.C.), we read (Jowett translation): "Let there be one man who has a city obedient to his will, and he might bring into existence the ideal *polity* about which the world is so incredulous."

polyhistor, see **polymath**

polymath   (POL ee math) *n*. A *polymath* is a person of great and varied learning. The same goes for a *polyhistor* (pol ee HIS tur). *Polymathic* (pol ee MATH ik) and *polyhistoric* (pol hee his TOR ik) are the respective adjectives. *Polymathy* (pol IM uh thee) and *polyhistory* (pol ee HIS tuh ree) both mean "great and varied learning." *Poly-* (much, many) is the familiar Greek prefix taken over into many of our words (*polygamous, polychrome, polygon*, etc.); the *-math* in *polymath* is based on the Greek verb *manthanein* (to learn), while the *histor-* in *polyhistor* is based on the Greek verb *historeein* (to inquire, learn). Note that the two meanings of that verb support the aphorism (St. Matthew 7:7): "Seek and ye shall find." The old radio quiz show *Information Please* (1932-1947; briefly on TV, 1952) involved a panel that included those famous *polymaths* Franklin P. Adams ("F.P.A.," the American author and columnist, 1881-1960), John Kieran (the American writer, naturalist, and sports columnist, 1892-1981), the American pianist Oscar Levant (1906-1972) and other wits and pundits who could answer almost any question on any subject. Then there was the general knowledge quiz program *The $64,000 Question* (a phrase that has passed into our language) which achieved notoriety when it was discovered that a "winner" had been fed the answers in advance, and became famous as a *pseudopolymath*. Current in Great Britain is a TV program similar—without the fraud—to *The $64,000 Question*, called *Mastermind*. *Polymaths* and *polyhistors* are convenient to have around if you lack encyclopedias.

polysyndeton, see **asyndeton**

porcine, see **accipitrine**

porlock   (POR lok) *vb*. To *porlock* is to interrupt an artist engaged in aesthetic creation. This word, as a verb, appeared in print for the first time in *Bruno's Dream* (Chatto & Windus, London, 1969), a novel by the great contemporary English novelist Iris Murdoch (b. 1919). This author suspected that *porlock*, as a verb, was an invention of Miss Murdoch, and dictionary research revealed only the following entry in Volume 3 (0 to Sez) of the Supplement (1982) to the Oxford English Dictionary:

> **Porlock** . . . The name of a town in Somerset [an English county], used allusively (see quot. 1816) in phr. *a person* etc. *from Porlock*, a person who interrupts at an inconvenient moment.
>   [1816 COLERIDGE *Kubla Khan* in *Christabel* 53 At this moment he [*sc.* Coleridge] was unfortunately called out by a person on business from Porlock, and detained by him above an hour.] **1959** *Listener* 1 Jan. 37/3 All the incidental distractions—the telephone-bell, the Christmas carollers at the door, the gentleman or lady 'from Porlock'—to which one is subject.

It seemed, therefore, that to *porlock* was to interrupt at an inconvenient moment. But correspondence with Miss Murdoch brought forth a graciously prompt fuller explanation, if a narrower definition (her letter posted February 7, 1985):

> The verb "to porlock" is my coinage. (I know of no other use of it.) It fills a terminological gap and I hope it will pass into general usage! The Coleridge story, upon which the idea entirely rests, and not on the characteristics of people in Porlock generally (!), is of course that Coleridge 'dreamt' *Kubla Khan* and on awaking started to write it down but was interrupted by the person on business from Porlock—and later on could remember no more of his 'dream poem'. Strictly, 'to porlock' should mean to interrupt an artist engaged in aesthetic creation. One *might* extend it to the interruption of any sustained serious theoretical or scholarly reflection or activity (e.g., that of a philosopher or historian). I would be against weakening it to mean any sort of unwelcome interruption. . . . One or two of my philosopher friends have already, with my encouragement, adopted it—in light-hearted conversation only. I haven't seen it yet in print!

This author can only express the hope that in this (and former) correspondence with Miss Murdoch, he has not been guilty of *porlocking*—and delaying even for a moment the completion of her next and eagerly awaited novel! A reference to the rather obscure village of Porlock appears in *The Kingdom by the Sea*, a travel book by the American writer Paul Theroux (b. 1946) (Hamish Hamilton, London, 1983):

> I left Lynton on the Cliff Railway, a cable car that descended to Lynmouth [incidentally, a short but terrifying ride experienced by this author and his wife many years ago]. I took a bus to Porlock, ten miles away. The road cut across the north of Exmoor, a rather brown forbidding place, and down the long Porlock Hill . . . Porlock, the home of the man who interrupted the writing of 'Kubla Khan', was one street of small cottages, with a continuous line of cars trailing though it. Below it, on the west side of the bay, was Porlock Weir . . . A hundred and seventy years ago a man came to Porlock and found it quiet. But he did not find fault. He wrote: 'There are periods of comparative stagnation, when we say, even in London, that there is nothing stirring; it is therefore not surprising that there should be some seasons of the year when things are rather quiet in West Porlock.'

Porlock seems to be on writers' minds, undoubtedly because of the Coleridge incident. In his *Diaries, 1920-1922* (Faber & Faber, London, 1981), Siegfried Sassoon (1886-1967) notes under dates April 27, 1921, ff.:

> ". . . Thinking of taking Gabriel [Gabriel Atkin, the English artist and Sassoon's great friend] to Porlock next week."

And he did so on May 5 following. Ten days later, he sent this poem to the English poet and critic Edmund Blunden (1896-1974):

> KNOW YOU EXMOOR? Have ye heard tell of PORLOCK?
> Whence started out, one morn in 1800 (?),
> A man, on *business* bent, at Nether Stowey.

Sought there one Samuel Coleridge; knocked and blundered
Through green-leaf-shuttered parloun into garden;
Coughed; made his errand palpable; surmised
Tomorrow's rain or rainlessness. 'Beg pardon
If I've disturbed your nap, sir!' Coleridge smiled;
Seemed half-attentive. Murmured like the stream
Descending Quantock, sloping toward the Channel.
And is he known in Hell—that oaf from Porlock?
Do flames attend him? Is he crucified
Upon Mount Abora? Plagued from feet to forelock
By parasitic friends? Or has he tried
To earn atonement? Did his phantom go,
With necroscopic cliches simplified,
To irritate poor Edgar Allan Poe?

postiche (paw STEESH) *n., adj.* A superfluous and inappropriate addition to a finished work, like a sculpture or other ornament stuck onto a building, may be described as *postiche*. More generally, *postiche* applies to things counterfeit or false. As a noun, a *postiche* is a superfluous and unbecoming addition, a sham, an imitation of or substitute for the real thing, a pretense, and in a special use, a wig or hairpiece, a particular type of replacement of the genuine article. *Postiche* was taken from the French, where it has all those meanings; they got it from the Italian *posticcio* or *apposticcio* (artificial, sham; *capelli posticci* means "false hair"); and they took it from Late Latin *apposticius* (false, put on).

postil, see **apostil(le)**

postliminy (pohst LIM uh nee) *n.* This is a term in international law, defined as the restoration to their original status of people or things captured in war, when they are returned into the power of their own nation. Under Roman law, the term covered the right of a war captive to resume his civil rights and privileges on his release and return to his native land, or of a banished citizen on his return after a pardon. The Latin term is *postliminium*, literally the condition of being "behind the threshold," i.e., at home, based on the prefix *post-* plus *limen* (threshold), the same *limen* that figures in *subliminal*, describing stimuli that operate *sub-* (under, below) the *threshold* of consciousness.

postpartum, see **parturition**

postprandial, see **preprandial**

potsherd (POT shurd) *n.* A *potsherd* is a fragment of broken pottery. It is a term commonly used to denote those that are of interest to archeologists, the kind found in digs all over the world, in ancient sites. It is from the gathering and piecing together of *potsherds* that the archeologists have been able to reconstruct samples of prehistoric and ancient pottery, which often reveals much about the respective cultures. A *shard*, also spelt *sherd*, is a fragment of broken earthenware, and, combined with *pot*, gives us *potsherd*. *Shard* is from Middle English, which got it from Old English *sceard*.

prandial, see **preprandial**

praxis (PRAK sis) *n. Praxis*, from the Greek for "deed, action," is practice as opposed to theory, the actual use of one's skills and knowledge. *Praxis*, the Greek noun, is related to the verb *prassein* (to do), and involves really *doing something* (Don't just sit there; *do* something!). But *praxis*, in English, can also mean "practice" in the sense of "convention" or "custom," i.e., the usual or accepted *practice* in a given profession or set of circumstances: what the British colloquially call the "drill," or the "right" or "usual drill," to denote the *praxis*, the usual and correct way of doing things, the normal and accepted procedure. *Parapraxis* (par uh PRAK sis), on the other hand, is an error, blunder, lapse, e.g., a slip of the tongue, a sudden blank in memory, and *parapraxia* is erroneous, faulty blundering action in general. *Parapraxic* (pair uh PRAK sik) is the adjective, and all three come from the Greek prefix *para-* (beside, amiss) plus *praxis*. The language of writers like the Irishman James Joyce (1882-1941) and the American Gertrude Stein (1874-1946) was intentionally *parapraxic*, employing invented words and unconventional constructions. This author, in his days as a student in Paris, under their influence, had a couple of *parapraxically* concocted poems accepted by the long-since defunct magazine *transition* (lower case *t* intentional), devoted to the "Revolution of the Word"; the compensation was $1.00 per page paid *to* the magazine *by* the poet. Hardly fair publishing *praxis*.

prelapsarian (pree lap SAIR ee un) *adj.* This adjective is descriptive of the time or state of things before the fall of man, the degeneration of the human race resulting from Adam's disobedience of the Lord's injunction forbidding the eating of the fruit of the tree of knowledge. Adam, the unredeemed man, is a symbol of original sin, for which he was cast out of the Garden of Eden and the state of innocence. We have been suffering from that sin ever since. Remember how sweet a time it was before we suffered from the knowledge of the power of the atom? *Prelapsarian* is from *pre-* (before) plus Latin *lapsus* (fall).

preprandial (pree PRAN dee ul) *adj. Preprandial* and *anteprandial* (an tee PRAN dee ul) mean "before a meal" and *postprandial* (pohst PRAN dee ul) means "after a meal"; the meal in question may be any meal, but the one referred to in all these words is usually dinner, despite the fact that the Latin noun *prandium* means "lunch" or "late breakfast," and the related Latin verb *prandere* means to "take lunch." This disparity probably has to do with the difference between the eating habits of the ancient Romans and those of our contemporary society. Even today, country people have "dinner" at midday, when city people eat "lunch." It is pleasant to have a *preprandial* apéritif or a *postprandial* liqueur (and even pleasanter to have both). Alcoholic beverages are not the only things *pre-* or *ante-* or *postprandial*: you can have a *preprandial* chat with a friend, or a *postprandial* business talk with an associate. *Postprandial* oratory or eloquence can be quite oppressive, or (much better) soporific after a heavy meal. The English novelist, poet, and dramatist Robert Williams Buchanan (1841-1901) wrote of enjoying "the sweet *post-prandial* cigar" (the British are lavish in the use of hyphens). A *postprandial* nap can be of great comfort. *Prandial*, without benefit of prepositional prefix, applies to anything pertaining to a meal, like *prandial* conversation, or *prandial* pleasure, but it is a word you won't come across often.

presbyopia   (prez bee OH pee uh, pres-) *n. Presbyopia* is farsightedness, not the good kind that wisely foresees future developments, but the annoying affliction of advancing age, when people develop the defect in vision in which near objects are hard to see clearly. There's the tired old joke: "My arms aren't long enough to hold the newspaper where I can read it." The remedy for *presbyopia* is, of course, reading glasses, which change the focus to accommodate the defect. *Presbyopia* is formed of the Greek prefix *presby-*, the combining form of the adjective *presbys* (old; also found in *Presbyterian*, based on *presbyteros*, older or elder) plus the suffix *-opia*, based on *ops* (eye; cf. *myopia*, formed of *mys*, muscle, plus *ops*).

prescriptive   (prih SKRIP tiv) *adj.* In law, a *prescriptive right* is one attained by long, unchallenged use or tenure of property, like an easement over land or title to land (the period of use conferring the right varies from state to state). *Prescriptive*, as opposed to *descriptive*, has a special application in the field of lexicography. A *prescriptive* dictionary is one that *prescribes* rules for the proper spelling, meaning, and use of words. A *descriptive* one "tells it like it is," to use the idiom of sports announcers, which in some cases has already earned the blessing of the descriptivists; it *describes* words as to current spelling, usage, etc. For example, *Webster's Unabridged*, Second Edition, lists and defines *chaise longue* with its proper pronunciation, while the *Random House Unabridged* does the same, but then adds (the unthinkable!) "Also **chaise lounge**." *Webster's* is *prescriptive*, *Random House* descriptive. Another example: *Webster* lists and defines *lingerie* with its correct pronunciation *à la française*, points out that it applies to women's linen underwear, and adds *prescriptively*: "Also, underwear of any fabric; as silk *lingerie*. This is a commercial misuse," while *Random House* descriptively gives, in its system what would be lahn zhu RAY (in this book as the preferred pronunciation, the "proper" one as the second choice, and the *j* sound in place of *zh* as the third). To sum up, if enough people do it wrong, it becomes right in a descriptive dictionary. Both these examples happen to involve aspects of the boudoir, but no sexual chauvinism is intended. *Prescriptive* is modeled after *descriptive*, which is from Late Latin *descriptivus*, based on Latin *descriptus*, past participle of *describere* (to describe). The Roman poet Horace (65-8 B.C.), in *De Arte Poetica* (On the Art of Poetry), favors the descriptive side: "Many terms that have fallen from use will be reborn, and some now honored will fall, if that is the will of usage, which controls the law and standards of speech." Well, Horace, you pays your money and you takes your choice.

prestidigitation   (pres tih dij ih TAY shun) n. *Prestidigitation* is sleight of hand, a synonym of **legerdemain** in its literal, good sense. This word was taken over intact from the French, where it means, literally, "ready-fingerness." The French got it from the Latin *praestigiae* (juggler's tricks), adding the *-digitation* from the Latin noun *digitus* (finger—whence we get *digit*). *Prestidigitation* is *not* light-fingeredness, which means, literally, "having nimble fingers," but is almost always used in the sense of "thievish," especially with reference to expertise in the art of pickpocketing. Thus, unlike *legerdemain*, which has both a good sense and a bad sense, *prestidigitation* has only a good sense, and is in fact a noble art, affording much enjoyment to children of all ages.

preterhuman, see **preternatural**

preterit, see **preternatural**

preterition, see **preternatural**

pretermit, see **preternatural**

preternatural   (pree tur NACH ur ul) *adj.* Anyone or anything so described is exceptional, outstanding, outside the ordinary course of nature, even abnormal. In context, this word can also mean "supernatural." It is from *praeternaturalis*, a Middle Latin adjective based on two Latin words, *praeter* (beyond) and *natura* (nature). *Praeter* has given us the prefix *preter-* (beyond, past, outside the range of, more than), as in *preterhuman* (beyond what is human, superhuman); *pretermit* (pree tur MIT), to disregard, neglect, leave undone, from Latin *praetermittere* (to let pass), based on *praeter* plus *mittere* (to send, to let go); *preterit* (PRET ur it), past tense, from Latin *praeteritus*, past participle of *praeterire* (to go by); *preterition* (pret uh RISH un), passing over, disregard—in law, the passing over, i.e., disinheriting of an heir, from Late Latin *praeteritio* (passing by). The general concept of *preter-* words is *going beyond*, exceeding (as in *preterhuman, preternatural*) or *passing by* or *over* (as in *pretermit, preterition*).

prevaricate   (prih VAR uh kate) *vb.* To *prevaricate* is to lie, to speak falsely with intent to mislead. A *prevaricator* (prih VAR uh kay tur) is a liar; a *prevarication* (prih var uh KAY shun) is a lie, a falsehood. The English poet and writer of hymns William Cowper (1731-1800) wrote of "the august tribunal of the skies, where no *prevarication* shall avail" (i.e., it won't do you any good to lie in heaven). In his mock-heroic satirical poem *Hudibras*, the English poet Samuel Butler (1612-1680—not the Samuel Butler, 1835-1902, who wrote *Erewhon*), with a fine disregard for pronunciation and the help of a terrible pun (*rat, cat*), wrote this couplet:

> Quoth Hudibras, I smell a rat;
> Ralpho, thou dost *prevaricate*.

Prevaricate comes from *prevaricatus*, past participle of Latin *prevaricari* (to lie; literally, to walk crookedly, as if straddling something).

priapean, see **priapic**

priapic (prye AP ik) *adj.* A *priapic* man is one exaggeratedly preoccupied with male sexuality and maleness generally. *Priapism* (PRYE uh piz um) is lascivious behavior, lewd display. The word is also used as a medical term for continuous erection of the penis, especially when due to a physical disorder. Priapus (prye AY pus), in classical mythology, was the god of male procreative power, who eventually came to be regarded as the principal deity of lasciviousness. The phallus was his chief symbol. He was the son of the great Aphrodite (af ruh DYE tee), the ancient Greek goddess of love and beauty (Venus in Roman mythology), and Dionysus (dye uh NYE sus), the classical god of fertility, wine, and drama, whose other name was Bacchus (BAK us). That was quite a family! A modern word for *priapic* is *oversexed* (sounds weak in comparison) or *macho* (MAH cho), describing one who is excessively virile, full of swagger and bravado. *Macho* is simply the Spanish word for "male." A *priapic* man has a one-track mind; his primary concern is with his virility and potency. Don Juan, the legendary Spanish nobleman, and the Italian sexual adventurer Giovanni Jacopo Casanova (1725-1798), famous for their many sexual exploits, are prototypes of *priapic* males, insatiable amorists, obsessed roués, rakes, and libertines. In Mozart's opera *Don Giovanni* (Don Juan), the hero's valet asserts that his master had "in Italy 700 mistresses, in Germany 800, in Turkey and France 91, in Spain 1,003." That's *priapic! Priapean* (prye uh PEE un) is a synonym of *priapic*. In the *New York Times* of October 10, 1984, there is a review of *Parachutes and Kisses* (NAL Books, New York, 1984) by Erica Jong (b. 1942), an author whose previous books were much concerned with sex. Says the reviewer: "In the new novel, the *priapean* Central Park West princess [Isadora Wing, Miss Jong's protagonist] has changed her venue but not her style . . . Miss Wing is one long sexual advertisement of herself . . . " It would seem that in his characterization of a female as "priapean," the reviewer showed a fine disregard for human comparative anatomy. Even the proposed Equal Rights Amendment doesn't go that far. Vive la différence!

pristine (PRIS teen, -tin, -tine) *adj. Pristine* is a much abused and misused word. It comes from Latin *pristinus* (former, earlier) and does *not* mean "spotless" or "pure" or "fresh." It is properly used to describe something still in its original state, with its original purity. The American historian William Hickling Prescott (1796-1859), in his *Conquest of Mexico*, wrote: "What, then, must have been the emotions of the Spaniards, when, after working their toilsome way into the upper air . . . they beheld these fair scenes in all their *pristine* magnificence and beauty! . . . " The Spanish historian Bernal Díaz del Castillo (c. 1492-1581), in his *Authentic History of the Conquest of New Spain*, tells us: "From this summit [Popocatepetl] could be seen the great city of Mexico, and the whole of the lake, and all the towns which were built in it."

prochronism, see **parachronism**

procrustean   (pro KRUS tee un) *adj*. This adjective, based on the legend of Procrustes (discussed hereafter) applies to anyone intent on promoting conformity at any cost, arbitrarily and even violently. According to classical mythology, Procrustes was an Attican robber who captured wayfarers and placed them on his iron bed. If they were longer than the bed, he amputated their overhanging limbs. If they were shorter, he stretched them until they fit the bed. Nasty chap! Thus, the attempt to reduce all people to a standard belief or pattern of behavior is known as placing them on Procrustes's bed, and *Procrustean* describes this radical type of enforced conformity. In his poem *Verbal Criticism*, the English poet David Mallet (c. 1705-1765) wrote:

> Tyrants more cruel than Procrustes old,
> Who to his iron-bed by torture fits
> Their nobler parts, the souls of suffering wits.

It does seem something of an exaggeration to label an attempt to procure conformity with a reference to old Procrustes. Would one thus characterize the legend at the bottom of a dinner invitation "Formal"?

procyonine, see **accipitrine**

prodrome   (PRO drome) *n*. A *prodrome* is a forewarning symptom of a disease, a warning signal, the way a scratchy throat is a *prodrome* of a cold. The word comes from the Greek *prodromos* (literally, running before), based on the prefix *pro-* (before) plus the suffix *-drome*, combining form of *dromos* (running), related to *dromein* (run). This word suggests comparison with the more familiar word *syndrome*, from Greek *syndrome* (combination), formed from the prefix *syn-* (with) plus *drom-*, a variant stem of *dramein* (to run) plus the noun suffix *-e* which explains why an alternative pronunciation of *syndrome* is SIN druh mee. A *prodrome* is a warning symptom; a *syndrome* is a combination of symptoms. There can, of course, be a *syndrome* of *prodromes*. Why not?

proem   (PRO em) *n*. A *proem* is an introductory piece, preface, or preamble to a book or speech. The adjective applicable to an introductory discourse is *proemial* (pro EE mee ul). *Proem* comes from Greek *prooimion*, based on the prefix *pro-* (before) plus *oime* (song) plus diminutive suffix *-ion*. Fowler characterizes *proem* and *proemial* as ". . . not having made their way like *poem* and *poetic* into common use," and says that they "remain puzzling to the unlearned and are better avoided in general writing." They are. The same would certainly go for *prolegomenon* (pro luh GOM uh non, -nun), a preface or prologue (though *prologue* is from *prologos*, based on *pro-*, before, plus *logos*, word or discourse). In *The Life and Opinions of Tristram Shandy*, the English writer Laurence Sterne (1713-1768) speaks of a "pithy *prolegomenon*" handed to Tristram by the commissary of the post office in France, regarding the rules and regulations of travel by post-chaise in that country.

prolegomenon, see **proem**

prolepsis   (pro LEP sis) *n. Prolepsis*, in Greek, means "anticipation," and is a **verbid** of the verb *prolambanein* (to anticipate), based on prefix *pro-* (before) plus *lambanein* (to take). In argument, *prolepsis* is the anticipation of objections from one's opponent in order to reply to them in advance. "But, you will complain, that cannot be because ... To that I can only reply ... " *Prolepsis* is used in other senses as well: the assignment of an event to too early a date (in this it is a synonym of **prochronism**); or the use of an adjective describing a condition which has not yet occurred. Fowler calls it the "anticipatory use of an epithet," and gives the example of a passage from *Isabella*, by the English poet John Keats (1795-1821):

> So the two brothers and their *murder'd* man
> Rode past fair Florence.

Murder'd was applied to one who was only later their victim. Other examples: He struck him *dead*, Fill *full* the cup, Paint the town *red*. In each case, the adjective anticipates something that will happen later, and is therefore used *proleptically*.

Promethean   (pruh MEE thee un) *adj.* A *Promethean* person is inventive, creative, courageously original. The adjective comes from *Prometheus*, a Titan in Greek mythology, a famous benefactor of mankind. His name means "forethinker" in Greek. Prometheus was a master craftsman who could construct men of clay and mud and water and bits of other animals. His creativity led to the meanings given above. Zeus had hidden fire from man, but Prometheus tricked him by stealing it and giving it to man, whereupon Zeus chained him to a mountainside and sent down an eagle to eat his liver by day. But his liver was wholly renewed at night. Prometheus remained in torment until Hercules slew the eagle and released him. An early form of match (1828) was called a "Prometheus." It consisted of a tiny glass bulb of sulphuric acid coated with potassium chlorate, sugar, and gum, wrapped in a twist of paper. One bit the bulb with the teeth and the chlorate set the paper on fire. Sounds dangerous! The English naturalist Charles Darwin (1809-1892), in his *Voyage of the Beagle*, wrote: "I carried with me some *promethean* matches, which I ignited by biting; it was thought so wonderful that a man strike fire with his teeth, that it was usual to collect the whole family to see it." In Shakespeare's *Othello* (Act V, Scene 2), Othello, finding Desdemona asleep, and deciding that she must die by his hand, cries:

> Yet she must die ...
> I know not where is that *Promethean* heat
> That can thy light relume ...

The "heat" was the *Promethean* fire with which Prometheus had given life to his figures of clay.

prosody (PROS uh dee) *n.* This word starts out looking like something that has to do with *prose*, but not so: *prosody* is the science or study of the metrical structure of poetry and verse form generally. The *prosody* of a particular poet is his distinctive form of versification. *The Divine Comedy* of the Italian poet Dante Alighieri (1265-1321) is written in a special, quite complex *prosody*, called "terza rima" (literally, third rhyme), in which the middle line of each triplet (series of three lines) rhymes with the first and third lines of the following triplet, with an odd line to complete the canto (main division of a long poem). It is a very difficult *prosody*, not to be recommended to lazy poets. In linguistics, the stress patterns of a statement are its *prosody*. The word is from Greek *prosoidia* (tone, accent, voice modulation, song), based on *pros* (toward) plus *oide*, a contraction of *aoide* (song), related to *aeidein* (to sing).

protasis, see **apodosis**

protopathic, see **epicrisis**

proximate (PROK suh mit) *adj.* By itself, *proximate*, from Latin *proximatus*, past participle of *proximare* (to come near, approach), in either the abstract or physical sense, describes something very near or close in time, order, or meaning, or immediately before or after. It has a special significance in legal parlance, in the expression *proximate cause*: a cause that, in the natural sequence of things, with no independent intervening agency, produces a specific effect or consequence. If A punches B on the nose and B, losing his balance, falls backward and dies of a broken skull, A is guilty of manslaughter even though never intended—there was no intervening act, and A's action was the *proximate cause* of B's death. In a 1930 case, a woman was waiting for a train. A different train came in and started to pull out. A man carrying a package ran for the departing train. A conductor leaned out in an attempt to help the running man jump aboard, dislodging the package, which fell to the track. The train wheels hit it, and, since it contained explosives, there was an explosion. The shock dislodged a heavy baggage scale from its hook and it dropped down onto the woman, who was injured. She sued the railroad company, and lost: no *proximate cause*. A plantiff suing for resulting damages must show that they were the *proximate* result of the defendant's act. Class dismissed.

psittacine, see **accipitrine**

pteropine, see **accipitrine**

pubescent, see **juvenescence**

puissant (PYOOH ih suhnt, pyooh IS unt; PWIS unt) *adj*. This is a literary adjective for "powerful, potent, mighty." It is a French word with all those meanings, and *le Tout-Puissant*, in French, means "the All-Powerful," i.e, "the Almighty." The ultimate source of *puissant*, via Vulgar Latin *possens*, is Latin *potens*, present participle of *posse* (to be able or powerful). In his *Areopagitica*, an attack on censorship and a stirring argument for freedom of the press, the English poet John Milton (1608-1674) wrote: "Methinks I see in my mind a noble and *puissant* nation rousing herself like a strong man after sleep . . . " The noun, with the same variations of pronunciation, is *puissance*.

pullulate (PUL yuh late) *vb*. As a special term in botany, to *pullulate* is to grow sprouts or buds. As a general term, to *pullulate* is to breed, to be fruitful and multiply (as enjoined by God in *Genesis* 1:28), or to exist in abundance, to teem. *Pullulate* is from Latin *pullulatus*, past participle of *pullulare* (to sprout), related to *pullulus* (sprout, young animal), diminutive form of *pullus* (young animal), which gave us *pullet*, a young hen. Excessive *pullulation* is a problem in many nations of the third world, a burden that the one-to-a-family campaign of China aims to curb; but no siblings . . . ?

pyknic, see **asthenic**

Pyrrhic, see **Cadmean**

Pyrrhonism, see **dubiety**

quarrel (KWOR ul) *n*. Besides its common use to denote an angry outburst of hostilities, *quarrel* has two other distinct meanings: a short, square-headed arrow used with a crossbow, or a small diamond-shaped or square pane of glass used in a latticed window. The narrow bar of lead that holds the *quarrels* together is known as a "came"—another example of a special and distinct use of a very common word, the past tense of *come*. *Quarrel*, in this use, is from Middle Latin *quadrellus*, the diminutive of Latin *quadrus* (square). *Came*, in this application, is a special use of *came* or *kame*, a term in physical geography meaning "ridge," especially one of detrital material left by a retreating ice sheet, from Middle English *camb* (comb). *Cames* are used in stained-glass windows as well as plain ones. One mustn't jump to conclusions about the meanings of English words: *quarrel*? *came*?

quasi (KWAY zye, -sye, KWAH zee, -see) *adj., adv., prefix*. As an adjective, *quasi* is the equivalent of "seeming (but real)," as in a *quasi revolutionary* (who

(who goes through the motions but really doesn't mean it). As an adverb, it means "seemingly (but not really)" and as such, is usually hyphenated as a prefix to an adjective, as in *quasi-authoritative*, *quasi-serious*, *quasi-historical*, like a "historical" novel that takes too many liberties. A *quasi-scientific* experiment is not the real thing; it pretends to be scientific, but there were no controls or checks providing a standard of comparison. *Quasi* is derived from the Latin *quam* (as) plus *si* (if): *quam si* became *quasi*, i.e., *as if* (but not actually). As to the use of the hyphen after *quasi*: treat it as a separate word before a noun (a *quasi alliance*, a *quasi authority*); use the hyphen when *quasi* is used with an adjective, adverb or verb: *quasi-authentic*, *quasi-willingly*; *quasi-believing*.

quiddity   (KWID ih tee) *n*. *Quiddity* has two remarkably distinct meanings. First, *quiddity* is the essence of a thing or person, the whatever-it-is that makes a thing or person what he, she, or it is. *Quid?*, in Latin, is *what?* and Middle Latin invented *quidditas* (quiddity; literally, "whatness"). The other meaning is "quibble," a nit-picking subtlety or nicety in argument. Shakespeare used it in the second sense in *Henry IV, Part 1* (Act I, Scene 2) in the scene where the Prince and Falstaff are having a boisterously nonsensical argument, and Falstaff says to Prince Henry: "How now, how now, mad wag! what, in thy quips and thy *quiddities?* what in a plague have I to do with a buff jerkin?" Again, in *Hamlet* (Act V, Scene 1), Hamlet, gazing at a skull (Yorick's, but Hamlet doesn't know that yet), says: "Why may not that be the skull of a lawyer? Where be his *quiddities* now . . . ?" But in *Hudibras*, the English poet Samuel Butler (1612-1680) used *quiddity* in the first sense, "whatness essence," whatever it is that differentiates a person or thing from all others:

> He knew
> Where entity and *quiddity*
> (The ghosts of defunct bodies) fly.

The English novelist Laurence Sterne (1713-1768) gave an example of *quiddity* without using the word: ". . . the *corregiescity* of Corregio." The English historian Thomas Carlyle (1795-1881), in *Frederick the Great*, quoted Sterne (without credit) but corrected his spelling: ". . . the *correggiosity* of Correggio." They were both referring to the *quiddity* of the Italian painter Antonio Allegri da Correggio (1494-1534), but they might as well have written of the Michelangelosity of Michelangelo or the Shakespeareosity of Shakespeare. Today, *quiddity*, in that sense, is a pet word of literary critics, who discuss the *quiddity*, for instance, of T.S. Eliot or John Updike, i.e., the special quality that makes Eliot Eliot and Updike Updike. In this sense, *quiddity* has a synonym: *haecceity* (hek SEE ih tee, heek-), denoting that which gives something its unique quality or characteristic. It is a "partial synonym," in that *quiddity* applies to persons as well as things, and *haecceity* appears to apply only to things. Its derivation is from Middle Latin *haecceitas* (literally, "thisness"), based on Latin *haecce*, a variant of *haec* (this—the feminine form of *hic*; feminine because it modifies the feminine noun *res*, thing, understood).

quidnunc (KWID nunk) *n*. A *quidnunc* is a gossip, a busybody, a nosy individual, a pretentious and over-eager collector and connoisseur of the latest tidbits of news. It comes from two Latin words: *quid nunc* (what now?). A *quidnunc* wants to know what's going on, and sometimes pretends to know it. John Lothrop Motley, the American historian and diplomat (1814-1877) wrote of "the idle stories of *quidnuncs*," and *Quidnunc* is the name of the hero of *The Upholsterer, or What News?* by the American playwright C.W. Murphy (d. 1931).

quincunx (KWING kungks, KWIN-) *n*. A *quincunx* is an arrangement of five objects, one at each corner of a square or rectangle and one in the center. The term is used mainly in landscaping, with reference to the arrangement of trees. The adjective is *quincuncial* (kwin KUN shul). *Quincunx* has an interesting derivation: *quinque*, Latin for "five" plus *uncia*, Latin for "twelfth." What have *five* and *twelfth* to do with the arrangement of trees, or anything else? Well, there was once a Roman coin called an "as," which originally consisted of a pound of copper (later reduced), and another Roman coin worth *five-twelfths* of an *as*, and that one was marked with a *quincunx* of spots, to indicate its value. Incidentally, *uncia* gave us *ounce* (one-twelfth of a pound) and *inch* (one-twelfth of a foot). The English writer Patrick Leigh Fermor (b. 1915), in *A Time of Gifts* (John Murray, London, 1977), made a dramatic use of *quincunx* in this passage: "Pruned to the bone, the dark vine-shoots stuck out of the snow in rows of skeleton fists which shrank to *quincunxes* of black commas along snow-covered contour-lines of the vineyards . . . "

quinquennial, see **lustrum**

quoin (koin, kwoin) *n*., *vb*. This little word has several uses, depending on context. In printing, a *quoin* is a wedge for locking type on a frame (called a "chase"). In architecture, it is an external angle of a wall or one of the stones forming the angle; a cornerstone (not necessarily the kind laid by governors and other celebrities), or a *voussoir* (vooh SWAR), a wedge-shaped stone forming part of an arch (derived, via French and Late Latin, from Latin *volutus*, past participle of *volvere*, to roll). Apart from these special uses, a *quoin* is any wedge-shaped piece of material used for a variety of purposes, like steadying a table in one of those restaurants where it's too dark to read the menu, keeping a door open, etc. To *quoin* is to wedge or secure or raise by wedging. *Quoin* is a variant of *coin* in the sense of "cornerstone," which is, via French *coin*, from Latin *cuncus* (wedge). *Cuncus* is the basis of the term *cuneiform*, as to which see **cuneal**, **cuneate**.

quondam (KWON dam) *adj*. *Quondam* means "former" or "sometime," describing something that used to be, or someone who once bore a certain relationship to a person, or a title to an office, that no longer exists. It was taken intact from the Latin, where it is an adverb meaning "formerly, once upon a time," although the Latin poets used it also in the senses of "some time in the future" and "at times." In English, *quondam* is not an adverb but an adjective that looks only at the past, pointing to something or someone that at one time had a certain role or character that now has ended, like a *quondam* dynasty or a *quondam* friend, associate, or partner. Shakespeare was fond of *quondam*. He used it twice in *Henry VI, Part 3*. In Act III, Scene 1, King Henry, in disguise, enters a chase (an unenclosed hunting-ground), where, unknown to him, two gamekeepers stand. He laments his fate. One of the keepers recognizes him and says: "This is the *quondam* king; let's seize upon him," and they finally arrest him. In Act III, Scene 2, the Earl of Warwick addresses King Henry's wife, Queen Margaret, as "our *quondam* queen." And in *Troilus and Cressida* (Act IV, Scene 5), Hector, addressing Menelaus, refers to Helen in these terms:

> Your *quondam* wife swears still by Venus' glove;
> She's well, but bade me not commend her to you.

quotidian   (kwoh TID ee un) *adj. Quotidian* means "daily," i.e, recurring every day, as in a *quotidian report*, and in that sense is synonymous with **diurnal** but only in the first meaning given under that entry, i.e. "daily," as opposed to "daytime" used attributively. By extension, *quotidian* has acquired the second meaning of "everyday" in the sense of "ordinary, commonplace," and in certain contexts, "trivial." In this extension, it follows its Latin antecedent *quotidianus* (daily), which acquired the meaning "common, ordinary." Things that go on day after day do become run-of-the-mill after a while. Variety is the spice, etc. The American poet Wallace Stevens (1879-1955), in *The Comedian as the Letter C*, wrote: ". . . The *quotidian* saps philosophers."

ralline, see **accipitrine**

rangiferine, see **accipitrine**

ranine, see **accipitrine**

rapscallion   (rap SKAL yun) *n.* This picturesque word means "rascal" or "rogue" or "scamp." It is based on *rascal*, which comes from Old French *rascaille* (rabble) and gave modern French *racaille* (rabble, riffraff, scum). In *The Adventures of Huckleberry Finn*, the American author Mark Twain (Samuel Langhorne Clemens, 1835-1910) tells us, "All kings is mostly *rapscallions*," a bird's-eye view of history, and rather a sweeping generalization. But don't let's get started on Richard III (1452-1485, king of England 1483-1485), who this author firmly believes was a good guy and whom he stoutly defends against the libels of the English statesman and writer Sir Thomas More (1478-1535 and only three years old when Richard died), the English chronicler Holinshed (died c. 1580—a firm follower of Sir Thomas More and a public relations man for Richard's foe and successor Henry VII (1457-1509), king of England 1485-1509, the first Tudor king), and William Shakespeare, who, after all, writing in the time of the Tudor Queen Elizabeth I, couldn't very well make Richard anything but a villain. Richard was *not a rapscallion*. Suggested reading on this disputed matter: *The Daughter of Time*, a most original piece of historical detection (first published by Peter Davies, London, 1951, by Penguin Books, Hammondsworth, 1954 and oft-reprinted by Penguin) by the Scottish writer and playwright Elizabeth MacKintosh under the pseudonym Josephine Tey (1896-1952).

raptorial (rap TOR ee ul) *adj.* A *raptorial* animal is a predator, one that preys upon other animals for its sustenance and that of its young. Eagles and hawks, for example, are *raptorial* birds; tigers and lions *raptorial* animals; almost all fish, reptiles, and insects are *raptorial. Raptorial* can apply as well to parts of the body adapted for seizing prey, like claws and teeth. Thus far, *raptorial* has not been used to describe those conglomerates that like to swallow defenseless corporations. It comes from Latin *raptor* (robber, plunderer, one who seizes), related to the verb *rapere* (to seize), *raptare* (**frequentative** of *rapere*), and *raptus* (tearing off, carrying off), from which we derive *rape*, a most unlovely crime.

ratiocinate (rash ee OS uh nate) *vb.* To *ratiocinate* (note the pronunciation of the first syllable) is to reason, and the process is *ratiocination* (rash ee os uh NAY shun). The Latin verb *ratiocinari* has a number of related meanings, all having to do with brainwork: to compute, consider, deliberate, infer, conclude, and it all goes back to *ratus*, the past participle of the verb *reri* (to think). The Latin noun *ratio* means "reckoning" and *accountant*, in Latin, is *ratiocinator*, which speaks well for the profession of accountancy. *Ratiocinatio* is Latin for "reasoning." It is only by discarding our biases and preconceptions that we can *ratiocinate*, and reach sane and *reason*able conclusions. Pure *ratiocination*, the exercise of the intellect alone, without interference from the emotions, is extremely difficult to achieve. The English novelist and satirist Samuel Butler (1612-1680), in his mock-heroic poem *Hudibras*—a venomous satire against the Puritans, represented by the "Presbyterian knight" Sir Hudibras——wrote:

> He was in logic a great critic,
> Profoundly skill'd in analytic.
> He could distinguish, and divide
> A hair 'twixt south and south-west side.
> On either which he would dispute,
> Confute, change hands, and still confute.
>
> He'd run in debt by disputation,
> And pay with *ratiocination*.

(This poem gave rise to the adjective *Hudibrastic* [hyooh duh BRAS tik], which came to describe anything written in a mock-heroic, sportively burlesque style.)

razzia   (RAZ ee uh) *n*. This is a word, not much heard these days, to denote a pillaging incursion or a plundering or slave-collecting raid of the sort we read about in the history books and romantic novels. *Razzia* also applies to a piratical takeover of a ship at sea. The term was used originally of the raids carried out by African Muslims, but would not be applicable to the October 1985 hijacking of the Italian cruise ship *Achille Lauro* by a small Palestinian force, because the four hijackers, though in cold blood they shot and killed an innocent crippled elderly gentleman as he sat in his wheelchair, were kind enough to refrain from plundering or slave-collecting. *Razzia*, via French and the Algerian Arabic word *ghaziah* or *gazia*, is from Arabic *gazwa*, related to the verb *gazw* (to make raids), the Arabic *ġ* being pronounced like the gutteral French *r*.

realpolitik   (ree AL paw lih teek) *n*. This is a word from the German, with the effect of "political realism, practical politics," international policy based on national interests and on material rather than moral considerations; a cynical term for the "might is right" school of international conduct that eschews any hint of idealism. The traditional policy of the "Drang nach Osten" (the thrust to the East), the age-old urge of German politicians to annex territories in the East, and *Lebensraum* (room for living), space for an expanding population, a Nazi slogan, have been German concepts and policies that have disturbed peace again and again. *Realpolitik* is only one of a series of words coined in Germany, alas.

rebarbative   (ree BAR buh tiv) *adj*. What is *rebarbative* is unattractive, annoying, irritating, distasteful, even repellent or downright repulsive. It comes, via French *rébarbatif* (stern, surly, grim, forbidding) from Old French *rébarber* (to be unattractive). The dictionaries all relate *rébarber* and *rebarbative* to French *barbe* (beard), based on Latin *barba*, but it is hard to see the connection, especially among the French who often wore beards long before they became as common as they are now in England and America; and in any case, beards can be attractive or unattractive, as the case may be. Whose beard are they talking about? Bluebeard's?

reboant   (REB oh unt) *adj*. Anything so described is resounding, reechoing, reverberating loudly. This is a poetical term, from Latin *reboans*, present participle of *reboare* (to echo, resound), based on prefix *re-*, indicating repetition, plus *boare* (to shout, roar, cry aloud; when describing places, to echo). The sound of a bass drum can be described as *reboant*. The voices of **spelunkers** shouting at one another in the far reaches of a huge cave are *reboant*.

rebus   (REE bus) *n*. A *rebus* is a riddle, wholly or partly hieroglyphical, an enigmatic representation of a word, phrase, or sentence by a series of pictures or symbols or a combination of both. A dot (*speck*) followed by pictures of a *tack* and a *yule* log and the letter *r* add up to *spectacular. I C U R Y Y 4* before a picture of a *hymn* book gives us "I see you are too wise for him." An English *rebus: If the B m t put: If it b.* means: "If the grate be empty, put coal on. If it be full, stop." Explanation (if needed): In British English, *great*, modifying a letter of the alphabet (now archaic in this sense), meant "capital, upper case," so that *B* was "great *b*"; and a period (punctuation ending a sentence) is usually called "full stop." *Rebus* is a form of Latin *res* (thing) and means "by means of things," i.e., represented by things rather than words.

recension　(rih SEN shun) *n. Recension* is the critical revision of a literary work based on close examination of both text and source material—the kind this author expected (and got) from his **diaskeuast** in the course of the writing of this book. *Recension* is derived from Latin *recensio* (reviewing), related to the verb *recensere* (to examine, review), based on prefix *re-* (again) plus *censere* (to assess, estimate). It is to be hoped that the *recension* of this manuscript will not result in too many changes and corrections.

redact　(rih DAKT) *vb.* To *redact* a piece of writing is to edit and revise it, work it into shape, put it into literary form suitable for publication. To *redact* a proclamation or a formal written statement is to frame it. *Redact* is from Latin *redactus*, past participle of the verb *redigere* (to bring back), based on *red-*, variant of *re-* before a vowel, plus *agere* (to drive). The editor is the *redactor* (rih DAK tur); the activity is *redaction* (rih DAK shun), and the adjective is *redactional* (rih DAK shun ul). *Redaction*, a vital step in the preparation of a writing for publication, can lead to serious disagreement between the *redactor* and an author who considers his every word sacred. In the case of writing that is too verbose, *redaction* can lead to *reduction*. Suffice it to say that there has been nothing short of peace and harmony between this author and his *redactrix*!

reify　(REE uh fye) *vb.* To *reify* an abstraction is to turn it into, or consider it as a concrete or material thing, to materialize it. *Space* is an abstract concept. It can be *reified* into a finite distance between two objects, and in that sense made concrete, or materialized. Time, too, can be *reified* from a concept to an objective, concrete thing, like the time between one event and another. *Reify*, and *reification* (ree if uh KAY shun), the act or result of *reifying*, are based upon the Latin noun *res* (thing) and its stem, *re-*. One can *reify* an endless number of abstract concepts, like *love* (think of Dante's love for Beatrice or Petrarch's for Laura), or hate (Macduff's for Macbeth, Lady Anne's for Richard III). One can *reify* the concept of communication into concrete systems such as speech, writing, the telephone, television, and all the other contemporary physical means of communicating information.

repine　(rih PINE) *vb.* To *repine* is to fret, complain, unhappily and nervously express discontent. The word is made up of the prefix *re-* (repeatedly) plus *pine* (to suffer and languish with yearning and longing, to waste away under emotional distress); via Old English *pinean* (to torment) and Latin *poena* (penalty, pain), from Greek *poine* (penalty). *Repine* may have been formed after the model of *repent*. In *Martin Chuzzlewit*, the English novelist Charles Dickens (1812-1870) has Mr. Pecksniff tenderly say: "Do not *repine*, my friends. Do not weep for me . . . " The American poet and essayist Ralph Waldo Emerson (1803-1882), in his poem *Sacrifice*, wrote:

> Though love *repine*, and reason chafe,
> There came a voice without reply—
> "'Tis man's perdition to be safe,
> When for the truth he ought to die."

restive (RES tiv) *adj*. A *restive* person is impatient and fidgety; he cannot easily bear control or restraint or delay, but always wants to get moving. A *restive* horse, on the other hand, stubbornly refuses to get moving, and keeps shifting sideways or backwards, jibbing and balking. Whether man or beast, *restive* indicates fidgeting and resistance to control; the person wants to get going, while the horse refuses to move. Fowler warns against the use of *restive* as a synonym of *restless*. "*Restive* implies resistance," says Fowler. The use of *restive* for *restless* would be an instance of **catachresis**. The derivation of *restive* is a complicated story. Originally it meant "at rest"; then, "obstinate"; then, "impatient," especially under restraint—the opposite of its original meaning. These things happen in language: *Egregious* originally meant "distinguished, noble, eminent, outstanding, out of the ordinary"; now, "glaring, flagrant," always pejorative, as in *an egregious blunder, an egregious liar. Restive's* predecessor is Middle English *restif* (stationary, or balking).

revanchism (rih VAN shiz um) *n. Revanche*, French for "revenge," has given rise to the noun *revanchism*, the policy of a nation seeking to regain territory lost to another nation, such as France's attitude and policy towards Alsace and Lorraine, lost to Prussia after the Franco-Prussian War of 1870-71. The adjective describing the policy is *revanchist* (rih VAN shist). The *revanchist* attitude of the Arab states as to territory lost to Israel after the Six Day War of 1967 has played a prominent part in causing the turmoil of the Middle East.

rhabdomancy (RAB duh man see) *n. Rhabdomancy* is another name for "dowsing," whether for water or metal ores, through the use of a forked rod. The source of the word is Late Greek *rhabdomanteia*, based on *rhabdos* (wand, rod) plus *manteia* (**divination**, prophecy). The rod in question is known as a "divining rod." This ancient form of divination, dowsing, or *rhabdomancy* was imported from Germany to Cornwall, England, for use in the Cornish mines, some time in the 16th century. People still discuss the question whether the use of *rhabdomancy* is an art, a skill, a gift, or a fake. If you are interested in the possibility of discovering oil under your lawn, there are available a number of modern scientific techniques.

rhinocerine, see **accipitrine**

rhotacism   (ROH tuh siz um) *n. Rho* is the equivalent of our letter *r* in the Greek alphabet. The Greeks had a word for just about everything, and came up with the verb *rhotakizein* (to make excessive use of the letter *rho*). Why the need for such a highly specialized word? Obviously, because the *r* sound was often unduly substituted for some other sound. *Rhotacism*, from Greek *rhotakismos* via Latin *rhotacismus*, based on that peculiar Greek verb, is the excessive use or misuse or mispronunciation of the letter *r*. The converse, i.e., the substitution of some other sound for that of *r*, is known as *pararhotacism*. In philology, the tendency to change *s* or *z* to *r*, especially between vowels, is a common form of *rhotacism*, as in the case of *lose* becoming *-lorn* in the word *forlorn*, and the genitive of the Sanskrit word *janasas* (race, people) taking the form *generis* in Latin. A common form of *rhotacism* in the way of mispronunciation or misarticulation is the burring sound of *r* in French speech and that of many inhabitants of Northumberland, a county in the northeast of England. In speaking English, the Japanese commonly practice *rhotacism* by substituting the sound of *r* for that of *l*, while the Chinese indulge in *pararhotacism* by substituting the sound of *l* for that of *r*. The verb is *rhotacise* (ROH tuh size). Talk about minding your *p*'s and *q*'s!

rodomontade   (rod uh mon TADE, -tad, roe duh-, -mun-) *n., adj., vb.* This interesting word, which can be used as an adjective (boastful) or a verb (boast, brag, talk big) is, however, almost always found as a noun, denoting extravagant boasting, vainglorious bragging, blustery self-glorification. The Italian fascist leader Benito Mussolini (1883-1945), whom the author saw (1926) in military trappings, addressing the multitudes from the balcony of the Palazzo Chigi in Rome, with jutting jaw and flailing arms, was the embodiment of *rodomontade*. His pal of later days, Adolf Hitler (1889-1945), wasn't bad at *rodomontade* either. That year, 1945, seems to have been a bad one for these two leading exponents of *rodomontade* following in the footsteps of Rodomonte, the vainglorious, bragging king of Algiers, who figured in the unfinished epic poem *Orlando Innamorato* by the Italian poet Matteo Maria Boiardo (1434-1494) and its sequel *Orlando Furioso* by his successor Ludovico Ariosto (1474-1553). Both works were based on Roland, the great French hero of medieval legend celebrated in the 11th century *Chanson de Roland*. The name *Orlando* is the Italian equivalent of *Roland*, but both Italian poets took advantage of their poetic license to transform Roland beyond recognition. What has survived of the *Chanson* and both *Orlandos* to become part of our language is *rodomontade*, nothing less than old Rodomonte with the *e* cut off and the suffix *-ade* stuck on, as often happens to nouns denoting action, like *fusillade*, *renegade*, *promenade* and *cannonade*. Cf. **braggadocio**, **fanfaronade**, **gasconade**, **thrasonical**. Next time you run into an irritating braggart, just point your finger and cry: "High time to stop your *rodomontade*, your *gasconade*, your *braggadocio*, your *fanfaronade*, you *thrasonical* churl!"

roorback (ROOR bak) *n.* A *roorback* is a smear, a defamatory lie published as a political "dirty trick" à la Nixon campaign. When James K. Polk (1795-1849, 11th president of the United States) was running for that office, a spurious and damaging article was published in 1844 purporting to be an extract from *Roorback's Tour through the Western and Southern States in 1836.* Baron von Roorback was a pretended traveler whose alleged notes included an account of an incident damaging to Polk's character. From this the word *roorback* (lower case *r*), sometimes *roorbach*, came to signify any damaging falsehood circulated for political effect.

Roscian (ROSH ee un) *n., adj.* As an adjective, *Roscian* may be used to describe anything having to do with actors or acting, but its special use is to describe a highly talented actor or performance. One can safely say of Laurence Olivier (b. 1907) that he is an actor of *Roscian* proportions, or that he always gives a *Roscian* performance. As a noun, a *Roscian* is an actor of uncommon, outstanding ability. John Gielgud (b. 1904) can be described as a *Roscian.* This word is derived from the name of the actor Roscius (126-62 B.C.), the sensation of the Roman stage. Shakespeare refers to him in *Henry VI, Part 3,* when (Act V, Scene 6) King Henry says to Gloucester, who is about to kill him, "What scene of death hath Roscius now to act?" (How am I to die?), and again, in *Hamlet* (Act II, Scene 2), when Hamlet, mocking the long-winded Polonius, who is about to announce the arrival of the players (which is old news to Hamlet) and make a long, long story of it, puts words into Polonius's mouth and starts to recite: "When Roscius was an actor in Rome . . . " It was the great fame of Roscius that gave us this interesting word *Roscian.*

rubric (ROOH brik) *n.* A *rubric* is a heading in a book or manuscript, a title or other distinguishing caption at the beginning of a chapter, section, etc. The *rubric* is written or printed in red or in special type that sets it apart from the general text. In older books and manuscripts it was customary for the *rubric* to be in red; hence its name, from the Latin *rubrica* (red earth, red ochre), based on *ruber* (red), from whose kindred adjective *rubeus* we get *ruby.* The adjective *rubrical* (ROOH brik ul) means "reddish" or "marked with red." To *rubricate* (ROOH bruh kate) something is to mark or color it with red. In the translation by the English poet and painter Dante Gabriel Rossetti (1828-1882), the opening words of *La Vita Nuova* (The New Life), an early work in prose and poetry of the great Italian poet Dante Alighieri (1265-1321), are these: "In that part of the book of my memory before which is little that can be read, there is a *rubric*, saying, 'Incipit Vita Nuova [The New Life Begins].'" Dante goes on to say, in the translation of Professor Mark Musa (Indiana University Press, Bloomington, Indiana, 1973): "It is my intention to copy into this little book the words I find written under that *heading*—if not all of them, at least the essence of their meaning."

rubrical, see **rubric**

rubricate, see **rubric**

rucervine, see **accipitrine**

ruddle (RUD ul) *n.*, *vb.* *Ruddle* is red ochre, used principally in sheep-marking for purposes of identification of the owner, a much less painful process than cow-branding. To *ruddle* is to mark sheep in that way. *Ruddle* has two variants, *raddle* and *reddle*. The latter is used as a pejorative for rouge and its application. *Raddled* is slang for the description of a face treated with an excess of makeup.

ruminant (ROOH mu nunt) *n.*, *adj.* *Ruminant*, as a noun, embraces all even-toed hoofed animals, comprising cloven-hoofed cud-chewing quadrupeds, including cattle, deer, camels, etc. As an adjective, *ruminant* means, literally, "cud-chewing," and figuratively, "meditative, contemplative." The related verb, to *ruminate*, means to "chew the cud"; figuratively, to reflect, meditate, ponder, muse. *Ruminant* is from Latin *ruminans*, present participle of *ruminare* (to chew over, chew the cud), and *ruminate* is from *ruminatus*, the past participle of that verb. All these words go back to Latin *rumen* (throat, gullet), which is English for the first of the two stomachs of a *ruminating* animal. The English novelist Charles Dickens (1812-1870), in *Pickwick Papers*, has Mr. Pickwick say: "I am *ruminating* on the strange mutability of human affairs." In Shakespeare's *Othello* (Act III, Scene 3), Othello says to Iago: "... Speak to me as to thy thinkings,/As thou dost *ruminate* ..." The German philosopher Friedrich Nietzsche (1844-1900) gave this advice in *Thus Spake Zarathustra*: "We ought to learn from the kine [cattle] one thing: *ruminating*." He was right.

rupicaprine, see **accipitrine**

rusticate (RUS tuh kate) *vb.* To *rusticate* is to live in the countryside or take a trip to the country. To *rusticate* someone is to send him to the country. To *rusticate* something is to give it a rustic finish, like *rusticating* the surface of a piece of furniture to make it look countryish, or *rusticating* a wall to produce a rural effect. *Rusticate* has a special meaning in Britain: to *rusticate* a university student is to suspend him as punishment for an offense; not to *expel* him, which, in British English, is to *send him down*. *Rustic*, *rusticity*, *rural*, etc., are all based on Latin *rus* (country); *rusticate* is from Latin *rusticatus*, past participle of *rusticari* (to live in the countryside).

ruth (roohth) *n.* Where do you suppose the common adjective *ruthless* comes from? Answer: from the uncommon noun *ruth*, meaning "pity, compassion," or "sorrow, grief"; from Middle English *ruthe*. Our verb and noun *rue* is from the related Middle English verb *ruen*. It often happens, as in the case of *ruth* and *ruthless*, that the negative is used far more commonly than the positive, and often has a positive effect. To describe the Macbeths as *ruthless* is to impart a quite positive impression. *Impeccable conduct* or *dress* presents a positive image; and how often have you run across *peccable*? *Impervious/pervious*: If you ran into the rarely used *pervious*, you might think it was a misprint for *previous*.

sabelline, see **accipitrine**

sacerdotal   (sas ur DOTE ul) *adj. Sacerdotal* means "priestly" and applies to anything having to do with priests and priesthood. *Sacerdotalism* (sas ur DOTE u liz um) is the spirit of the priesthood, devotion to priestly matters, priestcraft, and in context, the claim of excessive, even supernatural authority for the priesthood. *Sacerdotal* is from Latin *sacerdotalis*, based on *sacerdos* (priest), formed of *sacer* (sacred) plus *dare* (to give). When asked, in a test at school, "What is rabies, and what can be done about it?" a young student replied, "Rabies is Jewish priests and nothing can be done about it."

salamandrine, see **accipitrine**

salmagundi   (sal muh GUN dee) *n*. This peculiar word describes, in its narrow sense, a dish, usually served as a salad, consisting of a mixture of chopped cooked meat, onions, hard-boiled eggs, anchovies, pickled vegetables, radishes, olives, watercress, and other ingredients, with salad dressing, sometimes arranged in rows to form a color pattern. The term, however, is sometimes applied to a much simpler concoction: a meat and vegetable stew. It can also be spelt with a final -*y* instead of an -*i. Salmagundi* has a much wider figurative application, as a term denoting any heterogeneous mixture or miscellany, and in this sense it is a synonym for **gallimaufry** or *olio* or *hodge-podge*, a medley, a potpourri, a mishmash, a farrago. A painting, for instance, or any work of art, for that matter, revealing a mixture of many influences may be referred to as a *salmagundi* or pastiche. There is a jocular saying that a camel is a horse designed by a committee. That would make the poor beast a sort of *salmagundi* of an animal—a little of this and a little of that. Any creation in which too many cooks have had a hand may sadly turn out to be a *salmagundi*. The word is derived from the French noun *salmigondis*, said to be based, in turn, on the Italian for "pickled salami," known as *salami conditi*. Though it has nothing to do with the old nursery rhyme, the sound of *salmagundi* brings to mind the sad tale of

> Solomon Grundy
> Born on a Monday
> Christened on Tuesday

Married on Wednesday
Took ill on Thursday
Worse on Friday
Died on Saturday
Buried on Sunday
This is the end
of Solomon Grundy

and the end of *salmagundi*.

sanguinary (SANG gwuh nair ee) *adj. Sanguis* is Latin for "blood" and is the basis of several Latin adjectives having to do with *blood, bloodiness, bloodstained* and *bloodthirstiness*. We, too, have a number of derivatives having to do with *blood: sanguinary*, meaning "bloodthirsty, delighting in bloodshed or slaughter," or "characterized by bloodshed"; *sanguineous* (san GWIN ee us) or *sanguinous* (SANG gwuh nus), pertaining to blood, blood-colored, involving bloodshed; *sanguinolent* (sang GWIN uh lunt), pertaining to blood, tinged with blood; and finally *sanguine* (SANG gwin)—of all things, after this bloody mess, cheerful, hopeful, confident, disposed to thinking that all is going to go well. This nonconforming meaning arose from the belief, in old physiology, that there were four basic body fluids, known as "humors," blood, phlegm, black bile, and yellow bile or choler (see **choleric**), which determined, by their relative proportion, one's mental as well as physical make-up, and if blood predominated, that person was of cheerful disposition. This belief gave rise to the terms *sanguine, phlegmatic, melancholic*, and *choleric* and the theory that a good balance made for "good humor" and an imbalance for "ill humor." All this leads to the conclusion that one should not confuse *sanguinary* with *sanguine*, even though people out for bloodshed can, one supposes, be cheerful, hopeful, and confident about their mission and thus be *sanguinary* and *sanguine* at the same time. (See also **consanguinity**).

sanguineous, **sanguinous**, see **sanguinary**

sanguinolent, see **sanguinary**

sapid (SAP id) *adj. Sapid* describes anything having flavor, the implication being that it is agreeable flavor, palatable and appetizing. Applied to things other than food, like conversation, writing, etc., *sapid* takes on the flavor of "interesting," even "exhilarating." *Sapid* is, of course, the opposite of *insipid*, i.e., *not sapid. Sapid* is from Latin *sapidus* (flavored); *insipid* from Latin *in-sipidus*. The change from the *a* of *sapid* to the *i* of *-sipid* in *insipid* is an instance of **ablaut** in related words—in this case, antonyms.

saprogenic (sap roh JEN ik) *adj*. This is a word with unpleasant associations. *Sapro-* is the combining form of Greek *sapros* (rotten, putrid); *-genic* is an adjectival suffix meaning "producing," from the root of the Greek verb *gignesthai* (to produce). *Saprogenic*, then, means, "producing decay or putrefaction," as caused, for example, by certain bacteria; or "produced from putrefaction," like organisms growing on decaying matter, like maggots thriving on rotting flesh. Another form of *saprogenic* is *saprogenous* (suh PROJ uh nus). Other *sapro-* words are *saprophagous* (suh PROF uh gus), a biological term for a plant or animal feeding on dead or rotting animal matter, with suffix *-phagous* based on the Greek verb *phagein* (to eat, devour); *saprophyte* (SAP ruh fite), an organism, like certain bacteria and fungi, that lives on dead plant or animal matter, with suffix *-phyte* from Greek *phyton* (plant). Ugh!

saprophagous, see **saprogenic**

saprophyte, see **saprogenic**

sarcophagus   (sar KOF uh gus) *n.* A *sarcophagus* is a stone coffin, often adorned with sculpture and inscriptions. The ancient Greeks called limestone *lithos sarkophagos*: *lithos* (stone), *sarkophagos* (flesh-eating) based on prefix *sarko-*, combining form of *sarx* (flesh), plus suffix *-phagos* (eating), combining form of *phagein* (to eat, devour). *Lithos sarkophagos* meant "corrosive limestone," which was used to build coffins that would dissolve corpses. Later the *lithos* was dropped, and the *sarkophagos* was retained to mean "stone coffin" even after the Greeks began to use ordinary non-corrosive stone for their coffins. After all this gruesome stuff, let us get on to something a little less eerie—*subreption*. The use of *sarkophagos* is an example of *subreption*, a semantic change or shift occurring when a word continues in use though what it signifies undergoes change. *Subreption* denotes, literally, the obtaining of something by surprise, stealth, or misrepresentation. It comes from Latin *subreptio* (purloining), based on the verb *subrepere* (to crawl up from below), which has the variant *surrepere* and is related to the adjective *subrepticius*, variant *surrepticius*, from which we get *surrepticious*. Here are some examples of *subreption*: *pen* is derived from *penna* (feather) and was used originally when pens were made of quills. The name stuck even after the object underwent change. A *horn* was originally made of an animal's horn. A drinking *straw* was originally made of a straw. The word *volume* originated from the fact that, once, reading matter was in the form of a scroll or roll of papyrus or parchment, and the *vol-* of volume is related to *revolve*.

Sassenach, see **ilk**

satyriasis   (say tuh RYE uh sis) *n.* A *satyr* (SAY tur, SAT ur), in classical mythology, was a forest deity, lustful and riotous, an attendant on the god Bacchus, the god of wine (the Roman counterpart of Greek Dionysus). Satyrs were half man, half goat. *Satyr* has acquired the figurative meaning of "lecher," and so has *goat*, in slang usage. Hamlet didn't think much of satyrs. In the famous soliloquy "O! that this too too solid flesh would melt . . . " (Shakespeare's *Hamlet*, Act I, Scene 2), in his contempt of King Claudius, he cries that his father, compared with Claudius, " . . . was Hyperion to a satyr . . . " (Hyperion was a Titan, later identified with Apollo; his name was an epithet of the Sun god himself.) It will come as no surprise, then, that *satyriasis*, taken intact from the Greek, is the name for pathological uncontrollable lust among males. *Satyromania* (say tuh roh MAY nee uh) is a synonym of *satyriasis*.

satyromania, see **satyriasis**

saveloy (SAV uh loy) *n*. A *saveloy* is a highly seasoned, cooked, and dried sausage, originally containing pig's brains. The name comes, via French *cervelas* and Italian *cervellata* (a Milanese variety), based on *cervello* (brain), from Latin *cerebellum*, diminutive of *cerebrum* (brain). In the *Pickwick Papers* of the English novelist Charles Dickens (1812-1870), we read of "Mr. Solomon Pell . . . regaling himself . . . with a cold collation of an Abernethy biscuit [a hard biscuit flavored with caraway seeds, probably originated by John Abernethy, an English surgeon who died in 1831] and a *saveloy*." And in *Life and Labour*, by an English writer named Smiles—the book came out in 1887—we discover that "Sawyer, the gastronomist [see **gastronome**] . . . would stop at a stall in the Haymarket [a street in London] and luxuriate in eating a penny *saveloy*." As to the present status of the *saveloy*, a search through a large number of cookbooks in various languages has failed to produce any information. This must now be an obsolete delicacy.

sc. (no pronunciation given—used only in writing). *Sc.* is the abbreviation of Latin *scilicet*, a contraction of *scire licet* (it is permitted to know), an explanatory word meaning "namely." *Scilicet* is practically never used in full. If spoken, it is pronounced *SIL ih set*. *Sc.* is used to clarify, as in *I saw him (sc, the accused) running down the alley*, or *I had heard the opera (sc. Cosi Fan Tutte) in Milan*. Another use is to introduce a word to replace one already used, as in *I could (sc. couldn't) care less*, or *I couldn't of (sc. have) done that without your help*. In short, *sc.* explains an ambiguous word or introduces a word to be supplied, e.g., to establish the sense of a word used incorrectly.

scaphocephalic (skaf oh sih FAL ik) *adj*. A *scaphocephalic* person is one with a boat-shaped head. The unfortunate owner of this undesirable feature might also be described as *scaphocephalous* (skaf oh SEF uh lus), his head as a *scaphocephalus* (same pronunciation), and his condition as *scaphocephaly* (skaf oh SEF uh lee). These words are from Greek *skaphe* (boat) plus *kephale* (head). *Scaphocephalic* persons are rare, and if you come across one, don't stare, just mutter "scaphocephalic" to yourself, quietly.

scatology (skuh TOL uh jee) *n*. *Scatology* is obscenity, generally understood to be of the kind associated with aspects of excrement and obsessive interest in it. *Scatological* (skat uh LOJ uh kul) humor is based on some reference to excrement—"bathroom humor," as it were. *Scatological* language is the type preoccupied with excrement, but *scatology* has, in context, a more dignified meaning: the study of fossil excrement, also known as *coprology* (kah PROL uh jee). *Scatology* is derived from the Greek *skato-*, the combining form of *skor* (dung), plus the familiar suffix *-logy*, from Greek *-logia* used in the name of sciences, as in *geology*, *philology*, etc. *Coprology* comes from the Greek *kopro-*, the combining form of *kopros* (dung), a synonym of *skor*, plus the suffix *-logia*. *Coprology*, like *scatology*, can mean "obscenity" generally, but in particular the type preoccupied with excrement. *Scatological* sometimes drops the *-al* and is met with much more often than *coprologic(al)*. Whichever of these words is used, this type of humor is a consummation devoutly to be ditched.

sciamachy (sye AM uh kee, skye-) *n.* Based on the Greek nouns *skia* (shadow) and *mache* (battle), the Greeks formed *skiamachia* from which we took *sciamachy*, fighting with a shadow, a futile combat with an imaginary foe. Shadow-boxing, against an imaginary opponent in training for the ring, is a specialized form of *sciamachy*, a label which exponents of the art would be unlikely to recognize. When Don Quixote de la Mancha, in the novel by the Spanish writer Cervantes (1547-1616), tilted at windmills, he was engaging in *sciamachy*. His famous fight has become part of the language: To *tilt at windmills* is to contend with an imaginary enemy, or imagined injustices or wrongs. Paranoids, in mental conflict with the imagined hostility of others, are involved in involuntary *sciamachy* of still another sort.

sciolism, see **sciosophy**

sciosophy (sye OS uh fee) *n.* This term covers any field claiming to constitute knowledge, but without basis in proven fact. Astrology and numerology are prime examples of *sciosophy*, a word formed of two Greek words: *skia* (shadow) and *sophia* (wisdom)—in other words, "shadow-wisdom," i.e., unsubstantiated theory, hypothesis, supposition, and guess-work, posing as knowledge, as opposed to scientifically ascertained fact. It is different in both meaning and derivation from another "scio-" word: *sciolism* (SYE uh liz um), which is pretension to knowledge, and is derived via Late Latin *sciolus* (one with only a smattering of knowledge), from Latin *sciolus*, a diminutive of *scius* (knowing), based on the verb *scire* (to know). A *sciolist* (SYE uh list) is a pretender to knowledge or science; and *sciolistic* (sy uh LIS tik) and *sciolus* (SYE uh lus) describe such pretension. Palmists, phrenologists and readers of tea-leaves are all *sciolists*.

sciurine, see **accipitrine**

scot (skot) *n.* A *scot*, in olden times, was a charge, a fee, a payment, or a tax assessment. That explains why we say *scot-free*. (He got off *scot-free*, i.e., without penalty or other harm, or I got it *scot-free*, i.e., for nothing, without having to pay anything.) *Scot* is from Old Norse *skot* (contribution). There was also a Saxon coin called *sceat*, which gave rise to the term *church-scot*, a contribution in grain or poultry paid to support parish priests in those days. People who didn't chip in went *scot-free*, the cheapskates. See Falstaff's pun on *scot* mentioned under **termagant**.

scumble   (SKUM bul) *n.*, *vb.* To *scumble*, in painting or drawing, is to soften the brilliance of the finish by overlaying it with a thin coat of opaque or semiopaque color, applied with an almost dry brush. In the case of a drawing, this effect can be obtained by rubbing the surface lightly with a stump or a finger. As a noun, *scumble* is the act of scumbling, or its result, the softened effect thus produced. This technique is called *scumbling*. The word is believed to be a **frequentative** of the verb *scum* in the sense of to "form scum."

secern   (sih SURN) *vb.* To *secern* is to discriminate, separate in thought, distinguish, discern; from Latin *secernere* (literally, to sever, divide, separate), based on prefix *se-* (apart) plus *cernere* (to sift). The Roman poet Horace (65-8 B.C.) used *secernere* in the sense of "distinguishing" the just from the unjust, and a flatterer from a true friend. *Secernere* is synonymous with *discernere*, which gave us *discern*, one of the meanings of *secern*.

semiology   (see mye OL uh jee) *n.* Also *semeiology* (pronounced the same way), which, with the second *e*, is closer to its Greek source, *semeion* (sign), with the ubiquitous suffix *-logy*, from Greek *logos* (word, discourse, thought). *Semiology* is the science of signs and symbols or sign language itself. *Semiotic* (see mee OT ik, -mye-, sem ee-, sem eye-), *adj.*, means "relating to signs," and *semiotics* (treated as a singular noun, like *economics* or *politics*) is the theory of signs and symbols, which includes (and is not to be confused with) semantics (sih MAN tiks), the study of meaning, as well as pragmatics and syntactics—all quite complex and unnecessary to go into here. This is fairly technical stuff, but if you run into these words, don't think that the *semi-* part has anything to do with the prefix *semi-*, meaning "half," as in *semiannual*, *semicircle*, etc. Perhaps the spelling *semeiology* is preferable, because it would avoid any such misconception. And you will run into *semiology* and related words if you read the works of the English novelist Malcolm Bradbury (b. 1932). In *The History Man* (Specker & Warburg, London, 1975), we read: "The route to the children's school [daddy is driving them from home in the morning] is a track of familiar lanes, arrows and pointers, lines and halts, a routed *semiology*." And in *Rates of Exchange* (Secker & Warburg, London, 1983): "Some *semiotician* [Bradbury's concoction, but of obvious meaning; the scene is an airport terminal] has designed a system of wordless signs—arrows through squares, crosses in circles, ladders in oblongs—to guide bemused strangers through the labyrinth . . . " This lovely writing should give you a clear idea of the meaning of *semiology* and *semiotics*.

semiotic, see **semiology**

sempiternal   (sem pih TUR nul) *adj*. This is a literary term for "eternal, everlasting, imperishable," and is from Latin *sempiternus*, based on *semper* (always) plus *eternus* (eternal). It would seem that *eternal* should suffice and that *sempiternal* is tautological. How can something be "occasionally eternal"? "To gild refined gold, to paint the lily," says the Earl of Salisbury (*King John*, Act IV, Scene 2), " . . . Is wasteful and ridiculous excess." (Usually misquoted " . . . to gild the lily . . . ") The same may be said of *reiterate* (to "rerepeat," if you take your etymology seriously), and *sempiternal* is a clear case of painting the lily—too much of a muchness.

senescent, see **juvenescence**

seraglio, see **imbroglio**

seraph   (SER uf) *n*. We read in Isaiah 6:1-2 " . . . I saw . . . the Lord sitting upon a throne . . . Above it stood the *seraphims*: each one had six wings . . . " According to the *Heavenly Hierarchy* (*De Hierarchia Celesti*) popularized in the fifth century, these *seraphim* were superior angels, the highest of the nine choirs or orders. *Seraphim* is a Hebrew word (-im is a masculine plural ending) from which, by back formation, *seraph*, the singular form, developed. The form *seraphims* in the King James version has been corrected in the New English Bible with the dropping of the -s, *seraphim*, as is, being already plural. A *seraph* has three pairs of wings, one more than mere *cherubim*. In Isaiah's vision, as to each *seraph*: " . . . with twain he covered his face, and with twain he covered his feet, and with twain he did fly." The adjective *seraphic* (suh RAF ik) can be applied not only to *seraphs* but also, figuratively, to mortals of angelic or sublime character, those pure in heart. The English poet Thomas Gray (1716-1771), in *The Progress of Poesy*, praised John Milton (1608-1674) as one " . . . that rode sublime/Upon the *seraph*-wings of ecstasy." In the following century, the English novelist and poet George Meredith (1828-1909), in his poem *The Lark Ascending*, described the music of that bird celebrated in literature as "The song *seraphically* free/Of taint of personality."

seriatim   (seer ee AY tim, ser-) *adv., adj*. This is a word taken intact from Middle Latin, based on Latin *series* (row, chain, series), related to the verb *serere* (to connect, link). *Seriatim* means "point by point, taking up one subject or point after another in order." If you receive a letter covering a number of subjects, or hear an opponent's argument involving a series of points, you will do well to take them up *seriatim*, i.e., in the order in which they were served up. *Seriatim* can be used as an adjective (e.g., a *seriatim* listing, a *seriatim* response), but is most commonly used as an adverb, with verbs like *answer*, *consider, discuss, examine, look into, respond to*. The pattern of *seriatim* follows that of Middle Latin *litteratim* (letter by letter, i.e., literally), based on *littera* (letter of the alphabet).

serpentine, see **accipitrine**

sesquipedalian (ses kwih pih DAY lee un, -DAYL yun) *adj. Sesquipedalian* words are very long words. *Sesquipedalian* means, literally, "a foot and a half long." Julius Caesar (100-44 B.C.), in his *Gallic Wars*, wrote of *sesquipedalian* beams. The Roman poet Horace (65-8 B.C.) used this lovely adjective ironically when he wrote of *sesquipedalian words*, and another Roman poet, Catullus (c. 84-c. 54 B.C.) used it the same way, writing of *sesquipedalian teeth*. This adjective is applied ironically to pedantic words of inordinate length, like some of the entries in this book: e.g., **floccinaucinihilipilification**—a preposterous bit of *sesquipedalianism. Sesqui* is a Latin adverb meaning "half as much again"; *pedalis* (based on *ped*, the stem of *pes*, foot) means "a foot long"; hence *sesquipedalis* (a foot and a half long), and all perfectly logical. *Antidisestablishmentarianism* is often cited as a *sesquipedalian* word. (It means "opposition to a state's withdrawal of recognition or support of an established church," with special reference to the Anglican church in 19th-century England.) *Disarcivescovocostantinopolizzarsi* is a *sesquipedalian* Italian word meaning "to cease being the Archbishop of Constantinople," a word that you won't run into very often unless you do a lot of reading about ecclesiastical matters in that part of the world that happened before they changed the name of the city to *Istanbul*. The German language, of course, is full of *sesquipedalian* words because of the German habit of endless tacking on and making one word when other languages would use a phrase. Thus, *Feuerversicherungsgesellschaftspräsident* means "president of a fire insurance company"—and so on and so on. *Sesquipedalian* is itself a *sesquipedalian* word. In a learned article entitled "Learned Length and Thund'ring Sound: A Word-Lover's Panegyric" in Volume X, No. 3, of *Verbatim, The Language Quarterly*, Byran A. Garner invented a lovely *sesquipedalian* word: *sesquipedalophobia* ("hatred or fear of big words").

shallop (SHAL up) *n.* A *shallop* was a fore-and-aft rigged vessel, used in the 17th and 18th centuries for sailing in shallow waters. The term is now applied to any dinghy or small or light boat, used chiefly on rivers, propelled by oars or sails. *Shallop* comes from French *chaloupe* (launch), taken from German *Schaluppe*, archaic forerunner of *Schlup*, from which, together with Dutch *sloep*, we got *sloop*.

shivaree (shiv uh REE) *n.; vb.* This word has a number of variant forms and pronunciations: *charivari* and *charivaree* (shuh riv uh REE, sha ruh VAR ee), *chivari* and *chivaree* (shiv uh REE). *Charivari* was taken from the French (where the verb is *charivariser*), which got it from the Late Latin *caribaria* (headache); that came from the Greek *karebaria*, based on *kare* (head) plus *baria* (heaviness). However you spell or pronounce it, a *shivari* or *charivari* is a din or uproar, a cacophonous mock serenade produced by banging kettles, pans, trays, with the accompaniment of other noisemakers and hissing and shouting, for the purpose of expressing disapproval. The connection between its meaning and its derivation becomes abundantly clear. Originally, *charivari* was a common practice at weddings in medieval France, a bit of fun in the way of a noisy serenade to the newlyweds, but as time went on, the practice was continued only as an expression of derision and disapproval at unpopular weddings, and eventually, as a means of expressing ill will toward any unpopular person. Yet, according to Virginia writer Earl Hamner, Jr. (b. 1923), author of *Spencer's Mountain* and creator of the television series *The Waltons, shivarees*, as late as 50 years ago, were still a time-honored way to treat newlyweds in the rural Shenandoah. Another name for *shivaree* is *cat's concert. Charivari* was adopted as the name of a Paris satirical journal in 1832, and later, *The London Charivari* was taken as a subtitle for the English satirical weekly magazine *Punch*. As a verb, to *shivaree* is to engage in producing one.

sibyl (SIB il) *n.* A *sibyl* (often misspelt *Sybil*, as a girl's given name) is a fortune-teller, a prophetess, a medium, sometimes a witch. It was the name (*Sibylla* in Greek, *Sibilla* in Latin) given in ancient times to a number of women in various parts of the world who were thought to be qualified to make prophecies and utter oracles under the guidance of a god and pursuant to divine inspiration. The adjective *sibyllene* (SIB uh leen, -line, -lin), from Latin Sibyllinus, means "oracular, prophetic." The political and economic pundits of the day are much given to making *sibylline* utterances for our guidance, but where are the customer's yachts? The *Sibylline Books* were a collection of oracular pronouncements owned by the ancient Roman state and were consulted by magistrates, and in emergencies and times of disaster by the Roman Senate. When a prediction is characterized as *sibylline*, there is a strong implication that the utterance is considered cryptic and ambiguous, like those of the Delphic Oracle.

sic (sik, unless you prefer the Latin pronunciation, seek) *adv. Sic* has been taken over from Latin, where it means "thus," "so," "in this manner." It is found in two famous sentences: *Sic transit gloria mundi* ("Thus passes away the glory of the world." First written by Thomas à Kempis, 1380-1471, in *Imitation of Christ*, this sentence is included in the ceremony of the crowning of the pope.) and *Sic semper tyrannis!* ("Thus always to tyrants!" i.e., this is always the fate of tyrants. This anonymous Latin saying was adopted by John Wilkes Booth (1838-1865) after shooting Abraham Lincoln on April 14, 1865). However, used by itself in parentheses after a quoted word or passage, it indicates that the word or passage is being quoted (e.g., by a reviewer, or in an essay) exactly as it appeared in the original, where it was incorrectly used or spelt. *Sic*, thus used, calls attention to the error in the original and makes it clear that it is not the quoter's mistake. In short, *sic* means "Thus in the original; I found it this way, and am leaving it exactly as I found it, though I know it is incorrect. Don't blame it on me!" One receives a note reading: "You wernt in I'll try again tomorow" and wants to quote it in a letter to a friend. One writes, "I got a note from Jennie reading: 'You wernt (*sic*) in (no punctuation) I'll try again tomorow (*sic*).'" Thus one calls attention to the errors and makes sure that they are not attributed to him. Sometimes the phrase *sic passim* is used. *Passim* (PAS im) is Latin for "here and there, in various places." *Sic passim*, inserted in parentheses, means "Thus throughout the original," to indicate that the error in the original occurs repeatedly in the work referred to. If a student spelt James Joyce *James Joyse* repeatedly in an essay, a teacher quoting a passage in which the misspelling occurred would (or should) write "(sic passim)" after the error. The language quarterly VERBATIM, published by the eminent American lexicographer Laurence Urdang (b. 1918) of Old Lyme, Connecticut, and Aylesbury, Buckinghamshire, England, has a department listing errors in spelling, usage, grammar, etc., discovered in advertisements, public notices, etc., and sent in by readers. Mr. Urdang, a scholar much given to puns, heads the column "Sic! Sic! Sic!"

simulacrum   (sim yuh LAY krum) *n*. This word, in Latin, means "exact image, effigy, representation," or, figuratively, a "semblance, imitation, counterfeit, illusion, phantasm," depending on the context. Its principal use in English is to denote a superficial likeness or semblance, as might be expected from its relation to the Latin verb *simulare* (to imitate, pretend, counterfeit), from whose past participle, *simulatus*, we got *simulate*, to feign, make a pretense of (something—like knowledge or innocence). The English physician and writer Thomas Browne (1605-1682), in *The Garden of Cyrus*, wrote: "Life itself is but the shadow of death, and souls departed but the shadows of the living. All things fall under this name. The sun itself is but the dark *simulacrum*, and light but the shadow of God." In his *Religio Medici (Religion of the Physician)*, Browne attempted to reconcile religion and science, which is nice work if you can get it.

sinapism   (SIN uh piz um) *n*. *Sinapism* is mustard plaster, an old-fashioned medical remedy consisting of a black powdered mixture of mustard and rubber placed on cloth, applied to the body as a counterirritant. Via Latin *sinapsmus*, the word is from Greek *sinapismos* (application of mustard), based on *sinapi* (mustard), and related to *sinapizein* (to apply mustard). Incidentally, the *must-* in *mustard* is from *must* (new wine, pressed but not yet fermented): *must* is from the Latin adjective *mustus* (young, new, fresh), in the neuter ending *mustum*, short for *vinum mustum* (new wine). Originally must was used in mixing mustard paste.

sisyphean   (sis uh FEE un) *adj*. A *sisyphean* task is a never-ending, fruitless effort. This adjective derives from the sad legend of Sisyphus, in classical mythology the king of Corinth, a man famous for his trickery. For reasons varying with each of several sources, he was punished in Hades by being condemned to roll a huge stone up a steep hill, at the top of which the stone escaped him and rolled all the way down again—forever. Thus, his task was eternal, and totally unavaiing. A "labor of Sisyphus" or *sisyphean toil* is endless and heartbreaking. Literate mothers cleaning up the family room for the umpteenth time that day after the children have occupied it for a short while have been known to characterize their task as *sisyphean*. Recurring floods present riparian dwellers with *sisyphean* labors. The attempts of the authorities throughout history to stamp out prostitution would appear to be of *sisyphean* proportions. Penelope, the faithful wife of Ulysses, created for herself a *sisyphean* task: she was beset by suitors while Ulysses was away at the siege of Troy. To get rid of them, she promised to select one as soon as she had finished weaving a shroud for her father-in-law. Each night, she unraveled the work of the previous day, until Ulysses came home—and slew the suitors. Hence the expression *web of Penelope*, a never-ending task; a self-created *sisyphean* labor, as it were.

skimble-scamble, **skimble-skamble** (SKIM bul SKAM bul, SKIM ul SKAM ul) *adj*. This lively adjective describes things that are confused, rambling, incoherent, like a *skimble-skamble* narration of a frightening experience, or a *skimble-skamble* explanation of something somewhat beyond the speaker's power of comprehension. *Skimble-skamble* is said to have developed as a reduplication of the dialectal word *scamble* (to scramble, shamble, sprawl, struggle, or trample); or it may be simply a union of *scramble* and *shamble*. Shakespeare used it in *Henry IV, Part I* (Act III, Scene 1), when Hotspur, angrily mocking the long-winded Glendower, says:

> . . . sometimes he angers me
> With telling me of the moldwarp [mole] and the ant,
> Of the dreamer Merlin and his prophecies,
> And a dragon and a finless fish,
> A clip-wing'd griffon and a moulten raven,
> A crouching lion and a ramping [rearing] cat,
> And such a deal of *skimble-skamble* stuff
> As puts me from my faith . . .

(Hotspur goes on, and on, and on; it's well worth reading!) In later days, James Morris, in *Farewell the Trumpets* (Faber & Faber, London, 1978), used the expression "treated with *skimble-skamble* deference" to describe the way a throng might treat a great personage. *Skimble-skamble*, in its sound, is reminiscent of *crinkle-crankle*, a word described by this author in his *British English, A to Zed* (Facts On File, 1987) as follows: "A precious, or a least rare, adjective used to describe serpentine red brick garden walls, full of twists and turns . . . *Crinkle-crankle* is an informal variant of *crinkum-crankum*, which describes anything (not only walls) full of twists and turns and is sometimes used by itself as a substantive."

sleuth, see **slot**

slot (slot) *n*. Apart from its familiar meanings, a *slot* is an animal trail or track, especially that of a deer, marked out by hoofprints. This meaning is derived from

Old Norse *sloth* (trail, track), which also produced the noun *sleuth*, likewise a track or trail, or a bloodhound, a tireless tracker; hence a detective, the common meaning. Tireless tracker? A good name for an etymologist.

sockdol(l)ager, also **sockdol(l)oger**, **slogdollager**, **stockdol(l)ager**, etc. (sok DOL u gur) *n*. This is a slang word for "something sensational or exceptional," according to the English lexicographer Robert Burchfield (b. 1923) in *The English Language* (Oxford University Press, 1985). He includes it in a list of "American words that remain firmly unborrowed in British English, though they are encountered often enough in magazines like *Time*, *Newsweek*, and the *New Yorker* . . . Without them one cannot hope to understand the novels of modern American novelists like Bernard Malamud or Saul Bellow, or, for that matter the daily speech of most Americans." Also included in the list was "*honeyfuggle*" (to obtain by cheating or deception). According to the American dictionaries, a *sockdolager* is anything unusually big or heavy, or a heavy finishing blow, a word coined from the slang *sock* (hard blow) plus **doxology**, in the slang sense of "finish," i.e., the closing act of a church service. The English dictionaries include the definition "whopper," and add the meaning "decisive argument" (i.e., the "clincher").

soffit (SOF it) *n*. This is an architectural term for the underside of a building feature like a beam, arch, vault, cornice, staircase, or balcony. *Soffito* is "ceiling" in Italian, but its descendant *soffit* is usually limited to the ornamental underside of an architectural element. The ultimate source is Latin *suffixus*, past participle of *suffigere* (to fasten beneath), based on prefix *suf-*, a variant of *sub-* (under) plus *figere* (to fasten). *Suffixus* also gave us *suffix*, something "fastened on."

sol-fa, see **solmization**

solfeggio, **solfège**, see **solmization**

solidus (SOL ih dus) *n*. A *solidus* is an oblique stroke (thus: /) which has a variety of functions: in writing fractions (e.g., 3/4); to signify ratios (e.g. miles/minute); in the term *and/or*, used to indicate that either or both of the things enumerated may be involved (e.g., fine and/or imprisonment, or damage to persons and/or property); in Britain, under the former monetary system based on pounds, shillings, and pence, to denote the now obsolete shilling: 7/6 meant "seven shillings six pence"—the *solidus* or oblique stroke being descended from the lengthened form of the *s* that stood for "shilling(s)," the *s* of the still familiar, if now abandoned, L.S.D. (this has nothing to do with the hallucinatory drug *l*ysergic acid *d*imethylamide), L.s.d. or £ s.d., an abbreviation of the Latin *librae* (pounds), *solidi* (shillings), *denarii* (pence). *Solidus* has a number of synonyms: *diagonal*, *oblique*, *slant*, *virgule*, and in British English, simple *stroke*. *Virgule* (VUR gyoohl) is from Latin *virgula* (little rod).

solmization   (sol mih ZAY shun) *n.* This is the system of using the *do*, *re*, *mi*, etc., syllables to represent the tones of the scale. The set of syllables is known as *sol-fa* (sohl FAH, SOL fah), which is also used as a verb: to *sol-fa* is to sing a tune in these syllables. *Solfeggio* (sol FEJ oh, -FEJ ee oh), from the Italian, based on *sol* and *fa*, is another name for *solmization*, and for any vocal exercise using the *sol-fa* syllables, but the form *solfège* (sohl FEZH), the French equivalent, is more commonly heard. *Solmization* is derived, via French *solmisation*, from *sol* or *so* (the fifth tone of the diatonic scale—the basic scale in music—known as *G* in the key of *C*) plus *mi* (the third tone of that scale, *E* in that key).

solstice   (SOL stis) *n.* This is the astronomical term for either one of the two times each year when the sun is farthest from the equator, either north or south. In the Northern Hemisphere, the summer *solstice*, on or about June 21, the longest day/shortest night, marks the beginning of summer, and the winter *solstice*, on or about December 31, the shortest day/longest night, the beginning of winter. The *ecliptic* (ih KLIP tik) is the "track" in the heavens along which the sun appears to travel. It is, of course, the earth that does the traveling. On the two *solstices*, the sun reaches its north and south points in the ecliptic, i.e., the two points in the ecliptic farthest from the equator, and appears to be standing still. It is that illusion which gives the *solstices* their name, derived from Latin *solstitium*, based on *sol* (sun) plus *-stitium*, from *status*, past participle of *sistere* (to stand still). *Ecliptic* comes, via Old English and Latin, from Greek *ekleiptikos*, based on the verb *ekleipein* (to fail to appear—like the sun or moon during an *eclipse*).

somatic   (soh MAT ik, suh-) *adj.* *Somatic* means (among other technical senses) "physical" or "bodily," as opposed to *psychic*, having to with the mind. The combination of the two gives us *psychosomatic* (sye koh soh MAT ik -suh-), based on Greek *psyche* (literally, breath, based on *psychein*, to breathe; figuratively, soul, mind), describing a physical ailment resulting from a mental or emotional disturbance. *Somatic* is from Greek *somatikos* (pertaining to the body), based on *soma* (body, as opposed to soul). *Psyche* and *psychosomatic* have become fairly familiar terms nowadays, but one doesn't run into *soma* or *somatic* very often. A general practitioner friend who feels that *psychosomatic* is used all too glibly by his colleagues likes to greet his patients with a terrible pun: "What's *somatic* with you today?"

sonant, see **surd**

sopor   (SO pur) *n.* *Sopor* is a pathological condition of unnaturally deep sleep; from Latin *sopor* (deep sleep, slumber). We are more familiar with the noun and adjective *soporific*, (something) producing sleep, like a sleeping pill or political oratory or after-dinner speeches. ("You may be wondering why you were asked here tonight . . .") *Sopor* can also mean "lethargy," not actual sleep, in certain contexts. In this connection, if you are still awake, see **lethe**.

soricine, see **accipitrine**

sororicide, see **aborticide**

soteriology   (su teer ee OL uh jee) *n*. As a general term, *soteriology* is a discourse on health and hygiene, but in Christian theology, it is the doctrine of salvation through Jesus Christ. In Greek, a *soter* is a delivery or savior, and *soteria* is safety, salvation, or deliverance. *Soter*, in Greek religion, was an epithet of Zeus, Poseidon, and other gods. Ptolemy I (c. 367-285 B.C., king of Egypt 323-285 B.C.), known as Ptolemy *Soter*, was given that surname, meaning "Preserver," because he forced the Macedonian King Demetrius I (c. 337-283 B.C.) to raise the siege of Rhodes in 304 B.C. Saint *Sofer* was pope from c. 166 to 175. Whether they know it or not, today's born-again Christians are practicing *soteriology*.

speleology, see **spelunker**

spelunker   (spih LUNG kur) *n*. A *spelunker* is a cave explorer; to *spelunk* (spih LUNGK) is to do the exploring. *Spelaean* or *spelean* (spih LEE un) means "relating to caves," and serves as well to describe a cave-dweller. *Spelunk* comes, via Latin *spelunca*, from Greek *spelynx* (cave); *spel(a)ean* from New Latin *spellaeus*, based on Latin *spelaeum* (cave), which came from Greek *spelaion*. *Speleology* or *spelaeology* (spee lee OL uh jee) is the exploration of caves or, in other contexts, their study and science; likewise based on Latin *spelaeum*, plus *-logy*, from Greek *-logia* (study or science). *Spelunkers* take chances, and sometimes have to be rescued by search parties, experiences that usually make the headlines.

steatopygia   (stee uh toh PYE jee uh) *n*. *Stear*, Greek for "fat, grease," gave rise to the prefix *steato-*, while *pyge* is Greek for "buttocks, rump." Together, this prefix and noun gave us *steatopygia*, for fatty accumulation on the buttocks, and *steatopygic* (stee uh to PIJ ik) or *steatopygous* (stee uh toh PYE gus) fat-buttocked, as well as *steatopygy* (stee uh tuh PYE jee, -TOP ih jee), the condition of possessing a very fat rump. Cf. **callipygian**, **callipygous**, an endowment much to be preferred, except among certain South African peoples, perhaps, where *steatopygy* is very common, especially in women, and is very much admired, and *steatopygous* and *steatopygic* might be considered synonymous with *callipygian* and *callipygous*.

stereotropism, see **haptic**

stertor   (STUR tur) *n*. *Stertor* is snoring, the emitting of a rasping sound in breathing, as a result of obstruction of air passages in the head, in sleep or coma. *Stertorous* (STUR tuh rus) is the adjective. A *stertorous* condition is marked by deep snoring or very heavy breathing, especially in certain diseases, including apoplexy. *Stertor* is from the Latin verb *stertere* (to snore). *Stertor* is related to *stridor* (STRYE dur), which has the general meaning of a "harsh, grating sound," but in pathology is a heavy respiratory sound that comes, like *stertor*, from obstruction of breathing passages. *Stridor* is from Latin *stridor* (harsh noise, grating sound), related to *stridere* (to make a shrill sound, to creak, hiss or grate).

stich, see **stichomythia**

stichomythia   (stik uh MITH ee uh) *n*. Also *stichomythy* (stih KOM uh thee). This word, taken intact from the Greek, denotes a brief dialogue in verse drama in which each character usually utters a single line. This is common in classical Greek drama. Hallmarks of *stichomythia* are antithesis and repetition. There are such passages in all the Greek dramas. Here is an example from *Oedipus Rex* of Sophocles (c. 495-c. 406 B.C.), a dialogue between Oedipus and the seer Tiresias:

> Oedipus: Begone this instant! Away, away! Get you from these doors!
> Tiresias: I had never come but that you sent for me.
> Oedipus: I did not know you were mad.
> Tiresias: I may seem mad to you, but your parents thought me sane.
> Oedipus: My parents! Stop! Who was my father?
> Tiresias: This day shall you know your birth; and it will ruin you.

And so on, and so on; next stop, Sigmund Freud. In the *Prometheus Bound* of Aeschylus (525-456 B.C.):

> Io: Zeus fall from power?
> Prometheus: You would rejoice, I think, to see that happen?
> Io: How could I not, who suffer at his hands?
> Prometheus: Know then that it shall surely be.

And more, and more. *Stichomythia* is based on *stichos* (row, line, verse) plus *mythos* (speech, story). The word *stich* (stik), from Greek *stichos*, means "line of poetry."

stochastic   (stuh KAS tik) *adj*. Also **stochastical**. A *stochastic* study, opinion, or observation is a conjectural one, governed by the laws of probability. The English theologian and philosopher Ralph Cudworth (1617-1688), in a *Treatise on Freewill*, wrote: "We may . . . and often do proceed to make a judgment in the case one way or other, *stochastically* or conjecturally . . . There is need and use of this *stochastical* judging and opining concerning truth and falsehood in human life." Pollsters make their predictions *stochastically*, and are at times astonished at how wide of the mark they wind up (remember the headline DEWEY DEFEATS TRUMAN?). The source of this word is Greek *stochastikos* (skilled in aiming), based on the verb *stochasezthai* (to aim at, guess). Antistochastic advice: Don't count your votes before they're cast.

stock, see **talon**

storiology, see **genethlialogy**

strabismus   (struh BIZ mus) *n*. A person suffering from *strabismus* is cross-eyed, a vision disorder resulting from the turning of one or both eyes from the normal position. *Strabismus* is derived from Greek *strabos* (squinting) plus the suffix *-ismos*, which gave us our common suffix *-ism*, as in *baptism*, *criticism*, and nuisances like *rheumatism* and *communism*. There are several adjectives meaning "cross-eyed": *strabismal*, *strabismic*, and *strabismical*, all accented on the syllable *-bis-*. *Strabismal* rhymes with *dismal* and limericks are invited.

stridor, see **stertor**

strigine, see **accipitrine**

sturnine, see **accipitrine**

Stygian   (STIJ ee un) *adj*. *Stygian*, with an upper case *S*, describes anything relating to the River Styx, the river, according to classical mythology, over which Charon ferried the souls of the departed on their journey into the under-world. He charged a fee of one obol, a coin which was placed in the mouth of the deceased, for use in payment of that fee. From that dreadful river, the adjective *stygian* came to mean "dark, gloomy, forbidding," or "infernal," and one may speak of *stygian* night or a *stygian* cave or landscape, or a *stygian* room or hallway, dark, gloomy, forbidding. *Stygian* takes on an entirely different meaning in the expression *Stygian oath*: an oath "by the Styx" sworn by a god, a "Stygian oath," is inviolable. The Roman poet Virgil (70-19 B.C.), in *The Aeneid*, writes of "the swamp of the Styx, by which the gods take oath." The adjective in Latin was *Stygius*, in Greek *Stygios*. The English poet John Milton (1608-1674) starts his poem *L'Allegro* with the lines:

> Hence, loathed Melancholy,
>   Of Cerberus, and blackest Midnight born,
> In *Stygian* cave forlorn,
>   'Midst horrid shapes, and shrieks, and sights unholy . . .

subreption, see **sarcophagus**

sudorific   (sooh duh RIF ik) *adj*. This adjective describes anything that produces sweat, whether heat, fright, nervousness, medication, a message that the boss wants to see you, an unopened letter from the Internal Revenue Service, or simply one of those sweaty little afternoon naps. The related adjective *sudoriferous* (sooh duh RIF ur us) means "sweaty," describing a person secreting the stuff. A *sudarium* (sooh DAIR ee um) in ancient Rome was a hand-kerchief, or any piece of cloth, usually linen, for wiping one's face, and a *sudatorium* (sooh du TOR ee um) is a hot-air room to produce sweating. All these words are based on the Latin noun *sudor* (sweat) and verb *sudare* (to sweat). *Sudorific* has a synonym from the Greek: *diaphoretic* (dye uh fuh RET ik), which also means "sweat-producing," and comes from *diaphoretikos*; the noun *diaphoretic* means "sweat-producing medicine," and the related noun *diaphoresis* (dye uh fuh REE sis) is the medical term for perspiration, especially when it is artificially produced for health purposes. This batch are all based on the Greek verb *diaphorein* (to carry off). *Hidrosis* (hih DROH sis, hye), based on Greek *hidros* (sweat), is the term used in pathology for excessive sweating resulting from medication or illness. One must sweat one's way through all these ancient **etymons** (or, if you prefer, *etyma*) to find the *mot juste*.

suilline, see **accipitrine**

sumptuary (SUMP chooh air ee) *adj*. This adjective describes anything relating to or regulating expenditure. It comes from Latin *sumptuarius*, based on *sumptus* (expense), related to the verb *sumere* (to take, buy). Another Latin word stemming from *sumptus* is *sumptuosus* (very costly), from which we get *sumptuous*. *Sumptuary* is not a common word, but *sumptuous* is, and their etymologically related first two syllables should make it easier to get the sense of *sumptuary* when you run into it. The common use of *sumptuary* is in the term *sumptuary law*, one regulating and limiting personal budgets, especially expenditures for food, dress, and luxuries. Such laws have been enacted in various parts of the world from time to time. Some were in force in Greece and Rome in ancient times. Japan applied that type of regulation to the farming and commercial classes until the middle of the 19th century. In the 14th and 15th centuries, England enforced *sumptuary* statutes relating to dress and diet, imposing much more stringent limitations upon peasants than on the gentry, for the purpose of maintaining class distinctions and keeping the peasants in their place, lest they seek to pass as something superior to their actual status. The English laws were all repealed by James I, who ruled from 1603 to 1625. However, under the exigencies of World Wars I and II, there were returns to *sumptuary* laws for a time. There was food rationing, and limitations were imposed upon the cost and availability of other necessities of life. The alcoholic content of beer and whiskey was reduced, and restaurant meals were subject to a maximum cost of five shillings. This had nothing to do with class distinctions, but rather with the effectiveness of the enemy blockade. The author well remembers dining at the Savoy and the Ritz-Carlton for five "bob" (shillings)—then worth about $1.25—and not enjoying the food one bit!

suppositious, see **supposititious**

supposititious (suh poz ih TISH us) *adj*. This word, meaning "spurious, counterfeit," is not to be confused with its lexical close neighbor *suppositious* (sup uh ZISH us), meaning "hypothetical, assumed." They not only look alike;

they come from the same Latin source, *suppositus*, past participle of *supponere* (to substitute). But they mean quite different things, despite what some dictionaries say (e.g., the *Random House College Dictionary*, Revised, 1980, which rightly defines *suppositious* as "growing out of supposition," and then gives as a second meaning "suppositious [shortened form of SUPPOSITITIOUS])." As you might expect, Fowler has something to say about this troublesome matter, under the heading **suppositious, supposititious**: "It is often assumed that the first form is no more than an ignorant or wrong variant of the other. Ignorant it often is . . . , but there is no reason to call it wrong. There are two fairly distinct senses to be shared, viz. spurious, and hypothetical. *Supposititious* is directly from the Latin past participle *suppositus* = substituted . . . and therefore has properly the meaning foisted, counterfeit, spurious . . . *Suppositious* is from the English supposition = hypothesis, and therefore may properly mean supposed, hypothetical, assumed . . . *Supposititious* should not be given . . . senses proper to the synonyms of *suppositious*; it should be confined to those implying intent to deceive." This argument is supported by the *Oxford Guide to English Usage*, compiled by E.S.C. Weiner (Oxford University Press, 1983): "**suppositious**, hypothetical, conjectural; *supposititious*, fraudulently substituted (especially of a child displacing a real heir), e.g. *Russia . . . is the supposititious child of necessity in the household of theory* (H.G. Wells)." So does the *Chambers Twentieth Century Dictionary*, New Edition, 1973: "**suppositious** . . . usu[ally] a blunder for supposititious."

sural (SOOH rul) *adj. Sural* describes anything relating to the calf of the leg, from *sural* arteries to *sural* cramp to *sural* beauty as in classical Greek statuary, prima ballerinas, and the ladies of the ensemble. The word is from Late Latin *suralis*, based on Latin *sura* (calf).

surd (surd) *n., adj. Surd*, as an adjective, describes an unsounded or voiceless consonant, like the *k* in *knife*, the first *m* in *mnemonic*, the *t* in *whistle*. A *surd* is such a consonant. The word comes from Latin *surdus* (deaf, unheard, noiseless, silent, mute). Its opposite is *sonant* (SOH nunt), *n., adj. Sonant* describes a voiced sound, like the *b* in *boy*, the *m* in *man*, etc. *Sonant* is from Latin *sonans*, present participle of *sonare* (to sound, make a noise). *Consonant*, incidentally, is from *consonans*, present participle of Latin *consonare* (to sound together).

susurrant, see **susurration**

susurration (sooh su RAY shun) *n.* A *susurration* is a whisper, a murmuring, a rustling. *Susurrous* (soo SUR us) describes things with rustling or whispering sounds. *Susurrant* (soo SUR unt) means "whispering, murmuring." A *susurrus* (soo SUR us) is a whisper, a soft rustling or murmuring sound. All these words go back to Latin *susurrus* (whisper) and *susurrare* (to whisper), its present participle *susurrans* and past participle *susurratus*. Both the Latin and the English words are onomatopoeic—words formed by imitation of the sound made by the things they describe or denote, like *boom*, *buzz*, *hiss*, *sizzle*, *cuckoo*, and **tintinnabulation**.

susurrous, see **sussuration**

susurrus, see **sussuration**

syllepsis   (sih LEP sis) *n*. *Syllepsis* covers two rhetorical situations: where a word functions in a sentence in the same grammatical relation to two or more words but has a different sense in relation to each (example: he took the oath and his seat; for other examples, see **zeugma**), and where a word is applied to two others of which it grammatically suits only one (examples: neither you nor he knows; neither he nor they are happy). *Syllepsis* was taken intact from the Greek, based on the prefix *syl-*, variant of *syn-* before *l*, plus *lep-*, the stem of *lambanein* (to take).

syncope, see **aph(a)eresis**

syncretism   (SING krih tiz um) *n*. In philosophy and theology, *syncretism* is the attempt to reconcile or unify opposing schools of thought, principles, practices, etc. The word has been used as a pejorative term for inconsistency in accepting incompatible beliefs or principles. The term is applied especially to the attempt by the German theologian Georg Calixtus (1586-1656) to unite Christian churches, minimizing the importance of doctrine and emphasizing the basic principles of Christian living. The derivation is from Greek *synkretismos* (literally, confederation of Cretan communities; hence, a united front of opposing parties against a common foe), related to *synkretizein* (to unite, or attempt to unite opposing principles), based on prefix *syn-* (together) plus *Kret* (a Cretan).

syndic   (SIN dik) *n*. This word has a number of uses. In classical Greece, a *syndic* was a lawyer, a delegate, or a judge, depending on the context. At various places and times, a *syndic* was a mayor. The Italian word for mayor today is *sindaco*. *Syndic* is the title of a member of a special committee of the senate of Cambridge University, England. As a general term, a *syndic* can be an agent to transact business for others, especially an accredited legal representative of a town or corporation. *Syndicate* (SIN dih kate) has the special meaning of "body of *syndics*," but is generally understood to denote a commercial group of firms or individuals with a common interest, or a combined group of newspapers, or a criminal group. *Syndic*, via the French and the Late Latin *syndicus* (city official), is from the Greek *syndikos* (defendant's counsel), based on prefix *syn-* (with) plus *dike* (justice).

synecdoche   (sih NEK duh kee) *n*. This is the name of a figure of speech that uses a part for the whole or vice versa, or the general for the special or vice versa. It comes from Greek *synekdoche*, based on the prefix *syn-* (with, together) plus *ekdoche* (receiving from another). Examples: part for whole: 50 head (of cattle), lunch at five dollars a *head*; whole for part: *America* won 20 gold medals at the games; general for special: a nasty *creature* (man); a special for general: an *Einstein* (genius). *Synecdoche* is one of those things we use all the time without knowing it—the way M. Jourdain, the Bourgeois Gentilhomme in the play of that name by the French writer of comedies Molière (1622-1673), says to the Master of Philosophy: "Good Heavens! For more than forty years I have been speaking prose without knowing it."

synesis   (SIN ih sis) *n*. This is a term in grammar for a construction in which meaning takes precedence over strict grammatical form. An example is the use of a plural verb after a singular noun to indicate the action of the individuals who compose a group, like a committee, crew, university, company, athletic team, or political body, as opposed to the action of the entity as a whole. This is common usage in Britain, not usual in America. "Thus," quoting from this author's *British English, A to Zed* (Facts On File, 1987), "Harvard *plays* Yale, but Oxford *play* Cambridge . . . An American would be downright startled to see a sports headline reading 'JESUS ROW TO EASY VICTORY.'" (*Jesus* is the name of an Oxford college, and there is a *Jesus* at Cambridge as well, so we're not sure who won.) Fowler cites a good example of a choice between the singular and plural form of the verb: "*The Cabinet is divided* is better, because in the order of thought a whole must precede division; and *The Cabinet are agreed* is better, because it takes two or more to agree." *Synesis* was taken as is from the Greek, where it means "understanding, sense, intelligence."

synod   (SIN ud) *n*. *Synod* has a number of technical meanings in church parlance: an ecclesiastical council, an offical assembly of church dignitaries meeting to decide on matters of policy or religious doctrine; the entire body of a particular church or denomination; the region or district governed by a church council. *Synod*, however, quite apart from its technical uses in the ecclesiastical world, can be and has been used of any council, assembly, or convention. It has been used rather fancifully by some. The English lexicographer, critic, and poet Dr. Samuel Johnson (1709-1784), passing favorable judgment on a meal he had eaten, said: "Sir, we could not have had a better dinner had there been a *Synod of Cooks*." The Scottish soldier and poet James Graham, marquess of Montrose (1612-1650), used it in a poem addressed to "My Dear and Only Love":

> My dear and only love, I pray
> This noble word of thee,

> Be govern'd by no other sway
>   But purest Monarchy.
> For if confusion have a part,
>   Which virtuous souls abhor,
> And hold a *synod* in thy heart,
>   I'll never love thee more.

Synod is, via Latin *synodus*, from Greek *synodos* (meeting).

tabes, see **tabescent**

tabescent (tuh BES unt) *adj. Tabescent* describes anyone or anything wasting away, growing emaciated, becoming consumed. A person on a hunger strike becomes *tabescent*; so does a patient in terminal cancer. The noun *tabescence* (tuh BES uns), meaning "emaciation, shriveling," is sadly evocative of those starving millions in Ethiopia and other Third World countries we see on our television screens. *Tabes* (TAY beez) is the name of the pathological condition of progressive emaciation. *Tabes dorsalis* (dor SAY lis) is locomotor ataxia, syphilis of the spinal cord leading to loss of muscular control and paralysis. *Tabes* is Latin for "wasting, decay"; *tabescent* and *tabescence* are from *tabescens*, present participle of Latin *tabescere* (to waste away, decline, decay).

talion, see **condign**

talon (TAL un) *n.* Apart from its use to denote the claw of a bird of prey, *talon* has a special use in card games: the *talon* is the cards remaining after the deal. Thus, in cribbage, each of the two players is dealt a hand of six cards, and the thirteenth card is turned up and placed atop the remaining cards. That leaves 39 cards unused (52-13), and that is the *talon*, which comes from Latin *talus* (heel). In gin rummy, each player is dealt a hand of ten cards and one is turned up and placed to one side of the rest of the deck, which is the *talon* from which, in this game, unlike cribbage, the players draw in turn. A synonym of *talon* in this sense is *stock*, which, via Middle English, comes from Old English *stoc* (stump).

talpine, see **accipitrine**

tang, see **tinnient**

tantivy (tan TIV ee) *n., adj., adv.*; in the plural—**tantivies**—an *interjection.* A *tantivy* is a gallop. To *ride tantivy* is a hunting term for riding at full gallop. As an adverb, *tantivy* means "swiftly, headlong." *Tantivies* (plural) is a hunting cry when the chase is at full gallop, thought by some to be in imitation of the sound of the hunting-horn, by others in imitation of the sound of hoof-beats. The cry of *tantivies* brings to mind the definition of fox-hunting by the Irish poet and dramatist Oscar Wilde (1854-1900) in his play *A Woman of No Importance*: "The English country gentleman galloping after a fox—the unspeakable in full pursuit of the uneatable." In the late 17th century, *Tantivy* became slang for a High Church cleric or true-blue Tory, based on a contemporary caricature showing High Church clerics "riding *tantivy*" to Rome; sometimes *Tantivy Man* or *Tantivy Boy*.

tapirine, see **accipitrine**

tarn   (tarn) *n*. A *tarn* is a small mountain lake or pool. It got its name from Middle English *terme*, which came from Old Norwegian *tjörn* (pond). Weary mountain climbers delight in *tarns*, but one doesn't come across them often in speech or reading. The poets are fond of them. Wrote the English poet Walter de la Mare (1873-1956) in *The Scribe*:

> And still would remain
>   My wit to try—
> My worn reeds broken
>   The dark *tarn* dry,
> All words forgotten—
>   Thou, Lord, and I.

And the American poet Edgar Allan Poe (1809-1849), in *Ulalume*, wrote:

> It was down by the dank *tarn* of Auber,
> In the ghoul-haunted woodland of Weir . . .

Tarns are usually dark, dank, or deep, or all three, and always romantic.

Tarpeian, see **defenestration**

tatterdemalion   (tat ur deh MALE yun, -MAL-) *n*. A *tatter* is a bit of rag, any torn shred hanging loose from an article of clothing, a banner, a flag, a sheet of paper, etc., and anything *in tatters* like a battle-torn flag, a banner long exposed to the elements, long and arduously worn clothing, poorly laundered washing, is in shreds, about to fall apart. A *tatterdemalion* is a ragamuffin, someone in *tattered* clothes. The *tatter-* part, from Middle English, based on Old English *taetteca* (shred), is obvious; *-demalion* is claimed to be of unknown origin, though *-malion* suggests the Italian noun *maglia* (MAL yuh), meaning "undershirt," something that might well be visible through the *tatters*, no? Tramps, bag-persons combing through litter bins, panhandlers, bindlestiffs, beachcombers, vagabonds, and derelicts in general all fall within the genus *tatterdemalion*—a sad state of affairs.

taurine, see **accipitrine**

taxonomy   (tak SON uh mee) *n. Taxonomy* is the technique of classification generally, but it has a special application in biology: the science of identification and classification of animal and plant life. One engaged in this pursuit is a *taxonomist* (tak SON uh mist) or *taxonomer* (tak SON uh mur). *Taxonomy* came from the French *taxonomie*, based on the Greek noun *taxis* (order or arrangement in a physical science), related to the verb *tassein* (to arrange, put in order.)

tectonics   (tek TON iks) *n. Tectonics* (like *economics, physics, politics*, etc.) is treated as a singular noun; it is the name of the art and science of building in general, sometimes known as the "constructive arts," using *constructive* as an adjective meaning "pertaining to construction," i.e., building. *Tectonic* (tek TON ik), as an adjective, means "pertaining to construction or building." (It has other technical meanings in the field of geology, relating to the earth's crust.) Both words come from Greek *tektonikos* (relating to construction), based on *tekton* (carpenter).

telegony   (tuh LEG uh nee) *n.* In genetics, there is a theory, unsupported by reliable evidence, that a previous male mate exerts an influence upon offspring later born of the same female to a later mate. The word comes from Greek prefix *tele-* (far) plus *gonos* (begetting, seed). There is another unsupported theory, in stock breeding, known as "saturation," according to which the successive off-spring of the same parents increasingly resemble the sire. These terms apply to animal genetics, but there is no reason, if the theories are correct, why they shouldn't be effective in human affairs—or is *affairs* an injudicious word in this discussion?

teleology   (tel ee OL uh jee, tee lee-) *n.* This is the name applied to a philosophical doctrine serving to explain any series of events in terms of goals, purposes, or ends; the doctrine that final causes exist; the study of purpose and design in nature and the belief that they are a part of and apparent in nature. *Teleologism* (tel ee OL uh jiz um, tee lee-) insists that all phenomena are guided not only by mechanical forces but also by the aim of self-realization. In this sense, *teleology* is opposed to mechanism, the doctrine that all happenings are explainable by mechanical principles of causation. Our word came from New Latin *teleologia*, based on the Greek prefix *tele-* (end, from the noun *telos*, plus the suffix *-logia*). *Dysteleology* (dis tel ee OL uh jee, -tee lee-) is the opposite doctrine, negating the existence of final causes or purposes, and holding that life and nature are random, devoid of purpose. *Teleologists* have equated purpose or cause in the universe with God's will, arguing that since there is design in the universe, there must be a designer, who could only be God, and therefore God exists. The Spanish philosopher and poet Miguel de Unamuno (1864-1936) wrote, in the prologue of *San Manuel Bueno*: "I would say that *teleology* is theology, and that God is not a 'because,' but rather an 'in order to.'" (Unamuno is the man who said, in *The Agony of Christianity:* "Faith which does not doubt is dead faith.")

tellurian (teh LOOHR ee un) *n., adj. Tellurian* is descriptive of anyone or anything having to do with the planet earth, or characteristic of it; it is synonymous with *terrestrial* in that sense. As a noun, a *tellurian* is an earth-creature, a terrestrial, an inhabitant of this planet. *Tellurian* was formed from the Latin noun *tellus* (earth). *Tellus* was the ancient Roman goddess of earth, marriage, and fertility, the counterpart of the Greek goddess Gaea, who was also called *Ge, ge* being the Greek noun for "earth" and the basis of the prefix *geo-*, used in compound words having to do with the earth, like *geography, geology, etc. Tellus* is mentioned in the poem *Hyperion* of the English poet John Keats (1795-1821), when he writes of:

> Asia, born of most enormous Caf,
> Who cost her mother *Tellus* keener pangs,
> Though feminine, than any of her sons.

(*Caf*, also Kaf or Qaf, was the name of the mountain chain that encircled the earth, according to Moslem **cosmology**.)

telpherage (TEL fur ij) *n. Telpherage* is a system of overhead traction operated electrically, utilizing a cable along which cars or carriers travel suspended. These are known as *telphers*; the passage is known as a *telpherway* or *telpherline* and the operator as a *telpherman. Telpherage* and all these related words were coined in 1882 by the British electrical pioneer Fleeming Jenkin (1833-1885), who collaborated with the British physicist Lord Kelvin (1824-1907) in the development of submarine telegraphy cables. Jenkin, who knew his classical Greek, coined the word from the Greek prefix *tele-* (far, as found, e.g., in *telephone, television*, etc.) plus the Greek *pherein* (to bear).

tenebrous (TEN uh brus), rarely **tenebrious** (tuh NEB ree us) *adj.* A *tenebrous* place is dark and gloomy. *Tenebrae* is a Latin noun (plural in form, singular in meaning) that means "darkness," from which several Latin adjectives, including *tenebrosus*, were formed, all meaning "dark, gloomy." *Tenebrae* is the name given to a Catholic church ritual sung on Thursday, Friday, and Saturday of Holy Week, commemorating the Crucifixion. It is accompanied by the gradual extinguishing of candles, leaving the church in darkness. A landscape can be *tenebrous*; so can the interior of one of those Charles Addams (cartoonist, born 1912) houses. Murder mystery films often use *tenebrous* rooms and hallways for atmosphere. The Roman poet Catullus (c. 87-c. 54 B.C.) wrote of the *iter tenebricosum* (dark and gloomy road) whence, they say, no one returns, beating Hamlet's "bourn" whence "no traveller returns" by more than 16 centuries.

teratism, see **teratology**

teratoid, see **teratology**

teratology   (ter uh TOL uh jee) *n*. This is a term used in biology to denote the study and science of malformations and abnormal growths in animals and plants. The word is formed from the Greek noun *teras* (monster) and the suffix *-logia* which gave us the familiar *-logy* used in the names of sciences and bodies of knowledge, as in *biology, geology, theology*, etc. *Teras* gave us also a number of related words: *teratism* (TER uh tiz um), the worship of monstrosities, and *teratoid* (TER uh toid), monstrous, resembling, a monster. *Monster*, in these definitions, denotes any malformed animal, including man, that deviates grotesquely from the norm, with the implication that the effect is hideous, frightening, revolting. Ancient religions and legends often involve *teratological* concoctions. The Egyptian goddess Hathor was represented as a woman's body with a cow's head, and Bubashtis as a woman with the head of a cat or lioness, while the god Anubis was shown as a man with a jackal's face, and Thoth had the body of a man and the head of an ibis. Greek legend gave us the one-eyed Cyclops, the winged, snake-haired Medusa and her Gorgons, so hideous that one who gazed at them turned to stone; and the Sphinx, borrowed from Egyptian religion, was a winged lion with a human head, or sometimes the head of a ram or hawk. Hindu religion offers the god Siva or Shiva, a supreme deity endowed with multiple arms and, at times, three heads. Getting to later times, Gulliver, the traveler conceived by the English satirist Jonathan Swift (1667-1745), was faced by *teratoid* creatures, gigantic and infinitesimal. On the subject of actual human beings, though the word *teratology* didn't figure in the newspaper reports, the subject was deeply involved in the hideous results of radiation after the August 1945 A-bombings of Hiroshima and Nagasaki and the resulting malformation of Japanese babies, and later, in the birth of deformed babies as the result of the use of the tranquilizer thalidomide by pregnant women. *The Elephant Man*, the play by the dramatist Bernard Pomerance (b. 1940), concerned the tragic life of a *teratoid man*. Anyone who has braved freak shows at circuses has been exposed to *teratological* phenomena.

tergiversate   (TUR jih vur sate) *vb*. To *tergiversate* is to keep reversing one's opinion or attitude with regard to a subject, a theory, a cause, etc. More narrowly, it is to desert one cause or party for another, or become an apostate from one's religious faith. It can be used, as well, where one changes one's principles, equivocates, makes conflicting statements, is evasive. This rather tongue-twisting verb is derived from Latin *tergiversare* (to turn one's back), based on *tergum* (back) plus *versatus*, past participle of *versare* (to turn about often), related to *vertere* (to turn). The practice is *tergiversation* (tur jiv ur SAY shun). The adjective describing this type of behavior is *tergiversatory* (TUR jih vur suh tor ee, -torh ee)—an even greater challenge to the tongue, and one who practices *tergiversation* is a *tergiversator* (TUR jih vur say tur) or a *tergiversant*

(TUR jih vur sunt). After all this, one might prefer to remain consistent, but remember the American poet and essayist Ralph Waldo Emerson (1803-1882): "A foolish consistency is the hobgoblin of little minds . . . Speak what you think to-day (sic) in words as hard as cannon-balls (sic), and to-morrow (sic) speak what to-morrow (sic) thinks in hard words again, though it contradict every thing (sic) you said to-day (sic)." Please forgive all the (**sic**)s, but one must preserve the proofreader from criticism, at all costs.

termagant   (TUR muh gunt) *n.*, *adj.* A *termagant* is a shrew, a virago, an overbearing, violent, brawling woman (see **billingsgate**), and *termagant* as an adjective covers all those unlovely qualities. The word has an interesting derivation. With an upper case *T*, it was the name the Crusaders gave a legendary male deity supposedly worshipped by the Saracens who became a figure in the allegorical morality plays of the 15th and 16th centuries. As a character, *Termagant* was violent and rampageous, and dressed in flowing eastern robes that led the public to regard him as a turbulent female. In Shakespeare's *Henry IV, Part 1* (Act V, Scene 4), in the heat of battle Falstaff shams death in order to escape being killed, and when young Prince Hal, thinking him dead, makes the pun:

> Death hath not struck so fat a *deer* to-day,
> Though many *dearer*, in this bloody fray,

fat, old Falstaff puns back: " . . . 'twas time to counterfeit, or that *termagant Scot* [the rebellious Archibald, Earl of Douglas] had paid me *scot* [let me have it] . . . " (See **scot**.) *In Hamlet* (Act III, Scene 2), Hamlet advises the players: "Speak the speech, I pray you, trippingly on the tongue . . . O! it offends me to the soul to hear a robustious periwig-pated fellow tear a passion to tatters . . . I would have such a fellow whipped for o'er-doing *Termagant* . . . avoid it."

tertium quid   (TUR shum QUID, -shee um) *phrasal n.* This is the Latin translation of the Greek *triton ti* (literally, third what?) to denote a third something related to two known things but distinct from both, or intermediate between two things that are opposite or incompatible, like mind and matter, or, euphemistically, the third person in the eternal triangle, as a result of the new twist applied to the expression when the English poet and writer Rudyard Kipling (1865-1936), in *Wee Willie Winkie (At the Pit's Mouth)*, opened with "Once upon a time there was a Man and his Wife and a *Tertium Quid*." *Tertium quid* can also apply to something that escapes a dichotomy assumed to be exhaustive, or, jocularly, to anyone or anything whose status is anomalous or ambiguous, like a dependent living with the family and helping out—guest or servant?—or to a third thing resulting from the combining of two things but distinct from either, like the chemical result of two substances that produce a third, e.g., an alloy, or a neutral salt resulting from the mixture of an acid and an alkali, or a third party that shall be nameless. *Tertium quid* is said to be the invention of the Greek philosopher and mathematician Pythagoras (c. 582-c. 500 B.C.), who defined *biped* as follows: "A man is a biped, so is a bird, and a *tertium quid*," the last believed to be a reference to Pythagoras himself. Fowler says it has been applied to a "middle course, as the British Liberal Party . . . between the Conservatives and the Socialists." A lovely phrasal noun; choose your own interpretation.

test, see **carapace**

tetragram, see **Tetragrammaton**

Tetragrammaton   (teh truh GRAM uh ton) *n.* A *tetragram* is any word of four letters, like *love* or *hate*; from the Greek, based on *tetra* (four) plus *gramma* (letter). *The Tetragrammaton* is the Hebrew name of God, JHVH (transliteration of the four letters of the Hebrew alphabet, *yod* [yood], *he* [hay], *vav* [vov], *he*), too sacred to be pronounced, so that the Jews substituted *Adonai* (ah doh NOY) or *Elohim* (eh loh HIM; the plural of *eloh*, God). *The Tetragrammaton* was transliterated by scholars to *Yahweh* (YAH weh), and eventually corrupted to *Jehovah*. The English poet John Dryden (1631-1700), in *Britannia Rediviva* (Britain Renewed), wrote:

> Such was the sacred *Tetragrammaton*.
> Things worthy silence must not be revealed.

Getting back to *tetragram*, one might think that a *pentagram* is a word of five letters, but one would be mistaken. Though *penta-* is a combining form of *pente* (five), and *gramma* remains "word," a *pentagram* is not a five-lettered word, but a five-pointed star. And while we're at it, the next time you want someone to stop using four-letter words, tell him to cut out the *tetragrams* and see what happens.

tetralemma, see **lemma**

tetraonine, see **accipitrine**

thalassic, see **pelagic**

thaumatrope, see **thaumaturgy**

thaumaturgy   (THAU muh tur jee) *n. Thaumaturgy* is magic, the working of miracles or wonders. A *thaumaturge* (THAU muh turj) is a miracle-worker. *Thaumatology* (thau muh TOL uh jee) is the study of miracles. A *thaumatrope* (THO muh trope) is a "magic card," one with different pictures on the two sides, which appear to combine when the card is twirled rapidly. Examples: a horse on one side and a rider on the other, so that one gets the image of a rider on horse-back; a girl on one side and a boy on the other, giving the image of a couple embracing. All these words are based on the Greek noun *thauma* (wonder, wondrous thing, marvel), and the *-trope* in *thaumatrope* combines it with *tropos* (a turning). *Thaumaturgus* is Greek for "miracle-worker," and is a term applied to certain saints credited with the working of miracles. Bishop Gregory of Neo-Caesaria (c. 213-c. 270) was called "Thaumaturgus" because of the miracles he performed, including the moving of a mountain, no less. St. Bernard, abbott of Clairvaux (1090-1153), known as the "mellifluous doctor" for his wisdom and influence, was so effective in his work for the church that he acquired the title "Thaumaturgus of the West." The next time you employ a magician for a children's party, you may address him as "prestidigitator" (see **prestidigitation**), or *"thaumaturge,"* if you really want to compliment him.

theodicy (thee OD ih see) *n.* The German philosopher Gottfried Leibniz (1646-1716) coined the French word *théodicée,* based on the Greek prefix *theo-* (combining form of *theos,* god) plus *dike* (right, justice), for his theory of vindication of God's justice in permitting the existence of evil. Leibniz was try-ing to establish that this was the best of all possible worlds, despite the existence of evil, which is a necessary condition for the existence of the maximum moral good. If there were no evil against which to measure its opposite, how could there be moral good? It is not appropriate here to enter into an argument on this point. Suffice it to say that is what is meant by *theodicy,* for what it is worth.

thetic, see **nomology**

theurgy (THEE ur jee) *n. Theurgy* is miraculous divine action, the operation of a supernatural or divine agency in the management of human activities. The word is derived, via Late Latin *theurgia,* from Greek *theourgeia* (magic), based on *theos* (god) plus *ergon* (work), from which, incidentally, we get our word *erg,* a unit of work in the parlance of physics. The adjective is *theurgic, -al* (thee UR jik, -jih kuhl). One who believes that human affairs are governed by the inter-vention of a supernatural agency is a *theurgist* (THEE ur jist). The world is in such a mess that a bit (not too much!) of *theurgy* might be welcome.

thew (thyooh) *n.* This word, usually found in the plural, means "muscle" or "sinew"; figuratively, "strength." It comes from Middle English. The English poet Edmund Blunden (1896-1974), in his poem *Forefathers,* wrote:

> These were men of pith and *thew*,
> Whom the city never called;
> Scarce could read or hold a quill,
> Built the barn, the forge, the mill.

Shakespeare used *thews* frequently. In *Hamlet* (Act I, Scene 3), Laertes, advising his sister Ophelia not to take Hamlet too seriously, tells her:

> . . . nature . . . does not grow alone
> In *thews* and bulk; but as this temple waxes,
> The inward service of the mind and soul
> Grows wide withal.

Cassius, in *Julius Caesar* (Act I, Scene 3), bemoaning the weakening of the Roman character, says to Casca:

> . . . for Romans now
> Have *thews* and limbs like to their ancestors;
> But, woe the while! our fathers' minds are dead,
> And we are govern'd with our mothers' spirits.

And in *Henry IV, Part 2* (Act III, Scene 2), Falstaff asks Justice Shallow:

> Will you tell me . . . how to choose a man? Care I for the
> limb, the *thewes* . . . the bulk . . . ! Give me the spirit, Master
> Shallow.

The word is still alive: John Russell, the chief art critic of *The New York Times*, in an article on Brittany, writing rhapsodically about a country inn, tells us:

> The service is about as good as it could be, whether by
> strong-*thewed* young women from Moelan or by senior staff
> whose ways are anything but rustic.

Strong-*thewed* young women . . . ? Can't you see those muscles rippling? One can hardly wait . . . As might be expected, *thewless* means "timid, cowardly," or "weak."

thewless, see **thew**

thigmatropism, see **haptic**

thrasonical   (thray SON ih kul) *adj.* A *thrasonical* person is a braggart, a vainglorious boaster; a *thrasonical* statement is boastful, blustering, puffed-up, overweening. *Thraso* is the braggart in *Eunuchus* (*The Eunuch*), a comedy by the Roman comic dramatist Terence (c. 190-c. 159 B.C.). In Shakespeare's *As You Like It* (Act V, Scene 2), Rosalind, speaking to Orlando of the love-at-first-sight of Oliver and Celia, says: " . . . there never was anything so sudden but the fight of two rams, and Caesar's *thrasonical* brag of 'I came, saw and overcame.'" Shakespeare liked the word: In *Love's Labour's Lost* (Act V, Scene 1), there is a hilarious colloquy between the schoolmaster Holofernes and Sir Nathaniel, a curate. The curate starts: "I praise God for you, sir . . . " and goes on, in pompous language, to praise the schoolmaster, who responds: "Novi hominem tanquam te: [I know a man just like you:] his humour is lofty, his discourse peremptory, his tongue filed, his eye ambitious, his gait majestical, and his general behaviour vain, ridiculous and *thrasonical* . . . " For another adjective derived from another character in the same play, see **gnathonic**. Cf. **braggadocio**, **fanfaronade**, **gasconade**, **rodomontade**.

thremmatology, see **genethlialogy**

threnody   (THREN uh dee) *n.* A *threnody* is a lamentation, in the form of a speech, a poem, or a song, especially a dirge or funeral song, and in that sense it is a synonym of **epicedium**. **Threnody** comes from Greek *threnoidia*, based on *threnos* (dirge) plus *oide* (song). The observations with respect to contemporary funeral practices noted under **epicedium** apply here as well.

threpsology, see **genethlialogy**

thwart, see **umiak**

tigrine, see **accipitrine**

ting, see **tinnient**

tinnient   (TIN ee unt) *adj. Tinnient* describes anything that has a clear ringing or clinking sound; from Latin *tinniens*, present participle of *tinnire* (to clink, jingle). The bells around the neck of a horse trotting as it pulls a sleigh on a clear winter's day (shades of Currier & Ives) have a *tinnient* sound. Good crystal sounds *tinnient* when it is lightly tapped. Related words: a *ting* is a clear ringing sound, and *to ting* is to make such a sound; a *tang* is a sharper ringing sound, and *to tang* is to ring out or clang; *tinnitus* is a pathological ringing in one's ears, from *tinnitus*, past participle of the same *tinnire*. Tinging is pleasant, tinnitus isn't. (See also **tintinnabulation**.)

tinnitus, see **tinnient**

tintinnabulation   (tin tih nab yuh LAY shun) *n. Tintinnabulation* is the ringing or sounding of bells. This delightful onomatopoeic word comes from the Latin for *bell*; *tintinnabulum*. The adjective describing the sound is *tintinnabular* (tin tih NAB yu lur). The American writer Janet Flanner (1892-1978) wrote of " . . . church bells [tolling] . . . in a melancholy, quivering *tintinnabulation*." The word, by extension, can be applied to any bell-like sound. The English poet and novelist Sir Osbert Sitwell (1892-1969) used these lovely words: " . . . the splashing and *tintinnabulation* of a hundred countryscented showers," and in his poem *The Bells*, the American poet and short-story writer Edgar Allan Poe (1809-1849) tells of

> Keeping time, time, time
> In a sort of Runic rhyme
> To the *tintinnabulation* that so
>   musically wells
> From the bells, bells, bells, bells,
>   Bells, bells, bells.

(See also **tinnient**.)

titivate (TIT uh vate) *vb. Titivate* is colloquial for "spruce up, smarten up, put on the finishing touches"; sometimes written *tittivate. Tidivate* is an earlier form, giving rise, despite its initial short *i*, to a supposed derivation from *tidy*, plus the *-vate* from *elevate*, resulting in *tidy up*, or the *-vate* from *cultivate*, according to some authorities. Somehow, all this seems unlikely. A wholly distinct meaning, "titillate," which comes from Latin *titillatus*, past participle of *titillare* (to tickle), must have been the result of confusion, a powerful influence in etymology. In any event, do not confuse *titivate* with *titubate* (TIT ooh bate), meaning "to stumble, or stagger, or totter," from Latin *titubare* (to stagger) whose noun is *titubation* (tit ooh BAY shun), a medical term for "unsteadiness," especially when caused by a nervous disease. There is another *tit-* word that has to do with the way one moves: *tittup* (TIT up), *n., vb.*, that means, as a noun, "moving in an exaggeratedly bouncy way," like a frisky horse, and as a verb, to move in that way, supposedly derived, via *tit* (a dialectal term for "twitch"), from Middle English *tittle*, plus *-up*, taken from the *-op* of *gallop*. Maybe. In any case, all these *tit*-words have nothing to do with the *tit* or *titty* that means "teat," or the *tit* that you get for *tat* if you're lucky.

tittup, see **titivate**

titubate, see **titivate**

tmesis (tuh MEE sis) *n. Tmesis* is the grammatical term for the interpolation of a word between the parts of a compound word. *Be thou ware* for *beware*; *what things soever* for *whatsoever things*; the . . . greatness of his power *to us-ward* for *toward us* (*The Epistle of Paul to the Ephesians* 1;19) are examples of *tmesis* in olden use. It was done in Roman times: The Roman poet Ennius (236-169 B.C.) separated *cerebrum* (brain) thus: "Saxo *cere* comminuit *brum*" for "Saxo comminuit *cerebrum*." ("He smashed his brain against a rock.") *Tmesis* has been adapted into current slang, especially British: *abso-bloody-lutely, hoo-bloody-ray*, etc. A sort of *tmesis* (though this is, strictly speaking, an unwarranted extension of the term, because the interpolation is between two words, not the parts of one word) is heard in the departing husband's long speech in *Fumed Oak*, by the English dramatist Noel Coward (1899-1973), in which the finally resolute spouse condemns all the things in the dreary household he can't stand a minute longer, including the "A-1 bloody sauce." *No bloody good* is another example of quasi-*tmesis*. *Tmesis*, Greek for "cutting," was taken into Latin intact, and came to us likewise without change.

tolypeutine, see **accipitrine**

topiary (TOH pee air ee) *n., adj.* As an adjective, *topiary* describes shrubs and trees clipped into artificial shapes. As a noun, *topiary* is the art of performing such shaping into elaborate "sculpture," including animals, birds, urns, castellation (with turrets and battlements) and abstract geometrical forms. It is an old-fashioned art practiced mainly in older gardens, involving frequent clipping, at least twice a year, starting when a tree or shrub is young. Thickness and uniformity are the aims of such frequent clipping and trimming. The commonest plants used in *topiary* are box, privet and yew. Because of the constant and expert attention required, and the increasing cost and scarcity of the highly special skill involved, this type of gardening is growing ever rarer. *Topiary* is from Latin *topiarus* (pertaining to ornamental gardening), based on *topia* (landscape or landscape gardening—a plural noun, from Greek *topos*, place).

toponym (TOP uh nim) *n.* A *toponym* is not only a place name, but also a noun derived from a place name. There are many examples of such nouns. An extensive collection appears in an article entitled "Around the World by Dictionary", by Stephen E. Hirschberg, in the Spring 1984 edition of *VERBATIM, The Language Quarterly*, from which it is a pleasure to cull some illustrations. A 16th-century mint at Sankt Joachimsthal, in Bohemia, produced a coin called the "Joachimsthaler," which was shortened in German to *taler*, from which we got *dollar*. To *meander* is to roam or wander in a rambling course, because that is the way the River *Meandros*, in ancient Phrygia, wound its way; and *frieze*, a decorative feature of stately buildings, goes back to the embroidery of the same *Phrygia*. The Italian town of *Cerreto*, once famous for its quacks, gave the name *ciarlatano* to its natives—whence *charlatan*. *Taranto*, Italy, was a breeding place for big, hairy spiders, now known as *tarantulas*. *Angora* is based on *Ankara*, Turkey; *calico* on *Calicut*, East Indies; *damask* on Damascus, Syria. *Tuxedos* are named for the Tuxedo Park, New Jersey, country club where they first became popular. *Sherry* started in *Jerez*, Spain; *cos* lettuce came from the Greek island of *Kos*; *vichyssoise* from *Vichy*, France; *bourbon* from *Bourbon* County, Kentucky; *china* from China; *delft* from *Delft*, Holland; *bunk* from *Buncombe* County, North Carolina. *Toponym* comes from two Greek words: *topos* (place) and *onoma* (name), and is not to be confused with **eponym**, which is quite a different matter.

toxophilite (tok SOF uh lite) *n.* This is the name for one who uses the bow and arrow, a bowman or archer; *archer* is from Latin *arcarius*, based on *arcus* (bow). The English scholar and tutor of Queen Elizabeth I, Roger Ascham

(1515-1568), coined the word *toxophilus* (bow-lover) from the Greek noun *toxon* (bow) and suffix *-philos* (loving), based on the verb *phileein* (to love). A *toxophilite* is a devotee of archery; the study, practice, and love of that skill is *toxophily* (tok SOF uh lee). Archery, a method of hunting since time immemorial, and of primary military importance until the invention of gunpowder, was revived as a sport by King Charles II of England (1630-1685) and became a certified Olympic event in 1972.

traduce   (truh DOOHS, -DYOOHS) *vb.* To *traduce* someone is to slander him, vilify him, malign, defame, and calumniate him, speak falsely and with malice toward him or his character; from Latin *traducere* (to disgrace), a variant of *transducere* (literally, to carry over; figuratively, to expose, "show up"). In Shakespeare's *Othello* (Act V, Scene 2), Othello cries to Lodovico who has come to arrest him:

> . . . in Aleppo once,
> Where a malignant and a turban'd Turk
> Beat a Venetian and *traduc'd* the State,
> I took by the throat the circumcised dog
> And smote him thus.

Whereupon, he obeys Shakespeare's stage directions: *Stabs himself.* Things are tough all around and it's a bloody mess; but getting back to words and definitions, avoid the common error of identifying *slander* or *defame* with *libel*. Without going into legal minutiae and ramifications, *libel* is *slander* in written form and "published," i.e., communicated in that form to a third party or parties. Best advice: Keep your mouth shut and your pen in your pocket.

tra(ns)montane, see **cisalpine**

transalpine, see **cisalpine**

transitive   (TRAN sih tiv, -zih-) *adj.*; **intransitive** (in TRAN sih tiv, -zih-) *adj.* These are grammatical terms applicable to verbs. A *transitive* verb is one that can take an object, i.e., that expresses an action having a direct effect upon someone or something; examples: *love, hate, kiss, kick.* One doesn't just love or hate or kiss or kick; one loves, hates, kisses, or kicks someone or something. An *intransitive* verb does not take an object, but indicates a complete action by itself; examples: *go, stay, sit, lie.* The same verb, depending upon the use, can be both. After the battle of Marathon in 490 B.C., an unnamed courier ran almost 23 miles from the scene of battle to Athens to announce the victory—and fell dead on his arrival. His name was not Pheidippides, as often stated in error; that individual ran from Athens to Sparta (110 miles) before the battle to ask for help against the Persian foe. In the last two sentences, *ran* is *intransitive*; it is complete in itself, without an object. But when someone runs a business or a factory, *run*, in the sense of "operate" or "manage," is *transitive*. When you open in a play, *open* is *intransitive*; when you open a bottle of champagne (or a can of worms), *open* is *transitive*. To err is human, to forgive divine. Both verbs are *intransitive*. *Err* can't be used *transitively*, but *forgive* can, when, for example, we forgive them that trespass against us. *Transitive* verbs can form a passive; *intransitive* verbs cannot. One can be forgiven, but can't be "erred."

transmarine, see **cisalpine**

trebuchet, see **onager**

trencherman   (TREN chur mun) *n*. A *trencherman* is a heavy eater, a person endowed with a hearty appetite, one who would satisfy even the allegedly typical Italian mother who keeps crying, "Mangia, mangia!" or the caricature of the Jewish mother who endlessly inflicts cholesterol on her family. It is based on *trencher* (a plate, platter, or cutting-board; from French *tranchoir*, related to *trancher*, to cut or slice, and *tranche*, a slice or slab). In Shakespeare's *Much Ado About Nothing* (Act I, Scene 1), Beatrice describes Benedick: ". . . He is a very valiant *trencherman*; he hath an excellent stomach." *Trencherman*, in context, can also apply to a sponger, one who likes to feed at another's table.

tribade, see **tribadism**

tribadism   (TRIB u diz um) *n*. *Tribadism* is lesbianism; a *tribade* (TRIB ud) is a lesbian, usually in the sense of a homosexual female who assumes the male role, the "active" partner. *Tribadic* (trih BAD ik) is the adjective for the person and the practice. All these words go back to the Greek noun *tribas* (rubbing) and verb *tribein* (rub). In view of the anatomical limitations involved, the etymology is self-explanatory.

trigraph, see **digraph**

trilemma, see **lemma**

tringine, see **accipitrine**

triskaidekaphobia   (tris kye dek uh FO bee uh) *n*. This is fear of the number 13, and a person suffering from it is a *triskaidekaphobe* (tris kye DEK uh fobe). *Triskaidekaphobia* is from Greek *triskaideka* (13) plus the suffix *-phobia* (indicating fear or dread), while the suffix *-phobe*, applicable to the affected person, is the combining form of *phobos* (fearing). The superstition revolving around the number 13 is said to have originated from a banquet in Valhalla (in Scandinavian mythology, the hall that housed the souls of heroes slain in battle) where 12 were seated. When Loki, the Norse god of strife and spirit of evil, intruded (12 + 1 = 13), Balder, the Norse god of light, was killed. This was enhanced by the Last Supper, where Christ sat with the 12 Apostles (12 + 1 = 13 again). Friday the 13th is considered by *triskaidekaphobes* as a particularly unlucky day. The English essayist Joseph Addison (1672-1719) wrote in *The Spectator* (the English daily that ran from March 1, 1711 to December 6, 1772 and for a time in 1774) about being in a mixed group when an old lady caused panic by pointing out that it numbered 13. The day was saved when one of them, a friend of Addison, noticed that one of the ladies was pregnant. "Had not my friend found this expedient to break the omen, I question not but half the women in the company would have fallen sick that night." (13 + ? = ?)

triturate, see **comminute**

trochili(di)ne, see **accipitrine**

troglodyte (TROG luh dite) *n*. This is a technical name for a caveman, or one who lives in a cave. The term also covers anyone living in seclusion or in a primitive state, like a hermit. The adjective is *troglodytic* or *troglodytical* (trog luh DIT ik [al]). *Trogle* is Greek for "hole" and *dyein* is Greek for "get into"; hence *troglodyte*. The ancient Greeks gave the name *troglodytes* to uncivilized races who dwelt in holes in the ground or caves. The Greek historian and geographer Strabo (c. 63-c. A.D. 21) wrote of *troglodytes* living in Syria and Arabia, and the Roman naturalist and writer Pliny the Elder (23-79) asserted that *troglodytes* fed on snakes. Southern Egypt and Ethiopia were alleged to be the homes of the best known of the *troglodytes*. (The term has been applied in ornithology to wrens, because they build their nests, for the most part, in holes.) However, there was some confusion among the ancients between *troglodytes* and *Trogodytae*, a primitive people of northern Sudan. *Troglodytes* lived in caves because of the cold; the Trogodytae were located, according to some authorities, in Egypt and points south, where it isn't cold and there are no natural caves. There was predictable confusion because of the similarity of names: The inclusion of the *l* in ancient manuscripts was an understandable error. The Trogodytae went naked, it was said, ate not only the meat of cattle but the bones and hide as well, drank blood mixed with milk, squeaked like bats and kept their women in common. Whatever the case, a *troglodyte* is now understood to be a cave-dweller, a hermit, and in ornithological circles, a wren; and to complicate matters still further, *troglodyte* has gained the figurative sense of anyone primitive in character, coarse, brutal, or degraded in the way they look, live, or behave. To call someone a *troglodyte* is fightin' words.

troilism (TROY liz um) *n*. One ignorant of its pronunciation might have guessed that this had something to do with Troilus, the lovesick Trojan hero, whose exceptional obsession is attested by these lines from Shakespeare's *Troilus and Cressida*: "I am mad/In Cressid's love/ . . . Her eyes, her hair, her cheek, her gait, her voice:/ . . . her hand/In whose comparison all whites are ink,/ . . . to whose soft seizure/The cygnet's down is harsh/" . . . I am giddy, expectation whirls me round,/The imaginary relish is so sweet/That it enchants my sense./Even such a passion doth embrace my bosom:/My heart beats thicker than a fev'rous pulse . . ." and an amateur etymologist might be forgiven for his guess that *troilism* denoted love-enslavement. But no: according to the *Oxford English Dictionary* it is nothing nearly so romantic, but rather "sexual activity in which three persons take part simultaneously"; and the *Collins English Dictionary* defines it as "sexual activity involving three people" (they omit the *simultaneously*) with a reference to *ménage à trois* and *dualism*, apparently with the suggestion that the *-l-*, far from that in *Troilus*, is nothing more than an echo from the one in *dualism*. (No mention is made of *pluralism, idealism, materialism,* or for that matter, *feudalism*; and there must be many more *-al* adjectives that grew into *-ism* nouns.) So we see that *troilism* is based simply on *trois*, and we wonder, did the French invent it—for there is no such word as *threeism, treism, tresism* or *dreiism* that has come to this author's attention. Whatever the origin of the word, it is a far from common usage (we are not discussing the practice), and since in *Vita (The Life of Vita Sackville-West)* [Dame Victoria Mary, 1892-1962, English novelist and poet] (Weidenfeld and Nicholson, London, 1983) by the English biographer Virginia Glendenning (b. 1937) we find a quotation out of a communication from the English novelist Virginia Woolf (1882-1941) that includes the phrase "emotional troilism," one might conclude that *troilism* is (or was) nothing more than a bit of Bloomsbury cant. The *-l-* in *Troilus*, however seductive a clue to the amateur etymologist, turns out to be, alas, a red herring.

trope (trope) *n.* A *trope* is any use of language in other than its literal sense; a figure of speech, a rhetorical device such as a metaphor, **metonomy**, **synecdoche**, irony, etc. *Trope* is, via Latin *tropus* (figure of speech), from Greek *tropos* (a turning), related to *trepein* (to turn). *Tropology* (troh POL uh jee) is the use or study of figurative language or a treatise on the subject of figures of speech, from Greek *tropologia*. The overuse of *tropes* has been a frequent subject of satire. In *Hudibras*, the English poet and satirist Samuel Butler (1612-1680) mocked the subject of his satire in a number of different ways, including this:

> For rhetoric he could not ope
> His mouth, but out there flew a *trope*.

Another English poet, Matthew Prior (1664-1721), in the poem *Paulo Purganti and his Wife*, satirized his subject with:

> He ranged his *tropes*, and preached up patience;
> Backed his opinions with quotations.

tropology, see **trope**

trumpery (TRUM puh ree) *n., adj. Trumpery* is worthless stuff. In context, it can mean "nonsense, gibberish, twaddle." As an adjective, *trumpery* means "worthless, trashy," describing things of no real value, with the implication that the things so described are showy as well as worthless, as in *trumpery jewelry*, *trumpery arguments*. In Late Middle English, *trompery* was deceit, from Middle French *tromperie*, based on *tromper* (to deceive). Though the element of deceit is at the bottom of its etymological source, *trumpery*, in its literal sense of "rubbish, junk" or figurative sense of "stuff and nonsense," is simply one or the other, with hardly any reference to guile or duplicity, except that the showiness is, in a way, calculated to make a misleading impression.

turdine, see **accipitrine**

tutelage, see **tutelary**

tutelary (TOOHT uh lair ee, TYOOHT-) *n., adj. Tutelary*, as an adjective, describes someone acting as protector or guardian, like a *tutelary* angel or saint. As a noun, a *tutelary* is a saint or a deity, or a mere mortal in a *tutelary* position or relationship. The related noun *tutelage* (TOOHT uh lij, TYOOHT-) means "guardianship," the act or status of protecting or guiding, or "instruction," or the condition of being under a guardian. The Chinese revolutionary and political leader Sun Yat-sen (1866-1925) wrote of the three stages of revolution: "The first is the period of military government; the second, the period of political *tutelage*; and the third, the period of constitutional government." The words *tutor*, *tutorage*, and *tutorial*, as well as *tutelary* and *tutelage*, all go back to Latin *tutus*, past participle of the verb *tueor* (to look at, watch, and, by extension, to watch over, guard). *Tutus* (watched over), by extension, came to mean "safe, secure."

tyrannicide, see **aborticide**

U, Non-U (yooh, non yooh) *adj's*. This is primarily a matter of British sociolinguistics, but you may run into the terminology and the liberty is taken to quote from Appendix I.C.6. of this author's *British English, A to Zed* (Facts On File, 1987):

> For the subtleties of variations in the vocabulary of spoken (and to a much smaller extent, written) British English based on class distinctions, the reader is referred to *U and Non-U, an Essay in Sociological Linguistics*, by Prof. Alan S.C. Ross, of Birmingham University (England) . . . , later in *Encounter*, and still later in *Noblesse Oblige*, a collection of articles edited by Nancy Mitford (1904-1973; Hamish Hamilton, London, 1956; Penguin Books, Ltd., 1959). His article was commented on by Miss Mitford in *Encounter*, in a piece entitled *The English Aristocracy* . . . She, in turn, was

Encounter, by Evelyn Waugh in "An Open Letter to the Honorable Mrs. Peter Rodd (Nancy Mitford) On a Very Serious Subject." The Mitford and Waugh articles, too, are included in *Noblesse Oblige*. All these comments gave currency to the concept of U and Non-U as linguistic categories constituting "class-indicators." (The *U*, incidentally, doesn't stand for *You*, as in *While-U-Wait*, but for *upper class*.) It is felt that these distinctions would be lost on most Americans, whose ears are not attuned to English class differences based on accent or vocabulary and who suffer from a feeling of inferiority equally in the spoken presence of London cabbies and Oxford dons . . . It would be well to take the trouble to avoid some of the more glaring shibboleths, like *lounge* (for *living-room*), *serviette* (for *napkin*) . . . and *pardon*! (for sorry!).

Fowler says, of *U* and *Non-U*: "The English class system was essentially tripartite—upper, middle, and lower—and it was only by its language that the upper class (U) was clearly marked off from the others (Non-U)."

ubiety   (yooh BY ih tee) *n. Ubiety* is the quality or property of being in a definite place at any given time, "whereness," as it were, location. It comes from Middle Latin *ubietas*, based on Latin *ubi* (where), and should not be confused with *ubiquity* (yooh BIK wih tee), the property of being everywhere at the same time, from Late Latin *ubiquitas*, based on *ubique* (everywhere), from which we also get *ubiquitous* (yooh BIK wih tus), a familiar adjective. It may be said that the planets have ubiety, whereas, according to the British anthropologist Jacob Bronowski (1908-1974), man has *ubiquity*. In *The Ascent of Man*, Bronowski tells us that "Man is . . . the *ubiquitous* animal . . . "

ukase   (YOOH kase, yooh KAZE) *n.* Originally, in imperial Russia, a *ukase* was an order or edict handed down by the Czar, which automatically acquired the force of law, but the term has now come to denote any peremptory proclamation issued by an absolute or arbitrary authority without right of appeal. The use of the term need not be confined to duly constituted government authorities. It can be said that certain party bosses never make suggestions or call for them; they simply hand out *ukases*. Hollywood moguls, old style, operated by *ukase*. We took the word from the French, who based it on Russian *ukaz*.

ullage   (UL ij) *n. Ullage* is the quantity of liquid by which a container falls short of being full, i.e., the difference between the amount of liquid a vessel can hold and the amount it actually contains; from Old French *ouillage* or *eullage* (the amount of wine needed to fill a cask), related to *ouiller* or *oeiller* (to fill up). *Ullage* is used of a bottle of wine part of which has been lost by evaporation. In England, *ullage* was formerly used as a slang term for "dregs," and even more generally, "rubbish."

ulotrichous, see **cymotrichous**

ultramarine, see **cisalpine**

ultramontane, see **cisalpine**

ululate   (YOOHL yuh late, UL ool-) *vb*. Fowler suggests a different pronuncia-tion: ūlūl-, i.e., OOH looh-, saying, ". . . the imitative effect got by repeating the same sound should not be sacrificed; *ulul-* suggests howling much more vividly than *ŭlūl-* [i.e., ul ool] . . . " In any event, to *ululate* is to howl, like a dog or a wolf, to wail, to lament shrilly, without words; also, to hoot or screech like an owl. *Ululate* is derived from Latin *ululatus*, past participle of *ululare* (shriek, yell, howl), and also a noun meaning "howling, shrieking, wailing"; and *ulula* is Latin for "owl," and is involved in the derivation. The noun, *ululation* (yoohl yuh LAY shun, ul-) implies repeated, rhythmic wailing. *Ululate* is an onomatopoeic word, i.e., it imitates the sound it describes. To hear wolves *ululate* in the darkness sends shivers down one's spine, but to hear the *ululations* of professional mourners can be worse.

ululation, see **ululate**

umbrageous   (um BRAY jus) *adj*. *Umbrageous* has two entirely distinct meanings. Its principal meaning is "shady," in the sense of creating or providing shade, like the famous ". . . spreading chestnut tree . . . " (in the poem by the American poet Henry Wadsworth Longfellow, 1807-1882) under which ". . . the village smithy stands . . . " An *umbrageous* tree, then, is a shade tree. But an *umbrageous* person (*umbrageous* here refers back to the word *umbrage*, a feeling of offense, resentment, and annoyance, usually found in the expression to *take umbrage*) is one quick to take offense. When *umbrageousness* reaches the point of mental disorder, it becomes *paranoia*. *Umbrageous* is from Latin *umbratus*, past participle of *umbrare* (to shade or overshadow), and it may be the feeling of being overshadowed that creates the *umbrage*. *Umbrageous* trees provide shade; *umbrageous* people feel overshadowed.

umiak   (OOH mee ak) *n*. This is a Greenland Eskimo word for an open boat constructed of a wooden frame covered by animal skins, with a number of seats placed abeam for the rowers, exclusively women, who sit on opposite sides of the boat, each paddling with one oar. Such cross-seats in a boat are known as *thwarts*. *Umiaks* are used to carry passengers and freight, and are quite different from *kayaks*, Eskimo hunting boats, which are covered by flexible closures that fit around the waists of the crew.

unicameral, see **bicameral**

uninitiated   (un ih NEE shee ay tud) *n. pl*. The *uninitiated* are those not in the know, the "innocents," perhaps.˙ To *initiate* is, inter alia, to introduce (someone) into the knowledge and understanding of a subject, or into the secret rites of an organization, whether the Masons or a college fraternity. It comes from Latin *initiatus*, past participle of *initiare* (to initiate). There were various types of secret rites and "mysteries" in ancient Rome into which certain favored individuals were *initiated*. Those left out, the vast majority, were the *uninititated*. What goes on behind closed doors in governments, large corporations, political organizations, etc., is not shared with hoi polloi—the *uninitiated*—those in the dark and not privy to the inner workings, the wheels within wheels. In matters of art, the *uninitiated* are the opposite of the **cognoscenti**.

untoward   (un TORD) *adj. Untoward* is not an antonym of *toward* (in the direction of) and doesn't mean "away from." *Toward* has a number of rarely used meanings, one of which is "propitious, favorable," and *untoward* as the negative of *toward* in that sense means "unfortunate, unfavorable." Thus it can be said that *untoward* circumstances led to the downfall of Oscar Wilde. *Untoward* can also mean "improper," and it is in that sense that *untoward* behavior can be said to make people socially unpopular. The relation of *untoward* to *toward* is like that of *unsavory* to *savory*, where *unsavory* has the common meaning of "morally offensive" while *savory* commonly means "tasty." *Savory* has the rarely encountered meanings of "agreeable, pleasant, attractive" and it is in reference to those senses that *unsavory* is its negative. These are cases where an *un-* word is an antonym of only a rare sense of the positive form.

uranology, see **genethlialogy**

uriticaria, see **urticate**

ursine, see **accipitrine**

urticate   (UR tuh kate) *vb.* To *urticate* is to sting like a nettle. *Urtica* is *nettle* in Latin; the related Latin verb is *urticare* (to sting). *Urticaria* (ur tuh KAR ee uh) is an allergic condition of the skin causing severe itching, similar to that produced by nettles. It is called *nettle rash* as well, or *hives. Urtication* (ur tuh KAY shun) is the development of that condition, and an extremely unpleasant one it is. There is a belief, as rampant in the English countryside as nettles and dock themselves, that the stinging sensation produced by contact with a nettle is promptly relieved by rubbing the affected part with a dock leaf. (These weeds grow in close proximity, and are particularly prolific.) This belief, from the author's own painful experience, is without foundation.

usufruct   (YOOH zoo frukt, -soo-, yoohz yoo-, yoosh-) *n. Usufruct* is a term used in law primarily, to denote one's right to enjoy the use and benefits flowing from the use of another's property, without the ownership of it and without the right to harm or waste or destroy it. The word is from Late Latin, based on two Latin words, *usus* (use) plus *fructus* (fruit), and indicates the "fruit of the use." If A makes an arrangement with B for B to use A's estate or other asset and retain the profits and benefits of that use, on condition that A keeps it intact, B is said to have the *usufruct* of that asset, or to have a *usufructuary* (yooh zoo FRUK

FRUK chooh uh ree—same variations in pronunciation of first two syllables as shown above) right in it.

uxorial (uk SOR ee ul, ug-) *adj. Uxor* is *wife* in Latin, and *uxorial* means "wifely," describing the attitudes, devotion, responsibilities, and anything else pertaining to, befitting, or typical of wives. *Uxorilocal* (see **matrilocal**) and on a more somber note, *uxoricide* (see **aborticide**) are both based in part on *uxor*. Another *uxor* adjective, from Latin *uxorius* and not to be confused with *uxorial*, is *uxorious* (uk SOR ee us, ug-). The two words have nothing in common except the *uxor*. Whereas *uxorial* describes women in the marital role, *uxorious* applies only to the opposite sex, men who simply dote on their wives, are excessively and uncritically fond of them and lovingly submissive. *Uxorious* has the sense of overdoing it, and has a somewhat disparaging flavor. Sociological-cum-etymological note: There appears to be no Latin-derived adjective for a doting wife.

uxoricide, see **aborticide**

uxorilocal, see **matrilocal**

uxorious, see **uxorial**

vaccine, see **accipitrine**

vade mecum, see **ench(e)iridion**

valetudinarian (val ih toohd uh NAIR ee un, -tyoohd-), also **valetudinary** (val ih TOOHD uh ner ee, -tyoohd-) *n., adj.* A *valetudinarian* or *valetudinary* is an invalid, particularly one who is unduly concerned about his poor health. Both words are adjectives as well, describing the condition of one in poor health, or excessively anxious about it. These words are derived from Latin *valetudinarius* (sickly), based on the noun *valetudo* (state of health—good or bad), related to the verb *valere* (to be strong). *Valetudinarians* differ from hypochondriacs, in that *valetudinarians* really do have something to worry about, and may do so to excess, while hypochondriacs suffer from imaginary ills, and worry about them just as excessively, like *Le Malade Imaginaire* (The Imaginary Invalid) in the comedy by the French actor and comic playwright Molière (1622-1673). Do not confuse *valetudinarian* with *valedictorian*, the top student in a graduating class who delivers the *valedictory* address at commencement.

variorum (var ee OR um) *n., adj.* A *variorum* edition of a work is one that contains varying versions of the text, or annotations by scholars, as in a *variorum* edition of *The Divine Comedy* or an early Shakespearean printing. By itself, a *variorum* is a *variorum* edition. The term is a **compendious** form of the Latin phrase *editio cum notis variorum* (edition with notes of various people). The *variorum* in that expression is the masculine genitive plural of the Latin adjective *varius* (various) used as a noun, so that *variorum* means "of various people." *Variorum* is not the neuter nominative singular that, in the words of Fowler, ". . . the bookseller took it to be when he offered *a good variorum edition including variora from MSS in the British Museum."*

vatic, see **vaticinate**

vaticide, see **aborticide**

vaticinate (vuh TIS uh nate) *vb.* This verb is defined as "to prophesy" by dictionaries both American and British, but the admirable *Chambers Twentieth Century Dictionary* (W. & R. Chambers Ltd., Edinburgh) adds "(chiefly ironical)" and Fowler comments, "The verb, formerly equivalent to *prophesy*, now usually connotes contempt . . ." One who *vaticinates* is a *vaticinator* (vuh TIS uh nay tur). The practice is *vaticination* (vat ih suh NAY shun), and the related word *vatic* (VAT ik) means "prophetic, oracular, inspired." The derivation is from Latin *vaticinatus*, past participle of *vaticinari* (to prophesy), based on *vates* (seer). (Incidentally, note the difference in the English spelling of *prophesy*, verb, and *prophecy*, noun, as well as the difference in the pronunciation of the last syllable. The noun comes from Greek *propheteia*, and the verb is simply a verb use in variant form.) There is an etymological connection between these *vatic-* words and the *Vatican*, the papal palace, which got its name from its location atop the *Vaticanus Mons* (Vatican Hill) of ancient Rome, the former headquarters of the Roman *vaticanitores* (soothsayers). Don't take the utterances of *vaticinators* too seriously: remember Delphic ambiguity and the double-talk of Nostradamus, the French physician and astrologer Michel de Nostradame (1503-1566), which could go either way.

velleity (vuh LEE ih tee) *n. Velleity* is mere inclination or wish, without the effort to accomplish it; the weakest form of volition, unlike **conation**, which combines striving with volition. *Velleity* is from New Latin *velleitas*, based on Latin *velle* (to be willing, to wish). Fowler contrasts *volition* and *velleity* this way: "Volition . . . an exercise of will-power for a specific purpose . . . *Velleity* . . . an abstract and passive preference." The English biographer and critic Lytton Strachey (1880-1932) wrote: "Every wish, every *velleity* of his (Prince Albert) had only to be expressed to be at once Victoria's." The English jurist and philosopher Jeremy Bentham (1748-1832) wrote, in *Scotch Reform*: "In your Lordship, will is volition, clothed and armed with power—in me, it is bare and inert *velleity*." (Good characterization of *velleity*: bare, inert.) Jean Jacques

Rousseau, the French philosopher and author (1712-1778), in his *Prose Works*, wrote of mistaking ". . . emotion for conviction, *velleity* for resolve."

verbid (VUR bid) *n.* *Verbid* is a term used in grammar for a nonfinite verb form (infinitive—to say; gerund—saying; participle—saying or said) that has neither subject nor object, or a noun derived from a verb, also known as a *verbal.* To err is human, to forgive divine: *To err* and *to forgive* are used as nouns, subjects of *is*, and are *verbids* or *verbals.* Parting is such sweet sorrow: *Parting* is in the same boat—a *verbid* or *verbal.* The noun *aesthete* (or *esthete*), a person sensitive toward the beautiful, especially in the arts, is from the Greek *aisthetes* (one who perceives), a *verbid* of *aisthanesthai* (to perceive—or, as they say in the jazz world, to *dig*).

verism (VEER iz um, VER-) *n.* *Verism* is realism in the arts, whether literary or graphic. It is also the name for the proposition that literal representation of reality and truth is of the essence in literature and art. *Verism* requires the resort to the ordinary, everyday material of life, even if ugly or sordid, in art. The novels of the Russian writer Feodor Dostoyevsky (1821-1881), the paintings of the German artist George Grosz (1893-1959), the caricatures of the French cartoonist and lithographer Honoré Daumier (1808-1879), all showed life in the raw, products of *verism.* It is a theory, called *verismo* in Italian, that influenced much of early 20th-century Italian opera, like *La Bohème* of Puccini (1858-1924), *I Pagliacci* of Ruggiero Leoncavallo (1858-1919) and *Cavalleria Rusticana* of Pietro Mascagni (1863-1945). *Verism* comes from Latin *verus* (true), the source as well of a string of English words: *verify, verity, veritable,* etc.

verjuice (VUR joos) *n.* *Verjuice*, literally, is the sour juice of unripe fruits, especially crab apples and grapes. Figuratively, *verjuice* is sourness of temperament, disposition, or expression. It is the hallmark of a *curmudgeon*, itself an interesting word, generally described in dictionaries as of unknown origin, though Samuel Johnson (the English lexicographer, 1709-1784) says in his *Dictionary*: "It is a vitious [the old spelling, based on Latin *vitiosus*] manner of pronouncing *coeur méchant* [French for *wicked heart*] . . . "

vernissage (ver nih SAJ) *n.* This French word (literally, varnish, or varnishing-day) has been taken over in art circles to mean the "private viewing" of an art exhibition, by invitation only. The meaning of *vernissage* in French, originally "varnishing," was extended to include "varnishing-day," a day reserved for the painters to apply a coating of varnish or put finishing touches to their works, a function sometimes attended by critics. The term was first applied to this ritual at the Paris Salon, the annual exhibition of painting and sculpture by living artists, and extended to include the private view at the opening of any art exhibition. *Vernissages* are attended by critics, **cognoscenti**, collectors, and those who are more interested (as at the opera) in being seen than in seeing.

veronica (vuh RON uh kuh) *n*. *Veronica* is not only the name of a plant and a girl's name, but also, as every aficionado of bullfighting knows, a classic movement with the cape, where the matador stands stock still and slowly swings the cape away from the charging bull. The original *Veronica* was a woman of Jerusalem who wiped Jesus's forehead with a kerchief while He was on His way to Calvary. It was found to bear His likeness and was called the "Vera Icon" (True Image) and the woman later became Saint *Veronica*. The kerchief is kept as a relic at St. Peter's in Rome. The matador's pass is called the *veronica* because the cape slowly swung before the face of the charging bull is like the kerchief of St. *Veronica* wiping Christ's brow

vertiginous (vur TIJ uh nus) *adj*. *Vertigo* (VUR tuh go) is a fairly familiar word for "dizziness," a pathological condition in which a person feels that he or everything around him seems to be whirling around and that he is about to lose his balance. Not so well known is the adjective *vertiginous*, which some fail to relate to *vertigo* because the *g* is soft and the accent shifts from the first to the second syllable. *Vertiginous* can mean several things: "spinning" or "rotary," when it describes the movement of a top, or wind currents; "dizzy" or "giddy," of people affected with *vertigo*; "causing dizziness," like heights, a winding staircase, a rocking ship; or, figuratively, "unstable, subject to sudden change," in describing economic or social conditions. *Vertigo* was taken over from Latin, where it is related to the verb *vertere* (turn). *Vertiginous* comes from Latin *vertiginosus* (dizzy). In Latin, the accent of *vertigo* is on the second syllable (ver TEE go), and that used to be the pronunciation in English.

vespertine, see **acronical**

vespine, see **accipitrine**

viaticum (vye AT uh kum) *n*. According to Fowler, the use of *viaticum* for "provisions" is to be considered an example of "PEDANTIC HUMOR." The word is not often encountered, and when used seriously, denotes the funds and other necessities one takes along on a trip. The plural form is rare; some authorities supply the form *viaticals*, in the sense of "baggage." In ecclesiastical circles, *viaticum* has a special use: the Eucharist or Communion given to a dying person or one in danger of dying. In ancient Rome, *viaticum* was the travel allowance granted public officials sent out on a mission away from home, an advance "expense account." The word was taken intact from the Latin, where it means "money for a journey," and is the neuter form of the adjective *viaticus* (pertaining to a journey), based on *via* in the sense of "journey."

vigia (vih JEE uh) *n*. On a navigational chart, there are warning symbols called *"vigias"* indicating the approximate location of shoals or dangerous rocks. *Vigia* is a Spanish word meaning "lookout" or "watching"; in nautical parlance, "shoal" or "rock." Both Spanish and English are from Latin *vigilia* (keeping watch, guard; figuratively, watchfulness), from which we get *vigil*, *vigilance*, *vigilante*, etc. A chart full of *vigias* can make a helmsman quite nervous.

vinculum   (VING kyuh lum) *n.* A *vinculum* is a bond or tie, denoting unity. *Vinculum* is Latin for "cord, chain, bond," primarily in the sense of "fetters," related to the verb *vincire* (to bind, fetter, restrain). It has a special use in mathematics, as the name of a line drawn over a group of quantities to signify that they are to be treated as a unit, with the same effect as a set of parentheses around the group. Thus, $\overline{a+b}$ is the same as $(a+b)$. The vinculum comes in handy to denote a unit or units within a unit, thus: $(a+\overline{b+c})$ or $(\overline{a+b} + \overline{c+d})$. Brackets are used to show units within units within units, thus: $[(\overline{a+b} + \overline{c+d}) + (\overline{e+f} + \overline{g+h})]$. For units within units within units within units, use braces, thus: $\{[(\overline{a+b} + \overline{c+d}) + (\overline{e+f} + \overline{g+h})]\} + \{[(\overline{i+j} + \overline{k+l}) + (\overline{m+n} + \overline{o+p})]\}$. Incidentally, any of those plus signs, for the purpose of this discussion, could just as well have been minus signs. The *vinculum*, as used in mathematics, is still a tie or bond, serving a particular use.

viniculture, see **oenology**

viperine, see **accipitrine**

virgule, see **solidus**

viricide, see **aborticide**

virtu   (vur TOOH, VUR tooh) *n.* This word, taken intact from the Italian, where it means, inter alia, "virtue" and "merit," stemming from Latin *virtus* (excellence, worth), covers a range of meanings, all connected with objets d'art: excellence in such items; such objects collectively; a taste for them; knowledge in that field; love of fine arts generally. *Objects of virtu* are of interest because of their workmanship, rarity or antiquity. They are collected by connoisseurs, dealers, and museums. The works of the Russian jeweler and goldsmith Carl Fabergé (1846-1920) housed in the Hermitage, a museum in Leningrad, are prime examples of *objects of virtu*. Except for their ancestry (Latin *virtus*), *virtu* has nothing to do with *virtue* in the sense of "moral excellence" or "chastity."

vituline, see **accipitrine**

viverrine, see **accipitrine**

viviparous   (vye VIP uh rus) *adj.* Some animals give birth to living young. Others expel eggs which must hatch; still others produce eggs but instead of expelling them, hatch them inside the body so that the young are born alive. The first are *viviparous*; the second are *oviparous* (oh VIP uh rus); the third are *ovoviviparous* (oh voh vye VIP uh ruhs). Most mammals and some reptiles and fishes are *viviparous*. Birds, most reptiles, and a few species of mammals are *oviparous*. Certain reptiles and fishes are *ovoviviparous*. All these systems seem to work quite well. *Viviparous* is from Latin *viviparus* (giving birth to living young), based on the prefix *vivi-*, the combining form of *vivus* (alive) plus the suffix *-parus* (bearing), from the verb *parere* (to bear). *Oviparous* is from Latin *oviparus* (giving birth by means of eggs), based on prefix *ovi-*, the combining form of *ovum* (egg), plus the same suffix *-parus*. From the foregoing, the derivation of *ovoviviparous* is obvious.

volucrine, see **accipitrine**

voussoir, see **quoin**

vulpine, see **accipitrine**

vulturine, see **accipitrine**

widget (WIJ it) *n. Widget* is a colloquial alteration of *gadget*, the name for any small mechanical device whose name the speaker or writer doesn't know or can't remember at the moment. Examples: a switch, a cogwheel, a coil, a washer, an insulator, all those little things we can't live without. When you walk into a hardware store, don't confuse *widget* with *widgeon* (WI jun), or you'll have the man looking for a duck with a reddish-brown head and a yellowish-tan crown, and he may be out of them.

xyster, see **xystus**

xystus (ZIST us), **xyst** (zist) *n.* A *xystus* or *xyst* is a long covered portico, especially one used by ancient Greek athletes for exercising in bad weather or during the winter. The Romans applied *xystus* to any open colonnade or tree-planted walk. This noun comes from Latin *xystus*, which in turn came from Greek *xystos*, based on the verb *xyein* (to scrape, polish), because the floor of a *xystos* was smooth and polished. These words are related to the noun *xyster* (ZIST ur), a surgical instrument for scraping bones, taken intact from the Greek, where it means "graving tool," and is likewise based on their verb *xyein*.

zarf (zarf) *n*. A *zarf* is a cup-holder, usually a stand, for a cup without a handle. It is usually of decorative metal, sometimes precious, and usually richly ornamental. *Zarf* is an Arabic word for "vessel, container." The cup held by the *zarf* is called a *finjan* (fin JAN) or *fingan* (fin GAN). *Finjan* is Arabic, *fingan* Egyptian. The cup in question is usually a small coffee cup containing the thick concoction popularly known as "Turkish coffee." *Zarfs* are never used without *finjans* or *fingans*. The arrangement is a little like the tea-glass held in a metal holder used by our Russian brethren, who otherwise wouldn't be able to hold the superheated glass—except that the Russian glass can stand up by itself, unlike the *finjan* or *fingan*, which, incidentally, is also sometimes spelt *findjan* or *fingian*.

zebrine, see **accipitrine**

zeitgeist (TSITE gyest) *n*. *Zeitgeist* is a German word, based on a combination of two nouns: *Zeit* (time, era, age, epoch) and *Geist* (spirit). [Note: All nouns are capitalized in German; *Zeitgeist*, taken into English, may be spelt with either an upper or lower case *z*.] *Zeitgeist* (literally, time-spirit) is the spirit of the age, the typical attitude of the times, the characteristic moral or intellectual feeling of a particular era, the trend of culture and taste of a period in history. The *zeitgeist* of the Periclean age (c. 461-c. 431 B.C.) of ancient Greece was the attainment of greatness in the arts: architecture, sculpture, music, and drama. The *zeitgeist* of the Middle Ages operated against scientific investigation. The attempt to manage society through technocracy is part of the *zeitgeist* of the 20th century. The Women's Lib movement was definitely in tune with the *zeitgeist* of the 1970s.

zeugma (ZOOHG muh) *n*. *Zeugma* is a term used in grammar, rhetoric, or logic for a phrase in which one word governs or modifies two or more words not connected in meaning, as in the use of a verb with multiple subjects or objects, a preposition taking multiple objects, or an adjective modifying multiple nouns. In each case, the governing word is strictly applicable to one of the following words while the word appropriate to the other is omitted. The English novelist Charles Dickens (1812-1870) gives us a fine, jocular example in *Pickwick Papers*, when "Miss Bolo went home in a flood of tears and a sedan chair." The same *zeugmatic* situation occurs when, on a bitter, rainy day, a fisherman catches five fish and a cold, or funeral guests attend with weeping eyes and hearts, or a dinner party is spoiled by the host's bad wine and jitters, or an angry man leaves the house in high dudgeon and an overcoat. *Zeugma* is taken intact from the Greek, where it means "yoking," related to the verb *zeugnynai* (to yoke). (See also **syllepsis**.)

Part II

▼▼▼▼▼

1000
MOST OBSCURE
WORDS

For Marjorie, as always

Acknowledgments
(Written on my 81st birthday)

This is my fourth "1000 Word" book. In my previous works in this series (*1000 Most Important Words, 1000 Most Practical Words, 1000 Most Challenging Words*) I expressed my gratitude to kind and helpful friends. This time, I must add my thanks to three who have supported me throughout: Laurence Urdang, unarguably the best lexicographer I have had the good fortune to know; Paul S. Falla, a man of catholic knowledge, a genius in the world of words (I am deeply grateful not only for their help but for the friendships that have grown out of our common interest); and my son-in-law Eric Weber, a word expert in his own right, who many years ago urged me to enter the field. Without his help and encouragement I might have remained mute. I owe to Eric an unrepayable debt of gratitude for my enjoyment of a second career after a lifetime in the law. Thank you, Larry, Paul and Eric.

From time to time I have resorted to quotations given in various dictionaries, principally the *O.E.D.* and *Webster's Third*, as examples of the meaning and proper use of a headword. I am deeply conscious of the debt owed to those who have labored to uncover and amass those quotations, which might otherwise have been beyond the reach of one who toils alone.

Preface

I don't favor the use of complex words when simple ones will do. The main purpose of language is to communicate. Then why a book of obscure words? Mainly because they are fun and incidentally enlightening. I quote from a recent article by Joe D. Thomas, Professor Emeritus of English at Rice University: "One always refers to language as a tool; but after playing around with it for more years than there legitimately are, I tell you that it is also, in a vulgar phrase, *something else*. More precious than pearls of any price, it is a marvelous toy, a plaything of the mind."

The words in this collection are hardly ones you will run into, let alone use. But they are legitimate words, blessed by the cachet of established dictionaries that celebrate the wealth of our language, and the etymological material they evoke demonstrates our debt to the so-called dead languages, particularly those of Greece and Rome (though words from other sources appear as well). You may occasionally be surprised to find a familiar word among the entries, e.g., *aftermath, copy, dudgeon, ell, patriarch, relief, thesis*; they have been included only because they have certain unfamiliar, "obscure" applications.

I have written books that help in the expansion of vocabulary, books that aid, encourage and even challenge people to improve their verbal equipment. This book is different. It may have an incidental educational effect, but its main purpose is entertainment.

I take the liberty of quoting from the frontispiece of my *1000 Most Challenging Words*. First, the opening lines of a poem by Dryden:

> Latine is now of equal use become
> To Englishmen, as was the Greek to Rome;
> It guides our language, nothing is exprest
> Gracefull or true but by the Roman test.

Next, some lines from Samuel Butler's *Hudibras*:

> Beside, 'tis known he could speak Greek
> As naturally as pigs squeak:
> That Latin was no more difficile,
> Than to a black-bird 'tis to whistle.

(Obviously, *difficile* has to be pronounced di FIS il to conform to *whistle*.)

Finally, from the *Panegyric on Tom Coriate* by Lionel Cranfield, Earl of Middlesex:

> He Greek and Latin speaks with greater ease
> Than hogs eat acorns, and tame pigeons peas.

(Cranfield's couplet preceded Butler's *Hudibras* by a good many years. Would we could match the facility of Tom Coriate!)

That's the way it was once upon a time. Can we ever hope for a classical revival? (I am sure the reader understands that wherever the word *Greek* appears in the etymological discussion, I am referring to the Greek tongue of ancient times and that, to meet the needs of most contemporary readers, Greek words and combining forms are set forth in transliteration: the spelling of the words of one language in the more or less corresponding letters of the alphabet of another. Of the 24 letters of the Greek alphabet, only a few would be recognizable to those not versed in the classics, as the forerunners of their contemporary English equivalents.) Might a book like this spark some interest in those old, time-honored ancient tongues? If so, it would go to show that fun's not only fun but may sometimes produce unexpected results. I hope so.

Key to Abbreviations

Throughout the text abbreviations are used to refer to the following seven dictionaries:

CH	*Chambers Twentieth Century Dictionary*
C.O.D.	*Concise Oxford Dictionary*
LS	*Liddell and Scott Greek English Lexicon*
O.E.D.	*Oxford English Dictionary*
RH	*Random House Dictionary, Unabridged*
W II	*Webster's Second New International Dictionary*
W III	*Webster's Third New International Dictionary*

Key to Pronunciation

"a"   for "a" as in "hat"
"ay" or "a——e"   for "a" as in "hate"
"ah"   for "a" as in "bah," "o" as in gone
"air"   for "a" as in "dare," "ai" as in "air"
"a(r)"   for "a" as in "art"
"aw"   for "a" as in "awe," "ou" as in "ought"
"e" or "eh"   f or "e" as in "met"
"ee"   for "e" as in "meet"
"i" or "ih"   for "i" as in "bit"
"(e)ye" or "i——e"   for "i" as in "bite"
"o"   for "o" as in "got"
"oh" or "o——e"   for "o" as in "go" or "note"
"oo"   for "oo" as in "look"
"ooh"   for "oo" as in "boot," "u" as in "lute"
"o(r)"   for "o" as in "or"
"oy"   for "o" as in "boy" or "void"
"ou"   for "ou" as in "out"
"u" or "uh"   for "u" as in "but" and for schwa (an indefinite
                        "uh" sound of an unaccented syllable, like the "a"
                        in "woman," the "i" in "pencil," the "u" in
                        "focus," etc.
"u(r)"   for "u" as in "fur"
"th"   hard, as in "thing," "thistle," or "third"
"th"   soft, as in "this" or "that"

acatalectic   See **prosodion.**

acephalous   See **dolichocephal.**

acosmism, also **akosmism** (uh KOZ mis'm) *n.* From the Greek negative prefix *a-* (the *alpha privative,* equivalent to our *un-* and its variants) plus *kosmos* (cosmos, universe), the Greeks formed the term *akosmismus* to denote the theory that denies to the universe any absolute reality or any existence apart from God. It is the opposite of *pantheism* (PAN thee iz'm)—from the Greek prefix *pan-,* the combining form of *pan,* neuter of *pas* (all), plus *theos* (god)—the doctrine that identifes God with the universe or claims that God is only the combined forces of the universe as they manifest themselves. *Pantheism* has another distinct meaning—the worship of gods of various beliefs without distinction, as opposed to *theism,* belief in the existence of a god or gods, or *monotheism,* the doctrine that there is one God, the creator of mankind and the world, who transcends yet remains within the world. We are familiar with *atheism,* which opposes all the foregoing doctrines, denying the existence of any god. We must not omit mention of *polytheism*—from the Greek *polys* (many) plus *theos*—which denotes the worship of several gods, as practiced in ancient Egypt, Greece, Rome and many other early cultures. *Polytheism,* in some cultures, also involved the creation of a family relationship among these various gods through a kind of anthropomorphism, attributing quite human emotions and behavior to them, resulting in a rather cozy relationship between mankind and its pantheon. The same goes for *allotheism,* the worship of foreign, strange or unsanctioned gods, which is forbidden by the First Commandment.

acuate   See **acuminate.**

acuminate (uh KYOOH muh nuht) *adj.;* (uh KYOOH muh nate) *vb.* Note the difference in the pronunciations of the adjective and the noun. The noun *acumen* is familiar; it can be pronounced uh KYOOH muhn, a KYOOH muhn, AK yuh muhn or AK yuh men and is commonly understood to mean "keen perception" or "discernment" or "shrewdness," especially in matters of business. It has other technical meanings in botany and crustaceology, not relevant here. But *acuminate* is another matter. As an adjective, it means "pointed," and applies to anything that tapers to a fine point. As a transitive verb, it means "to sharpen"; as an intransitive verb, "to taper," i.e., "to come to a point." *Acuminous* (uh KYOOH muh nuhs) can be either the adjectival form of *acumen,* meaning "possessing (or characterized by) *acumen*" or can serve as a synonym of *acuminate* in the adjectival sense. *Acumination* (uh kyooh muh NAY shuhn) means either "sharpening" or "tapering point," depending on the context. *Acuminulate* (uh kyooh MIN yuh luht) is another adjectival form, as you might expect from the inclusion of the syllable *-ul-,* from the Latin diminutive suffix *-ulus, -a, -um,* meaning "slightly pointed" or "tapering to a minute degree."

All of these words stem from the Latin *acumen* (point), related to the verb *acuere* (to sharpen). It is well to note, too, that Latin *acus* means "needle," and *acutus*, from which we get *acute*, is the past participle of *acuere*. English also has the adjective *acuate* (AK yuh wate), meaning "sharply pointed" or "needle-shaped," derived from an assumed Middle Latin *acuatus*. *Acuity* ("acuteness," "keenness" or "sharpness," whether applying to a physical object or the mind, the understanding or the senses) is dealt with in my *1000 Most Challenging Words*, while *acumen* is fully discussed in my *1000 Most Practical Words*. They, too, go back to our old friends *acus* and *acuere*. Don't credit them, however, with *accurate*; that is from the Latin *accuratus*, the past participle of *accurare* ("to take care of," "do carefully," "prepare with care"), which is derived from the Latin prefix *ad-* (to, toward) plus *curare* (to take care of). Be acute, proceed with acumen and acuity and you'll be accurate, especially with words.

acumination   See **acuminate**.

acuminous   See **acuminate**.

acuminulate   See **acuminate**.

adscititious (ad sit ISH uhs) *adj*. Anything worthy of this impressive adjective is "added, supplemental, originating or acquired from something extrinsic, adventitious," the opposite of *inherent*. The word is derived from the Latin *adscitus* or *ascitus* (derived, foreign), the past participle of the verb *a(d)sciscere* (to approve, appropriate), built of the preposition *ad-* (toward—indicating tendency or addition) plus *sciscere* (to seek, to find out). This brings up a point quite incidental to the main entry, but let's have it out now. We just mentioned *sciscere*. That word is the inchoative of *scire* (to know). But what is an *inchoative*? *Inc(h)oare* means "to begin" or "to begin to treat of" something. Its past participle is *inc(h)oatus*, and that gave us *inchoate*, which is discussed in my earlier *1000 Most Important Words* and is described as denoting "things just begun, undeveloped ..." The lengthened form, *inchoative* (in KOH uh tive), is the name given to verbs in Latin and Greek that express the concept of "beginning an action" rather than performing one. Their first person singular forms end in *-sco* in Latin and *-sko* in Greek. Thus, to swipe some examples from Fowler, in Greek, *gignosko* means "to learn," i.e., "begin to know," while in Latin, *calesco* means "to grow warm" rather than "be warm." So—at long last—*sciscere*, whose first-person singular is *scisco* (there's the *-sco* ending), means "to seek to know" rather than "to know." (Incidental moral: Seek and ye shall find.) Getting back to our headword: John Evelyn, in *Numismata; a Discourse on Medals Ancient and Modern* (1697)—*numisma* is Latin for "money, coin," from the Greek *nomisma* (custom, usage, currency, coin, akin to *nomizein*, to observe, recognize, and *numismatics* is our word for "the study of coins and medals")—writes of "... such *adscititious* Habits as may be contracted by Institution, Discipline and custom." After all this, the simplest definition of *adscititious* is "additional," in the sense of "supplemental." Forgive the anticlimax.

adytum (AD ih tuhm) *n*. The Greek word *adyton* (not to be entered), composed of the negative prefix *a-* (the "alpha privative," as in *amorphous, amoral, apolitical*, etc., meaning "not") plus *dytos*, a verbal adjective from the verb *dyein* (to enter), was Latinized to *adytum*, denoting the innermost section of a temple, the secret shrine whence oracles were uttered, and later, the chancel of a church. It acquired the figurative meaning of "sanctum." Samuel Taylor Coleridge, in *Essays on His Own Times* (1800), criticized a politician as one who carried with him "the habits of a disputing club into the *adyta* of the Cabinet." Everyone should have his own *adytum*, for solitary contemplation and search for the truth. Think of all those poor souls who don't have a roof, let alone an *adytum*!

aftermath   See **rowen.**

akratisma   See **chittering-bite.**

alieniloquy (ay lee en IL uh kwee) *n*. The *O.E.D.* quotes the definition "a talking wide from the purpose, or not to the matter at hand" from the early British lexicographer Nathan Bailey's *Universal Etymological English Dictionary* (1731 edition—first edition 1721; they preceded the publication of Samuel Johnson's *Dictionary of the English Language* (1755); the 1731 edition was published as *Dictionarium Britannicum: or a More Compleat Universal Etymological English Dictionary*; Bailey's definition was adopted by John Ash in his *New and Complete Dictionary of the English Language*, 1775, trailing Johnson by 20 years). The word is characterized as "obsolete" by the *O.E.D.*, but its Latin ancestor, *alieniloquium*, shows up in Professor Elizabeth Dipple's exhaustive study of the novels of Iris Murdoch (*Iris Murdoch, Work for the Spirit*). In a discussion of Murdoch's *The Sea, The Sea* Dipple points out that Charles Arrowby is the ostensible protagonist, "but, as in the case of the medieval idea of the *alieniloquium* (a speaking of things other than those it purports to do...) there is a sustained questioning of the spiritual life ... a profound psychic landscape whose symbolic quality very slowly, in small, subtle steps unfolds. James [Arrowby, the protagonist's brother] is its vehicle, and on him rests the deep infrastructure of the book." Dipple's definition varies somewhat from Bailey's, but the underlying meaning is the same in both. Profound stuff, in both Murdoch's novel (as in all her novels) and Dipple's analysis. In a recent letter, Professor Dipple tells me that "... *alieniloquium* seems to me a splendid way of talking about the secret agenda of many texts, and I much prefer it to coarser and more simplistic words like *allegory*." So do I.

allele (uh LEEL) *n*. This word is a shortened form of *allelomorph* (uh LEE luh morf, uh LEL uh-), a term in Mendelian genetics for any of several forms of a gene responsible for hereditary variation. The longer form, *allelomorph*, is formed from the Greek *allelo-*, the stem of *allelon* (of one another) plus *morphe* (form). Gregor Johann Mendel was an Austrian monk (1822–84) who pioneered in experimental studies of heredity, carrying out independent scientific investigations on plants, mainly garden peas, by means of controlled pollination and statistical analysis of the results, especially hybridization. Mendel's basic conclusion was that an inherited characteristic is determined by the combination of two hereditary units (now known as *genes*), one from each of the parental reproductive cells. These genes are known as *alleles* or *allelomorphs*. If you want to investigate further, see K. R. Lewis's book entitled *The Matter of Mendelian Heredity* (1964) and R. C. Olby's *Origins of Mendelism* (1966), and if they disagree with what I have said on the subject, better side with them.

allelomorph   See **allele**.

alloch(e)iria (ah loh KEYE ree uh, -KIH-) *n*. Since *allo-* is the combining form of the Greek adjective *allos*, meaning "other," and *cheiro-* the combining form of *cheir*, meaning "hand," one might jump to the (as usual, erroneous) conclusion that *alloch(e)iria* had something to do with "on the other hand," as in "on the one hand, on the other hand." Actually, *alloch(e)iria* is the name for the attribution of a sensation to the wrong part of the body. How often have you been surprised to hear from your dentist that it isn't your canine but your first premolar that has the abscess? You've been suffering not only from the abscess, my dear, but also from a case of *alloch(e)iria*. My dentist tells me it happens all the time and that the confusion can involve not just two neighboring teeth but often neck and even shoulder pains. Even with a supply of Greek combining forms at your command, be careful.

al(l)odium (ul LOH de uhm) also **al(l)od** (AL od) *n*. This word, in any of its forms, was used in feudal times to denote an estate in which the holder had absolute possession and control free of any subjection by way of rent, service or acknowledgment to a superior. The term was applied particularly in Anglo-Saxon society of the 11th century. It was the antithesis of a *feod* or *feud* (pronounced FOOHD—and this *feud* is not the Montague and Capulet type), the name then applied to an estate held of a lord or other superior on condition of the rendering of certain services by the tenant or vassal to the superior. This type of fiddledeedee has long been obsolete, but if you settle down with one of those interminable historical novels set in that distant era, you'd better be acquainted with it. *Al(l)odium* is a Middle Latin term, derived from two Old High German words: *al* (all) and *od* (property).

allotheism   See **acosmism**.

alnage (OL nij) *n*. The practice of *alnage* and the office of *alnager* have long since faded from the scene, but you might bump into these terms if you were reading fact or fiction involving life in England in days of yore. *Alnage* and the office of *alnager* were introduced into English law in 1320 during the reign of Edward III. *Alnage* was the official inspection and measurement of woolen cloth by an *alnager* appointed by the court, who also declared its quality and value. The practice and office were abolished during the reign of King William III (1689–1702). *Alnage* was also the official name of the fee paid the *alnager*. Geoffrey Chaucer must have had something to do with this function since he was the comptroller of the customs on wool and hides at the port of London from 1374 to 1386. (Geoffrey held lots of important jobs and did all kinds of things besides writing *The Canterbury Tales* and other notable works that set the course of English literature.) *Alnage* and *alnager* owe their names to the fact that the measurement of the cloth was by the *ell*, which in turn got its name from Old French *aulnage*, from *aulner* (to measure by the *ell*), and which can ultimately be traced back to Latin *ulna* (elbow, and by transference, a measure of length). *Ell* has had a great diversity of meanings as a measurement, including the distance from the elbow to the wrist, from the shoulder to the wrist, from either to the fingertips—usually the middle finger—and so forth. Some Latin poets used *ulna*, for instance, to mean "as much as a man can span with both arms," others to mean "a fathom" (which is etymologically the same thing). *Ell* finally crystallized, in England, as a unit of length (chiefly for cloth) equal to 45 inches and is now no longer in use. It designated different lengths in different countries: in Holland, approximately 27 inches, in Scotland, about 37—all very confusing in earlier days, nowadays happily obsolete. It reminds one of the *cubit*, from Latin *cubitum* (elbow), which was used in olden times as a unit of length equal to the span from the elbow to the tip of the middle finger—anywhere from 18 inches to 21 or even more, based on natural variations in the length of forearms. Midgets and giants were undoubtedly omitted from consideration. Just imagine, if *ells* and *cubits* were still current in the age of basketball players. Good riddance, I say: So long to *alnage, alnagers, ells* and *cubits*!

alnager   See **alnage.**

alphonsin (al FON sin) *n*. Named after its inventor, Alphonsus Ferrier of Naples, Italy, in 1552, an *alphonsin* was a surgical instrument consisting of a forceps equipped with three elastic branches closed together by means of a ring. The purpose of this ingenious apparatus was the extraction of bullets from the body. Any follower of the Korean War television series "M.A.S.H." has watched Hawkeye and his colleagues extract bullets from wounds countless times. These excellent surgeons weren't using *alphonsins*, however. There are many different types of forceps in use these days for the extraction of foreign objects from bodies, among them the Allison and the Crile. Do not confuse *alphonsin* with the adjective *Alphonsine*, pronounced the same way but descriptive of certain astronomical tables prepared by a group of Jewish, Arabian and Christian astronomers in 1252 under the patronage of Alfonso X (the Wise), King of Castile and León. The result of such confusion in a hospital operating room would be too horrible to contemplate.

altricial   See nidicolous.

altrigenderism (al truh JEN duh riz'm) *n. Alter*, in Latin, means "other of two," as opposed to *alius*, "other of more than two." The distinction was not always maintained by the Roman writers, but that is the general rule. From *alter* we get the prefix *altri-*; from *gener-*, the stem of *genus* (class, kind—especially as applied to living beings), we get *gender*. Add the suffix *-ism* and we have *altrigenderism*, which has naught to do with change of sex but rather the happy, if often unnerving, state of development when one becomes interested in, nay, attracted to members of the opposite sex. This is an experience shared by most of us and the subject of a good deal of literature—whether poetry, short story, novel or drama. It leads to romance, elation, perplexity, suffering; but this is a book about obscure words, not psychiatry, so we'd best end the discussion right now.

alveary (AL vee uhr ee) *n.* An *alvearium*, in Latin, is a "beehive." The historian Pliny used the words *alvus* and *alveus* as synonyms of *alvearium*. *Alveary* is also the name, in anatomy, for the hollow of the external ear—a kind of pun, because that, as well as a beehive, is where wax collects. Strangely, the word has an altogether distinct meaning: an early dictionary of English, French, Greek and Latin. This is another sort of pun, as indicated by an early (1580) scholar named John Baret, who wrote: "Within a yeere, or two, they had gathered together a great volume, which (for the apt similitude between the good Scholers and diligent Bees in gathering their waxe and honie into their Hiue) I called then their Alvearie." In Latin, an *alveus* is any hollow or socket, and in English, *alveated* means "vaulted," like a beehive.

amathophobia (am uh thuh FOH bee uh) *n.* Since *amathos* is Greek for "sand," and we all know the meaning of *phobia*, one would suppose that *amathophobia* was a learned term for "fear of sand," like the dread of sandstorms that must beset denizens of desert lands. But no: It is defined by W III as "fear of *dust*," like the obsession that beset Craig's wife in the play of that name and ruined her marriage. Strangely, the word is missing from *W II* and is not to be found in any of my other dictionaries, including the *O.E.D.* and its Supplement. Lexicographers move in mysterious ways. I suppose that just about every-thing in the world is subject to somebody's phobia, even something as seem-ingly benign as health. How about hypochondriacs, who obviously suffer from *sanitaphobia*? (*Sanitas* is Latin for "health.") What about *divitiphobia* (*divitiae* is Latin for "wealth"), the fear of wealth by those devout readers of the Bible who take literally the usually misquoted statement of Paul in his First Epistle to Timothy: "The love of money is the root of all evil?" And Keats enjoined *scientiphobia* (*scientia* is Latin for "wisdom") when he wrote: "O fret not after knowledge—I have none ..." So what good does it do to go to bed early and get up early? And I beg to be forgiven for having concocted the silly hybrids *sanitaphobia*, *divitiphobia* and *scientiphobia*. But it does seem that *-phobia* can be attached to every noun in the dictionary.

ambidexter (am bee DEK stur) *n., adj.* As an adjective, *ambidexter* describes a person able to use both hands equally well. The word is built of the prefix *ambi-*, the combining form of Latin *ambo* (both), which is found in a number of familiar words (including *ambiguous* and *ambivalent*), and *dexter* (right), which came to mean "skillful" and gave us *dextrous* or *dexterous*. *Sinister* means "left" in Latin and by transference came to mean "wrong, unfavorable." It was taken intact into English to mean "ominous, threatening." In adjectival use, *ambidexter* is now archaic, having given way to the familiar term *ambidextrous*, and that word has been extended in meaning to denote versatility, as used, for instance, by T. S. Eliot in describing a writer equally at home in verse and prose. *Ambidexterity*, literally the ability to use both hands equally well, acquired the figurative meaning of "superior skill" generally, and, by extension, "double-dealing." It was so defined by the good Doctor Johnson in his *Dictionary* (1755) and used in that sense by Isaac D'Israeli (father of Benjamin) in *Amenities of Literature* (1841), where he wrote of " ... that intricate net of general misery, spun out of ... crafty *ambidexterity*." But, getting back to *ambidexter* in its use as an adjective, it came to mean "double-dealing" in legal parlance, of a person who takes bribes from both parties to an unlawful transaction. It's bad enough to take a bribe from either party, but *both*? And if we ever run across an ambidextrous *ambidexter*, good heavens, he'd have it four ways, wouldn't he, and that would be quadruply sinister!

ambry (AM bree), also **aumbry** (AWM bree) *n.* This word has been spelled in many different ways, including *armary*, *almary* and *awmry*. It came from the Latin *armarium* (cupboard, chest) and at various times has meant "repository," "a place for keeping things," "treasury," "storehouse," "safe," "locker," "press" and "cupboard," either a wall recess or a separate piece of furniture of whatever nature. It has also been applied to a pigeonhole type of compartment. In churches it has been used to designate a closed recess for keeping books, vestments, sacramental plates, consecrated oil and other ritual accessories, and in the home, a place for keeping food, a pantry, a dresser or what the British call a "meat-safe"—a compartment in which to store meat (in the days before refrigerators)—most recently made of wire gauze, but in the old days, with sides of haircloth (also known as *cilice*, itself an interesting word from Greek *kilikion* via Latin *cilicium*, so called because it was originally made of goat hair from Cilicia, an ancient country in southeast Asia Minor that became a Roman province). Additional uses of *ambry* include the following: a place for books and archives, a library, a livestock hutch. Has there ever been a more versatile word? Still another use: In Richard Stanyhurst's 1582 translation of *The Aeneid*, we see the words: "In this od hudge *ambry* [the Trojan horse] they ramd a number of hardye Tough knights." The word still showed up much later. In William Beckford's *Recollections* (1835) we read of "a press or *ambery* elaborately carved" and William Morris's poem *The Life and Death of Jason* (1867) mentions "a little *aumbrye*, with a door o'er-gilt." Anything more you'd like to know about *ambry*?

ambs-ace (AMZ ase) *n.* From the Latin *ambo asses* (both aces) comes the term *ambs-ace*, meaning "both aces" or "double ace." (*Ace* is a dice term, meaning "one," i.e., the side of the die marked with a single dot.) Two aces, in this sense, are known by the slang term "snake-eyes" and as a first throw constitute a crap. The game of dice is known as "craps"; a first throw of two ones, a one and a two, or two sixes is a crap and loses the bet, and the dice pass to an opponent. Since a throw of two aces, or *ambs-ace*, is the lowest possible throw, *ambs-ace* came to denote, figuratively, "bad luck, worthlessness, next to nothing or nothing," and the expression *within ambs ace of* was an emphatic form of *within an ace of*, i.e., on the very edge (or verge) of. *Ambs-ace* has been spelled in many different ways, one of which was *ames-ace*, a form found in *All's Well That Ends Well*, when Lafeu speaks the line: "I had rather be in this choice than throw *ames-ace* for my life." (Act II, Scene 3.) In *Among My Books*, James Russell Lowell writes of "a lucky throw of words which may come up the sices [*sixes* as a dice term] of hardy metaphor or the *ambs-ace* of conceit." An elegant turn of phrase if ever there was one!

amphiscian (am FISH ee uhn) *n., adj.* Two related words, also both nouns and adjectives, are *heteroscian* (het uh ROSH ee uhn) and *periscian* (puhr ISH ee uhn). There are endless ways of categorizing the inhabitants of this planet: by color, culture, nationality, physical traits, intellectual prowess, moral codes and so on; but did you know that there are categories based on the direction in which one's shadow is cast? And that this necessarily depends on which zone one inhabits? Let me explain: An *amphiscian* is "one who dwells in the torrid zone"; thus, his or her shadow is thrown both ways: to the north part of the year, to the south the rest of the year. Simple enough: *amphi-* is a Greek prefix meaning "on both sides," and *skia* means "shadow." *Heteroscians* are inhabitants of a temperate zone, whose noon shadows fall in one direction, either north or south. Here we have the Greek prefix *hetero-*, meaning "one or the other," plus *skia*. And finally we come to *periscian*, one who resides in a polar circle, whose shadow moves around him or her in a complete circle on those days on which the sun does not set. The Greek prefix *peri-*, meaning "around," is attached to our old friend *skia*. In this age of rapid travel from zone to zone, you should always know which of these nouns or adjectives applies. There may be more important criteria, but I can't imagine what. See also **macroscian** for more on this subject.

ampollosity   See **ampulla.**

ampulla (am POOL uh) *n.* After running into the word *ampollosity* in Browning's *The Ring and the Book* (*o* rather than *u* in *CH* as opposed to the *O.E.D.*, and the word being defined as "pretentious inanity, turgidity, bombast"), my eye leapt to *ampulla* and its plethora of definitions, of which the following are only some: "a small two-handled flask"; "a pilgrim's bottle"; "a vessel for holy oil, as at coronations"; "a cruet for the wine and water used at the altar"; "a small glass container for a hypodermic dose." These were followed by uses in biology and anatomy. To add to the confusion, variant spellings are *ampoule* and *ampul*. *Ampulla* is an irregular Latin diminutive of *amphora*—the Roman and Greek two-handled jar ubiquitous in museums of classical antiquities—a word derived from the Greek prefix *amphi-* (both, on both sides), seen in words like *amphibious*, plus *phoreus* (bearer). Derivation notes in dictionaries also credit the influence of Old English *ampulle*, Old French *ampo(u)le* and Italian *ampolla* (phial, vial). Browning's spelling must have been the result of his long romance with Italy (where the rascal was in April when he wrote "O to be in England/Now that April's there ... "—a time when the weather in England is usually wet and rainy).

Amyclaean (am ih KLEE uhn) *adj.* Like the adjective **moazagotl**, which modifies only one noun, *cloud*, this adjective modifies only the noun *silence*. Just what is an *Amyclaean Silence*? *Amyclae* (uh MEYE klee) is the name of an ancient town of Laconia, the country in the southeast Peloponnesus, Greece, of which Sparta, three miles north, was the capital. At one time it was the principal city of Laconia. Again and again it was beset by false rumors of impending invasion by the Spartans, so often that the authorities issued a decree prohibiting any mention of the subject. The Spartans finally arrived, but the decree was respected and no one dared give warning. Amyclae was taken. This curious incident gave rise to the expression "more silent than Amyclae." Somehow, it brings to mind the converse legend of the boy who cried "Wolf!"

anaclitic (an uh KLIH tik) *adj.* Freud coined the German word *Anlehnungstypus*, literally, "leaning-on type," to describe one whose choice of a love object was based on dependence of the libido on another instinct, such as hunger. (This brings to mind the old vulgar, nay, repellent aphorism: "The way to a man's heart is through his stomach." Ugh!) Freud based his term on the Greek adjective *anaklitos* (reclining), from the verb *anaklinein* (to lean back, recline), built of the prefix *ana-* (back) plus *klinein* (to lean). *Anaclitic* was later extended to signify dependence on another or others generally. In Joan Riviere's translation from Freud, *S. Freud's Introductory Lectures on Psychoanalysis* (1922), she writes about " ... The *anaclitic* type (*Anlehnungstypus*) in which those persons who become prized on account of the satisfactions they rendered to the primal needs of life are chosen as objects by the Libido also."

In Howard Warren's *Dictionary of Psychology* (1934), *anaclitic object-choice* is defined as "taking one's earliest attachments (to mother or nurse) as a model for the selection of the first love object." Pretty dangerous, those "earliest attachments."

anadiplosis   See **anaphora.**

anagoge (an uh GOH jee), also **anagogy** (AN uh goh jee) *n. Anagoge* or *anagogy* (the *O.E.D.* calls the latter "a better English form") is "the elevation of the mind to things celestial," "mystical interpretation," especially the interpretation of the Bible in the "fourth or mystical" sense. The "four senses" of Scripture are defined as the historical or literal, the allegorical, the moral and the *anagogical* (an uh GOJ ih kuhl). According to the *Schaff-Herzog Encyclopedia of Religious Knowledge* (Philip Schaff, 1819–93, edited the first edition of the *Realencyclopaedie* of Johann Jakob Herzog, 1805–82), "Jerusalem is *literally* a city of Palestine, *allegorically* the Church, *morally* the believing soul, *anagogically* the heavenly Jerusalem." The adjective *anagogic* (an uh GOJ ik) is applied to things pertaining to mystical interpretation and the strivings of the unconscious toward morally high ideals. The more of that the merrier!

analemma (an uh LEM uh) *n.* Although the Greek verb *lambanein* (to take) and its extended form *analambanein* (to take up—the prefix *ana-* having the force of *up*) figure in the derivation of this word, it has nothing to do with *dilemma*, the *lemma* part of which is also derived from *lambanein*. We know (all too well!) what a *dilemma* is, but how about an *analemma*? That is the Latin word for a "sundial pedestal," or the sundial itself, derived from the Greek noun *analemma* meaning "support, prop," which explains the pedestal idea. Thomas D. Nicholson, in the December 1987 issue of the magazine *Natural History*, defines the word as follows:

> The *analemma* we see on globes records how the point on the earth directly below the sun at clock noon changes during the year. The sun moves north of the equator in summer and south of the equator in winter. It is ahead of clock noon from September 1 to December 26, falls behind from December 26 to April 15, then moves ahead again until June 15, and falls behind again until September 1, alternately speeding up and slowing down with respect to clock time. It is exactly even with the clock four times a year—on December 26, April 1, June 15, and September 1.

This definition is followed by a diagram in the shape of an elongated eight, much like a child's drawing of a pussycat from the rear, missing ears and whiskers. In short, an *analemma* is a scale of the sun's daily declination drawn from tropic to tropic on artificial terrestrial globes.

anaphora (uh NAF uh ruh) *n.* This word would appear to have, among its several meanings, two that are antithetical. Thus, it is a term in rhetoric for the device of beginning successive sentences or lines with the same word or phrase for the purpose of emphasis. Example: In the 29th Psalm we read: "The voice of the Lord is upon the waters ... The voice of the Lord is powerful; the voice of the Lord is full of majesty. The voice of the Lord breaketh the cedars ... The voice of the Lord divideth the flames of fire. The voice of the Lord shaketh the wilderness ... The voice of the Lord maketh the hinds to calve ..." Another example: In Pope's *Elegy to the Memory of an Unfortunate Lady* we find these lines: "By foreign hands thy dying eyes were closed,/By foreign hands thy decent limbs composed,/By foreign hands thy humble grave adorned ..." So far so good, but *anaphora* can also mean the opposite: the avoiding of repetition of a preceding word or phrase through the use, for example, of *it* or *do*, as in : My father speaks French; I speak *it* and my mother *does* too. *Anaphora* is taken from Greek, meaning "carrying back," based on the prefix *ana-* (back) and the verb *pherein* (to carry, bear). It has a variant form, *epanaphora* (ep uh NAF uh ruh). It also denotes the central prayer sequence of the Eucharist. A related term in rhetoric is *epistrophe* (uh PIS truh fee), also known as *epiphora* (uh PIF uh ruh—which also means "involuntary weeping"!), the repetition of a word or phrase at the *end* of successive clauses or sentences. Example: Antony to the Citizens in *Julius Caesar*, Act III, Scene 2: "I should do Brutus wrong, and Cassius wrong ... I will not do them wrong ... " A further rhetorical device is *symploce* (SIM ploh see), the combining of *anaphora* and *epistrophe*. This term is derived, as so often happens, via Late Latin, from Greek *symploke* (intertwining, combination), based on the prefix *epi-* (upon) plus *strophe* (twist, turning around). A more exhaustive (and brilliant) list of obscure words having to do with rhetoric and grammar, followed by brief definitions, can be found in the Glossary/Index of Arthur Quinn's exquisite little book *Figures of Speech*, published in 1982 by Gibbs M. Smith, Inc., Salt Lake City. Included in his list and beautifully treated in the text with copious examples are the following (I omit some dealt with in my *1000 Most Challenging Words*): *anadiplosis* (repitition of an end at the next beginning); *antimetabole* (an *epanados* which is also an *antithesis*); *auxesis* (arrangement in ascending importance); *diacope* (repetition with only a word or two between); *epanados* (repetition in the opposite order); *epanalepsis* (repetition of the beginning at the end); *gradatio* (repeated *anadiplosis*); *hypozeuxis* (omission of a *zeugma*—a term dealt with in my above cited work) and *inclusio* (repetition of the beginning of a passage at its end). There will be a brief period of study before the examination.

anaptotic   See **aptote.**

anaptyxis   See **metaplasm.**

androgenesis   See **androgenous.**

androgenous (an DROJ uh nuhs) *adj*. At first glance, this word might well be mistaken as a misspelling of its homophone *androgynous*, an error confessed by the ever-entertaining William Safire in his weekly column "On Language" in the *New York Times Magazine* of January 15, 1989. The admirable Mr. Safire has always been willing to admit the error of his linguistic, if not his political, ways and is indeed the champion of the "Mea Culpa Stakes." *Androgynous* is defined in my *1000 Most Challenging Words* as "applied to man and other animals, describing specimens having the characteristics of both sexes. This can refer to sexual organs or other physical characteristics, or to personality or temperament." That word is derived from a combination of Greek *andros* (man) and *gyne* (woman). *Androgenous*, on the other hand, is differently derived, in that the *-genous* element has nothing to with the female sex but is based on the Greek suffix *-genes* (born), from the root of the verb *gignesthai* (to be born), and has the force of "generating." This word, then, means "pertaining to the production of exclusively male offspring." For those who want to go more deeply into the subject, *androgenous* is the adjectival form of *androgenesis*, which is male *parthenogenisis*, i.e., a development whereby the embryo contains only the male parent's chromosomes because of the failure of the nucleus of the ovum to participate in fertilization. As you might suspect, there is also such a thing as *gynogenesis*, and since you now know all about those Greek prefixes and suffixes, you will easily recognize that phenomenon as the situation whereby the embryo contains only the female parent's chromosomes because the sperm that activated the ovum degenerated, poor chap, before it could combine with the egg nucleus. You thought this was a book about words? Well, a little excursion into biology never hurt anyone.

aniconic (an eye KON ik) *adj. Icon*, from Greek *eikon*, in its general sense means "image" and frequently denotes—particularly in the Orthodox church and art and museum circles—a religious portrait of Christ or a saint, in oil or mosaic. In the art world, *iconic* decribes works executed in the conventional or traditional mode. Putting *an-* (the Greek prefix known as the "alpha privative," shortened to *a-* before a consonant, as in *amoral, atypical*, etc., and used to express negation) before *iconic*, we get *aniconic*: descriptive of things that are symbolic or suggestive rather than representational. For example, objects of worship or veneration in primitive religions, such as trees and rocks symbolic of gods without being images of them, can be said to be *aniconic*. The noun *aniconism* (an EYE kuhn iz'm) denotes that type of worship, and an *aniconist* (an EYE kuhn ist) is a follower of that form of religion. Animals were widely used as sacred objects in ancient religious systems. The wolf, griffon and crow represented Apollo; the stag, Diana; the heifer, Isis; the peacock and the lamb, Juno; the eagle, Jupiter; the bull, Neptune; the dove, the swan and the sparrow, Venus. How much more exciting the symbol can be than the representational image!

anicut, also **annicut** (AN uh kut) *n*. This is the name of a dam which, for irrigation purposes, is built across a river, storing up water, which in turn is drawn off into channels running in different directions to regulate and control the supply. It is an Anglo-Indian word, from Tamil *anai* (dam) and *kattu* (building); the procedure it denotes is common in southern India, primarily in Madras, as an efficient alternative to the canal system of the northern regions.

anlaut (AN lawt) *n*. There are three related terms in philology having to do with the position of a sound in a word or syllable: *anlaut*, *inlaut* (IN laut) and *auslaut* (AW slaut). They denote, respectively, the first, medial (or internal) and final sound in a word or syllable. Example: In the word *flute*, *f* is the *anlaut*, *u* is the *inlaut* and *t* is the *auslaut* (not the final letter, but the final sound). All three words are of German origin; *Laut* (pronounced lout; n.b.—all German nouns are capitalized), as a substantive, means "sound"; the prefixes *an*-, *in*- and *aus*- mean, respectively (and inter alia): "to," "to the edge or beginning of"; "in," "inside of"; "out of," "at the end of." Some philologists distinguish two types of *anlaut*: absolute, denoting the position of a sound at the beginning of a phrase, and relative, denoting a sound at the beginning of a word. None of these terms has anything to do with the more familiar *umlaut* (OOM lout), a diacritical consisting of two dots placed over a vowel. It resembles in form, but not in function, the dieresis, written over the second of two adjoining vowels to indicate that they are to be pronounced separately, not as a diphthong. In German, the *umlaut* alters the sound of the vowels *a*, *o* and *u* in ways that cannot be expressed in terms of English pronunciation and are not material to this discussion. The *um*- prefix in this word has the force of "about, around," as in "change about, change around," i.e., "convert."

anonyma (uh NON ih muh) *n*. For years, *The New Yorker* regaled us with a department headed "What Paper D'Ya Read?" juxtaposing newspaper reports on the selfsame item in (sometimes) hilariously different versions. Now, how about a "What Dictionary D'Ya Read?" We are dealing with the noun *anonyma*, and here go the dictionary definitions: *CH*: "a showy woman of easy morals"; *W III*: "the innominate artery"; and the same authority defines the innominate artery as "a large artery arising from the arch of the aorta and dividing into the right common carotid and the right subclavian arteries" and goes to great lengths to tell us all about common carotids and subclavian arteries and other anatomical doodads of interest only to medical personnel; and the impartial *O.E.D.* plays both sides of the field with: "1. A woman of the demi-monde. *Obs*. 2. *Anat*. The innominate artery." Well, if I had to choose between spending a free evening with the *Chambers* type and the *Webster*... *RH* solves the dilemma: it ignores *anonyma*.

anopisthograph   See **opisthograph**.

anthelmint(h)ic   See **helminth**.

anthropopsychism (an thruh poh SEYE kiz'm) *n. Anthropomorphism* (an thruh puh MOR fiz'm, -poh-) is a fairly familiar word. *Anthropomorphic* is defined in my *1000 Most Important Words* as descriptive of "any act or statement that ascribes human characteristics to gods, animals or objects." Obviously, *anthropomorphism* is that type of ascription. *Anthropopsychism* is a more restrictive term, denoting the ascription of spiritual faculties or traits characteristic of the human race to God or to the agencies of nature: *spiritual*, as contrasted with *physical*, to be specific. In *The Unity of Nature* (1884) the Duke of Argyll says of *anthropopsychism*: "It is not the Form of man that is in question. It is the Mind and Spirit of man—his Reason, his Intelligence, and his Will." He speaks of a "fundamental analogy ... between the Mind which is in us and the mind which is in Nature" and goes on to tell us that "the true etymological expression for this idea ... would be, not *Anthropomorphism* but *Anthropopsychism*." Consider the etymology—*psyche*, the Greek for "soul, spirit," as opposed to *morphe*, the Greek for "form, shape"—and you will more clearly understand the Duke's distinction.

antibacchius   See **bacchius.**

antilegomena (an tih leg OM ih nuh) *n. pl.* This noun is the neuter plural, used as a substantive, of the Greek adjective *antilegomenos*, the present passive participle of the verb *antilegein*, built of the prefix *anti-* (against) and the verb *legein* (to speak). The *antilegomena* were the books of the New Testament that were not at the outset accepted but were eventually admitted into the Canon (Greek word for "rule"): the books of the Bible accepted by the Christian church as having divine authority. These contested books were The Second Letter of Peter, A Letter of James, A Letter of Jude, A Letter to Hebrews, the Second and Third Letters of John and The Apocalypse (The Revelation of St. John). They are customarily contrasted with the *homolog(o)umena* (hom ol o GOO mih nuh), the books of the New Testament universally accepted as authentic in the early Church. This word, too, is a plural noun, the neuter plural of *homolog(o)umenos*, the present passive participle of the verb *homologein* (to agree), from *homologos* (agreeing), built of the prefix *homo-* (same) plus suffix *-logos*, from the same verb *legein*. The name *antilegomena*, sometimes capitalized, was first used by Eusebius of Caesarea (263?–c.340), the Christian theologian and historian who was bishop of Caesarea from c. 315 to his death. Few Christians realize that the authenticity of these books was ever disputed.

antimetabole   See **anaphora.**

antiphrasis (an TIF ruh sis) *n.* From the Greek verb *antiphrazein* (to speak the opposite), based on the preposition *anti-* (opposite of, reverse of) plus *phrasis* (speech), from *phrazein* (to speak), we get *antiphrasis*, the rhetorical device of using a word in a sense opposite to its common or literal meaning, usually for humorous or ironical purposes. Thus, when Liberace was panned by the critics after his Carnegie Hall recital, he " ... *cried* all the way to the bank." In his preface to the *Concise Oxford Dictionary*, H. W. Fowler (he of *Fowler's Modern English Usage*) said: "A dictionary-maker, unless he is a *monster* of omniscience, must deal with a great many matters of which he has no first-hand knowledge," (the older, and Latin sense of "monster" was "anything extraordinary"). Old-time jazz cognoscenti say about a great performer in that medium, "He's *bad!*" meaning "He's good." *W III* gives the example: "a *giant* of three feet, four inches." A mean-spirited acquaintance of mine can't see an unattractive man or woman go by without muttering, "I think you're *pretty*, too!" *Antiphrasis* is an effective rhetorical usage but one must make sure, by inflection or gesture, that one is not taken literally.

antiscian   See **amphiscian; macroscian.**

aphesis   See **feck; hyleg.**

apheta   See **hyleg.**

aphetic   See **feck.**

aposematic   See **epigamic.**

aptote (AP toht) *n.* This is a term in grammar for an indeclinable noun, i.e., one that does not change by virtue of its function in a sentence. The adjective describing such nouns is *aptotic* (ap TOT ik). A related adjective, *anaptotic* (an ap TOT ik), describes nouns that were once inflected but have given up inflectional modifications (case endings) as a result of what some linguists call "phonetic decay," the function of such endings being performed by rules of position in the sentence and the use of "relational words" like prepositions. *Aptote* is derived, via Latin *aptotum*, from the Greek *aptoton*, formed of initial *a-*, the "alpha privative" expressing negation, plus *ptotos* (falling), cognate with *ptosis* (case), from *piptein* (to fall); while *anaptotic* is built of the prefix *an-* (alpha privative again) plus *aptotos*, though some say it is formed of the prefix *ana-* (back) plus *ptotikos* (belonging to case). (While we're at it, *case* is simply a category in inflection; eg., nominative for the subject, possessive or genitive to indicate ownership, origin, etc.) Chinese is a language without inflection, hence *aptotic*. English is *anaptotic*, i.e., a language that has lost most of its original inflections, relying rather on *relational words*, usually prepositions, and position in the sentence. Latin, Greek, Arabic and (in a different way) Eskimo are much more highly inflected than English. In Latin, for example, we have a dative case, one that expresses "indirect object," to indicate the position of a donee or a listener. If I give something *to a boy*, or tell a story *to a man*, the Latin noun *puer* (boy) changes to *puero*, and the noun *homo* (man) to *homini*. In English, *boy* and *man* remain unchanged, and the preposition *to* does the trick. French would use the preposition à, but in German, the nouns, adjectives and articles would be inflected. English, of course, inflects for the plural of nouns (*sister, sisters*). You might well be aware of all this simple grammatical lore, but it does help to illustrate *aptote* and *anaptotic*.

aptotic   See **aptote**.

arbalest   See **matrass**.

archimandrite   See **hegumen**.

arsis   See **hemiola**.

attaccabottoni (uh TAK uh baw TOH nee) *n*. In Italian, *attaccare* can mean "to attach" or "to attack." *Bottone* means "button"; its plural is *bottoni*. *Attaccare un bottone* is literally "to attach (or attack) a button," figuratively "to buttonhole." An *attaccabottoni*, then, is a "buttonholer," or in short, a bore, the type of person that more or less imprisons, or at least immobilizes, you and recounts long, pointless tales, usually relating to sad experiences that he or she well deserved. In his excellent daily column in the *Times* (London), "Word-Watching," from which I appropriated this admirable entry, Philip Howard says, "It rhymes with a lot of baloney." Pretty close, Philip! My father arrived in this country from Germany about a century ago, speaking a very correct and unidiomatic British-accented English. When met on the street and asked, "How are you?" he took the question quite literally and went to great lengths (especially on cold, windy days, or when the greeter was in a palpable hurry) to narrate just about everything that had happened to him during the previous few months. This wasn't a case of spontaneous buttonholing but one (according to my father's lights) provoked by the victim.

aumbry   See **ambry**.

auslaut   See **anlaut**.

auxesis   See **anaphora**.

axiopisty (aks ee AH pih stee) *n*. This word comes to us from the Greek *axiopistia* (trustworthiness, credibility), based on the adjective *axiopistos* (trustworthy), built from *axios* (worthy, deserving—which gave us *axiom*, in the sense of "worthy of belief"), plus *pistis* (faith, belief). *Axiopisty* means "trustworthiness, credibility," the quality that makes someone or something deserving of trust, an endowment devoutly to be wished. The American statesman Henry L. Stimson believed in trust. "The only way to make a man trustworthy," he said, "is to trust him; and the surest way to make him untrustworthy is to distrust him and show your distrust." Another saying of his: "The only deadly sin I know is cynicism." Apparently, he felt that *axiopisty* could be built by *pistis* and destroyed by *apistia* (mistrust: that little alpha privative, *a-*, rears its powerful head again!)

azyme (AY zime) *n.* From the Greek alpha privative (negating prefix *a-*) plus **zyme** (leaven, substance added to dough to produce fermentation, usually yeast) we get *azyme* (unleavened bread, bread that has not risen). This is the *matzo* (a Yiddish word, from Hebrew *massah*) that is eaten by Jews during Passover. In Exodus we read: "And the Lord spake unto Moses, saying ... (12:8) And they shall eat ... unleavened bread ... (12:15); Seven days shall ye eat unleavened bread ... (12:17); And ye shall observe the feast of unleavened bread ... (12:20); Ye shall eat nothing leavened ... (12:34); And the people took their dough before it was leavened ... (12:39); And they baked unleavened cakes of the dough which they brought forth out of Egypt, for it was not leavened; because they were thrust out of Egypt, and could not tarry ... (13:6); Seven days thou shalt eat unleavened bread ... (13:7); ... and there shall no leavened bread be seen with thee ... " The Lord was surely insistent on this matter of *azyme*, which is also consecrated by Christians of the Western Church in celebrating the Eucharist. *Azymous* (AZ ih muhs) is the adjective for "unleavened," and an *azymite* (AZ ih mite) is a member of any church that uses unleavened bread, i.e., wafers, in the Eucharist. Incidentally, *azyme* is now sold quite unceremoniously in food stores as a vehicle for transporting dips to the mouth at cocktail parties.

bacchius (buh KEYE uhs) *n.* This is a term in Greek and Latin prosody (meter), denoting a foot of two long or stressed syllables preceded by one short or unstressed one. Examples: *belabor, enticement, reluctance.* The adjective for such a foot is *bacchiac* (buh KEYE uhk). The reverse is an *antibacchius* (an tih buh KEYE uhs), a foot of two long or stressed syllables followed by a short or unstressed one; the adjective is *antibacchic* (an tih BAK uhk), as you mightn't expect. Examples: *lethargy, proofreader.* All of these terms are related to the prosody of the verse sung or recited at the festivals in honor of Bacchus (the *anti-* in *antibacchius, -ic* is the Greek prefix meaning "opposite to.") These festivals were known as *bacchanalia* (bak uh NAY lee uh), a term that was later applied to all drunken revels, as is *dionysiac* from Dionysus, the Greek name for Bacchus.

bahuvrihi   See **tatpurusha.**

bambocciade (bam boh CHAHD) *n.* The Dutch painter variously known as Pieter van Laar and Peter de Laer (1592–c.1675) was known for his grotesque scenes of everyday working-class and peasant life, including realistic studies of country wakes and penny-weddings among the poor (where guests paid trifling sums to defray the expenses of the feast, with anything left over going to the newlyweds to help furnish their homes). The painter's nickname was

Bamboccio (bam BAW cho), an Italian word meaning, literally, "chubby little child" or "puppet" but used figuratively to mean "simpleton." *Bamboccio* was derived from the Italian *bambino* (baby boy) plus the intensive suffix *-occio*, giving it the sense of "big booby," and the name *bambocciade* applied to this type of rustic genre painting came, via French *bambochade* and Italian *Bambocciata*, from *bamboccio*.

banausic (buh NOS ik, -NOZ-) *adj*. This word somehow irritates me, as it runs counter to my early teachings. My wise father told me all about the laborer being worthy of his hire. "All work must be respected," he said, "provided it is honest and good. The shoemaker is worthy of your respect and appreciation, as worthy as your doctor, your professor, your famous artist, your great physicist." Well, *banausic*, derived from Greek *banausikos* (relating to artisans, from *banausos*, artisan) came to mean more or less, "practical." Wrote John Buchan (Baron Tweedsmuir, Scottish novelist, historian and governor general of Canada 1935–1940): "My approach to this literature was ... *banausic*. I wanted advice, instruction, not aids to reflection." He was using *banausic* to mean "governed by utilitarian purposes." So far so good. But the word, sadly, developed pejorative connotations: "common, dull, menial," and even "moneymaking," and "materialistic" in a disapproving, condescending, demeaning sense. I don't like that sort of elitist attitude toward the noble horny-handed sons of toil.

bebung (BAY boohng) *n*. This term in music for a maneuver on the clavichord: fluctuating the pressure of the finger on the key to produce a tremolo effect. For the benefit of those who may not be familiar with early musical instruments, a clavichord is a keyboard in a small rectangular box containing a sounding board and a set of strings. Pressure on a key causes a small metal wedge, called a *tangent*, to strike a string. The clavichord was supplanted by the piano at the end of the 18th century, but here and there specialists in ancient instruments play it at intimate recitals for the cognoscenti. The instrument makes very soft sounds and requires rapt attention: no talking (or heavy breathing). The tremolo can be performed on certain musical instruments, particularly the strings (as well as by the human voice, in which case it is known as *vibrato*), to produce an emotional effect. *Bebung* is a German word, based on the verb *beben* (to shake or quiver); it means "vibration" and in music "tremolo."

bellet(t)rist (bel LEH trist) *n*. *Belles-lettres* (bel LET'R), literally, in French, "fine letters," has been assimilated into English to denote elegant literature, or literature regarded as a fine art, having a purely aesthetic, as opposed to a utilitarian, function. The term embraces poetry, fiction, criticism and literary studies. The *O.E.D.* calls it a "vaguely used term ... now generally applied (when used at all) to the lighter branches of literature or the aesthetics of literary study." This term gave rise to *bellet(t)rist*, "a person devoted to *belles-*

lettres," and the adjective *belletristic* (bel let TRIS tik), describing anyone or anything in that category. Coleridge said, "I wish I could find a more familiar word than *aesthetic*, for works of taste and criticism. It is, however, in all respects better, and of more reputable origin, than *belletristic*." Matthew Arnold referred to himself as "an unlearned *belletristic* trifler." The word still bore its somewhat pejorative connotation when the English writer Mark Pattison wrote (1868), "We have risen above the mere *belletristic* treatment of classical literature."

benison   See **catmalison.**

bicorn   See **chichevache.**

biretta   See **zucchetto.**

bombus (BOM buhs) *n.* A *bombus*, in Latin, is "any hollow sound," and more specifically, "a humming, a buzzing, a booming, a trumpet blast." Its Greek antecedent, *bombos*, denoted any deep, hollow sound. Quite obviously, the word is onomatopoeic in both languages. We have taken it over in a variety of senses. As a medical term, it denotes both *tinnitus*, a humming or buzzing noise in the ears (a source of great discomfort to many people), and a rumbling of the intestines, which can be most embarrassing at dinner parties. In entomology, *bombus* is the name of the insect genus that includes the bumblebee, whose everyday name comes from *bomblen* (to boom), the Middle English descendant of *bombus*. Finally, and rather strangely, *bombus* is a term applied to an orchestral conductor's technique: the movement of the hands indicating the rhythmic flow and harmonic pattern of the buzzing of bees. This must be the only instance where an ancient source has given us a medical term, an entomological classification and the name of an orchestral conductor's technique. Dead languages indeed!

borborygmic   See **borborygmus.**

borborygmus (bawr buh RIG muhs) *n.* Taken intact from the Latin, based on Greek *borborygmos*, from the verb *borboryzein* (to have a rumbling in the bowels), we get this almost onomatopoeic word denoting the sound of flatulence in the intestines. In his *Zoonomia, or the Laws of Organic Life* (1794), Erasmus Darwin called it *borborigmi* and defined it as "rumbling of the bowels," and in 1880, Lionel S. Beale, in his book *On Slight Ailments*, used it in the plural, stating, "*Borborigmi* ... are a serious annoyance." He didn't say precisely to whom, but I would imagine the sufferers included near neighbors at a dinner party. The adjective describing one producing these unlovely sounds, and the sounds themselves, is *borborygmic* (bawr buh RIG mik), and it can be found in Vladimir Nabokov's *Ada* (1969), where we come upon this dramatic sentence: "All the toilets and waterpipes in the house had been suddenly seized with *borborygmic* convulsions." Some sentence, especially for a man writing in an acquired tongue! Seems Nabokov liked *borborygmi*. In his *Introduction to Pushkin's Poetry* (1988), he expressed his concern about the loss of the original Russian in translation. He tried to put Pushkin's lines into French, and this is what happened, in Nabokov's words:

> Even though all the words are there, I do not believe these lines [the translation] can give an idea of the ample and powerful lyricism of our poet ... [I tried] to put myself into a kind of trance so that ... the miracle of total metamorphosis might occur. At last, after several hours of these internal mutterings, of those *borborygmi* of the soul that accompany the composition of poetry, I felt the miracle had been accomplished. But ... the distance separating the Russian text from the translation ... was now evident in all its sad reality ...

So here we have *borborygmi* of the soul as well as those of the toilets! Of course, Nabokov's experience brings to mind the sad but realistic Italian pun about translation: *"Traduttore traditore"* ("Translator traitor"—and how well my poor translation from the Italian illustrates the point!).

boreen (boh REEN) *n*. When I run across a two-syllable word ending in *-een*, I sense the spirit of Ireland: *colleen, poteen* (illicitly distilled Irish whiskey), *shebeen* (an illicit liquor store). So with *boreen*, "a narrow country lane, especially in hilly country," according to *W III*, and by transference, "an opening passage through a throng." The derivation is from the Irish *bothar*, pronounced BOH uhr, plus the usual diminutive ending *-een*, from Irish *-in*. Some authorities offer the suggestion that the *bo-* element is from Old Irish *bo* (ox, cow), going back to Latin *bos* (ox, bull, cow). An especially charming term of endearment is *mavourneen* (muh VOOHR neen), "my dear one, my darling," which comes from the Irish words *mo mhurnin*. One can almost smell the peat. Both senses of *boreen* appear in Samuel and Anna Hall's *Ireland: Its Scenery, Character, etc.* (1841). At one point, we find the phrase, "At my brother's, a piece down that *boreen*," and later on, "Wheresomever he went, the people made a *boreen* for him." A sweet word, describing at first the lovely prospect of a remote narrow country road, and, by an imaginative extension, an aisle made through a crowd of people deferentially permitting the passage of a personage.

Borough-English *n*. The word *borough* has a confusing (and here irrelevant) multiplicity of meanings that depend largely on the geographical or chronological context. In all cases, it is a political subdivision of one sort or another. *Borough-English* is another matter: a custom in certain English counties (Kent, Sussex, Surrey, Somerset), abolished in 1925, whereby real estate passed to the youngest sister, and failing a sister, to the youngest brother, and so on to the youngest collateral relative of whatever degree of consanguinity. This arrangement, obviously, flew in the face of the system of primogeniture. The name was derived in a curious manner, as a partial translation of the Anglo-French *tenure en Burgh Engloys* (tenure in English borough). According to Blacksone (i.e., Sir William Blackstone, 1723–80, English jurist and author of the then-definitive *Blackstone's Commentaries*), the Normans gave it that name to distinguish this purely English custom from the universal French system of inheritance. Real estate held by those inheriting under the *Borough-English* system was occasionally known as "Cradle Land" or "Cradle Holding," an obvious reference to inheritance by the "baby" of the family. (The *O.E.D.* differs, saying that *cradle-land* means "a land in which a people dwell in their earliest times.") According to Sir Frederick Pollock, an authority on the land laws of England, in an 1882 issue of *Macmillan's Magazine*, "The custom of *borough-English* abounds in Kent, Sussex, Surrey, the neighborhood of London, and Somerset. In the midlands it is rare, and north of the Humber [the estuary between Lincolnshire and Yorkshire in the north of England] ... it does not seem to occur." Another system of inheritance in Kent that went into effect after the Norman Conquest was *gavelkind*, whereby primogeniture was replaced by the division of the deceased's property equally among his sons, and the laws of inheritance by widows and widowers differed from the general customs of England. Note that all of the above relates to the case of intestacy (the absence of a will) and that changes could be effected by will.

bothros (BOTH ruhs) *n.* The only mention of *bothros* in the *O.E.D.* that I could find was a reference to "G[reek] *bothros* pit" in the etymology of a botanical term of no great interest, and in the *Supplement*, the same reference in another botanical term of little concern here; but there is no listing of *bothros* as a v. ord. *W III* does list it, as a term in archaeology, with the definition "a hole or pit into which drink offerings to the nether gods were poured by the ancient Greeks"; and the etymological information is that it is Greek, "perhaps akin to Latin *fodere* to dig." (*W II* had listed it, characterizing it with the reference "Gr[eek] Antiq[uity]" but with no etymological material, and defining it as "a hole or pit made in the earth, esp[ecially] one in which drink offerings to the nether gods were poured." One wonders what happened in the interim before *W III* was published to cause the dropping of the "esp[ecially]" and the introduction of the etymological link to *fodere*. Obviously, the *W III* staff had come to the conclusion that the *only* function of *bothroi* [the plural form of the noun] was to receive those libations, and somebody came up with the possible kinship with *fodere*.) On the other hand, many entries or parts of entries in *W II* were dropped from *W III* for reasons of space; the new edition was confined to 5 inches in thickness for technical reasons of production. *RH* mentions Greek *bothros* in the etymology of a zoological term of no interest here but ignores it as an English word. What are we to do? All I can do is to hope that since the gods who got the libations were "nether," the Greeks didn't waste any vintage wines on them, and let it go at that.

bothy, also **bothie** (BOTH ee) *n*. The *O.E.D.* characterizes this word as Scottish, *W III* as chiefly Scottish, and *CH*, in one of its definitions, refers to Scotland but apparently accepts it as belonging to the English language. (Remember that *CH* is published in Edinburgh, and its editor is named MacDonald.) In any event, a *bothy* is "a hut, a humble abode, one-roomed and sometimes affording only temporary shelter." *CH* says it is "a barely furnished dwelling for farm-servants in the north-east of Scotland"; *W III* adds "a shepherd's or hunter's shelter" and says that the *o* can be either long or short; and *RH* says that the first two letters can be pronounced as in *thin* or *that*; the *O.E.D.* tells us that *bothies* (however pronounced) were used as collective lodgings by masons and quarrymen as well as farm laborers and makes mention of *bothies* for female servants as well. *CH* adds the information that a *bothy ballad* is a folk song, "dealing with country matters, usu[ally] bawdy" (sounds like fun), and gives us *bothyman* without bothering to define it, because the meaning is obvious. Take your choice of pronunciation and scope of function, but you get the general idea. All of these sources relate it to the noun *booth*.

bothy ballad   See **bothy.**

bothyman   See **bothy.**

brachiate (BRAKE ee ate) *adj., vb*. If you happen to remember *bracchium* (arm) from Latin 1, you would guess correctly that *bracchiate* was an adjective meaning "having arms." What you mightn't know is that as a term in botany, it describes trees that have paired branches pointing so as to form approximately right angles and crossing each other alternately. If you had had no Greek, you wouldn't know that the Romans got *bracchium* from the Greek *brachion*. It happens that *brachiate* is also a verb, describing the practice of anthropoids like apes, chimpanzees, gibbons and orangutans of swinging from branch to branch by their arms. Julian Huxley, in *Problems of Relative Growth* (1932), tells us that man "is undoubtedly descended from *brachiating* ancestors with relatively long arms." *Brachiation* is the act or practice of *brachiating*, and an anthropoid that engages in that activity is a *brachiator*. If I remember rightly, Tarzan was a pretty good *brachiator* and helped to prove Huxley's point.

brachycatalectic   See **ithyphallic.**

brachycephal   See **dolichocephal.**

breviate (BREE vee ate) *n*. At first glance, *breviate* looks like an abbreviation of *abbreviate*, but it has a life of its own as a noun meaning "brief statement, compendium, summary." It comes from *breviatum*, the neuter of the past participle of Latin *breviare* (to shorten—from which we get *breviary*), from the adjective *brevis* (short), which may be familiar from the Roman philosopher Seneca's aphorism *Vita brevis, ars longa* (Life is short, art enduring), first said three centuries earlier by the Greek physician Hippocrates (the "Father of Medicine"). One P. B. Power wrote a book entitled *Breviates: or Short Texts and their Teachings* (1862). Thomas Fuller, in *A Pisgah-sight of Palestine* (1650), wrote: "What we read in St. Luke was onely the *breviate*, sum, and abridgement of his Sermon." (*Pisgah* is the name of a mountain ridge in ancient Palestine, now in Jordan. It was from one of its peaks, Mt. Nebo, that Moses viewed the Promised Land.) Thomas Tryon used the word figuratively in *A Treatise of Dreams and Visions* (1695): "God made him [man] ... a *breviate* [epitome] of the nature of all things divine and humane." *Breviate* was once used to denote a brief dispatch, a note or a lawyer's brief, but those uses are now obsolete.

bunraku (boohn RAH kooh) *n.* This term, transliterated from the Japanese, has become the generic term for the Japanese puppet theater. Originally, it was the name of a type of traditional puppet manipulation practiced by the *Bunraku-za* puppetry company in its theater. There are two schools of Japanese puppet art, the Yuki and the *Bunraki*. The former manipulates the puppets by strings, the latter by people holding the dolls. In the *Bunraku* technique, the puppets measure about three feet high and are manipulated by men who remain visible throughout the performance. The chief characters are each handled by three persons. This form of entertainment, known variously as the "puppet theater" or "doll theater," is a uniquely Japanese form requiring a high degree of expertise. Somehow, the visible manipulators seem to fade into the background so completely as to impart an uncanny realism to the puppets.

burgage   See **soc(c)age.**

ca'canny (kuh KAN ee), occasionally **-conny** *n., vb. Ca'* is a Scottish variant of *call,* and *canny* is a familiar word with some rather unfamiliar meanings, including, as an adverb, "cautiously, carefully." Put together, *ca'canny,* as a verb, means "to proceed cautiously," but in labor terms it means, "to go slow," i.e., to adopt a "go-slow policy" as an antimanagement tactic. As a noun, a *ca'canny* is "a slowdown, a deliberate slackening of the work rate or quantity produced." *Ca'canny* began as a general term for "caution" or "moderation" but soon acquired the special meaning of the labor tactic described above. As long ago as 1896, an issue of the *Westminster Gazette* described a British labor leader as the first "to reduce to a fine art the *ca'conny* policy so well known in Western America." In the same year, the *Seamen's Chronicle* discussed the subject in question-and-answer form: "What is *ca'canny*? It is a simple and handy phrase which is used to describe a new instrument or policy which may be used by the workers in place of a strike." A 1958 issue of *The Economist* contains this amusing sentence: "The teaching staff defends itself skilfully from battle to battle with cynicism and *ca'canny*." The rather awkward forms *ca'cannyism* and *ca'cannyness*, to describe the policy, or used to denote caution generally, have also been introduced. A 1963 issue of *The Economist* spoke of " ... the entrenched forces of *ca'canniness*." The use of the term may be restricted to England and Scotland—but not the practice.

cacodemon   See **evancalous.**

cacography   See **evancalous.**

cacohydrophobia   See **xenodochiophobia.**

caconym (KA kuh nim) *n*. *Kakos*, in Greek, means "bad" and gives us the prefix *caco-*, as in *cacophony, cacography* (bad handwriting or spelling), *cacology* (bad choice of words or incorrect pronunciation), etc. Add *-nym*, the suffix formed from *onoma* (name), as in *antonym, pseudonym*, etc., and you wind up with *caconym*, a "bad name," "bad nomenclature" or "bad terminology," especially in biology and botany. O. F. Cook, in *The American Naturalist*, states: "A name rejected for linguistic reasons [is] a *caconym*." *The National Cactus and Succulent Journal* tells us: "A name may qualify as a *caconym* in different ways. First, from sheer length. Second, from the clash of consonants making it difficult (for a European at least) to articulate." Perhaps *mesopterygium* (part of the fin in some fishes) and *mesopterygoid* (part of the pterygoid that articulates with the palatine bone of the basipterygoid process of the splenoid, or with both—bet you didn't know that!) or *blastophthoria* (the hypothetical degeneration of germ cells caused, for example, by alcoholism) or *pseudolamellabranchiate* (relating to certain mollusks such as some scallops and oysters—the definition goes on and on) might be classified as *caconyms* and candidates for rejection. Arise, a new Linnaeus!

cacorrhaphiaphobia (kah koh rahf ee uh FOH bee uh) *n*. A strange word, this, for, though the *caco-* element, from the Greek *kako-*, the combining form of *kakos* (bad), and the familiar *-phobia* suffix are straightforward enough, the central element, *rhaphia*, meaning in this context "planning, devising," is based on the verb *rhaptein*, whose literal meaning is "to sew" but which is here used metaphorically in the sense of "to plan" or "to devise." How a verb meaning "to sew" gets to be used figuratively to mean "to plan" remains something of a mystery to me. I have been unable to discover any explanation of this strange departure. Well, putting it all together, we arrive at "fear of failure" (literally, bad planning dread, from *caco-* plus *rhaphia* plus *phobia*). Fear of failure is indeed a not uncommon human experience, one that has doubtless inhibited many a promising career, but it took those Greeks to have a word for it. Shades of Zoe Akins! If you think the Germans have a genius for concocting sesquipedalian jawbreakers by stringing word elements together, just browse through a Greek dictionary when you have time on your hands. Have time on your hands? They had *two* words for that: *hesukhazein* and *skholazein*.

cacotopia See **dystopia**.

cacuminal (ka KYOOH muhn uhl) *adj*. This is a term in phonetics. *Cacumen* is Latin for "top, tip." *Cacuminal* describes sounds produced with the tip of the tongue curled upward toward the hard palate or roof of the mouth. Synonyms, in this field, are *retroflex, inverted, cerebral* and *coronal*, all with special uses. The phonologist A. J. Ellis gave as an example of a "corona" phoneme, "The ... *d* in *do* with the tip of the tongue free from the gums, and approaching the 'crown' of the arch of the hard palate." Other examples are *l* and *n*, in the pronunciation of which the upward curl of the tongue occurs at the end of the sound, rather than the beginning, as in the case of *d*. All the adjectives mentioned above can be used alone, as substantives. A word etymologically related to *cacuminal*, but with a different meaning and application, is *cacuminous* (ka KYOOH muhn us), describing trees having pyramidal tops. In fact, in Latin, *cacumen*, by itself, can mean "treetop." Mortimer Collins, in *Pen Sketches by a Vanished Hand* (1876), wrote the lines: "Luminous books (not voluminous)/To read under beech-trees *cacuminous*." Some of the meanings of *luminous* are "clear," "lucid" and "intellectually brilliant." Lucky reader!

cacuminous See **cacuminal**.

caduceus See **petasus**.

caesura See **dolichurus**.

caitiff (KAY tif) *n*. To call a man a *caitiff* is to say that he is a mean, base, despicable person. *Caitiff* can be used as an adjective as well: a *caitiff* person is mean, vile, base. Originally, the word meant "captive," a sense now obsolete but one that explains its derivation from Latin *captivus* (captive). The term took expectable forms in the Romance tongues: Old French *chaitif*, whence came modern French *chétif* (puny, pitiful, mean, worthless), Spanish *cautivo* (captive), Italian *cattivo* (bad, wicked, nasty). The word then took on a different meaning, also now obsolete: "wretched, miserable, pitiable." It is easy to see how this development came about: After all, a captive is a wretched soul, a person in a piteous situation. Eventually, *caitiff* acquired the connotation of contempt and finally, of moral disapprobation, so that it now means "villain," base, mean and despicable, totally dissociated from the "captive" sense, like *chétif* in French and *cattivo* in Italian. The same development occurred in its adjectival use. In 1501 Richard Arnolde could write, in his *Chronicle*: " ... he is kepte as a *kaytyf* in myserable seruitude," and in 1678 Samuel Butler, in *Hudibras*: "I pity'd the sad Punishment/The wretched *caitiff* underwent." Edward A. Freeman, in *The History of the Norman Conquest* (1867), described "Two *caitiffs* whose names are handed down to infamy." What a clear and interesting demonstration of the evolution of the sense of the word! There are even instances of transformation from commendatory to pejorative: *awful*, from "awe-inspiring" to "very bad"; *egregious*, from "distinguished, illustrious" to "outrageous, shocking"; *dreadful*, from "reverential, awe-inspiring" to "horrid." A case in reverse: *terrific* from "terrifying" to "excellent, (colloquially) great." As my college English professor used to say, "To be sure of the meaning, take note of the date!"

calcinate   See **phlogiston.**

calenture (KAL uhn chuhr) *n. Calere* means "to be hot" in Latin; the present participle is *calens*, of which the stem is *calent-*, and from that the Spanish took *calentar* (to be hot) and *calentura* (fever). The French turned that into *calenture*, and we took it over intact, to designate an illness affecting sailors in the tropics, causing delirium that leads the victims to believe the ocean to be green fields into which they wish to jump. The word came to mean "fever" generally, and sometimes "sunstroke." In *Robinson Crusoe*, Defoe writes: "In this voyage ... I was continually sick, being thrown into a violent *Calenture* by the excessive Heat." Swift's poem *The Bubble: a Poem (Upon the South Sea Project)* contains these dramatic lines:

> So, by a *calenture* misled,
> The mariner with rapture sees,
> On the smooth ocean's azure bed,
> Enamell'd fields and verdant trees.

The word was eventually used metaphorically to mean "burning passion, ardor." Donne wrote: "Knowledge kindles *Calentures* in some." Jeremy Taylor (*Of the Sacred Order and Offices of Episcopacy*, 1642) wrote of " ... the *Calenture* of primitive devotion." So you see, there are good and bad *calentures*, fevers that burn your body, and fevers that burn your soul.

calepin (KAL uh pin) *n.* An Augustine friar named Abrosio (no, this isn't the first line of a limerick) was born in Calepio, Italy, and thus acquired the surname Calepino, in the same way that the painter Paolo Cagliari became *Veronese* and Domenico, whose real surname we don't know, is known as *Veneziano* because of their geographical, rather than familial, associations. Ambrosio brought out a polyglot Latin dictionary in 1502. Edition after edition appeared, and it became the leading Latin dictionary of the 16th century—so much so that his geographical cognomen became generic in Italian for "dictionary," entering the French language as "calepin," in which form it was taken into English. The word then acquired the figurative meaning of "notebook, memorandum book, reference book." In earlier times people spoke of "my *Calepin*" in the same way as devotees of classical Greek have been referring to "my *Liddell & Scott*" since its appearance in 1846. Here are some lines from Donne's *Fourth Satire*:

> Whom do you prefer
> For the best linguist? And I sillily
> Said that I thought *Calepine's* Dictionary.

Calepins were highly valued in the old days, so much so that there is on record a 1569 Lancastrian will that makes one the subject matter of a specific bequest: "I wyll that Henry Marrecrofte shall have my *calapyne* ... " We must forgive the linguistically inclined testator for his fanciful spelling of *calepin*.

calotte   See **zucchetto.**

calx   See **phlogiston.**

canephor(e) (KAN uh for), also **canephora, -ros, -rus** (kan EF uh ruh, -ros, -rus) *n.* In ancient Greece, this was the name of a maiden who carried on her head a basket containing the sacred objects used at the feasts of Demeter, Dionysus (Bacchus) and Athena. In architecture, the term was applied to a sculptured figure of a young person of either sex carrying on the head a basket containing materials for the offering of sacrifices, or a caryatid (kar ee AT uhd) (a sculptured figure used as a column) supporting a basketlike member serving as a capital. According to an 1849 issue of *Fraser's Magazine*, "to be chosen *canephor* was as if 'Beautiful' were stamped on the lintel of a woman's door." Encomium indeed! Shades of the Miss America contest! The Greek noun was *kanephoros* (basket bearer), built of *kaneon* (basket) and *phoros* (bearing), akin to *pherein* (to carry).

cangue, also **cang** (KANG) *n.* This delightful object was a portable pillory consisting of a broad heavy wooden frame or board borne with the top beam supported on the shoulders by petty offenders in China in the old days. The device was 3 or 4 feet square, weighed 50 or 60 pounds and prevented any use of the hands above the shoulders, so that the poor soul had to be fed by others. It couldn't have been much fun. The related Portuguese word is *cango*, a variant of *canga*, a porter's yoke or a yoke for oxen. A letter to the Chinese embassy in Washington inquiring as to the date of the abolition of the *cangue* and the nature of its replacement in the current criminal system is awaiting an answer.

cardophagus (kar DOF uh guhs) *n. Kardos*, Greek for "thistle," became *carduus* in Latin. *Phagos* is Greek for "eater, glutton" and is related to *phagein* (to eat). Putting the pieces together we got *cardophagus*, which means literally "thistle-eater," and, in the bargain, "donkey." *Chardon* is French for "thistle," and the French idiom *bête à manger du chardon* (literally, silly enough to eat thistles) means "as silly as an ass," and an ass is a donkey, isn't it, so that somehow we get to *donkey* from *thistle-eater*, don't we? *Cardo* is both Italian and Spanish for "thistle"; my, how that dead Latin does persist! In Thackeray's novel *The Virginians* we read: "Kick and abuse him, you who have never brayed; but bear with him, all honest fellow-*cardophagi*." Is there a "Be Kind to Donkeys" week? In British English, *donkey's years* means "a long time." Example: "They've lived there for donkey's years," or "I haven't seen Archie for donkey's years." Some say that this picturesque expression is a pun on *donkey's ears*, which, as you know, are very long. Others say that it is an allusion to the great age to which donkeys live, based on the tradition that nobody ever sees a dead donkey. After all this, if you want to tell a friend he's silly, call him a *cardophagus* and let him think it's a compliment. Do donkeys eat thistles? I've never seen it happen, and I invite information from donkey-buffs or thistle-buffs.

catalectic   See **prosodion.**

catholicon (kuh THOL uh kuhn) *n.* At first blush, this word might appear to have some application to religious matters, but that is not the case. The derivation here has to do with the adjective *catholic* in the sense of "universal, all-encompassing," as in "catholic tastes" or "catholic interests," from which sense the ecclesiastical use derived: the Church Universal. A *catholicon* is "a panacea, a universal remedy, a cure-all." Thus, Sir Thomas Browne, in *Religio Medici* (1643), could write: "Death is the cure of all diseases. There is no *Catholicon* or universal remedy I know but this." *Catholic* comes from the Greek adjective *katholikos* (universal), and *catholicon* from *katholikon*, the neuter form of the adjective. The *O.E.D.* begins its definition with the words "An electuary supposed to be capable of evacuating all humours ... " That leads us to wonder a bit about *electuary, evacuate* and *humours*, does it not? *Electuary* (ih LEK tyooh air ee) is from the Late Latin *electuarium*, which seems to stem from the Greek verb *ekleichein* (to lick out) and is the pharmaceutical term for medicines sweetened with honey or syrup, to be licked off a spoon. *Evacuation* is used in physiology for the emptying of waste matter, especially through the bowels. *Humours* (the British spelling) were considered by the ancients to be the principal fluids of the body: blood, phlegm, choler and black bile or melancholy, the balance of which determined a person's physical and mental makeup. Would that we could find a *catholicon* for the disorders of today's world!

catholicos   See **hegumen.**

catmalison (KAT mal uh z'n, -s'n) *n.* This peculiar dialectal word is based on what is probably a misconception concerning cats. The word is constructed of *cat*, the familiar domestic pet, and *malison* (MAL uh z'n, -s'n), meaning "curse," from Old French *maleison*. A *malison* is a doublet of malediction. (*Doublet* has various meanings, one of which denotes either of a pair of words in the same language derived from the same source but divergent in meaning: e.g. one directly from Latin, the other via Old French. *RH* gives the example of *quiet* and *coy*, the former coming directly from Latin *quietus*, the latter via Old French *quei*.) *Malison* is the opposite of *benison* (BEN ih suhn), an archaic word for "blessing," which is a *doublet* of *benediction* (Latin *benedictio*, Old French *beneiçun*). But we've come a long way from *catmalison*, which means "cupboard in or near the ceiling" and therefore a "curse" to cats, for the simple reason that they can't find a way of getting into it. The misconception mentioned above is the rash underestimation of a cat's ability to get into *anything*, based on my lifetime of experience and admiration of their persistence and ingenuity. My cats, anyway!

catoptric (kat OP trik) *adj.* This adjective describes anything relating to reflection, part of the science of optics, which deals with the properties of light and vision. The word is derived from the Greek *katroptikos* (relating to a mirror), based on *katropton* (mirror), formed of the preposition *kata* (against) plus *op*- (the stem of *oran*, to see) plus *-tron* (the suffix of instrument, as in, e.g., *cyclotron*). Ansted and Latham, writing about the Channel Islands in 1862, spoke of "the light-houses each having a *catoptric* light of the first order." *Catoptrics* is the branch of optics covering reflection generally. *Catoptromancy* (kat OP troh man see) is divination by means of a mirror, the suffix *-mancy*, from Greek *manteia* (divination), being a combining form meaning "divination," as, for example, in *necromancy*. Edward Smedley, writing in 1855 about the occult sciences, described *catoptromancy* as "a species of divination by the mirror." This science didn't do Snow White's stepmother much good.

catoptromancy   See **catoptric.**

cecity (SEE sih tee) *n. Cecity* is "blindness." The word comes from the Latin *caecitas*, and like its ancestor, encompasses blindness of the mind as well as the eye. "None so blind as those that will not see," wrote Matthew Henry in *Commentaries: Jeremiah*, echoing Jer. 5:21: " ... O foolish people, and without understanding; which have eyes, and see not ... " Anthony Burgess (*Earthly Powers*) used the word figuratively, too: " ... my love ... induces a *cecity* to your inefficiency and your bad behavior." The metaphorical use appears to be more common than the literal. Incidentally, going back to the derivation of *cecity*, the ending *-ity* is our equivalent of the Latin *-itas* in abstract nouns: *capacitas, ferocitas, simplicitas* and lots more; thus, *cecity* from *caecitas*. *Cecutiency* (sih KU shun see), "tendency to blindness," is derived from *caecutiens*, the present participle of the verb *caecutire* (to be blind), and this leads me to observe that our ending *-ency* comes from the Latin *-entia*, which in turn is based on the Latin present participial endings: *dependency, emergency, exigency*, from *dependens, emergens*, etc. Disraeli wrote of "the *cecity* of superstition," and Matthew

Arnold, in *Ode to Westminster Abbey*, wrote: "After light's term, a term of cecity."

cenacle (SEN uh k'l) *n*. Though this word has the general meaning of "supper room," it is usually understood to refer to the room in which Christ and the apostles ate the Last Supper on the night before the crucifixion. It has also been given the meaning of a "coterie" or its meeting place. Via Late Latin *cenaculum*, the diminutive of Latin *cena* (dinner, meal), the word comes from the French *cénacle* (a guest chamber where the Lord's supper was eaten; figuratively, literary society or coterie). The scene of the Last Supper in the *cenacle* has been painted by a number of masters, the most famous by far being the one Leonardo da Vinci painted on a wall of the refectory of the convent of Santa Maria delle Grazie in Milan. In World War II, allied bombs reduced the refectory to ruins, but da Vinci's wall was practically undamaged and the painting left intact, *mirabile dictu*, though time had worn it badly. It is now, thank heaven, protected against further deterioration.

Chasid   See **Mitnagged.**

chasuble   See **phelonion.**

chernozëm (chair nuh ZYOM) *n*. Also transliterated from the Russian as *tschernozem* and *tschernosem*; but note the pronunciation of the last syllable, following the same system that requires the spelling of Gorbachev, pronounced Gorbachov. Why is this? Why not spell it the way it is pronounced? (Because the *e* in the last syllable is topped by a sort of umlaut and therefore takes the stress.) Be that as it may, *chernozëm* is the Russian word for "black earth," based on *cherno-* the combining form of *cherny* (black) [I must interpolate: Remember the stock Russian song *ochi chorniya*, meaning "black eyes," sung along with *The Two Guitars*, tremulously, with balalaika accompaniment, on the tiniest provocation, wherever Russians congregate? Well, here's old friend *cherny*, pronounced *chorny*, once again.]—now getting back to etymology—plus *-zem*, the combining form of Russian *zemlya* (earth). *Chernozem* is a soil extremely rich in humus and carbonates, found in cool and temperate subhumid climates, notably in central Russia and central North America. I first ran across the word in my friend Lement Harris's fascinating memoir *My Tale of Two Worlds*. In a chapter entitled "Soviet Farms and Life" (the year was 1929 and the place Egorlikskaya, near Rostov) he writes: "With the harvest completed, I spent a day driving around the countryside ... The whole region is black earth, *chernozem*, the richest soil that exists ... the black-earth band in North America runs north and south, roughly from Winnipeg, Canada, to the panhandle of Texas. The Soviet black-earth band runs east and west, from the Ukraine across the Volga River into the arid parts of Central Asia." Well, now you know about *chernozem*: what it is, where it is and why it's a blessing wherever it is.

chersonese (KUR suh neez, -nees) *n. Chersonese* means "peninsula." Whereas *peninsula* is derived from the Latin *paene* (almost) plus *insula* (island), *chersonese* comes from the Greek *chersonesos*, formed of *chersos* (dry land) plus *nesos* (island). Apparently, the Romans thought of a peninsula as "almost an island" and the Greeks as a "dry island," both rather imaginative terms. You don't see *chersonese* these days, but it was once much used in literature. In *Paradise Lost* Milton wrote: "Thence to Agra and Lahor of Great Mogul, Down to the golden *Chersonese*," and in his *Tour Through the Whole Island of Great Britain*, Defoe wrote of "this little *Chersonese*, called The Land's End." Washington Irving wrote of "that great *chersonese* or peninsula ... known by the name of Arabia." The English poet Patrick Shaw-Stewart, rereading *The Iliad* on the way to Gallipoli during World War I, according to Michael Wood in *In Search of the Trojan War* (Facts On File, New York, 1985), " ... felt a dreadful sense of *déjà vu* at the sight of ... Troy ... " and wrote a poem containing these lines:

> Achilles came to Troyland
> And I to *Chersonese*:
> He turned from wrath to battle,
> And I from three days' peace.

So *chersonese* caught the attention of writers both English and American and is therefore worthy of our attention; it is a pretty and interesting word, and, particularly in view of its derivation, right up there with *peninsula*.

chiasmus (keye AZ muhs) *n. Chi* is the 22nd letter of the Greek alphabet; its symbol is X. *Chiasmus* is a rhetorical term, taken from Greek *chiasmos*, the noun akin to the Greek verb *chiazein* (to mark with a *chi*, i.e., an X). A *chiasmus* is a device in rhetoric based on the scheme of parallelism in reverse order, i.e., a grammatical figure in which the word order in the first of two parallel clauses is reversed in the second. The word is based on the fact that a *chi*, or *X*, is a symbol of *crossing*, i.e., dividing in crossed form. Examples are given in the various dictionaries. *CH*: "Do not eat to live, but live to eat." *C.O.D.*: "To stop too fearful, and too faint to go." *W III*: "A superman in physique but in intellect a fool." The *O.E.D.* gives us one in Latin, quoting an 1871 book by A. S. Wilkins on Cicero's attack on Catiline in which Cicero, in one of the Catilinarian Orations, uses the *chiasmus*, "Frequentia sustentatur, alitur otio" (By abundance he is sustained, nourished by leisure). Wilkins comments: "This is a good instance of the ... figure called *chiasmus* ... in which the order of words in the first clause is inverted in the second." *W II* gives: "Burns with one love, with one resentment glows." These examples ought to give you a pretty good idea of what a *chiasmus* is.

chichevache (CHICH uh vash) *n. Chicheface*, a French word (*chichefache* in northern France), means literally "niggardly-face, thin face, ugly face." Chaucer changed the word to *chichevache*, meaning "lean cow, ugly cow," and used it in *The Clerk's Tale* as the name of a fabulous monster that fed only on good, patient women, and who, because there were so few of them, was always lean and hungry, all skin and bones. In the Chaucer poem, we read: "O noble wyuys ful of heigh prudence/Let noon humilytee youre tongè naille/Ne let no clerk have cause or diligence/To write of yow a storie of swich mervaille/As of Grisildis, pacient and kynde,/Lest *Chichevache* yow swelwe in hire entraille." (Freely: Noble wives, don't let anyone proclaim your virtues, comparing you to patient Griselda [the model of enduring patience and wifely obedience, heroine also of the last tale in Boccaccio's *Decameron*], lest *Chichevache* swallow you into his entrails.) That monster was the very converse of *Bicorn* or *Bycorne* (BEYE korn), a fabulous beast who was well nourished by his diet of virtuous and patient husbands. The English monk and poet John Lydgate, a younger contemporary of Chaucer, wrote a poem entitled *Chichevache and Bicorn*, in which we read: "*Chichevache* etith wymmen goode." What a pair of misogynists those English poets were; how different from their Italian contemporary!

chinook   See **moazagotl.**

chi-rho (KEE roh, KEYE-) *n*. The first two letters of the name of Christ in Greek, *kh* and *rho*, are known as *chi* and *rho* in the English language. (In the Greek alphabet they are *X* and *P*.) The monogram formed of *chi* and *rho*, *chi-rho*, also called the *Christogram*, constitutes a symbol of Christ, often embroidered on altar cloths and clerical vestments. After the conversion of the Emperor Constantine I to Christianity, he adopted a standard consisting of a purple silk banner that hung from a crosspiece on a pike, adorned with a golden crown bearing the *chi-rho*, a *P* surmounting a *X*. Known as a *labarum* (LAH buh ruhm), it became the imperial standard of the later Roman emperors, taking the form of a gilded spear bearing an eagle at its top and a cross-staff from which hung a purple streamer adorned with a fringe of gold, decorated with precious gems. *Labarum* was the Latinization of the Greek word *labaron*, of unknown origin, and came to signify any symbolic banner. It is suggested, however, that one should not apply the word to a banner bearing representations of a hammer and a sickle ...

chittering-bite (CHIT uh ring bite) *n*. *Chitter* is a British dialectal verb meaning, among other things, "to shiver with the cold," "to tremble." The *O.E.D.* calls it "a parallel form to *chatter*." What, then, is a *chittering-bite*? It is "a bit of bread (or something else that comes to hand) taken to prevent shivering or chattering of the teeth." It is also known as a *chittering-crust* or a *chittering-piece*. "The Greeks," according to a mid-19th-century writer named Charles Badham, " ... appear to have begun the day with a sort of 'chittering crust.'" The *O.E.D.* ends this observation with the Greek word *akratisma*, which is defined in my *Liddell & Scott* as "breakfast." It must have been cold early in the morning in Greece, causing enough shivering to require a chittering-bite.

chrematistics (krem uh TIS tiks) *n.* (*pl.*—treated as singular). *Chremat-* is the stem of the Greek *chrema* (thing, possession), akin to the verb *chresthai* (to use, need). From the adjective *chrematistikos* we got *chrematistics*, the "study of wealth," and *chrematistic*, "pertaining to money making." The *O.E.D.* includes in its definition "political economy" and defines *chrematist* as "political economist." In Henry Fielding's *Amelia* (1751) we find the sentences: "I am not the least versed in the *chrematistic* art ... I know not how to get a shilling, nor how to keep it in my pocket if I had it." William T. Brande's *Dictionary of Science, Literature and Art* (1842) states that the Continental writers "consider *political economy* as a term more properly applicable to the whole range of subjects which comprise the material welfare of states and citizens, and *chrematistics* ... as merely a branch of it," but William Ewart Gladstone, in *Homer* (1858), says: "The phrase ... 'political economy' cannot be defended on its merits. The name '*Chrematistic*' [sic] has been devised in its stead." You pays your money and ...

chrism (KRIZ'm) *n., vb.* Late Latin took the noun *chrisma* from the Greek word for "ointment," based on the verb *chriein* (to anoint). *Chrism* is "holy or consecrated oil," usually mixed with balm and various spices, used in some churches in the administering of certain sacraments, such as baptism, confirmation, ordination and the consecration of altars and churches. The term also has the meanings of "unguent" or "ointment" generally, "sacramental anointing" and "unction." Capitalized, it is a term used in the Eastern Orthodox Church for a sacrament analogous to confirmation in the Western Church. A variant, *chrisom*, is the name of a white robe or cloth worn by a person being baptized, white being the symbol of innocence. A *chrisom child* is an "innocent child," or more specifically, one still wearing the *chrisom cloth*; or one that died in its first month, often buried in that cloth; also, more generally, any infant. Shakespeare used the form *christom* in *Henry V* (Act II, Scene 3), when the hostess of the Boar's Head Tavern, formerly Mistress Quickly, on learning from her husband Pistol that Falstaff is dead, says that he " ... made a finer end, and went away an it had been any *christom child* ... " The related word *chrismal*, besides its use as an adjective meaning "pertaining to *chrism*," means "a vessel containing *chrism*." *Chrismation* (kriz MAY shun) is a synonym of *Chrism* (uppercase *C*) in the sense mentioned above. *Chrismatory* (KRIZ muh toh ree) can mean either the "vessel containing *chrism*" or the "sacramental anointment with *chrism*." In addition to all of the above, *chrism*, as a verb, means "to anoint with *chrism*." The connection between *chrism* and *Christ* is that *Christos*, the Greek name for *Christ*, is derived from *christos* (anointed), used as a substantive, from *chriein* (to anoint—as explained above), and Christ is the Messiah, from Hebrew *messiach* (anointed), and the Lord's *Anointed*.

chrismal   See **chrism.**

chrismation   See **chrism.**

chrismatory   See **chrism.**

chrisom   See **chrism.**

christom   See **chrism.**

chunda   See **chunter.**

chunder   See **chunter.**

chunner   See **chunter.**

chunter (CHUN tur) *vb. To chunter* (also *chunner, chunder*) is "to murmur, mutter, grumble, complain." As to derivation, all the dictionaries I have consulted state that it is (or probably or apparently is) "imitative," or "of imitative formation," but they don't tell us what it is "imitative" of. One of the meanings of *imitative* is "onomatopoeic," and I suppose that is what the dictionaries are trying to tell us. Does *chunter* sound like the noises of murmuring, muttering, grumbling or complaining? A little, but it could evoke other images as well: huffing? puffing? panting? The variant *chunder* does sound a little like "grumbling," perhaps, but to me, despite the seeming agreement of all the lexicons, "imitative" gives the impression of groping, to avoid the dread "origin unknown." In 1863 Mrs. Toogood's *Specimens of the Yorkshire Dialect* contained the entry: "He is a *chuntering* sort of fellow, never contented." Francis K. Robinson's *A Glossary of Words Used in the Neighborhood of Whitby* [Yorkshire] (1876) defines a *chuntering bout* as "a fit of sulkiness with impertinence." But the word didn't remain confined to Yorkshire. D. H. Lawrence, in *Sea and Sardinia* (1921), speaks of "a thin old woman ... *chuntering* her head off because it was her seat," and Christopher Fry's *The Lady's Not for Burning* (1949) gives us: "You fog-blathering, chin-*chuntering*, liturgical ... base old man!" In *On the Beach* (1957) Nevil Shute writes: "The baby stirred, and started *chuntering* and making little whimpering noises." Be careful not to confuse the variant *chunder* with the Australian slang *chunder*, used as both a verb and a noun meaning "vomit." It has a variant, *chunda*. Ugly-sounding word; no "imitative" here, just plain outspoken "origin unknown." Nevil Shute used this *chunder* (and its variant *chunda*) too. In *A Town Like Alice* (1950) we read: "The way these bloody Nips go on. Makes you *chunda*." And in his *Beyond the Black Stump* (1956): "But I gets sick at the stomach. I *chundered* once today already." The London magazine *Private Eye* uses *chunder* in the Australian slang sense in two different 1970 issues. I won't quote: We've had enough of this nasty kind of *chundering* already.

Churrigeresque (chu rig ur ESK) *adj.* José Benito Churrigera (1665–1725) was a Spanish architect and sculptor renowned for his ornate *retables* (rih TAY buhlz), decorative structures raised above the backs of altars. He designed palaces, churches and cathedrals in the baroque style, and his name gave rise to this adjective as descriptive of the architectural idiom of the late 17th and early 18th centuries in Spain, notable for its extravagant design, extreme richness and exuberance. That style greatly influenced Spanish colonial architecture in both the United States and Mexico, but the work there is naive in comparison with the original because of poor workmanship. In his writings on Spain in the 1840s and 1850s, Richard Ford made frequent use of this adjective, calling one building "vile *churrigeresque*" and the ornaments of an enormous organ "*churrigeresque* and inappropriate." *Churrigeresque* has found a place in many architectural writings of the 19th and 20th centuries. I wonder, if he came back today, whether Churrigera would say, as he cried all the way to the bank, "I don't care what they say about me, as long as they spell my name right."

cicisbeo (chee cheez BAY oh, chih chiz-) *n.* Taken from the Italian, this mouthful of a word denotes a married woman's gallant, also known as a *cavalier servente* (literally, a "serving cavalier") in Italy, especially in the 18th century. There are various theories about the term's origin: It may be an inversion of *bel cece* (beautiful chick-pea, in Italian), or come from *chiche beau*—*pois chiches* are "chick-peas" in French. The modern French equivalent of *cicisbeo* is *sigisbée*, which is defined in French dictionaries as "*cicisbeo*, lover." The French are quite blunt in their definition of the relationship. *The Annual Register* of 1773 says: "The *Chichisbeo* is an appendix to matrimony." That's telling it like it is, no? But John Wesley, the English theologian and founder of Methodism (1703–91), stated flatly: "English ladies are not attended by their *cicisbys* yet; nor would any English husband suffer it." Definitions go all the way from "dangler about women" to "professed gallant" to "escort" to "gigolo" to the aforestated "appendix to matrimony" to "lover." Who knows? It might be anything from Dante's innocent long-distance adoration of Beatrice to Louis Armstrong's "(Just a) Gigolo" to the institution euphemistically known as "escort service" (by the male attendant) to hubbie's "best friend." Byron, in *Beppo*, said that *cicisbeo* had … grown vulgar and indecent … *Cavalier servente* is the [proper] phrase." I prefer *cicisbeo*.

cilice See **ambry.**

cinquain (sing KANE) *n.* This word was taken over from the French and denotes a five-line stanza arranged as follows: two syllables in the first line, four in the second, six in the third, eight in the fourth and two again in the fifth. This eccentric form is reminiscent of the Japanese *tanka* (TAHNG kuh), also a five-line stanza but with a different arrangement: the first and third lines have five syllables and all the others seven. This brings us to another Japanese verse conformation, the *hokku* (HAW kooh or HAH kooh), with three short unrhymed lines, the first and third consisting of five syllables, the middle line of seven. The *hokku* is generally epigrammatic in content and is formed of *hok* (beginning) plus *ku* (hemistich—see **hemistich**). A 19th-century development of the *hokku* is the *haiku* (HEYE kooh), also an unrhymed three-line poem with the same syllable scheme as the *hokku*. The *haiku* refers in one way or another to one of the seasons of the year. It is a term that applies as well to a poem written in a language other than Japanese and can include some modification of the original *haiku* form. Now that we know all about *cinquains* and three different Japanese verse forms, why don't you try your hand at composing one or more of each? Here's my *haiku*:

> I love to think of
> The summer with its green leaves
> And dazzling blossoms.

Terrible poetry, and terribly easy to invent, but they say Hirohito was a master at it.

cippus (SIH puhs) *n*. This word has a variety of meanings. In Latin, it means a "post" or "stake"; in Late Latin and English, "the stocks"; in architecture, a "small low column" with or without a base or capital, usually bearing an inscription and used by the ancient Romans and Greeks as a gravestone, a landmark or the memorial of a notable event. In 1862 De Quincey wrote the following: " ... in Ceylon, a granite *cippus*, or monumental pillar, of immemorial antiquity." Baroness Frances Bunsen, in 1860, described "the inscription on the *cippus* placed over the remains of ... two children." The dictionaries include the meaning "stocks," but from the illustrations I have seen of stocks and pillories, I think "pillory" would be more appropriate, because that form of public punishment was built on a *post* or *stake* (cf. the definition above), whereas stocks consisted of a seat placed behind a frame or low wall of timber having holes for the feet, and sometimes the hands, of offenders deserving public punishment, with nothing resembling a post or stake. All this is old stuff, but these details are (or should be) of concern to lexicographers. Stocks and pillories were quite different in form, though they served the same purpose.

circadian (sur kuh DEE uhn, sur KAY dee uhn) *adj*. *Circa* is a Latin adverb and preposition; in the latter capacity, relating to time, it means "about." The *c*, *c*., or *ca*. in dates given in encyclopedias and other works of reference—for example, the dates of the birth or death of a historical figure or the date of an event—are all abbreviations of *circa*. *Dies* is Latin for "day." From the combination of the two we get *circadian*, denoting a physiological activity or cycle repeated approximately (*circa*) every 24 hours. *Circadian* also describes the rhythm of any such activity. The term does not pretend to mean "exactly every 24 hours." Halberg says, in *Zeitschrift für Vitamin- Hormon- und Fermentforschung* (Journal of Vitamin, Hormone and Enzyme Research, 1959): "'*Circadian*' might be applied to all '24 hour' rhythms, whether or not their periods … are different from 24 hours, longer or shorter, by a few minutes or hours." This definition quite emphatically stresses the *circa*.

circumambages (sur kuhm am BAY jeez) *n. pl. Ambages*, in Latin, means "going round, winding, roundabout way," and by extension, "circumlocution, ambiguity, obscurity." In English, *ambages* is treated as a plural meaning "indirect, roundabout paths," in both literal and figurative senses, and can also, in context, mean "delays." The adjective *ambagious* is dealt with in my *1000 Most Challenging Words*, where it is defined as "circuitous." It can also mean "tortuous" and, in context, "circumlocutory." So much for *ambages* and *ambagious*. Now we come to *circumambages*, which looks a little like a case of painting the lily ("to gild the lily" is a misquotation: see Shakespeare's *King John*, Act II, Scene 2: "To gild refined gold, to paint the lily … /Is wasteful and ridiculous excess.") It isn't, however, because the use of the Latin prefix *circum-* (around) gives us a new word, which most dictionaries treat as a plural, meaning "instances of deviousness or indirectness in speech or writing," or, in a more general sense, according to the *O.E.D.*, "round-about methods," as well as "round-about modes of speech." The same dictionary lists the participial adjective *circumambaging* as meaning "using methods to get round people." The meaning "circumlocution" for *ambages* in the Latin dictionary brought to mind the wonderful bit in *Little Dorrit* where Dickens coins the term "Circumlocution Office": "Whatever was required to be done, the Circumlocution Office was beforehand with all the public departments in the art of perceiving—How not to do it," calling for the comment in *Brewer's Dictionary of Phrase and Fable*, "A term applied in ridicule … to our public offices, because each person tries to shuffle off every act to someone else; and before anything is done it has to pass through so many departments with such consequent delays that it is hardly worth having bothered about it." "*Our* [i.e., British] public offices … "? How about *universal*?

circumbendibus (sur kuhm BEN dih buhs) *n.* Jocularly formed of the Latin prefix *circum-*, the English word *bend* and the Latin ablative plural ending of certain classes of nouns, *-ibus*, a *circumbendibus* is a "roundabout method, or a roundabout expression in the nature of a circumlocution." In *The Art of Sinking*, by Alexander Pope and others (1727), we find: "The Periphrasis, which the moderns call the *circumbendibus* … " (Incidentally, *periphrasis*, in case you aren't familiar with it, is only another word for "circumlocution, roundabout way of expressing oneself." This word is fully discussed in my *1000 Most Challenging Words*.) Sir Walter Scott, in *The Waverley Novels* (1814), uses these words: "Partaking of what scholars call the periphrastic and ambagitory [Scott's version of *ambagious*: see **circumambages**], and the vulgar the *circumbendibus* … " Phony Latinization is not all that rare: e.g., *omnium gatherum*, meaning "mixture" or "open house," which I characterize in my *British English, A to Zed* as "Mock Latin," explaining that *omnium* is the genitive plural of *omnis* (all), and *gatherum* is a "phony Latinization of 'gather.'" Said to have been invented

by a group of Eton boys, *floccinaucinihilipilification* is a word meaning "belittling," consisting of a series of genitives of four Latin nouns meaning "trifle"
or "nothing," fully discussed in my *1000 Most Challenging Words*. And how
about the horrible mutilation of *De gustibus non disputandum* (There is no
accounting for tastes): *Disgustibus non disputandibus?* Here that tempting *-ibus*
rears its ugly head twice.

circumforaneous (sur kuhm fuhr AY nee uhs) *adj*. This adjective comes from
the Latin *circumforaneus*, built of the preposition *circum* (around) plus *-foraneus*
(relating to the *forum*, market). The Latin adjective was used in various ways:
Its general meaning was "around the forum"; modifying *aes* (literally, copper
ore, bronze, but by extension, money), it meant "borrowed from the Forum
bankers"; with *pharmacopola* (drug vendor, but by extension, quack), it meant
"attending at markets." The English form means, literally, "wandering about
from market to market"; figuratively, "wandering, vagrant, roving,
vagabond" and by extension, "quack." Apparently, there is something about
merchants setting up stalls from market to market that smacks of quackery
and calls for *caveat emptor* in loud accents.

clapdish   See **clapperdudgeon**.

clapperdudgeon (KLAP uhr duj uhn) *n*. The *O.E.D.* says that " ... the origin
of the appellation is unknown" but mentions the suggestion of one Collier that
the word comes from the act of knocking a *clapdish* with a *dudgeon*. A *clapperdudgeon* is a "beggar"; a *clapdish* is a "wooden dish with a lid," once carried by
lepers and beggars from the *lazar-houses* (hospitals for the diseased poor,
especially lepers) which were later called *lazarets* or *lazarettos*, to announce
their approach and receive alms; and *dudgeon* is the name of a type of wood
used by wood turners, expecially for handles of knives, daggers and the like.
Dudgeon is generally believed to be the root of the box shrub. This *dudgeon*
hasn't a thing in the world to do with the *high dudgeon* in which irked persons
walk out of rooms. Incidentally, has anybody ever walked out of a room in
low dudgeon? *Clapperdudgeon* has also been used as a term of reproach or
insult. George Augustus Sala, in *The Strange Adventures of Captain Dangerous*
(1863), tells us that "Rogues, Thieves ... and *Clapper-Dudgeons* infested the
outskirts of the Old Palace," and writes of "A perfect chaos of *clapdishes* ...
Impostors ... cripples, and gambling bullies." The word may be archaic, but
the next time you want to reproach somebody, call him a *clapperdudgeon* and
see whether he or she walks out of the room in you-know-what.

clerisy (KLER uh see) *n*. In German, *Klerisei* means "clergy" but is used
colloquially to mean "hangers-on," a not very complimentary extension of the
literal meaning. In the Middle Ages, the clergy were the only intelligentsia;
hence the evolution of *clerk* from *cleric*, the dual meaning of *clerical*, etc. This
clerisy came to signify "intelligentsia, scholars, learned men, the well-educated
or academic class." This use was introduced by Samuel Taylor Coleridge, who

wrote, in *Literary Remains* (1818): "After the Revolution ... a learned body, or *clerisy*, as such, gradually disappeared." In *Specimens of his Table Talk* (1834) he discussed "the *clerisy* of a nation, that is, its learned men, whether poets, or philosophers, or scholars." Ralph Waldo Emerson, in *Essay on Manners* (1841), wrote of "the artist, the scholar, and in general, the *clerisy*." But it must be remembered that the term *cleric* means "clergyman," from Late Latin *clericus*, and that as late as 1858 *The Times* (London) used *clerisy* in the sense of "clericism" in writing about "the restrictions of *clerisy* and celibacy." In 1870 James Russell Lowell, in *Among My Books*, wrote of "a layman, alike indifferent to *clerisy* and heresy," a nice turn of phrase. I think, however, that nowadays, *clerisy* is used to denote the literati, the intelligentsia, and no longer refers to the church. This would seem to be borne out by the definitions given in the abridged dictionaries of Britain and America, as exemplified in both *RH* and the *C.O.D.*

cochlea (KOK lee uh) *n.* Definitions of this word vary, depending on your choice of dictionary. One is content with the anatomical meaning: the "spiral-shaped cavity forming the division of the inner ear"; the *O.E.D.* adds "spiral staircase, screw, Archimedes's water-screw [of which more later]," "spiral univalve shell, snail-shell"; *CH* goes all the way: "anything spiral-shaped" (that covers a lot of territory!), adding "snail-shell, medick-pod [*medick* is a type of clover or trefoil with spiral pods], winding stair, spiral cavity of the ear." They all agree that via Latin *coc(h)lea* (shell, screw), the word goes back to Greek *kochlias* (snail, screw). To add to the confusion, *cochlear* (KOK lee uhr) means not only "pertaining to the *cochlea* of the ear" but also "spoon" (French *cuiller*) from Latin *coc(h)leare* and *coclearium* (spoon, in the shape of a snail shell). As to the water-screw mentioned above, we have to look into the remarkable career of our old friend Archimedes (287–212 B.C.), the Greek mathematician, physicist and inventor, famous for the "Eureka!" incident and the lever with which he could "move the world." One of his many inventions was the water-screw, consisting of a cylinder containing a continuous screw the same length as the cylinder. With the lower end placed in the water, by revolving the screw, water is raised to the top. This principle is applied to drainage and irrigation machines, and the device can also handle light, loose materials like sand and grain. One must be careful with *cochleariform* (kok lee AIR uh form), which means "spoon-shaped," and *cochleiform* (ko LEE uh form) meaning "shaped like a snail shell."

cochlear   See **cochlea.**

cochleariform   See **cochlea.**

cochleiform   See **cochlea.**

cocqcigrues (KOK see groohs) *n. pl.* This is how Charles Kingsley spelled it in *The Water Babies*, when the fairy Bedonebyasyoudid said, "That is one of the seven things I am forbidden to tell you till the coming of the *Cocqcigrues*." In French *coquecigrue*, accented on the second syllable, is a colloquialism meaning "fiddle-faddle, stuff and nonsense, idle story," and Kingsley misspelled it. *His* phrase *till the coming of the Cocqcigrues* was a translation from the French *à la venue des coquecigrues*, meaning "never," similar to *when the cows come home*. The *coquecigrues* were mythical animals of French legend and, since they were legendary, they'd never show up, hence the French idiom and the words Kingsley put into the mouth of Mrs. Bedonebyasyoudid.

coctile (KOK tuhl, -tile) *adj. Coquere* is Latin for "to cook, bake, boil, roast, heat," i.e., to prepare by cooking of any sort. Its past participle is *coctus*, from which the Romans formed the adjective *coctilis*, meaning "baked," used by Ovid in describing the walls of Babylon in the sense of "made of baked brick." *Coctile*, then, means "made by baking or exposure to heat," as a brick, which is hardened by fire. The related Latin noun *coctio* gave us *coction*, "boiling, cooking," which in the old days denoted the attainment of a more nearly perfect, more mature or generally more desirable state, either through natural processes or through human processes such as the application of heat, and, more specifically, the digestion of food. Another archaic meaning was "suppuration," a phase of wound healing or the development of any disease. The combining form *cocto-* has the force of "boiled" or "altered by heat," as in *coctostable* (kok toh STAY b'l—at boiling point). The verb *concoct* and the noun *concoction* are obviously products of the prefix *con-* (together) plus *coction*. *Concoquere* is Latin for "to boil together," with the predictable past participle and related substantive and adjectival forms. Our *concoct* and *concoction* have lost all reference to heat, now meaning simply "to devise" and "fabrication," with pejorative connotations, as in "concocting an alibi."

coction   See **coctile**.

coctostable   See **coctile**.

coenesthesia, also **cenesthesia** (see nis THEE zuh, -zee uh, sen is-); **coenesthesis**, also **cenesthesis** (see nis THEE sis), *n*. However you choose to spell it, this term denotes the totality of impressions you get from organic sensations forming the basis of your awareness of your bodily state, such as the feeling of health, vigor or apathy. Without *coenesthesia* you wouldn't be able to answer the question "How are you?" or even "How's tricks?" *Coenesthesia* is derived from two Greek words, *koino-*, the combining form of the adjective *koinos* (common), and *aisthesis* (perception), which gave us our word *esthesia* (also *aesthesia*), meaning "sensitivity, the capacity for feeling or sensation." Next time you wake up feeling just great or simply lousy, remember that you wouldn't feel anything without *coenesthesia*.

coistril   See **custrel**.

colporteur (kol POR tur) *n*. No, this is not intended as a representation of the way the French say "Cole Porter," though it must be pretty close to it. *Colporteur* was taken over intact from the French, where it means "peddler," and figuratively, "spreader of news." But in American English it means "peddler of books" and secondarily, "one employed to travel about distributing Bibles and religious tracts gratuitously or at a very low price." *Colportage* is the activity of such a person and is likewise accented on the second syllable, while in British English it can refer to peddler (they spell it *pedlar*) generally, especially one selling religious tracts and books. It all goes back to Latin *collum* (neck) and *portare* (to carry), presenting the image of one carrying a tray of books suspended from the neck and hanging in front, or more likely in back, in view of the French expression *porter à col* (to carry on one's back, though *col* means literally "neck"). Whether in front or in back, these *colporteurs* were missionary types and were generally respected as intrepid individuals. *Colportage* was a common 19th-century practice, now generally confined to the Gideons, an international association of Christian business and professional persons founded in 1899, now active in over 65 countries, distributing Bibles to hotel bedrooms and hospitals and New Testaments to schools. The name is derived from Gideon's men who overthew the Midianites (*Judges* vii).

consuetude (KON swih tyoohd) *n*. *Consuetude*, from Latin *consuetudo* (custom, usage, habit), is a "custom so established in human dealings as to have acquired the legal force of law." The Latin verb *consuescere* (to accustom, habituate) has an intransitive usage: "to accustom oneself." *Consuetude*, then, specifically denotes an unwritten law, never enacted by a legislature but derived from immemorial custom. If things have been done a certain way in commercial transactions over the ages, the rules governing such dealings become as fixed as though they were inscribed in black and white in the law books, and a violation of those rules and regulations cannot legally be sidestepped on the basis that they do not appear in statute form. In case of dispute, history, not enactment, governs. *Desuetude* (DEZ wih tyoohd) means "disuse" from the Latin *desuetudo*, related to the verb *desuescere* (to become unaccustomed), and its past passive participle *desuetus* (disused). When customs of long standing have passed into a state of *desuetude*, they no longer have the force of law. Before relying on *consuetude*, make sure *desuetude* has not set in. If in doubt in a commercial matter, consult the merchants as well as your lawyer.

coprophagous   See **merdivorous.**

copy   See **heriot.**

copyhold   See **heriot.**

coronal   See **cacuminal.**

corroboree (kuh ROB uh ree) *n.* You might well think that this word denotes a person who makes a statement that, needing corroboration, gets it; or, on hearing the word (note its pronunciation), that it signifies a robbery engaged in by two or more. But no: A *corroboree* is nothing more or less than a "native dance of Australian aborigines, held by moonlight or the light of a bush fire, and either festive or warlike in character." In travel accounts the word appears in a variety of forms: *caribberie, corob(b)ory, -berri,* etc. It is also used as a verb signifying the performance of the dance. It has been used, as well, as a song for such a dance or for any festive occasion among those natives. In his writings, Darwin used the form *corrobery* to describe a "great dancing party" in that part of the world. One who *corroborates* is a *corroborator,* and one who receives *corroboration* would logically be called a *corroboratee,* but there's no such word, I'm happy to say.

corsned (KORS ned) *n.* In Old English law, this was the name for "ordeal by swallowing a piece of bread or cheese." If it stuck in the throat, that proved guilt. The morsel was "consecrated by exorcism" and was known as *panis coniuratus* (sworn bread). In his *Commentaries,* the great work of early law, Sir William Blackstone wrote (1769): "*Corsned* or morsel of execration: being a piece of cheese or bread, of about an ounce in weight, which was consecrated with a form of exorcism; desiring of the Almighty that it might cause convulsions and paleness, and find no passage, if the man was really guilty; but might turn to health and nourishment, if he was innocent." *Corsned* is from the Old English *corsnaed,* formed of *coren,* the past participle of *ceosn* (to choose), plus *snaed* (piece), from *snidan* (to cut). Today we use *ordeal* in the sense of any severe test or experience. In the old days, ordeals were primitive trials to determine guilt or innocence by exposing the accused to various types of physical danger, the result being left to divine judgment, since God would defend right even by miracle if necessary. There were ordeals by battle, by fire (e.g., walking barefoot over red-hot ploughshares), boiling water (plunging the hand into boiling water), cold water (sink or swim) and the cross (the parties stood upright before a cross; the first to move was guilty). Most were abolished in favor of jury trial in the early part of the 13th century. As a practicing lawyer for more than half a century, I never cared much for juries …

coryphaeus   See **epirrhema.**

costerdom (KOS tur duhm) *n.* The little suffix *-dom* is indeed versatile. It can indicate condition: *freedom, martyrdom, stardom;* groups having something in common: *officialdom, dogdom;* rank or office: *earldom, dukedom;* realm: *Christendom, kingdom;* and geographical area: *Anglo-Saxondom.* In *costerdom,* the suffix has the force of designating a group identifiable because of a common pursuit: *costers* or *costermongers,* those who sell fruit, vegetables, sometimes fish, etc., from barrows or pushcarts on the street. The origin of *coster* is *costard,* a large apple, indicating perhaps that at one time the wares were restricted to that commodity, and *monger,* a British word for "dealer," almost always found in combination with the particular article dealt in, as in *cheesemonger, fishmonger* or *ironmonger.* (*Monger* is found as well in other combinations of a pejorative nature, like *scandalmonger* and *warmonger.* There is a new derogatory term: *peacemonger,* for *dove,* a term of abuse in warlike quarters.) A special sector of *costerdom* is the realm of those wearing *pearlies*—costumes decorated with mother-of-pearl buttons. There are pearly kings and queens, who show up at gala occasions as buskers performing on the streets, but this, alas, like so many traditional customs, is fast disappearing from the streets of England.

cothurnus (koh THUR nuhs) *n.* From the Greek *kothornos,* this is a buskin: a thick-soled laced boot reaching halfway to the knee, worn by Greek and Roman actors in the staging of ancient tragedies. Edgeworth and Richard's *Practical Education* (1798) states: "The actor on the stage is admired whilst he is elevated by the *cothornus.*" Actors on stage always seem taller than they really are, and the *cothornus* enhanced this illusion. The word eventually acquired the figurative sense of the grave, tragic and lofty style characteristic of tragedy, as evident in a passage in Frederic W. Farrar's *Life and Work of St. Paul* (1879): "St. Paul cannot always wear the majestic *cothornus,* yet his lightest words are full of dignity." Virgil used the figurative sense in describing some verses as "Sophocleo ... digna *cothurno*" (worthy of Sophoclean tragedy).

cowan (KOU uhn) *n.* It is always a disappointment, to one interested in etymology, to find the words *origin unknown* after a dictionary entry, and all too often one keeps hunting for clues and grasping at straws—to no avail. And so it is with *cowan,* which is a Scottish word for "dry-stone diker." And what is a *dry-stone diker*? In Scotland, a *dike* is a wall, and a *dry-stone* (or *dry-stane*) *dike* is one built without mortar. Thus a *dry-stone diker* is one who builds walls without the use of mortar (or nowadays, cement). But *cowan* has other meanings as well: It is a pejorative term for a person who works as a mason without having served an apprenticeship in that occupation or having been bred to it. This is made clear in these words from Robert Forsyth's *Beauties of Scotland* (1806): "The men who are employed in building walls for inclosing fields are called ... *cowans,* to distinguish them from the regular masons." Stretching the use of the word, *cowan* came to denote a person who is uninitiated into the secrets of Freemasonry, i.e., one who is not a member of that society. In a *Text-book of Freemasonry,* published in 1881, certain officials are described as "armed with a drawn sword, to keep off all *Cowans* and intruders to Masonry." They took things pretty seriously in those days. *CH* stretches the word a little further: " ... one who tries to enter a Freemason's lodge, or the like, surreptitiously." Finally, *cowan* became a slang term for any sneak, or "prying or inquisitive person," according to John C. Hotten's *Dictionary of Modern Slang, Cant, and Vulgar Words* (1859–74). John Strang's *Glasgow and its Clubs* (1856) used the word attributively to describe "outsiders," writing about a tavern "shut off from the observation and the ken of the *'cowan'* world." We have come a long way from an unapprenticed mason to a snooping outsider.

Cradle Holding   See **Borough-English.**

Cradle Land   See **Borough-English.**

cramponée   See **fylfot.**

cubit   See **alnage.**

custrel (KUS trel) *n. Custrel* was the title of a knight's attendant. The word came from the Old French *coustillier,* a soldier armed with a *coustille,* a two-edged dagger. The normal transmutation into English would have produced *custeler,* but metathesis intervened, and the *l* and *r* got switched around to form *custrel.* The term was applied as well to a knight's groom and eventually developed the secondary meaning of "knave, base fellow." This was probably the result of association with *custron,* meaning "scullion," and one in that position would have been a boy of low birth, a base-born fellow and very likely a vagabond in the bargain. A common variant of *custrel* is *coistrel* (KOY strel). The *O.E.D.* points out that "an interchange of *u* and *oi* in words from French is frequent." *Coistrel* was used for "groom" at first, but, like *custrel,* degenerated into "knave, varlet." In Scott's *The Betrothed* we read: "Nor can you fly from your standard without such infamy as even *coistrels* or grooms are unwilling to incur." We find *coistrel* (or a variant spelling) in its pejorative sense in Ben Johnson's *Every Man in his Humor:* "You whorson, bragging *Coystril?*"; and in *Twelfth Night:* "He's a Coward and a *Coystrill* that will not drinke to my Neece"; and again in *Pericles, Prince of Tyre:* "Thou'rt the damn'd doorkeeper to every *coistrel* that comes inquiring for his tib [girl—in the context of this brothel, whore]." Try to imagine an Elizabethan spelling bee!

custron   See **custrel.**

dabchick   See **didapper.**

dactyl   See **dolichurus.**

dactyliography (dak til ee AW gruh fee) *n.* In Greek, *daktylos* means "finger" and *daktylios* "finger ring." In zoology, the word *dactyl* means, inter alia, "finger" or "toe," and in classical prosody it denotes a foot of three syllables, one long and two short; in English and other modern languages, a stressed syllable followed by two unstressed ones; thus, as in the opening syllables of *The Aeneid* and *Evangeline*, respectively: *Arma vi/rumque ca; This is the/forest pri.* From *dactyl*, we get the adjective *dactylic* (dak TIL ik), and from *daktylos* a number of nouns: *dactyliography* and *dactyliology* (dak til ee AWL uh jee), both meaning "the study or lore of finger rings or engraved gems"; *dactyliomancy* (dak TIL ee uh man see), combining *dactylio-* with *manteia* (divination), "divination by means of finger rings"; *dactylogram* (dak TIL oh gram, DAK til uh gram), "fingerprint"; *dactylography* (dak tih LAW gruh fee), "the study of fingerprints"; and *dactylology* (dak tih LAW luh jee), "talking with the fingers, as with the manual language of the deaf." *Dactylion* (dak TIL ee uhn) means "tip of the middle finger," and a *dactyliotheca* (dak til ee uh THEE kuh), from Greek *daktyliotheke*, combining *daktilio-* with *theke* (box, chest), is a case for a collection of rings, gems or seals. In addition, there are a good many *dactyl-* terms in the field of biology. I may have missed one or more uses, so I'm keeping my *dactyls* crossed.

dactyliology   See **dactyliography.**

dactyliomancy   See **dactyliography.**

dactylion   See **dactyliography.**

dactyliotheca   See **dactyliography.**

dactylogram   See **dactyliography.**

dactylography   See **dactyliography.**

dactylology   See **dactyliography.**

daddock (DA duhk) *n. Daddock* means "rotten wood." The *dad-* is said to be of uncertain origin; the *-ock* is thought to be a diminutive suffix, as in *hillock* and *bullock.* An obsolete word, *doddard*, may offer a clue. It once denoted a tree that had lost its branches as a result of decay, and *dod* is an obsolete verb that meant "to lop," e.g., a tree. Whatever the etymology, Dryden, in a 1693 poem entitled *Persius*, wrote the words: " ... Rots like a *doddard* oke, and piecemeal falls to ground." The participial form *dodded* is still in use in some parts of England, describing plants, trees and animals that have lost their heads, as in *dodded* trees, those that have been polled, stalks of corn that have lost their beards or awns, sheep and cattle that have lost their horns and so forth. Several old glossaries define *daddock* as "rotten wood." In *Margaret, a Tale* (1845), Sylvester Judd wrote: "The great red *daddocks* lay in the green pastures where they had lain year after year, crumbling away." A glossary of terms current in Upton-on-Severn (Worcestershire) dated 1884 defined the adjective *daddocky* as "flimsy, unsubstantial, soft with decay," indicating that the obsolescence of *daddock* didn't occur that long ago, in dialect, anyway.

daddocky   See **daddock.**

dahabeeyah, also **dahabiah** (day hah BEE ah, dah uh BEE uh) *n.* Like so many words transliterated from Arabic, this word can be spelled and pronounced in a variety of ways. It is the name given to a long shallow-draft houseboat used on the Nile, which, though lateen-rigged, is frequently propelled partly or wholly by engine. (For the benefit of landlubbers, a *lateen* sail is triangular in shape and is set on a long sloping spar. It is used commonly in the Mediterranean area.) *Dahabeeyah* has an interesting etymology, for Arabic *dhahabiyah* means "the golden one," and one might well wonder what that has to do with a Nile houseboat. Explanation: It was the name given to the golden state barge used by the Muslim rulers of Egypt. In the preface to her book *A Thousand Miles up the Nile* (1877), Amelia B. Edwards tells us: "The *Dahabeeyah* hired by the European traveller reproduces in all essential features the painted galleys represented in the tombs of the kings." As one who has looked long and enviously at the paintings of the galleys in those tombs, I can assure you that they must have afforded an extremely luxurious means of travel. The simple Nile *feluccas* (fuh LUK uhs) used nowadays are pretty crude in comparison.

dalmatic (dal MAT ik) *adj., n.* As an adjective with an uppercase *D, Dalmatic* is a rarely used synonym of *Dalmatian*. Both refer to *Dalmatia*, a region in western Yugoslavia along the Adriatic coast. In my experience, *Dalmatian* is most commonly used as the name of a familiar breed of short-haired dog, white with irregular black (sometimes liver-colored) spots, also known as a *coach dog*, often attached to fire-engine companies (or "fire brigades," as they are known in Britain). But as a noun with a lowercase *d*, a *dalmatic* is a "vestment worn over the alb (a long-sleeved ecclesiastical linen garment) by a deacon or a bishop on certain liturgical occasions." It has a slit on either side of the skirt, wide sleeves and two stripes. A similar garment is worn by sovereigns at coronations and certain other ceremonies. An ancient Latin text tells us that the *"Dalmatica* vestis" (*Dalmatian* garment, i.e., the *dalmatic*) was first made in the province of Dalmatia and was a *tunica sacerdotalis candida cum clavis ex purpurea* (a priestly sleeved garment with purple stripes). This explains the term, which is the feminine form (modifying *vestis* understood) of Latin *Dalmaticus* (Dalmatian).

dandiprat, also **dandyprat** (DAN dih prat) *n.* This was originally the name of a small coin worth three halfpence, current in 16th-century England. In *Guevara's Familiar Epistles* (1574), by Edward Hellowes, we find this reference to the coin: " ... they aske an halfpenie for spice, a penie for candels, a *dandiprat* for an earthen pot ... " William Camden, in *Remaines of a Greater Worke*

Concerning Britaine (1605), tells us that "K. Henry the 7th stamped a small coine called *dandyprats.*" Somehow the term was applied to an insignificant or contemptible fellow, or one of small physical stature, like a dwarf or a pygmy. We find in Peter A. Motteux's translation of *Cervantes' History of Don Quixote* (1733) these words: "I saw a little *Dandyprat* riding about, who, they said, was a hugeous great Lord," and in Josuah Sylvester's translation of *Du Bartas his Divine Weekes and Workes* (1606): "Am I a dog, thou Dwarfe, thou *Dandiprat?*" The word was also used of a lad or urchin, though rarely a young lass. In Scott's *Kenilworth*, we find: "It is even so, my little *dandieprat,*" and in Charles S. Calverley's *The Cock and the Bull* (a parody of Browning's *The Ring and the Book*) (1875): "It's a thing I bought of a chit of a boy ... 'Chop' was my snickering *dandyprat's* own term." (*Chop* was the boy's term for "exchange" or "price.") Thomas Heywood applied the term to a female, in *The Wise-Woman of Hogsdon* (1638): "Her name is Luce. With this *Dandiprat*, this pretty little Apes face, is yon blunt fellow in love." The development of *dandiprat* from the name of a coin of little worth to a contemptuous term for an insignificant person is reminiscent of the history of the word *picayune*. Originally, it was the name of a coin equal in value to half a Spanish real or six U.S. cents that circulated in Louisiana, Florida and other southern states. The name was based on *picaillon*, a copper coin of Piedmont and Savoy. It is easy, as in the case of *dandiprat*, to see how *picayune* became an adjective meaning "trifling, of little account, paltry, measly," as in *a picayune amount, a picayune effort*. If inflation continues at the current dizzying pace, it won't be long before *dollar* will go the way of *dandiprat* and *picayune*. "He's a pipsqueak, a *dollarish* sort of chap." Perish the thought!

dandyfunk   See **dunderfunk.**

dandyprat   See **dandiprat.**

daven (DAH vuhn, DAW-) *vb.* Taken over from Yiddish, *to daven* is "to pray," in accordance with the ritual prescribed for the daily and holiday Jewish liturgies. Orthodox Jews *daven* three times a day, adding supplementary prayers on the Sabbath, holy days and special occasions. During morning prayers, males usually wear the *tallis* (TAH luhs), "a rectangular or square shawl" with *zizis* (TSIH tsis), "tassels," attached to the four corners. The shawl, with blue or black stripes across the lower edge, is made of wool or silk and is worn over the head or around the shoulders. The congregant prays silently or barely murmers, while standing and usually swaying. In the West, he faces east, toward Israel, just as the Muslim faces Mecca wherever he or she prays. Prayers are recited in classical Hebrew (not the Hebrew of contemporary Israel), quite rapidly. Unhappily, as is sometimes the case with Catholic praying in Latin, they are often recited by rote with little understanding of the literal meaning of the words. There are many Yiddish stories about *davening*, such as the following: A devout Jew is lost in the forest. The time for evening prayer is at hand, but he has forgotten to bring along his prayer book. He tells God his memory is so poor that he can't recite the prayer by heart; he'll just recite the alphabet, and God, who knows all the prayers, will simply put the letters in proper order. God is so touched by the man's sincerity that he tells the angels: "That was the worthiest prayer I've heard all day!" Then there is the tale of the youngster who arrives, breathless, at the synagogue on Yom Kippur, the holiest day of the year. As he runs toward the door, the *shamus* (SHAH mus), or "sexton," stops him and says, "You can't go in there, dressed like a slob and without a *yarmulke!*" (YAHR m'l keh, a skullcap: the head must be covered in an Orthodox synagogue; see **zucchetto**). "But you have to let me in," cries the youth, "I have a message for Mr. Levine, my boss, and if I don't deliver it I'll lose my job!" "Go in then," says the *shamus*, "but God help you if I catch you *davening!*"

dawk-wallah (DAWK wo luh), also **dak-wallah** (DAHK wo luh) *n*. Both components, *da(w)k* and *wallah*, are Anglo-Indian terms (this does not mean "Eurasian," but pertains to the Raj, the period of British rule in India). In the old days, *dawk* was the name given in India to relays of men, on foot or horseback, used to carry mail and baggage, or people in palanquins. It was the common term for the mail system. *Wallah* was a general term for a servant or employee performing a particular service. Thus, a man in charge of the ice supply would be the *ice-wallah*, and the person who worked the punkah (the ceiling fan, made of cloth in a rectangular frame and operated by pulling a rope) was the *punkah-wallah*. (Incidentally, variants of *punkah* and *wallah* dropped the *h*.) The *dawk-wallah*, then, was a "letter carrier or mailman." We read in Edward Braddon's *Life in India* (1872): "The arrival at any village of the *dak-walla* (letter carrier) with a letter is an event to be remembered and talked of." The mail bag was known as the *dak bag*. With the independence of India and the exodus back to England, Anglo-Indian terminology was carried home, but as the years passed, it naturally died out. One hears it from the lips of old India hands, less and less, of course, and it is considered chic in some quarters to come out with a bit of the old idiom somewhat for the fun of it, but not without a twinge of nostalgia.

deblaterate   See **quisquilious**.

deblateration   See **quisquilious**.

decollate (dee KOL ate) *vb*. To *decollate* is "to behead"—it's as simple as that—and the word is derived from the Latin verb *decollare* (to behead), based on the gruesome combination of the preposition *de-* (from) and *collum* (neck). A *decollation* (dee kuh LAY shuhn) is a "beheading or decapitation," the latter synonym involving the Latin noun *caput*, whose stem, *capit-*, is seen in such words as *capital*. *Decollation* is not a case of *lallation*, also known as *pararhotacism*, the pronouncing of *r* like *l*, the converse of *rhotacism*, the pronouncing of *l* like *r*; for a discussion of these twists of pronunciation, see my *1000 Most Challenging Words*, under the entry *rhotacism*. *Decollation* means not only "beheading" but also denotes any picture of one, especially the grim painting of the head of St. John the Baptist on a *charger*—a word archaic in American English and, according to my British dictionaries, questionably not so in British English, where it denotes a flat dish capable of holding a large joint (*joint* being the British English equivalent of American English *roast*, as in *roast of beef*, according to my *British English, A to Zed*). The *decollation* of St. John at Salome's request is all too vividly related in Matt. 14:6–11.

decubitus (dih KYOOH bih tuhs) *n*. This is a medical term for one's "posture in bed"—that is, the way one lies down. It is taken from Late Latin, formed from the verb *decumbere* (to lie down), a word, built on the prefix *de-* (down) plus *-cumbere*, that is not found in classical Latin and used only in Late Latin compounds, such as *discumbere*. *Ventral decubitus* denotes lying on one's belly; *dorsal decubitus* is lying on one's side. Flint's *Principles of Medicine* (1880) warns against dorsal *decubitus*: "The dorsal *decubitus* should not be constantly maintained; changes of position are important." This advice doubtless relates to avoiding bedsores. If you ever saw Robert Benchley's hilarious short film "How to Sleep," about a constantly twisting insomniac, you would have been treated to the spectacle of whirlwind changes of *decubitus*!

decuman (DEK yuh muhn) *adj., n.* As an adjective, *decuman* means "huge, immense," or in context, "main, principal." Meaning "immense," its chief use is to modify *wave*: A *decuman* wave is a huge one. This usage is based on the popular (and baseless) notion that the tenth wave in a series is the largest and most dangerous to shipping. *Decuman* comes from the Latin *decumanus*, a variant of *decimanus* (relating to the tenth part of something), from *decimus* (tenth). On the subject of the erroneous belief as to the tenth wave, Sir Thomas Browne, in *Pseudodoxia Epidemica, or Enquiries into Very Many Received Tenets [Vulgar Errors]* (1646), included this old wives' tale in his treatment of "Vulgar Errors," and De Quincey gave it the same short shrift in *Pagan Oracles* (1862). No less an authority (?) than *Fraser's Magazine*, in an 1838 issue, declared: "The tenth, or *decuman*, is the last of the series of waves, and the most sweeping in its operation." In a wholly different context, the *Decuman Gate* was the name given to the main entrance to a Roman military camp, located on the farthest side from the enemy. It got that name because it was guarded by the *tenth* cohort (division of 300 to 600 men) of a legion. Used by itself, as a noun, a *decuman* is a great wave, one capable of wreaking great damage, but, as we have seen, it can do so not because it is tenth, but because it is big.

deipara   See **theotokion**.

dendrophilous (den DRAW fil uhs) *adj*. *Dendron* is Greek for "tree," and *dendro-* is its combining form. Attaching it to *-philous* (loving), we get *dendrophilous*, meaning "tree loving," and who among us isn't *dendrophilous*? (Except possibly those dreadful real estate developers who ruthlessly demolish our beautiful trees to make way for their dreadful assembly-line abodes or shoe-box commercial structures.) *Dendrophilous* has a special use in botany, to describe plants growing on or twisting around trees, like many vines, some of which are "loving" in a sense but eventually kill their hosts with too much of a good thing. We've all seen what a clinging vine like ivy can do to a tree. Combining both effects of -*philous*, and echoing Oscar Wilde's " ... each man kills the thing he loves," how fortunate that only some vines kill the trees they love!

deodand (DEE uh dand) *n. Deo* (the dative case of *deus*, Latin for "god," though in the case of *deodand* the god was the Christian God) means "to God," and *dandum* is the neuter of *dandus*, the gerundive of *dare* (to give), meaning "something that must be given." Thus, a *deodand*, in English law up to 1846, was a "thing forfeitable to God," but in practice forfeited to the crown and then put to pious uses (i.e., sold and its proceeds distributed in alms). The term was applied to a chattel (a piece of personal, as opposed to real, property) that had been the immediate cause of the death of a person, and the forfeiture to God, actually to the crown, was an expiatory offering. Here are some examples: Sir Henry Finch, in *Law, or a Discourse thereof, in Fours Bookes* (1636) wrote: "If a man being upon a Cart carrying Faggots ... fall downe by the mouuing of one of the horses in the Cart, and die of it; both that and all the other horses in the Cart, and the Cart it selfe, are forfeit ... And these are called *Deodands*." Here is a rather extreme case, from Sir William Blackstone's *Commentaries* (1765): "If a man falls from a boat or ship in fresh water, and is drowned, it hath been said, that the vessel and cargo are in strictness of law a *deodand*." Pretty sweeping judgment! What if the drownee had been drunk, or simply careless? Or someone who didn't like him pushed him overboard? And incidentally, why the restriction to "fresh water"? Okay on the bounding main?

desquamate (DES kwah mate) *vb. Squama* means "scale" in Latin (the animal kind, not the weighing or musical kind), and *desquamare* is a transitive Latin verb meaning "to scale," as a fish. From its past participle *desquamatus* we get the verb *desquamate*, which is used both transitively and intransitively. Thus, one *desquamates* a fish, or simply *desquamates*, i.e., "peels," as after a sunburn or sometimes after an attack of scarlet fever. The noun *desquamation* (des kwah MAY shuhn) covers both the transitive and intransitive uses. The adjective *desquamative* (DES kwah may tiv) can be used to describe a condition resulting in peeling or something that causes the skin to peel. Prudent people use various lotions to avoid *desquamation*, and even more prudent people stay out of the sun altogether to avoid skin cancer.

desuetude   See **consuetude.**

dharna, also **dhurna** (DUR nuh) *n.* Taken from the Hindi, *dharna* is a "method of appealing for justice, of forcing payment of an obligation or compliance with a just demand or of calling attention to an injustice, by sitting and fasting at the door of the offender until the wrong is admitted and justice done." Complainants have been known to fast even to the point of death. This procedure is known as *sitting in dharna* or *sitting dharna*, and the offending party is said to be *put in dharna.* Horace H. Wilson, in *History of British India* (1844), wrote of soldiers "detaining their commanders in the sort of arrest termed *dharna,*" and others have regarded *dharna* as a form of arrest. It must have been an effective method, putting one's case before the court of public opinion, as it were. I hardly think it would work in the western world: The party *sitting dharna* would probably be arrested for trespass.

diacope   See **anaphora.**

diastrophism (deye AS troh fiz'm) *n.* This is a general term in geology for the various processes whereby the crust of the earth is deformed. The word is based on the Greek *diastrophe* (distortion, dislocation), from *diastrephein* (to twist about, turn in different directions) and is built of the prefix *dia-* (aside) plus *strophe* (turning). The sinking and rising of regions of the earth, subsidence and upheaval, together constitute *diastrophism*, which comprises *orogeny* (oh ROJ uh nee) and *epeirogeny* (ep eye ROJ uh nee). *Orogeny* is the process of mountain formation, from *oros* (mountain) plus suffix *-geneia* (producing). *Epeirogeny* is the process of the formation of continents resulting from the deformation of the crust of the earth, which also produces ocean basins; the word is formed of the Greek *epeiros* (mainland, continent) plus the same suffix *-geneia*. All of these terms and processes are dealt with in *tectonics* (tek TON iks), the science of structural geology, dealt with briefly in my *1000 Most Challenging Words*. Since the Earth is the only planet we occupy at the moment, one ought to have at least a tiny bit of familiarity with all these geological shenanigans that shape the dear old thing.

didapper (DEYE da pur) *n.* A *didapper* is a "small diving water bird," also known as a *dabchick* or *little grebe*, which generally frequents rivers and fresh waters. The term *dive-dapper*, now obsolete but still heard in some dialects, was once used as the name of a small diving fowl, and the *di-* element in *didapper* is a relic of that *dive-*, or, as the *O.E.D.* says, a "reduced form" of it. Apart from all this ornithology, *didapper* has been applied jokingly and pejoratively to the kind of person who disappears for a while and suddenly pops up again. Alexander Pope collaborated on *The Art of Sinking* (1727), which included this satirical passage on writers: "The *didappers* are authers (sic), that keep themselves long out of sight, under water, and come up now and then, where you least expected them." Charles C. Colton, in *Lacon: or Many Things in Few Words* (1851), described a man named Wilkes as " ... one of those *didappers*, whom, if you had stripped naked, and thrown over Westminster bridge, you might have met on the very next day, with … a laced coat upon his back, and money in his pocket." Most of us have met such people; now you see them, now you don't; they vanish, they're gone forever, and whoops! here they are again, as though nothing had happened. *Didappers*, every one of them.

digamy (DIG uh mee) *n. Digamy* is a "second marriage." It rhymes with *bigamy* but is legal after a divorce, an annulment or the death of a first spouse. Dr. Johnson correctly defined it in his dictionary, but according to Boswell, when a gentleman who had been very unhappy in marriage remarried immediately after the death of his first wife, Johnson called it "the triumph of hope over experience." *Digamy* comes via Latin *digamia*, from Greek *digamia*, formed of the prefix *di-* (twice) plus *gamos* (marriage). *Trigamy*, as you might reasonably expect, is a "third marriage," and that word does exist, but even the *O.E.D.* makes no mention of the anticipatable (there is no such word as *anticipable*, which would be more euphonious) *quadrigamy*, *quinquigamy*, *sexigamy* or *septigamy* (a word to take care of the cases of Tommy Manville, Mickey Rooney and, I'm sure, others). To get back to the simpler matter of *digamy*, one who practices it is a *digamist* (DIG uh muhst), and the adjective for the resulting state is *digamous* (DIG uh muhs). You may remember a Marx Brothers film in which, on bended knee, Groucho, though already married, proposes to the surprisingly unflappable, or at least insufficiently outraged, Margaret Dumont. "But that would be bigamy!" says she. "Big o' *you*?" cries Groucho, "It would be big o' *me*!"

dimeter   See **ithyphallic**.

dioscuric (deye oh SKYOOHR ik) *adj.* This is a very fancy way of saying "twin," as in *twin brothers* or the *twin crises*, e.g., of starvation and disease after a natural catastrophe. The word arises out of Greek mythology, which is full of the complex family relationships of the gods. Leda was the wife of Tyndarus, sometimes known as Tyndareus. The wily Zeus, in the form of a swan, came upon her one day while she was bathing and seduced her. In due time she gave birth to twin sons known in Greek mythology as Castor and Polydeuces and in Roman legend as Castor and Pollux, who became demigods. Other sources tell it differently: She brought forth two eggs, from one of which Castor and Clytemnestra were hatched and from the other, Pollux and Helen of Troy. According to still other authorities, the first two were the legitimate children of Leda and her husband. Whatever the "facts" may be, the popular legend is that Castor and Pollux were the offspring of the union of Leda and Zeus, an event celebrated in a 1925 poem by William Butler Yeats. (Yeats's theme is that the "union" caused, through Helen, the war and the destruction of Troy.) They were known to the Greeks as the *Dioskouroi*, from *Dios*, the genitive of *Zeus*, plus *kouroi*, plural of *kouros* (boy, son). Thus, *dioscuric*, literally "like Castor and Pollux," came to mean "twin" generally, without reference to those two boys. When I first came across this word, I jumped to the conclusion that the *dio-* element was simply the Greek prefix *dia-*, which drops the *a* when it is attached to a word beginning with *o*, as in *diorama*, formed of *di-*, a variant of *dia-*, plus *orama* (view). In etymology, look before you jump.

dipody   See **ithyphallic.**

diptych   See **polyptych.**

dodded   See **daddock.**

dolichocephal (do li koh SEF'l) *n*. One so called is a person with a long head. *Dolichos* means "long" in Greek, and *kephale* "head." With a bit of Greek at your command, you might figure out that a *brachycephal* (brak ee SEF'l) is a person with a short head, for *brachys* means "short" in Greek, and good old *kephale* tags along. These two Greek prefixes are found in other anatomical terms relating to size. *Kephale* developed into our word element *cephalo-* as in *cephalometry* (sef'l OM eh tree), "the science of measuring the dimensions of the head." *Cephalate* (SEF uh late) or *cephalous* (SEF uh luhs) means "having a head" as opposed to *acephalous* (without a head) like, presumably, Washington Irving's famous horseman, or the queen in the old English music-hall ditty who walked the bloody tower at the midnight hour "with 'er 'ed tucked underneath 'er arm." The *a-* in *acephalous* is a prefix known as the "alpha privative," with the negating effect of *un-*, *dis-*, *-less*, etc. *Acephalous* is used figuratively to describe a nation or organization that has lost its "head" in the sense of "leader," like our country after the assassination of a president, or Monsarrat's *Tribe that Lost Its Head.*

dolichurus (dol ih KOOH ruhs) *n*. The Greek adjective *dolichouros* means "long-tailed" and is built of the prefix *dolicho-*, the combing form of the adjective *dolichos* (long), plus the noun *oura* (tail). The resulting noun is the name of a *dactylic hexameter* with a redundant syllable at the end, but that definition, in turn, may need a bit of clarification. *Dactylic hexameter* may be considered redundant, because *hexameter* alone is usually defined as "a *dactylic* line of six feet," as in Greek and Latin epic poetry (*The Iliad*, *The Aeneid*, etc.). The first four feet are *dactyls* (a *dactyl* is a foot of three syllables, one stressed followed by two unstressed, as in *terribly*) or *spondees* (a *spondee* is a foot of two syllables, both stressed, as in *split screen*), the fifth is a *dactyl* and the sixth is a *spondee* or a *trochee* (a *trochee* is a foot of two syllables, one stressed followed by one unstressed, as in *spinach*). A *caesura* (sih ZHOOHR uh), or "pause," usually follows the stressed syllable in the third foot. In the unlikely event that the foregoing isn't entirely clear, here is an example of a dactylic hexameter: *This is the forest primeval. The murmuring pines and the hemlocks* ... After all this, just remember that a *dolichurus* is simply a dactylic hexameter with a redundant syllable at the end, as would have been the case if Longfellow (perish the thought!) had had the bad taste to write *conifers* rather than *hemlocks*.

donzel (DON zuhl) *n.* This term, meaning a "squire, esquire, an attendant to a knight, a page," designated a young gentleman not yet knighted but an aspirant to that office. The office is obsolete; the word is included here not only because it has a nice sound but also because it illustrates that sloppiness in language is nothing new. In a delightful, hilarious little book entitled *Anguish English* by Richard Lederer, subtitled *An Anthology of Accidental Assaults Upon Our Language*, there is a final section headed "Howta Reckanize American Slurvian," bewailing the sad state of pronunciation and articulation in the United States; examples: *guvmint, hafta, "Jeetjet?"* Lederer tells us that in a 1949 *New Yorker* article, John Davenport labeled this kind of sublanguage *"Slurvian."* More examples: *The mill of the room; a few mince;* and so on and so on. Well, there's nothing new about Slurvian. *Donzel,* way back there, is a medieval example. Late Latin produced *domnicellus,* a diminutive of Latin *dominus* (Lord); *domnicellus* gave the Italians the Slurvian *donzello;* that gave the English the Slurvian *donzel.* People have been *slurring* their way through language for centuries. Sorry, I have no early Egyptian examples. So truzme.

dor   See **dumbledore.**

dos   See **pollicitation.**

doseh (DOH seh) *n.* This is the name of a festival that was held each year at Cairo, by the followers of the sheikh of the Sa'di dervishes, celebrating the birth of the Prophet Muhammad. The main feature was the sheikh's riding on horseback over the prostrate bodies of his devotees. Mercifully, the authorities abolished this jolly event in 1884. The name of the festival derives from the Arabic word *dowsah* meaning "treading." This brings to mind the word *juggernaut* (JUG er nawt), which has come to denote any overpowering destructive force or object, such as a giant battleship, an unbeatable football team, an overwhelming political machine or anything monstrously huge and irresistible. In England, the term has been applied to those enormous trailer trucks that have caused a great controversy about their use on country lanes and city streets, where they make a deafening noise, shake the fabric of ancient buildings and annoy the citizens no end. In my *British English, A to Zed,* I point out that "The word is related to *Jagannath,* an idol of the Hindu god Krishna, which was drawn in processions on vast carts under whose wheels fanatics threw themselves in their ecstasy, to be crushed to death."

dossil (DOS il) *n.* This little noun has a number of meanings that are only loosely related. In Late Latin, a *ducillus* was a "spigot" or "plug," and that was what *dossil* meant. Later, it came to mean a surgical dressing for wounds, also known as a "pledget," which is a kind of "plug," and which may explain this second meaning. *Pledget* (PLEJ it) also means an "oakum string for caulking ship seams," another kind of plug. *Dossil* took on still another meaning: a "cloth roll" for wiping excessive ink from engraved plates, usually of copper, of the type used in the printing process. *Dossil* is pronounced the way Americans pronounce *docile* (the British make the *o* long or short and pronounce "ile" as EYE'l), which comes from Latin *docilis* (easily taught), from *docere* (to teach), but the two words are unrelated, as are their etymologies. It might be said that the cloth roll used in printing is also a kind of "plug" in that it "stops" the flow of excessive ink, but that seems a bit farfetched. However, it must be admitted that *dossil* has a legitimate claim to versatility. As for *oakum* (OH kum), if you are not familiar with the word, it is "string or fiber obtained by untwisting and teasing or picking apart old ropes"; *picking oakum* used to be a typical convict's occupation.

doublet   See **catmalison.**

doulocracy   See **dulia.**

draegerman (DREE gur muhn) *n.* At first blush, this word looked to me like a variant or a corruption of *dragoman* (DRAY guh muhn), one of the headwords in my *1000 Most Challenging Words*. A *dragoman* is an "interpreter, sometimes also a guide," according to that learned tome. "The term is usually applied," I say in that book, "to persons who professionally interpret Near Eastern languages, particularly Arabic, Turkish, and Persian, for government offices, tour companies, and the like." But a *draegerman* doesn't interpret; he is a "member of a crew trained for underground rescue work," and his title comes from one A. B. Draeger, a German scientist who invented a certain type of breathing apparatus. The *-man* in this word is simply English for *homo*, whereas the final syllable of *dragoman* hasn't a thing in the world to do with our word *man*; it's a development from the penultimate syllable of Medieval Greek *dragomenos* that finally wound up as French *dragoman*, which we adopted. The plural of *draegerman* is *draegermen*, but the plural of *dragoman* should be *dragomans*. However, English-speaking people, assuming that the *-man* of *dragoman* was our *man*, formed the errroneous plural *dragomen*, which has now become an acceptable variant. "Insistence on *-mans*," says Fowler, "is didacticism." The April 20, 1937 issue of of the *Ottawa Journal* speaks of the "Stellanton Draeger crew" and refers to "Stellanton's *draegermen*—a crew of rescue men trained to enter a colliery after an explosion." A little investigation in *Webster's Geographical Dictionary* revealed that there is indeed a town of Stellartown, not Stellantown, in Nova Scotia, pop. 5,575, in the heart of a coal-mining region, so it appears that the *Ottawa Journal* was guilty of a typographical error, a sin not unknown in journalistic circles. *The Times* (London) in its October 25, 1958, issue informs us that "the *draegermen* ... carry about 45 lb. of oxygen equipment on their backs." Stout fellows!

draggle (DRA g'l) *vb. Draggle* is a diminutive and frequentative (a verb expressing the frequent repetition of another verb, e.g., *drip/dribble, spark/sparkle*—fully discussed in my *1000 Most Challenging Words*) of *drag* and means "to drag or trail on the ground," as through dirt, bog or mire, and thus make limp and sodden. This is the sort of thing that used to happen when skirts were long and reached well below the ankles—a problem solved by raising hems and dramatically solved by the miniskirt. As an intransitive verb, *to draggle* means "to get dirty and wet by being trailed along damp ground." By extension, the verb has been used as a pejorative description of one shuffling along in a slovenly manner. *Draggled* is a participial adjective meaning "sodden, wet, limp and muddy." Israel Zangwill wrote of "scarecrows in battered harts or *draggled* skirts." *Draggle-tailed* took on the meaning of "sluttish, slatternly," and *draggle-tail* was used to denote a slattern. Partridge (*A Dictionary of Slang and Unconventional English*) goes further and defines a *draggle-tail* as a "nasty, dirty slut" and hence a "low prostitute." There is a couplet in John Gay's *Trivia; or the Art of Walking the Streets of London* (1717) that reads: "You'll see a *draggled* Damsel here and there/From Billingsgate her fishy Traffick bear." Unsightly image, but good, substantial John Gay! (Billingsgate, discussed in that same book of mine, was for centuries a London fish market, notorious for the foul language spoken by its vendors and porters, especially the fishwives who worked there. It gave rise to the term *billingsgate* for particularly offensive language of vituperation and vilification.)

draggle-tail   See **draggle**.

draggle-tailed   See **draggle**.

Drawcansir (draw KAN sur) *n*. This name for a swaggering, blustering, overbearing bully, based on a character of that name in *The Rehearsal*, a burlesque of which George Villiers, second duke of Buckingham (1628–87), was coauthor and producer. Villiers, a courtier of Charles II, was responsible for this satire on heroic drama, which appeared in 1671. *Drawcansir* was a parody of the character Almanzor in Dryden's *Conquest of Granada*. In the final scene of Villiers's satire, he joins in a battle and kills all the fighters on both sides. Sometimes his name is spelled *Draw-can-sir*, and that is thought to be based on "drawing a can of liquor," since his great drinking capacity is mentioned earlier in the play, in which he is described as " ... a fierce Hero, that ... does what he will, without regard to good manners, justice, or numbers." In 1880 Justin McCarthy (*A History of our Own Times*) described a politician named Layard as " ... a very *Drawcansir* of political debate, a swashbuckler, and soldado [Spanish for "soldier"] of Parliamentary Conflict." Abraham Tucker, in *The Light of Nature Pursued* (1852), referred to the original character's feat of exterminating all the combatants on both sides by describing a character as " ... such a *Drawcansir*, as to cut down both friend and foe." Given his propensity to world-class drinking, I would hardly invite a *Draw-*

cansirish acquaintance of mine to use my extra ringside ticket to a prizefight, even if he favored one of the gladiators.

drogulus (DRAW gyooh lus) *n.* Talk about obscure words! A *drogulus* is, according to the *O.E.D. Supplement A–G*, "an entity whose presence is unverifiable, because it has no physical effects." Have we finally met the man who wasn't there?

> As I was going up the stair
> I met a man who wasn't there.
> He wasn't there again today.
> I wish, I wish he'd stay away.

Had Hughes Mearns, who wrote that poem, heard about the *drogulus*? No, he came up with that bit of poesy before A.J. Ayer coined *drogulus* "on the spur of the moment" and, *A–G* hypothesizes, "perh[aps] by subconscious association with DRAGON + L[atin] *-ulus* as in DRAGUNCULUS." Ayer himself said, in 1957, "Suppose I say 'There's a *drogulus* over there,' and you say 'What?' and I say '*Drogulus*,' and you say 'What's a *drogulus*?' Well I say 'I can't describe what a *drogulus* is, because it's not the sort of thing you can see or touch, it has no physical effects of any kind, but it's a disembodied being.'" Two years later, L. S. Penrose (*New Biology*) said: "I had difficulty in finding a suitable name for the activated complexes produced in ... [certain] experiments. On showing one of these to Professor A. J. Ayer, I inquired whether it might perhaps be a '*drogulus*' ... He replied that it was undoubtedly a *drogulus*." Is this obscure enough for you?

dry-stone-diker   See **cowan.**

dudgeon   See **clapperdudgeon.**

dulia, also **douleia** (DOOH lee uh) *n. Douleia*, in Greek, is "servitude," *doulos* "slave" and *doulosis* "enslavement." *Dulia* or *douleia* denotes the inferior or minor form of veneration, which under the code of the Roman Catholic Church is accorded to saints and angels, as opposed to *hyperdulia* (hy per DOOH lee uh), the form accorded to the Virgin Mary, and *latria* (LAH tree uh), that reserved for God alone. More *d(o)ul-* words: *Dulosis* (dooh LOH sis) denotes the type of enslavement imposed by certain ants upon, poor chaps, other ants; and *d(o)ulocracy* (dooh LOH cruh see) is "government by slaves," a word explained by Thomas Blount in his *Glossographia, or a Dictionary Interpreting Such Hard Words ... as are Now Used* (1656). "We should be the sport of chance and caprice," wrote Julius and Augustus Hare (was there a third brother named *September*?) in *Guesses at Truth* (1867), "as has ever happened to a people when fallen under a *doulocracy*." Blount explained Such Hard Words as are Now Used, whereas Schur explains Such Hard Words as are Now Not (or Hardly Ever) Used. *Useful*?

dulosis   See **dulia.**

dumbledore (DUM b'l dor) *n. Dumbledore* is the name of two different insects: the bumblebee, which the British also call *humblebee,* and the cockchafer, a large grayish-brown scarabaeoid beetle extremely destructive to forest trees and vegetation. Strange, that the same word can apply to the helpful bumblebee, so important in pollination, and the harmful cockchafer. The *hum-* of *humblebee* is undoubtedly onomatopoeic, while the *bumble-* of *bumblebee* is built on the verb *bumble,* which means "to buzz, make a humming sound" as well as "to bungle" or "muddle." As to the *-dore* in *dumbledore,* that comes from the noun *dor,* which applies to any insect that flies with a humming or buzzing sound. The *cock-* of *cockchafer* is a reference to the bird and implies size or vigor, and *chafer* is the name applied to any large, slow-moving beetle, or in Britain, to any scarabaeoid. John W. Robberds wrote *A memoir of the Life and Writings of W. Taylor of Norwhich, Containing his Correspondence with Southey* (1843), in which he quotes from Southey: "Is it not the *humble-bee,* or what we call the '*dumbledore*', a word whose descriptive droning deserves a place in song?" Indeed, what is more melodious, on a green lawn in midsummer, than the droning of Isaac Watts's " … little busy bee" improving "each shining hour"?

dunderfunk (DUN dur funk) *n.* This rather expressive word is the name of a ship biscuit, soaked in water, mixed with fat and molasses, then baked in a pan. An alternative name is *dandyfunk.* It sounds awful, and its origin and effect are unknown. From the sound of it, the *O.E.D.* appears to be quite right in spurning it, and it seems a good reason for avoiding the profession of seaman.

dunnage (DUHN ij) *n., vb.* To prevent cargo in the hold of a ship from moving around and to keep it dry, pieces of wood, brush, mats and other miscellaneous articles are placed under or among the cargo. The term for such material is *dunnage.* The term is applied as well to bracing installed by shippers in the hold, or in a freight car or truck, to protect goods while in the course of shipment. *Dunnage* also refers to padding in shipping containers to prevent the breakage of fragile merchandise. It is a remarkably versatile term, for it applies as well to baggage generally, personal effects and lumber of such low quality as to be unsalable. It is also a colloquial term in British English for miscellaneous baggage of any sort, and British slang for sailors' or tramps' clothes. The *C.O.D.* traces it to the Anglo-Latin word *dennagium,* of unknown derivation. (*Anglo-Latin* is the term for the Latin current in medieval England.) In addition to all this, *dunnage* is used as a verb meaning "to secure or stow with *dunnage.*" There would appear to be no connection between *dunnage* and *dun,* itself an extremely versatile little word that covers a color, variations in the color of horses, drabness, a method of curing codfish, keeping after a person to pay his debts and fortified dwellings in Ireland and Scotland protected by two or more earthen mounds enclosing deep moats.

duniwassal (DOOH nih wos'l), also **dunniwassal** (DUHN-) *n*. From Gaelic *duine* (man) and *wasal* (gentle, well-born) came the noun *duniwassal*, also *duinnie-wassal*, a "gentleman of the Scottish Highlands," particularly a younger son of a noble family. Sir Walter Scott, in *Bonny Dundee*, wrote the stirring lines: "There are wild *Duniewassals* three thousand times three/Will cry hoigh! for the bonnet o' Bonny Dundee." Bonny Dundee was John Graham of Claverhouse, Viscount Dundee, a Stuart supporter killed in 1689 at the battle of Killiecrankie. Scott wrote of these Highland gentlemen of lesser rank in the *Waverley Novels*: "His bonnet had a short feather, which indicated his claim to be treated as a *Duinhé-Wassell* [note different spelling] or sort of gentleman." *The Times* (London) in 1884 wrote of " ... *duinniewassals*, or small gentry." One had to be careful about the size of the feather in one's bonnet in those days, for the all-important matter of rank was involved.

dvandva   See **tatpurusha.**

dysgenic   See **evancalous.**

dyslogistic (dis luh JIS tik) *adj*. We are familiar with the adjective *eulogistic* and the noun *eulogy*, having to do with praise. The Greek prefix *eu-* has a positive effect and is found in such words as *eugenics*, *euphemism* and *euphonious*. In each case the *eu-* conveys the sense of "good," "well," "nice." *Eu-* is the combining form of the adjective *eus* (good), the neuter of which, *eu*, is used as an adverb meaning "well." *Dys-*, on the other hand, is a Greek prefix with the opposite sense: "bad" or "ill." Thus, we have *dyspepsia* (bad digestion), where *dys-* is joined to *pepsis* (digestion), and *dystrophy* (faulty nourishment), as in the all too familiar term *muscular dystrophy*. Here, the *dys-* is joined to the Greek noun *trophe* (nourishment). *Dysentery* is a combination of that ill-omened prefix with *enteron* (intestine). You can be sure that *eu-* something is infinitely preferable to *dys-* anything. (Don't worry about *eunuch*: that *eu-* is not a prefix but simply the first syllable of *eune*, "bed," joined to *ouchos* "keeping," a word related to the verb *echein*, "to hold," resulting in the noun *eunouchos*—eunuch, but as indicated by its formation, used by the Greeks to mean "chamberlain" or "steward," an official who kept his eye on the ladies and was carefully castrated before assuming that august office.) After all that, it would seem appropriate to inform you that *dyslogistic*, which has nothing to do with *logistics*, means quite the opposite of "laudatory": "uncomplimentary, indicating disapproval or censure" and is formed of *dys-* plus *logos* (word). A *dyslogistic* eye cast upon you can be quite *dis*concerting, but the *dis-* in that word was borrowed not from Greek but from Latin.

dysphasia   See **evancalous.**

dysphonia   See **evancalous.**

dysphoria   See **evancalous.**

dyspnea   See **evancalous.**

dysthymia   See **evancalous.**

dystocia (dih STOH shee uh, -shuh), also **dystokia** (dih STOH kee uh) *n.* Under certain headwords in this book I have discussed the Greek prefixes *eu-* and *dys-*; see, for example, **dystopia**. *Dystocia* and *eutocia* present a good example of these opposing prefixes. *Dystocia* is "slow or difficult labor or childbirth," from the Greek *dys-* (hard, bad, ill) plus *tokos* (childbirth), related to *teknon* (child). *Eutocia* (yooh TOH shee uh, -shuh) is "normal childbirth," without complications, from the Greek prefix *eu-* (good, well) plus the same *tokos*. If you happen to know the meaning of the underlying noun (in this case *tokos*), you can figure out the meanings of the compounds using these prefixes. It's as easy as that.

dystopia (dis TOH pee uh) *n.* As any dictionary will show you, there are a great many words that begin with the prefix *dys-*, taken from the Greek, where, to quote *Liddell & Scott*, it is an "insepar[able] Prefix, opp[osite] to *eu*, like our *un-* or *mis-* in *un-lucky, mis-chance*, always with a notion of *hard, bad, ill*, etc., destroying a word's good sense or increasing its bad sense." You can find a fair number of examples in my discussion of **evancalous**. *Dystopia* is a prime example, being the opposite of *Eutopia*. *Cacotopia* (KA ko toh pee uh)—using the Greek prefix *caco-*, from *kakos*, bad—is characterized in the *C.O.D.* as a "nonce-word" based on the mistaken notion that *Utopia*, the imaginary island described in Sir Thomas More's *Utopia* (1516) as a place blessed with perfection in law, politics, etc., was a misspelling of *Eutopia*. We must straighten this out. *Eutopia* was a play on *Utopia*, which was based on Greek *ou* plus *topos*, meaning "nowhere" (because there was no such place), while *Eutopia* was built from Greek *eu* plus *topos*, *eu-* being a prefix based on the adjective *eus* (good), used in its neuter form *eu* as an adverb meaning "well," so that *Eutopia* means "a place of ideal happiness and good order." If we look at *Utopia* and *Eutopia* closely, we can see that far from being synonyms, they should be used in antithesis: A region of ideal happiness and order is—nowhere! Obviously, if *cacopia* can be called a "nonce-word," so can *dystopia*. Whether or not you agree with my argument, *Dystopia* is an imaginary place where everything is as bad as possible, as imaginary as More's *Utopia*, or, with a lowercase *d*, a condition in which everything is as bad as possible. John Stuart Mill, as reported in an 1868 issue of *Hansard* (the British equivalent of our *Congressional Record*), said: "It is, perhaps, too complimentary to call them [his political opponents] *Utopians*, they ought rather to be called *dys-topians*, or *caco-topians*. What is commonly called *Utopian* is something too good to be practicable; but what they favour is too bad to be practicable." A 1967 issue of *The Listener* (the BBC radio and television journal) contained this sentence: "The modern classics— Aldous Huxley's *Brave New World* and George Orwell's *Nineteen Eighty Four*—

are *dystopias*. They describe not a world we should like to live in, but one we must be sure to avoid." Agreed!

dysuria   See **evancalous**.

ebionism   See **theandric**.

ebionite   See **theandric**.

ebionize   See **theandric**.

eccaleobion (eh kal ee oh BEYE uhn) *n*. Even if you were up on your Greek, you'd never guess what this strange word means: "egg-hatching apparatus," a contraption for hatching eggs by artificial heat instead of brood hens. It was invented circa 1839 by a man named Bucknell. Either the inventor or a scholarly friend coined the name from the Greek sentence *Ekkaleo bion*, meaning "I evoke life," a pretty fancy name for a hatchery. *Ekkaleo* is the first person singular of the verb *ekkaleisthai* (to evoke), and *bion* is the accusative of *bios* (life). In 1839 Bucknell wrote an article entitled *Eccaleobion: A Treatise on Artificial Incubation*. The term was used metaphorically in an 1880 issue of *Harper's* magazine: "Willis's *Home Journal* was at one time a very *eccaleobion* for young writers." I wonder how many readers of the magazine knew what *eccaleobion* meant. When you buy a chicken or other fowl these days, the overwhelming likelihood is that it is the product of one sort of *eccaleobion* or other. Brood hens are very much the exception.

eclosion (ih KLOH shuhn) *n*. From the Latin prefix *ex*- (out of, from) plus *clausum*, the neuter of *clausus*, itself the past participle of *claudere* (to shut) used as a noun meaning "an enclosed place," the French got *éclosion*. We took it over (without the accent) meaning "emergence from concealment," with a special meaning in entomology denoting the emergence of an imago from the puparium (the pupal case) or the emergence of a larva from an egg. (This is hardly the place to go into these entomological phenomena. There are lots of books on the subject. And remember: *etymology* is about words; *entomology* is about *ents* and other insects.) In a 1906 letter of William James, found in his *Letters*, edited by brother Henry (1920), we read: "It is queer to be assisting at the *éclosion* of a great new mental epoch, life, religion, and philosophy in one." William used the French word, not yet adopted into English.

ecmnesia (ek MNEE zhee uh, -see-) *n*. A long look at this word will find the *-mnesia* familiar from the word *amnesia*, the common word for "loss of

memory," built of the Greek negative prefix *a-* (known as the "alpha privative," as found in words like *amoral, asexual, apolitical*) plus *mnesis* (memory).
In *ecmnesia* we have, instead of *a-*, the prefix *ec-*, from the Greek *ek-* (out), and
we get a word that limits the loss of memory to the events of a particular
period, as opposed to the wiping out of the entire past. The *Billings Medical
Dictionary* defines *ecmnesia* as "a form of amnesia in which there is normal
memory of occurrences prior to a certain date, with loss of memory of what
happened for a certain time after that date." This is a common condition
following a concussion, which knocks out recollection of the accident and
subsequent events for a limited period thereafter. It may aptly describe as well
the condition of the mind on "the morning after the night before," during
which the boys had gotten together for a little serious drinking at, for instance,
a bachelor party. *Chambers's Dictionary of Psychiatry* calls the condition "amnesia with poor memory [as opposed to 'loss of memory'] for recent events,
but with relatively intact memory for events in the remote past." Perhaps the
latter definition was concocted by a lexicographer who had suffered a milder
concussion or attended a somewhat less boisterous party the night before. As
Einstein said, everything is relative.

eddish   See **rowen.**

egeria, also **aegeria**, usually capitalized (ee GEE ree uh, e-, ih-) *n.* An *egeria* is
a "female adviser." *(A)egeria* was the name of a nymph, one of the four
Camenae, the wise and prophetic fountain nymphs revered in Roman religion:
Carmentis, Egeria, Antevorta and Postvorta, later identified with the Muses.
Egeria was the nymph who advised and instructed Numa Pompilius (753–673
B.C.), second king of Rome, in his sage lawmaking, and, according to legend
was his companion and wife. From her role as adviser and instructor, her name
became generic for any female counselor. Disraeli, in *Vivian Grey*, wrote the
following lovely sentences: "It is in these moments that we gaze upon the
moon. It is in these moments that Nature becomes our *Egeria.*"

electuary   See **catholicon.**

eleutherian   See **eleutherism.**

eleutherism (uh LYOOH thuh riz'm) *n.* This is the commendable emotion of
"zeal for freedom," the very opposite of the suppressive practices so painfully
evident in totalitarian regimes. *Eleutheros* is Greek for "free," and it is easy to
see how *eleutherism* was constructed. *Eleutherian* (el lyooh THEH ree uhn) was
the title of Zeus in his role of protector of political freedom, one of his more
gracious aspects. *Eleutheromania* (uh lyooh thuh roh MAY nee uh) is mad zeal
for freedom (*-mania* can be tacked onto just about anything, as in *Anglomania,
bibliomania, Beatlemania*, etc.) and can lead to anything from playing hooky to
hippyism to anarchy. One must be all out for *eleutherism*, but excessive zeal or

fanaticism is to be deplored. It was Barry Goldwater, when he campaigned for the presidency, who favored "extremism in the cause of liberty." This is a pretty good definition of *eleutheromania* and made good old conservative Barry too radical for many.

eleutheromania   See **eleutherism.**

ell   See **alnage.**

emblements (EM blih muhnts) *n. pl.* Dictionaries vary in their definitions of this word. Most confine its meaning to the products, and ensuing profits, from land that has been sown or planted or cultivated. Thus, *RH* provides an etymology based on Middle Latin *imbladare* (to sow with grain), built on prefix *im-*, a variant of *in-* (in) plus *blada* (grain). *W III* defines it as "the growing crop ... resulting from annual cultivation as distinguished from old roots (as pasturage) or from trees (as timber or fruit)" or the profits from a crop so sown, and attributes it to Middle French *emblaer* (to sow a field with grain). *CH* goes along with that distinction: "crops raised by the labour of the cultivator, but not tree-fruits or grass" and traces it back, via Old French *emblaer*, to Late Latin *imbladare*, from *in-* plus *bladum* (wheat). But the *O.E.D.*, after going along generally with that derivation and defining the word as "the profits of sown land" (short and sweet), tells us that "the word is sometimes used more largely for any products that arise naturally from the ground, as grass, fruit, etc.," attributing the broader definition to Tomlins's *Law Dictionary Greatly Enlarged and Improved* over that of one G. Jacobs. To play it safe, skip the grass and the fruit trees.

empolder (em POHL dur), also **impolder** *(im POHL dur) vb.* To *empolder* a piece of low-lying land is "to reclaim it from the sea by the erection of dikes." A *polder* is such a piece of land. This is a Dutch word, taken into English, and a term not generally applied outside of Holland. It was used of French land, however, in an 1894 issue of the *Westminster Gazette*: "Much of the asparagus eaten in London is grown in the *polders* reclaimed from the sea near Mont St. Michel." *Blackwell's Magazine*, in a 1922 issue, advised that some acres of low-lying land had been cleared and *"empoldered* with mud-dams." In 1951 *New Biology* reported that "an area of 100 acres ... was *empoldered* (i.e., surrounded by earth walls)." *Impoldered* showed up in an 1899 issue of the *Pall Mall Gazette*, which spoke of "*impoldering* and pumping, the raising and keeping of dykes," and in the 1929 edition of the *Encyclopedia Britannica* we find the following: "A great part of the Netherlands has now been *impoldered* ... The largest *impoldering* scheme on record has now been commenced." I discussed *polder* in my *1000 Most Challenging Words*, saying that the reclaiming of *polders* and their protection by a system of dikes is "an operation that occurs quite frequently in the Netherlands, where so much of the land is nether."

emunctory (ih MUNGK tuh ree) *n., adj.* As an adjective, *emunctory* describes anything pertaining to the conveying of waste matter from the body, especially nose blowing. As a noun, it denotes any bodily cleansing organ or canal, such as the excretory ducts, kidneys and pores. The word is derived from Late Latin *emunctorius* (excretory) and *emunctorium* (a means of cleaning through excretion; in classical Latin, a pair of nostrils). It all goes back to the Latin verb *emungere* (to clean a nose, and with the reflexive pronoun—*se emungere*—to wipe one's nose) and its past participle *emunctus*. The Latin phrase *emunctae naris* (literally, "with a clean nose") was used figuratively to mean "shrewd, discerning," and taking it a step further, as the poet Horace used it, "with a keen scent for other people's faults" ("Why beholdest thou the mote that is in thy brother's eye, but considerest not the beam that is in thine own eye?"—Matt. 7:3—or, as the *New English Bible* puts it, "Why do you look at the speck of sawdust in your brother's eye, with never a thought for the great plank in your own?"); but some say all Horace meant by *homo emunctae naris* was "a man of keen perception." You can take your choice of bibles and interpretations of Horace. In *Tristram Shandy* (1767), Laurence Sterne advises: "Blow your noses,—cleanse your *emunctories*,—sneeze, my good people."

enallage (en AL uh jee) *n.* It sounds like *analogy* (uhn AL uh jee) when you say it, but its meaning is quite different. *Enallage* is the "substitution of one grammatical form for another, the exchange of one tense, mood, case, number for another," e.g., singular for plural, present for future or past. The important aspect is that the "mistake" is intentional, at least when the author is manifestly literate. When the prizefight manager Joe Jacobs yelled, "We wuz robbed!" in 1932, it must be remembered that it was the same Joe Jacobs who said, instead of " ... and may the best man win!" the immortal words: " ... and may the superior gladiator emerge victorious!" Joe's *wuz* (*was*) wuz no mistake, in my opinion. And wuzn't it effective! And it is to be assumed that when the magazine *Punch* came out with "You pays your money and you takes your choice," the use of the singular verb was a conscious deviation from correct grammar. It is no secret that James Joyce was well up on his grammar, so that when he had Molly Bloom declare, "My patience are exhausted," Joyce was quite aware that his little pun involved a singular noun. For all these examples I am indebted to Professor Arthur Quinn of the University of California and his charming and learned little book *Figures of Speech*. Here's one of my own: "The old gray mare, she ain't what she used to be." Wouldn't *isn't* have made that time-honored statement insipid?

enantiomorph (en AN tee oh morf) *n., adj.* This word was first used in a German text, C. F. Naumann's *Elemente der Theoretischen Krystallographie* (1856). It is formed of the Greek *enantios* (opposite) and *morphe* (form) and means "mirror image." It gave rise to the adjectives *enantiomorphic* and *enantiomorphous* and the nouns *enantiomorphism* and *enantiomorphy*, all accented on the "MOR" syllable. In the 1885 edition of the *Encyclopedia Britannica*, A. C.

Brown provided a good example of *enantiomorphism*: " ... our two hands ... the one of which resembles in figure the mirror image of the other." *Enantiopathy* (en an tee AW puh thee), from *enantios* plus *pathos* (feeling), is the treatment of disease by an agent that is opposite to it, rather than one that is similar to it, as in the "like-cures-like" basis of homeopathy; the word is sometimes used as a synonym of *allopathy*. Another word from *enantios* is *enantiosis* (en an tee OH sis), a figure of speech using the antonym of what is meant. Remember "Oh What a Lovely War"? Among jazz musicians, *bad* means "good"; I have heard half-swooning aficionados exclaim, after a virtuoso improvisation by Louis Armstrong or Oscar Peterson, "That's *bad*, man!" You can't be more *enantiopathic* (permissible coinage?) than that. Enantiomythic?

enantiopathy   See **enantiomorph.**

enantiosis   See **enantiomorph.**

encaenia (en SEE nyah) *n*. From the Greek *enkainia* (consecration festivities), the neuter plural of *enkainios*, built of the prefix *en* (in) plus *kainos* (new), we get this word, construed as a plural, meaning "festive ceremonies commemorating the founding of a city or the consecration of a church or temple," in Jewish circles, the Temple of Jerusalem. Construed as a singular, and often capitalized, the word more specifically denotes the annual commemoration of founders and benefactors at Oxford University, held in June, a ceremony at which prize poems and essays are recited and honorary degrees conferred. This ceremony, held in the Sheldonian Theatre, concludes the academic year. The Sheldonian Theatre is the Senate House at Oxford, named after Gilbert Sheldon (1598–1677), Archbishop of Canterbury, who provided the funds for the building, which was designed by Sir Christopher Wren and opened in 1699. In my experience, it has come as a surprise to a number of Oxford men that *encaenia* ever had any meaning wider than that of the annual Oxford rite, but none of them had "read" (British English for "majored in") "Greats" (Oxford idiom for "classics").

endogamy (en DOG uh mee) *n*. We are familiar with certain -*gamy* words: *bigamy, monogamy, polygamy*. The suffix -*gamy* is derived from the Greek noun *gamos* (marriage). *Endogamy* and *exogamy* (ex OG uh mee) are antonyms also relating to marriage. *Endogamy* is "marriage between individuals of the same group as required by law or custom"; *exogamy* is "marriage to a person outside a specific group" (likewise as required by law or custom). The prefix *endo-* is the combining form of Greek *endos* (within); *exo-* that of Greek *exo* (outside of). These terms relate primarily to the social customs or regulations of primitive societies, but we all know that *outbreeding* and *inbreeding* are terms applicable to the social customs and in some cases, the religious requirements of modern times. The respective adjectives are *endogamous* (en DOG uh muhs) and

exogamous (ex OG uh muhs). *Romeo and Juliet* demonstrates the tragic consequences of an *exogamous* union between members of groups as small as
feuding families. The requirements of *endogamy* within Orthodox Jewish
society have led to the gruesome custom of the recital of prayers for the dead
by parents over any child of the family who marries "outside the faith."
Miscegenetic (mis ej uh NET ik) marriages (those between members of different
races; in particular, between white and black—from Latin *miscere*, to mix, plus
genus, race) were long forbidden by many states of the American South, and
even after the repeal of the restrictive laws, ostracism by both sides, blacks as
well as whites, has made most of such unions unsuccessful in the United
States; they are still difficult in many European societies as well. The dream of
"one world" is still far from realization in ways quite apart from political
considerations.

engastrimyth (en GAS truh mith) *n.* This word means "ventriloquist." What
a debt we owe to the classical languages! Here we have the beautiful word
engastrimyth, with a lovely derivation: via French *engastrimythe*, from Greek
engastrimythos, formed of the prefix *en* (in) plus *gastri*, dative of *gaster* (belly),
plus *mythos* (speech), and how do we define it? With another word of classical
ancestry, *ventriloquism*, from Latin *ventri*, the combining form of *venter* (belly),
plus *loqui* (to speak). We were much too "refined" to use anything as vulgar
as "belly speaker," and as so often happens, preferred the nearer Latin to the
more remote Greek. Somehow, belly *dancer* got through, and we were spared
any such prissy and revolting concoction as *ventrisaltant* (*saltare* being Latin
for "to dance," and *saltant*- the stem of its present participle).

enoplion   See **prosodion.**

enthymeme (EN thuh meem) *n.* Latin *enthymema* was taken over intact from
the Greek, which derived it from the verb *enthymeisthai* (to consider, keep in
mind), built of the prefix *en-* (in) plus *thymos* (mind), and we wound up with
enthymeme. It can mean either of two things: a "syllogism in which one of the
propositions, usually a premise, is understood but not stated," or in Aristotelian philosophy, a "rhetorical syllogism which, though probable and persuasive, may not be valid." You know what a *syllogism* is: "All horses have four
legs; Dobbin is a horse; therefore Dobbin has four legs." "All horses have four
legs" is the major premise; "Dobbin is a horse" is the minor premise; "Dobbin
has four legs" is the conclusion. In an *enthymeme*, a premise is understood but
missing. Example: "All horses have four legs; therefore Dobbin has four legs."
The minor premise "Dobbin is a horse" is implied but not set down. The
Aristotelian sense is different: The conclusion may not be justified. "The gods
are all-powerful; Jove is a god; therefore Jove is all-powerful." But *are* all gods
omnipotent? If not, Jove may not be. Whichever sense may be involved, the
adjective is *enthymematic* (EN thee muh MAD ik). All the words in this book
are obscure; therefore *enthymeme* is obscure. No longer, I hope.

eonism (EE uh niz-m) *n.* An *eon* is an indefinitely long period of time, and one might be pardoned for jumping to the conclusion that *eonism* had something to do with paleontology, archaeology or prehistory, but no. The *eon* in this word comes from the name of the Chevalier Charles d'Eon (1728–1810), a French diplomat and adventurer who wore women's clothes. *Eonism*, then, is "transvestism," especially by a male, and an *eonist* is a "transvestite." *CH* is kind to the Chevalier. It omits the "adventurer" and tells us that Charles "chose female dress as a disguise," making him appear to have been a daring Scarlet Pimpernel sort of diplomat. Havelock Ellis calls it " ... clearly a typical case of what Hirschfeld later called 'transvestism' and what I would call 'sexo-aesthetic inversion,' or more simply '*Eonism.*' ... The *Eonist* (though sometimes emphatically of the apparent sex) sometimes shows real physical approximations towards the opposite sex." The September 5, 1970, issue of *The Times* (London) had this to say: "Today we can see that the Chevalier was an a-sexual transvestite. From his name Havelock Ellis coined the term *eonism* to describe this minor deviation." Minor deviation? I suppose so: no harm done, but that does seem to have been an extraordinarily permissive view.

epanados See **anaphora.**

epanalepsis See **anaphora.**

epanaphora See **anaphora.**

epeirogeny See **diastrophism.**

epenthesis See **metaplasm.**

epeolatry (ep ee OL uh tree) *n. Epeolatry* is "the worship of words," and is derived from the Greek nouns *epos* (word) and *latreia* (worship). A *-latry* word more familiar to us is *idolatry*, which comes from Greek *eidolatres* (idolater) based on *eidolon* (idol) and *latreuein* (to worship). *Worship* may seem to be an excessive way of describing love of words but may not be too far from one's obsessive interest in words and language generally, a condition of mind to which I have been subject since an early age. "Words," my father told me when I was about 12, "distinguish us from animals, are God-given, and we must cherish and never abuse them." Recent experiments with some species of apes demonstrate that we are not unique among the animals in knowing and using words, the distinction being more in the nature of laryngeal equipment. The writer William Gaddis (*The Recognitions*) said, explaining about his choice of unusual words: "[I] can't often comment on reasons for their selection except in some cases (as Eliot) plain homage." Worship? Idolization? Homage? Same thing.

epexegesis (ep eks uh JEE sis) *n. Exegesis* is "critical interpretation or explanation," especially of the Bible. It is a Greek word taken into English, meaning "explanation," formed of the prefix *ex-* (out of, from) plus *ege-*, the stem of the verb *hegeesthai* (to guide). A practitioner of *exegesis* (eks uh JEE sis) is an *exegete* (EKS ih jeet), and *exegetics* (eks uh JET iks) is the science of *exegesis*. Now when we put still another prefix, *ep-* (in the sense of *in addition*) in front of *exegesis*, we get *epexegesis*, denoting the addition of one or more words to clarify the import intended, or the specific sense intended of a preceding word, phrase or sentence, and as you might expect, there is the adjective *epexegetic* (ep ex uh JET ik), or *epexegetical*, which gives rise to the adverb *epexegetically*. I fear that *epexegesis* can be overdone. To give a homely example: My dear father arrived in this country from Germany as a lad of tender years, speaking extremely good, but not entirely idiomatic, English. He therefore took many phrases literally that weren't quite meant that way. I have been told that in his early years in Boston, when someone met him and said, "How are you?" after responding "Fine" he went on and on and *epexegetically* really told them how he was, in tremendous detail involving just about every aspect of life: health, progress on the job, marital status, plans for the future, *und so weiter und so weiter*, totally ignoring his listener's obvious straining at the leash. Daudin's plea "passons au déluge" in Racine's *Les Plaideurs* was never more appropriate. Poor dad: His eager but unwarranted *epepepexegesis* made him less popular than he deserved to be.

ephod   See **ethrog.**

epieikeia (ep ee eye KEYE uh), also **epikeia** (ep ee KEYE uh) *n. Ekipy* is an obsolete form. *Epieikeia* was taken intact from the Greek, meaning "reasonableness" or "equity," as opposed to rigid legal rules. *Equity* is the name of a branch of English and American law that overrides and supplements common or statute law and is designed to protect rights, do justice and enforce duties determined by substantive law. The Greek word is based on the adjective *epieikes* (suitable, reasonable), built of the prefix *epi-* (according to) plus *eikos* (reasonable, likely). Having got this far, what does it mean? In the Roman Catholic church, *epieikeia* is such interpretation of a canonical law as excuses compliance in a case of any hardship that violates natural and reasonable law, as when a wife, for instance, honestly presumes that she may miss Mass rather than leave the bedside of a seriously ailing husband, or in a situation where to attend, she would have to leave an infant baby alone. *Epieikeia* allows the individual to act in accordance with that type of reasonable presumption. I know that when fasting on Yom Kippur results in severe physical distress or harm, a rabbi will excuse an individual from compliance with the law. In the case of the Jewish religion, the person does not presume exoneration but takes the precaution of obtaining rabbinical permission. I am advised that there are similar procedures in other religions, and how could it be otherwise?

epigamic (ep ih GAM ik) *adj.* This adjective describes a person or animal attractive to the opposite sex. The word is derived from the Greek prefix *epi-*

(upon) plus *gamos* (marriage), which together formed the Greek adjective *epigamos* (marriageable). The term is used with respect to the mating of people and animals and the characteristics that are effective in attracting the opposite sex during courtship. In his *Essays of a Biologist* (1923), Julian Huxley writes: "The human species ... has *epigamic* characters of both kinds. Some, like voice and moustache, are different in the two sexes, others, such as colour of eyes and lips, are common to both." *Chambers's Encyclopedia* (1959) speaks of " ... display in which a sexual element is involved; aposematic or threat display, and distraction or diversionary display." *Aposematic*, a zoological term formed of the Greek prefix *apo-* (away, from, off) plus *semat-*, the combining form of *sema* (sign), is applied to markings such as colors that serve as warning signals to repel attacking enemies. Muster your *epigamic* arsenal, boys and girls; choose carefully, and you may land the mate of your dreams.

epigraphy   See **pseudepigraphy.**

epimeletic (ep ih muh LET ik) *adj.* This adjective is used to denote the care of young animals by their parents and other members of the same species. In most of those fascinating television films dealing with wildlife, a great deal of attention is paid to the extraordinary activities of parents in the gathering of food for the young, the protection of them from predators and the actual instruction given them in matters of hunting and self-protection. Of course this has to do with the instinctive concern for the preservation of the species, but it is easy to commit the "pathetic fallacy" (discussed in my *1000 Most Challenging Words*) of attributing conscious altruism to the concerned, protective and seemingly affectionate parents. The oft-repeated scenes are really touching. *CH* cites the worker bees as a conspicuous example of a group exhibiting *epimeletic* behavior. The word comes from the Greek adjective *epimeletikos* (fitted for care, management, etc.), based on the noun *epimeletes* (one who has charge of [something], a trustee, manager, overseer) and related to the verb *epimeleomai* (to take care of, have the charge or management of, pay attention to). Child abuse, so horrifyingly and inexplicably frequent in the news these days, is rare in animal society, though the fish in my pond do seem to eat lots of their young, and there are examples in some species of mothers who have to protect the kiddies from being gobbled up by dear old dad.

epinicion   See **epinikion.**

epinikion (ep i NIK ee uhn), also **epinicion** (ep ih NIS ee uhn, -NISH-) *n.* This word, taken intact from the Greek, is the name given to a song of victory, an ode written and sung to honor a victor in war or a winner in games, like those at Olympia in honor of Zeus and at Delphi in honor of Apollo. The word is built upon the prefix *epi-* (on, after) plus *nike* (victory). If you have been to the Louvre, you have seen the massive sculpture known as the *Winged Victory* (or *Nike*) *of Samothrace*, and you may remember an American guided missile that some classically oriented denizen of the Pentagon (one supposes) christened the *nike*, a public relations gesture that would have appealed, it is to be presumed, to a learned minority. Euripides wrote an *epinikion* for the Athenian politician and general Alcibiades after his victory over Sparta in the Peloponnesian War. Anyone familiar with the Book of Isaiah must rejoice with him in his sublime *epinikion*. At college football games today, the cheerleaders urge the spectators to indulge in cheers and songs, but these are only pleas for victory, not *epinikia*. *Happy Days Are Here Again*, the Democrats' paean sung at political rallies before, as well as after, victory, can turn out to have been a premature *epinikion*.

epiphonema (ep ih fuh NEE muh) *n.* The Greek verb *epiphonein* (to mention), constructed from the prefix *epi-* (upon, after) and the verb *phonein* (to speak), from *phone* (sound), was taken, via Latin, into Engligh, giving us *epiphonema*, an "exclamatory sentence, a succinct summarization of the content of a discourse, a striking, emphatic peroration." One of the most memorable *epiphonemas* of all time was that with which Cato the Elder (234–149 B.C.), the Roman statesman and senator Marcus Porcius Cato, concluded every speech he made in the Roman senate after his visit to Carthage in 157 B.C. Cato was a stern moralist who disapproved of the extravagance of Carthaginian life and saw in its revived prosperity a standing threat to Rome. His *epiphonema* was "Delenda est Carthago" ("Carthage must be destroyed"), a slogan that was instrumental in bringing on the Third Punic War in which Carthage was destroyed. This *epiphonema* became proverbial and was taken to mean that "anything standing in the way of our greatness must be removed at all costs." Patrick Henry came up with a pretty good *epiphonema* in his speech in the Virginia Convention of March 23, 1775: "Give me liberty, or give me death!" They don't come much better than that.

epiphora   See **anaphora.**

epirrhema (ep ih REE muh) *n.* This is a technical aspect of classical Greek comedy. We are somewhat familiar with classical Greek writers of tragedy—Aeschylus, Sophocles and Euripides—whose works are occasionally revived for the benefit of their woefully inadequate numbers of devotees. Less familiar are the ancient Greek writers of comedy—Aristophanes and Menander; and those who pursued that craft between the two—Cratinus and Eupolis—of whom we have only fragments. In Greek comedy, the *epirrhema* was the "address of the leader of the chorus, known as the *coryphaeus* (kor ih FEE uhs—from Greek *koryphe*, head), to the audience" after the chorus had come forward and addressed the audience on behalf of the author, a part of the program known as the *parabasis* (puh RAB uh sis). So, if anybody asks what *epirrhema* means, just tell him, no, it isn't a dread and loathsome disease like *gonorrhea, diarrhea* or *logorrhea*. (I suffer from only the last-named of these; and *-rrhea* is a Greek suffix meaning "flow" or "discharge" and has nothing to do with the *-rhema* of *epirrhema*, which is constructed of the prefix *epi-* "after," plus the aforesaid *-rhema*; and why the double *r*?)

epistaxis (ep ih STAK sis) *n*. This is a fancy word, taken intact from the Greek, meaning "nosebleed." The Greek word is related to the verb *epistazein* (to bleed at the nose), formed of the preposition *epi-* (upon) and the verb *stazein* (to let fall in drops). I can't quite picture a sports announcer exclaiming that the challenger in a boxing match has caused the champ to sustain an *epistaxis*, but you never know. The great radio boxing announcer Joe Humphries one evening replaced the usual "And may the best man win!" with "And may the superior gladiator emerge victorious!" Incidentally, Joe scorned the microphone, even at the old Madison Square Garden. *Stentorian* was the word for Joe. But he should have said *better* instead of *best*, since one mustn't use a superlative in comparing only two. Next time you are moved to anger by your collocutor, advise him that if he continues in that vein, you will act upon the veins inside his proboscis in such a way as to bring about an *epistaxis* and then celebrate his hasty retreat.

epistrophe See **anaphora.**

epithumetic (ep i thooh MED ik), also **epithymetic** (ep i thim ET ik) *adj*. The form with the *u* is the preferred American spelling, the one with the *y*, the British. The 20th letter of the Greek alphabet is called *upsilon* in American English and *ypsilon* (although *upsilon* is a permissible variant) in British English. In this headword, the first form is an American dictionary listing, the second a British dictionary listing, hence the *u* and *y* in the respective variants. But let's get to the definition, which in either case is "pertaining to appetite or desire." The word is a synonym for *sensual*, as in a phrase such as *the epithumetic aspect of human nature*. The derivation is from the Greek verb *epithymein* (to long for, desire), based on the prefix *epi-* (upon) plus the noun *thymos* (desire, mind, soul). Sensual desire is something that is certainly *epi-* one's *thymos* a good deal of the time, and as usual, the Greeks had a word for it.

epithymetic See **epithumetic.**

epopt (EP opt) *n*. Literally a "beholder, overseer, watcher," *epopt* was the name given to one initiated into the highest grade of the Eleusinian mysteries of ancient Greece. The Greek noun was *epoptes*, from the verb *epopteuein* (to look upon, observe), built from the preposition *epi-* (upon) plus *opteuein* (to see). By extension, *epopt* came to denote anyone instructed in any secret system. Mysteries, in Greek and Roman religion, were secret cults, requiring elaborate initiations that included purification rites, the observing of sacred objects and the acceptance of occult knowledge. The Eleusinian were the most important mysteries. They were taken over by the Athenians circa 600 B.C. The ritual purification in the sea took place before the procession to Eleusis, 14 miles away. The initiates were sworn to secrecy, so that we know almost nothing about the details of the ritual. In general, it celebrated the abduction of Persephone by Dis, king of the Underworld, and her return to her mother Demeter, the goddess of the fertility of the earth, identified by the Romans with Ceres, their goddess of agriculture, from whose name we got the word *cereal*. And away we go, all the way from *epopt* to Corn Flakes and Post Toasties!

ergophobia (ur goh FOH bee uh) *n*. This is a somewhat jocular word invented in 1905, as reported by the *British Medical Journal* in the February 11 issue of that year, where we read that " ... it often pays better to idle and loaf about than to work, and the consequence is that a new disease has been engendered, which I [W. D. Spanton] have termed '*ergophobia*.'" This is a rather neat concoction: the Greek noun *ergon* (work) plus the familiar suffix -*phobia*. A note in the *Daily Chronicle* a little later that year (issue of May 5/7) reads: "*Ergophobia* ... means a hatred or terror of work. It is a new disease which a medical paper has recently called attention to." The *ergon* so deftly used in inventing the name of this new "disease" was the source of the physical term *erg* adopted in 1873 for a unit of work or energy: the amount of work done when a force of one dyne (the force that produces an acceleration of one centimeter per second per second on a mass of one gram) moves its point of application one centimeter in the direction of the force. Don't worry about this technical terminology—it's inserted so that you get the general idea of the *erg-* in *ergophobia* and understand that the *o* inserted between *erg-* and -*phobia* has nothing to do with the *o* in *ergo*, meaning "therefore," and was put there purely for reasons of euphony. *Ergophobia* was defined by some wag as " ... a recognized if not a notifiable disease." Notifiable? That's a British English adjective for a disease that must be reported to public health authorities. The November 24, 1960, issue of the *Daily Mail* (London) carried the headline "*Ergophobics?*" and followed that with this definition: "Boys suffering from *ergophobia* (the dilemma of having to choose between working and stealing)." Seems a bit unkind, if one is concerned about sociological problems. Perhaps the dilemma is having to choose between working and welfare—*if* jobs are available.

estovers (es TOH vurz) *n. pl*. The usual meaning of *opus* in Latin is "work, labor." There.is a special use in the phrase *opus est*, or *est opus*, literally "there is work" (for someone to do) and by transference, "there is need," "it is necessary." From *est opus* came Old French *estovoir* (to be necessary), also used as a noun (a necessary, a need), and eventually *estovers*, meaning "necessaries allowed by law," and "the right to such necessaries." The term was used especially of the wood that a tenant had the right to take from the landlord's estate as needed for the repair of his house, tools, implements, hedges, etc. It also covered the needs of a widow or a wife separated from her husband and the sustenance of an imprisoned felon for himself and his family, taken from his property during the term of his confinement. The phrase *common of estovers* denoted the right to take wood from another's estate for the use or furnishing of a house or farm. Sir William Blackstone's *Commentaries on the Laws of England* (1765), commonly referred to by lawyers as *Blackstone's Commentaries*, defined it in these terms: "a liberty of taking necessary wood." It is interesting to read of so humanitarian a system prevailing as far back as 1523 in John Fitzherbert's treatise of that date, *A ryght frutefull mater: and hath to name the boke of surueyeng* (some title!), which contains this provision: "The Lorde may giue or selle the resydewe of the sayde woodes or wastes, Except that [unless] a manne haue *commen of Estouers*." To each according to his needs?

ethrog (EH throg), also **etrog** (ET rog) or **esrog** (ES rog) *n*. An *ethrog*, from the Hebrew *ethrogh*, is the "fruit of the *citron*," a small, shrublike citrus tree (*Citrus medica* to botanists) used by Orthodox Jews with the palm branch (known in Hebrew as the *lulab, lulal* or *lulov*, from the Hebrew *lulabh*, meaning "branch") during the festival of *Sukkoth*, or *Succoth*, the Feast of Tabernacles, a seven-day commemoration of the dwelling of the Jews in tents in the wilderness, and the celebration of harvest. Sukkoth is a festive occasion, and some Orthodox Jews erect little temporary structures festooned with palm fronds and fruits wherein food is eaten and songs are sung. This happens in the early autumn. I remember, as a child, confusing *ethrog* and *ephod*, which had nothing whatever to do with each other. An *ephod* (EH fod), in early Hebrew times, was a religious garment, an ornate apronlike vestment worn by Hebrew high priests, hanging from the shoulders and fastened with a band. By specifications ordained in Exod. 28:6, the apron was to be "of gold, of blue and purple and scarlet stuff, and of fine twined linen, skillfully worked." I remember my grandfather, who drilled me on this stuff, laughing at the thought of a high priest wearing an *ethrog*, which resembles an enormous lemon, suspended from his shoulders and topped by a palm branch. All of this is old stuff now but was taken seriously in the not-so-distant past.

eudemonia   See **evancalous.**

eupepsia   See **evancalous.**

euphuism   See **gongorism.**

eupnea   See **evancalous.**

eurybathic   See **stenobathic.**

euryhaline   See **stenobathic.**

eurythermal   See **stenobathic.**

eutocia   See **dystocia.**

Eutopia   See dystopia.

evancalous (uh VAN kuh luhs) *adj. Agkalos* is Greek for "armful," related to *agkale* (the bent arm; used mostly in the plural), which in turn is based on *agke* (arm). *Eu-* is a Greek prefix meaning "good, well," the combining form of *eus* (good) or the neuter of *eus* used as an adverb (well). *Eu-* is found in many English words, imparting the concept of *good* or *well*: *eudemonia* (happiness); *eugenic* (improving offspring); *eulogy* (high praise); *eupepsia* (good digestion; the opposite of the all-too-familiar *dyspepsia*); *euphemism* (pleasant substitute to avoid a harsh word or expression); *euphonious* (pleasant-sounding); *euphoria* (a feeling of well-being, often with no basis in reality); *eupnea* (easy breathing, as opposed to *dyspnea*, labored breathing); and *eurhythmic* (characterized by pleasant rhythm). Our little *eu-* spreads a lot of happiness in the world. Away with *caco-*, from Greek *kakos* (bad: *cacodemon; cacography; cacophonous*) and *dys-* (bad: *dysentery; dysfunction; dysgenic; dyslexia; dyspepsia; dysphasia*, inability to speak or comprehend words; *dysphonia*, poor vocal function; *dysphoria*, dissatisfaction, anxiety, restlessness; *dyspnea; dysthymia*, despondency; *dystrophy*, all too familiar in *muscular dystrophy*, disorders marked by degeneration or abnormal development of muscle; and *dysuria*, difficulty and pain in urination—a great big pile of misery. Now, back to our lovely *evancalous*: with the sweet *eu-* (sometimes pronounced *ev-*), attached to *agkalos* (in case you've forgotten: "armful"), you've got a cheerful combination: "good (or pleasant) to embrace," and what could be nicer? *Cheerful little armful* is a phrase out of my all-too-distant past, evoking those nostalgic reminiscences of enthralling adolescent love. Ah, me! "Youth's the season made for joys, Love is then our duty ... "

évolué (ay vol yooh AY) *adj. n.* This word is the past participle of the French verb *évoluer* (to evolve) and is used as both an adjective and a noun. As an adjective modifying the word *nation*, it means "advanced" (as opposed to *backward*); modifying *person*, it means "enlightened" or "progressive." But it has come into use as a noun, rather chauvinistically, it would appear, to designate an African from a part of the continent that was formerly under French or Belgian control, who has been educated along European lines and has thus become Europeanized in his or her thinking and reactions. In this context, it is used adjectivally to mean, in effect, "Europeanized." J. Parker, in *Apes and Ivory* (1953), gives a rather class-ridden definition: "Exactly what is an *évolué*? A Native of some education—a clerk or an office worker." In 1956 K. Hulme, in *A Nun's Story*, writes: "A first generation to work with whites ... that queer lonely society of the *évolués* which was neither black nor white." In 1961 P. Mason wrote, in *Common Sense about Race*: "The man who had become entirely '*évolué*' or assimilated to Western ways," and nine years later, in *Fanon*, D. Caute wrote of "the Black French *évolué* (the relatively educated, Europeanized and privileged native)." As time goes on, the term will, it is to be hoped, be deemed racist and pejorative and be considered of historical interest only.

exclaustration (eks klos TRAY shuhn) *n. Claudere* in Latin means "to shut." The neuter of its past participle, *clausum*, is used as a noun meaning "enclosed place." The related noun *claustrum* means, inter alia, "enclosure" and is the source of our *cloister*. When monastic vows are taken, one retires from the outside world and enters a monastery or a convent, but those vows are sometimes renounced and the individual re-enters the world outside the walls. Latin *ex-* (from) and *claustrum* (enclosure; in this case, cloister) plus the noun ending combine to give us *exclaustration*, the "resumption of secular life by one who has been released from his or her vows." This doesn't happen very often, and that may explain why *CH* appears to be the only dictionary that deals with the word.

exequies (EKS ih kweez) *n. pl.* There is a singular, *exequy*, but *CH* comments "usually in plural," while the *O.E.D.* states "now always in plural," and that's the way I've always seen it, except in the fine poem by Bishop Henry King (1592–1665), "*Exequy* upon His Wife." *Exequies* are "funeral rites." The word comes from the Latin *exsequiae*, taken from the verb *exsequi*, meaning literally "to follow (a corpse) to the grave" and formed of the prefix *ex-* (from) and *sequi* (to follow), the principal component in the derivation of *consequent, subsequent,* etc. Note the dropping of the *s* in *exequies*, which sometimes happened in the Latin as well (*exequiae*). We are more familiar with *obsequies*, a word whose meaning "came about by accident," to quote from the comment in my *1000 Most Important Words*. The "accident" was the confusion of *exsequiae* with *obsequium*, the Latin word for "compliance, submission," which had nothing to do with funerals and resulted in the Late Latin error *obsequiae*. Strange, that we went along with the error and the "accident" and hardly ever use the "right" word, *exequies*. Our word *obsequiousness*, in the sense of "servile deference," the kind shown at funerals we never wanted to attend but felt we had to, probably had something to do with our attraction to *obsequies*.

exogamy   See **endogamy.**

expiscate (eks PIH skate, EKS-) *vb.* If you knew that *piscis* meant "fish" in Latin, you might jump to the conclusion that to *expiscate* was to "rid (e.g., a body of water) of fish," but you would have jumped in the wrong direction. *Expiscate* comes from the Latin *expiscatus*, the past participle of *expiscari* (to fish out), based on *ex-* (out) plus *piscari* (to fish), from the *piscis* mentioned at the outset of this etymological exercise. It sounds slangy, but to *expiscate* is exactly that, to "fish out" in the sense in which *fish* is used in the colloquialism *fishing expedition*, a phrase cried out by politicians who are quite properly being investigated. In this context, then, our verb means to "find out by skillful examination and close scrutiny." The activity is called *expiscation* (eks pih SKAY shuhn), and the adjective describing it is *expiscatory* (eks pih SKAT uh ree, eks PIH skuh toh ree). An 1829 issue of *Blackwell's Magazine* used the expression *"expiscatory curiosity,"* and Thomas Carlyle wrote of *"expiscatory questions."* As a nonce-word, *expiscate* has been used in the "wrong" sense warned of above: to "rid" or "exhaust of fish": An 1858 issue of the *Saturday Review* stated that *"Norway is nearly expiscated."* With the reckless methods of contemporary fishing, the nonce use might well be revived and put into circulation by conservationists.

extrapunitive   See **intropunitive.**

famulus (FAM ooh luhs) *n.* In the first stages of the study of Latin, we learn about the declension of nouns. *Puella* is the model of the "first declension," nouns ending in *-a*. *Servus* is the usual model of the "second declension," masculine nouns ending in *-us*. *Puella* means "girl" and *servus* "slave." *Servus* is related to the verb *servire* (to be a slave), and we learn that our words *serve, servile*, etc., stem from the Latin root *serv-*. What has this to do with *famulus*? Well, a *famulus* in old Roman times was a special kind of slave, a "household servant, an attendant, especially one attached to a scholar or a magician"— very special indeed. In some dictionaries, *famulus* is defined as a "private secretary or factotum." In others, he is simply an "attendant." They all stress the relationship to magicians and scholars, a rather restricted function. Domestic slaves were a feature of Roman society. Some were well educated and became instructors. Except for their status as owned chattels, the *famulus* class had little in common with the ordinary *servus*. Incidental intelligence: Did you know that our word *slave* comes from the *Slavs*, who lived on the banks of the river Dnieper, and in Eastern Europe called *Slavi* and, who, as captives, spread through many parts of early medieval Europe as *slaves*?

farthingale (FAR *thing* gale) *n.* Except in films about the Old South, *farthingales* aren't much in evidence these days. They were frameworks made of hoops, generally constructed of whalebone worked into textile of some sort, or otherwise padded rolls, used to bell out women's dresses to form a hoop skirt or crinoline. The word could also mean "hooped petticoat." In Old French it was called a *verdugale* or *vertugalle*, a corruption of the Spanish word *verdugado*, based on *verdugo*, a word with a great many meanings, including "hoop" or "ring." John Ray, in *Observations Made in a Journey through Part of the Low Countries, Germany, Italy and France, with a Catalogue of Plants Not Native of England* (1673) wrote: "The Women wear great *Vardingales*, standing ... far out on each side." In Charles Reade's *The Cloister and the Hearth* (1860), we read:

"Whatever he [Gerard, the hero of the novel, the father of Erasmus] was saying or doing, he stopped short at the sight of a *farthingale*," and well he might have, for that attire is very fetching, don't you think? And come to think of it, isn't *fetching*, the present participle of *fetch*, a strange extension of the usual meaning of that verb?

fartlek (FART lek) *n*. I assure you that this word has nothing to do with gastric disturbances, the kind that embarrass one at dinner parties, even though *The Oxford Pocket Book of Athletic Training* (Duncan and Bone, 1957) defines it as " … a pleasant … form of *wind* sprints across country" (emphasis mine). The truth is that *fartlek* is the Swedish training technique for middle- and long-distance running, in which the athlete runs cross-country in a mixture of fast and slow pace. The August 18, 1958, issue of *The Times* (London) refers to it as " … the *Fartlek* or run-as-you-please training which originated from Sweden in the 1940s." The word is made up of Swedish *fart* (speed) and *lek* (play), and the running manual *Tulloh on Running* defines it in these terms: "*Fartlek*, meaning 'speed play' … is a continuous run in which patches of fast striding are interspersed with jogging." It does sound like fun and is said to be an effective form of training. The common meaning of the German noun *Fahrt* is "journey," but in nautical parlance, it is the equivalent of "speed," as in *halbe Fahrt* (half speed), *kleine Fahrt* (slow speed), etc., so we see that Swedish *fart* has impeccable connections. As to the American variety, most authorities trace it to Middle English, and some to Greek *porde*. Its German equivalent is *Furz*, which, like the American term is marked "vulgar" in the respective dictionaries. (And I hope I have offended nobody's sensibilities in this learned discussion.)

fauve   See **favism**.

fauvism   See **favism**.

fauvist   See **favism**.

favism (FAH viz'm) *n*. *Favism* is an "acute, extremely severe allergic reaction caused by eating broad beans or inhaling broad-bean pollen." The reaction takes the form of acute hepatitis, hemolytic (i.e., causing the breaking down of red blood cells and the releasing of hemoglobin) anemia, jaundice, diarrhea, fever, etc., and is said to be suffered particularly in southern Italy. The word was taken from the Italian *favismo*, from *fava* (bean, especially broad bean); *fava* figures in the Italian expression *prendere* (or *pigliare*) *due colombi a una fava*, meaning "to kill two birds (literally "doves") with one stone"; *fava* is from Latin *faba*, "broad bean," a word used by the Roman writer of comedies Terence in the sentence *Istaec in me cudetur faba*, meaning literally, "That broad bean of yours will be threshed in me," and idiomatically, "I shall have to suffer for this." The broad bean, according to my *British English, A to Zed*, is the approximate equivalent of our *lima bean*, and its identity is clarified (?) by the following comment: "Similar, but larger, darker and with a coarser skin. The British variety is the seed of a vetch known as *Vicia faba*; the American, that of the plant known as *Phaseolus limensis*." When I said "The British variety ... ," as I later discovered, I should have said, "The British and European (and for all I know, the South American and other) varieties." "A dictionary-maker," in the immortal language of Fowler, " ... must deal with a great many matters of which he has no first-hand knowledge." Be all that as it may, the *Vicia* in *Vicia faba* is Latin for "vetch," a word dear to the hearts of those who concoct (I might have avoided the **circumbendibus** "those who concoct" by using the word *concocters*, but that sounds like the plural of the word for a highly specialized component of a complex piece of automatic industrial machinery and in any case has a nasty sound) American (as opposed to British) crossword puzzles. I say " ... as opposed to ... " because there is a vast difference, and Americans who tangle with the British variety run the risk of premature death from frustration *cum* exasperation. If you care to know what a *vetch* is, you can look it up in any standard dictionary and become entangled in enough Linnean terminology to take a day's untangling. Caution: Never confuse *fava* or *favism* with *favus* or *favose*, *favus* being a fungal scalp disease resulting in a honeycombed appearance; and *favose* means "honeycombed." These come from Latin *favus* (honeycomb). Second caution: Never, never confuse any of the foregoing terms with *fauve*, *fauvist* or *fauvism*. A *fauve* is member of a group of early-20th-century painters (Matisse was the most prominent) who conceived a painting primarily as a two-dimensional colored decoration, rather than as an imitation of nature. *Fauvist* is a synonym of *fauve*, and *Fauvism* is the label applied to that school of painting. All of those words come from French *fauve* (wild beast). We've come a long way from broad beans, but that's how things go at times.

favose   See **favism.**

favus   See **favism.**

feck (FEK) *n.* We often use negative words, quite common ones, without stopping to think that they are based on positive words that are uncommon and unfamiliar. Everyday examples are words like *impeccable, untoward, ruthless, uncouth* and *disgruntled*. We almost never give a thought to the positive terms in the senses that form the basis of the familiar negatives: *peccable* (liable to error), *toward* (propitious), *ruthful* (compassionate). So it is with *feckless*, meaning "ineffective, incompetent, feeble, helpless." It must be obvious that there would be no such word unless there were also the word *feck*, and there is such a word, as unfamiliar or obscure as it may be. *Feck*, a mainly Scottish term that is also heard in the north of England, has a number of meanings, including "efficacy, efficiency," and by extension, "energy, vigor." It is deemed to be an aphetic form of *effect* (*aphetic* being the adjective from *aphesis*, the linguistic phenomenon of the loss of an unstressed initial vowel or syllable). *Feck* gives rise to the adjective *feckful,* meaning "vigorous, efficient, powerful." In Robert Willan's *List of Ancient Words at Present Used in the Mountainous District of the West Riding of Yorkshire* (1811), *feckful* is defined as "strong and brawny." Hence our word *feckless;* and it all goes back to *feck.* This is a different term from the slang *feck* (origin unknown) used by James Joyce in the sense of "swipe" or "pinch." In *Portrait of the Artist as a Young Man* (1916) he describes persons who " ... *fecked* cash out of the rector's room," and in *Ulysses* (1922) he writes of "*fecking* matches from counters." Nothing to do with the *feck* we've been discussing. A word about *aphesis* (AF uh sis) and *aphetic* (uh FET ik): *Aphesis* comes from the Greek, meaning "letting go," based on the verb *aphienai* (to set free), built of the preposition *ap-,* a variant of *apo-* (away) plus *hienai* (to send); cf. *aph(a)eresis* in my *1000 Most Challenging Words.*

feckful   See **feck.**

fetial, also **fecial** (FEE shul) *n., adj.* In ancient Rome, there was a college of priests known as *fetiales* who were charged with conducting the rites involved in the declaration of war and the conclusion of peace. A member of that group was known in Latin as a *fetialis,* from which we got the noun *fetial.* As a Latin adjective, *fetialis* means "pertaining to the *fetiales,*" and by extension, "ambassadorial." The *fetial law* is the Roman law pertaining to the declaration of war and to peace treaties. The *O.E.D.* tells us that the form *fecial* came from an erroneous spelling of the Latin word and that the latter is of unknown origin. *W III* suggests that *fetial* comes from an "assumed" Old Latin noun, *fetis,* meaning "statute" or "treaty." Its definition of *fetial* as a noun is somewhat wider than the above, ascribing to that college of priests the responsibility for overseeing diplomatic relations in general and giving *diplomatic* as a synonym for the adjective. Sir William Segar, in *Honor, Military and Civil* (1602), tells us that "It was not lawful for ... any Souldier to take Armes, until the *Faecials* had so commanded or allowed." One wonders, did the *Consules* of the *Respublica* (the two annually elected chief executives of the republic of Rome) ever bypass the *fetiales* the way President Truman initiated the "police action" in Korea or President Johnson used the Tonkin Gulf Resolution to justify the bombing of North Vietnam, in each case bypassing Section 8 of the Constitution, which gives "The Congress ... [the] power ... To declare war ... "? There is no record of a "War Powers Act" in the annals of Rome. Suggested reading: *Original Intent and the Framers' Constitution,* by Leonard W. Levy (New York: Macmillan Publishing Company, 1988).

fidimplicitary   See **quisquilious.**

flabellate   See **flabellum.**

flabellation   See **flabellum.**

flabelliform   See **flabellum.**

flabellum (fluh BEL uhm) *n. Flare* is Latin for "to blow" and can be used transitively, as in "blow a horn," or intransitively, as in "the wind blows." The related noun *flabrum* means "breeze," and its diminutive is *flabellum*, "small fan," which we took intact into English to denote a ceremonial fan of the sort used in religious rites or formerly displayed on state occasions as an appurtenance of the pope, a bishop or a royal personage. *CH* says that it was "anciently used to drive away flies from the chalice during the celebration of the eucharist." *Flabellum* has certain uses in biology far too technical to go into here. Related adjectives are *flabelliform* and *flabellate*, meaning "fan-shaped," and *flabellation* is "the act of fanning."

fletcherism (FLEH chuh riz'm) *n.* There is also the word *fletchery*, and though the two are often confused, they have nothing whatever to do with each other. An American author named Horace Fletcher (1849–1919) preached the virtues of small bites and thorough mastication, 32 to the mouthful, if I correctly remember my mother's urgent pleas. Followers were known as *fletcherites* (FLEH chuh rites). Whether or not *fletcherization* (fleh chuh reye ZAY shun) contributed to health, it certainly prolonged mealtimes. In *Strictly Business*, O. Henry used the verb metaphorically, writing of a certain Annette who " ... *Fletcherized* large numbers of romantic novels." *Fletchery* (FLEH chuh ree), on the other hand, is the name given to the wares made or sold by a *fletcher*, a maker or vendor of arrows or bows and arrows. It is derived from *flèche*, French for "arrow." It is never safe to guess; such are the snares and pitfalls of amateur etymology.

fletcherite   See **fletcherism.**

flincher   See **vellinch.**

flitch (FLICH) *n.* Like so many words of Teutonic, rather than Greek or Latin ancestry, *flitch* has been found in a number of different spellings. The word goes back to Old English *flicca* and Old Norse *flikki* and designates a side of hog that is salted and cured, i.e., a side of bacon. One must be careful, in discussing *bacon*, to differentiate between British and American usage. To a Briton, *bacon* is what an American would call "Canadian bacon," and what we in America call "bacon" is generally referred to as "streaky" (a right descriptive name!) in Britain. We read, in Jephson and Reeve's *Narrative of a Walking Tour in Brittany* (1859): "From ... the ceiling hung a ... row of ... *flitches* of bacon," and Robert Herrick, in his poem *Hesperides*, applied the word jocularly to the human frame when he wrote (1648): "He ... walks with dangling breeches ... /And shewes his naked *flitches*." In days of yore, a *flitch* could be claimed once a year at Dunmow, Essex, by a man and wife who could present proof that they had lived in married peace for a year and a day. A 1615 record indicates that a certain Richard Wright claimed the "Bacon of Dunmow," and "there was delivered unto [him] one *fleech* of Bacon"; and in 1820 William Combe, in *The Tour of Doctor Syntax in Search of Consolation*, wrote: "They might have claim'd or I'm mistaken/ With conscience clear one *Flitch* of Bacon." We are mostly concerned here with bacon and conjugal harmony and need not dwell on other uses of *flitch* as applied to the cutting of whale blubber or halibut, the sawing of timber and carpentry. Sufficient unto the *flitch* is the reward of marital peace!

florilegium (flohr ih LEE juhm), also **florilegy** (floh RIL uh jee) *n.* A *florilegium* is an "anthology, a collection of choice pieces of literature." Literally, it is a "collection of flowers," formed of Latin *flor-*, the stem of *flos* (flower) and *legere* (to collect, gather, cull). *Florilegium* is a literal translation of Greek *anthologia*, built of *anthos* (flower) plus *logia* (collection), akin to *legein* (to gather), cognate with Latin *legere*. Originally, *anthology* was applied to a collection of the "flowers of verse," i.e., small select poems, especially epigrams, but the term was extended to cover any collection of literary pieces. James Russell Lowell, in *My Study Windows* (1871), wrote: "We have made but a small *florilegium* from Mr. Hazlitt's remarkable volumes," referring to the writings of the English critic and essayist William Hazlitt (1778–1830). The *O.E.D.* tells us that *florilegium* was formed "after the analogy of *spicilegium*." When we get to that word, we find that it is formed of Latin *spica* (ear of corn; but caution: *corn*, in British English, is a generic term analagous to American *grain*, and definitions in the *O.E.D.* are set forth in British English) plus *legium* (see above) and means "gleaning," literally, but "collection" or "anthology" figuratively. It also turns out that *spicilegium* has not been "naturalized" (i.e., taken into English), that its equivalent *spicilegy* is obsolete and that the proper form now is *spicilege* (SPIH suh lej). Somewhat complicated; better stick with *anthology*.

foehn   See **moazagotl.**

forisfamiliation (for is fah mil ee AY shuhn) *n.* This term denotes the procedure under Scottish law by which it is recognized that a child has flown the family nest and is prepared to set up on his or her own account. The verb is *forisfamiliate* (for is fa MIL ee ate), and it can be used both transitively and intransitively. When a parent *forisfamiliates* a child, the parent emancipates the heir from parental authority and in effect portions the heir off so as to exclude him or her from any claim to future inheritance; when the heir *forisfamiliates*, it amounts to the acceptance of a present gift and renunciation of any share of future parental inheritance. In short, *forisfamiliation* amounts to "exclusion from inheritance," whether by act of heir or parent. Both noun and verb stem from the Late Latin verb *forisfamiliare*, constructed of the adverb *foris* (outside) plus *familia* (family). This is all to warn you that if the subject arises, play it safe and consult your Scottish lawyer, especially since there are not only lots of subsidiary wrinkles, but, as I have recently (June 15, 1988) been informed by the Deputy Secretary of the Law Society of Scotland, many of the wrinkles are " ... in the melting pot at the moment [how's that for mixing metaphors—wrinkles in the melting pot?] as the Scottish Law Commission has the question under review."

fricatrice (FRIK uh truhs) *n. Fricare* means "to rub" in Latin, and the noun *fricatrix*, which the *O.E.D.* describes as "a word or form not actually found, but of which the existence is inferred," means, literally, "female rubber," i.e., "a female who rubs"; hence, the *O.E.D.* defines *fricatrice* as "a lewd woman." It is defined the same way in *W III*, which goes on to include "harlot" and "female homosexual," calling attention to the Latin and Greek noun *tribas*. Under *tribadism*, in my *1000 Most Challenging Words*, I dealt with the words *tribadism* (lesbianism), *tribade* (a lesbian, "usually in the sense of a homosexual female who assumes the male role, the 'active partner'"), *tribadic*, the adjective for the person and the practice, the Greek noun *tribas* (rubbing) and the Greek verb *tribein* (to rub). If all this brings to mind the implications of the modern institution known as the "massage parlor," so be it. In *Volpone* (1605), Ben Johnson puts these words into the mouth of "A patron": "To a lewd harlot, a base *fricatrice*." Robinson Ellis's translation of *The Poems and Fragments of Catullus* (1871) contains the line "Like slaver [saliva] abhorr'd breath'd from a foul *fricatrice*." Some dictionaries state that the word is archaic; others do not. The practice certainly isn't.

frippery   See **frippet**.

frippet (FRIH puht) *n.* This is a slang term for a "flashy or frivolous young woman." W. Chetham Strode's novel *Sometimes Even Now* (1933) gives us this sentence: "I'll invite him—and he can bring all his 'lovelys' and '*frippets*' with him." Apparently, the term, though pejorative, did not connote too harsh a judgment upon the young person in question. In *Sick to Death* (1971), David Clark writes: "Quite a nice bit of *frippet*. But too young for me. I like a mature woman." The phrase "rather enticing bit of *frippet*" appears in Sheed's *Middle Class Education* (1960). Both the *C.O.D.* and *O.E.D. Supplement* say "origin unknown" about this word. It would seem to me, however, to have something to do with the noun *frippery* (FRIH puh ree), the immediately preceding entry in the *C.O.D.*, defined there as "finery, needless or tawdry adornment esp[ecially] in dress ... "; in the *O.E.D.* as (inter alia) "finery in dress, *esp*[ecially] tawdry finery ... tawdry ornamentation in general ... tawdry style; frivolity" and as an adjective "trifling; frivolous ... "; and in *CH* as (inter alia) "tawdry finery; foppish triviality," all of which have some connection (even if remote) with "flashy and frivolous" young women. But who am I to argue with the beloved *W III* and *O.E.D.*?

frondeur (fron DUR) *n. Fronde* is French for (inter alia) "sling," and *frondeur* is French for "slinger, fault finder, rioter, dissident, member of the *Fronde*." *Fronde* was the name given to as series of civil wars in France (urban riots, peasant revolts, battles, etc.) during the minority of Louis XIV, and by extension, it was applied to any malcontent party or to any violent political opposition. The name *frondeur*, in the sense of "slinger," was given to the "parliamentarians" (really lawyers) who participated in the revolt, because they were compared to schoolboys who used their slings only when the teacher wasn't looking. In other words, they were sneaky. An article in the *Daily Telegraph* (London) of September 22, 1880, inquired: "Are the French, then, incurable *frondeurs*? incorrigible revolutionists, who must attack a Minister simply because he is 'in'?" *Fronde* and *frondeur* have nothing to do with the botanical term *frond*, denoting the leaf of a palm or fern.

fustigate (FUS tuh gate) *vb*. You think you've never *fustigated* anybody? Well, probably not, in the literal sense. In Latin, a *fustis* is a stick, especially a knobbed stick, a cudgel or a club, and the unpleasant word *fustuarium* meant "clubbing to death," a common punishment for desertion. *Fustigare* meant "to cudgel to death" (this is a very disagreeable subject), and its past participle *fustigatus* gave us *fustigate*, but our verb by no means implies capital punishment: just a "beating, or another sort of severe punishment." So far, so literal. The figurative meaning is much attenuated: "to criticize harshly, to castigate," with no hint of corporal, let alone capital, consequences. Somehow, the clubbing aspect got lost in the Romance descendants of the Latin ancestor. In French *fustiger* means "to whip"; the Italian *fustigare* and the Spanish *fustigar* have the same effect: no sticks, clubs or cudgels, just whips, though I wouldn't want to be forced to choose; and the figurative sense seems not to have caught on in those tongues. The *O.E.D.* takes the "sting" out of *fustigate* by characterizing it as "now humorously pedantic."

fusuma (FOOH suh mah) *n*. A house in the Occident, whatever its size, has a finite number of rooms, anywhere from 1, in a shanty, to the 375 or so in Knole, the Sackville-West castle in Sevenoaks, Kent, England—and there are palaces with even more. Not so in Japan, where the houses are equipped with *fusamas*, sliding screens of opaque paper that run along grooves in the floor and ceiling and divide a single space into a number of rooms. E. S. Morse, in *Japanese Homes* (1886), defined *fusamas* as "movable partitions between the rooms." Very useful, one would think, in case of the arrival of unexpected guests, provided they didn't make too much noise.

futhork, also **futhorc** or **futhark** (FOOH thork) *n*. I suppose most people realize that the word *alphabet* got its name from *alpha* and *beta*, which are the first and second letters of the Greek alphabet and the basis of the Greek word *alphabetos*. We generally think of the alphabet in terms of *a, b, c*, etc., but there are many different alphabets, such as the Hebrew, Arabic, Russian, German (before the adoption of Western-type characters), Sanskrit (Devanagari) and others. *Futhork* is the name given to the Runic alphabet, fashioned from its first six letters: *f*, *u*, *th*, *o*, *r* and *k*. In the variant name *futhark*, *a* takes the place of *o*. What is the Runic alphabet? *Runic* describes anything written in *runes*, i.e., letters of the ancient Germanic alphabet, which was used by Scandinavians and Anglo-Saxons from the third to the twelfth centuries. *Runes* were formed by modifying Roman or Greek characters to facilitate carving them in inscriptions on wood or stone. *Rune* has other meanings as well: a secret, a mystic symbol, spell or song, any song or canto. There aren't many about who can write or read *futhork*, but *rune* and *runic* were no strangers to the poets of the last century. Wrote Dante Gabriel Rosetti (*The Sybyl*):

> 'I saw the Sibyl at Cumae'
> (One said) 'with mine own eye.
> She hung in a cage, and read her *rune*
> To all the passers-by ...'

and Matthew Arnold (*The Grande Chartreuse*):

> ... Thinking of his own Gods, a Greek
> In pity and mournful awe might stand
> Before some fallen *Runic* stone ...

while Poe (*The Bells*) gave us the chilling lines:

> Keeping time, time, time
> In a sort of *Runic* rhyme ...

and Emerson (*Woodnotes II*) told us that

> ... nature beats in perfect time
> And rounds with rhyme her every *rune* ...

fylfot, also **filfot** (FIL fot) *n.* A *fylfot* is a type of swastika, also known as a *gammadion* and a *cross cramponée*. First, some derivations: *Swastika* comes from the Sanskrit *svastika*, which is in turn based on *svasti* (well-being), from *su* (good) plus *asti* (he is). *Gammadion* (guh MADE ee uhn) gets its name from its resemblance to four Greek uppercase *gammas* set at right angles. *Cross cramponée* (kross kram pah NAY) is a term in heraldry, based on the French noun *crampon*, a metal bar bent in the form of a hook and used as a grappling iron; thus, *cramponée* describes a cross with a square hooklike bend at the end of each of its four limbs. So much for *fylfot*'s other names, but how about *fylfot* itself? This word appears to have occurred only once, in a 15th-century manuscript known as the *Lansdowne*, but, judging from its context in the manuscript it is believed to be a nonce spelling of *fill-foot*, a pattern or device for "filling the foot" of a painted window. The *fylfot* or swastika is a mystical symbol that is found worldwide and goes back to prehistoric times. It has been discovered on Etruscan tombs, Celtic monuments, Buddhist inscriptions, Greek coins, Byzantine architecture and American Indian artifacts and was the hateful badge of Nazism.

galdragon (GAL druh guhn) *n.* If you saw this word and didn't know where the accent was, you might think it was a slang term for a female dragon, but you'd be wide of the mark, unless you want to stretch a point. To end the suspense, *galdragon* is what the people of the Shetland Islands used to call a sorceress or witch. The word has nothing to do with dragons in the sense of the legendary fire-breathing variety. The Shetlanders took the word from Old Norse *galdra-kona*, a combination of *galdra* (incantation, crowing, or witchcraft generally) and *kuna* (woman). A crowing woman may resemble a "dragon" in the slang sense of an intimidating beady-eyed old female, but the etymology is as stated.

galligaskins (gal ih GAS kinz) *n. pl.* This was the name given to a kind of wide hose or breeches worn by men in the 16th and 17th centuries. It degenerated into a humorous name for any type of loose breeches. The word was a corruption of the 16th-century French adjective *garguesque*, a variation of *greguesque* resulting from metathesis (transposition of letters), which itself was taken from the Italian noun *grechesca*, based on the feminine form of the adjective *grechesco* (Greek), this fashion having been described in the 16th century as *alla gregescha* (in the Greek manner). *Grègues* is still French for "breeches" of any variety; in Spanish it is *griega*. The English poet John Philips (1676–1709), a pioneer in blank verse at a time when the standard form was the heroic couplet, wrote these lines in "The Splendid Shilling," a parody of Milton:

My *galligaskins*, that have long withstood
The winter's fury and encroaching frosts ...

Philips also wrote the poem "Cyder" about apple growing and cider pressing, in imitation of Virgil's *Georgics*. Laurence Sterne 1713–68) in *Tristram Shandy* wrote naughtily: "His whole thoughts ... were taken up with a transaction which was going forwards ... within the precincts of his own *Galligaskins*." The article of attire is mentioned as well in Trollope and Browning. If you come across a pair in the attic, hold on to them: Old styles keep coming back. You never know.

gammadion   See **fylfot.**

gavage (gah VAHZH) *n.* This word, which in French means "cramming (of poultry)" or "gorging," has been taken into English to mean "forcible feeding (generally)" by means of a force pump through a tube leading into the stomach. *Gaver* is the French verb for "to cram with food," and *gave* is the French word for a "bird's crop." The French origin of the word has obviously to do with the production of *pâté de foie gras*, which is produced by a rather brutal process of stuffing food into geese so as to enlarge their livers unnaturally. It is a treat for gourmets but doesn't do the geese much good. Lawrence Durrell, in *Holiday* (1963), wrote: "In goose country, where the practice of force-feeding geese (*gavage*) is in operation, there are always a goodly number of casualties." A Doctor Turnier of Paris, according to *Buck's Handbook of Medical Science* (1889), "advocated the method of *gavage* in infants prematurely born." Sir William Osler, the Canadian physician and professor of medicine, in the 1905 edition of his *Principles and Practice of Medicine*, recommended *gavage* in cases of persistent anorexia. History records some ghastly cases of the *gavage* of hunger-striking British women in their struggle for women's voting rights. Ugh! And today they have not only suffrage, but *Mrs.* Thatcher!

gavelkind   See **Borough-English**.

gematria (guh MAY tree uh, gee muh TREE uh) *n.* From Rabbinical Hebrew *gee mah TREE yah*, taken from Greek *geometria* (geometry), came the term *gematria*, denoting a cabalistic system of interpretation of the Hebrew Scriptures. The *cabala* (spelled in a variety of ways) was a mystical system of scriptural interpretation developed by Hebrew religious scholars of the Babylonian academies from the sixth to the eleventh centuries. In both the Greek and Hebrew alphabets, the letters had numerical equivalents (Greek alpha=1, beta=2, etc.; Hebrew aleph=1, beth-2, etc.) By adding the numerical equivalents of the letters of a word in the Hebrew scriptures, the scholars arrived at a total and found another word the numerical equivalents of whose letters added up to the same total. Then, by interchanging the words, they arrived at a mystical interpretation of the original word and thus found its "hidden meaning." In his *Astro-meteorologica, or Aphorisms and Discourses of the Bodies Celestial, their Natures and Influences* (1686), John Goad wrote: "I am persuaded … that there may be something in Cabala, *Gematry*, something in the mysterious Force of Numbers, in Critical Days, Climacteric Years & c." I have a sneaking suspicion that those early scholars were much akin to today's numerologists and readers of tea leaves.

gemel   See **gemellion**.

gemellion (juh MEL ee uhn) *n.* This word, taken from medieval Latin *gemellio*, based on the Latin adjective *gemellus* (twin), is one of a number of words that go back to that Latin source. It is the name of either of a pair of usually identical basins used for washing the hands before a meal. The water is poured over the hands from one *gemellion* into the other. It was applied especially to one of a pair of basins so used for the ritual washing of hands at the Mass. The word is sometimes spelled *gemellione*, giving it an Italian twist. *Gemellus* gave the French *jumeau* (male twin) and *jumelle* (female twin) and shows up closer to the Latin in such terms as *grossesse gémellaire* (twin pregnancy) and *école géminée* (coeducational school); in such Italian words as *gemello* and *gemella* (male twin, female twin); and similarly in Spanish *gemelo* and *gemela*. Getting back to English, a *gemel* is a pair of bottles blown individually and then fused together with the necks pointing in different directions, so that the halves can contain different liquids, such as oil and vinegar. As an adjective, *gemel* means "paired" or "twin." A *gemel window*, for example, is one that fills two openings. How that Latin keeps rearing its lovely head!

Geneva bands (juh NEE vuh bands) *n. pl.* You doubtless know that *Geneva* is a city in Switzerland, but you may not know that its name is often used attributively with reference to matters connected with Calvinistic doctrine, because it was to Geneva that Calvin (a Frenchman) went, in 1536, to devote his life to the work of the Reformation. *Geneva bands*, to those unfamiliar with the customs of the Swiss Calvinist clergy, might at first blush be taken for those Swiss musical groups that play rather noisy brass instruments, featuring selections of the oompah variety. In fact, *Geneva bands* are part of the ecclesiastical dress of some Protestant clergymen, consisting of a pair of narrow white cloth strips that hang down from the front collar of the robe. English barristers also wear bands. These *bands* or strips are modeled after those worn by the Swiss Calvinist clergy. The *Geneva gown* is a flowing large-sleeved black gown of the academic model worn as a vestment for preaching by the Calvinistic clergy of Geneva and widely adopted by Protestant ministers. What, then, does *Geneva movement* mean? A religious crusade? Wrong again: It is a device for producing intermittent motion, whereby a cam on a driving wheel engages slots on a driven wheel; also known as *Geneva motion* or *bar movement*, an old type of watch movement too complex to go into here. And speaking of *movement*, we certainly have moved far from *bands* on ecclesiastical dress, though we've managed to stay in Geneva.

Geneva motion   See **Geneva bands.**

Geneva movement   See **Geneva bands.**

geotaxis (jee oh TAX is) *n. Geotaxis* applies to *motile* cells, spores, etc.—i.e., organisms capable of spontaneous movement—and denotes their response to the stimulus of gravity, whether toward or away. *Geotaxis* is formed of the Greek nouns *ge* (earth, as in *geology, geography*, etc.) and *taxis* (arrangement). It is synonymous with the biological term *geotropism*, "movement or growth with respect to the force of gravity," based on *ge* plus *tropos* (turning). Getting back to *motile*, that word is used as a noun in psychology for a person whose mind creates distinct motor images, as opposed to auditory or visual images, motor images being those involving muscular movement. (I'm not sure what this is all about, either. "A dictionary-maker," said H. W. Fowler in his preface to the *C.O.D.*, "unless he is a monster of omniscience, must deal with a great many matters of which he has no first-hand knowledge." I am not a monster of omniscience.)

geotropism   See **geotaxis.**

gephyrophobia (GUH fye ruh FOH bee uh) *n.* We are acquainted with *phobia* as both a noun and a ubiquitous (these days, anyway) suffix indicating fear or dread or terror of something or other, as in *acrophobia* (dread of heights), *agoraphobia* (fear of open areas), *claustrophobia* (dread of confined places) and *xenophobia* (fear—or hatred—of foreigners or strangers or of anything foreign or strange, a morbid condition that accounts for lots of the troubles in our world). *Gephyrophobia* is formed of the Greek noun *gephyra* (bridge—the kind that crosses rivers and valleys, not the card game that makes evenings at cousin Harriet's bearable, or the contraptions installed by dentists or the raised structure on ships) and our old friend *phobia*. An example of this rare condition is set forth in the following news item in *The Times* (London) of October 3, 1987, which is my authority for the spelling of this headword.

'BRIDGE TOO FAR' STOPS DRIVER
By Thomson Prentice, Science Correspondent
Gephyrophobia—a terror of crossing bridges—brought traffic to a halt for 45 minutes on the A45 yesterday.

The prospect of crossing the three-quarters of a mile long Orwell Bridge, near Ipswich, Suffolk, was too much for a middle-aged woman driver. She came to a halt in the middle of the A45 approach road and refused to budge.

The woman told police that she was terrified of crossing bridges and had planned her route to avoid them, but had taken a wrong turning on her 100 mile journey from Felixstowe to London.

Rush-hour traffic built up into a long tailback while police tried to find a solution.

Eventually PC Ian Lankester took over at the wheel and the woman, whose identity has not been disclosed, crouched in the back seat with her hands over her eyes during the fearful crossing.

The bridge is Britain's longest single-span concrete bridge and has a drop of 150 feet. However, the woman's problem was not caused by a fear of heights, but by gephyrophobia, one expert said.

Mr Norman Lee, president of the National Council of Psychotherapists, said: "The sufferer cannot bear the responsibility of crossing from one side to another, and opts out of the decision."

Ghibelline   See **Guelph.**

glebe (GLEEB) *n.* This is a term having to do with British ecclesiatical life, denoting a portion of land that is part of a clergyman's benefice and furnishes him a revenue. In Britain, *benefice* (BEN eh fis) is used to designate a "church living," i.e., a position granted to a clergyman, especially a rector or vicar, that guarantees a fixed amount of property or income, or the revenue itself. *Glebe* is also used poetically to mean "earth," "land" or "field" in Britain, but in that sense, it is archaic in American English. The term comes from Latin *gl(a)eba* (clod, land) and is sometimes expanded to *glebe land*. *Glebe* can also denote a parsonage without the real property appurtenant. Thackeray tells us in *The*

Virginians (1859): "Virginia was a Church of England colony; the clergymen were paid by the State and *glebes* allotted to them." Using the word poetically in the sense of "cultivated land" or "field," Tennyson, in an 1833 poem, wrote of "Many an ... upland *glebe* wealthy in oil and wine." In that use, the term had no ecclesiastical connotation whatever. If you run across the word, before deciding how it is being used, better look over the territory and see if there are any clergymen lurking about.

glossolalia (glos oh LAY lee uh), also **glossolaly** (glos oh LAY lee) *n.* From Greek *glosso-*, the combining form of *glossa* (tongue), plus *-lalia* (-speaking), from *laleein* (to speak), we get *glossolalia*, also known as the "gift of tongues." In Frederic W. Farrar's *Life and Work of St. Paul* (1879), we read of " ... those soliloquies of ecstatic spiritual emotion which were known as *Glossolalia*, or, 'the Gift of Tongues.'" In *Early Days of Christianity* (1882), Farrar wrote: "In Corinth the terrible abuses of *glossolaly* had led to outbreaks which entirely ruined the order of worship." William S. Lilly, in an 1898 issue of the monthly review *The Nineteenth Century*, discussed " ... those of the disciples who possessed that singular gift of *glossolaly*, or speaking with tongues." Practitioners of *glossolalia* were known as *glossolalists* (glos oh LAY lists), who are referred to in Farrar's *St. Paul* in these words: " ... the rivalry of unmeaning sounds among the *glossolalists*." The *gift of tongues* is more explicitly defined as "unintelligble ecstatic 'speech'" uttered in religious services of various denominations that assign more importance to emotional fervor than to intelligibility, although the worshipers may have some notion of what they are "talking" about. I would imagine that their thoughts flow heavenward together with their sounds, thus improving on the prayers of King Claudius at the end of Act III, Scene 3 of *Hamlet*, who rises and says: "My words fly up, my thoughts remain below: / Words without thoughts never to heaven go."

glossolaly   See **glossolalia**.

gongorism (GONG gor iz'm) *n.* This word comes from the name of the Spanish poet Luis de Góngora y Argote (1561–1627) and denotes a florid, pedantic, affected style of writing introduced into Spanish literature in the 16th century. Góngora was roughly contemporary with the English writer John Lyly (1554–1606), the father of *euphuism* (YOO fyuh iz'm), a "flowery, affected, precious, high-flown style of language," written or spoken. Lyly was much imitated at the end of the 16th century. He was best known for his two-part didactic romance *Euphues, or the Anatomy of Wit*, and *Euphues and his England*, a work advocating a reform of education and manners. *Euphuism* utilized preciosity, alliteration, antithesis and other similar devices. A literary review in 1886 noted that "Euphuistic language corresponded in date and character with *Gongorism* in Spain." The name of Lyly's protagonist was fashioned after the Greek adjective *euphues* (well-bred), formed of the Greek prefix *eu-* (well) and *phue* (growth). I have not succeeded in learning whether these two writers knew each other. Probably not, in view of the difficulty of traveling in those days. Strange, the way these innovations seem to pop up simultaneously in distant places.

gradatio   See **anaphora**.

grager (GRAH guhr—rough *r* as in French) *n.* We know from the Book of Esther that the villainous Haman, a prince in the court of King Ahasuerus (better known as Xerxes I), plotted to kill all the Jews in the kingdom. Seems he was particularly eager to get rid of Mordecai, the cousin and guardian of Ahasuerus's beautiful Jewish Queen Esther, and built a gallows 50 cubits (about 85 feet) high for the purpose. But Mordecai, who had become popular with Ahasuerus by foiling a plot to assassinate the king, found out, and told Esther, and she told the king. He not only overruled Haman but ordered him hanged on those very gallows. (See my discussion of *petard* in *1000 Most Challenging Words* for an explanation of Shakespeare's *hoist with his own petard*, where I mention Haman's fate as an illustration.) The deliverance of the Jews is celebrated in the annual Hebrew festival of Purim. During the religious service, children use a rattle or other noisemaking contrivance to drown out the hated name of Haman whenever it is mentioned. That apparatus is known as a *grager*, a Yiddish word derived from the Polish noun *grzegarz*, meaning "rattle." *Gragers* come in various models, the usual form having a handle around which some form of noisemaking contraption is swung with great gusto. For once, the kids have a lot of fun during the service instead of the usual wiggling around and the struggle to stay awake.

graveolent (gruhv EE oh luhnt) *adj.* You would want to stand as far away as possible from anything (or for that matter, anybody) that could be so described, for *graveolent* means "rank-smelling, fetid" and applies to whatever or whoever emits a strong offensive odor. This wonderfully dignified substitute for *stinky* is composed of Latin *grave*, the adverb formed from the neuter of *gravis* (heavy) plus *-olent*, the stem of *olens*, the present participle of the verb *olere* (to smell). Rotten eggs are as good an example as any of a *graveolent* substance, and the next time you are tempted to say, "Something smells fishy around here!" you might with more dignity exclaim, "I detect something *graveolent* hereabout!"

griffin (GRIH fin) *n.* A good many Anglo-Indian words have found their way into the vocabulary of people, especially Englishmen, who have never been within a thousand miles of India. A few examples: *bungalow, dhobi* (washerman/woman), *dhoti* (loincloth), *guru, pukka(h)* (genuine), *punkah* (ceiling fan), *sahib* (gentleman; term of respect); *swami, walla(h)* (-man, person employed in something, as in *typewriter-wallah*, a person who repairs typewriters). *Griffin* is such an Anglo-Indian word, of uncertain origin, meaning "greenhorn" as applied to a European newly arrived in India (in the old days, when India was the Jewel in the Crown), a "novice, newcomer" who had to get used to Indian ways. "Quiz" (a pseudonym), in *The Grand Master; or Adventures of Qui Hi? in Hindustan* (1816), wrote: "Young men, immediately on their arrival in India, are termed *griffins*, and retain this honour until they are twelve months in the country." In a letter (1834) he included a note reading: "N. B. *Griffin* means a freshman or freshwoman in India." *Griffinage* is the term for the condition of being a *griffin*, or a person's first year in India. Edward H. D. E. Napier (not the famous general), in *Scenes and Sports in Foreign Lands* (1840), wrote: "A large detachment who, like myself, all in their *griffinage*, had but lately landed in Madras." *Griffin*, in this sense, is usually explained as a figurative use of the same word as the name of a mythical beast with the head and wings of an eagle and the body and hindquarters of a lion, but the *O.E.D.* says that " ... there is no evidence for this." Yet the hybrid nature of an Anglo-Indian is a tempting basis for this bit of popular etymology, no?

griffinage   See **griffin**.

grimthorpe (GRIM thorp) *vb.* To *grimthorpe* an ancient building is "to remodel or restore it without proper grounding or knowledge of its authentic character or without exercising care to remain faithful to its original quality and uniqueness." *Grimthorping* implies lavish expenditure without appropriate skill or decent taste. The eponym of this peculiar word is Sir Edmund Beckett, first Baron *Grimthorpe* (1816–1905), an English lawyer and architect whose restoration of St. Albans Cathedral generated severe censure and a storm of controversy. The July 23, 1892, issue of *The Athenaeum* (the literary review founded by James Silk Buckingham in 1828 that was incorporated with *The Nation* in 1921, which merged with *The New Statesman* in 1931, which merged with *New Society* in 1988), spoke of " ... St. Albans and other great national fabrics that have been '*Grimthorped*,'" and the July 28, 1900, issue used the expression " ... *grimthorping* with a vengeance." Prince Charles is a champion of ancient monuments and would be the first to be concerned about the dreadful practice of *grimthorping*. Poor Baron Grimthorpe: What a way to be remembered!

Guelph (GWELF) *n.* If anyone at all familiar with the political scene during the late Middle Ages hears the word *Guelph*, the word *Ghibelline* (GIB uh leen, -lin) springs to mind, because the *Guelphs* and the *Ghibellines* were major opposing political factions during that period. The Guelphs got their name from the German dukes, named *Welf* or *Guelph*, who ruled in Saxony and Bavaria. They were rivals of the Hohenstaufens, whose center was a castle named *Waiblingen*, which was garbled into *Ghibelline* when both factions showed up in Italy, where they kept fighting, with the *Guelphs* on the side of the Pope and the *Ghibellines* favoring the great noble families, each party seeking political dominance. After a while, these party names lost their original connotations. In Florence, the Guelphs expelled the Ghibellines and themselves split like an amoeba into Black and White Guelphs. The curious and sad fact is that they kept feuding more or less for the hell of it, because neither faction represented any special ideology or social stratum. The magnificent Dante Alighieri (1265–1321), author of *The Divine Comedy* and other prose and poetic gems, whose writing fixed the character of modern Italian, joined the White Guelphs, and when the Black Guelphs rose to power, he was banished, at the age of 37, and spent the rest of his life, 19 years, wandering throughout Italy. His unhappiness gave rise to these immortal lines from the *Inferno*: "There is no greater sorrow than to recall a time of happiness in misery," echoing the doleful lines of the Roman philosopher and statesman Boethius (?475–525) from his *Consolation of Philosophy*: "For truly in adverse fortune the worst sting of misery is to *have been* happy." Gone and mostly forgotten are the *Guelphs* and the *Ghibellines* and the Whites and the Blacks and their senseless warring and feuding and banishments, while Dante's moving words remain immortal.

gynogenesis   See **androgenous.**

Habdalah, also **Habdala, Havdala, Havdallah** (hav DAY luh) *n.* Orthodox Jews take the Commandment regarding the Sabbath very seriously: " ... the seventh day is the Sabbath of the Lord thy God ... the Lord blessed the Sabbath day, and hallowed it ... " In the household of my childhood, the Sabbath, from nightfall Friday to nightfall Saturday, was truly a time of rest. The house was thoroughly scrubbed, no work was done (and *work* was a most inclusive term) and special prayers were said. The Sabbath so differed from the other days that it was truly "separated" from them; hence the Hebrew word *habdalah* (separation, division) was the source of the *Habdalah*, the Jewish religious rite that celebrates the conclusion of the Sabbath, and the name of the prayer recited at that ceremony. Michael Friedländer's *The Jewish Religion* (1891) tells us: "On Sabbath evening, after the close of the Sabbath, we recite the *Habdalah*, in which God is praised for the distinction made between Sabbath and the six week-days." In Israel Zangwill's *Children of the Ghetto* (1893), we find the words: "*Havdalah*, ceremony separating conclusion of Sabbath ... from the subsequent days of toil." Beth-Zion Abrahams, in her translation of her own *Life of Glüchel of Hameln 1646–1724* (1962), writes of an incident that occurred " ... at the close of Sabbath, while my husband was reciting the *Habdalah* ... " Yes indeed, the Sabbath was quite distinct from the subsequent days of toil in my youth, and I still miss the distinction.

haboob (hah BOOHB) *n.* Like so many words transliterated from the Arabic, this word is found in a variety of spellings: *habbub, haboub, hubbob, hubbub,* etc.

I ran into it, or it ran into me, when a fellow passenger on a tour told me about an awful *hubbub* that he experienced in northern Africa. I wondered why he put the stress on the second syllable of this familiar word for "tumult" or "uproar" and asked what the trouble had been about. After a bit of confusion, he explained that this *hubbub* was a sandstorm that had blinded him and his fellow travelers. Eventual reference to the dictionaries revealed that a *haboob*, in whatever spelling, is a "violent windstorm that occurs principally in the Sudan," bringing with it desert sands. *Haboobs* also occur in Arabia, on the plains of India and in the United States as well. The word is from the Arabic *habu*, meaning "blowing furiously" or "violent wind." The *Daily News* (London) in 1897 described a *haboob* as "a tornado of sand and small stones," and Ralph E. Huschke's *Journal of Meteorology* (1959) defines *haboob* as "a strong wind and sandstorm or duststorm in the northern Sudan, especially around Khartum, where the average number is about 24 a year." As to those nearer home, a 1973 issue of *Scientific American* tells us: "The American *haboobs* are not so frequent as the Sudanese (two or three a year at Phoenix as compared with perhaps 24 a year at Khartoum)." I experienced one in 1953 on the way from Santa Fe to the oil fields of southeastern New Mexico. It brought our car to an instantaneous halt, pitted the windshield, got into our hair, eyes, ears and mouths and scared the daylights out of us. Incidentally, the Arabic word *habu* has nothing to do with its Japanese twin, which is the name of a poisonous pit viper *Trimeresurus flavoviridis* native to certain Pacific islands. However, it has one thing in common with the *haboob* described above. According to an 1895 issue of the *Geographical Journal*, "The poisonous Trimeresurus ... , called *habu* by the natives ... is an object of universal fear."

haecceity   See **proprium.**

haiku   See **cinquain.**

hamesucken (HAME suk'n) *n.* In Old English this was spelled *hamsocn*, from *ham* (rhymes with *game*), meaning "home" plus *socn*, meaning "seeking" or "attack." *Hamesucken* is the crime of "assaulting a person in his or her own house or wherever he or she resides." This is a specific offense only under Scottish law (which is quite distinct from English law). Laws of other countries lump it with assault generally. The word has been spelled in various ways through the years. Thus, we read in John Erskine's *Institute of the Law of Scotland* (1773): "Haimesucken ... is the crime of beating or assaulting a person within his own house." There is a German word, *heimsuchung*, which is variously defined as "visitation" or "affliction," but a German friend tells me that this seldom-heard word means something much closer to "retribution" or "punishment" for past offenses." One is "sought out" by one's nemesis and "gets what he deserves." The German word appears not to involve anything in the nature of beating or assault per se, though retribution might on occasion happen to take that form.

hammada, also **hamada(h)** (huh MAH duh) *n.* Most people think of the desert as a sea of sand, undulating and marked by dunes. It is so pictured in painting, song and story. But many parts of it are flat rocky areas from which the sand has been stripped by the winds. This is typical of the Sahara. Such an area is known as a *hammada*, an Arab word taken intact into English. The *McGraw-Hill Encyclopedia of Science and Technology* (1966) describes it in these terms: "Ordinarily, a *hammada* is a bare rock surface composed of relatively flat-lying consolidated sedimentary rocks from which overlying softer sediments have been stripped, principally by wind erosion." The 1886 edition of the *Encyclopedia Brittanica* speaks of " ... undulating surfaces of rock (distinguished as *hammada*)." Some travel writers have described the *hammadas* as "plateaus," but from other authorities one gets the impression that this is true of only some of the rocky areas. In my travels in Egypt I noticed, to my surprise, that my romantic notion of the desert as an unbroken sea of spotless sand was anything but justified: In many areas, the desert was strewn with pebbles and larger bits of blackish stone that belied what I remembered from my youth as background of *The Sheik of Araby* ("Into your tent I'll creep,/At night when you're asleep ... " etc.). Nor was the sand spotless, alas.

hanap (HAN ap) *n.* From Old French *hanap*, Old English took *hnap*, related also to Old High German *(k)napf* and Dutch *nap*, and in all those languages the meaning was "wine cup, goblet." In antiquarian circles, a *hanap* is a "richly carved medieval goblet, often with a cover or lid." From Robert Fabyan's *Newe Cronycles of England and of Fraunce* (1494), we learn that "Kyng Rycharde gaue vnto the Frenshe Kyng a *hanap* or basyn of golde ... ," and Alexis Soyer tells us, in his *Pantropheon: or History of Food and its Preparation* (1853), that "Charles the Bald gave to the Abbey of St. Denis a *hanap*, said to have belonged to Solomon." (After looking in vain for *Pantropheon* in all my dictionaries, the best I could come up with was the Greek noun *trophe* (nourishment) and a number of *tropho-* words having to do with aspects of nutrition, all very technical and specialized.) One Charles Dickens, Jr., wrote a *Dictionary of London* (1884) in which he spoke of "a ... collection of mazers and *hanaps* and cups." A *mazer* (MAY zer) was a bowl or goblet without a foot, originally made of "mazer" wood [maple or other hard wood], often richly carved and mounted with silver or gold or other metal, but the term was also applied more generally to a bowl made entirely of metal or anything else. The related word *hanaper* (HAN uh per) was the name of a case for one or more *hanaps*, or a baize-lined plate basket in which silver flatware was kept, or a container for valuables or money. The name was also applied to a round wicker case or small basket for keeping documents. Up until 1832, *hanaper* was the name of a department of the Chancery in London to which fees were paid for the sealing and filing of charters and other documents. *Hanaper* gave rise to the modern word *hamper*, the familiar wickerwork container, usually equipped with a cover, for laundry or picnic fare.

hanaper   See **hanap.**

hapax   See **hapax legomenon.**

hapax legomenon (HAH pahks leg GO muh non) *n*. This phrase, taken from the Greek and literally meaning "(something) said once," is used to denote a word, or form of a word, of which only one instance has been recorded in the entire work of an author or a whole literature. *Hapax* means "once" and *legomenon* "said." In *Poetic, Scientific & Other Forms of Discourse* (1956), Joshua Whatmough points out: "The *hapax legomenon*, although statistically it hardly differs from a word of very low occurrence ... is nevertheless anomalous just like the *scazon* (SKAY zon) in Greek comedy." To understand what he is driving at, I must tell you that a *scazon* (from Greek *skazon,* a nominative use of the present participle of *skazein,* to limp), is an alteration of the commonest Greek iambic meter (a line of six iambs—an *iamb* being a foot consisting of an unstressed followed by a stressed syllable) in which a *spondee* (i.e., two stressed syllables) or a *trochee* (i.e., a stressed followed by an unstressed syllable) replaces the final *iamb.* There were those who disapproved of *scazons,* like Obadiah Walker, who said, in *Of Education, Especially of Young Gentlemen* (1673), "Archilochus and Hipponax two very bad Poets ... invented those doggerel sorts of Verses, Iambics and *Scazons.*" Well, you can't please everybody. To go back to our headword for a moment, *hapax legomenon* is sometimes shortened to just *hapax.*

haplography (hap LOG ruh fee) *n*. I discuss *haplology* in my *1000 Most Challenging Words,* as denoting the loss of a syllable from the middle of a word (*conservatism* for *conservativism, syllabication* for *syllabification,* etc.) I should have added that *haplology* relates to the spoken word: It is an "omission in utterance." A related phenomenon is *haplography,* the "inadvertent omission in writing of one of two or more adjacent similar letters, syllables, words or passages." *CH* defines it tersely: "the inadvertent writing once of what should have been written twice." But that definition doesn't cover the case of the stenographer or copyist whose eye wanders in the following circumstance (an experience I have encountered more than once in my legal career): A paragraph of a contract begins, "If the parties agree on the price and the date of delivery ... " The next paragraph begins, "If the parties agree on the price but leave the date of delivery open ... " The stenographer types those initial words of the first of the paragraphs and is then interrupted by, for example, a telephone call. The call ended, she goes back to the draft and her eye catches the first few opening words of the second paragraph; she continues with that one and omits the first one in its entirety. Alas! (But the boss is a kindly soul and all is forgiven; happy ending.) The *haplo-* element is the combining form of *haplous* (single), and the familiar *-graphy* is from *-graphia,* the combining form of *graphe* (writing). *Caveant scriptores!*

Hasid   See **Mitnagged.**

hebenon   See **posset.**

heeltap   See **supernaculum.**

hegemon   See **hegumen.**

hegumen (hih GYOOH muhn) *n.* This is a general term in the Greek Orthodox (or Eastern) Church for a leader of a religious community. More specifically, a *hegumen* is the "head of a minor or second-class monastery." *Hegumen* can also denote the second in authority in a major monastery in the Greek Orthodox Church, corresponding to a prior in the Western Church. The word comes from the Greek *hegoumenos,* the present participle of *hegeisthai* (to lead, command) used as a noun, and is sometimes used as a title of honor for certain monks who are also priests, known as *hieromonks* (HEYE roh muhnks). Further up in the hierarchy of the Greek Orthodox Church is the *archimandrite* (ark uh MAN drite), a word composed of the prefix *archi-,* from the Greek verb *archein,* related to the nouns *arche* (beginning) and *archos* (ruler), plus *mandra* (monastery) (literally, "fold"). *Archimandrite* is the title of the superintendent or abbot of a major monastery. It may also be bestowed by a *patriarch, catholicos* (kuh THA luh kos) or bishop upon monks who are heads of a group of monasteries (corresponding to *superior abbots* or *provincial fathers* in the Western Church), and upon prominent *hieromonks.* Some definitions: In the Eastern Church, a *patriarch* is the spiritual head of certain independent churches, such as the Russian, Syrian and Coptic churches. A *catholicos* has the same position in certain other independent churches, like the Armenian Church. Neither of those titles is used in the Greek Orthodox Church. It's as clear as mud to me but was clear as a bell to a priest of an Eastern Church who explained it all to me over a plate of hot borscht in the basement of his church. In any case, do not confuse *hegumen* with *hegemon* (HEE juh mon, HEH-), meaning "paramount power" in international politics, from the familiar word *hegemony* (he JEH muhn nee), and taken intact from the Greek, where it means "leader" and is thus related to *hegumen,* though only in derivation.

helminth (HEL minth) *n.* A *helminth* is a "worm," especially a parasitic worm, like a tapeworm. The word comes from the Greek noun *helmins,* with *helminth-* as its stem. The adjective is *helminthic* (hel MIN thik), and the science of worms, especially of the parasitic type, is *helminthology* (hel min THAH lo gee). The pathological condition caused by the presence of worms in the body is *helminthiasis* (hel min THEYE uh sis), a word taken, via New Latin, from the Greek verb *helminthian* (hel MIN thee in), "to suffer from worms." Medicine administered to rid the body of parasitic, especially intestinal, worms, is described as *anthelmint(h)ic* (an thel MIN t(h)ik), composed of the prefix *anti-*

(*ant-* before a vowel or *h*, against) plus *helminth*, followed by the usual -*ic*. *Worm* is a peculiar word, in that as a noun, a *worm* is, zoologically speaking, a "long, slender, soft-bodied, legless bilateral invertebrate," but as a verb, *to worm*, apart from *worming* one's way out of a situation or into someone's favor, or *worming* a secret out of a weak-willed soul, is really "to free from worms," i.e., to *deworm*. If you have pimples, you don't *pimple* them, and if you have a rash, you don't *rash* it. With *worm*, the same little word covers both the problem and the remedy. Think about this linguistic aberration next time you take Fido to the vet.

helminthiasis   See **helminth.**

helminthic   See **helminth.**

helminthology   See **helminth.**

hemeralopia   See **nyctalopia.**

hemiepes   See **prosodion.**

hemiola (heh mee OH luh) *n.* This was the term in medieval music (sometimes spelled *hemiolia*) for a perfect fifth, based on the fact that it was produced by shortening a string to two-thirds of its length. It also denoted a triplet, i.e., a rhythmic alteration of three notes in place of two, or vice versa. The word was taken intact via Late Latin from the Greek, being the feminine of *hemiolos* (in the ratio of 1 ⅓ to 1), based on the prefix *hemi-*, "half," plus -*olios*, from *holos*, "whole." The adjective *hemiolic* (heh mee OL ik) in classical prosody described an accent characterized by the proportion of 3 to 2, a *hemiolic* foot being one distinguished by that ratio between *thesis* and *arsis*, which mean, respectively, (1) "downbeat," the accented part of a musical measure, taken intact via Latin from the Greek, where it meant, inter alia, "downbeat of the foot in keeping time," from the verb *tithenai* (to place or lay down); and (2) "upbeat," the unaccented part of a musical measure, taken via Late Latin from the Greek, where it meant "lifting of the foot in keeping time," from the verb *aeirein* (to lift). A foot where three notes take the place of two is called a *paeon* (PEE uhn) in prosody, consisting of one long or stressed syllable and three short or unstressed ones that take the place of two, and this is known as a *paeonic* foot. Via Latin *paeon*, the word comes from Greek *paion*. There is some question about the derivation of *paeon*. It is generally thought to be an Attic variation of *paean*, a hymn of thanksgiving to Apollo after a victory or a war song addressed to Ares (the Roman Mars), but the first-century Roman rhetorician Quintilian derived it from the alleged inventor of the form, a physician named Paeon. Hard to settle the argument at this late date. I hope this little discussion has not diminished your interest in classical prosody. If so, I apologize and hope to be forgiven.

hemiolia   See **hemiola.**

hemiolic   See **hemiola.**

hemistich (HEM ih stik) *n. Stich,* from the Greek *stichos,* means "verse" or "line of poetry," and a *hemistich,* as you might suspect, is half (or approximately half) of such a line, as divided by a *caesura* (a break or pause between words within a metrical foot—discussed briefly under **dolichurus**). *Hemistich* can also be applied to any line of verse of lesser length than that of the poem generally. Abraham Cowley, in *Davideis* (1638), included a note to the effect that he disagreed with those "who think that Virgil himself intended to have filled up these broken *Hemestiques.*" In *The Spectator* (issue 39, 1711), Joseph Addison wrote: "I do not dislike the Speeches in our English Tragedy that close with an *Hemistick* or Half Verse." Henry Hallam, the literary and constitutional historian, expressed the opinion (1847) that "the occasional *hemistich* ... [broke] the monotony of [measures]." It would appear, then, that *hemistichs* had the approval of English literati, and why not, pray?

heresiarch (huh REE zee ark, he-, -see-, HER uh see-) *n.* We get this word via Late Latin *haeresiarcha* from Greek *hairesiarches* (leader of a sect or school), based on *hairesis* (heresy) plus the suffix *-arches* (-arch, ruler). It means "originator or chief advocate of a heresy" or "leader of a group of heretics." In Horace Walpole's *Anecdotes of Painting in England, with Some Accounts of the Principal Artists; Collected by G. Vertue* (1786), we read: "Jargon and austerities are the weapons that serve the purposes of *heresiarcs* (sic) ... " A related word is *heresimach* (huh REE zee mak, he-, -see-, HER uh see-), an "antiheretic," using the Greek suffix *-machos,* from the verb *machesthai* (to fight). *Heresiography* (huh ree zee AH gruh fee) is "a treatise on heresies or a description of them," and a *heresiologist* is "one who writes about heresies or against them." The word *heresy* itself has an interesting etymology. It is based, via Late Latin *haeresis,* on Greek *hairesis,* which has a number of meanings, among them "taking, choice, school of thought, philosophic principle or sect, religious sect," all going back to *haireisthai* (to take for oneself, choose), that being the "middle voice," a verbal "voice" not found in Latin or English, of the verb *hairein* (to take). *Heresy* is used in the realm of science as well as religion. Many "scientific *heresies*" are now accepted as scientific truths.

heresimach   See **heresiarch.**

heresiologist   See **heresiarch.**

heresiology   See **heresiarch.**

heriot (HEH ree uht) *n.* This is an English legal term that dates back to feudal times, when it denoted a death duty payable to the lord of the manor upon the death of a tenant. Originally, the duty or tribute so payable consisted of the horses and arms that had been lent by the lord to his tenant, but later the duty consisted of the best beast or chattel owned by the tenant. Later, in the case of *copyhold tenures* (of which more later), the death duty consisted of whatever chattel the custom of the particular manor provided or of a payment of money. *Heriot* comes from Old English *heregeatwe* (military equipment, from *here*, army, plus *geatwe*, equipment), which was shortened in Middle English to *heriet* or *heriot*. In exceptional cases, the duty might be payable on a change of tenant or even a change of lord. The word was used figuratively (and imaginatively) by Bishop John Hacket in *Scrinia Reserata, a Memorial Offer'd to the Great Deservings of John Williams, Archbishop of York* (1692) in these words: "His body was interred ... in Langeday, the *heriot* which every son of Adam must pay to the Lord of the Mannor of the whole Earth." (*Scrinia reserata* means literally, in Latin, "cases of papers opened," freely, "files examined.") In relatively recent times, an 1896 issue of the *Daily News* reported this item: "In the Court of Appeal yesterday ... Sir Thomas claimed that either by *heriot* custom or *heriot* service he was entitled to a *heriot* of the best beast of the deceased tenant." As to *copyhold*, that was a type of tenure or holding of land constituting a parcel of the manor at the will of the lord in accordance with the customs of the particular manor as inscribed in the *copy*, i.e., the transcript of the manorial court roll, which contained the names of the tenants and the customs of the manor affecting such tenure. *Heriot* was clearly distinguished from *relief*, a system whereunder a sum of money was paid by the heir of a deceased tenant to the lord for the right to assume the estate, which otherwise would have reverted to the lord. A special form of *heriot* was *thirdings*, which consisted of one-third of the corn or grain growing on the tenant's parcel at the time of his death. Historical novels are replete with terms like these.

hermitage   See **supernaculum**.

hesychasm   See **hesychast**.

hesychast (HEH zuh kast) *n. Hesychast* was the name given to a member of an Eastern Orthodox sect of ascetic mystics that arose in the 14th century among the monks of Mount Athos, the easternmost prong of the peninsula of Chalcidice, in northeastern Greece. They formed a school of *quietists* practicing a method of contemplation for the purpose of attaining a beatific vision or a like mystical experience. Their practice was known as *hesychasm* (HES uh kaz'm); the adjective describing their method of solitary meditative mysticism is *hesychastic* (heh see KAS tik). *Hesychast* is derived via medieval Latin *hesychasta*, from ecclesiastical Greek *hesychastes* (quietist, hermit), related to the verb *hesychazein* (to keep quiet, be still) and the adjective *hesychos* (quiet, still). As early as the sixth century, the term *hesychastic*, in addition to describing their practices, took on the meaning "soothing, calming," without reference to any order of monks; it was also an ancient Greek musical term descriptive of a melodic system that tended to calm and appease the mind. Getting back for a moment to *quietism* (KWEYE eh tiz'm), that is the general term for a type of religious mysticism founded on the doctrine that the essence of religion is the withdrawal of the soul from all external objects and the fixing of the mind solely on the contemplation of God. Followers, known as *quietists* (KWEY eh tists), subscribed to the tenet that when one has attained the mystic state by inner, mental prayer, his transgressions will not be considered sins, since his will has been extinguished in the course of the contemplation of God to the exclusion of all externals. This would appear to be a comfortable way of avoiding retribution for all one's transgressions. The monk Gregorius Palamas, later canonized as St. Gregory Palamas, an intellectual leader of the *hesychasts*, pled the cause of his party at the councils of Constantinople in 1341 and 1351 with such fervency that his fellow sectarians acquired the name of *Palamites* (PAL uh mites), now considered synonymous with *hesychasts*. According to the *Oxford Dictionary of the Christian Church* (1959, 2d ed. 1974), in the second half of the 14th century, *hesychasm* was accepted by the entire Greek Church, and its adherents were also known as *Palamites*.

hesychastic   See **hesychast.**

hetaera (heh TEER uh), also **hetaira** (heh TIRE uh) *n.* This word, from the Greek *hetaira*, the feminine form of *hetairos* (companion), has several shades of meaning. It is generally understood to have meant "courtesan" or "mistress" in ancient Greece. *RH* defines the term as a "female paramour" or "concubine" but goes on to widen the definition to include "any woman who uses her charm to gain wealth or social position." *CH* starts off with a different slant: "in Greece, a woman employed in public or private entertainment" (a female somewhat like a geisha in Japan, especially the "private entertainment" aspect, the audience consisting, in both cases, of men); but *CH* goes on to include "paramour, concubine, courtesan (especially of a superior class)" as well. *W III* equates the term with "demimondaine" and then defines that term as "a woman of the demimonde; a kept woman." The *O.E.D.* definition includes "a female companion or paramour, a mistress, a concubine; a courtesan, harlot." That definition covers a lot of distance, all the way from "female companion" (seems innocent enough) to "harlot" (not so innocent). The *O.E.D.* quotes *LS*: "In Attic [Greek] mostly opposed to a *lawful wife*, and so with various shades of meaning, from a *concubine* (who might be a wife in all but the legal qualification of citizenship) down to a *courtesan*." It is evident that the word must be understood in context and used carefully, in view of the variety of its meanings. There were *hetaerai* who acquired great renown. Phryne, an Athenian *hetaera* of the fourth century B.C. famous for her beauty (she was the model for Praxiteles's Cnidian Venus), became so rich that she offered to rebuild the walls of Thebes if the authorities agreed to put on them the inscription: "Alexander destroyed them, but Phryne the *hetaera* rebuilt them." The offer was not taken up. The story goes that when the defense was doing badly during her trial on a capital charge, she was acquitted on the spot when she bared her uniquely beautiful bosom to the judges. One offshoot of the word comes as a surprise: Going back to the original Greek root, *hetairos* (companion), the term *hetairia* means a "club" or "society"; but another related word *hetearocracy* (heh teer AH cruh see), also *hetairocracy* (heh tire AH krah see), which can mean the "rule of courtesans" (cf. **pornocracy**), has another meaning as well: the "rule of fellows (of a college)"! James Bowling Mozley, in *Essays, Theological and Historical* (1878), wrote of "the '*hetairocracy*' of Oriel Common Room." (Oriel is an Oxford College, and a *common room* is a room in a college available to members for business or social purposes.) Based on its Greek origin, one might be forgiven for guessing that still another related word, *hetaery* (heh TEE reye), denoted a sort of Playboy Club, teeming with Bunnies, but no: It comes from *hetaireia* (companionship) and means an "oligarchical club" formed in ancient Athens principally for political and judicial purposes—nothing the least bit naughty.

hetaerocracy   See **hetaera**.

hetaery   See **hetaera**.

hetairia   See **hetaera**.

heteronomous   See **heteronym**.

heteronomy   See **heteronym**.

heteronym (HET ur oh nim) *n*. Most of us are familiar with *synonym, homonym* and *antonym*, but how about *heteronym*, built of the Greek prefix *heter-* (other, different) plus *-onym*, the combining form of *onoma* (name)? A *heteronym* is a "word of the same spelling as another but with a different pronunciation and meaning." Examples: *lead* (to conduct) and *lead* (a metal); *sow* (to scatter seed, to plant) and *sow* (an adult female swine); *desert* (arid region) and *desert* (to abandon); *refuse* (to decline to accept) and *refuse* (rubbish, trash). Be careful not to confuse *heteronym* with *heteronomy* (het uhr OH noh mee), the state of being under the rule or control of another, as opposed to the more familiar term *autonomy*. The adjectival form of *heteronym* is *heteronymous* (het uh RON uh muhs), to be carefully distinguished from *heteronomous*, the adjectival form of *heteronomy*, meaning "subject to different laws." Note that *heteronymous* and *heteronomous* do not qualify as a pair of *heteronyms*, because they are *not* pronounced differently, unlike the *heteronymous* examples shown above.

heteronymous   See **heteronym**.

heteroscian   See **amphiscian**.

heterozetesis (hed uh roh zuh TEE sis) *n*. This word was found only in *W III*, which gave as its derivation the Greek prefix *hetero-*, the combining form of *heteros* (other, different) plus *zetesis* (search, inquiry), related to the verb *zetein* (to seek, inquire), and gave as its definition simply *"ignoratio elenchi,"* letting it go at that. If we look up that phrase, we find: "L[atin], lit[erally], ignorance of proof; trans[lation] of G[reek] *elenchou agnoia.*" Under the headword *elenchus* in my *1000 Most Challenging Words*, after explaining that an *elenchus* is a "logical refutation, an argument that refutes another argument," I say that *ignoratio elenchi* means "ignoring the argument ... the fallacy of ignoring the point in question and arguing to the wrong point," which is pretty close to the *W III* definition: "a fallacy in logic of supposing that the point at issue is proved or disproved by an argument based on such a fallacy." There is a passage in Vita Sackville-West's *Pepita* about a will contest in which her mother testified against the charge of undue influence. The judge was Sir Samuel Evans, and counsel for the contestants was the able F. E. Smith. Here is a bit from the transcript:

> The Judge: You are fencing with each other prettily, but these are all speeches to the jury.
> Mr F. E. Smith: My Lord, the lady puts it on me.
> The Judge: Your experience ought to enable you to cast it off.
> Mr F. E. Smith: If I do, my Lord, I shall get no answer, because the lady answers another question every time, which I have not asked.

I cannot remember coming across a prettier example of *ignoratio elenchi*, i.e., *heterozetesis*.

hierodule (heye AIR uh dyoohl) *n*. From the combining form of the Greek adjective *hieros* (holy, sacred) came the prefix *hiero-*, which (dropping the *o* before a vowel) is found in words like *hierarchy* and *hierocracy* (the latter denoting government or rule by ecclesiastics, like what is going on in Iran these days). *Doulos* is Greek for "slave," so that a *hierodoulos* was a "slave (of either sex) who dwelled in a temple and was dedicated to the service of a god." According to *LS* the term *hierodoulos* "was especially applied to the public courtesans or votaries of Aphrodite at Corinth." The Greek geographer and historian Strabo (63 B.C.–A.D. 21, but the dates are uncertain) was the authority for that special application. The April 27, 1893, issue of *The Nation* would appear to have been somewhat off base in its use of *hierodule*, when it spoke of "The Amazons ... the warrior priestesses, or *hierodules*, of the Cappadocian Hittites." Warriors? Courtesans? What's going on here? Anyway, I'd love to know just what went on when a devotee of Aphrodite paid a visit to that temple at Corinth.

hieromonk   See **hegumen.**

hip(s)   See **hypo.**

hippiatric (hip ee AY trik) *n., adj. Hipp-* is a combining form of Greek *hippos* (horse), and *-iatric* comes from *iatros* (physician); together they formed *hippiatrikos*, the adjective from *hippiatros*, meaning "horse doctor," although the *O.E.D.* definition, "veterinary surgeon," would appear to indicate that the practice of a *hippiatros* was not necessarily limited to the treatment of equine ailments. The plural form, *hippiatrics*, means "treatment of diseases of horses," or, in context, "farriery," which denotes anything from the mere shoeing of horses to the treatment of horse diseases to veterinary surgery in general; but *hippiatrics* can cover, as well, a study or treatise on the diseases of horses. *Hippiatry* is a synonym of *hippiatrics* (hip ee AY trix) and *hippiatrist* (hip pee AY trist) is another word for *hippiatric* used as a substantive to mean "horse doctor." None of the above has anything to do with hippies.

hippocamp See **hippodame.**

hippocampus See **hippodame.**

hippocrene (HIP uh kreen) *n.* Usually capitalized, *Hippocrene* was the name of a fountain in ancient Greece that burst forth, according to legend, at the spot on Mount Helicon (the abode of the Muses) struck by a hoof of Pegasus, the winged horse ridden by Bellerophon when he rode against the Chimera, a monster, according to Homer, with a lion's head, a goat's body and a dragon's tail. (*Chimaira* is Greek for "female goat.") *Hippocrene* was known as the Fountain of the Muses and was believed to be a source of poetic inspiration, whence it acquired the meaning "poetic or literary inspiration." George Daniel, in *Polylogia; in Severall Eclogs* (1638–48), wrote: "And *Hippocrene* it selfe is but a Tale/To countenance dull Soules who drinke not Ale." Keats, in *Ode to a Nightingale* (1820), cried, "O for a beaker ... Full of the true, the blushful *Hippocrene*." In *The Goblet of Life* (1841), Longfellow wrote of "maddening draughts of *Hippocrene*." In 1880 James Russell Lowell complained, "We shrink from a cup of the purest *Hippocrene* after the critics' solar microscope," and Oliver Wendell Holmes (the elder), in 1891, wrote of "a loiterer by the waves of *Hippocrene*," so we see that the fabulous spring was on the minds of poets over the centuries. It got its name from Greek *hippokrene*, composed of *hippos* (horse) and *krene* (fountain). Fortunate are those who have found it and drunk of its waters.

hippodame (HIP uh dame) *n.* This is a word erroneously used by Spenser in *The Faerie Queene* for *hippocamp*, a shortened version of *hippocampus*, when he wrote of "Infernell Hags, Centaurs, feendes, *Hippodames*," and later of "His [Neptune's] swift charet ... Which foure great *Hippodames* did draw." *Hippocampus* is also the term in ichthyology for the sea horse, and in anatomy for a certain part of the brain that supposedly resembles the sea horse. I have gone into all this lest, in reading *The Faerie Queene*, you ran into *hippodame* and thought it denoted a female horse, or mare, and got confused. In fact, *hip-*

podame is an obsolete form of *hippodamist* (hih POD uh mist), which means "horse tamer," i.e., one who breaks in horses, taken from the Greek word based on *hippos* (horse) plus the stem of *damazein* (to break in). Samuel Warren, in *Ten Thousand a Year* (1841), wrote: "The present famous *hippodamist* at Windsor, by touching a nerve in the mouth of a horse, reduces him to helpless docility." That's not the way I've seen it done out West!

hippodamist   See **hippodame**.

hipps   See **hypo**.

hircine (HUR sine, -sin) *adj. Hircus* is Latin for "billy goat"; the adjective *hircinus* means "goatlike," and more specifically, "smelling like a goat," which isn't a very good way to smell. From *hircinus* we get *hircine*, with both those meanings, as well as a meaning of its own: "lustful," in view of that legendary aspect of a goat's character. Cf. "old goat," a slang pejorative for an aged lecher. *Cervus* is Latin for "stag" (cf. French *cerf*, Italian *cervo*, Spanish *ciervo* and our adjective *cervine*), and the combination of *hircus* and *cervus* gave us *hircocervus* (hur coh SUR vuhs), the name of a fabulous beast, half goat, half stag. This was a translation from the Greek *tragelaphos*, built of *tragos* (billy goat) and *elaphos* (stag), from which the Romans got *tragelaphus*, a kind of antelope, and we got *tragelaph* (TRA juh laf), the name of a large African antelope, also called *strepsiceros* (strep SIS uh ruhs), from the Greek *strephein* (to turn) plus *keras* (horn), indicating that this particular type of antelope has twisted horns. Apparently the ancients thought that an antelope was part goat, part deer. It's a long way from smelly goats to antelopes with twisted horns, but this is the sort of thing that happens once you begin delving into dictionaries, especially in the field of biological classification.

hircocervus   See **hircine**.

hirple (HUR p'l, HIR-) *n. To hirple* is "to walk or run lamely, to drag a leg, to hobble." As a noun, a *hirple* is a "limping or crawling sort of gait." It is a chiefly Scottish word but is heard as well in the north of England, or, as the British put it, south of the border. (That phrase, *south of the border*, to American ears, means "south of the border with Mexico," i.e., south of the Rio Grande. *The border*, in Britain, refers to the one with Scotland, and the British generally use *frontier* for an international border.) The dictionaries present those doleful words "origin unknown" for this word. This may be a wild guess, but the Greek verb *herpein* (to move slowly, to creep) which is cognate with Latin *serpere* (to creep, crawl), whose present participle *serpens* gave us *serpent*, may somehow have crept into *hirple*. (The cognate relationship may become clearer if we compare the first-person singular present indicative forms of the verbs: *herpo/serpo*.) The *O.E.D.* gives a rather feeble assent in saying of *hirple*: "Its coincidence in sound and sense with Gr[eek] *herpein* is noticeable." In Sir

Walter Scott's *The Pirate* (1821), we find the sentence: "They will be waiting for him, *hirpling*, useless body." Lord Cockburn's *Memorials of his Time* (1821–30) speaks of " ... a slow stealthy step—something between a walk and a *hirple*." *Shamble* may be as good a synonym as any.

hokku   See **cinquain.**

hominist   See **hominization.**

hominization (hom uh nih ZAY shuhn) *n.* This word was taken from the French *hominisation*, as used by P. Teilhard de Chardin in his *Le Phénomène Humaine* (1948). Latin *homin-*, the stem of *homo* (man), is the basis of the word, which denotes the development, through evolution, of traits, particularly those mental and spiritual characteristics that distinguish man from the rest of the animal world. In Julian Huxley's *Evolution in Action*, we are told: "The original stock of pre-human apes differentiated into many species, all showing a trend toward what has been called *hominization*—the acquisition of more human characters." In Bernard Wall's translation of de Chardin's work, entitled *The Phemenon of Man* (1959), we find these words: "*Hominisation* (note British alternative spelling with *s*) can be accepted in the first place as the individual and instantaneous leap from instinct to thought, but it is also ... the progressive phyletic spiritualisation in human civilisation of all the forces contained in the animal world." [*Phyletic* means "relating to a line of descent."] In the same translation, Wall uses the participial adjective *hominized*: "Are not the artificial, the moral and the juridical simply the *hominised* (note *s* again) versions of the natural, the physical and the organic?" A 1973 issue of the *Times Literary Supplement* spoke of the " ... *hominized*, secularized world." *Hominization* has nothing to do with *hominist* (HOM uh nist), as used by Bernard Shaw (1903) in the preface to his *Man and Superman* (1903): "The wildest *hominist* or feminist farce is insipid after the most commonplace 'slice of life.'" *Hominist* is the word for one advocating equal rights for men, the way their opposite numbers, the feminists, seek them for women. The poet Rupert Brooke (1887–1915) wrote, in a letter published in 1968: "If feminists are 'women' trying to be men, I suppose 'men' trying to be women are *hominists*."

homolog(o)umena   See **antilegomena.**

horn-mad (horn MAD) *adj.* The *O.E.D.* tells us that this word applied originally to beasts equippled with horns and in that context meant "enraged so as to be ready to horn anyone," i.e., to gore the offender. But it was extended to describe persons "enraged, furious, boiling over with anger." An earlier form was *horn-wood*, now obsolete. Examples are given in which the *horn-* element was spelled *horne-*, and the *Shorter Oxford English Dictionary* explains the *-wood* by listing *wood* as an obsolete adjective meaning, inter alia, "violently angry," or "irritated"; "enraged, furious," giving as an example an excerpt from the speech of Demetrius in *A Midsummer Night's Dream* (Act IV, Scene 1): " ... and here am I, and wood [*wode*, in my edition] within this wood, because I cannot meet my Hermia." Thomas Nashe, the English dramatist, novelist and satirical pamphleteer, in *Have with you to Saffron-Walden* (1596), wrote of "a bull ... bellowing and running *horne mad* at every one in his way," and Robert Louis Stevenson, in *Catriona: a Sequel to Kidnapped* (1893), tells of a lady who "would be driven *horn-mad* if she could hear of [something or other]." But this adjective also has an altogether different meaning, involving *horn* as a symbol of cuckoldry. This goes all the way back to Latin *cornu* (horn), which is reflected in Italian *cornuto*, Spanish *cornudo* and French *cocu*, all names bestowed upon the poor deceived husband. In this context, *horn-mad* means "enraged at being cuckolded," a sense that the *O.E.D.* attributes to "word-play." Both senses show up in *The Comedy of Errors* (Act II, Scene 1), when Dromio of Ephesus says to Adriana, "Why, mistress, sure my master is *horn mad* ... I mean not cuckold-mad; but sure, he's stark-mad." And in *The Ring and the Book* (1868), Browning uses the *cuckold* sense: "Somebody courts your wife, Count? Where and when? How and why? Mere *horn-madness*: have a care!" In his delightful little book *The Whole Ball of Wax and Other Colloquial Phrases* (1988), the American lexicographer Laurence Urdang (William Safire calls him "America's Samuel Johnson") deals with *horn-mad* and has (as is his usual practice) interesting things to say. I urge the reading of his book for supplementary information about this curious term, as well as all sorts of fascinating data about our wonderful language.

humuhumunukunukuapuaa (HOOH mooh HOOH mooh NOOH kooh NOOH kooh AH pooh AH uh) *n.* Yes, this *is* a word, the name of either of two triggerfishes that swim among the coral reefs of the tropical Indian and Pacific oceans. The lovely name is generally applied to one of the two species known to ichthyologists as *Rhinecantus aculeatus*. Beyond that, it is the name of the state fish of Hawaii. Each of our 50 states has a state flower, a state tree and a state bird. Some have a state insect, dog, grass or even fossil, and a fair number have a state fish. If you say *humu* ... etc. fast, you can almost hear the steel guitars twanging and see the wahines swaying. A few examples of other state fishes: Alaska, the king salmon; California, the golden trout; Pennsylvania, the brook trout—but they all sound rather prosaic alongside Hawaii's *humu* ... If your state lacks a state fish and that bothers you, select one and send a specimen of your nominee to your congressperson, senator or governor along with your complaint.

hydria   See **krater**.

hyle (HEYE lee) *n. Hyle* is Greek for "wood" and "matter" in the sense of physical substance in general as opposed to incorporeal things such as mind, spirit, qualities and actions. *Hyle* figures in numerous compounds: *hylic* (HEYE lik), "material, corporeal"; *hylicism* (HEYE luh siz'm) and *hylism* (HEYE liz'm), "materialism"; *hylicist* (HEYE luh sist) and *hylist* (HEYE list), "materialist"; *hylogenesis* (heye loh JEN uh sis), "the origin of matter"; *hylopathism* (heye LOP uh thiz'm), built of *hyle* and Greek *pathos* (sensation), the doctrine that matter is sentient (a case of *pathetic fallacy*, as discussed in my *1000 Most Challenging Words*?); *hylopathist* (heye LOP uh thist), denoting a follower of that doctrine; *hylophagous* (heye LO fuh guhs), built of *hyle* and *phagein* (to eat), "wood-eating," as applied, e.g., to termites; *hylotheism* (heye LOH thee iz'm), built of *hyle* and *theos* (god), "the doctrine that God and matter are identical"; *hylotheist* (heye LOH thee ist), denoting one who follows that doctrine; *hylotomous* (heye LOT uh muhs), built of *hyle* and *temnein* (to cut), "wood-cutting," as applied to insects; *hylozoism* (heye loh ZOH iz'm) built of *hyle* and *zoe* (life), "the doctrine that all matter is endowed with life" (more pathetic fallacy? Incidentally, there is a technical term used in psychology for the pathetic fallacy: *psychomorphism* (seye koh MORF iz'm), from Greek *psyche*, soul, plus *morphe*, form, meaning the "attribution of mental and spiritual processes, such as feeling, knowledge and purpose, to animals or inanimate objects); *hylozoist* (heye loh ZOH ist), denoting a follower of that doctrine; and *hylozoical* (heye loh ZO uh kuhl) and *hylozoistic* (heye loh zoh IST ik), adjectives descriptive of that doctrine. There are more *hylo-* compounds, but they would get us into philosophical concepts and doctrines too abstruse for even this book.

hyleg (HEYE leg) *n.* This is a term in astrology, the "science" that claims to interpret the influence of the heavenly bodies on human affairs. The astrology and horoscope business beguiles millions of people and relieves them of millions of dollars (pounds, francs, lire, etc., but not rubles, as far as I know). *Hyleg* is variously defined (a multiplicity of dictionaries can cause a combination of enlightenment and confusion). It is said to be the "ruling planet at the moment of birth," the "astrological position of the planets at the hour of birth," etc. *Hyleg* appears to be a modification of Persian *hailaj* (which means "material body," according to *W III*, but "calculation of astrologers by which they obtain evidence of the length of an infant's life" according to the *O.E.D.* Persian lexicographers, according to the *O.E.D.*, say the word is originally Greek and means "fountain of life.") Some dictionaries give *apheta* (AH fuh duh) as a synonym of *hyleg*. When we investigate that word, we find it to be a New Latin word taken from Greek *aphetes*, literally "one who lets go"; figuratively, "heavenly body determining the vital quadrant," from the Greek verb *aphienai* (to send forth), meaning in English "the ruler of life in a nativity." Phew! This has nothing to do with *aphetic*, the adjective from *aphesis*, also derived from *aphienai*, denoting the loss of a short unaccented vowel (i.e., "one let go") at the beginning of a word, as in *lone* from *alone*, *special* from *especial*, *squire* from *esquire*, etc. *Aphesis* is synonymous with *aph(a)eresis*, discussed at length in my *1000 Most Challenging Words*. (My astrologer assured me that this was an ideal day to write up this entry.)

hylic   See **hyle.**

hylicism   See **hyle.**

hylicist   See **hyle.**

hylism   See **hyle.**

hylist   See **hyle.**

hylogenesis   See **hyle.**

hylopathism   See **hyle.**

hylopathist   See **hyle.**

hylophagous   See **hyle.**

hylotheism   See **hyle.**

hylotheist   See **hyle.**

hylotomous   See **hyle.**

hylozoical   See **hyle.**

hylozoism   See **hyle.**

hylozoist   See **hyle.**

hylozoistic   See **hyle.**

hyp(s)   See **hypo.**

hypaethral (hi PEE thrul, heye-), also **upaithric** (ooh PYE thrik) *adj.* Any structure without a roof is *hypaethral*, i.e., "roofless, open to the elements." The Harvard Stadium, the Yale Bowl, the countless meeting places of those stalwart college and professional football teams, are *hypaethral*, with the exception of those few covered arenas like the Astrodome. How we have shivered and suffered in those *hypaethral*, or if you prefer, *upaithric* structures in the late autumnal and early winter contests! The noun for one of those open stadia is *hypaethron* (hi PEE thron, hye-) but I can't think of any one of them that calls itself that. The adjective comes from two Greek words: *hypo* (beneath) and *aether* (sky), which gives us *ether, etherial,* etc. The other form in the headword is simply a matter of spelling, having the same root and the identical meaning.

hyperbaton   See **metaplasm.**

hyperborean (heye pur BOH ree uhn, -buh REE uhn) *n., adj.* In both Latin and Greek, *boreas* means "north"; in classical mythology, *Boreas* was the god of the north wind. By combining *hyper-,* from Greek *hyper* (over, beyond) with *borean,* formed from *boreas* by adding the English *-an* ending, we get *hyperborean,* meaning "pertaining to, or inhabiting an extreme northern region"; also used as a noun denoting, literally, an inhabitant of the extreme north, and, informally and figuratively, one who lives in any northern climate. According to Greek legend, the *Hyperboreans* were a happy race who enjoyed perpetual sunshine and plenty in the realms beyond the north wind. In Maurice Keating's *Travels through France and Spain to Morocco* (1816), we read: "At six in the morning the yokes of oxen were going to their work a field; and nearly three hours advantage ... of active life is possessed [in France] over us *Hyperboreans.*" As an ethnological term, a *hyperborean* (sometimes capitalized) is a "member of an Arctic people," like the Eskimos, or the Koryak and Chukchi of northeastern Asia. The 17th-century Puritan clergyman John Davenport used the adjective figuratively to mean "frigid" when he wrote of being "dragged ... out of our *hyperborean* gloom into the South." Davenport was one of the founders of New Haven, Connecticut, and those of us who suffer through winters in that part of the world know what he was talking about.

hyperdulia   See **dulia.**

hypnagogic   See **hypnopedia.**

hypnobate   See **hypnopedia.**

hypnogogic   See **hypnopedia.**

hypnology   See **hypnopedia.**

hypnopedia (hip nuh PEE dee uh) *n. Hypnos* is mentioned in **thanatism,** but only briefly. He was the Greek god of sleep, the twin brother of Thanatos, the god of death. *Hypno-* is the combining form and has served as a prefix in a number of words in our language. *Hypnosis* is the most familiar of them. *Hypnopedia,* combining *hypno-* with the *paid-* of Greek *paideuein* (to teach, instruct), is "learning or conditioning by repetitive recorded sound during sleep" (sometimes semiwakefulness). A *hypnobate* (HIP nuh bate) is a "sleep-walker." Here, the prefix is combined with *-bates* (walker). *Hypnology* (hip NOL uh jee) is the "scientific study of the phenomena of sleep and hypnosis." *Hypnopompic* (hip nuh POMP ik), using *pompe* (sending away), means "dispelling or disturbing sleep" or "having to do with the condition of semiconsciousness preceding sleep." *Hypnophobia* obviously means "dread of sleep."

Hypnogogic (sometimes *hypnagogic*, built of *hypn-*, omitting the *o* before a vowel plus *-agogos*, from *agein*, to lead), the opposite of *hypnopompic*, means "relating to the drowsiness preceding sleep." A *hypnagogic* or *hypnogogic* image is a hallucination occurring when one is falling asleep or extremely fatigued. A *hypnoscope* (HIP nuh skope), using the suffix -scope, from *skopos* (watcher), is an "instrument used by hypnotists to ascertain whether the subject is capable of being hypnotized." It is to be hoped that this discussion has been more *hypnopompic* than *hypnogogic*.

hypnophobia   See **hypnopedia.**

hypnopompic   See **hypnopedia.**

hypnoscope   See **hypnopedia.**

hypo (HEYE poh) *n*. This word takes a number of forms: *hypo, hyp* (usually, *the hyp* or *the hyps*), *hip* and *hipps*. They all go back to *hypochondria*, a familiar word, but perhaps you don't know its origin; via Late Latin, from the Greek neuter plural of *hypochondrios* (pertaining to the upper abdomen, once believed to be the seat of melancholy). I dealt with the archaic word *hip* in *British English, A to Zed*, giving as its American equivalent "the blues," and said: "As a noun, it is sometimes spelled *hyp*, revealing its derivation (hypochondria)." *Hypo* and its variants mean "pathological depression," and it is found in the plural as well. Herman Melville, in *Moby Dick, or the Whale* (1851), used it in the expression "when my *hypos* get the upper hand of me," and in *Oldtown Folks* (1869), Harriet Beecher Stowe used it the same way: " ... alleging as a reason that' 'twould bring on her *hypos.*'" In the introduction to *Polite Conversation* (1738), Jonathan Swift writes sarcastically: "Some Abbreviations exquisitely refined; as ... *Hypps*, or *Hippo*, for Hypochondriacks." Robert P. Ward, in *Tremaine; or the Man of Refinement* (1825), has this to say: "Belmont was a melancholy place, and I was dying there of *hyp*!" A 1710 issue of *The Tatler* contains this bit of tattling: "Will Hazzard has got the *Hipps*, having lost to the Tune of Five Hundr'd Pound." In *John de Lancaster* (1800), Richard Cumberland has a character say: "You have caught *the hip* of [i.e., from] your hypochondriac wife," thus clearly revealing the derivation of *hip*. Whether *hypo, hypos, hyp, hyps, hip* or *hips*, it is (or they are) a condition much to be deplored. So, cheer up!

hypocaust (HEYE poh kawst) *n*. The Greek verb *hypokaiein* means "to light (a fire) under (something)"; it is built of the prefix *hypo-* (under) plus *kaiein* (to burn). *Hypokaustos* (heated by a *hypocaust*) has the neuter form *hypokauston*; used as a noun, it led to Latin *hypocaustum* or *hypocauston*, which is the name given to the central heating system of an ancient Roman building, usually a villa or public bath, consisting of a space below the floor containing a furnace and a series of flues for the distribution of the heat. Every ancient Roman villa excavated thus far in Britain contains the remains of a *hypocaust* that follows the pattern described by the first-century Roman architect and engineer Vitruvius. The sense of the word was extended, by transference, to include the meaning "stove," as indicated by a passage in Scott's *Anne of Geierstein* (1829): "The *stube* [room, chamber, apartment] of a German inn derived its name from the great *hypocaust*, or *stove*, which is always strongly heated, to secure the warmth of the apartment in which it is placed." But the original meaning of *hypocaust*, and Vitruvius's description, just go to show that there is nothing new under the floor.

hypocorism (hip OK ur iz'm, hipe-), also **hipocorisma** (hip ok uhr IZ muh, hipe-) *n*. From Greek *hupokorisma, -mos* (pet name), built of *hypo* (in the sense of "somewhat" or "slightly") plus *koros* (boy), *kore* (girl), and related to the verb *hypokorizesthai* (to act like a child, to use child talk), we get *hypocorism*, meaning "pet name"; and from *hypokoristikos*, as used in the phrase *onoma hypokoristikon* (pet name, diminutive), we get *hypocoristic* (hip ok uhr IS tik), meaning "like a pet name," and by extension, "pertaining to the inclination to use endearing terms and euphemisms." Thus, Samuel Pegge (the elder) in *Anonymiana; or Ten Centuries of Observations on Various Authors and Subjects* (1809) wrote: "Harry ... is the free or *hypocoristic* name for Henry." (Strangely enough, the *Oxford Dictionary of English Christian Names* says that *Harry* is the original English form of the name.) That seems obvious but is a clear example of the use of *hypocoristic* and its noun. *Abe, Ben, Chet, Don*—one could run through the alphabet and come up with *hypocorisms* all the way to *Zeke*.

hypocorisma   See **hypocorism**.

hyponoia (heye puh NOY uh) *n*. Occasionally one runs into a word on whose definition dictionaries differ—usually narrowly, on a matter of nuance, once in a while widely, because of divergent etymologies. *Hyponoia* is a case of the latter. *RH* defines it as "dulled mental activity; diminished function of thought" and is satisfied with "HYPO- + -NOIA" as its etymological background. In that dictionary, *hypo-* is traced to Greek *hypo* (under, below), and *-noia* to *no-*, the stem of *noos* or *nous* (mind) + *-ia*; and *-ia* is described as a noun suffix applying in various fields, including diseases. I set great store by *RH*, but I always turn to the *O.E.D.* for support and additional etymological material. Lo and behold: *Hyponoia* is tucked away in a very long list of *hypo-* words and is defined as "underlying meaning." The derivation given is Greek *hyponoia*, from the verb *hyponoein* (to suspect). *CH* tells us that *hypo-*, in composition, means "under; defective; inadequate," and if you connect "defective" with Greek *noos* (mind) you get "defective mind," in harmony with the *RH* definition. But if you then go to *LS*, you find *hyponoia* defined as "a hidden meaning or sense: a suspicion, conjecture, guess, supposition, fancy: the true meaning which lies at the bottom of (a thing)," and see that it comes from the verb *hyponoeein*, meaning, inter alia, "to think covertly, suspect." If you look up *suspicion* in the Woodhouse *English-Greek Dictionary*, you find its Greek equivalent to be our old friend *hyponoia*, supporting the *O.E.D.* and differing from *RH* and *CH*. There used to be a department in *The New Yorker* magazine entitled "What Paper D'ya Read?," in which wildly differing versions of the same news event were quoted from various newspapers. I propose (timidly) to our leading American lexicographer, Laurence Urdang, editor of the language quarterly *Verbatim*, a column entitled "Which Dictionary D'ya Read?," but I suspect (*hyponoeo*) that my proposal will be politely (Laurence is always polite) rejected because of the dearth of material.

hyponymy (heye PON uh mee) *n*. This is a term for a relationship between a pair of words or concepts, one of which is included in the other but the other of which is not included in the first. Example: *horse/quadruped; horse* is included in *quadruped*, in that the term *quadruped* includes *horse*, but it doesn't work the other way around. *Hyponym* (HEYE puh nim) will be discussed later. In *Structural Semantics: An Analysis of Part of the Vocabulary of Plato* (1963) by John Lyons, who has written a number of instructive works in the fields of linguistics in general and semantics in particular, we find a definition of *hyponymy* and some examples: "*Hyponymy* is the relation that holds, for instance, between *scarlet* and *red*, or between *tulip* and *flower* ... It may be defined in terms of unilateral implication [a very helpful phrase: *tulip* implies *flower*, but *flower* does not imply *tulip*; the key word is *imply*]. Thus X *is scarlet* will be understood (generally) to imply X *is red*; but not conversely." To put it another way, *hyponymy* is not a vice-versa relationship. *Hyponym* and *hyponymy* are formed from the Greek prefix *hypo-* (under, shortened to *hyp-* before a vowel) plus *onoma* (name), which figures in *antonym* and *synonym* and other -*nym* words. In another part of his book, Lyons says: "I say that *scarlet* is a *hyponym* of, or is included in, *red*." Note that here, Lyons uses the word *include*, rather than *imply*. In view of the meaning of *hyp(o)-* given above, I would tend to modify the *O.E.D.* definition of *hyponym*: "One of two or more words related by *hyponymy*" so as to make it clear that *hyponym* applies to the word that is *included* (i.e., by *implication*), not the *including* (i.e., general or generic) word. Thus, *scarlet* and *tulip* are *hyponyms*, being *included* in *red* and *flower* respectively, while *red* and *flower* are not *hyponyms*. And note the *two or more* in that definition, which is very helpful, because one might infer, from the examples and quotations under *hyponymy*, that only two words are involved. Obviously, that is not the case: The examples might just as well have been *red, scarlet* and *vermilion*, or *flower, tulip* and *rose*, with the latter two words in each case serving as *hyponyms*.

hypos   See **hypo.**

hypotaxis (heye poh TAX is) *n*. In my *1000 Most Challenging Words*, I discussed *parataxis* (par uh TAX is), the "omission of a connective between clauses or sentences," and gave examples like "Don't worry, I'll see to everything." Here is a famous one: "I came, I saw, I conquered." In *parataxis* (taken intact from the Greek noun meaning "placing side by side"), there are no connectives indicating the relation between the clauses, i.e., whether they are coordinate or subordinate. *Hypotaxis* is the opposite construction, in which a connective is used to indicate the relationship between clauses, which is one of subordination, a dependent arrangement. Example: *I went to Venice because I love the place.* In *parataxis*, it would have been put this way: I went to Venice, I love the place. *Taxis* is "arrangement" in Greek; *para-* is "beyond," *hypo-* is "under," whence we get *subordination.* Don't confuse *hypo-* and *hyper-*, meaning "excessive." Thus, *hypertension* is high blood pressure; *hypotension* is low blood pressure.

hypozeuxis   See **anaphora.**

hypselotimophobia   See **xenodochiophobia.**

ichabod (IK uh bod) *interj.* The first thing that comes to mind on meeting this word (usually capitalized), unless one is unusually familiar with I Sam. 4:21, is Ichabod Crane, the headless horseman of Washington Irving's *Legend of Sleepy Hollow.* But there was a much earlier *Ichabod.* When the pregnant daughter-in-law of the priest Eli heard of the Philistines' defeat of Israel, the deaths of Eli and her husband Phineas and the taking of the ark together with the Torah, her labor pains began, and on giving birth, she named the infant *Ichabod*, from the Hebrew word *i-khabhodh*, meaning "The glory is departed." That word has ever since been used as an exclamation of regret for the good old days. The adjective *Ichabodian* was later coined to mean "regretful" or "lamentable."

ichnite (IHK nite) *n. Ichnos*, in Greek, means "track, footprint"; its combining form is *ichno-*, *ichn-* before a vowel. *Ichnite* means "fossil footprint," especially that of an animal preserved in a rock. The synonym *ichnolite* (IK noh lite) comes from a combination of *ichno-* with *lithos* (stone). *Ichnology* (ik NOL uh jee) and *ichnolithology* (ik noh lith OL uh jee) both mean the "study of fossil footprints," a subsection of paleontology, but they can also denote the *ichnological* features of a given area, i.e., the fossil footprints characteristic of a district, in the same way *flora* and *fauna* are used. *Ichnomancy* (IK noh man see), according to Edward Smedley in *The Occult Sciences* (1855), "is the art of finding out the figure, peculiarities, occupations, &c. of men or beasts by the traces of their posture, position and footsteps." That word combined *ichno-* with a suffix derived from Greek *manteia* (divination). One might think that *ichnography* (ik NAW gruh fee) was the written lore pertaining to fossil footprints, but that is not so: It means "groundplan" or "plan or map of a place." Charles Merivalle, in *A History of the Romans under the Empire* (1865) wrote about "the *ichnography* of the wall of Antoninus," and the word was used in a figurative sense in an 1830 issue of *Fraser's Magazine*: "The theatre is, as it were, the *ichnography* (ground-plan) of a people."

ichnography   See **ichnite.**

ichnolite   See **ichnite.**

ichnolithology   See **ichnite.**

ichnology   See **ichnite.**

ichnomancy   See **ichnite.**

ignoratio elenchi   See **heterozetesis.**

impolder   See **empolder.**

impunitive   See **intropunitive.**

inchoative   See **adscititious.**

inclusio   See **anaphora.**

infangthief (IN fang theef) *n.* In Old English, this was spelled *infangentheof*, and the word was built of the adverb *in-* (in), plus *fangen*, the past particple of the verb *fon* (to seize) plus *theof* (thief). Its literal meaning was thus "thief seized within." *Infangthief* denoted the jurisdiction over a thief caught within the territorial limits of the lord of the manor and the lord's right to try and punish him. This was distinguished from *outfangthief*, the lord's right to pursue a thief, if the miscreant were attached to the manor, bring him back to the lord's own court for trial and keep his forfeited chattels on conviction. This latter right was defined in various ways and circumscribed in the 13th century, by which time its meaning became arguable. Of course, all this is old stuff, and these practices are obsolete. This leads me to make a point: A practice or an artifact may be obsolete, but the word denoting it may not necessarily be so. Thus, a chariot is an obsolete vehicle, but the word *chariot* isn't. The same applies to a penny farthing (the old bicycle with an outsize front wheel), or a biplane or a battle-axe. I make this point to demonstrate that there is a difference between *obscure* and *obsolete* and that a word like *infangthief* may be obscure but isn't obsolete. Otherwise, writers would be unable to produce those interminable historical novels in which people exclaim "Egad!" and "Gadzooks!" and "Tush! Tush!," which are obsolete but not obscure.

inlaut   See **anlaut.**

intimism (IN tuh miz-m) *n.* According to Peter and Linda Murray, in their *Dictionary of Art and Artists* (1959), *intimism* is "a form of Impressionist technique applied to the depiction of everyday life in domestic interiors rather than to landscape. The work of Bonnard and Vuillard is usually meant." This form of painting is based on the selection of intimate and familiar scenes and occasions from the daily routine of the painters themselves, and the term was obviously based on the adjective *intimate.* Another word for the same type of painting is *genre*, which I define in my *1000 Most Important Words* as "an artistic style," which, as applied to painting, "has the special meaning of 'scenes of everyday life,' that tell a story in realistic terms." An *intimist* (sometimes *intimiste*) is a "painter who practices *intimism.*" One meets the term in newspaper art criticism and reviews of painting exhibitions, and it is occasionally used attributively or adjectivally as well.

intimist   See **intimism.**

intinction (in TINK shuhn) *n.* This is the term for a manner (especially in the Eastern Church) of administering Holy Communion by means of dipping the bread into the wine and giving it, thus moistened, to the communicant. This custom was followed in the Western Church from the seventh to the twelfth centuries. Gasquet & Bishop, in their *Edward VI and the Book of Common Prayer* (1890), called *intinction* a "purely oriental rite" but in 1965, it was once more authorized by the Roman Catholic Church as a permissible method. Meaning no disrespect, this practice would appear to be a timesaving but soggy method of delivering the ingredients. The word comes from Late Latin *intinctio* (immersion), based on Latin *intinctus*, the past participle of *intingere* (to dip in), based on the prefix *in-* (in) plus *tingere* (to dip, wet, moisten).

intropunitive (in troh PYOOH nuh tiv) *adj.* Three relatively modern terms in psychology end in *-punitive* and deal with blame, in the sense of censure, reproach: *intropunitive* (sometimes *intrapunitive*), *extrapunitive* and *impunitive*. The *-punitive* ending comes from the Latin *punitus* (the source of our *punitive*), the past participle of *punire* (to punish, chastise); the prefixes are self-explanatory. *To be intropunitive* is "to blame oneself rather than others or external events; to give way to an excessive feeling of responsibility for frustrations or other misfortunes." *Extrapunitive* (ek strah PYOOH nuh tive) applies to persons who blame other people or events unreasonably and react aggressively to frustration. *Impunitive* describes those who are resigned to frustration and blame neither themselves nor others unreasonably. Henry Alexander Murray discussed these psychological problems in *Explorations in Personality* (1938):

> ... He [the patient] may react with emotions of guilt and remorse and tend to condemn himself as the blameworthy object. This type of reaction

may be termed *"intropunitive ."* … He may manifest the emotion of anger and condemn the outer world … for his frustration, adopting an attitude of hostility toward his environment. This type of reaction may be termed *"extrapunitive."* … He may experience emotions of embarrassment and shame, making little of blame and emphasizing instead the conciliation of others and himself to the disagreeble situation. In this case he will be more interested in condoning than condemning and will pass off the frustration as lightly as possible by making references, even at the price of self- deception, to unavoidable circumstances. This type of reaction may be termed *"impunitive."*

John Michael Argyle, in *Religious Behavior* (1958), sums it up this way: "A … personality variable is that of *punitiveness*: people are said to be *extrapunitive* if they react to frustration by aggression directed outwards, *intropunitive* if the aggression is directed inwards, and *impunitive* if they do not react aggressively at all." That's putting it in a nutshell.

iotacism   See **mytacism.**

ipseity   See **proprium.**

isagogic (eye suh GOJ ik, -GOG-) *adj.* This adjective means "introductory." Add an *s* and you have *isagogics*, a plural noun treated as a singular (like *economics, physics*, etc.), which is a division of theological study *introductory* to exegesis, which is defined in my *1000 Most Important Words* as "interpretation, especially of Scripture, but applicable generally." In the context of *isagogics*, we are of course speaking of Biblical interpretation. *Isagogic* is derived from the Greek noun *eisagoge* (introduction), based on the prefix *eis-* (into) plus the verb *agein* (to lead); while *exegesis* (ek suh GEE sis) was taken over intact from the Greek, which was based on the verb *exegeisthai* (to explain), formed of the prefix *ex-* (out) plus *hegeisthai* (to guide). There is no point to studying *isagogics* unless you are going into Biblical *exegesis*.

isodomon (eye SOD uh mon), also **isodomum** (eye SOD uh mum) *n.* This is a form of classical Greek masonry in which uniform blocks are laid in courses of equal height in such a way that the vertical joint between two blocks is placed exactly over the middle of the block below. I remember a film of Churchill in his garden building a brick wall in just that way, and my question to a contemporary bricklayer about this method evoked the reply, "Natch." It does seem logical. The adjective is *isodomous* (eye SOD o muhs) or *isodomic* (eye so DOM ik). *Isodomos* is Greek for "equal-coursed." *Isodomon* is its neuter form, and the word is built on the prefix *iso-*, the combining form of Greek *isos* (equal) plus *domos* (course), related to the verb *demein* (to build).

itacism   See **mytacism.**

ithyphallic (ih thee FAL ik) *adj.* An *ithyphallus* is an "erect penis," from the Greek *ithys* (straight) and *phallos* (penis). As an adjective, *ithyphallic* has a number of meanings. Most commonly, it applies to statues and graphic representations displaying that part of the anatomy in that state or to meter employed in hymns sung at ancient festivals honoring Bacchus, the Greek and Roman god of revelry. The technical description of that meter is *trochaic dimeter brachycatalectic*, as to which we shall attempt to enlighten you without introducing too many new terms: *Trochaic* (troh KAY ik; discussed under **dolichurus**) applies to a foot of two syllables, one stressed followed by one unstressed, as in *spinach*; a *dimeter* (DEYE mee tur) is a verse containing two measures; *brachycatalectic* (brak ee kat uh LEK tik) designates the omission of two syllables at the end of a verse composed of larger metrical units like *dipodies* (DIP uh deez), measures of two feet in which the stress of one is stronger than that of the other—but, unless you're about to write poetry in the classical manner, enough already! Getting back to *ithyphallic* for a moment: It can also apply to the Bacchic festivals of yore or the gigantic phallus carried in those processions. However, getting away from festivals and Bacchus, the adjective, used in a more general or literal way, can apply to the erect phallus itself, and from there it was extended (the meaning, not the phallus) to mean "lustful" and "obscene," which hardly seems fair, for where would the animal world be (nowhere!) without the *ithyphallus*? Incidentally, *ithyphallic* can be used as a noun denoting a poem in *ithyphallic* meter, or more widely, any licentious poem, like (if they can be called poetry) so many of our best limericks.

jabble (JAB'l) *n., vb.* This is British English for "turbulance on the surface of water, choppiness, rippling, splashing" and figuratively, "emotional turmoil, agitation of the mind." As a verb, *to jabble* is "to splash or splatter liquid," whether water in a usually placid pool or tea in a saucer, where, of course, it shouldn't be if you're careful and well mannered. The figurative use to denote emotional disturbance or mental agitation brings to mind the colloquial expression "Don't make waves," meaning "Don't start trouble," often given as advice to someone to avoid bringing up a certain subject that will cause "troubled waters." That, in turn, is an image that brings to mind the hideous old joke about a group of sinners in hell, punished (in the manner of the ingenious tortures fashioned by Dante in *The Divine Comedy*) by having to stand eternally in a brimming cesspool, the surface of which reaches just below their lower lips. A visitor (it might be Dante, led by Virgil) approaches and hears a constant murmuring, almost inaudible, issuing from the cesspool. As the visitors near, the murmur becomes louder and louder, and finally becomes intelligible. They are murmuring to one another: "Don't make waves! Don't make waves!" People in that position, then, shouldn't *jabble*.

jack-leg, jackleg (JA kleg)*n., adj*. A *jack-leg* is an "incompetent person," lacking not only ability and skill but scruples as well. As an adjective, *jackleg* describes such a person, and both noun and adjective express contempt. The British use the term *cowboy* in much the same vein. I define that term in my *British English, A to Zed*, as a "self-employed workman ... who undercuts a skilled man and does a job of awe-inspiring incompetence," a quite different application from the American usage: a "reckless driver." The *O.E.D. Supplement* tells us that it is "freq[uently] used [in American] of lawyers and preachers," and this is borne out in a number of examples supplied, relating to those professions and to carpenters and army officers as well. (The term seems to have originated in Texas.) In a 1974 issue of *American Speech*, we read: "One innovation possibly attributable to population shift is *jackleg preacher* ... " In R. Ottley's *New World A-Coming* (1943), the author tells us about a cult that was " ... augmented by a number of herb doctors, clairvoyants and '*jackleg*' preachers." The *jack-* part of the word seems to come from the name *Jack*, the common nickname for the ubiquitous *John*, hence a generic term for the "common man," while the *-leg* appears to be an echo of that in the pejorative term *blackleg* for "scab." The *Decca Book of Jazz* (1958) speaks of "wandering evangelists and '*Jack-leg*' preachers," and from what we have discovered in recent days about evangelists—those who wander not on foot but by television——*jackleg* seems much too mild a pejorative.

jampan (JAM pan) *n*. In the hill country of India, a vehicle of transportation for ladies is the *jampan*, a type of sedan chair carried by four men. The chair is large and clumsy; it has poles attached to the sides and sometimes a top from which curtains are hung. This contrivance is not nearly as elegant as the sedan chair once used by the French aristocracy before the revolution, with richly attired carriers on either side. The Indian carrier is known as a *jampani* or *jampanee*. *Jampan* and its several variants (*jampaun, jompon*, etc.) come from Bengali *jhampan* and Hindi *jhappan*. John Lang, in *Wanderings in India* (1859), describes "ladies and gentlemen on horseback, and ladies in *janpans* [sic]—the *janpanees* dressed in every variety of livery," and *The Times* (London) of August 17, 1879 tells us: "Every lady on the hills keeps her *jampan* and *jampanees*, just as in the plains she keeps her carriage and footmen." India fanciers, including my wife, tell me that transportation by *jampan* is a very comfortable way of mounting staircases.

jampani   See **jampan.**

jerque (JURK) *vb*. This term may be related to the Italian verb *cercare*, meaning "to search." In view of its form and sense, it seems like a pretty good guess. The *O.E.D.* says that "historical evidence is wanting," but it's the best we can do. *To jerque* is "to search a vessel for smuggled goods" or "to examine its papers in order to ascertain whether its manifest and the custom office's cargo lists are in agreement, and to make sure that all the cargo has been properly entered and accurately described." A *jerquer* is a "custom-house officer charged with the duty of examining a ship's papers to verify that all is in order with respect to the manifest." An 1867 *Sailor's Word-book* defines *jerquing a vessel* as "a search performed by the *jerquer* of the customs, after a vessel is unloaded, to see that no unentered goods have been concealed." Nowadays a lot more *jerquing* might well be in order, with respect to aircraft as well as vessels, to root out the importation of narcotics.

jumart (JOOH mart) *n.* Fabled monsters of many descriptions have long existed in legend, mythology and the imagination of people throughout the world. They "exist" in many ancient religions, especially Egyptian and Greek. The sphinx is probably the best known in the world; the griffin, with the head and wings of an eagle and the body of a lion, and the unicorn are familiar legendary monsters. The *jumart* was at first taken quite seriously: a hybrid, the offspring of a bull and a mare or a female ass, or that of a horse or ass and a cow. No less a person than the philosopher John Locke (*An Essay Concerning Human Understanding*, 1690) considered such a union possible: "We have Reason to think this not impossible, since Mules, and *Gimars* [Locke's spelling], the one from the mixture of an Horse, and an Ass, the other from the mixture of a Bull, and a Mare, are so frequent in the World." Locke erred, of course, and by 1809 an article in *The Philosophical Transactions of the Royal Society* mentioned "a *jumart* [JOOH mart; taken from the French; formerly *jumare*, an adaptation of modern Provençal *gemerre, gemarre*, origin unknown] ... the *pretended* offspring of the mare and the bull." Except for rare aberrations by man, animals are pretty fussy in their choice of mates.

kalyptra See **zucchetto.**

karakia (ka ra KEE uh) *n., vb. Karakia* is a Maori incantation. The word comes up in a number of books about Maori customs and culture. The clearest definition appears in Peter Henry Buck's *The Coming of the Maori* (1949):

> The priests established oral communication with their gods by means of *Karakia*. A *Karakia* may be defined as a formula of words which was chanted to obtain benefit or avert trouble ... They cover a range which exceeds the bounds of religion. It is therefore impossible for one English word to cover adequately all the meanings of *Karakia*. All *Karakia* are chants but there are a number of chants ... which are not *Karakia* ... Probably incantation is the nearest in general meaning.

It might be well to define *incantation*: "magical formula, spell, charm; the chanting of words purporting to have magical power." This word comes to us via Late Latin *incantatio*, from Latin *incantare* (to chant, enchant, bewitch). Such incantations are of course not peculiar to Maoris; they are used and heard in many, if not most, primitive cultures. Stage "magicians" (to go from the sublime to the phony) use them all the time: *hocus-pocus* is a pretended incantation used in magic and juggling shows; *toutous talontus* and *vade celerita jubes* were additional ridiculous mock Latin incantations reeled off by conjurors in the old vaudeville days, and though I can't find it in the dictionaries, *abracadabra* was favored as well. These silly "incantations" are not intended to denigrate the serious *Karakia* or the incantations of any culture. *Karakia* is used as a verb as well: intransitively, "to chant *karakia*"; transitively, "to put a spell on (someone) by so doing."

kelebe   See **krater.**

klismos (KLIZ mos, -muhs) *n*. In ancient Greece, this was the name of a chair designed with a concavely carved back rail that curved forward from the back and with legs that curved upward and inward from the floor, in the form of a shallow letter *c*. The name was taken intact from Greek *klismos* (chair, couch), akin to the verb *klinein* (to lean, recline). The style of the *klismos* was often imitated during periods of classical Greek revival and was popular in the early 19th century. Specimens of the revival imitations can still be found in antique shops and at auctions. I have sat in one and found it rather uncomfortable, but then, though I don't like the way they look, I like to snuggle into the over-stuffed variety.

kobold (KOH bold) *n*. We have taken this word intact from the German, where a *Kobold* is a "hobgoblin, elf or sprite." The etymology is uncertain, but some relate the word to Dutch *kabouter* and Middle Dutch *cobout*. A *kobold*, a character in German folklore, is a household sprite, sometimes rather tricky and slippery, and not always to be trusted. He is akin to a brownie, who can be very helpful when nobody's looking and assist a great deal with the household chores, scoring "brownie points" in recognition of services rendered, like a good husband who does the dishes or bathes the kids even after a hard day at the office. Another version of the *kobold* in folklore is that of the gnome that dwells undergound, haunting caves and mines. James Russell Lowell, in *Among My Books* (1870), used the term in a quite dramatic figurative sense; "There in the corner is the little black *kobold* of a doubt making mouths at him." Doubts *can* be as disturbing as little black imps making mouths at one.

krater, also **crater** (KRADE ur, KRAH tur) *n*. The Greek word *krater* means "mixing bowl" for mixing wine and water, i.e., diluting the wine. The bowl was used in ancient days by Greeks and Romans. Unlike the more or less familiar amphora, the *krater* had lower handles, a much wider mouth, a much more capacious body and a flat round base. It came in various sizes. One variety of *krater*, known as a *kelebe* (KEL uh bee), was ovoid in shape, with handles that dropped straight down to the shoulder of the jar from horizontal extensions of the rim. That word came from the Greek *kelebe*, which R. M. Cook, in *Greek Painted Pottery* (1960), called "a conventional name for a *column crater*." Our word *crater*, in the sense of "volcano opening," came from the Latin *crater* or *cratera* (mixing vessel, wine or punch bowl), which in turn came from the Greek *krater*. Other types of Greek jars were the *hydria* (HEYE dree uh), based on *hydros* (water), a large jar in which water was carried, having two, sometimes three handles; and the *stamnos* (STA mnos), based on *sta-*, the combining form of *istanai* (to cause to stand), a two-handled jar with a neck shorter than that of the *hydria*. One finds examples of some of these jars not only in the museums but while wandering in Greek villages, a highly recommended form of exercise.

kwashiorkor (kwah shee OR kur) *n.* This is a term native to Ghana denoting those terrible cases of malnutrition in infants and children, causing stunting, skin and hair color changes, edema (abnormal puffy swelling), liver degeneration, anemia and the type of apathy one sees in those horrifying television films of starvation in African countries. The underlying cause is a diet lacking in protein and excessively high in carbohydrate. No doubt there are as many obscure words to designate this condition as there are regions where it exists (there's not much point in going into Ethiopian and Sudanese dialects), but the very fact that there is even a word for it is horrifying in itself. Let's hope that this word (and its equivalents in other regions) will one day be not only obscure but obsolete, or at least of only historical interest. An article in *The Times* (London) as far back as December 2, 1959, wrote of a " … hospital doctor [who] described the incidence of *kwashiorkor* as 'needless slaughter' which could easily be prevented by funds for milk and other proper nourishment." In 1971 a Cape Town journal called *Progress*, writing of a medical research organization, wrote: "One of the unit's major achievements was to prove that the cure of *kwashiorkor* … could be initiated by the administering of a synthetic skimmed milk." Need more be said?

labarum   See **chi-rho.**

lallation   See **psellism.**

latria   See **dulia.**

lazaret   See **clapperdudgeon.**

lazaretto   See **clapperdudgeon.**

lazar-house   See **clapperdudgeon.**

levirate (LEV uh ruht, LEEV-, -rate) *n. Levir* is Latin for "brother-in law" but only in the restricted sense of "husband's brother," as opposed to "sister's husband." It was compulsory among the ancient Hebrews for a brother, or if none existed, the next of kin of a deceased husband, to marry a childless widow. This curious custom, known as the *levirate*, prevailed in certain other nations as well. The word can be used attributively, as in *levirate marriage*, but the adjective *leviratic* (lev uh RAT ik) or *leviratical* (lev uh RAT uh kuhl) is used as well; and the term *leviration* (lev uh RAY shuhn) denotes such a marriage. We find these words in Renan's *Life of Jesus* (1863) which reads in translation: "The Mosaic code had consecrated this patriarchal theory by a strange institution, the *levirate* law." Matt: 22:24 is cited as the authority for the ancient rule that the firstborn son of such a marriage is deemed the son of the deceased brother: " ... Moses said, If a man die, having no children, his brother shall marry his wife, and raise up seed unto his brother." When a younger brother of the deceased marries the widow, the marriage is known as a "junior *levirate*." *Polygyny* (the custom of having multiple wives) was common in ancient societies, including the Hebrew. *Sororal polygyny* from Latin *soror* (sister) is one in which the wives are sisters. Another custom quite apart from *levirate* is *sororate* (suh ROH ruht) denoting marriage with two or more sisters, usually successively, after a first wife has been found to be barren, or after her death. These ancient marriage arrangements so alien to modern societies were considered quite normal in ancient times.

leviratic(al)   See **levirate.**

leviration   See **levirate.**

lickerish (LIK ur ish) *adj.* It sounds like that chewy black stuff that comes in long strips and blackens your tongue, but it isn't. That's *licorice* or *liquorice*. *Lickerish* describes one fond of good food, not necessarily a gourmet or an epicurean: just somebody who likes good eating and is rather eager to savor the experience. Its meaning has been expanded to reflect the desire for other things, such as wine, women and song—i.e., "desirous" generally—and in context, subject to lustful cravings, even to the point of serving as a synonym for *lecherous*, with which it appears to have an etymological connection. There was a time when *lickerish* meant "tempting" (to the appetite) and "dainty," but those uses are now obsolete. The word appears to have come from the obsolete adjective *lickerous*, from Old North French, as a variant of Old French *lechereus*. There are a number of variant spellings, the most frequent of which is *liquorish*. In connection with the enjoyment of fare, we find in W. E. Heitland's *Quintius Curtius* (1879) the description of one who drank "rather by good fellow-ship than from a *liquorish* appetite." In the sense of "desirous" or "greedy" generally, Jonathan Swift, in *A Tale of a Tub* (1704), wrote of "a *liquorish* affection to gold." In *The First Part of King Edward the Fourth* (1600), Thomas Heywood wrote: "Go to Hell … ye may be caught, I tell ye: these by *liquorish* lads," using this versatile word in the sense of "lecherous, lustful." A useful and dramatic word; too bad it has gone out of style.

liquorish   See **lickerish.**

literal (LIT uh ruhl) *n.* In its common function as an adjective, *literal* is hardly an obscure word. A *literal translation* is a "word-for-word translation." The *literal meaning* of a word is its "primary or strict meaning," as opposed to its figurative or metaphorical sense. Thus, *thunder* is the loud, explosive noise resulting from the expansion of air heated by lightning; that is its *literal* meaning. But the *thunder* of hoofs or of applause has nothing to do with this meteorological phenomenon; there, *thunder* is used in its figurative sense of a resounding noise like the one associated with lightning. But *literal* has another, entirely distinct use as a noun. A *literal* is a "misprint of a letter in type or writing," the kind proofreaders are supposed to ferret out when they *reed* a *manuescript*. This is a usage that appears more often in British than American English. In either sense, *literal* comes, via Late Latin *litteralis*, from Latin *littera* (letter of the alphabet; in the plural, *litterae*, an epistle, or "letters" in the sense of "literature").

lithodipyra (lith oh duh PEYE ruh) *n.* In 1769 the Coade family took over a factory in Lambeth, a borough of South London, where a type of artificial stone had been made and continued to be made until about 1837. They gave it the name *lithodipyra*, forming the word from *litho-*, the combining form of Greek *lithos* (stone), plus *di-*, the combining form of *dis* (twice), plus *pyr* (fire): stone twice fired. This was the process of manufacture of the artificial stone made in that factory, which was also called *Coade Stone*. The manufacturer claimed that the artificial stone was more resistant to both heat and frost than natural stone. The product was used quite extensively for monuments, statues and fancy stone work in general. The firm advertised in 1778: "Coade's *lithodipyra* or artificial stone manufactory. For all kinds of statues, capitals, vases, tombs, coats of arms, & architectural ornaments &c. &c." A monument to Edward Wortley Montagu (d. 1761), the ambassador to Turkey and husband of the English writer Lady Mary Wortley, is in the cloisters of Westminster Abbey. Friends who have have seen the statue say that it is in excellent condition and looks like natural stone. The name *lithodipyra* attests to some knowledge of classical Greek on the part of the Coade family, an attribute far more common in those days than would be the case today.

lithonthryptic   See **lithotrity.**

lithontripist   See **lithotrity.**

lithontriptic   See **lithotrity.**

lithontriptor   See **lithotrity.**

lithotripist   See **lithotrity.**

lithotripsy   See **lithotrity.**

lithotripter   See **lithotrity.**

lithotriptic   See **lithotrity.**

lithotriptor   See **lithotrity.**

lithotrite   See **lithotrity.**

lithotritic   See **lithotrity.**

lithotritist   See **lithotrity.**

lithotritize   See **lithotrity.**

lithotritor   See **lithotrity.**

lithotrity (lith OT rih tee), also **lithotripsy** (LITH oh trip see) *n.* These nouns are alternative terms for the surgical operation of crushing stones in the bladder into particles small enough to be passed through the urethra. *Lithotrity* is formed of the Greek noun *lithos* (stone) plus *tritus*, the past participle of the Latin verb *terere* (to rub, wear away), thus forming a hybrid word, one formed from elements taken from different languages. *Lithotripsy* comes from the same *lithos* plus Greek *tripsis* (rubbing). The surgical instrument used in this operation has a variety of names, formed from the above sources: *lithotrite* (LITH oh trite), *lithotritor* (lith oh TREYE tuhr), *lithotriptor* (lith oh TRIP tuhr) and *lithontriptor* (lith on TRIP tuhr; *lithon* is the genitive plural of *lithos*). The adjectives are *lithotritic* (lith oh TRIT ik), *lithotriptic* (lith oh TRIP tik), *lithontriptic* (lith on TRIP tik) and *lithonthryptic* (lith on THRIP tik; *thryptika* means "breakers," related to *thryptein*, to shatter). All four adjectives are also used as substantives denoting medicines that produce the same result. To *lithotritize* (lith OT ruh tize) a patient is to perform the operation on him or her. *Lithotritist* (lith OT rih tist), *lithotripist* (lith oh TRIP ist) and *lithontripist* (lith on TRIP ist), as you might predict, are all terms for the surgeon performing the operation. Now that we have gone into all those variations relating to a surgical procedure practiced since the 19th century, we must introduce the term *lithotripter* (note the *e*), an instrument currently in use for reducing kidney stones to tiny particles, using shock waves instead of resorting to surgery to produce the same result. The derivation is the same as that of *lithotriptor* (note the final *o*), the vowel being changed merely to distinguish between the old surgical device and the new technique.

litotes (LEYED uh teez, LID-, leye TOHD eez, and some authorites prefer *t* to *d* in all cases) *n. Litotes*, however you choose to pronounce it, is one of the many kinds of figures of speech, i.e., expressive or fanciful forms of language using words in other than their literal sense, as in "apple of his eye," "a horse of a different color," "a different kettle of fish," and "forever chasing rainbows." There are many different kinds of *tropes* as such figures are called. In previous books I have dealt with some of them: In *1000 Most Important Words* I discussed *euphemism, hyperbole, metaphor* and *simile*; in *1000 Most Challenging Words, hyperbaton, metonymy* and *synecdoche*. Now comes *litotes*, meaning an "understatement, especially one in which an affirmative is expressed by the negative of its contrary" (the opposite of *hyperbole* or exaggeration). Examples: *Not bad*, meaning "very good"; *not easy*, for "very difficult." The British use their own brand of *litotes*: *not half*, which is discussed in my *British English A to Zed*, from which I quote: " ... In describing the boss's reaction when he came in and found everybody out to lunch, a porter might say, 'He *didn't half* blow up,' meaning that he did blow up about as completely as possible. In other words, *not half* is used ironically, meaning 'not half—but totally.'" *Litotes* was taken, via New Latin, from the Greek, where it was a diminutive of *litos* (simple, plain, meager). It might be said that some of the discussion in this book is *not at all brief*.

locofoco (loh koh FOH koh) *n*. This peculiar concoction appears to have been fashioned from the *loco-* of *locomotive* (under the mistaken notion that *locomotive* meant "self-propelled") plus a rhyming corruption of the Italian word *fuoco* (fire). Says the *O.E.D.*: " ... the inventor would hardly think of Latin *focus* (hearth), which is the source of the modern Roman word for 'fire.'" Whatever the source, the word is the name of a match or cigar invented in the 19th century which could be ignited by being rubbed against any rough surface. It was described in the Springfield, Massachusets, *Union* as "a decided improvement over the lucifers," matches tipped with antimony sulfide and potassium chloride, which could be ignited by friction against a hard surface. But now comes the amusing part: *Locofoco*, usually capitalized, became the name of the "Equal Rights" or radical section of the American Democratic Party as a result of an event at a meeting on October 22, 1835, of New York City Democrats.

The radical members were forewarned of a plot by the opposition to break up the meeting by putting out the lights; they came armed with *locofoco* matches and candles and thus foiled the plot. This happened at Tammany Hall, and immediately after the event the *Courier and Examiner*, a Whig newspaper, and the *Times*, a Democratic journal, gave the name *"Locofoco Party"* to the radicals, and the label soon thereafter was applied to the whole Democratic party. This is, of course, fairly ancient American political history, but one must be fond of words that come to designate things as disparate as self-igniting matches (or cigars) and political parties.

longanimity (long uh NIM uh tee) *n.* This word denotes patience, fortitude, forbearance and especially the long-suffering endurance of hardship. The adjective that describes one exhibiting such qualities is *longanimous* (long AN uh muhs), and that is surely an apt description of Job in his hardship and patience. The derivation is from Late Latin *longanimitas*, built on Latin *longus* (long) and *animus* (mind, spirit, soul). Another word involving *animus* is *parvanimity* (pahr van IM it ee), meaning "meanness," the quality of having a little or ignoble mind or spirit, and this word involves Latin *parvus* (little). *Parvanimity* is obviously the antithesis of the more familiar quality of mind known as *magnanimity*, but nowhere do I find a listing of *"parvanimous"* as the antithesis of *magnanimous*. Nonetheless, I hereby coin the adjective *parvanimous* and without publishing their names, hereby confer it upon several people I know.

longanimous   See **longanimity.**

lorimer (LAWR ih mur) also **loriner** (LAWR ih nur) *n.* We start with Latin *lorum* (thong, strap), then via Late Latin *loramentum* (harness) proceed to Old French *loremier*, French *lormier* (from obsolete French *lorain*, the straps, often studded with metal or gems, that were used in the harness and trappings of a horse), and arrive, finally, at *lorimer*, "one who makes metal parts of horse harnesses," like bits, metal mountings for bridles, spurs and, more generally, small ironware and works of wrought iron. (Those who specialize in the making of spurs are known as *spurriers*.) People don't commonly speak of *lorimers* by that name today, and it persists only in the title of one of the livery companies. And what are livery companies? They are the descendants of the old city of London craft guilds. (The City of London, presided over by the Lord Mayor, and sometimes known as the "square mile," is the financial district of London.) The name *livery company* derives from the fact that their members used to wear distinctive livery, i.e. uniforms, on special occasions. These companies date back to the early 14th century. I have attended a number of annual livery company dinners, very formal affairs involving evening dress, huge dinners, speeches and loving cups—large drinking vessels with two or more handles, unhygienically passed around at banquets. There are 12 "great companies" and more than 70 "lesser companies." Many of them still maintain halls in the City and contribute to charities, almshouses and schools. The *Lorimers'* Company is one of the lesser category. John Holland wrote a book entitled *A Treatise on the Progressive Improvement and Present State of the Manufacture in Metal* (1833) in which he informs us that "The manufacture of all the metallic parts of horse furniture was carried on ... by artisans, incorporated under the denomination of *loriners* and *spurriers*." (Note the alternative spelling *loriners*.) This was the *Company of Lorimers*.

lulab   See **ethrog.**

lulal   See **ethrog.**

lulov   See **ethrog.**

lumpectomy (lump EK tuh mee) *n.* This quite unpleasant-sounding medical term for the excision of a lump from the body, usually involving the female breast, is a horrible example of a hybrid word, i.e., one built of components taken from different languages. (*Hybrid* itself comes from the Latin *hybrida*, a variant of *hibrida*, and applies to anything composed of elements from heterogeneous sources, like the offspring of animals or plants of different species, or persons whose parents come from different ethnic groups, or words like *lumpectomy*.) Hybrid words are unpopular among linguistic purists, who commonly offer *television* as an example, *tele-* being of Greek origin (*tele*, far) and *vision* of Latin origin (*visio*, view). In the case of *lumpectomy*, we have *lump-*, from Middle English *lumpe*, and believed to be cognate with Early Dutch *lompe* (piece) and certain Scandinavian words, while *-ectomy* is a combining form meaning "excision," taken from New Latin *-ectomia*, based on Greek *ek* (out of) plus *-tomos* (cutting). I have no objection to hybrids, whether in the animal world (I love mules), the plant world (I am a hybrid rose fancier) or the world of language, provided that the result has a pleasant sound. Would all-Latin *proculvision* or all-Greek *teleopsis* roll off the tongue more smoothly than good old *television*? But *lumpectomy*? No, especially when *tylectomy* (*tulos*, Greek for "lump") might fill the bill. Let's excise the *lump-* from *lumpectomy* and fill the space with *tyl-*.

lungi, also **lungyi, longye** (LOON gee, -jee) *n.* From the Hindu word, which in turn came from Persian, a *lungi* is a type of cloth, usually cotton, used for such articles of attire as sarongs, skirts and turbans, as seen especially in India, Pakistan and Burma. In India it also has the special meaning of a piece of cotton cloth between two and three yards long, wrapped around the waist several times and worn as a loincloth. It lends a particular grace to the body that somehow cannot be imitated by Western people. Strangely, on a Western man or woman, no matter how young, slim and graceful, it just doesn't look right; in fact, it looks conspicuously wrong. *Lungis* have changed over the years. In 1634 Sir Thomas Herbert (*A Relation of Some Yeares Travaile Begunne Anno 1626*, *into Afrique and the Greater Asia*) described it in these terms: "A *lung* to conceale their privy members." Not long thereafter, in a 1662 travel book that included a translation of *"the travels of J.A. de Mandelslo from Persia into the East-Indies,"* John Davies of Kidwelly wrote of "Some Common-cloaths ... of those kinds which are commonly called ... *Longis* ... &c." In 1698 John Fryer (*A New Account of East India and Persia*) wrote: "The Peer as well as Peasant, wrapping only a *Lunga* about his middle ... " and (not quite consistent about his spelling—or was it the printer?) a little later in the same book wrote: "The Men and Women came down together to wash, having *Lungies* about their wastes only." Things got somewhat more elaborate by 1727 when, in *New Account of the East Indies*, Alexander Hamilton wrote: "His Dress was only a Silk *Lungie* or Scarf made fast by a Girdle of Gold Plate, about his Middle." Silk, mind you! And by 1901 an item in the *Daily News* (London) told of "Indian soldiers ... wearing *lungis* of beautifully woven silk." The *lungi* hangs down only to the knee, leaving the legs exposed, and presents a much neater appearance than the *dhoti*, the long loincloth worn by Hindu men. As for Hindu ladies, I'll take the sari any day.

lycanthropy   See **zoanthropy.**

macaronic   See **swasivious.**

macroscian (ma KROH shee uhn) *adj., n.* As an adjective, this word describes anyone or anything casting a long shadow. It comes from the Greek *makroskios*, built of *makro-*, the combining form of *makros* (long) and *skia* (shadow). As a noun, it means (according to the *O.E.D.*) "one having a long shadow, an inhabitant of the polar regions." See **amphiscian**, where I discuss *periscian* and define it as "one who resides in a polar circle, whose shadow moves around him in a complete circle on those days on which the sun does not set." Here we have a bit of a conflict, i.e., between *macroscian* and *periscian*, unless it be the case that the *periscian*'s shadow not only moves around him but is also a long one. Osbert Sitwell used *macroscian* metaphorically in the expression "that *macroscian* day which I had dreaded for so long," apparently a day far ahead on which something dire was bound to happen. *W III* tells us that *macroscian* has to do with long shadows but is silent on the matter of polar regions. Under *macroscian*, the kindly *O.E.D.* refers us to the entry *antiscian*, an adjective pertaining to the *antiscii*, who are those who dwell on the same meridian but on opposite sides of the equator, with the result that their shadows at noon fall in opposite directions. (The derivation of *antiscian* is surely obvious.) Better study this discussion together with that covering **amphiscian** to get the whole thrilling story.

macroscopic (mak ruh SKOP ik) *adj.* You ought to be able to figure this one out, but you never can tell. It's really quite simple: Since *microscopic* is an everyday word whose everyday meaning is "tiny," literally, "so tiny that you can't see it without the use of a microscope," but loosely just "very small," *macroscopic* is an antonym whose meaning is what you might expect: "large enough to be visible to the naked eye." It has a synonym, *megascopic*, which happens to be used especially in the study of rocks, and denotes those whose physical features are visible to the unaided eye. Why so? Nobody knows, as far as my pumping of geologists could determine. Anyway, it should be predictable that the *micro-* in *microscopic* is the combining form of Greek *mikros* (small) and that the *macro-* in *macroscopic* bears the same relationship to Greek *makros* (long). As for *megascopic*, we are all too dismally familiar with the prefix *mega-*, the combining form of Greek *megas* (large, great), from the terrifying word *megaton*, which has to do with the destructive force of the H-bomb. (A megaton—pay attention, class—is an "explosive force equivalent to that of a million tons of TNT.") All of these *-scopic* words make use of the combining form of the Greek verb *skopein* (to look at). The *-ton* in *megaton* is just plain old *ton*, from Middle English *tonne*, so that *megaton* is one of those hybrid words (words composed of elements drawn from different languages, like *television*) that outrage linguistic purists. (Television outrages me for other reasons as well.)

malapert (MAL uh purt) *adj.* A *malapert* person is "impudent, bold, saucy, forward, presumptuous"—quite a collection of unpleasant traits. In Old French, it meant "unskillful," based on *mal*, from Latin *malus* (bad) plus *appert* (a modification of *espert*, from Latin *expertus*, "tested, approved, experienced," but understood in English as if *apert*, old French for "open, outspoken," from Latin *apertus*, frank, straightforward). Shakespeare liked the word. In *Twelfth Night*, Act IV, Scene 1, Sir Toby Belch and Sebastian are having it out. Says Sebastian: "If thou dar'st me further, draw thy sword." Sir Toby answers: "What, what! Nay then, I must have an ounce or two of this *malapert* blood from you." (*Draws.*) In Act V, Scene 5 of *Henry VI, Part 3*, George, Duke of Clarence, chides Prince Edward: "Untutor'd lad, thou are too *malapert*." Queen Margaret, in Act I, Scene 3 of *Richard III*, tells Dorset: "Peace! Master marquess, you are *malapert* ... " In each case, it was impudence that was being checked. In Scott's *The Bethrothed* (1825), a lass is told: "You are too *malapert* for a young maiden." Ben Jonson used the word as an adverb in *Epicaene: or the Silent Woman* (1609): "It angred me to the soule, to heare hem beginne to talk so *malapert*." Steele, in *The Tattler* (1709), used it as a noun: "The *Malapert* knew well enough I laughed at her." In his *Comedies of Terence Translated into Blank Verse* (1765), George Colman (the elder) made the same use of the word: "Away, you *malapert*! Your forwardness/Had well nigh ruined me." However the word is used, the person in question obviously deserves to be taken down a peg or two.

malison   See **catmalison**.

malversation (mal vur SAY shuhn) *n*. The general meaning of this word is "breach of trust in public office, or in any position of trust; corrupt administration," details of which have been filling many a news column these troubled days (but wasn't it always thus?). According to all the dictionaries I have consulted, the term covers just about every aspect of misbehavior (extortion, bribery, embezzlement, misappropriation, disloyalty) in positions of public or private trust. The word was taken over intact from the French, where it appears to mean "peculation" or "embezzlement" generally, with no particular reference to public office or trust. The French took it from two Latin words: *male* (badly) and *versatus*, the past participle of *versare* (to keep turning about, twist around), whose passive form, *versari*, means "to behave, keep busy, occupy oneself." *Versare* is itself an interesting word, in that it is the frequentative of *vertere* (to turn). And what, pray, is a frequentative? As explained in my *1000 Most Challenging Words*, a *frequentative* is a verb that "serves to express the frequent repetition" of an action covered by another verb. In other words, to *versare* (as it were) is to *vertere* (as it were) repetitiously, i.e., to keep on *vertere*-ing. Even the innocent-sounding verb *vertere* itself had a sinister extended meaning as used by Cicero, in the expression *vertere ad se* (to turn [something] to oneself; in other, more direct, words, to appropriate, or in less delicate terms, to steal, swipe, snitch or pinch [somebody else's property]). If you keep doing that you qualify for the frequentative, and jail.

Manichaean (man ih KEE uhn) *adj., n*. This is a somewhat overworked, voguish, little understood and both loosely and improperly applied adjective and noun that stem from the Persian religious teacher Manichaios, also known as Mani and Manes (c. 215–275), who began his teaching c. 240. Properly, this word applies to his doctrine holding that the world was controlled by two antagonistic powers, Good (light, God and the spirit) and Evil (darkness, Satan or chaos and the body.) Only through total asceticism could the pure spirit be freed from physical sensuality. He claimed that Jesus Christ had been sent into the world to banish darkness and restore light (i.e., to do away with evil and make goodness triumphant), but that his apostles had perverted that doctrine and he, Manicaios, had been sent to Earth as the Paraclete (the intercessor—a term applied to the Holy Ghost) to set matters right. Manichaeism influenced many Christian sects (St. Augustine was a Manichaean for nine years) and was denounced as a heresy, though it survived into the 13th century in Asia and elsewhere. In his "On Language" column in the *New York Times* of June 12, 1988, William Safire had much to say about the unrestrained and oversimplified use of *Manichaean* by American political pundits in phrases like "an unending *Manichaean* East-West death struggle," "a *Manichaean* view of the world that he [Nixon] sees as divided between the bad Soviet Union and the good United States" and "Reagan's *Manichaean* division of the world into the Good and Evil Empires." "Whence," asks Safire, "this voguish evocation of an obscure figure fogbound in the mists of history?" (Admirable Safirian evocative eloquence, if I may say so!) He quotes William F. Gavin as follows: "We all know that politicians don't have a clue about the esoteric complexities of *Manichaean* theology ... Accusing a politician of harboring a *Manichaean* view of the world is a shorthand way of saying this poor chucklehead lacks sophistication, is ignorant of nuances, and doesn't know—yokel that he is—that there is no black or white, but only shades of gray." Gavin suggests " ... a moratorium on applying theological labels to political figures who, poor souls (so to speak), have enough trouble with ordinary language ... " Amen.

maniple   See **phelonion.**

manticore (MAN tih kor) *n.* This is the name of a mythical beast, part lion, part scorpion, with the head of a man. Also in the form *manticora*, the word comes, via Latin *manticora*, from Greek *mantichoras*, apparently an erroneous reading of *marti(o)choras*, an old Persian word for "man eater." In some versions, the beast is equipped as well with porcupine's quills, and in heraldry, with dragon's feet and spiral horns: however you look at it, a complex and terrifying beast. In *The Water Babies*, the English novelist and clergyman Charles Kingsley writes of "unicorns, firedrakes, *manticoras*." A *firedrake*, in Germanic mythology, was a fiery dragon; in *Beowulf*, we read of "fyr-draca," and in *Hereward the Wake* the same Kingsley wrote: "He expected the enchanter to enter upon a *fire drake*." Obviously, Kingsley liked mythical beasts, especially *firedrakes*, and why not?

manualiter   See **pedaliter.**

mast   See **pannage.**

matrass (MA truhs) *n.* This word, pronounced, as you can see, just like the *mattress* of a bed, has two distinct meanings. The principal one is a "glass flask with a round or oval body and a long neck, once used to dissolve substances by heating the bottle, or for distilling." The other meaning is "bolt" or "bolt head," also called "quarrel," a short, thick, square- or blunt-headed arrow to be shot from a crossbow. (The strange use of *quarrel* in this connection derives from Old French *quar(r)el*, which the C.O.D. relates to a conjectural Romanic noun *quadrellus*, diminutive of Late Latin *quadrus*, square.) *W III* gives only the first definition but adds "—also called *bolt head.*" The O.E.D. gives both definitions, "quarrel or bolt for the cross-bow" and one similar to the first one given above (the glass vessel with a long neck ...) and adds the note: "By some considered to be a transferred use of *matrass* [in its meaning of 'bolt' or 'quarrel' to be shot from a crossbow] with reference to the shape of the vessel." Other possible derivations are suggested, but I like the "transferred use" bit, which goes a long way to explain how one word, which sounds like a bed mattress but isn't one, can have two such wildly disparate meanings. The byways and back alleys of etymology never cease to amuse and bemuse. By the way, a special type of crossbow is the *arbalest* (AR buh luhst), which had a steel bow instead of a string. It was used in medieval times as a weapon and was capable of shooting balls and stones as well as quarrels. This word was derived from the *ar-* of Latin *arcus* (bow) plus Latin *ballista*, a Roman military device for projecting large stones and the source of our term *ballistics*.

matroclinous (mat roh KLEYE nuhs), also **matroclinal** (mat roh KLEYE nuhl), **matroclinic** (mat roh KLIN ik) *adj.* All of these forms mean the same thing (in the field of genetics, not the inheritance of worldly goods): "inherited from the mother or the maternal line." The derivation is from either Latin or Doric Greek *mater* plus Greek suffix *-klines* (leaning), from the verb *klinein* (to lean) or Latin *clinare* (to lean). In any event, put the Latin and Greek elements together; don't mix them and get a hybrid word like *television*, in which the prefix *tele-* is from the Greek and the rest is from the Latin. As you might expect, dad is not neglected, for we have as well *patro-* words matching those *matro-* forms listed above, with the derivation based on Latin or Greek *pater* and the same suffixes. In the case of both *matro-* and *patro-* types, we also have the words *matrocliny* and *patrocliny*, each accented on the third syllable, *-KLEYE-*, and denoting, respectively, resemblance to mother or dear old dad.

matrocliny   See **matroclinous**.

mazer   See **hanap**.

megascopic   See **macroscopic**.

melisma (muh LIZ muh) *n.* The original meaning of *melisma* was "song, melody, air." Grove's *Dictionary of Music* excludes from its definition "recitative or any passage of purely declamatory nature," and says that it is not entirely correct to use *melisma* in the sense of "fioritura" (florid musical embellishment) or "cadenza" (a parenthetic flourish that interrupts an aria or other solo, usually performed by the soloist toward the end of a concerto, sometimes improvised and always technically brilliant regardless of authorship). *Melisma* was taken intact from the Greek meaning "song" or "melody," and is based on the verb *melodein* (to sing), from *melos* (song), which plays a part in the etymology of *melody*: *melos*, plus *-oidia*, from *adein* (to sing; the Greeks had more than a word for it). But usage changes: *W II* included in its definition "a grace or melodic embellishment ... less correctly, a cadenza," and *W III* extended its definition to include "melodic embellishment or ornamentation" and "cadenza," as well as a "group of notes or tones sung to one syllable in plainsong," defining *plainsong* in various ways, including "nonmetrical monophonic chant ... used today in some liturgical churches," viz., *Glo-o-o-ria in Excelsis Deo*, the Christmas hymn. Grove based its definition on the Greek, but, based on further investigation and discussions with a number of musician acquaintances, it is safe to say that *melisma* now has as its principal meaning "musical ornament," or "ornamental melody," an affectation particularly common in the Renaissance/Baroque transition, as heard often in the music of Monteverdi (1567–1643) and his contemporaries. The *C.O.D.* cautiously steers a middle course, content with "melodic music or tune." The Grove definition is understandable in view of the etymological background of the word, but is now too limited in view of the extensions that have crept in over the years.

mendacious   See **mendicity.**

mendacity   See **mendicity.**

mendicancy   See **mendicity.**

mendicity (men DIS ih tee), also **mendicancy** (MEN dih kan see) *n.* Both terms mean "beggary," i.e., the state of being a begger or *mendicant* (MEN dih kuhnt), or the practice of begging. *Mendicity* is from Latin *mendicitas* (beggary), *mendicancy* from Latin *mendicans*, the present participle of *mendicare* (to beg), which is also the basis of *mendicity*. One must avoid confusing these words with *mendacity* (men DAS ih tee), which is "untruthfulness," from Late Latin *mendacitas* (falsehood), a synonym of *mendacium*. The sweet little Latin noun *mendaciunculum* (a little lie) is the sort we might call a "fib" or in certain cases a "white lie," as when you tell Aunt Elizabeth that her horrible new hat suits her beautifully. These *mendac-* words go back to Latin *mendac-*, the stem of *mendax* (lying, untruthful), which gave us *mendacious*, a rather high-class way of saying "lying, false" when you want to seem less blunt, though it all amounts to the same thing. What you say is either true or false; a little bit false is like a little bit pregnant: you is or you ain't. These words should not be all that obscure, but I thought it well to include them to make sure you never confuse them. Archbishop Frederick Temple (1821–1902) certainly knew the difference when he observed, at a meeting of the Ecclesiastical Commissioners (as quoted in *Years of Endeavor* by Sir George Leveson Gower, 1902): "There is a certain class of clergyman whose *mendicity* is only equalled by their *mendacity*."

menhir (MEN heer) *n.* A *menhir* is an "ancient (usually prehistoric) single standing stone or monolith." The word comes from two Breton words: *men* (stone) and *hir* (long). *Men* has kindred words in Welsh (*maen*) and Cornish (*men* with a long *e* or *medn*), and *hir* has one in Old Irish (*sir* with a long *i*). *Menhirs*, the *O.E.D.* tells us, have been discovered in "various parts of Europe, and also in Africa and Asia." In my *1000 Most Challenging Words*, I deal with *dolmens*, which are Celtic prehistoric structures generally considered to be tombs, constructed of a capstone laid on top of two or more large vertical stones, and *cromlechs*, their Welsh counterparts (though that term applies equally to any circular group of large upright stones lacking a capstone). There are many *dolmens* and *cromlechs* in Britain. Although the *C.O.D.* omits "Britain" specifically as one of the locations where *menhirs* are found, a 1904 book by Sir Bertram C.A. Windle, *Remains of the Prehistoric Age in England*, tells us that "The Dartmoor row begins with a circle and ends with a *menhir.*" Apparently the *O.E.D.* must have meant to include *England* in the term "Europe" in its list of *menhir* locations, thus anticipating England's actual participation in the E.C. by some years.

menology (min OH luh jee) *n.* This is the name given to a calendar of saints' days, especially of the Greek Church, giving biographies of the saints. The word comes via Late Latin *menologium* from Greek *menologion*, formed from *men* (month) plus *logos* (account). Philemon Holland, in his 1610 translation of William Camden's 1586 *Britannia siue Florentissimorum Regnorum, Angliae, Scotiae, Hiberniae, Chorographia Descriptio*, entitled in English *Britain, or a Chorographicall Description of England, Scotland, and Ireland*, wrote: "They report ... upon the authority ... of the Greeks *Menology*, that St. Peter came hither." The term has been applied to an Anglo-Saxon metrical church calendar that was first printed in 1705. The word *menologium* (min uh LOH juhm) is often substituted for *menology*. A *menologist* (muh NOL uh jist) is a compiler of a *menology*.

merchet, also **marchet** (MAHR chuht), **marcheta** (mahr KAY duh) *n.* In feudal times, all sorts of restrictions were placed by the overlord upon the vassal's freedom to act. One of these was the limitation of the vassal's right to marry off a son or daughter, especially when the marriage was to one outside the overlord's jurisdiction. In addition, the vassal had to contend with the lord's *droit du seigneur* (right of the lord), also known as the *jus primae noctis* (right of the first night), a handy little arrangement that gave the lord the right to deflower the bride of a vassal or the vassal's daughter in prospect of her wedding. The *merchet* was a "fine imposed upon the vassal for marrying off his child or for waiving the *droit du seigneur.*" One wonders what the lord's wife thought about that *droit* or *jus*, but that's just a passing thought. What the vassal thought about it didn't matter, and customs being customs, especially in those days, he probably took it in his stride, as did his womenfolk—and in any case nobody could do anything about it. The derivation is, via Middle English and Anglo-French, from Latin *mercatus* (trade). Some trade!

merdivorous (mur DIV uh ruhs) *adj.* When I looked into *RH* to make sure of the meaning of this word, I found the definition "coprophagous," and the same thing happened when I peeked into *WIII*. Why such delicacy, since when one gets to *coprophagous* (koh PROF uh guhs), one's educated guess is confirmed: Both mean "dung-eating," *merdivorous* from Latin *merda* (dung, excrement) plus *vorare* (to eat, devour, swallow greedily), and *coprophagous* from Greek *kopros* (dung) plus *phagein* (to eat, devour). In *RH*, the definition is qualified by the phrase "as certain beetles," and the *O.E.D.* skips the Greek equivalent and is content with "(said of insects)," but *W III* tells the awful truth under the related entry *coprophagy*: "the ... eating of dung ... that is normal behavior among many insects, birds and other animals but in man [aha!] is a symptom of some forms of insanity." Why didn't these fine lexicons come out with an English definition in the first place, instead of giving us the term derived from Greek, and why didn't *RH* go on to inform us of the human aberration? Let's not dwell on this esoteric subject; nothing about the human race surprises me; *de gustibus* etc. But this little exercise in etymology shows us that if you knew your Latin stems you needn't have wandered into Greek territory—and vice versa, or as the old Greeks said it, *enantios, empalin, toumpalin* or *anapalin*. Did I hear anyone say, "The Greeks had *four* words for it?"

merry-andrewize   See **pantropragmatic.**

metacism   See **mytacism.**

metaplasm (MET uh plaz'm) *n.* Apart from a special use in biology not relevant here, this word has a number of applications in rhetoric and grammar. It comes from Greek *metaplasmos*, defined by *LS* as "the formation of noun cases or verb tenses from stems that vary from those of the nominative or present," as the case may be. An example is found in the Latin verb *fero*: infinitive *ferre*, perfect tense *tuli*, supine *latum*. (Don't worry about irregular Latin verbs: This example is given simply to support dear friends *LS*.) *Metaplasmos* was built from the prefix *meta-*, which has lots of meanings and most often denotes change, and *plasma* (something molded), akin to the verb *plassein* (to form, mold). In rhetoric, *metaplasm* is the "shifting of the position of words from their normal order," also known as *hyperbaton* (heye PUR buh ton), fully discussed in my *1000 Most Challenging Words*, where I give examples, to which I now add *By Love Possessed* and *God Almighty*. In grammar, *metaplasm* is the "changing of a word by adding, extracting or transposing letters or syllables." The erroneous insertion of a sound is also known as *anaptyxis* (an ap TIK sis), applying only to vowels—both terms relating to insertions within the mutilated word—and *paragoge* (PARE uh goj'), covering additions of sounds at the end of mangled words. In the case of the transposition of sounds in words, we find the synonym *metathesis* (me TA thuh sis). I shouldn't belabor the point, but *epenthesis, anaptyxis, paragoge* and *metathesis* are all dealt with in that same previous work of mine, complete with examples. If you've exhausted your funds by buying this book, you can get the other one out of the library. (Is that okay with you, Dear Publisher?) (Ed. note: Certainly.)

metathesis   See **metaplasm.**

metaxy (meh TAK see) *n. Metaxu* is Greek for "between." The Greek upsilon can be either *u* or *y* in transliteration, so when I found the word in Professor Elizabeth Dipple's profound work on the novels of Iris Murdoch (*Iris Murdoch, Work for the Spirit,* the University of Chicago Press, Chicago, and Methuen & Co. Ltd., London, 1982; see also a reference to that book in **alieniloquy**) and came to the conclusion that *metaxy* meant "betweenness," or "indecision" or "confusion," I thought that Dipple had coined the word and wrote her to that effect. But she hadn't, she told me. I quote from her letter: "*Metaxy* is a word used by the political philosopher Eric Voegelin in his *Anamnesis* and elsewhere. Obviously a Platonic realist, Voegelin sees humankind existing in an inescapable middle place between materiality and spirituality, and he names this condition *metaxy*." As to Voegelin's title *Anamnesis,* that word is dealt with in my *1000 Most Challenging Words,* where I say, inter alia: "In Platonic terms, it is the recollection of a previous existence. *Anamnesis* comes intact from the Greek, where it means 'remembrance' generally ... Anything that recalls to mind earlier experiences may be described as *anamnestic.*" *CH* includes in its definition "the recollection of the Platonic pre-existence." Please don't jump to the conclusion that I believe in transmigration or previous existences; once is enough!

misapodysis   See **tyrosemiophile.**

Misnagid   See **Mitnagged.**

Mitnagged (mit nah GED), also **Misnagid** (mis NAH guhd) *n.* These terms are taken from Hebrew *mithnagged* and Yiddish *misnaged,* meaning "opposing, opponent," and denote an Orthodox Jew opposed to the creed of the Chasidim or Hasidim. The latter is a Jewish sect founded in Poland about 1750 by Rabbi Israel ben Eliezer to revive the practices of the earlier Chasid sect, itself founded about the third century B.C. to counter Hellenistic influences. They were then known as the *Assideans* or *Hasideans* and were devoted to strict observance of purification and adherence to Hebrew law. (*Chasid* is pronouced CHA sid, the plural cha SEED im; the *ch* being pronounced as in German. *Hasid* is a common alternate spelling.) They are found in many countries and are conspicuous for their costumes and hair styles. The usual attire is a broad-brimmed black hat and a long black cloak; the hair style is characterized by long, curled sideburns known in Yiddish as *peyes* (PAY uhs, from Polish *pejsy*). Today's Chasidim, on the theory that if you're not with us you're against us, apply the term *mitnagged* or *misnagid* to any Jew who is not a Chasid, which is true of the vast majority of Jews.

mixobiosis   See **phylacobiosis.**

mizmaze (MIZ maze) *n. Mizmaze,* a reduplication of *maze* (for a full explanation of *reduplication* see **nid-nod**), means "labyrinth or maze." In John

Harman's translation of Master Beza's *Sermons upon the Three First Chapters of the Canticle of Canticles* (1587) we read: "Solomon ... hath walked us through the whole labyrinth and *mizmaze* of this life." The poet John Davies of Hereford wrote in *The Muses Sacrifice* (1612): "Errors *misse-maze*, where lost is Veritie, / Or blinded so, that still wrong course it takes." Thus far, the examples indicate that the word was used in an abstract sense, rather than to denote a physical maze of the sort one gets lost in at Hampton Court. Again, in the 1624 collection of the *Sermons* of Bishop Miles Smith, the word is found in its figurative sense: "In this distraction, and *miz-maze*, I think the middle-way to be the best way." Bishop Thomas Percy, in his *Reliques of Ancient English Poetry* (1794), uses the word in its literal sense: "On the top of Catharine-hill, Winchester (the usual play-place of the school), was a very perplexed and winding path, running in a very small space over a great deal of ground, called a *Miz-maze*"; but *mizmaze* is usually found in the figurative sense of "confusion, perplexity, bewilderment." An 1875 issue of the *Quarterly Review* speaks of " ... the physico-theological *mizmaze* which ... clouded the perception of those who were following immediately in the wake of Newton." Louisa Parr, in *Adam and Eve* (1880), treats us to this sentence: "I want to be a bit quiet—my head seems all of a *mizmaze* like." In Margaret A. Courtney's *Glossary of Words in Use in Cornwall* (West Cornwall by Miss Courtney; East Cornwall by Thomas Q. Couch), Couch defines *mizmaze* as "bewilderment." It's an unintentionally almost onomatopoeic word for the buzzing that goes on in one's head when in a state of confusion, with a distant accidental cousin in *mishmash* (another reduplicative, this time of *mash*, one of whose meanings is "muddle"). These etymological treasure hunts can leave one in a thorough (the British would say "proper") *mizmaze*.

mizpah (MIZ pah) *n. Mizpah* is the name of the place in ancient Palestine where, according to Gen. 31, 41–49, Jacob and Laban built a cairn, a heap of stones to memorialize their covenant, after they had settled the quarrel between them. Laban said, "This cairn is witness today between you and me." *Mizpah* is Hebrew for "watchtower"; that is why the cairn was named *Mizpah*, "for Laban said, 'The Lord watch between me and thee.'" That word is now used as a term or token of agreement and remembrance, either as an adjective or attributively as a noun, to identify an ornament with the inscription *Mizpah*, given, for example, by a lover to signify remembrance. Hence the term "*Mizpah* ring, bracelet, brooch, etc." H. G. Wells, in *Babes in the Darkling Wood* (1940), uses the expression "*Mizpah*, as they say inside the engagement rings ... Like most English people they thought that was a pledge between two young lovers." An 1898 catalogue of T. Eaton & Co., a jewelry firm, listed the item "*Mizpah* ring." In *Images and Shadows: Part of a Life* (1970) Iris Origo writes: "He gave me the gold Victorian locket—engraved with the word *Mizpah*, 'God watch between us two'—which he had given to his fiancée." I remember a silver brooch worn by my mother bearing the inscription *Mizpah* engraved in Hebrew letters. When I asked her what it meant (this was long after my father's death), she answered something like "I'll never forget (or forsake) you" and said he wore a ring with the same inscription, though I don't remember ever seeing it.

Mizrachi (miz RACH ee—*ch* as in German, e.g., *machen, lachen,* or Scottish, e.g. *loch*) *n.* This is the name of an Israeli religious and political group created in 1902 as the Orthodox wing of the Zionist movement. The group strives to promote traditional Judaism within the Zionist movement and to protect Hebrew fundamentalism against secularization. Many followers of events in Israel are familiar with the *Mizrachi* movement but ignorant of the derivation of the name. *Mizrach,* sometimes spelled *mizrah,* is from Hebrew *mizrah,* meaning "east, the place of sunrise," based on *zarah* (to rise, come forth), and has a number of meanings: "the east," "the direction of Jerusalem," "facing toward Jerusalem in prayer," and more tangibly, a "sacred picture" hung on the eastern wall of a house, i.e., toward Jerusalem; also, the "eastern wall of a synagogue." Israel Zangwill, in *Children of the Ghetto* (1892), writes of " ... a crudely-coloured *Mizrach* on the east wall, to indicate the direction towards which the Jew should pray." A 1911 issue of *The Zionist* states: "The *Mizrachi* profess to see in such work [ardent secular Zionism] a danger to orthodox Judaism of which they claim to be the bulwark in Zionism." James Joyce was familiar with *Mizrach* (and just about everything else!); in *Ulysses* we read: "His gaze turned in the direction of *Mizrach,* the east." Though relatively small in numbers, the *Mizrachi* members of the Knesset, under the proportional representation system in Israeli elections, wield disproportionate influence. In the Antwerp home of an ardent *Mizrachi* aunt of mine, I was found reading the *Divine Commedia* in bed one night. (I had majored in Italian literature at Harvard.) "Why," she asked, "do you read a Catholic work when there is so much to find in our Talmud?"

moazogotl (moh aw tsuh GAW duhl) *adj.* This mouthful of an adjective can claim two distinctions: It serves exclusively as a modifier of the noun *cloud,* and it is not to be found in any dictionary that I have come across except *W III* and that includes the *O.E.D.* Well, what is a *moazagotl* cloud, and whence comes this lovely word? A *moazagotl* cloud is a "cloud bank that is created under foehn conditions on the lee side of a mountain." And what, pray, are foehn conditions? *Foehn* shares with *moazagotl* the distinction of appearing in no other dictionary than the same old *W III,* which informs us that it comes to us from Latin *favonius* (warm west wind—related to *fovere,* to warm), via the tortuous route of Vulgar Latin *faonius,* Old High German *phonno* and German *föhn,* in which form it does appear in the *O.E.D.* and its supplement. Fair enough, but what is *foehn*? It is a "warm, dry wind that blows down the side of a mountain" and is like a *chinook,* which is a "warm, dry *foehnlike* wind that blows down the eastern slopes of the Rockies." So back we go from *chinook* to old friend *foehn,* also known as square one. *Moazagotl* and *Chinook* are usually capitalized.

motile   See **geotaxis.**

mousmee, mousmé (MOOHS may) *n.* This comes from the Japanese word *musume* and means "unmarried girl." It is applied especially to a waitress or tea girl and is by no means a disrespectful term of address. Quite the contrary: Henry C. St. John, in *Notes and Sketches from the Wild Coasts of Nipon* (1880), writes of "the gentle kindness and pretty ways of the *mousmees.*" In Pierre Loti's *Madame Chrysanthème*, it means what you would expect: a girl hired as a temporary wife à la *Butterfly*. From what I have been told by those who have traveled in Japan, and from my recollection of the old days in Britain, *mousmee* is close to the obsolescent British slang term *nippy*, a word originally confined to the nimble waitresses at Lyons Corner Houses, a restaurant chain that (alas!) has gone the way of so many cozy institutions, but then became generic for *waitress*. In my *British English, A to Zed* (1987), I observe that "*Nippy* is just about on its way out." One summons a waitress in Germany as *Fräulein*, in France as *mademoiselle*, in Italy as *signorina* and in Spain as *señorita*, but all we can muster is the rather pale *miss*, and that's about all that's left in Britain. I like *mousmee*; it sounds affectionate.

moxa   See **moxibustion.**

moxibustion (moks uh BUS chuhn) *n.* A *moxa* (MOK suh) is a "cone- or cylinder-shaped mass composed of the downy surface of the dried leaves of wormwood, sunflower pith (similar to the white inner skin of an orange) or a similar substance such as absorbent cotton or spider's web," burned on a patient's skin as a counterirritant in the treatment of gout and other ailments. Modeled after *combustion* because of the burning process, *moxibustion* is "cauterization by the application of a burning *moxa*." *Moxa* is from the Japanese *mokusa*, which is pronounced MOK sah. There is also the synonym *moxocausis* (moks uh KOW suhs), formed by combining *moxa* and the Greek noun *kausis* (burning), akin to *kaein* (to burn). Could there be a better example of a hybrid word than this—the union of a Japanese noun with a Greek one? A July 1965 issue of the *New Scientist* refers to *moxibustion* as "the burning of a herbal [the *h* is sounded in Britain] mixture on part of the body to transfer the site of irritation from one place to another." In an April 1974 issue of *Scientific American*, mention is made of the adoption by the West of "certain traditional [Chinese] techniques: the use of herbal preparations ... and of two related treatments, *moxibustion* and acupuncture." I shuddered at the thought, but my doctor says they both work.

moxocausis   See **moxibustion.**

multipara   See **primipara.**

multiparity   See **primipara.**

multiparous   See **primipara.**

mumpsimus (MUMP sih muhs) *n.* No, this has nothing to do with the infectious disease whose main symptom is the swelling of the parotid and other glands. It is a word taken from an old story about a priest who, in conducting the Mass, always read "quod ore *mumpsimus*" instead of "sumpsimus." The correct Latin expression means "which we have taken into the mouth," *sumpsimus* being the first-person plural perfect of the verb *sumere* (to take, receive). When the old illiterate priest's error was pointed out, he is alleged to have replied, "I will not change my old *mumpsimus* for your new *sumpsimus*." In one version, the old priest referred to his missal, which was incorrectly printed. In another, a fly speck in the missal made the first *s* in *sumpsimus* look like an *m*. In any event, the old man had read it that way for 40 years or more and just wasn't going to go in for any newfangled alterations. In *Impenetrability*, Robert Graves gives *mumpsimus* as an illustration of the coining of new words by simple declaration. In a speech from the throne in 1545, Henry VIII gave *mumpsimus* his blessing as signifying "an erroneous doctrinal view obstinately adhered to," stating: "Some be too stiff in their old *mumpsimus*, others be too busy and curious in their *sumpsimus*." Although *Brewer's Dictionary of Phrase and Fable* gives *mumpsimus* the narrow definition "an established manuscript-reading that, though obviously incorrect, is retained blindly by old-fashioned scholars," modern dictionaries define it variously and much more generally as "an error cherished after exposure; stubborn conservatism; an antiquated person" (*CH*); "one who obstinately adheres to old ways, in spite of the clearest evidence that they are wrong; an ignorant and bigoted opponent of reform; ... an old fogey; ... a traditional custom or notion obstinately adhered to however unreasonable it is shown to be; ... (as a quasi-adjective) stupidly conservative" (*O.E.D.*); "a bigoted adherent to exposed but customary error; a custom or tenet adhered to by a *mumpsimus*" (*W III*). Would anybody agree to coining a Latin verb *mumere* by back formation: *mumo, mumere, mumpsi, mumptum*, from which we derive *mummify* (to preserve)?

mutualism   See **phylacobiosis.**

myrmecoxene   See **symphile.**

mytacism (MITE uh siz'm) *n.* You mightn't think there would be a word denoting the erroneous or excessive use of the letter *m* in writing or of the *m* sound in defective speech, but there it is, in all its glory and obscurity: *mytacism*. *W II* is content to give as its derivation the Greek *mytakismos* but warns us to "cf. *metacism*," which we'll get to in a moment. *W III* omits reference to *metacism* but adds the information that *mytakismos* is "irregular from *my* [*mu*, the Greek letter] plus *-ismos* -ism" (this seems somewhat obscure); it doesn't offer *myism*, which isn't listed in that dictionary (or any other, so far as my explorations indicate), so apparently there ain't no such animal. Let's first get rid of *metacism*, which cannot be found in *W III* but shows up in *W II*, with the pronunciation MET a siz'm and the derivation "Late Latin *metacismus*, from Greek *mytakismos* [same as for *mytacism* in both *W*'s]: fondness for the letter *m*," and the alternative meanings "putting a word ending in *m* before one beginning with a vowel—considered an error in Latin prose"; and "pronunciation [in Latin] of a final *m* that precedes a word beginning with a vowel, in which case the *m* should be elided [i.e., not pronounced]." *W II* has the decency to warn us to take a look at *mytacism*. Enough, now (if not too much) of *metacism*. *Mytacism* is one of several cases of **psellism**, but in my comment on that word, defined as "any defect in pronunciation," I include several examples of types of *psellism* but omitted both *mytacism* and *metacism*. I find *mytacism* particularly obscure, expecially because my efforts to find an example of it have thus far met with no success. Any exemplification will be most welcome.

I feel it is time to point out that in transliteration from Greek into English via Latin, the letter *upsilon* (20th in the Greek alphabet) becomes *y*. (Thus, for example, Greek *muthos* is English *myth*; Greek *lura*, English lyre.) As to its form, the *upsilon* in uppercase resembles *Y*, in lowercase *u*.

LS defines *mutakismos* as "fondness for the letter *mu*," and the verb for this mysterious abuse is *mutakizein*, defined as "to be fond of the letter *mu*," with the explanation "formed like *iotakizein*." Going to that verb, one finds it defined (predictably) as "to lay too much stress upon the *iota*," and the next entry is *iotakismos*, "the above fault in pronunciation." In the definition of the verb, examples are given: *Troiia* for *Troia*, *Maiia* for *Maia*. *Iota* is the ninth letter of the Greek alphabet, and the smallest; for this reason it is used in Greek, as well as English, French, Italian and German—possibly also in other languages unfamiliar to me—to mean a "very small bit (of something)." It corresponds to Hebrew *yodh* and is the origin of English *jot* (cf. "jot or tittle" in Matt.5:18). As long as we are discussing *iota*, we might as well (irrelevant though it may be) mention the fourth-century ecclesiastic Arius (d. 336), the founder of Arianism. This doctrine states that God is alone and separate from every created being, while Christ is a created being and so not fully God, though as maker of all other creatures he might be worshiped as a secondary divinity, who assumed a body but not a human soul and thus was neither truly God nor truly man. Arius was excommunicated for his pains. He and his followers (who for a time included a large part of the Church and several Germanic rulers) held that Christ was not of the same nature or essence (*homoousios*, rendered in Latin as *consubstantialis*) as God the Father but only of similar nature (*homoiousios*). The dispute may be compared to that between Trinitarians and Unitarians. It aroused much violence, and some mockery in subsequent ages, at the shedding of blood "for the sake of an *iota*." Arius's doctrine was condemned at the Council of Nicaea in 325, presided over by the Emperor Constantine, who was not yet a Christian. According to William J. Turner, in the winter 1988/89 edition of the magazine *Free Inquiry*, the slight spelling variation between the two Greek words gave rise to the saying "I don't care an *iota*." Maybe, but to me it sounds apocryphal. The use of *iota* in the sense of "jot" is good enough for me. Getting back to more mundane matters, for abuses of the sounds of certain other letters of the alphabet, see **psellism** and **lallation** in this book and *rhotacism* and *pararhotacism* in my *1000 Most Challenging Words*. (I still find myself wondering why some ancient Greeks "were fond of" or "laid too much stress on" *mus* and *iotas*.) From *iotakismos* we get *iotacism* (excessive use of *i*) and the variant *itacism* used especially for the tendency, which has prevailed in modern Greek, to pronounce several vowels like *i* (English *ee*] instead of with their original value. Come to think of it, a fair number of not-so-good-English-speaking people tend to make excessive use of poor little *i*: cf. mischievious, ancilliary, heinious, municipial.

nasute   See **phylacobiosis.**

niddle-noddle   See **nid-nod.**

nidicolous (nih DIK uh luhs) *adj*. From Latin *nidus* (nest) and *colere* (to inhabit, dwell) we get *nidicolous*, which denotes young birds that linger for some time in the nest. This condition is common to birds whose young are hatched in a state so immature and helpless as to need tender loving care for quite a time. Birds with that habit are known as *altricial* (al TRISH uhl), an adjective derived from Latin *altrix* (female nourisher) and *altor* (male nourisher), both from *altus*, the past participle of *alere* (to nourish). The opposite of *nidicolous* is *nidifugous* (nid DIF yuh guhs), from *nidus* and *fugere* (to flee), an adjective that describes birds that abandon the nest soon after hatching—such as the chicks of chickens and other gallinaceous birds—because they can do without parental care at a very early stage. Such birds are also known as *precocial* (pree KOH shuhl), formed, via Latin *praecox* (early ripening, precocious), from New Latin *precoces*. So, in the avian department, *nidicolous* youngsters are *altricial* and *nidifugous* kiddies are *precocial*, and if you can't resist concocting a limerick whose first line ends with *nidicolous* and whose second or final line terminates in a misspelling of *ridiculous*, go ahead; and remember, there's always *pediculous* (puh DIK yuh luhs), meaning "infested with lice," from Latin *pediculus*, diminutive of *pedis* (louse), a happy coincidence because it can apply to fledglings.

nidifugous   See **nidicolous.**

nid-nod (NID nod) *vb*. To *nid-nod* is "to keep nodding, from drowsiness, boredom or sheer fatigue." This is a reduplicative form, based on *nod*. In *reduplication*, a word formation that occurs quite frequently, the initial element is joined to a rhyming element (as in *helter-skelter, hocus-pocus, hurly-burly* and *mumbo-jumbo*) or a second element in which the vowel changes (as in *fiddle-faddle, flimflam, seesaw, skimble-skamble* and *zigzag*). This occurs in other languages as well: cf. French *zigzag*, German *zickzack*. Robert Burns used *nid-nod* effectively: "We're a' noddin, We're a' noddin, *nid nid noddin* ... at our house at hame." Like *nod*, *nid-nod* may be used transitively, with *head* as the object. Susan Ferrier used *nid-nodding* as a participial adjective in *The Inheritance* (1824), writing of " ... that odd little *nid-nodding* face." The word was used figuratively as a gerund in an 1896 issue of *Blackwell's Magazine*: "The *nid-nodding* of the red rose ... " A related word is *niddle-noddle*, meaning "to nod rapidly or unsteadily back and forth." It, too, may be used transitively, with *head* as the object. This sentence appears in an 1845 issue of *Punch*: "He continually *niddle-noddles* his head like a toy mandarin." Writing about obscure words and reduplicatives in my quiet country study may at times be drudgery, but I much prefer it to the *hustle-bustle* of the big city.

noctivagant (nok TIV uh guhnt) *n., adj*. A *noctivagant* is "one who wanders in the night"; as an adjective, the word applies to any such person—a "night wanderer." It is formed of Latin *noct-*, the stem of *nox* (night) plus *vagant-*, the stem of *vagans*, the present participle of *vagari* (to wander), which gave us *vagabond* and *vagary*. There is a synonym, *noctivagous* (nok TIV uh guhs), formed of *nocti-* plus *vagus* (wandering), which gave us *vague*, but it is used only as an adjective, never as a noun. *The Pageant* (1843) by Francis E. Paget contains this amusing sentence: "Beasts of prey, burglars, and ladies of fashion are the only three kinds of *noctivagous* mammalia." Thomas Adams, in *The Sinner's Passing-Bell; or a Complaint from Heaven of Man's Sins* (1614, reprinted in his *Works*, 1861), wrote: "The lustful sparrows, *noctivagant* adulterers, sit chirping about our houses."

noctivagous   See **noctivagant**.

nolt-tath   See **tath**.

nosocomial (nos oh KOH mee uhl) *adj*. Anything pertaining to a hospital may be described by this adjective, from the Greek *nosokomeion* (hospital), built on *nosos* (disease) plus *komein* (to tend). A *nosocomial* sickness is one originating in a hospital, like the frightening Legionnaires' disease contracted by a number of hospital patients, which has resulted in numerous fatalities. This type of phenomenon brings to mind the adjective *iatrogenic*, with which I deal in my *1000 Most Challenging Words*, in connection with the headword *iatric*. *Iatros* means "physician" in Greek, and the suffix *-genic* means "producing," so that *iatrogenic* describes any illness "produced" by a doctor (wrong treatment, mistaken diagnosis, etc.). This discussion is not intended as a charge leveled against the medical profession or hospitals, but accidents do happen, and they have to have a name.

noyade (nwah YAHD) *n.* Jean Baptiste Carrier was a French revolutionist, a member of the National Convention that proclaimed the Republic on September 22, 1792 and was the governing body of France until October 1795. He was notorious for the brutality with which he carried out the sentences of the revolutionary tribunal in Nantes and was himself guillotined in 1794. His method was *noyade*, wholesale drowning, and the ferocity of the measure was referred to in an 1822 issue of *Blackwell's Magazine*: "They choked their rivers with their *noyades*." John Adams, in one of his *Familiar Letters*, made a peculiar use of the word in commenting on " ... The *noyade* of the tea in Boston harbor." Thomas Carlyle, in *The French Revolution*, used the word correctly in writing (1837) of "sounds of fusillading and *noyading*." *Noyade* means "drowning" in French and is based on the verb *noyer* (to drown), which came from the Latin verb *necare* (to kill, put to death), which acquired the sense of "drown" in Late Latin. Carrier's practice on the Loire was to cram boats full of the condemned and then have the plugs pulled. There is no record of anybody's escape by swimming. (The victims were bound together.)

nunatak (NUN uh tak) *n.* This is an Eskimo word for a "rock peak that protrudes above the inland ice of a region." It was first mentioned by the Swedish arctic explorer and geologist Baron Nils Adolf Erik Nordenskjöld (1832–1901), whose work was carried on by his nephew Nils Otto Gustav (1869–1928) and extended to the antarctic regions. An 1877 issue of the *Quarterly Journal of the Geological Society* speaks of *nunataks* in various parts of Greenland. J. D. Whitney, in *Climatic Changes* (1882), describes a *nunatak* rising almost a mile above sea level. Six years later, an article in the *Times* (London) contained this bit of poetic prose: "The '*nunataks*' which rise like skeletons above the frozen waste." A 1900 issue of *Time* spoke of " ... *nunataks*, or ... sea-cliffs, with *talus* beaches here and there." *Talus* (TAY luhs), from Late Latin *talutum*, from Latin *talus* (ankle), is a geological term for a sloping mass of fragments of rock at the foot of a cliff. In *South with Scott* (1921), E. R. G. R. Evans wrote about a *nunatak* 2,800 feet high. The word appears in a number of works of exploration and geology in various regions, including Norway. This Eskimo word is now a respected geological term in our language.

nuppence (NUH pens) *n.* This is British slang for "no money" or "nothing," as in *It's worth nuppence*, or *He's living on nuppence*. The word is fashioned after *tuppence*, on which I comment as follows in my *British English, A to Zed*: "*Twopence* and *twopenny* are pronounced TUPPENCE and TUPPENNY, and are sometimes slangily spelled that way." There have been a number of changes in British coinage in the last 20 years, most notably the decimalization of the currency on February 15, 1971, when shillings were abolished and the pound thenceforth consisted of 100 "new pence." The pound formerly consisted of 240 pence; hence, the new penny was worth 2.4 times as much as the old penny. Nowadays *two pence* is written, "two pence" or "two pee" but the term *tuppence* stays on, without reference to its actual cash value, in the figurative sense of a "trifle." An 1886 issue of *Longman's Magazine* complained: "The Americans can get our books, and do get them, and republish them and give us nothing—that awful minus quantity, *nuppence!*" In 1964 *The Observer* used the expression "Living on *nuppence*." But even after the old penny became the new penny, or *p.*, the *Times Literary Supplement*, in 1973, contained the sentence: "For the appreciation of the novel, this information matters little more than *nuppence*." Partridge, in his *Dictionary of Slang and Unconventional English* (7th edition—1970) has the entry: "**nuppence**. No money: from ca. 1885; ob[solete]. Ex *no pence* after *tuppence*." *Nuppence* was still alive in 1973, but it may well be obsolete now: I had to explain it to an English friend in 1988.

nyctalopia (nik tuh LOH pee uh) *n.* One shouldn't encumber a book of this sort with those weird medical terms for all sorts of rare diseases, but this one hits home, because I suffer from it, and so do many of my coevals. *Nyctalopia* is what is vulgarly known as "night blindness," but the term covers any degree of reduced vision in low light indoors or out. There was a time when ... were sadder words e'er spoken? But things could be worse, thanks to Mr. Edison. The term comes intact from New Latin, from Middle Latin, from Latin *nyctalops* (incapable of seeing at twilight), in turn taken intact from Greek, based on the Greek prefix *nyct-*, the combining form of *nyx* (night), plus *alaos* (blind) plus *ops* (eye). *Hemeralopia* (hem uhr uh LOH pee uh) is related but quite different: a visual defect causing reduced vision in bright light, a condition vulgarly known as "day blindness." This term was taken intact from New Latin, from Greek *hemeralops*, based on *hemera* (day) and the same *alaos* and *ops*. Predictably, the adjectives are respectively *nyctalopic* (nik tuh LOP ik) and *hemeralopic* (hem uhr uh LOP ik). Here, too, things could be worse: One can always wear dark sunglasses or stay indoors. If these remedies prescribed by Dr. Schur don't help, see your eye doctor.

nystagmic   See **nystagmus.**

nystagmiform   See **nystagmus.**

nystagmoid   See **nystagmus.**

nystagmus (nuh STAG muhs) *n.* Via New Latin, from Greek *nystagmos* (drowsiness), related to *nystazein* (to sleep, doze), we get this term in pathology denoting involuntary rapid oscillation of the eyeballs, usually accompanied by dizziness, occurring during and after bodily rotation or after being struck on the back of the brain or the central cavity of the labyrinth of the ear. The oscillation is usually lateral but can be vertical or rotatory. This condition is most frequently found among miners. The movements of the eyeballs are ceaseless and give the impression that the eyes are vainly attempting to glimpse the light. The adjective is *nystagmic* (nuh STAG mik), *nystagmoid* (nuh STAG moyd) or *nystagmiform* (nuh STAG muh form). In view of the condition's frequent occurrence among miners, the Greek *nyx* (night) may enter into the derivation. Wherever it's found, and whatever the cause, it's a good thing not to have.

obmutescence (ob myooh TEH sens) *n*. The -*mute*- in this word might give you a hint of its meaning: "the act of becoming mute or speechless," with the implication that it is a stubborn, willful act, or "remaining silent, unreasonably and obstinately." The Latin preposition -*ob* can either mean "toward" or "to" or simply act as an intensive; *mutescere* is Latin for "to become silent," from *mutus* (silent), and *mutescens* is its present participle; hence, *obmutescence*. The adjective is *obmutescent*, and it describes perfectly the willful, obstinate witness who keeps his or her mouth firmly shut, or the stubborn child who won't 'fess up. William Paley, in *A View of the Evidence of Christianity* (1794), wrote of "the *obmutescence*, the gloom and mortification of religious orders," and an 1827 issue of *Blackwell's Magazine* described someone as "subject to habitual and invincible *obmutescence*." I like that "invincible"; it puts one in mind of the Mafia code of *omertà* (literally, a legal term in Italian, meaning "connivance," but applied by the Mafia to the "pledge of silence" when a member is questioned by the authorities about the activities of any other member).

obnounce (ob NOUNS) *vb*. The Latin prefix *ob*- is the combining form of the preposition *ob* and has many uses in combination with Latin verbs. One of these is to indicate that the action is "against" something or "objectionable" or "unfavorable." *Nuntiare* is Latin for "to announce"; *obnuntiare* is an intransitive verb meaning, in the idiom of *augurs* (soothsayers), "to report an unfavorable omen" for the purpose of avoiding or stopping some action of the state. That, in turn, gave us *obnounce*, with the same meaning. *Obnunciate* (ob NUN see ate) is a synonym of *obnounce*, and *obnunciation* (ob nun see AY shuhn) is the noun. Henry Cockeram's *The English Dictionarie, or an Interpreter of Hard Words* (1623) contains the item: "To Tell ill newes, *Obnunciate*; a Telling thereof, *Obnunciation*." ("Interpreter of Hard Words" sort of rings a bell, in this here book!) A listing in Thomas Blount's *Glossographia, or a Dictionary Interpreting Such Hard Words … As Are Now Used* (1656—there goes that bell again, folks) reads: "*Obnunciation* … as the ancient Romans were wont to dissolve their Assemblies (which dissolution they called *obnunciation*) when soever any evil token was seen or heard, either by the Magistrate or Augur." Did Blount have that right—that the Romans called the *dissolution* an *obnunciation*? According to Cockeram, the *telling* of bad news was the *obnunciation*, not the *dissolution*; and that makes more sense, if you go back to *obnuntiatio*, which my Latin dictionary defines as "in the language of augurs, the *announcement* of an unfavorable omen." Blount either disagreed with Cockeram or failed to read him; in either case, his Latin must have been somewhat shaky.

obnunciate   See **obnounce.**

obnunciation   See **obnounce.**

obreption (ob REP shuhn) *n.* Somehow, this word looks like a misprint, but it isn't. It denotes the attempt to obtain or the actual obtaining of something by making a false statement or expression of deceit. It is derived from Latin *obreptio* (stealing or creeping upon), related to the verb *obrepere* (to creep or crawl up to, steal up on). The word has a special meaning in ecclesiastical and Scottish law, where the object sought to be obtained in this way is a dispensation or gift, as the case may be. Randle Cotgrave's *Dictionarie of the French and English Tongues* (1611) defined it as "the creeping, or stealing to a thing by craftie meanes." McDouall's *Institute of the Laws of Scotland in Civil Rights* (1752) speaks of " ... checks against subreption or *obreption, i.e.* their [speaking of dispensations] being obtained by concealing a truth, or expressing a false-hood." This introduces the somewhat related word *subreption*, which differs from *obreption* in that the former involves concealment, the latter outright falsehood. I dealt with *subreption* in my *1000 Most Challenging Words*, under (of all things) the headword *sarcophagus*. There, I explained the use of *subreption* in the sense of the semantic change or shift that occurs when a word continues in use, though what it signifies undergoes change; the example given in that book was: " ... *pen* is derived from *penna* (feather) and was used originally when pens were made of quills. The name stuck even after the object underwent change." That, however, is a special use of *subreption*. Its general meaning is the gaining of a gift or an advantage by concealing the truth. Both these "craftie meanes" are equally reprehensible; there's little to choose between them. *Subreption* is from Latin *subreptio*, related to the verb *subrepere* (to creep under, steal into). But note: Whereas *obreption* comes from the combination of the preposition *ob-* (toward, to, against) and *reptus*, the past participle of *repere* (to creep), *subreption* is obtained by yoking the preposition *sub-* (under) and *raptus*, the past participle of *rapere* (to snatch). Talk of minding your *p*s and *q*s? How about *a*s and *e*s?

occamy (OK uh mee) *n.* This appears to be a corruption of *alchemy*, which meant, inter alia, an "alloy imitating gold," known as "alchemy gold." *Occamy* was an "alloy imitating silver." Thomas Nashe, in *Have with you to Saffron-walden* (1596), writes of " ... a tongue of copper or *ochamie* (meerly counterfetting silver) such as organe pipes and serjeants maces are made of." Sir Richard Steele (of Addison and Steele) in *The Guardian* (1713) described a " ... thimble and an *occamy* spoon." In Sir Francis Palgrave's *History of Normandy and of England* (1857) the word is used figuratively in the sense of "sham" or "counterfeit": "the dawning spirit of conventional honour gilding the *ockamy* shield of Chivalry." This *occamy* is in no way related to *Occamism*, the doctrine of the English philosopher William of Occam (d. 1349), the *Doctor Singularis et Invincibilis* known popularly as the "Invincible Doctor," who is fully discussed in my *1000 Most Challenging Words* under the headword *Occam's razor*. (He "dissected" all questions as with a razor, hence the term *Occam's razor*.) Thus, an *Occamist* was a disciple of Occam, not a counterfeiter of silver.

ochlocracy (ok LOK ruh see) *n*. There are a fair number of words ending in *-cracy* that are quite common and familiar—*aristocracy, autocracy, democracy, plutocracy,* etc.—each with its concomitant ending in *-crat* and each built of a word derived from the Greek (*aristos*, best; *autos*, self; *demos*, people; *ploutos*, wealth) plus the suffix *-kratia*, from *kratos* (power). There are less familiar words such as **pornocracy**, *ochlocracy* and *stratocracy*, each with its related terms utilizing suffixes from the Greek. *Ochlocracy* is "mob rule," from *ochlok-ratia*, built of *ochlos* (crowd) and *kratos*. Related words are *ochlocrat* (one who advocates mob rule); *ochlocratic* (describing that attitude) and *ochlophobia* (dread of crowds). *Stratocracy* from *stratos* (army) and *kratos*, is "rule by army, military despotism." A *stratocrat*, predictably, is an adherent of that type of government, and *stratocratic* is the adjective. These words are included because they *are* obscure. Should they be? No: The problem is the elimination of the classics from our curricula, a condition much to be deplored.

ochlocrat   See **ochlocracy.**

ochlophobia   See **ochlocracy.**

omadhaun (OM uh don, -thon) *n*. This is (or was) an Irish term of abuse: To call a person an *omadhaun* is to label him a fool. In Irish, the spelling is simpler: *amadán*, cognate with Latin *amens*, i.e., "mindless." Hall Caine spelled it differently in *The Manxman* (1894) when a character accused another in these terms: "You dobmouthed *omathaun*" (perhaps it is a Manx form), and Jane Barlow used still a different spelling in *Strangers at Lisconnel* (1895), writing of "Hugh McInerney, whom people were apt to call an *omadhawn*." An Irish friend of advanced years tells me that the term is rarely heard, and in his experience, the final syllable is always pronounced *-thon* (soft *th*). It is a very abusive term, he says, and is equivalent to "blithering idiot" or even "mad-man."

onychocryptosis (on nee koh krip TOH sis) *n*. *Onyx* is the Greek for "nail"—as in fingernail, toenail—or "claw," as well as the veined gem used in semipre-cious jewelry. *Kryptos* is the Greek for "hidden." *Onycho-* is the combining form of *onyx*; thus, *onychocryptosis* is the logical form for "ingrown toenail," since the ingrown sides, the parts that cause the pain and sometimes the infection, are "hidden." There is a shorter word—*onyxis*—denoting the actual ingrowing of the nail. We also find other *onycho-* combinations: *onychomancy*, "divination by observation of the nails," the *-mancy* coming from *manteia* (divination); *onychophagy*, "nail biting," *-phagy* being the combining form from *phagein* (to eat); and *onychophagist*, a "nail biter." It seems the Greeks suffered from the kind of nervous attack that prompted Noël Coward to deduce the armlessness of the famous statue of Venus de Milo as the terrible effect of long-term nail biting.

onychomancy   See **onychocryptosis.**

onychophagy   See **onychocryptosis.**

onyxis   See **onychocryptosis.**

opisthograph (uh PIS thuh graf) *n*. This is a "manuscript written on both sides of the paper, parchment or papyrus." The term includes as well a tablet inscribed on both sides. Via Latin *opisthographus*, from Greek *opisthographos* (written on the back), built of the prefix *opistho-*, the combining form of *opisthen* (behind) plus *graphos* (written), related to the verb *graphein* (to write), we got the noun *opisthograph* and the adjective *opisthographic*. The *Encyclopedia Britannica* in 1876 commented, with respect to slabs with a pagan inscription on one side and a Christian one on the reverse, "These are known as *opisthographs*." In his 1816 *Researches into the History of Playing Cards*, Samuel W. Singer used the phrase " ... *opisthographic*, or printed on both sides of the vellum." The adjective *anopisthograph* (an uh pis thuh GRAF), formed of the Latin and Greek prefix *an-* (not, without, lacking) plus *opisthograph*, means "without writing or printing on the back; inscribed on one side only." There is also the form *anopisthographic* (an uh pis thuh GRAF ik), which would seem the more usual form for an adjective. E. G. Duff, in *Early Printed Books* (1893), discussed certain books printed "on one side only ... or, as it is called, *anopisthographically*.

opsigamy (op SIG uh mee) *n*. You've heard of *bigamy*, an illegal second marriage, and there is **digamy**, a legal second marriage, and even **trigamy**, the meaning of which you can guess. Then what is **opsigamy**? *Opse* means "late" in Greek, and *gamos* means "marriage." From these the Greeks concocted *opsigamia*, "marriage late in life," from which we got *opsigamy*. In his 1824 book *The Highlands and Western Isles of Scotland*, John Macculloch wrote: "Nor is there any danger of Donald's being flogged for *opsigamy* by the Highland nymphs as the Spartans were of old." Flogged for *opsigamy* in Sparta of old? You learn something every day!

opsimath (OP sih math) *n*. From Greek *opsimathes* (late in learning) we get this lovely word for "one who acquires knowledge late in life." It is based on Greek *opse* (late) and *mathe* (learning). *Opsimathy* (op SIM uh thee) is the learning thus acquired. An 1883 issue of the *Church Times* contains these words: "Those who gave the name were not simple enough to think that even an *opsimath* was not something better than a contented dunce." An issue of the *Saturday Review* of the same year had this to say: "[He] is what the Greeks called an *opsimath*: not ignorant, but a laggard in learning." Back in 1656, one John Hales, in *Golden Remains*, wrote: "Therefore *Opsimathie*, which is too late beginning to learn, was counted a great vice, and very unseemly." In 1889 *Harper's Weekly* proclaimed: "The figures alone betray the inevitable weakness of *opsimathy*." Why all this denigration? How about "better late than never?" And "adult education?" And Cato the Elder, the great Roman statesman, soldier and writer, who in very advanced age took up the study of Greek and two years later was proficient in it? I'm all for *opsimathy* and am still adding to my store of lore, such as it is, at an age when wheelchair catalogues are many persons' most important reading.

opsimathy   See **opsimath.**

opsomania   See **opsophagy.**

opsony   See **opsophagy.**

opsophagy (op SAW fuh jee) *n. Opson* is Greek for "cooked meat, relish, rich food generally, delicacies of all sorts," and *phagein* means "to eat," from which came the suffix *-phagos* (eating, eater). Thus, *opsophagy* is the "eating of delicacies" and in most cases, especially fish. There are related words: *opsony* (OP suh nee), denoting anything eaten with bread to give it flavor, in Greece and Rome of old chiefly fish, from Greek *opsonion* and Latin *opsonium*; and *opsomania* (op suh MAYE nee uh), taken as is from the Greek, a "pathological or morbid yearning for delicacies or for some specific food." Pregnant women are said to acquire acute longings for delicacies like grapefruit or pickles or almost any arbitrary selection. In Robley Dunglison's *Medical Lexicon* (1842, 1858, 1867, 1874, 1893), *opsomaniac* was defined as "One who loves some particular aliment to madness." Well, we do say things like "I'm simply *crazy* about olives" (or caviar or oysters or whatever). Thus, there's nothing new about *opsomania*.

oreo (OH ree oh) *n.* This is U.S. slang for a "black person with a 'white' mentality," who thinks like a white or tries to join white society. It is, of course, a derogatory term, especially as used by other blacks who spurn such pretensions. *Oreo* is the name of a popular commercially prepared cookie consisting of two round chocolate wafers enclosing a white sugar-cream filling—"black" on the outside, "white" on the inside. The application of the name of that cookie to a black person with a "white mentality" is apt but cruel. Thoughtful blacks heartily dislike and reject the term. An article in the magazine *Black*

World, June 1971, stated: "Every Black man or woman who refers to his Black brother or sister by a derogatory label such as *Tom*, *nigger* or *oreo* is deliberately walking into the enemy's trap." It's a sad world that has to invent such derisive labels. This one is reminiscent of the days when a secretly dissident Nazi was called "rare roast beef"—brown on the outside, red on the inside—and they were "rare" indeed, in more senses than one.

orihon (OH ree hon, AW-) *n.* This is the name of a Japanese form of book produced by the accordion-folding of strips of paper, vellum or other material in such a way as to divide the written or printed text on one side into columns or pages. It is usually provided with covers and laced down one side with some type of cord. The entire text appears on one side of the paper or other material, leaving the reverse side blank. The etymology is uncertain, but most dictionaries agree that it is "probably" from Japanese *ori* (fold) plus *hon* (book), and a "fold book" it surely is. The Chinese follow a similar procedure in the production of *orihons*. The *O.E.D.* calls it "the link between the roll and the book." In a book entitled *Greek Papyri* (1968) E. G. Turner tells us that "books of this kind (termed *orihon*) are still in everyday use in China and Japan." The Japanese are adept at the art of folding paper into intricate shapes. This craft is known there as *origami* (awr ih GAH mee) and has been handed down from generation to generation for ages. In the *Manchurian Candidate* (1960), Richard Condon writes of one expert who "amused them [his audience] or startled them or flabbergasted them with the extent of his skill at *origami*." I have watched one of my sons engage in this art, producing all kinds of things, from houses, bridges, chairs, animals of various species, boats and flowers to birds that could be made to flap their wings by pulling their beaks. Many books have been published on the art of *origami*, a word of Japanese origin formed of *ori* plus *kami* (paper).

orogeny   See **diastrophism.**

outfangthief   See **infangthief.**

Paduanism   See **Patavinity.**

paenula   See **phelonion.**

paeon   See **hemiola.**

paeonic   See **hemiola.**

Palamite   See **hesychast.**

pancratian   See **pancratium.**

pancratiast   See **pancratium.**

pancratic   See **pancratium.**

pancratium (pan KRAY shuhm), also **pancration** (pan KRAY tee uhn) *n.* This is the name of a sport combining boxing and wrestling from the Greek *pankration*, combining the prefix *pan-* (all) and *kratos* (strength). The adjective is *pancratian*, and the noun *pancratiast* denotes a competitor or victor in the sport. The related adjective *pancratic*, literally "pertaining to the *pancratium*," means, by extension, "excelling in all types of athletics," and by further extension, "excelling in all types of accomplishment," a pretty broad territory indeed. Nathan Bailey's *Universal Etymological English Dictionary* (1731) defines *pancratick* (sic) as "all-powerful, almighty." James Russell Lowell's *Bigelow Papers* (1848) spoke of " ... the advantages of a *pancratic* ... education." A special use of *pancratic* is found in the field of optics: A *pancratic* eyepiece is one capable of various degrees of power. It was invented in the early 19th century and was brought out under the name of *Pancratic Eye Tube.* Edward H. Knight's *Practical Dictionary of Mechanics* (1884) described the *Pankratic* microscope as having " ... a sliding tube containing the eye-piece, by which its distance from the object glass may be changed, and various degrees of enlargement ... obtained without change of glasses." It is interesting to see how *power*, which goes all the way back to Latin *posse* (to be able), has a special use in optics, in the way Greek *kratos* developed a special use in the same field. Janet Van Duyn, in her excellent book *The Greeks, Their Legacy*, in the McGraw-Hill *Early Cultures Series* (1972), gives us a vivid description of the *pankration* as it was fought in the Olympic Games in ancient Greece:

> The *pankration*, a blend of wrestling and boxing, was probably one of the most brutal legally sanctioned sports on record. In this contest the two opponents punched, kicked, and strangled each other until one of them raised a finger to acknowledge defeat. Nearly every kind of maiming blow man could deliver was allowed, with the exception of gouging and biting. Breaking an opponent's fingers, easy enough under the circumstances, was also frowned upon. If further rules existed, they have not come down to us.

(Don't you like that "frowned upon?") Today's "professional" wrestling seems to have taken *pankratium* a step or two further. A bit later in her book, Ms. Van Duyn tells us: "Wrestling the *Pancratium* was a feature of the Olympic Games. A rough and brutal form of athletic contest in which almost no holds were barred, it was a favorite with Greek audiences." There is a marvelous bas relief of two contestants in this "sport" exhibited in the National Archaeological Museum in Athens.

pannage (PAN uhj) *n.* This word has a number of meanings, all associated with the pasturing of swine (sometimes other animals as well). *Pannage* is the "pasturing of swine (or other animals) in a forest" or the right or privilege to do so. It can also denote the payment made to the owner of the forest for that privilege, or the profit made by the owner of the woodland. It is a term that relates to the customs of medieval England and covers as well the material on which the swine fed: mainly acorns and beechnuts, known collectively as *mast*. An 1882 issue of *The Athenaeum: Journal of Literature, Science, and the Fine Arts* speaks of " ... herds of wild ponies and droves of wilder pigs thriving on the *pannage*." A little-used meaning of *mast* is "nuts, especially beechnuts and acorns, amassed as detritus on the forest floor; the accumulation of such matter used as feed for hogs and other animals." In this usage, *mast* is derived from Middle Dutch and Old high German *mast*, meaning "food," and Old English *mete* with the same meaning. One of Charles Lamb's essays that appeared under the signature *Elia* in an 1822 issue of *The London Magazine*, entitled "In Praise of Roast Pig," speaks of " ... the swineherd, Ho-ti, having gone out into the woods ... to collect *mast* for his hogs." As for *pannage*, the derivation is from Latin *pascio* (pasturing), related to the verb *pascere* (to feed, lead to pasture) and its past participle *pastus*, which led to medieval Latin *pas(ti)naticum*.

panpharmacon (pan FAR muh kon) *n.* This is a synonym of *panacea*, a "universal remedy, a medicine for all poisons and diseases." It was taken intact from the Greek, built of the prefix *pan-* (all) plus *pharmakon* (drug), and related to the adjective *panpharmakos* (skilled in all drugs). It was defined in Thomas Blount's *Glossographia, or a Dictionary Interpreting Such Hard Words ... as are Now Used* (1661) as "a medicine for all diseases," and William Salmon, in *Pharmacopoeia Bateana, or Bate's Dispensatory* (1694), in describing a certain remedy, was careful to say: "It is used by some as *Panpharmacon*, but what Diseases it will absolutely cure I think is scarcely determin'd." *Panacea* is a familiar word, but a little discussion may be of use. It was taken, via Latin, from Greek *panakeia*, based on the adjective *panakes* (all-healing), built of *pan-* plus *akos* (cure), akin to the verb *akeisthai* (to heal). In Greek mythology, Panacea was the daughter of Aesculapius, the Latin form of Greek Asklepios, the god of healing and medicine. His symbol is a snake entwined around a staff, based on his legendary introduction to Rome, during a 293 B.C. plague, in the form of a serpent. Alchemists in the Middle Ages searched for panaceas, and legend has given us a variety: Achilles's spear, which could heal wounds; Promethean unguent, which made the body invulnerable to fire and military arms; Prince Ahmed's apple, a remedy against all ills (superior to those others, which were effectively only against certain ailments—but you can't win 'em all), to name a few. A *panpharmacon* that could handle AIDS would be welcome.

panspermatism (pan SPUR muh tiz'm), also **panspermism** (pan SPUR miz'm), **panspermy** (pan SPUR mee), **panspermia** (pan SPUR mee uh) *n.*

Panspermatism is derived from the Greek prefix *pan-* (all), plus *spermat-* (root of *sperma*, seed) plus *isma* (state, condition). In opposition to the theory of spontaneous generation, a biogenetic theory was propounded in the 19th century holding that the atmosphere teems with germs that develop whenever and wherever they meet a favorable environment. Believers were known as *panspermists*. In the words of the *Sydenham Society Lexicon of Medicine and Allied Sciences* (1893), *panspermia* is "the physiological system according to which there are germs disseminated through all space which develop when they encounter a suitable soil." In ancient times, the Roman poet and philosopher Lucretius (99–55 B.C.), in *De Rerum Natura* (On the Nature of Things), wrote: "Nil posse creari de nilo" (Nothing can be created from nothing), and the Roman satirist Persius (A.D. 34–62) agreed: "De nihilo nihilum, in nihilum nil posse reverti" (Nothing can come out of nothing, nothing can go back to nothing)—beating the *panspermists*, in their opposition to spontaneous generation, by a good many centuries. It's difficult to say what those old boys might have thought of the "germs everywhere" doctrine, but they certainly would have agreed in disbelieving in spontaneous generation. The *panspermists* theorized that life could be diffused throughout the universe through germs carried by meteorites. We haven't discovered life on any other planet yet, but who knows?

panspermia   See **panspermatism.**

panspermism   See **panspermatism.**

panspermy   See **panspermatism.**

pantagamy (pan TAG uh mee) *n.* This is the term for a marriage practice in certain communities, a "free-for-all," in which every man is considered the husband of every woman and vice versa. Sounds pretty messy, but it has a history. One of the more amusing aspects of the word is the disagreement among dictionaries as to its derivation from Greek components. *W III* gives it as *pant-* plus *-gamy*, short and sweet. *Pant-* is a combining form of *pas* (all, every), and *-gamy* is from *-gamia*, based on *gamos* (marriage). *RH* omits the entry (out of delicacy?). When we get to the *O.E.D.*, we find something quite elaborate: "An illiterate formation for *pantogamy*, from Greek *PANTO-* all plus *-gamia*, from *gamos*, marriage. (*Pantagamy* is etymologically, from Greek *agamia* celibacy, 'universal or total celibacy.')" (Note: The *a* of *agamia* means, literally, "no marriage," i.e., "celibacy.") In its definition, the *O.E.D.* refers to the practice of "the Perfectionists at Oneida Creek in U.S." More about them later. *CH* gets the prize for its pawky Scottish humor. (*Pawky* gets the following treatment in my *British English, A to Zed*: " … Its usual application is to Scottish humor. The Scots have spread two legends about themselves which are not borne out by the facts: 1. that they are stingy; 2. that they are humorless. Simple jokes are sometimes referred to by the English as 'easy jokes for Scotsmen.' *Pawky humor* is Scottish humor according to their own *pawky* legend, the kind that encourages the victim to make a fool of himself." Note the address of the *CH* publisher: "No. 11 Thistle Street, Edinburgh. The thistle is the national emblem of Scotland.) All that *CH* has to say about the derivation of *pantagamy* is: "Greek *gamos*, marriage, *agamia*, bachelorhood." Its definition: "A word that ought to mean universal bachelorhood applied with unconscious irony to the universal marriage of the Perfectionists, in which every man is the husband of every woman." It is now time to get to the *Perfectionists*. They were a sect founded in 1839 by John Humphrey Noyes, who lost his license to preach because of his "perfectionist" doctrine, a name taken from Matt.5:48: "Be ye therefore perfect, even as your Father which is in heaven is perfect." Beginning in 1846, his sect began the practice of "complex marriage," so arousing the neighborhood (Putney, Vermont) that in 1846 they fled to Oneida, New York. By 1879, internal problems and outside hostility forced Noyes to emigrate to Canada, where he spent the rest of his life. Noyes's basic premise was that man's innate sinlessness could be regained through communion with Christ, and such communion made communal marriage sinless. The sect was dissolved in 1881. The Mormons were established in 1831. It was only 15 years later that Noyes out-Mormonized them, combining polyandry and polygamy. Must have been confusing.

pantaleon (pan TAL ee on), also **pantalon** (PAN tuh lon), **pantalone** (PAN tuh lun), **pantaloon** (pan tuh LOOHN) *n.* Despite the ultimate variant, this word has nothing to do with lean old dotards wearing spectacles low on the nose, slippers or pantofles and tight trousers—i.e., the character that originated in the *commedia del' arte* of Venice. The word, which denotes a type of stringed instrument, comes from the unusual first name of *Pantaleon* Hebenstreit. And who was he? A German musician who, in 1705, invented a musical instrument, a large dulcimer with from 100 to 250 strings of gut and metal wire, struck by wooden mallets held by the player. Hebenstreit died in 1750. The instrument that bears his name is described in the venerable *Grove's Dictionary of Music* (1880 edition) under the heading *Pantaleon* or *Pantalon* as follows: "A very large Dulcimer invented and played upon in the early part of the last century by *Pantaleon* Hebenstreit, whose name was transferred to the instrument by Louis XIV. The name was also given in Germany to horizontal pianofortes with the hammers striking downwards." So far, so good; but why would anyone name a son *Pantaleon*? (All I have been able to dig up is that *Pantaleon* figures in the Roman Missal at July 27, and *Pantileimon* in the Byzantine one at the same date.)

pantopragmatic (pan toh prag MAT ik) *n., adj.* Thomas Love Peacock, the English novelist and poet who was one of Shelley's closest friends and eventually his executor, wrote satirical novels full of wit and eccentricity. One of them, *Gryll Grange* (1860), concerned an imaginary society devoted to *pantopragmatics*, the "'science' of universal benevolent interference." As an adjective, *pantopragmatic* describes one who meddles in everybody's business; as a noun, it denotes a universal busybody. The word is derived from Greek *panto-*, the combining form of *pas* (all), plus *pragmatikos* (active and skilled in business, businesslike). From Peacock's book: "Two or three ... arch-quacks have taken to merry-andrewizing in a new arena, which they call the Science of *Pantopragmatics*." (*Merry-andrewize* is a nonce verb made from *merry andrew*, a buffoon, a clown; originally a quack or charlatan's assistant.) Peacock gave the president of his society the name "Lord Facing-both-ways." I'm sure you've run into a *pantopragmatic* or two; I have, and they are to be avoided like the plague, though they mean well. They have nothing else to do; their "advice" is spontaneous, thoughtless, generally irritating. It's lovely to have a word for their kind.

pantoum (pan TOOHM) *n*. *Pantoum* is an erroneous French spelling of the Malay word *pantun*, which is the name of a complicated verse form consisting of a series of quatrains built as follows: in the first, let's say the rhyme is *abab*; in the next, the second rhyme (*b*) recurs as the first, so that the rhyme is, say, *bcbc*; and in the next, the same system is followed, giving *cdcd*, and so on and so on, until we get to the final quatrain, where the initial rhyme of the series (*a*) recurs as the second rhyme, thus: *xaxa*. Complicated, isn't it? The August 2, 1897, issue of the *Daily News* contains a reference to this verse form: "Very few people know what a *Pantoum* is; it ... is a Malay form of verse patented by Mr. Austin Dobson [English poet, biographer and essayist, 1840–1921]." The *Encyclopedia Britannica* of 1883 defines this verse form, under the heading *pantun*, thus: "improvised poems, generally of four lines, in which the first and third and the second and fourth rhyme. The meaning intended to be conveyed is expressed in the second couplet, whereas the first contains a simile or distant allusion to the second, or often has, beyond the rhyme, no connexion with the second at all." This "explanation" seems even more complicated than the rhyme scheme set forth above, based on the definition given in *W III*, which is an expanded version of the one in *W II*. To muddle the situation, *RH* says that the second and fourth *lines* (not *rhymes*) of each quatrain are repeated as the first and third *lines* of the following one. Anyone desiring to improvise a *pantoum* please raise his hand.

pantun   See **pantoum.**

paphian (PAY fee uhn) *n., adj.* Paphos is the name of an ancient city in Cyprus that was the center of worship of the Greek goddess of love Aphrodite (Venus in the Roman hierarchy of gods) and the site of a great temple to that deity. *Paphos* gave rise to the Greek adjective *paphios*, which became Latin *paphius* andour *paphian*, usually capitalized. The adjective describes anything or anyone relating to *Paphos* or characteristic of the place or its people. In view of this city's devotion to the cult of Aphrodite, the adjective came to be used of anything relating to love, especially illicit love, so that it eventually took on the meaning of "wanton." As a noun, it meant, at first, "a native of Paphos," later "a worshiper of Aphrodite" and eventually, "prostitute," hardly a way to show one's repect to the lovely goddess.

parabasis   See **epirrhema.**

paragoge   See **metaplasm.**

paragraphia (par uh GRAF ee uh) *n*. This word, which might be mistaken for an exotic plural form of the common word *paragraph*, has nothing to do with paragraphs except for its derivation. It is, to make matters a bit more confusing, variously defined as a "condition of mental disorder or brain injury in which the sufferer writes words or letters other than those intended" or (in British) the "actual writing of wrong words or letters resulting from disease or brain injury." Either way, it's a sad state of affairs. The adjective is *paragraphic*, but that is also the adjective from *paragraph*. Both *paragraphia* and *paragraph* are derived from the Greek prefix *para-* (beside or beyond) and the verb *graphein* (to write). An example of *paragraphia*: When a friend of mine staying with me arrived at the breakfast table having had (as proved to be the case) a slight stroke in the night, he found himself unable to articulate. On being offered pencil and paper, he wrote, "Is there anything *right* with me?" We departed quickly to the nearest hospital. (This sturdy fellow was fine the next day.)

parallelepiped (par uh lel uh PEYE puhd, -PIH-, -le LEH puh ped, -luh LEH puh ped), also **parallelepipedon** (par uh leh luh PIH puh dawn, -duhn), **parallelopipedon** (par uh leh luh PIP uh dawn, -duhn) *n*. I didn't think enough people used the word to involve that many pronunciations or spellings! Anyway: This word, in the first spelling given above, was taken intact from the Greek, based on *parallelos* (parallel) plus *epipedon* (plane surface), the neuter of *epipedos* (level), from prefix *epi-* (upon) plus *pedon* (ground). May I say "Whew!?" So what is it? It is nothing more or less than a "six-faced polyhedron (a multfaced solid figure), all faces of which are parallelograms (quadrilaterals, i.e., four-sided figures with four sides and four angles) placed in pairs of parallel planes." So—why all the geometry all of a sudden? Two reasons: It's a wildly obscure word that you will never meet, let alone use, in all likelihood (that alone qualifies it for inclusion); and it was a term of abuse, meaning "blockhead," arbitrarily hurled at his students by a high school mathematics teacher, according to a telephone call that came in while I was broadcasting about obscure words on a talk show. Happy now? In his *History of Ancient Pottery and Porcelain* (1858), Samuel Birch wrote of bricks that were " ... *parallelopipeda*, of Nile-mud or clay of a dark loamy colour, held together by chopped straw." Note the plural in *-a* and the spelling with *o* after the third *l*, said by the *O.E.D.*, like one with *i* in that position, to be incorrect. I wonder how many readers caught this egregious error.

pararhotacism   See **psellism.**

paroemia (puh REE mee uh) *n.* A *paroemia* is a "proverb, adage, old saw"—though *old* would appear to be equally applicable to *proverb* and *adage,* or superfluous in all cases, because you don't run into new *paroemiae.* They're all old, except some that Ambrose Bierce invented and listed under the heading *Saw* in his *Devil's Dictionary,* some examples of which follow:

> A penny saved is a penny to squander.

> A bird in the hand is worth what it will bring.

> Think twice before you speak to a friend in need.

> Strike while your employer has a big contract.

> Where there's a will there's a won't.

Bierce also invented some beautiful examples under his rubric *Epigram.* *Paroemia* is derived, via Latin, from Greek *paroimia,* based on the prefix *par-* (near, beside) plus *oimos* (road), i.e., "heard commonly, in small talk by the road." Incidentally, I have something in common with Ambrose Bierce, who commented on his "famous obscurity," a lovely oxymoron, when he wrote: "My, how my fame rings out in every zone—/A thousand critics shouting: 'He's unknown!'"

parvanimity   See **longanimity.**

pataphysics (PAT uh fiz iks) *n.* This is the name of the "science of imaginary solutions," an invention of the French dramatist Alfred Jarry (1873–1907). Jarry wrote symbolic farce, which led to the theater of the absurd, which I dub "murder mysteries," because it is a mystery to me how the authors of that type of theater get away with that kind of murder. Jarry was a familiar Paris figure, famous for his eccentric and dissolute behavior. He preached the superiority of hallucinations over rational thought. The hero of his satirical farce *Ubu Roi* (Ubu the King) is cowardly and repulsive, an authentic antihero. His surrealistic verse narratives are witty, blasphemous and scatological. The system of *pataphysics* is ludicrous but amusing, if your tastes run in that direction.

Patavinity (pat uh VIN uh tee) *n.* This word comes from Latin *Patavinitas,* from *Patavinus,* the adjective relating to *Patavium,* the Latin name for what is now Padua. That was the birthplace of the Roman historian Livy (Titus Livius, 59 B.C.–A.D. 12). His writings revealed dialectal characteristics peculiar to Patavium, and *Patavinity* came to mean "provincialism" in writing generally. Hence arose the noun *Paduanism* (PAD yooh un iz'm) as well, denoting the dialectal peculiarities of that part of the country, and a term that became a synonym for "patois." Certain Roman critics censured Livy for *Patavinity* in his historical writings. They considered it a stylistic weakness, especially compared with the elegance of the work of the more sophisticated city fellers of Rome.

patriarch   See **hegumen.**

patroclinous   See **matroclinous.**

patrocliny   See **matroclinous.**

pawky   See **pantagamy.**

pedaliter (peh DAL uh tuh, -tur) *adv.* This is a direction in organ music meaning "to be played on the pedal keyboard"; *manualiter* (man yuh WAL uh tuh, -tuhr) is in the same category, meaning "to be played on the manual keyboard." If you have watched an organist perform on a large organ fitted with a pedal keyboard, you will have noticed that while most notes are played on the manual keyboard, operated by the musician's fingers, some very low notes issue from the pedal keyboard, operated by the player's feet. *Pedalis* in Latin, means, literally, "a foot long (or wide)," based on *ped-*, the stem of *pes* (foot), but it was used in the more general sense of "relating to the foot." In New (i.e., postmedieval), Latin the adverbial suffix *-ter* was added to form the organ direction first mentioned. Latin *manualis*, based on *manus* (hand), meaning literally "fitted to the hand," used as well in the general sense of "manual," got the same treatment, resulting in *manualiter*, the other organ direction described above. The playing of an organ fitted with pedals requires an extraordinary degree of bodily coordination, and the sight of a gifted organist playing one of Bach's great preludes and fugues always fills me with wonder at not only the musicianship but also the sheer physical dexterity of the performer, using all four appendages in wondrous coordination.

perdurable   See **perdure.**

perdurance   See **perdure.**

perdurant   See **perdure.**

perdure (pur DYOOR) *vb.* The *O.E.D.* originally marked this verb as "now *rare*," but the *Supplement* says, "Delete now *rare* and add later examples," which it does. *To perdure* is "to continue, last, keep going, endure," but, unlike its close relative *endure*, *perdure* can be used only intransitively. The *per-* element is here used as an intensive; the *-dure* is from Latin *durare* (to harden, endure), based on the adjective *durus* (hard). *Perdure* is somehow more forceful than *endure*. The same goes for the participial adjective *perduring*. In *A Dissertation on Metaphysics* (1890), John Skinner writes, "The Soul is revealed intuitively as a *perduring* living agent or entity." In M. León-Portilla's *Time and*

Reality in the Thought of Maya, translated by Boilès and Horcasitas (1973), it is stated that "For longer than a millennium and a half, not a little of Maya symbolism has *perdured*." The Summer 1977 issue of the magazine *Daedalus* contains these words: "The assignment and reassignment of meaning must be investigated as processes in the domain of resilience possessed by each population recognizing itself to be culturally *perduring*." Predictably, we have the adjective *perdurable* (pur DYOOR uh bl, PUR dyoor-), "lasting a long, long time or indefinitely." The English novelist and critic Sir Arthur Quiller-Couch declared that "our literature is going to be our most *perdurable* claim on man's remembrance." *Perdurance* is "persistence, permanence," and *perdurant* is a synonym of *perdurable*. Shakespeare used *perdurable* twice. In *Henry V* (Act IV, Scene 5), the Dauphin, on learning of his defeat, cries, "O *perdurable* shame!— let's stab ourselves!" Incidental note: This comes only a few lines after Orleans shouts, "*O seigneur! le jour est perdu, tout est perdu.*" ("O Lord! the day is lost, all is lost.") In the innocence of youth I somehow connected *perdurable* with *perdu* and for years thought of *perdure* as a French word meaning "loss." Now I—and you—know better. Iago says to Roderigo in *Othello* (Act I, Scene 3): "I have professed me thy friend, and I confess me knit to thy deserving with cables of *perdurable* toughness." *Perdurably* shows up as well. In *Measure for Measure* (Act III, Scene 1), after Isabella refuses to yield her body to Angelo to save her brother Claudio from the death sentence imposed upon him for getting the fair Juliet with child, he exclaims: "Why would he for the momentary trick [trifle]/Be *perdurably* fin'd?" (Death is certainly *perdurable*, if anything is!)

Perfectionist   See **pantagamy.**

periscian   See **amphiscian.**

perispomenon   See **properispomenon.**

perissology (pehr uh SOL uh jee) *n. Perissology* is "redundancy, superfluity of words, pleonasm." I discuss *pleonasm* in my *1000 Most Challenging Words*, with many examples (*free gift* and *obviate the necessity of* are two of my pet hates), but I must now add *the hoi polloi*, an all-too-frequently heard bit of *perissological* illiteracy. If you're going to go in for a little fancy Greek, please remember that the *hoi* in *hoi polloi* is the definite article, making the *the* a *perissology. Fowler's Modern English Usage* has something to say about this: "These Greek words for the majority, ordinary people, the man in the street, the common herd, etc., meaning literally 'the many,' are equally uncomfortable in English, whether *the* (= *hoi*) is prefixed to them or not. The best solution is to eschew the phrase altogether, but it is unlikely to be forgotten as long as *Iolanthe* is played. "Twill fill with joy and madness stark the *Hoi Polloi* (a Greek remark.)'" *Perissology* is formed via Late Latin *perissologia*, taken intact from the Greek, based on the adjective *perissologos* (speaking too much), built on *perissos* (redundant) plus *logos* (word). George Campbell, in *The Philosophy of Rhetoric* (1776), says: "If we should say *the alcoran* we should fall into a gross *perissology*." Campbell is right, of course, *al* being *the* in Arabic, but just as *Fowler* regrets that *the hoi polloi* is here to stay, *the Alcoran* shows up in high literary places. In *The Hind and the Panther*, Dryden writes: "The jolly Luther, reading him, began/T'interpret Scriptures by *his* Alcoran" (the *his* constituting as much a *perissology* as a *the* would be). And before that, Francis Bacon, in his *Essay on Atheism*, said: "I had rather believe all the fables in the legend, and the Talmud, and *the* Alcoran, than that the universal frame is without a mind." And how about these words, all of which contain the Arabic definite article: *alchemy, alcohol, alcove, alembic, algebra, alkali, arsenal, artichoke, azimuth* and even *lute*, which goes back, via Middle English, Middle French, Old English and Old Provençal *laut* to Arabic *al ud* (the wood); and as an effect of the Muslim conquest, the Spanish words *alcalde* (mayor), *alcázar* (castle, fortress), *Alhambra, almacén* (shop, warehouse) and many more? Despite Dryden, Bacon and all the users of *the hoi polloi*, never use a redundant, pleonastic, tautological, *perissological* word if you can help it, because it is needless, unnecessary, plethoric, superfluous, entirely *de trop* and in bad taste.

perjink (puhr JINGK), also **perjinkety** (puhr JINGK uh tee), a Scottish word, *adj.* To call a person *perjink* or *perjinkety* is to praise him or her for being precise or minutely accurate, or to complain that he or she is prim or finical. The context must decide whether praise or criticism is intended. The word is sometimes spelled *prejink*, and its origin is unknown. John Jamieson's 1808 *Etymological Dictionary of the Scottish Language* has this entry: "*Perjink*, 1. Exact, precise, minutely accurate ... 2. Trim, so as to appear finical." In *The Life of Mansie Wauch, Taylor in Dalheith* (1839), David M. Moir described a character as looking " ... as *prejinct* as a pikestaff [a walking-stick with a spike at the bottom to prevent slipping]." That would seem to indicate primness to the point of finicalness. To be *on one's perjinks* is to be "on one's best behavior," "meticulous about details." *Perjinkities* or *prejinkities* means "niceties, proprieties," or "exact details," depending again on the context. John Ruskin, in *Praeterita: Outlines of Scenes and Thoughts ... in my Past Life* (1887) wrote: "[She] had always what my mother called '*perjinketty* ' ways, which made her typically an old maid in later years." That may give the exact flavor: fussy, prim, insistent on precise details and niceties; spinsterish. The *Praeterita* in Ruskin's title means "things past"; it is the neuter plural of the past participle *praeteritus* of the Latin verb *praeterire* (to pass by). Ah, those Latin elegancies!

perjinkety   See **perjink.**

perjinkities   See **perjink.**

per stirpes   See **stirp.**

petasus (PET uh suhs) *n.* Hermes, whose Roman counterpart was Mercury, was a most versatile god: god of science, commerce, eloquence, games and feats of skill; patron of thieves, rogues, travelers and vagabonds. He is represented as wearing a low, broad hat, sometimes winged, known in Latin as a *petasus* and in Greek as a *petasos;* also *talaria* (tuh LA ree uh), winged sandals or wings attached to the ankles, from the neuter plural of the Latin adjective *talaris* (pertaining to ankles), based on *talus* (ankle); and carrying a *caduceus* (kuh DYOOH see uhs, -shee uhs), a wand or staff of the sort borne by heralds (often pictured with two serpents twined around it and two wings at the top—in addition to his many other attributes, he was the messenger of the gods). So if you happen to run into a good-looking chap wearing a *petasus* and *talaria* and sporting a *caduceus*, and if you are a thief, rogue or vagabond or happen to be traveling, you couldn't be in better company.

petrology   See **Zingg.**

pharmakos   See **polypharmacy.**

phelonion (fuh LOH nee uhn) *n.* This is a vestment worn by priests of the Eastern Orthodox Church, similar to a *chasuble* (CHAZ yuh buhl) worn by the celebrant at Mass in the Western Church. *Phelonion* was taken intact from Late Greek, where it had a variant *phailonion*, an alteration of *phainolion* resulting from an erroneous transposition of consonants. The term *phainolion* came from Latin *paenula* (cloak), a sleeveless garment with an opening for the head alone, covering the entire body. The 1753 Supplement to Ephraim Chambers's *Cyclopedia; or, an Universal Dictionary of Arts and Sciences* describes the *paenula* as " ... among the Romans, a thick garment fit for a defence against cold and rain," but by 1868, it was more fully described in Wharton B. Marriott's *Vestarium Christianum: the Origin and Gradual Development of the Dress of Holy Ministry in the Church*, particularly as to " ... its gradual exaltation from the garb of slaves or of peasants to one which even emperors might wear in travelling, and which was expressly prescribed in the fifth century of our era as the dress of senators." Thus, the *paenula* eventually rose from its humble origin to an ecclesiastical vestment, and was taken into English.

phenakistoscope (fen uh KIST uh skope) *n.* This is the name of a scientific toy that produces the illusion of moving pictures. It consists of a disk with figures representing a moving person or object arranged about the center in successive positions. When the disk is turned around rapidly and the figures are viewed through a fixed slit, or their reflections are seen in a mirror through a series of slits cut into the rim of the disk itself, the continuity of the successive images produces the illusion of actual motion. The name of the gadget is derived from Greek *phenakistes* (deceiver), based on the verb *phenakizein* (to deceive) and the noun *phenax* (deceiver). According to the 1838 edition of the *Encyclopedia Britannica*, the device was invented by a Dr. Roget and then improved by a succession of people. It has been called by various other names, including *stroboscope* (STROH buh skohp) and *magic disk*. Another optical toy based on the same principle is the *zoetrope* (ZOH uh trope), from Greek *zoe* (life) plus the suffix *-tropos* (turning), based on the verb *trepein* (to turn); also called *zootrope* (ZOH oh trope), *zoo-* (ZOH oh) being the more normal combining form of *zoe*. With this optical toy, successive figures on the inside of a rapidly revolving cylinder are viewed through slits in its circumference and give the appearance of a single animated object or person. This toy was also known as the "wheel of life." In the *"Bab" Ballads* (1869), W. S. Gilbert wrote these lines: "And also, with amusement rife/ A 'Zoetrope, or Wheel of Life ...'" An 1881 edition of *The Athenaeum* explained: "By a *zoetrope* ... figures are projected on a screen ... exhibited as in motion ... with all ... changes of position." Ah, the simple pleasures that preceded the movies and television!

philologaster (fil OL uh gas tur) *n.* In my *1000 Most Challenging Words*, I explain that the suffix *-aster* forms nouns denoting "inferior versions of the real thing." Thus, a *poetaster* (POE uh tas tuhr) is a "second-rate poet; a rhymester, a versifier"; and I give other examples of *-aster* nouns. One I omitted is *philologaster*, a lovely mouthful, and as you have already guessed, it means an "incompetent philologist," a mere "dabbler in philology," a "petty philologist" or a "would-be philologist." While the Latin *philologus*, taken from the Greek *philologos* means "student of literature" or "scholar," *philologist* has a narrower meaning: "one versed in *linguistics*, the science of language." *Linguist* used to mean (and still can, in context) "one skilled in a number of languages, a polyglot," but with the development of *linguistics*, it has taken on the meaning of "specialist in linguistics," or "linguistician," and the result can be somewhat confusing, expecially to older people who grew up before *linguistics* developed. I prefer *linguistician*. I pray that *-aster* will never be attached to any noun denoting an activity of mine. *Philologaster* and *etymologaster* (I just made that one up) is fightin' words.

phit See **phut**.

phlogiston (flo JIST on, -GIST-, -uhn) *n.* Until the 1770s and the development of the theory of oxygenation, *phlogiston* was believed to be an element, a material substance, that separated from any combustible body in the course of burning. Metals were supposed to be created from the union of their *calces*, the *friable*, i.e., ashy, residue left after *calcination* (i.e., heating to a high temperature), with *phlogiston*. In short, *phlogiston* was a nonexistent chemical thought to be released during combustion. The chemist James B. Conant (he was my organic chemistry professor at Harvard in 1924–25, and president of Harvard from 1933 to 1953) asked, logically enough, "What manner of substance or principle could *phlogiston* be that when it was added to another material the total mass or weight diminished?" The French scientist and pioneer in chemistry Lavoisier (1743–94) disproved the *phlogiston theory*, which had held that every combustible substance was a compund of *phlogiston*, liberated through combustion, leaving the other constituent as a residue. The word was taken via New Latin from the neuter of Greek *phlogistos* (burnt, inflammable), a verbal adjective from *phlogizein* (to set afire), based on *phlog-*, the stem of *phlox* (flame), related to *phlegein* (to burn). It was from *phlegein* that *Phlegethon*, the river of liquid fire in Hades that flowed into the river Acheron, took its name. In *Paradise Lost*, Milton writes of "Fierce *Phlegethon*/Whose waves of torrent fire inflame with rage." My memory may be faulty, but I remember wearing a little sack, hanging by a loose cord around my neck and containing a bit of substance smelling of camphor, as a preventive during the influenza epidemic of 1918. The substance was called, unless I am much mistaken, "antiphlogiston," though I can't see any earthly connection with the long-discarded *phlogiston theory*; but mother insisted, and I didn't get influenza. As to *friable*, mentioned above. I quote from my *1000 Most Challenging Words*: " ... like *ply* and *pliable, fry* and *friable* are unrelated. *Friable* describes anything easily crumbled or broken ... from ... Latin *friabilis*, based on *friare* (to crumble) ... Col. Sanders should not come to mind when you see ... *friable*."

phrontist   See **phrontistery**.

phrontistery (FRON tis tur ee) *n*. The Greeks gave the name *phrontisterion* to a "place for thought and study," a "thinking-shop," according to one of the *O.E.D.* definitions; would the modern "think tank" be such a place? Aristophanes applied it in ridicule to the school of Socrates. It may now be used to denote any institution of learning, though it is rarely in evidence. The Greek noun was derived from *phrontistes* (philosopher, profound thinker, one with intellectual pretensions) from the verb *phrontizein* (to reflect), based on *phrontis* (thought, reflection). The word *phrontist* applies to a "deep thinker," a "person involved in study, reflection, meditation," and it, too, in its Greek form, was applied ironically by Aristophanes to Socrates. In the early days of its history, Oriel, the Oxford college founded in 1326, was called "the *phrontisterion*," half in earnest, half in ridicule. The ridicule part shows that anti-eggheadism is nothing new.

phut (FUT) *adv., n., interj*. This is the way it is pronounced in the expression *to go phut* (more later, in the discussion of other uses). *To go phut* is "to break, become useless, unserviceable, to come to nothing. According to the *O.E.D.*, *phut*, in this use, comes from Hindustani *phatna* (to split). There is yet another *phut*, pronounced differently (F'T): an imitative or onomatopoeic word indicating a thud, a dull sound, as of the impact of a bullet or the explosion of a distant shell. It has been used, for example, to indicate the thud of a tennis ball against the racket. As an interjection, it indicates a feeling of hopelessness: "We'll do all we can to help, but if it doesn't work, *phut*!" The *O.E.D.* calls it "echoic; an imitation of a sound" and gives an example from Steevens's *With Kitchener to Khartoum* (1898): "Thud! went the first gun, and *phutt*! came faintly back, as its shell burst on the zariba." But the *O.E.D. Supplement* corrects the *O.E.D.*'s etymology, stating that the two *phuts* are one and the same. So much for *phut*; as for **zariba**, see that entry. A related word is *phit* (FIT), which is an imitation of various sounds. An 1894 issue of the American magazine *Outing* describes a bear that " ... gave a soft *'phit!'* of startled recognition, pricked up his ears and turned his head askew." An 1896 issue of the *Daily Chronicle* wrote of "the pert crack of the Lee-Metford, the *'phit'* of whose bullet is lost in the whirr of a lead-coated stone from the Matabele arsenal." If you hear *f't!* or *fit!* from fairly close by, duck!

phylacobiosis (FIL uh koh beye OH sis) *n.* This is a term in entomology for the arrangement whereby a particular species of ant dwells in a termite nest and apparently performs the service of the soldier class of termite known as the *nasute* (NAY sooht) caste, whose function is to guard the nest against predator insects. *Phylacobiosis* comes from *phylak-*, the stem of Greek *phylax* (guard), plus *-biosis*, a suffix denoting "way of life," from *bios* (life), related to *bioun* (to live). We are more familiar with the prefix *bi-* or *bio-*, from the same Greek source, as in *biology, biopsy*, etc. *Phylacobiosis* is one type of *mixobiosis*, a general term (you guessed it) that denotes a form of relationship known as *mutualism*, in which organisms (such as ants) of different species live together in common or composite colonies, in an arrangement benefiting both. *Mixobiosis* is built of *mixo-*, the combining form of *mixis* (mixing), from the verb *mignunai* (to mix), plus *-biosis*. *Nasute*, from Latin *nasus* (nose), describes any organism with a well-developed proboscis and applies specifically to the class of modified soldier termites mentioned above, so called because their jaws have receded, and the tops of their heads form a type of snout which ejects a sticky fluid that entraps attacking insects. Now that the linguistic exegesis has somehow developed into a short entomological sermon, you can stop worrying about those vulnerable termites and begin worrying about your vulnerable wooden house.

phyle   See **taxiarch.**

piacular (peye AK yooh lur) *adj.* This adjective would appear to have two antithetical meanings: "expiatory," i.e., atoning for; and "requiring expiation," i.e., extremely bad, atrocious, sinful, wicked. In other words, a *piacular* act is either one that is good, in the sense that it atones for a bad act, or one that is bad, in that it requires an act of atonement. The word comes from Latin *piacularis* (atoning, expiating), based on *piaculum* (a means of atoning for sin, for appeasing a deity—but Horace and Livy both used it in the opposite sense: an act requiring expiation, i.e., a sin or crime). It all goes back to the verb *piare* (to propitiate, to seek to appease by an offering) and the adjective *pius* (dutiful; more generally, honest, upright). It is obvious that care must be taken to make clear the sense in which *piacular* is being used (if you care to use it!). John R. Macduff, in *Memories of Patmos* (1871), wrote of " ... the great brazen altar of burnt offering, where *piacular* or bloody offerings were alone presented," using the adjective in the sense of "expiatory," while De Quincy, writing on *Whiggism* (1857), used the word in the opposite sense, describing a politician in terms of "[leaving] no stone unturned to cleanse his little ... fold from its *piacular* pollution." Strange (and dangerous!) for a word to signify two opposite things.

Pierian (peye EER ee uhn) *adj*. Literally, this adjective applies to *Pieria*, a district in northern Thessaly in Greece, the reputed home of the Muses and by extension, to the arts, expecially poetry and learning. To refresh your recollection, there were nine muses in Greek mythology, patron goddesses of the arts, daughters of Zeus and Mnemosyne (memory): Calliope (epic poetry and eloquence), Euterpe (music and lyric poetry), Erato (love poetry), Polyhymnia (oratory and sacred poetry), Clio (history), Melpomene (tragedy), Thalia (comedy), Terpsichore (dance and choral song) and Urania (astronomy). Paintings at Herculaneum show them in their special attributes. Early in Greek history the Muses were worshiped in *Pieria*, for which reason they were also known as the *Pierides*, and there were springs in various districts considered sacred to them. Pope's famous line "A little learning is a dang'rous thing" is followed by "Drink deep, or taste not the *Pierian* spring"; and John Addington Symonds wrote: "*Pierian* Muses! hear my prayer." A *pierid* (PEYE uh rid) is any butterfly of the family *Pieridae*, typical of which is the *Pieris* (PEYE uh ris), the cabbage butterfly.

pilliwinks (PIL ee winks) *n*. This word, which sounds carefree and charming, like a children's game or a mischievous prank, is actually the name of a hideous instrument of torture designed to crush fingers—ugh! The *O.E.D.* lists a fantastic variety of spellings of this delightful gadget, 16 of them, in fact, all the way from *pyrwykes* to *pinniwinkis* to *pirliewinkles*, and notes that one of the variant forms, *pyrewinkes*, "coincides with the contemporary spelling of *periwinkle* (the flower)" but hastens to assure us that "there is no obvious connexion [note spelling] of sense." "Origin unknown" is the final verdict—an observation maddening but not unfamiliar to etymologists. Specialists in this category of artifact state that the *pilliwinks* were supposed to resemble thumbscrews, also known in the good old days as "thumbikins" or "thumbkins," another name that sounds like delightful woodland sprites beloved of little children.

pilpul (PIL poohl) *n*. This is an Aramaic word for "vigorous, keen argumentation and debate among rabbinical scholars" on the subject of proper interpretation of Talmudic principles and rules, particularly with respect to moral and religious matters. The word is related to the verb *pilpel* (to search, debate). *Aramaic* is a Semitic tongue that goes back to at least the ninth century B.C. It spread all over southwest Asia as a commercial lingua franca. After the Babylonian Captivity, it was adopted by the Jews and replaced Hebrew. The

Talmud, the focal point and the most important influence in Jewish life over its long history, is a collection of civil and religious laws, moral doctrine and ritual. There were two editorial revisions, the Palestinian, produced in the mid-fourth century A.D., and the Babylonian, completed at the end of the following century. The later revision was three times as large as the earlier one and is considered the more important version. The study of the Talmud and Talmudic disputation were for centuries the focal point of Jewish education and life.

pimp (pimp) *n.* Well you may wonder at the inclusion, in a dictionary of obscure words, of such a simple and familiar term, until you learn that there are two vastly dissimilar types of *pimp* in this world, or at least in that part known as the southern counties of England—or some of them. The familiar *pimp* is the pander or procurer, who lives off the earnings of prostitutes. The other type is—well, let me explain. Some years ago, as I entered the ironmonger's [British English for *hardware store*] in the village in the County of Kent, England, where I live about half of the time, I noticed a sign in the window: Pimps—2 for 5 d. (that was before the radical change, on February 15, 1971, in the British currency system, when *d*, the symbol of "pence," was changed to *p*). Naturally, that stirred not only my curiosity, but also my amazement. The shop was run, in the occasional absence of the young manager, by a somewhat slow-witted elderly couple, and this was one of those days. Setting aside, for the moment, the original object of my visit, I innocently asked for two *pimps*. After a certain amount of chin scratching, the old woman announced that they were out of them. That put me in a difficult position, but I forged ahead and asked, "What *are* pimps? The not-so-slow-witted woman stared at me for a moment or two and asked, intelligently enough, "Begging your pardon, sir, but if you didn't know what they were, how did you know you wanted them?" Trapped, I confessed, "I didn't really want any *pimps* and was only trying to find out what they were." At this juncture, the old man emerged through a little door saying, "I found one; here it is," and displayed a little bundle of kindling in cylindrical form, about ten inches long and eight inches in diameter, tied with wire. "A *pimp*, sir, is a bung o' firewood, and you can have this one for nothing if you want it." *Bung*, in this context, was a new one on me as well, and I hadn't heard *firewood* used to mean "kindling" before, but I let that pass and asked the old gentleman whether *pimp* was heard all over England or only locally. (I was sure the innocent twain hadn't run into the other kind of *pimp*.) "Oh, no, sir, not everywhere, only here in Kent, and maybe in Sussex, but only just across the border." The border between those two counties has always seemed rather vague in that part of the country. So I accepted the gift, and since I was writing an Anglo-American dictionary at that period of my life, hastened home to make some notes. Later on, reading Vita Sackville-West's *The Edwardians*, I found a passage in which the young nobleman, Lord of the manor, " … looked into the *pimping-shed*, where old Turnour [one of the domestic staff] was chopping faggots." I rejoiced in this confirmation of the philological advice supplied by the sweet old couple at the ironmonger's.

pisé   See **tapia.**

plagiary   See **plagium.**

plagium (PLAY jee uhm) *n. Plagium* is Latin for "kidnapping," and it was taken intact into the English language to denote that felony. It was based on the Latin *plaga* (net for hunting). The Romans coined the word *plagiarius* for "kidnapper," and the Roman poet Martial used it in jest for "literary thief," i.e., "plagiarist." Another English word for "kidnapper" is *plagiary*, taken directly from *plagiarius*. What has come down from all this in modern usage are the words *plagiarism* and *plagiarist*, based squarely on Martial's jocular metaphorical extension. Samuel Johnson, in a 1758 issue of *The Idler*, wrote of "compilers and *plagiaries* ... who give us again what we had before," a wonderfully succinct gibe at "literary thieves."

pledget   See **dossil.**

pollicitation (puh lis ih TAY shuhn) *n.* The Latin noun *pollicitatio* means "offer" or "promise"; the verb *polliceri* means "to make an offer"; *pollicitari* means "to keep promising" and is the frequentative of *polliceri*. (A *frequentative* of a verb, as explained under that heading in my *1000 Most Challenging Words*, is a related verb that "expresses the continual repetition of the action of the original verb.") *Pollicitatus* is the past participle of *pollicitari* and is the origin of *pollicitatio*, the Latin ancestor of our headword. Why *pollicitatus* was preferred to *pollicitus*, the past participle of *polliceri* (which would have produced *pollicitio* in Latin and *pollicition* in English) is hard to explain, except for reasons of pronunciation. As to *polliceri*, that arose by combining *pro* (forth) with *liceri* (to bid). In Roman times, a *pollicitation* was "an informal offer, not yet accepted by the promissee and unenforceable, except in the case of a promise of *dos*," the property contributed to the husband by the wife or by a third party on her behalf. That contribution originally became the husband's absolutely but was later made legally returnable to the original donor on the termination of the marriage by death or divorce. In English law, *dos* (Latin for "dowry, marriage portion") denoted the property settled by or on behalf of a wife upon her husband at the time of the marriage; it is the origin of the term *dower*, which could mean either the "property settled by the wife upon the husband," or the converse, as the case might be. These practices are now obsolete. (The way things are going these days, the same is beginning to be true of marriage itself!)

polypharmacy (pah lee FAR muh see) *n. Poly-* is the combining form of Greek *polys* (many), and *pharmakon* is Greek for "drug, medicine," so that the combination *polypharmacon*, New Latin from Greek *polypharmakon*, designated a remedy consisting of many ingredients. *Polypharmacy* denotes the administering of numerous drugs concurrently, especially for the treatment of the same ailment. In current health officers' slang the word is used to indicate a situation whereby a patient has been administered such a multiplicity of drugs that it is impossible to ascertain which drug is causing what or the overall effect of the combination. This definition comes from Dr. Melvin Konner's *Becoming a Doctor* (1987). Allegedly overheard: "Well, Freddy's really ridin' the roller-coaster of *polypharmacy*, an' I don't know what's doin' what to what." This tendency of some doctors today is known as "pill-happiness" (meaning no offense—some of my best friends and saviors are doctors). And while we're at it, look out for *pharmakos* (FAR muh kos), somehow and probably irregularly derived from *pharmakon* but having nothing whatever to do with pharmacology. It is a word for a "scapegoat" of a rather specialized variety, in the form of a person, usually one already condemned to death for some crime or other, sacrificed according to ancient Greek custom as a means of purification or atonement for a community or city. Though *pharmakos* is technically unrelated to *pharmakon*, I suppose that the purification involved was somehow felt to be "remedial" in a way, since atonement and purging are at least metaphorically related.

Polypheme (POL ih feem) *n*. This is the anglicized form of *Polyphemus*, one of the Cyclopes (from the Greek *kyklops*, formed of *kyklos*, circle, plus *ops*, eye), a fabled race of giants who inhabited chiefly Sicily. They had one eye in the middle of the forehead and figured in *The Odyssey*. *Cyclops*, with a lowercase *c*, is used allusively to mean "giant" or "monster" generally. Their occupation was the forging of iron for the god Vulcan. According to Ovid's *Metamorphases*, Acis, beloved of Galatea, a sea nymph (not the Galatea beloved of Pygmalion), was the rival of *Polyphemus*, who in a jealous rage crushed him to death with a huge rock. Acis was then transformed into the river Acis. (*Metamorphoses*, as the name indicates, relates tale after tale about mythical transformations, which intrigued Ovid.) The bereaved Galatea threw herself into the sea, joining her sister nymphs. Handel composed an opera entitled *Acis and Galatea*, first performed in 1720 but rarely heard these days, like (sadly) so many of his operas. Homer tells us that when Odysseus landed in Sicily, *Polyphemus* captured him and twelve of the crew and ate six of them. Odysseus managed to blind him and get away with the survivors. *Polyphemus* has lent his name to the *Polyphemus moth*, a large yellowish-brown silkworm species (*Telea Polyphemus*) with a prominent eyelike spot on each of its hind wings, and to certain one-eyed animals. The name *Polyphemus* was taken from the Greek adjective *polyphemos*, meaning literally "figuring in many tales or legends, much spoken of," and, as we have seen, the adjective suited him.

polyphloisbic (pol ee FLOIS bik) *adj*. We all know that the prefix *poly-* indicates muchness, being the combining form of the Greek adjective *polys*, meaning "many," "much," "heavy," "great," "large," "wide" or "long" (I must stop somewhere), as the context requires. *Phloisbos* is Greek for "din," and the combination of the two plus the usual adjectival suffix *-ic* gives us the delightful adjective *polyphloisbic*, modifying anything that makes a hell of a noise. Homer used it to describe the sea (*thalassa*) as "loud-roaring" (*polyphloisboio thalasses* in the genitive case), and Thackeray concocted *poluphloisboiotatotic* as though from a Greek superlative form with the ending *-otatos*. But there is no reason why you shouldn't use it to describe the rush of a New York subway express train or the "music" of a frantic rock group who, in the deathless prose of Woody Allen (*Hannah and Her Sisters*) "looked as though they wanted to stab their mothers."

polyptych (POL uhp tik) *n.* A work of art, often an altarpiece, consisting of four or more panels that are hinged and fold together, is called a *polyptych*, from Greek *polyptychos* (having many folds, folded a number of times), built of *poly-* (many) plus *ptyche* (fold, layer). The reason this term applies only to a work of four or more panels is that there are specific terms for those consisting of a smaller number, viz., *diptych* and *triptych*. A *diptych*, as you might have guessed from the prefix *di-* (two, in both Latin and Greek), consists of two pictures, also usually forming an altarpiece, hinged and folding together. But *diptych* has several other meanings as well. The ancient Romans used waxed tablets on which they wrote with a pointed instrument called a *stylus*. They sometimes used a two-leaved hinged tablet that folded together to protect the writing on the easily damaged waxed surfaces. That double tablet was known in Late Latin as *diptycha*, a plural noun, from the neuter plural of Greek *diptychos*. *Dyptychs*, from the Latin plural *diptycha*, became the name of a two-leaved tablet with a list of the names of the living on one side, and on the other, the names of the dead commemorated in eucharistic services. *Dyptych* is applied also to a literary work with two contrasting parts (e.g., the same tale from two different points of view, as in the Japanese classic *Rashomon*, which, however, included the versions of more than two persons). Finally, the same word is used for any work consisting of two matching parts covering complementary or contrasting illustrations of two aspects of a single general topic—e.g., the flora and fauna of a particular region. Then we get to *triptych* (also *triptich*), the three-leaved waxed writing tablet used by the ancient Romans; or a picture (sometimes a carving) with three hinged and folding parts, usually an altarpiece, consisting of a central panel and two side panels each half its size that fold over it. The term can also apply to a literary or musical work with three matching or contrasting sections. Of the same origin is *triptyque* (also *triptique* or *tryptyque*), from the French *triptyque*, taken from Greek *triptychos*, denoting a customs pass for the temporary importation of a car into a particular country, or a general international pass for a car. What is the explanation of that use? Do those passes consist of three leaves, or is it a pun on "trip-ticket?"

polysemant (pol ee SEE muhnt) *n*. From Late Greek *polysemantos* (having many meanings), based on the prefix *poly-* (many) plus *semainein* (to mean), from *sema* (sign), we get *polysemant*, meaning a "word with more than one meaning." The adjective is *polysemantic* (pol ee suh MAN tik), and that puts us on somewhat more familiar ground, since *semantic* and *semantics* are met with quite frequently. A related adjective, *polysemous* (pol ee SEE muhs, puh LIS uh muhs), describing words having many meanings, comes from Late Latin *polysemus*, taken from Greek *polysemos*, built of *poly-* plus *sema*. *Polysemy* (pol ee SEE mee, puh LIS uh mee), from New Latin *polysemia*, means "multiplicity of meanings." You will find many words in this book that qualify as *polysemants*. It is my habit to describe them as *versatile*. One doesn't have to search for *polysemants* among obscure words: Just look up *cow* and *how* in any unabridged dictionary, and you'll be amazed at their *polysemia*!

polysemantic See **polysemant.**

polysemous See **polysemant.**

polysemy See **polysemant.**

pornocracy (por NOK ruh see) *n*. We are all quite familiar with the noun *pornography*, but few of know how that word came about. Here's the story: *Porne* is Greek for "whore," and *graphein* is the Greek verb for "to write." That led to the noun *pornographos* (describing prostitutes and their profession), so that the original force of *pornography* was literature on that interesting subject. But the scope of the word grew to include obscene writing, art, photography, etc., especially that without artistic merit or "redeeming social value," as the courts put it. Then what about *pornocracy*? We know that the suffix *-cracy*, as in *democracy, autocracy, technocracy*, etc., indicates ruling force; it comes from Greek *kratos* (rule). And *porne* is our old friend "whore." The rule of whores? Actually, their influence, especially over (for shame!) the papal court in the early half of the tenth century. History says so, and who are we to deny it?

posset (POS uht) *n*. Once upon a time, a *posset* was served either as a delicacy or as a medicinal potion to people suffering from colds or other ailments. It was a warm drink of milk curdled with a liquor, usually ale or wine, sweetened with sugar and spices and sometimes thickened with bread or eggs. The poet Robert Herrick, in *Hesperides: or the Works both Humane and Divine of R.H.* (1648), says in a poem to Phillis: "Thou shalt have *possets*, wassails fine;/Not made of ale, but spiced wine!" In that case, Phillis wasn't ill; the *posset* was a delicacy, not a medicine. But Frances E. Trollope (sister-in-law of *the* Trollope), in *A Charming Fellow* (1876), expresses concern about an invalid: "I do wish he would try a hot *posset* of a night, just before going to bed." The word was used as a transitive verb meaning "to make curdle" or, as Oliver

Wendell Holmes used it, "to pamper, with delicacies," writing of one "cosseted and *posseted* and prayed over"; and intransitively meaning "to make a *posset*," as George Meredith used it in *The Ordeal of Richard Feverel* (1859): "She broke off to go *posseting* for her dear invalid." *Posset* pots are two-handled vessels used in making *possets*, and *posset* cups have two handles, usually a cover and a spout for feeding *possets* to invalids. They are rare now and are sought after by collectors of 17th- and 18th-century curios. In *Hamlet*, the ghost, in Act I, Scene 5, tells Hamlet how he was poisoned by Claudius:

> Upon my secure hour thy uncle stole,/With juice of cursed hebonon [a drink containing a poisonous juice, possibly henbane (*Hyoscyamus niger*), a poisonous plant of the deadly nightshade family or of the German *Eibenbaum*, yew-tree]/in a vial,/And in the porches of mine ear did pour/The leperous distilment; whose effect/Holds such an enmity with blood of man/That, swift as quicksilver, it courses through/The natural gates and alleys of the body;/And with a sudden vigour it doth *posset*/And curds ... /The thin and wholesome blood: so did it mine...

A happier kind of *posset* is mentioned in *Merry Wives of Windsor* (Act I, Scene 4), when Mistress Quickly says to Simple: "Go; and we'll have a *posset* for't soon at night, in faith, at the latter end of a sea-coal fire." And in the same play (Act V, Scene 5), Page says to Falstaff: "Yet be cheerful, knight: thou shalt eat a *posset* to-night at my house ..." Eat? That *posset* must indeed have been greatly thickened with bread! Delicacy or remedy, the *posset* sounds like a good drink. It came from Middle English *posschote, poshote, possot*; origin unknown, though there may be some connection with *posca*, a mixture of weak wine, water and vinegar once used as a remedy.

posslq (POS 'l kyooh) *n.* One evening, a dinner guest was telling us about his recent Christmas party. In listing the guests, he got to: "Then there was my son Bert and ... er ... the ... er ... woman he's living with and my daughter Anne and ... er ... the ... er ... man she's living with—but surely, there must be a better way of saying this!" That brought on a general discussion in which all the guests took a hand at trying to concoct a less awkward term for the person one's child is ... er ... living with. *Boyfriend* and *girlfriend* were dismissed without hesitation for inexactitude, as not necessarily implying cohabitation. His *woman*? Her *man*? Too crude; too suggestive of Tarzan and Jane. *Mistress, lover*? Too much like *Madame Bovary* or *La Bohème*. *Live-in companion, live-in friend, housemate, partner* and Lord knows what else were turned down as inexact or tasteless or stiff or loose or whatever. One of those present, well versed in Briticisms, including archaisms, came up with *tally-husband* and *tally-woman*, based on the obsolete slang or dialect expression *to live in tally*, and that caused general derision until this trustworthy fellow swore that the expression was defined by the *O.E.D.* as "to cohabit without marriage." That suggestion was, understandably, howled down. However, despair not. The California tax authorities have come to the rescue: *posslq*! This is an official term, an acronym considerably more difficult to pronounce than *Nato* or *Opec*, constructed as follows: *Person of the Opposite Sex Sharing Living Quarters.* It is officially defined as "either of two persons, one of each sex, who share living quarters but are not related by blood, marriage or adoption"; in other words, a man and a woman who have forgone "the benefit of clergy" (in popular but inexact meaning of that phrase). This rather quaint acronym, however, would seem not to cover the case of a homosexual ménage (note the "one of *each* sex" in the official definition). To remedy that situation, simply change the *O* (for *opposite)* to *S* (for *same*) in *posslq,* and you come up with *pssslq*) (PSS 'l kyooh), which is even harder to pronounce than *posslq.* If, to avoid the rather ominous hissing sound of *psssql,* you substitute *identical* for *same,* you wind up with *pisslq,* which is easier to pronounce but might prove embarrassing. To cover the case of a bisexual housemate, we would have to change *posslq* to *bpslq*—which has the advantage of being one letter shorter but the disadvantage of being unpronounceable—or to *possdcslq* (person of the opposite or same sex depending on circumstances sharing living quarters), which may be all-embracing (no pun intended) but is self-evidently unacceptable, leaving the alternative *peossslq* (person of *either* the opposite or same sex sharing living quarters), but that may be unclear and in any event involves excessive hissing. When it comes to a *ménage à trois,* we would get two *posslqs* in one package, if you follow me, which I'm having a hard time doing myself. In the rare case of the live-in buddy's being a hermaphrodite, whom the relevant authorities might designate a person of *indeterminate* sex, we would once more be stuck with the awkward *pisslq,* but surely there would be a creative linguist languishing somewhere in the labyrinthine quarters of the authority who would be quick to replace *identical* with *unclassified* or *unclassifiable* or something or other beginning with *u* and come up with *pusslq.* Not to worry, as the British say.

poteen　　See **boreen.**

pradakshina (prah dah KSHEE nah), also **pradakshna** (prah DAH kshnah) *n.* This word is taken from Sanskrit, where it is built of *pra* (in front) plus *dakshina* (right, cf. Latin *dexter*, English *dexterous*, etc.) and is the name of the Hindu and Buddhist religious rite of walking around something in a clockwise direction. In *Sinhalese Social Organization: The Kandyan Period* (1956), Ralph Pieris writes of one who "reverentially performs *pradakshina* three times to the diagram." Monier Monier-Williams, in *Religious Thought and Life in India* (1833), narrates an elaborate instance of this form of worship: "A pilgrim ... sets out from the source of the Ganges ... and walks by the left bank of the river to its mouth ... ; then, turning round, he proceeds by the right bank to [the point] ... whence he departed. This is called *Pradakshina.*" There is a moving scene in the film of M. M. Kaye's *The Far Pavilions* where the widow circumambulates her dead husband's funeral pyre clockwise, reciting the words "Ram Ram" over and over, preparing herself to join the corpse in the rite of suttee. In my *British*

English, A to Zed, I include the headword *withershins, widdershins*, meaning "counterclockwise," with the comment: "It is said to be bad luck to walk around a church *withershins*, a practice that sounds like one of those tiresome routines developed in black magic or withcraft." Somehow, the preference for the right over the left extends to favoring clockwise to its opposite. The Latin adjective *sinister* literally means "left, on the left," but figuratively "wrong, improper, unlucky, unfavorable." And there are more than 80 British dialectal terms, all of them more or less pejorative, for *left-handed*, including *bawky-handed, coochy-gammy, cow-pawed, scroochy* and *cuddy-wifted*, to name a few. No such prejudice prevails against *southpaws* in baseball.

praecipitatio   See **virga.**

precentor (pree SEN tur, prih-) *n.* This was the title of a person who led or directed the singing of a church choir or congregation. In some cathedrals, he was a member of the chapter (general assembly of canons, who attended to the business of the cathedral) ranking next to the dean (head of the chapter), and his duties were deputed to a *succentor* (suhk SEN tuhr), sometimes known as a *subchanter* (sub CHAN tuhr), who acted as the *precentor*'s deputy. We read in Walter A. Hook's *Church Dictionary* (1871): "Formerly the *precentor* in most of the Cathedrals ranked next to the Dean. Now he is usually a minor canon." Things do change, even in ecclesiastical hierarchies. All of these terms are based on the Latin verb *canere* (to sing), preceded by the appropriate prefix *prae-* (before, in front) or *sub-* or *suc-* (under), as the case may be. Now, if you find yourself in a cathedral and want to present yourself to the choir director, you'll know how to address him or her, and won't bungle.

precocial   See **nidicolous.**

prejink   See **perjink.**

presbycusis (prez buh KYOOH sis, pres-) *n.* This is the technical term for "loss of hearing in advancing age" and a good example of a word containing an element with which we are more familiar in other combinations: *presby-*, as in *Presbyterian. Presby-* is the combining form of Greek *presbys* (old). Thus, a *presbyter*, an "elder in the Presbyterian church," is based on Greek *presbyteros*, from *presbys* plus *-teros*, the comparative suffix. I have already dealt with *presbyopia* in my *1000 Most Challenging Words*. It means "farsightedness," another annoying ocular affliction of old age, and involves the suffix *-opia*, from Greek *ops* (eye). What about *-cusis*, then? Here we combine *presby-* with *(a)kousis*, Greek for "hearing," related to the verb *akouein* (to hear), the source of our *acoustic(s)*. These things do come together if you look far enough. *Presbyopia, presbycusis*, ah me! "Last scene of all,/That ends this strange eventful history,/Is second childishness, and mere oblivion,/Sans teeth,*sans eyes*, sans taste, sans everything." Shakespeare (end of Jaques's speech in *As*

You Like It, Act II, Scene 7) left out the *ears* by name, but *everything* includes them, doesn't it?

primipara (preye MIP ur uh) *n.* From Latin *primus* (first) plus *parere* (to bring forth, bear) we get *primipara*, a "woman who has given birth to her first child or is about to do so." Some dictionaries define the word as applying to female animals as well. Others include the definition a "woman who has given birth to only one child," with the implication that there aren't going to be any more. This would describe the majority of women in China, which now favors the one-child family. The adjective is *primiparous* (preye MIP uhr uhs), the condition *primaparity* (preye mih PAR uh tee). As you might expect, a *multipara* (mul TIP uh ruh) is a "woman who has borne more than one child," and *multiparous* (mul TIP uh ruhs) and *multiparity* (mul tuh PAR uh tee) are the corresponding adjective and noun, except that they include as well the phenomenon of giving birth at any one time to multiple offspring and clearly apply to animals as well as women. *Multiparity* in women has become fairly frequent in recent days as the result of the administration of fertility drugs to women previously incapable of conception—variously described, in the joke about the group of recently arrived refugee German gynecologists, as "inconceivable," "unbearable," "impenetrable," "impregnable," and (climactically) "insurmountable." You have to supply the exaggerated phony accents.

primiparity   See **primipara**.

primiparous   See **primipara**.

proceleusmatic (proh suh loohz MAT ik) *n., adj.* This word has two distinct yet interestingly related meanings. As an adjective, it means "inciting, animating, rousing," and its Greek derivation explains this use. It comes, via Late Latin *proceleusmaticus*, from Greek *prokeleusmatikos*, based on *prokeleusmat-*, the stem of *prokeleusma* (incitement), from the verb *prokeleuein* (to urge on, give orders to), built of the prefix *pro-* (for—as opposed to against; cf. *pros* and *cons*) plus *keleuein* (to urge, command, drive on). As a noun, a *proceleusmatic* is a term denoting a metrical foot consisting of four short syllables, and it is used as an adjective as well, describing such a foot. The connection between the two meanings is found in the fact that in ancient times, such four-syllable or *proceleusmatic* feet were used in songs by which, according to Dr. Samuel Johnson in *A Journey to the Western Islands of Scotland* (1775), "the rowers of [ancient] galleys were animated." In *The History of the Crusades*, by Charles Mills (1818), we are told that "In an army ... there were as many *proceleusmatick* words as there were banners." Carl Engel, in *Introduction to the Study of National Music* (1866), confirming Johnson, writes of "the oar song of the Hebridians, which resembles the *proceleusmatic* verse by which the rowers of Grecian gelleys were animated." As to the two "distinct meanings" first mentioned, the "inciting" or "urging" came first, as specifically relating to the rhythmic beat inflicted, as it were, on those poor galley slaves, and the general prosodic application followed.

properispomenon (proh per ih SPOH muh non) *n., adj.* If you are not interested in classical Greek grammar, you might do well to sit this one out, because we're going to go on to discuss *perispomenon* (pa rih SPOH muh non) as well. But you never know: You might just bump into one or even both of them. A *properispomenon* is a term in Greek grammar for a "word having a circumflex on its penult," and the same term serves as an adjective describing such a word. It is the neuter of the passive participle of the verb *properispan* (to put a circumflex on the penult). You know, of course, that the penult is the next-to-the-last syllable of a word, like the *-tan-* in *titanic*. A *perispomenon*, on the other hand, is a "word with a circumflex on its *last* syllable." It is formed of the Greek prefix *peri-* (around) plus the verb *span* (to pull, stretch), which we have already met in the discussion of our old friend *properispomenon*, and like that word, it can function as an adjective as well. Since I'm sure you know what a circumflex is, we don't have to go into that. If you need any more information about *properispomena* or *perispomena* and want to find examples of them, please consult your *O.E.D.*.

proprium (PROH pree uhm) *n.* This word, the neuter of the Latin adjective *proprius* (literally, one's own special, particular, peculiar; by extension, peculiar to, characteristic of, a person or thing), means a "distinctive characteristic," an "attribute that is essential to someone or something." It is "selfhood," or "essential nature" or "individuation in personality." I went into the meaning of *quiddity* in my *1000 Most Challenging Words* and called it "the essence of a thing or person, the whatever-it-is that makes a thing or person what he, she, or it is." I spoke, too, of its synonym *haecceity*, "that which gives something its unique quality or characteristic," pointing out that *haecceity* was a "partial synonym," in that *quiddity* applied to both persons and things while *haecceity* was used only of things. I could have included a related word with which, at the time, I was unfamiliar: *ipseity* (ip SEE uh tee), from Latin *ipse* (self), meaning "individual identity." As many have pointed out, true synonyms do not exist, since although two or more words may mean just about the same thing, the connotations of a word may make any one of the "synonyms" inappropriate in a given situation. A search through the dictionaries and thesauri and books like the Rodale *Synonym Finder* (Laurence Urdang, editor in chief) will help to set you straight. *Proprium, quiddity, haecceity, selfhood, ipseity*—each has its place, but heed the warning.

proseuche (pro SOOH kee, pro SYOOH kee), also **proseucha** (pro SOOH kah, pro SYOOH kah) *n.* A *proseuche* or *proseucha* was an "oratory, a place of prayer"; a word taken from the Greek, based on the verb *proseuchesthai* (to offer prayers), constructed of the prefix *pros-* (toward) plus *euchesthai* (to pray), from the noun *euche* (prayer). Among the ancient Hebrews, the *proseuche* was usually a roofless structure, as distinct from a synagogue of orthodox construction. In the *Works* of Joseph Mead or Mede (1672) a *proseucha* was described as " ... a plot of ground encompassed with a wall or ... other ... inclosure, and open above ... A Synagogue was ... a covered edifice ... Synagogues were within the Cities, as *Proseucha's* were without." But a translation of *Father Didon's Jesus Christ* (1892) says that the Jews "built synagogues and *proseuchae* at the entrances of towns." Whether within cities or at the entrances to cities, the Jews could say their prayers in synagogues or *proseuches*. On visits to Israel, I saw many offering their prayers at the Wailing Wall, which had neither enclosure nor roof. I can't imagine it makes any difference to the Deity, as long as the words are accompanied by thoughts. See the king's concluding speech in *Hamlet*, Act III, Scene 3: "Words without thoughts never to heaven go."

prosodetic   See **prosodion.**

prosodiac   See **prosodion.**

prosodic   See **prosodion.**

prosodion (pruh SOH dee on) *n.* At first glance, this word appears to have something to do with *prosody* (the art or science of meter), but its proper meaning is "processional hymn," the kind sung by ancient Greeks as they approached a temple or the altar of one of their many gods. *Prosodios* is Greek for "processional," from *prosodos* (procession, formed of *pros*, "toward," and *hodos*, "way"). *Prosodion* is its neuter form, used as a noun. *Prosody* is another matter, formed of *pros* and *oide* (song). However, *prosodiac* (pruh SOH dee ak) is used as a synonym of *prosodic* (pruh SOD ik), meaning "relating to prosody," and also as a noun denoting the verse sung in a *prosodion*, this verse being an *enoplion* (eh NOP lee uhn) followed by a long or short syllable. An *enoplion* is an "*acatalectic hemiepes* preceded by one or two short syllables or one long one"; its name is formed from the neuter of *enoplios* (martial), based on *enoplos* (armed). As to *acatalectic* (a kad'l EK tik), that is a term in prosody meaning "a foot of verse complete in the number of its syllables," as opposed to *catalectic*, meaning "incomplete, lacking a syllable in the last foot." In this instance, I shall spare you the derivations but provide an illustration: "Tell me not in mournful numbers,/Life is but an empty dream!" This is a trochaic tetrameter, the first line *acatalectic*, the second *catalectic* (it drops a syllable). Warning: Never confuse *acatalectic* with *acataleptic* (ay kad'l EP tik), a term applied to one who refused to make a judgment, on the principle that certainty is impossible. Now we must deal with *hemiepes* (heh mee EP eez): a "dactylic tripody with a spondaic third foot or without the two short syllables of the third foot." (*Dactylic*, dak TIL ik: describing a metrical foot of three syllables, one stressed followed by two unstressed. *Tripody*, TRIP uh dee: in prosody, a group of three feet. *Spondaic*, spon DAY ik: describing a *spondee*,

SPON dee, a foot consisting of two stressed syllables.) Now that you have digested all the foregoing, caution: *Prosodetic* (pros uh DED ik) has nothing whatever to do with any of it. All it does is to describe the ligament of a bivalve mollusk. Forgive me: I got carried away. Dictionaries *are* distracting—and if you aren't bored, you haven't been listening.

prosopopoeia (pruh soh puh PEE uh) *n.* From Greek *prosopopoiia* (personification), built of *prosopon* (face, person), plus *poiein* (to make), we get this noun signifying two distinct rhetorical devices: (1) in which an absent or imaginary person is portrayed as speaking or acting—usually where a plausible but invented speech is put into the mouth of a real character; and (2) one in which an abstract quality is represented as a person or as having personal traits—a personification or embodiment of a quality or other abstraction. In category (1), characters who existed long before the age of video and tape recorders are quoted, particularly in historical novels, in words that seem to fit the occasion. "I am dying, Egypt," says Antony to Cleopatra in the play that bears their names, and he goes on to make quite a long speech before he dies. (Dying characters in drama and opera often take a long time dying and seem quite verbose on their deathbeds.) Antony's was a dramatically justified *prosopopoeia* if there ever was one. Here's another of my favorites: "One day, Abe, you'll grow up to be the finest president of these United States," said his stepmother Sarah Bush, "and it'll be you who'll keep them united!" That one is from a children's biography of the Great Emancipator, read many years ago and long since vanished from my bookshelves, but well remembered. And nobody will convince me that Napoleon ever said, "Not tonight, Josephine." In his novel *Ragtime*, E.L. Doctorow introduced a mixed bag of real people (long since dead) and fictional characters and put words into the mouths of both. But it remained for Iris Murdoch to present us with the most absorbing examples of *prosopopoeia* that I have ever come across introducing pretended speakers and putting words into the mouths of Socrates and Plato, in *Acastos, Two Platonic Dialogues*, "imagined dialogues between wise old Socrates and wild young Plato, with help from Acastos [Plato's fictional friend] and other friends," to quote from the dust jacket. *Art and Eros* is a dialogue about art; *Above the Gods* is a dialogue about religion. Dame Iris invented half a dozen participants who have much to "say" in these wonderful dialogues. *Prosopopoeia* has never been put to better use. Dr Robert Lowth, in *Lectures on the Sacred Poetry of the Hebrews* (G. Gregory's translation from the Latin, 1787), gave the following explanation of this type of *prosopopoeia*: "Of this figure there are two kinds: one, when action and character are attributed to fictitious, irrational, or even inanimate objects; the other, when a probable but fictitious speech is assigned to a real character." In category (2), a spotless character is represented as a knight in shining armor, or versatility as a Renaissance figure like da Vinci. In *Alciphron, or the Minute Philosopher* (1732), Bishop George Berkeley speaks of "Sentiments, and vices, which by marvellous *prosopopoeia* he converts into so many ladies." (It was not unusual for such figures to be ladies.) Sir George A Macfarren, in *Six Lectures* *on Harmony* (1876), describes a person who was "everywhere at once ... the *prosopopoeia* of ubiquity." Somewhat hard to pronounce, but a useful word nonetheless.

protreptic (proh TREP tik) *n., adj.* A *protreptic* is "an exhortation" or "pep talk" (which it rather sounds like), and the adjective means "hortatory, urging." The derivation, via Late Latin *protrepticus*, is from Greek *protreptikos*, related to the verb *protrepein* (to turn forward, urge on), based on the preposition *pro-* (forward) plus *trepein* (to turn). (The *-hort-* in *exhort* and *hortatory* is from the Latin verb *hortari* "to urge, encourage.") A stirring example of this form of address in literature is the opening speech of the king in *King Henry V*, Act III, Scene 1:

> Once more unto the breach, dear friends, once more ... imitate the action of the tiger; Stiffen the sinews, summon up the blood ... lend the eye a terrible aspect ... set the teeth, and stretch the nostril wide, Hold hard the breath ... On, on, you noblest English ... upon this charge/Cry "God for Harry, England and Saint George!"

That was some *protreptic*! And it worked!

proxemics (prok SEE miks) *n.* This is a new term in sociology coined by Dr. Edward T. Hall, concerning spatial relationships arranged by human beings. In *The American Anthropologist*, vol. 65 (1963), Dr. Hall defines it as follows: "The study of how man unconsciously structures microspace—the distance between men in the conduct of daily transactions, the organization of space in his houses and buildings, and ultimately the layout of his towns." The September 29, 1969, issue of *The Guardian* (London) had this to say: "Though territoriality and its effects has been studied for many years now in connection with animal life, Dr. Hall is ... the first person to link the concept direct with human beings and ... has coined a purely human word for it: *proxemics*." There is now also an adjective, *proxemic*, as in "*proxemic* behavior." The *Times Literary Supplement*, issue of June 4, 1971, states: "In man, '*proxemic*' behavior ranges from the distance two people maintain while engaged in conversation or the way a group of people arrange themselves, to architecture and city planning." Please bear all this in mind the next time you find yourself in a crowded elevator or in the subway during rush hour, and especially when planning a new condominium.

pschent, also *p-skhent* (PSKENT, SKENT, PSCHENT—*ch* as in German *ich*). *n.* This is an Egyptian word for the double crown worn by the pharaohs after Menes (fl. c. 3200 B.C.), the king of Upper Egypt, conquered Lower Egypt and unified the two countries. Despite the unification and centralization of Egypt that followed, the memory of the two former ancient kingdoms was preserved, especially in certain formalities of government and customs. Since the Nile flows from south to north, please remember that *Upper* Egypt is the name of the *southern* part of the country, and *Lower* Egypt the name of the *northern* part. This can be quite confusing but becomes clear when one remembers that *Upper* refers to the part near the source (or *lower* end) of the Egyptian part of the Nile (the Blue Nile) and *Lower* to the *upper* end, where the river flows into the Mediterranean. Before Menes's conquest and the unification, the pharaohs of Upper and Lower Egypt wore different types of crowns. After the unification, the pharaohs wore the double crown, or *pschent*. (If you want to see what the former separate crowns and the double crown looked like, there is an excellent diagram on page 1,829 of *W III*.) The word is formed of Egyptian *p* (the, the definite article) plus *skhent* (double crown, from the Greek transliteration of the demotic, i.e., the simplified form of ancient Egyptian hieratic writing, consisting of simplified hieroglyphics, used by the priests in record keeping; more about *demotic* and *hieratic* in my *1000 Most Challenging Words*). The word became known through the discovery of the Rosetta Stone in 1798. If you have ever been on a tour of Egypt and been blessed by a guide who told you all (or more than) you wanted to know about paintings on royal tomb walls, you undoubtedly often heard: " … and this is a representation of the pharaoh wearing the crowns of Upper Egypt and Lower Egypt, seen here smiting his enemies … " Those old pharaohs certainly did a lot of smiting, a polite Egyptian-guide-ism meaning "beating the hell out of."

psellism (SEL iz'm, PSEL-) *n*. From Greek *psellismos* (stammering—the verb is *psellizein*, the adjective *psellos*), the French got *psellisme*, though their common word is *bégayer*, and we got *psellism*, though our common word is *stammering*. *Psellism* covers any defect in enunciation, including lisping, **rhotacism** (substitution of the *r* sound for some other sound, the way the Japanese, for example, substitute *r* for *l*) and pararhotacism (the converse: substitution of some other sound for that of *r*, the way the Chinese pronounce *r* as *l*, for example). *Lallation* is another name for *pararhotacism*, but it denotes childish speech generally, as might be guessed from its source: Latin *lallare*, "to sing a lullaby." *Psellism* can result from malformation of the vocal organs or from nervous ailments (especially after attending Oxford?). I happen to find the "Oxford stammer" rather attractive, particularly in women, though it drives some people (probably Cantabrigians, i.e., students at Cambridge University) crazy.

psephism See **psephology.**

psephology (see FOL uh jee, seh-) *n. Psephology* is the "statistical and sociological study of election results, isues and trends"; also known as *psephoanalysis* (see foh uhn AL uh sis). A related word, *psephism* (SEE fiz'm), denotes a decree of the Athenian assembly of classical times. Why *psephology* and *psephism*? Because the Greek noun *psephos* means "pebble," and the Athenian legislators voted with pebbles. The technical name for a pundit who specializes in the study of this aspect of the democratic process is *psephologist* (see FOL uh gist), as you might have suspected, but most of them would not be aware of that lofty label, I fear. We are all familiar with the ubiquitous suffix *-logy*, tacked on in this headword to our now, by this time, familiar *psephos*.

pseudepigraphy (syoohd uh PIG ruh fee) *n*. This is the word for the ascription of a written work, especially a book, to one other than the true author. Thus *The Pseudephigrapha* is the name of books ascribed to Old Testament characters but rejected as such by scholars versed in the subject. This headword is based on the Greek prefixes *pseud-* (or *pseudo-* before a consonant), from the adjective *pseudes* (false) and *epi-* (upon), plus *graphein* (to write). An *epigraphy* (eh PIG ruh fee) without the *pseud-*, or *epigraph* (EH pig graf), not to be confused with *epigram*, is "an inscription, especially on a building," or a "citation or motto at the beginning of a book or section of a book." Authors like to cite poetic or prose passages before the text proper as apposite introductions to what's ahead. Sometimes, alas, the *epigraph* is the best part of the book.

pseudocyesis (syooh doh sye EE sis) *n*. You doubtless know from familiarity with other *pseudo-* words, like *pseudonym* and *pseudointellectual*, that something phony or deceptive is afoot, but if you don't know that *-cyesis* comes from Greek *kyesis*, "pregnancy" (*kyein* means "to be pregnant"), you can't guess that *pseudocyesis* is "false or imaginary pregnancy in women," attributed by psychologists to an exceptionally strong desire or need for motherhood. In *pseudocyesis*, despite the lack of conception, many of the phenomena of actual pregnancy develop: Menstruation stops, the abdomen and breasts swell, lactation occurs and urine tests may even be falsely positive. Some women in this condition report the sensation of fetal movement. When finally the *commedia è finita*, the disappointment often causes severe depression. "Bloody Mary" (Mary Tudor, daughter of Henry VIII and queen of England, 1553–58) underwent this disastrous experience. Elizabeth I's accession would not have happened, and the history of England would have been quite a different story, but for the *pseudo-* in that *-cyesis*!

psilanthropism (psil AN throh piz'm) *n*. This word, taken from the ecclesiastical Greek adjective *psilanthropos* (merely human), based on the prefix *psilo-*, the combining form of *psilos* (bare, mere), plus the familiar *anthropos* (man), is the name given to the theological argument or doctrine that Christ was a mere man, and not divine. This book is not the vehicle for the discussion of that hotly contested dispute, which has plagued theologians for centuries. A *psilanthropist* (psil AN throh pist) is one who adopts this doctrine; the theological sense of *humanitarian* is synonymous with *psilanthropist*, and *anthropomorphite* is still another synonym for one who affirms the humanity but denies the divinity of Christ and claims that the Deity possesses a material body. *Psilanthropism* or *humanitarianism* (in this sense) has been a charge leveled at Unitarians for many years.

psychomorphism   See **hyle.**

psychopannychy (seye koh PAN uh kee) *n.* This is the "all-night sleep of the soul," the theological doctrine that the soul falls asleep at the time of death and does not wake until resurrection, the day of judgment. It comes from Greek *psych-*, the combining form of *psyche* (spirit, soul) plus *pannychios* (all night long), built of *pan-*, the combining form of *pan*, the neuter of *pas* (all), plus *nychios* (nightly, pertaining to night), from *nykt-*, the stem of *nyx* (night). This sleep of the soul is known as *psychopannychistic slumber* and the supporters of the doctrine as *psychopannychists*. The doctrine was much disputed. Calvin rejected it. Bishop John Gauden, in *Ecclesiae Anglicae Suspiria* [Sighs of the Anglican Church], *The Tears ... of the Church of England* (1659) wrote: "No more ... than the Saducees might deny and overthrow the resurrection against Christ; or the *Psychopannuchists*, the souls immortality." In Joseph Glanvill's *Lux Orientalis, or an Enquiry into the Opinion of the Eastern Sages Concerning the Prae-Existence of Souls* (1682), we find: "Unless we will be so dull as to fall into the drouzie dream of the *Psychopannychites!*" Carl W. Buch's (1847) translation of Hagenbach's *Compendium of the History of Doctrines* speaks of " ... a revival of the earlier notion of the death of the soul ... under the milder form of the sleep of the soul (*Psychopannychy*)." Death of the soul, sleep of the soul, existence of the soul, nature of the soul? Upon my soul, I don't know the first thing about it.

putto (POOH toh) *n.* There are several words in Italian for "boy" in the ordinary sense: *fanciullo, figlio, ragazzo;* but *putto*, from Latin *putus*, is the term for the representation of a child in Italian Renaissance painting and sculpture. The child is shown nude, sometimes in swaddling clothes, sometimes winged, often in the attitude of a cupid. The word is found more often in the plural, *putti*, than the singular, since it was customary for works of art to show them in groups. In an 1894 issue of *The Nation*, the art critic and collector Bernard Berenson wrote: "It was his passion ... for the expression of the joyful feeling that led Correggio to seize every chance to paint *putti*." A February 1973 issue of the *Daily Telegraph* (London) wrote of a painting "on one side [of which] are two coats of arms ... held together by ribbons in the hand of a flying *putto*." *Putti* are still a common sight on the walls and ceilings of great concert halls and other large rooms in public buildings.

pyrrhonism   See **zetetic.**

pyrrhonist   See **zetetic.**

pyrrhonize   See **zetetic.**

pyx (PIKS) *n., vb.* In Roman Catholic (and High Anglican) practice, the *pyx* is the "vessel or container in which the Host is contained after consecration, or in which it is carried to the sick." In the sixth century it took the form of a small round box with a conical lid and was usually suspended within the church. In about 1500 it took the shape of a standard box with a flat lid. In England it usually hung above the altar. The bishop determined its size, shape, color and material, whether lapis lazuli, iron, silver, brass or whatever else took his fancy, as well as its decoration, and that prevailed for the entire diocese. Antique church *pyxes* are hard to come by and are much sought by dealers and collectors. *Pyx* has another distinct meaning: the chest at the Royal Mint in London in which gold and silver coins are deposited for testing as to weight and purity at an annual ceremony known as the *trial of the pyx*, conducted by a jury of the Goldsmiths' Company. There is a similar chest in the United States Mint. *Pyx* also serves as a verb meaning "to put into a *pyx*" and more specifically, "to place the host into a *pyx*"; or "to place specimen coins into a *pyx*" and by extension, "to test coins as to weight and assay." Eventually, *pyx* came to mean "box" generally, but this is only a literary use. The container in the British Mint is usually known as the *pyx chest*. *Pyx* comes, via Latin, from Greek *pyxis* (box). Our word *box*, in the sense of "container" or "receptacle" comes, via Late Latin *buxis*, from Greek *pyxis*; and as the name of an evergreen shrub, it comes via Latin *buxus*, from Greek *pyxos*—lots of tricky little vowel changes to worry about. *Pixie* and *pixy* have nothing to do with *pyx* and are of "origin unknown," "origin obscure" or "[?]," depending on which dictionary you consult.

quean (KWEEN) *n.* At first sight, this word looks like a misprint, especially when you find out that it is a term for one or another type of female; but no, it is (or was) a perfectly good word, with a different ancestry from that of *queen*. The *C.O.D.* calles it an "impudent or ill-behaved woman" and labels it "archaic"—rightly so, as we shall see. Not so *CH*, which gives it a variety of meanings: "saucy girl"; "woman of worthless character"; and in Scots, just plain "girl." *W III* defines it as "disreputable woman" and in context, "prostitute." The *O.E.D.* lists a string of meanings: "female"; in early Middle English, "a term of disparagement or abuse"; "a bold, impudent, or ill-behaved woman"; "jade, hussy"; and specifically, "harlot, strumpet"; and in Scots, "a lass, usually denoting one of a robust and healthy appearance." *RH* gives "bold, impudent woman, shrew, hussy, prostitute," and in British dialect, "girl or young woman, especially a robust one." Not a hint of archaism in any of those save the good old *C.O.D.*, but wait: The *O.E.D. Supplement* says "Now archaic" and quotes Edith Sitwell in *Sleeping Beauty*: "My eyes are dim,—I yet can see You, lazy *quean*! Go work!" It also mentions Eric Partridge's definition: "a homosexual, especially one with girlish manners and carriage";

he calls it "low." I mentioned different derivations: *quean* is from Old English *cwene*, *queen* from old English *cwēn*—undoubtedly related, but not identical.

quiddity   See **proprium.**

quietism   See **hesychast.**

quietist   See **hesychast.**

quisquiliary   See **quisquilious.**

quisquilious (kwis KWIL ee uhs) *adj. Quisquiliae* is a Latin plural noun meaning "rubbish, refuse, sweepings," from which we get *quisquilious* and *quisquiliary* (kwis KWIL ee air ee), "of the nature of rubbish or refuse," i.e., "trashy, worthless." The Latin noun applies to people as well as things. An 1857 issue of *Fraser's Magazine* contained the sentence: "Besides garden fruit, insects and worms, the Jay's diet is sufficiently *quisquilious.*" Jeremy Bentham's *Rationale of Judicial Evidence* (1827) declared: "The science is overloaded by the *quisquilious* matter they rake together." The author of an article in an 1817 issue of *Blackwell's Magazine* preferred the form *quisquiliary.* The piece, caricaturing the Scottish author and translator Sir Thomas Urquhart (1611–60), spun out this magnificent bit of prose, using two other words we shall have to deal with now: "Those shallow and *fidimplicitary* coxcombs, who fill our too credulous ears with their *quisquiliary deblaterations.*" The *O.E.D.* characterizes *fidimplicitary* as a "nonce-word" (a word coined and used only for a particular occasion). It is based on the ecclesiastical Latin phrase *fides implicata* (implicit faith) and describes those who swallow whole whatever the other fellow says. (Urquhart had used the word in a work entitled *The Discovery of a Most Exquisite Jewel* (1652): "*Fidimplicitary* gown-men ... satisfied with their predecessors' contrivances ... ") For *deblaterations* we have to start with *deblaterate* (dih BLAT uh rate), meaning "to prate, blab," based on Latin *blaterare* (to babble, chatter), and go on to the noun. I trust that I will not be charged with *deblaterating* too much *quisquilious* matter in this brief treatise.

reckling (REK ling) *n.* A *reckling* is the "runt of a litter," or the "youngest or weakest child in a family." It has also been used as a synonym of "weakling" generally, without regard to litters or families, and as a synonym of "puny" in adjectival use. *Wreckling* is a variant spelling, but there would seem to be only the weakest connection with *wreck*, and no authority has attempted to explain its derivation. Tennyson used the word in *Vivien* (later renamed *Vivien and Merlin; Idylls of the King*, 1859): "On returning found/ Not two but three [babes]; there lay the *reckling one*/ But one hour old!" Sir Henry Taylor used the noun attributively in *Philip van Artevelde; a Dramatic Romance* (1834): "A mother dotes upon the *reckling* child/ More than the strong." I timidly suggest a connection between *wreckling* and a fusing of *wreck* and *weakling*, but you are entitled to your own flights of fancy.

relief   See **heriot.**

remugient (ruhm YOOH juhnt) *adj.* *Mugire* is Latin for "to roar, bellow" (cognate with Greek *mukasthai*), and *remugire* is "to bellow again, bellow back," with the Latin, like English, indicating repetition by the prefix *re-.* *Mugire*, by transference, took on the meanings "roar, rumble, groan." Its present participle is *mugiens*; the plural, *mugientes*, was used by Horace as a substantive meaning "oxen," literally "the bellowing ones." *Remugire*, by extension, took on the meaning "to resound." Its present participle *remugiens*, whose stem is *remugient-*, gave us *remugient*, meaning "resounding" (literally, "rebellowing"). Virgil used the verb in the sentence "Vox adsensu nemorum igeminata *remugit*" (The voice *resounds* magnified by the echo of the woods). Henry More, in *An Explanation of the Grand Mystery of Godliness* (1660), used the word in a dramatic passage when he wrote of "Trembling and tottering Earth-quakes accompanied with *remugient* Echoes and ghastly murmurs from below." Were *mugire* and *mukasthai* onomatopoeic in their first syllables?

retable   See **Churrigeresque.**

rhotacism   See **psellism.**

rhyparography (reye puh RAW gruh fee) *n.* From Greek *rhyparos* (filthy) plus *-graphos* (writing, painting; related to *graphein*, to write), we get *rhyparography*, meaning "painting, drawing, or writing about mean or sordid subjects." But the word has another meaning that has nothing to do with unworthy subject matter: "still-life or genre painting." It is hard to see the connection between the two meanings, since genre painting is simply a category that depicts scenes from everyday life, and still life includes anything from fruit or vegetables to guitars or tablecloths, and what's mean or sordid about them? So one must be careful to distinguish between the two meanings when meeting up with *rhyparography*. The faint connection might be that genre and still-life painting are removed from the romantic or elegant, but that hardly bespeaks filth or grossness. As has been noted before, strange are the ways of language and meanings; and as might be expected, there is an active noun, *rhyparographer* (reye puh RAW gruh fur), for a painter who practices *rhyparography* (again presumably in either sense of the word). The Greek ancestor *rhyparographos* means simply "painting sordid subjects"—nothing to do with genre or still life generally. In the early days, *rhyparography* was defined in the narrow sense. Sir William Smith's *Dictionary of Greek and Roman Antiquities* (1842) speaks of

"*Rhyparography*, pornography and all the lower classes of art," but a few years later John Leitch's translation of Mueller's *Ancient Art and its Remains* (1850) mentions " ... *rhyparography* (so-called still life ...)." Yet the taint of the seamy side of life remained, as seen in George Saintsbury's article in an 1886 issue of *The Academy*, where he criticizes a writer who " ... takes a sort of Naturalist delight in describing the most sordid ... features of the least attractive kind of English middle class life, and never misses a *rhyparographic* touch when she can introduce one"; and in 1885 J. E. Harrison, in *Studies in Greek Art*, wrote of the " ... mire of *rhypography*." Note the shorter form: *rhypography* (reye PAW gruh fee), from Greek *rhypos*, not to be confused with *rhypophagy* (reye PAW fuh jee), the "eating of filth," from *rhypos* plus *-phagia*, related to *phagein* (to eat).

rhypography   See **rhyparography**.

rhypophagy   See **rhyparography**.

rondel   See **sirvent(e)**.

roquelaure (ROK uh lore) *n*. If you were in charge of the costuming of the male members of the cast in a play set in the 18th or early 19th century, you might dress one or more of them in a *roquelaure*, a "short cloak reaching to the knee," named for a fashion set by Antoine-Gaston, Duc de Roquelaure (1656–1738), a marshal of France. Laurence Sterne, in *Tristram Shandy*, referred to this garment in two passages: "I have a project ... of wrapping myself warm in my *roquelaure*, and paying a visit to this poor gentleman." Again: "Your honour's *roquelaure* ... has not once been had on since the night before your honour received your wound." Frederick Marryat, in *Japhet in Search of a Father* (1836), evidently conceived of the *roquelaure* as reaching some way below the knee, for he wrote, "I went out and purchased a *roquelaure*, which enveloped my whole person." In his *Biographical History of England; being a Continuation of J. Granger's Work* (1806: that work being James Granger's *Letters between G. and Many of the Most Eminent Literary Men of his Time*, 1805), Mark Noble noted: "The *roquelaure* cloak ... displaced the surtout." The *surtout* was a "man's overcoat," which, according to the *O.E.D.*, was a name taken from the French (*sur*, above, plus *tout*, everything) "applied c[irca] 1870 to a kind of single-breasted frock-coat with pockets cut diagonally in front." Getting back to this play and your job of dressing the male members of the cast, you might well be confused: If the *roquelaure* was worn only until the early part of the 19th century, how could it "displace" the *surtout*, which was not known as such until circa 1870? Wasn't it the other way around? And how about the dictionary definitions that describe the *roquelaure* as reaching *to* the knee, and Marryat's telling us that it enveloped the "whole person?" It may be this sort of thing that results in the distasteful practice of doing period plays in modern dress, for fear of the carping of nitpicking critics.

roskopf (ROS kopf) *n.* This word denotes the type of watch described below. It is sometimes capitalized, as a sign of respect to G. S. Roskopf, a Swiss watchmaker (d. 1889) who designed it. It is a watch with a barrel (the flat cylindrical metal container that encloses the mainspring of a watch or clock) of greater diameter than the radius of the watch. This is a most unusual design, not especially attractive, but interesting. Horological friends have tried, without much success, to explain the advantages of Roskopf's innovation— something to do with greater accuracy, etc.—but the design itself hasn't much to recommend it.

rosmarine (ROZ muh rine) *n.* Three meanings are given for this word by the *O.E.D.*: "rosemary," "sea-dew" and "walrus." These three would appear to be pretty far apart: an herb, dew from the ocean and a marine animal. The walrus is a marine mammal of the genus *Odobenus rosmarus*, which does give us some connection with *rosmarine*. The word is used in the second sense mentioned above, "sea-dew," in Jonson's *Queenes Masque* (1616): "You shall ... steep Your bodies in that purer brine, / And wholesome dew call'd Ros-marine." It is used in the third sense in Spenser's *Faerie Queene* (1590): "The horrible Sea-satyre ... And greedy *Rosmarines* with visages deforme ... " Incidentally, *rosmaro* is Spanish for "manatee, sea-cow," and *rosmarino* in Spanish means "rosemary"; *ros* by itself is Latin for "dew," but *ros marinus* or *rosmarinus* in one word means "rosemary," and *ros maris* (dew of the sea) seems to be reserved for "sea-dew." Confusing. *CH* gives the definitions "rosemary," referring to Spenser; "sea-dew," referring to Jonson; and again referring to Spenser, "a walrus, or a sea-monster supposed to lick dew off the rocks." In "Word-Watching," the admirable definition-guessing game appearing daily in *The Times* (London), Philip Howard gives the definition "walrus." He goes on to explain: " ... once thought by old wives of both sexes to climb rocks by its teeth to feed on dew" and follows with the above chilling quote from Spenser. His "old wives of both sexes" echoes a quotation from *Tristram Shandy* that I used in my *1000 Most Challenging Words* under the headword *anile* when I ended the comment with: "Despite the remark in *Tristram Shandy* ... about 'the nonsense of the old women' (of both sexes), you can call an old woman *senile* but you can't call an old man *anile*." I don't know whether walruses like the taste of rosemary. If you run into *rosmarine*, I suggest you go along with Philip Howard and settle for "walrus."

rostrocarinate (ros troh KAR uh nate) *n., adj.* As an adjective, *rostrocarinate* is an archaeological term describing flint objects that resemble an eagle's beak, especially those found in East Anglia (i.e., the counties of Norfolk and Suffolk in southeast England, which were once an early English kingdom). They were at first believed to be artifacts of the late Pliocene era but are now recognized as natural, not man-made, formations. The term is derived from *rostro-*, the combining form of Latin *rostrum* (literally, that which gnaws; as an ornithological term, beak; as a nautical term, the curved end of a ship's prow, used for ramming) plus *carinatus*, from *carina* (keel); *carinatus* gave us *carinate*, meaning "keel-like" or "shaped like the keel or prow of a ship." As a noun, *rostrocarinate* means an object having the shape described above. *W III*, in an edition with a 1986 copyright, defines the word in terms of an artifact, whereas the *O.E.D. Supplement O to Scz*, copyright 1982, had already revealed that these flints, once believed to be hand tools, were now considered "natural formations." As to the *W III* definition, one must remember the enduring statement of H. W. Fowler in his preface to the *C.O.D.*: "A dictionary-maker, unless he is a monster of omniscience, must deal with a great many matters of which he has no first-hand knowledge." Forgiveness is in order. Back in 1934 the *Journal of the Royal Anthropological Institute* contained these words: "Among these large *tools* ... a number of well-made *rostro-carinate* forms is to be distinguished"; and J. K. Charlesworth's *Quaternary Era* (1957) states (referring to certain "Cromerian *implements*," i.e., artifacts of a period dating a million years back): "These *tools* ... include *rostrocarinates*." It was natural for the *W III* staff to rely on those authorities and very clever of the *Supplement* not to. Incidentally, in using the term "monster of omniscience," Fowler may well have had in mind the Latin noun *monstrum*, which means, inter alia, "wonder" or "miracle," not simply "monster."

rowen (ROU uhn) *n*. Also **rowan, rowing, rawing, rawn** and numerous other variants. Among other things, this word is interesting because of its synonyms, of which more later. Its general meaning is "second crop (e.g., of hay) in a season." It is Middle English, from Old French (and modern French as well) *regain*, meaning "second crop." In old French, *gain* meant, inter alia, "crop, harvest," and the prefix *re-* had the same force of "repetition" as in a number of modern languages (English and various Romance tongues). *W III* defines *rowen* as "a stubble field left unplowed till late in the autumn to be grazed by cattle" and gives "aftermath" as a second meaning, while *RH* tells us that a *rowen* is "the second growth of grass or hay in a season; and *CH* and the *C.O.D.* are content with merely "aftermath." The *O.E.D.* speaks of "second growth" and adds not only "aftermath" but also "eddish" and goes on to explain, in its usual helpful way, that "The precise application of the term (esp[ecially] with regard to the cutting of the aftergrowth or leaving it for pasture) varies to some extent in diferent localities." In a sense, "precise applications" of many terms "vary in different localities," do they not? As to *eddish*, the *O.E.D.* gives us "an aftergrowth of grass after mowing" and "stubble." I said above that *rowen* was interesting because of its synonyms. *Eddish* is a new one on me, but I found *aftermath* quite a surprise, because I had never run across that familiar word except in its generally understood meaning of "consequences," almost always with dire implications, as in "the aftermath of war," "the aftermath of widespread drought," epidemic, a stock market crash, etc. In their definitions of *aftermath*, most American dictionaries speak of "consequences" first and "second growth" second, while the British dictionaries do the reverse. In any event, I tried *aftermath* on a number of friends both British and American, and not one of them mentioned anything to do with second growths or crops. And only one American dictionary, *W III*, put the farming definition first and the "consequences" definition second. What's more, in its example of the second meaning, it mentioned "gratifying" effects rather than dire ones. Confusing, but interesting, I hope, to word buffs. As to the derivations of these synonyms, the *O.E.D.* tells us that *eddish* is "of obscure etymology," while in the case of *aftermath* in the agricultural sense, the *after-* is simple enough, but the *-math* is less obvious. *Math*, now dialectal British English meaning "mowing of a grass or hay crop" or the "gathered crop" itself, is an *assumed* Middle English term, from Old English *maeth* (crop of hay, grass mowing), derived from the root of the Old English verb *mawan* (to mow). The more familiar meaning "consequences" or "effects" is obviously a figurative extension, whether dire or gratifying.

rune   See **futhork.**

runic   See **futhork.**

scazon   See **hapax legomenon.**

scholiast   See **scholium.**

scholion   See **scholium.**

scholium (SKOH lee uhm), also **scholion** (SKOH lee uhn) *n.* A *scholium* or *scholion* is a "marginal notation in the nature of an explanatory note or comment," especially by an early grammarian on a Greek or Latin text. The word can also signify a note added by the author illustrating or developing a point discussed in the text and has been incorrectly used to mean a "trite saying" or "maxim," such as "familiarity breeds contempt," or, as a waggish friend of mine said about goings-on between male members of the staff and attractive females in a business office: "Familiarity breeds attempt." A *scholiast* (SKOL ee ast) is a "commentator" or "annotator." Another friend of mine collaborated on a *Key to Finnegans Wake*, with more text devoted to the *scholia* than Joyce allotted to the original. *Scholium* comes, via Modern Latin, from Greek *scholion*, a diminutive of *schole* (school).

scrag (SKRAG) *n., vb. Scrag* is a small word with an uncommonly large number of meanings. It is thought to be a modification of the obsolete *crag* in the senses of "neck, throat, neck of mutton or veal, a skinny person." The *O.E.D.* suggests that the initial *s* was added "due to some feeling of phonetic expressiveness" (to lend a touch of onomatopoeia?). In any event, *scrag* means "sheep's neck," "the lean, inferior part of a veal or mutton neck," "human neck" (slang) or "skinny person or animal" (pejorative); as a verb, it means, "to hang on the gallows" (slang), "to throttle," "to wring the neck of (a person or fowl)," "to tackle by the neck" (in soccer), "to kill, murder"; and to "bend" (a sheet of metal, for testing). A *scragger* or *scrag-boy* is a "hangman"; a *scragging-post* is "the gallows"; a *scrag-whale* or *scrag-tailed whale* is one with a knobbed back (i.e., any of a number of small whales without a dorsal fin but with protruberances on the dorsal ridge near the tail). A *scraggy* person, animal or limb is skinny and bony (pejorative); *scraggy* meat is lean meat; *scraggy* rocks are rugged rocks; a *scraggy* branch is knotted and full of projections; *scraggy* trees are stunted, ragged and of scanty growth. Getting back to this versatile noun, *scrag* can also mean "tree stump," a "rough projection on a tree trunk, a stump, a rock" or a "piece of rough, rocky, barren ground." Lots of work for a little word!

scrag-boy   See **scrag.**

scragger   See **scrag.**

scragging-post   See **scrag.**

scraggy   See **scrag.**

scrag-whale   See **scrag.**

scrutable   See **scrutate.**

scrutate (SKROOH tate) *vb.* *Scrutiny, scrutinize* and *inscrutable* are familiar words, owing their origin to Late Latin *scrutinium* (close examination) and Latin *scrutari* (to examine). Both these words are thought to come from *scruta* (broken bits, trash, rags), on the theory that *scrutari* implied a search so thorough that it even included an examination of rags and trash, reminiscent of the deseprate hunt for clues in modern detective stories. But *scrutate*, meaning "to search out, investigate," from *scrutatus*, the past participle of *scrutari*, is a quite unfamiliar form. So, too, is *scrutable* (SKROOH tuh b'l), meaning "decipherable, comprehensible, legible," while *inscrutable* is not quite its opposite, but means rather, "not quite comprehensible" and is generally understood as "mysterious," as in phrases like "the inscrutable East" and the popular character "the inscrutable Mr. Moto," of detective-story fame. I have in the past written about the peculiarity of usage in our language whereby the negative adjective is much more often used than the positive from which it is taken and is frequently not the exact opposite in meaning. Thus, for example, *impeccable* is used generally in the sense of "faultless, irreproachable," as applied to dress, conduct and manners, while the rarely used *peccable* denotes liability to sin or gross error, though they both stem from Latin *peccare* (to go wrong, err, sin). The same goes for *steady* in its ordinary uses and *unsteady*, generally denoting shakiness of gait; and there are many more examples of this phenomenon. From Latin *scrutatio* we get *scrutation* (skrooh TAY shuhn), "minute search, examination, investigation," and we take Latin *scrutator* intact into English, meaning "investigator" generally, and more specifically "scrutineer," one who acts as inspector of votes at an election. *Scrutatory* comes into the picture as well, meaning "examining, searching, investigating." That about does it, except for the peculiar and apparently unrelated term *scruto*, a theatrical term of undetermined origin, meaning "trapdoor," flush with the stage, usually constructed of strips of wood or whalebone, and also known as *scruto-piece, sloat* or *slote*. A possible explanation of *scruto* or *scruto-piece* might have to do with "something one should have investigated," i.e., *scrutinized*, before falling into the trap; and *sloat* and *slote* may have had something to do with *slot*, the kind of opening things slip through—but, as I always say, beware of etymological guesswork.

scrutation   See **scrutate.**

scrutator   See **scrutate.**

scrutatory   See **scrutate.**

scruto   See **scrutate.**

scruto-piece   See **scrutate.**

securiform (sih KOOH rih form) *adj.* You might well be forgiven for thinking that this adjective has to do with *security*, but not after reading what follows. Our words *secure* and *security* are derived from Latin *securus* and *securitas*, which mean, respectively, "free from care, untroubled, secure" and "freedom from anxiety," "safety, security." Those Latin words are in turn based on the Latin prefix *se-* (without) and *cura* (care). Well and good; then how about *securiform*? Here we have a different story, for this word means "axe-shaped" (surprise!), because it is based on a different Latin word: *securis* (axe), based in turn on the verb *secare* (to cut) plus *forma* (form, shape). One may feel more secure carrying an axe than not, but that has nothing to do with the lack of etymological relationship between *securus* and *securis*. Mustn't let these little accidents fool you; appearances can be deceiving, particularly in etymology.

sermuncle (SUR munk'l) *n. Sermo* is Latin for "talk, discourse," and its diminutive *sermunculus* was formed in the usual way, by adding the diminutive suffix *-culus*, which incidentally caused the change of the *o* of the stem *sermon-* to *u*. (Cf. *carbuncle*, from Latin *carbunculus*, which originally meant "live coal," formed from *carbon-*, the stem of *carbo*, meaning "burned wood," plus the same diminutive suffix -*culus*, with the same change from *o* to *u*; *carbunculus* came to denote any red object and was applied to an inflamed tumor.) Latin *sermo* became *sermon* in English—a particular type of "discourse"—and, in more modern times, a short one became known as a *sermonette* (ocasionally *sermonet* or even *sermonettine*) with the addition of the familiar diminutive suffix -*ette*. It is a more readily recognizable synonym of *sermuncle*. By whatever name, these short sermons were devised to correspond to the shorter attention span of those members of the congregation endowed with much less patience than that of their forefathers.

sestet   See **sixain.**

sestina   See **sixain.**

sextain   See **sixain.**

sharia (shah REE uh) *n*. Taken from Arabic *shariah*, like most words of Arabic source this word has a number of variant spellings, always characteristic of transliterations from Eastern languages: *shariah, shariat, sheria, sheriah, sheriat,* etc. *Sharia* is the "Islamic religious law": the body of established law based primarily on the commandments of Allah as found in the Koran and revealed through the *sunna* (SOO nah)—the "words and deeds of Muhammad." Though this is the sacred law, it covers not only religious matters but also political, economic, civil and criminal areas and the general field of social and domestic affairs in Muslim countries. The *sharia* is usually supplemented by the traditional practices of a given region. A March 1979 issue of the *Guardian* (London) described the *shariah* as "a way of life remarkable for its homogeneity ... meaning simply the way or path," but doubtless the advent of the Ayatollah and the mullahs has brought about changes in the way of increasingly rigorous interpretation and enforcement. With every dispatch from some of the Islamic countries, we must evermore cherish our constitutions, whether written, as in America, or unwritten, as in Britain.

shebeen   See **boreen.**

Shekinah (shih KEE nuh), also **Schechinah** (shih CHEE nuh) *n*. This is a theological term, taken from Hebrew (*shuh CHEE nah*—*ch* as in *ach, loch*), signifying God's presence on earth or a manifestation thereof; also, a "refulgent light symbolizing the Divine Presence." *Shechinah* is used in the *Targums* in place of *God*; e.g., when He is said to dwell among the cherubim, in order to avoid any hint of anthropomorphism. *Targum* (TAR guhm) is Chaldean for "exegesis, interpretation," denoting an Aramaic translation or interpretation of a book of the Old Testament made after the Babylonian captivity (in the sixth century B.C.). That word gave rise to the verb *targum* (to interpret or paraphrase Scripture); the adjective *targumic* (tar GOOM ik), the noun *tar-*

gumist (TAR guhm ist, a translator and commentator who assisted in the compilation of, or one one versed in the literature of, the *Targums*), the adjective *targumistic* (tar guhm IS tik, pertaining to the *targumists*) and the verb *targumize* (TAR guhm ize, to make a *Targum* of a book of the Old Testament). George Eliot, in *Scenes of Clerical Life* (1858), wrote: "The golden sunlight beamed through the dripping boughs like a *Shechinah,* or visible divine presence." The term has also been applied to the presence of Jesus Christ on earth. It could be manifested by any natural or supernatural phenomenon, like the burning bush or the cloud on the summit of Mt. Sinai, by a mystical intervention in human affairs or through a sense of personal communion with God sensed by man.

shive   See **vellinch.**

sirvent(e) (seer VAWNT—the *A* pronounced nasally as in French) *n.* The ancestor of this word was Provençal *sirventes,* which was mistakenly taken to be a plural form, so that both the French and English form became the erroneous singular *sirvent(e).* (I once heard someone say that so-and-so's accomplishments deserved a big *kudo;* same mistake!) Be that as it may, a *sirvent* is a "troubador's poem or lay, usually of a satirical nature." In *Ivanhoe* we read: "The knight ... asked his host whether he would choose a *sirvente* in the language of *oc,* or a *lai* in the language of *oui.*" *Oc* was *yes* in the Romance dialects of southern France, and *Langue d'oc* was the name given to them. *Oil* or *oui* was *yes* in the Romance dialects of northern France, and *Langue d'oil* and *Langue d'oui* were names given to them. Bishop William Stubbs, in *Seventeen Lectures on the Study of Mediaeval and Modern History* (1886), writes of " ... some few *sirventes* or satiric lays that entitle Richard [I] to the name of a trouvère [a medieval narrative poet of northern France]." (Trouvère is the northern French form of the word, more familiar to us as *troubadour.*) In Browning's *Sordello* we find the couplet: "A notion of the Troubador's intent/In rondel, tenzon, virlai or *sirvent.*" A *rondel* is a verse form of thirteen or fourteen lines on two rhymes, the seventh and thirteenth being identical with the first and the eighth, and the fourteenth (if present) with the second. A *tenzon* or *tenson* is a verse competition between two troubadors before a court of love (a judicial court to determine affairs of the heart in Provence in the days of the troubadors). A *virlai,* more commonly *virelay,* is a song or short lyric piece originating in 14th-century France, consisting of short lines in stanzas with two rhymes, the end rhyme of one stanza being the chief one of the next. Back to Browning for a moment: He had to pronounce *sirvent* in his own, arbitrary, way, to rhyme with *intent.* Things like that don't matter much to poets; they have enough troubles as it is.

sis(s)erary (sis ur AY ree), also **sassarara** (sas uhr AY ruh) *n.* Originally, this was a popular corruption of *certiorari,* the name of a writ issuing from a superior court calling for the record of a proceeding in an inferior court on an appeal. A petition for *certiorari* is the document filed with the Supreme Court of the United States on an appeal to that court. *Sis(s)erary, sassarara* and a large number of variant spellings are now all obsolete in this sense. *Certiorari*, incidentally, is the passive infinitive of the Latin verb *certiorare* (to inform), related to *certior* (surer), the comparative of *certus* (sure, certain). *Sis(s)erary* and its variants acquired the following meanings: "Severe rebuke," "scolding," "sharp blow," "torrent (of language)," "loud clang." The expression *with a siserary* (however spelled) means "with a vengeance," as used, for example, by Laurence Sterne in *Tristram Shandy*: "It was on a Sunday in the afternoon, when I fell in love all at once *with a sisserara*." In *The Vicar of Wakefield*, Oliver Goldsmith used it this way: "'As for the matter of that,' returned the hostess, '... out she shall pack *with a sassarara*.'" Smollett used it in the sense of "rebuke," Scott in the sense of "torrent" (a *siserary of Latin*) and others with the meaning of "clang." In all its spellings, a versatile word!

sixain (suh ZANE, sik SANE) *n*. This is a term in poetry meaning a "stanza of six lines," taken over from French, where *sixain* is an alternative to the more frequently found *sizain*, which came from Old French *sisain*, based on *sis* (six). *Sextain* (SEK stane) is another word for a "six-line stanza." The related word *sestina* (seh STEEN uh) denotes a much more complicated form, a lyrical arrangement contrived by the troubadors of Provence in the 12th century consisting of six stanzas, each of six lines, originally unrhymed, with the six end words repeated in different order in each of the stanzas, and an envoy (sometimes spelled *envoi*; a short concluding stanza) of three lines, in which three of these end words occur in the middle of the line and the other three at the end of the line—a very elaborate scheme indeed! The *sestina* is not to be confused with the *sestet*, the last six lines of a sonnet in the Italian form, considered as a unit. This takes some explaining. A sonnet consists of fourteen lines, usually in iambic pentameter (each line containing five feet of two syllables, the first syllable unstressed, the second stressed). A sonnet in the Italian form, also known as the *strict form*, is divided into a group of eight lines considered as a unit and known as the major group or *octave*, followed by a group of six lines, the minor group, or *sestet*. The looser "Shakespearean" form of sonnet consists of three quatrains (groups of four lines) followed by a couplet (two lines), with a less exacting rhyme scheme. Look at the first quatrain of one of the most beautiful of Shakespeare's sonnets (number 18):

> Shall I compare thee to a summer's day?
> Thou art more lovely and more temperate:
> Rough winds do shake the darling buds of May,
> And summer's lease hath all too short a date ...

and read the rest.

sjambok (SHAM bok) *n*. Also found in the forms *sambock, shambok, jambok*, etc., this is the name of a heavy whip made of rhinoceros or hippopotamus hide, used in South Africa for driving cattle and whipping people—lovely thought! As a verb, *to sjambok* is "to flog with such a whip." This delightful instrument is described in a number of South African travel books (e.g., Thomas Pringle, *African Sketches*; Frederick Selous, *Travels and Adventures in South-east Africa*). The word originated in Cape Dutch, fashioned after Malay *samboq* and Persian and Urdu *chabouk* or *chabuk* (horsewhip). We have seen lots of pictures on television of South African police using heavy-looking whips on protesters. Do you suppose the whips were made of rhinoceros or hippopotamus hide? *Sjamboks*? Or is everything plastic these days?

skelder (SKEL dur) *vb.*. *To skelder*, used intransitively, is "to beg, to live by begging, especially by passing oneself off as a wounded or discharged soldier." Shackerley Marmion (there's a name for you!), in his comedy *A Fine Companion* (1633), penned these words: " ... wandering abroad to *skelder* for a shilling." Transitively, *to skelder* is "to swindle, defraud, obtain (money) by cheating." Ben Jonson, in *Poetaster, or the Arraignment* (1601), said: "A man may *skelder* yee, now and then, of halfe a dozen shillings, or so." Sir Walter Scott, in *Woodstock, or the Cavalier* (1826), wrote: "I have lived in a *skeldering* sort of way myself." The dictionaries agree that the origin of *skelder* is shrouded in mystery, differing only in whether to characterize it as "unknown," "obscure" or simply "cant." Perhaps *cant* needs an apostrophe and is simply short for "can't help you"?

skimmington (SKIM ing tuhn) *n*. *To skim* is "to clear a liquid" (of scum or any other unwanted floating substance). This is usually done with a skimming ladle, also known as a *skimmer*. A *skimmington* is a "boisterous, ludicrous procession, once common in the countryside, to ridicule or heap odium upon an unfaithful or abusive spouse," and the term was applied as well to the person in the procession who impersonated the cuckolded or abused spouse, whether the henpecked or cuckolded husband or his unfaithful or shrewish wife. To *ride (the) skimmington* was to hold such a procession. A *skimmity* (SKIM uh dee) or *skimmity ride* was another name for that kind of procession. Well may you wonder, what is the connection between *skimming* scum off the top of a liquid and boisterous processions shaming abusive spouses? Believe it or not, there is a simple explanation: The shrewish wife in the procession was usually represented as beating her unhappy spouse with a *skimming* ladle. Farfetched? Nothing in language is farfetched. Elementary, as Sherlock Holmes would have put it, on coming across the frontispiece of a 1696 publication entitled *Diveres Crabtree Lectures*, showing a woman beating her husband with a *skimming* ladle and bearing the caption "*Skimmington*, and her Husband." In *The Mayor of Casterbridge* (1886) Thomas Hardy wrote of "the rude music of the *skimmington* and the *skimmington ride*," and an 1865 issue of *St. James' Magazine* asserts: "The '*skymington*' (sic) is still in use for henpecked husbands and shrewish wives." Cf. *shivaree*, another type of noisy procession expressing disapproval, fully discussed in my *1000 Most Challenging Words*.

skimmity   See **skimmington**.

sloat   See **scrutate**.

slote   See **scrutate**.

smogger (SMOG ur) *n*. This is the tramps' cant word for their special road-sign code, said to have been initiated in England during the reign of Henry VIII (first half of the 16th century). Communication among vagabonds was achieved by chalk marks, which they called *"smogger"* (origin unknown), made on gateposts. For example: Two large overlapping or intersecting circles meant "tell a sob story, a sad tale of woe"; three circles in a row meant "soft touch for money here." Tramps read *smogger* as easily as Egyptologists read hieroglyphics. The symbols were usually taken by householders to be naive children's drawings. No one has demonstrated any connection between *smogger* and the much later *smog*, a portmanteau combination of *smoke* and *fog*.

smoot (SMOOHT) *n*. This is a unit of linear measurement equivalent to approximately 5 feet 7 inches. Its origin is one of the more esoteric bits of Harvard College history. Oliver R. Smoot was an M.I.T. (Massachusetts Institute of Technology) freshman in 1958. As a bit of fraternity hazing, he had to lie down 365 times as friends (?) painted *"smoot* marks" every tenth time to measure the length of the Harvard Bridge over the Charles River. It comes to about a half mile; i.e., 10 *smoots* = 1/2 mile. Not long ago (this is March 1989) *smoot* marks were threatened with obliteration. The bridge was to be renovated and the *smoots*, maintained and repainted over the years by freshmen, eradicated. However, bridge authorities ruled that the *smoots*, now a tradition, must stay. Indeed, a plaque honoring the *smoot* will be installed on the bridge this spring. Bravo! So far, the *smoot* has not been taken into everyday English, but in view of the multiplicity of Harvard men gaining high positions in our government, it may be adopted, and as a Harvard '27 man myself, two of whose older brothers were M.I.T. men, '16 and c. '19 respectively, I shall do my best to keep the *smoot* alive.

snuff (SNUFF) *n*., *vb*. In addition to denoting a preparation of powdered tobacco inhaled through the nostrils, *snuff* has a number of entirely distinct meanings: the "sooty, partly consumed, ill-smelling end of a lamp or candle wick that has to be trimmed:' a "candle end"; figuratively, "anything of no value"; a *"heeltap"* (see **supernaculum**); in Scotland, "umbrage, a huff or pet"; as a verb, "to sniff, to smell at something doubtfully, to remove the *snuff* from, to brighten"; *to snuff out* is "to put out (a lamp or candle) with *snuffers*." As slang, *to snuff it* or *snuff out* is "to die." The derivation is from German *Schnuppe* (snuff of a candle), and, in the sense of "something of no value," cf. German *Das ist mir ganz Schnuppe* (I don't care a rap). In Trollope's *He Knew he was Right* (1869) we read the words "going out like the *snuff of a candle*," i.e., on the way out, dying. Pepys used *snuff* in the sense of "umbrage" in his *Diary* (a 1662 entry): "Mr Mills ... I expect, will take it in *snuffe* that my wife did not come to his child's christening the other day." Stevenson used it in the sense of "huff" or "pet" in *Kidnapped*: "Dinnae flew up in the *snuff* at me." A very versatile word, *snuff*, quite apart from *snuff*-taking.

soc(c)age (SOK ij) *n*. This is one of those technical terms having to do with social and economic arrangements under the feudal English legal system. *Soc(c)age* was the "tenure of land for agricultural service fixed in amount and kind or by payment of rent in money," but in either case free of any obligation to render military service to the owner. *Soc* was a variant of *soke*, which denoted, among other things, jurisdiction over a defined territory or group of people; and a *sokeman* was a "tenant by *socage*," also known as a *socager*. The origin of these various terms was Old English *socn* (jurisdiction). Another form of tenure was *burgage*, in which royal land or that owned by the nobility in English *burghs* (boroughs) was held for an annual rent, and in Scottish boroughs for the service of "watching and warding," i.e., overseeing and guarding. The most distinctive feature of *socage* was freedom from "knight-service" (military service) in the lord's armed forces. Our conscientious objectors never suggested that type of proposition.

socager   See **soc(c)age.**

soke   See **soc(c)age.**

sororate   See **levirate.**

spicilege   See **florilegium.**

spiggoty, also **spiggity, spigotti,** etc. (SPIH guh tee) *n*. I disapprove of all ethnic pejoratives, but one does run into them, and I suppose they have to be explained. *Spiggoty*, then, is a derisive term for a Spanish-speaking native of Central or South America. The name seems to have originated during the digging of the Panama Canal, from the broken English "speekee (or spikka) de" in the expression "no speekee de Inglish," which was supposedly all the Panamanians could muster when addressed in English. Rex Stout, in *Fer-de-Lance* (1934), used the word in this passage: "'He's a dirty *spiggoty*.' 'No. Archie, Mr. Manuel Kimball is an Argentine.'" In *Harbor Nights* by H. Klemmer (1937) we see this unhappy sentence: "*Marijuana* is a popular *spiggoty* drug which has spread rapidly into the North during recent years." Harry La-Tourette Foster's *The Adventures of a Tropical Tramp* (1922) contains this bit of prose: "Just stood around the dock and jabbered a lot of *spiggoty* talk at me, like I could understand *spiggoty*. I don't know a word of this damned Spanish, and I'm glad of it!" We can see from these passages that *spiggoty* was a contemptuous term, and I'm happy to say that, so far as I can ascertain, it's extinct. But unhappily, *spic* or *spick*, also derived from *spiggoty*, still issues from the mouths of thoughtless people.

spondee   See **dolichurus.**

spurrier   See **lorimer.**

stamnos   See **krater.**

statocracy   See **ochlocracy.**

statocrat   See **ochlocracy.**

stenobathic (sten oh BATH ik) *adj*. From Greek *stenos* (narrow) we get the combining form *steno-*, which, combined with *bathos* (depth), gives us this term relating to aquatic life and describing those species capable of life within only a narrow range of depths. Combining the same *steno-* with *hals* (salt), we get the aquatic term *stenohaline*, designating a species capable of living only within a narrow range of salinity. *Steno-* plus *therme* (heat) produces *stenothermal*, describing animals capable of existing only within a narrow range of temperature. Greek *eurys* (wide) has the combining form *eury-*, which is combined with *bathos, hals* and *therme* to produce *eurybathic* and *euryhaline* to describe aquatic life capable of existence within wide rangers of depth and salinity, respectively, and *eurythermal* to designate animals that can survive within a wide range of temperature. One could, I suppose, combine additional Greek prefixes and environmental terms to increase the scope of biological terminology much more widely, but sufficient unto the day is the homework thereof.

stenohaline   See **stenobathic.**

stenothermal   See **stenobathic.**

stillicide (STIL ih side) *n*. This might well be taken for the name of one of those heinous crimes like *fratricide, matricide* or *regicide* whereby somebody gets killed, but people don't go around killing *stills*, except perhaps those mean "Feds" who destroyed the apparatus used in the moonshine industry romanticized in old movies. Actually, *stillicide* has nothing whatever to do with killing. The confusion arises because there are two distinct Latin verbs, *caedere* and *cadere*, from which we get the suffix *-cide*. *Caedere* means "to kill," *cadere* "to fall." The *-cide* of all those killing words comes from *caedere*; the *-cide* of *stillicide* comes from *cadere*. Now, *stilla* is Latin for "drop," as in *drop of water* (or any liquid), and *stillicidium* means "dripping moisture" generally, and in a special usage, "rain water dropping from eaves of houses." *Stillicide* developed as a legal term denoting the dropping of rain water from one's eaves upon the roof or land of a neighbor and was then applied to an easement (called a *servitude* in Scots law) permitting such dropping, which would otherwise be actionable. If your eaves protrude far enough to cause rain water dropping from them to moisten your neighbor's land, better talk it over with him and ask for an easement, but if he's stubborn, consult your lawyer, and if he can't work it out, get your carpenter to fit gutters and downspouts. Otherwise, the *stillicide* might result in a *vicinicide*, a word I just concocted to mean "killing of a neighbor," from *vicinus*, Latin for "neighbor," and the murderous type of -*cide*.

stirp (STURP) *n*. In Latin, *stirps* means literally the "stock or stem of a tree or plant," and by transference, figuratively, "stock, source, origin" relating to human beings; particularly, the "stock of a family, a line of descent." It is in the latter sense that the legal phrase *per stirpes* (pur STUR peez; *stirpes* is the plural of Latin *stirps*) is used in testamentary or trust documents. Distribution *per stirpes* is one that follows the lines of descent. For example, if a bequest is qualified as made *per stirpes* (as opposed to *per capita*) and the testator is survived by three children and the two children of a deceased child, the bequest would go initially four ways because there are four *stirpes*: one share to each surviving child and one share to the two grandchildren collectively, so that each of them would receive one-eighth of the bequest. In effect, the testator is saying: "I loved my four children with equal affection while they were all alive, and therefore allot that last fourth to the children of the one that died during my lifetime." As a practicing lawyer for more than half a century, I had to explain the shortcut technical term *per stirpes* a couple of thousand times or thereabouts. It was sometimes hard to keep the attention of the client, and I frequently had to resort to diagrams, but all in a good cause.

strangury (STRANG yur ee) *n*. This book contains few medical terms, which exist in the thousands and certainly are obscure to the layman, whom they generally terrify rather than inform, yet this word not only has an interesting derivation but also exemplifies one of those cases of dangerous etymological association. *Strangury* is the "painful retention of a difficulty of discharging urine." Via Latin *stranguria*, it comes from Greek *strangouria*, composed of *stranx* (drop, trickle) plus *ourein* (to urinate), from *ouron* (urine). It amounts to a slow, painful discharge, a drop at a time, caused by spasmodic contraction of the bladder and urethra. Our word *strain* is associated with *stranx* and the Greek adjective *strangos* (twisted, flowing drop by drop). This disorder goes back a long way, as indicated by the Greek and Latin nomenclature mentioned above, and as long ago as 1398 there appeared the following graphic description of the disease in John de Trevisa's translation of Bartholomeus de Glenville's *De Proprietatibus Rerum* (On the Properties [Peculiarities?] of Things): "He that hath that dysease ... that hyghte *Stranguria*, pysseth ofte ande lytyll." Laurence Sterne, in *The Life and Opinions of Tristram Shandy*, gives us this sentence: "I hope they have got better of their colds ... fevers, *stranguries*, [etc.]." Now comes the dangerous jump-to-conclusion exercise in association-type etymology: Some have believed that *strangury* is a disease caused by *strangling* (!) or choking, as a result of which it has been used figuratively (and erroneously) by no less great figures than George Farquhar in *Love and a Bottle*: "Is my countenance strain'd, as if my head were distorted by a *Stranguary* [sic] of thought?" and Thackeray in a contribution to *Punch*: "Everybody stopped. There was a perfect *strangury* in the street." The adjective is *strangurious* (strang YUR ee uhs), and damned be him who cries "I hold too much!"

strappado (struh PAH doh, -PAY-) *n.* This is the name of a terrible form of torture, in which the victim's wrists were tied behind his back and fastened to a pulley, by means of which he was hoisted and then let down partway with a jerk. The word served as well to denote the procedure and the instrument involved. In the bad old days, it was used to force confessions, evidencing, like the rack, catherine wheel, thumbscrew and a variety of other instruments of torture, the delightful combination of man's ingenuity and inhumanity to man. *Strappado* was a modification of Italian *strappata* (sharp tug), related to the verb *strappare* (to pull sharply), with the addition of the common quasi-Spanish suffix *-ado*. In H.C. Lea's *History of the Inquisition* (1888) we learn that "in some witch trials of 1474 in Piedmont the oath to tell the truth was enforced with excommunication and '*tratti di corde*' [literally, tugs of cords] or infliction of the torture known as the *strappado*." I have been unable to ascertain the number of wrists broken, or shoulders separated, in the course of this delectable exercise. The device was used in the Inquisition and for some time thereafter. It is mentioned as a contemporary form of torture in numerous works, some as late as 1688. Shakespeare was familiar with the term (what *wasn't* he familiar with?). In *Henry IV, Part I*, Act II, Scene 4, in the course of a hilarious and protracted argument at the Boar's Head Tavern involving Prince Hal, Coins, Francis, Bardolph, Peto, other rough characters and Falstaff, whose veracity in recounting a valorous deed is challenged by the Prince, Falstaff exclaims: "What, upon compulsion? 'Zounds! an I were at the *strappado*, or all the racks in the world, I would not tell you on compulsion."

strepsiceros   See **hircine**.

strigil (STRIJ uhl) *n.* The ancient Romans and Greeks used the *strigil*, a curved skin-scraper of metal or ivory, to scrape the sweat and dirt from the skin after exercise or a hot bath. The term was later applied to any type of flesh-scraping brush used for that purpose. *Strigil* was taken from Latin, based on the verb *stringere* (to touch lightly). A *strigil* was, so to speak, a "currycomb" used on human beings by themselves or others. The Italian noun *striglia*, the German *Striegel* and the French *étrille* all mean "currycomb" and attest to the persistent influence of the Latin term. John Evelyn's *Diary* has an entry for June 1645, telling of "being rubbed with a kind of *strigil* of seal's-skin, put on the operator's hand like a glove," and Richard Chandler, in *Travels in Asia Minor*

(1775), provides this information: "We were rubbed with a mohair-bag fitted to the hand, which, like an ancient *strigil*, brings away the gross matter perspired." *The Civil Engineer and Architect's Journal*, in an 1843 issue, tells this sad story: "One day Hadrian recognized an old companion in arms in poverty, scraping himself with a tile instead of the *strigil*." D. Maguire's *Art of Massage* (1887) shows that this scraping technique persisted well into the 19th century: "Our masseurs of to-day use an instrument similar to the *strigil* made of box or any other hard wood, and call it sometimes *strigil* or *raclette*." (*Raclette* is French for "scraper," synonymous with *racle*; *raclage* is "scraping," *racler* means "to scrape" and a *racleur* is a "scraper," and colloquially a "poor violinist," i.e., a bad "scraper of catgut.")

subchanter   See **precentor.**

subreption   See **obreption.**

succentor   See **precentor.**

sunna   See **sharia.**

supernacular   See **supernaculum.**

supernaculum (sooh pur NAK yuh luhm, syooh-) *n., adv., adj.* Before analyzing this word, you should know that it's a term of praise, something wonderful, a treat, and then you'll be on the right track (but perhaps for the wrong reason). As an adverb, *supernaculum* means "to the last drop" (which happens to be a phrase familiar from the extensive national advertising of an American brand of coffee). It is used chiefly in the expression "drink to the last drop," and this is why: The word is constructed of Latin *super* (over, above, upon) plus New Latin [*CH* says "sham Latin"; the *O.E.D.* "Modern Latin"; *W III* "New Latin"] *nagulum* or *naculum* (nail), meaning, literally, "on the nail." This curious expression arises from the German idiom *auf den Nagel trinken*, literally, "to drink upon the nail," figuratively, "to drink [liquor] to the last drop." The reference here is to the practice of turning the emptied glass upside down onto the left thumbnail, to demonstrate that all the liquor has been drunk, i.e., drunk to the last drop. In Disraeli's *Vivian Grey* (1827) we find the sentence: "As he withdrew the horn from his mouth, all present ... gave a loud cry of '*Supernaculum!*'" In Thomas Nash's *Pierce Pennilesse his Supplication to the Diuell* [Devil] (1592) there is a passage that makes the procedure absolutely clear: "Drinking *super nagulum*, a deuise of drinking new [newly] come out of Fraunce [wasn't it in fact Germany?]; which is, after a man has turned up the bottom of the cup, to drop it on his naile, & make a pearle with that is left; which, if it shed, and he cannot make stand on, by reason ther's too much, he must drinke againe for his pennance." (Not a harsh penance, by any means!) *Supernaculum*, as a noun, means an "alcoholic drink of the finest quality," or as *CH* puts it, "a liquor of the best kind, too good to leave heeltaps." *Heeltap* is a fine word itself, meaning a "bit of liquor left in the glass after drinking." We have to get back to *supernaculum* for a moment: There would seem to be a bit of uncertainty as to whether there should be nothing at all on the thumbnail or one drop that must "stand on" without "shedding," according to Thomas Nash. The only way to resolve this seeming inconsistency is to remember that *to* in the expression *to the last drop* might mean "up to" or "to and including," a dilemma that has worried legal draftsmen for centuries. In America, lawyers avoid the ambiguity by using *through* when the sense is "to and including" and the circumlocution seems cumbersome. There is an adjective from our fine headword: *supernacular*, said of excellent drink. Thackeray, in *The Book of Snobs* (1848) writes: "Some white Hermitage at the Haws (by the way, the butler only gave me half a glass each time) was *supernacular*." And what is *hermitage*? Apart from a "hermit cell" or any "retired abode," it is the name of a white wine made near Valence (Drôme) in France, the locality of a supposed hermit's cell. By the way, I wish that Thackeray had placed the "only" immediately before the "half" in his sentence. The position of *only* in our sentences is a matter of great distress to some. There is a popular song entitled "I only have eyes for you." It doesn't mean "I alone of all the people in the world," or "only eyes," as opposed to ears or other parts of the anatomy, which wouldn't have been true by any means, but "only you of all the inhabitants of this planet." The poor lyricist had to fit the words to the melody, with that unpardonable result.

surtout   See **roquelaure.**

swasivious (swa SIV ee uhs) *adj.* To my regret, this delightful word is marked "obs[olete], rare" in the *O.E.D.*, and the only etymological note is "f[rom] It[alian] SUASIVO plus -IOUS." The meaning is "agreeably persuasive," and *swasivious* deserves to be resurrected to take the place of that circumlocution. In any event, it rhymes with *lascivious*, and that would be of great convenience to limerick makers, especially in view of its meaning. The only reference to literature offered by the *O.E.D.* is "1592. R.D. *Hypnerotomachia* ... With pleasurable actions, maydenly iestures, suasiuious behauiours." The initials *R. D.* turn out, after some confusion, to be those of Sir Robert Dallington, of whom we shall have more to say later. It develops that *Hypnerotomachia* is an Italian work in macaronic Latin (more about *macaronic* below) written by a Dominican friar, Francesco Colonna, under the pseudonym Poliphilus some time before 1479 and published in Venice in 1499. The work is a mysterious allegorical romance with the full title *Hypnerotomachia Poliphili*. In 1592 the aforesaid Dallington published an English translation of part of it entitled *The Strife of Love in a Dream*, edited by Andrew Lang in 1890. The explanation of *Hypnerotomachia* is in the definition of three Greek elements: *hypn-* (the combining form of *hypnos*, sleep), *eroto-* (the combining form of *eros* (erotic love), and *mach* (conflict, battle). The more literal meaning of *hypnerotomachia* would be the "struggle between sleep and sexual desire," a problem most healthy males will quickly recognize. I promised to come back to *macaronic*. It is fully discussed in my *1000 Most Challenging Words*, where I explain it as "applied, in a narrow sense, to language characterized by a mixture of Latin and non-Latin words ... " The word has broader applications not relevant here. An up-to-date work about the good friar's book is a German tome by Linda Fierz-David published in Zurich in 1948 under the title *Der Liebestraum des Polifilo*. *Liebestraum* means "love-dream," and *Polifilo* is the Italian spelling of *Poliphilus*. Come back, *swasivious*. As to the *w*, Shakespeare used it in *King John*, Act V, Scene 5, when the Messenger says: "The count Melun is slain; the English Lords,/By his perswasion, are againe falne off," and in *Twelfth Night*, Act III, Scene 4, where Antonio says to Viola: "Isn't possible that my deserts to you/Can lacke perswasion?" Of course, it depends on which folio you read. *Perswaisive(ly)* appears often in 17th-century literature, including Milton. The Italian *suasivo* mentioned in the etymology is one of a group of three adjectives (*suadente, suasivo, suasorio*) meaning "persuasive," all going back to Latin *suadere* (to present in a pleasing manner), and the "pleasing" element clearly justifies the *O.E.D.* definition. There are a great many *sua-* words in Latin having to do with persuasion, recommending, advising, etc., and the *per-* of Latin *persuadere* is the intensive prefix, giving the effect of "thoroughly, utterly," suggesting that the *persuasive* effort has been so strong as to result in *convincing*.

symphile (SIM file) *n.* You wouldn't think that ants or termites kept guests in their nests, would you? Well, they do. A *symphile* is an "insect of another species, such as any of various beetles, living in the nests of social insects like ants or termites who feed and guard them for the value of their secretions, which are consumed as food by the hosts." This is an example of *commensalism*. (*Commensal* is discussed at length in my *1000 Most Challenging Words*, from which I quote: "When it is used of animals or plants, *commensal* describes types living together, or a type living on or in another, without harm to either.") *Symphile* is from Greek *symphilia*, formed of the prefix *syn-* (together) plus *philos* (friend), and has a synonym, *myrmecoxene* (mur muh KOK seen), from *myrmec(o)-*, the combining form of Greek *myrmex* (ant) plus *-xene*, the combining form of *xenos* (stranger, alien—from which we get our unhappy word *xenophobia*). In view of that bit of etymology, I am puzzled to find *myrmecoxene* defined, in the discussion under *symphile* in *W III*, as "true guest." I suppose every accommodating beetle in an ant's nest is a "true guest," but not every "true guest" is an ant's beetle.

symploce   See **anaphora**.

tabby   See **tapia.**

tabia   See **tapia.**

talaria   See **petasus.**

talion (TAL ee uhn) *n. Talion* means "like for like, retaliation" from Latin *talio* (like punishment, retaliation), based on the adjective *talis* (such, of such a kind), and it figures in the derivation of our word *retaliation.* In Exodus: 21:23–25, we read " ... life for life / Eye for eye, tooth for tooth, hand for hand, foot for foot / Burning for burning, wound for wound, stripe for stripe ... " This system of condign punishment is discussed under the headword *condign* in my *1000 Most Challenging Words,* where I also mention Gilbert's " ... punishment fit the crime ... " in *The Mikado.* In Roman times, this primitive penal code was known as the *Lex Talionis* (Law of Retaliation), freely (very freely, and quite crudely) translated "tit for tat," and that childish-sounding phrase has been variously traced to Dutch *dit voor dat* (this for that) and French *tant pour tant.* An extension of the *Lex Talionis* was the infliction on an unsuccessful plaintiff of the very punishment that the accused would have suffered if found guilty. In the Rollin-Tilton translation of Edmundo De Amicis's *Morocco* (1879) there is a tantalizing account (because the *O.E.D.* quotation doesn't tell us what went before) of a vindictive lady who " ... demanded that in virtue of the law of *talion* he [presumably the judge] should order the English merchant's two front teeth to be broken." A teeth for a teeth?

tallis   See **daven.**

talus   See **nunatak.**

tanka   See **cinquain.**

tantara   See **taratantara.**

tapette (ta PET) *n., adj.* In French, *tapette,* aside from its literal meanings "tap, type of hammer to push corks in, engraver's pad, marble game," is slang for "homosexual." The word has been taken into English by a number of writers. In Evelyn Waugh's *Vile Bodies* (1930) we find "My dear, he looks terribly *tapette.*" Rebecca West, in *The Thinking Reed* (1936), has a character declare: "It will make my room look as if I were a *tapette!*" In *Another Country* (1963), James Baldwin describes a character who " ... had lived by his wits in the streets of Paris, as a semi-*tapette* and as a *rat d'hôtel* [hotel thief]." *Tapette* means "passive male homosexual," or in (objectionable) slang pejorative usage, "pansy." Its use has been widened to denote any effeminate man whose sexual tastes may be totally heterosexual, or "straight." I detest all derogatory labels in this area; some of my best friends ... etc.

taphephobia (ta fee FOH bee uh) *n*. In view of all the frightening news about earthquakes in the last few years, I'm sure *taphephobia* is on the increase. It means "morbid fear of being buried alive" and is based on Greek *taphe* (burial, grave), akin to *thaptein* (to bury, inter), plus Late Latin *-phobia*, indicating fear of something, from Greek *phobos* (fear, terror). (Does the derivation of Late Latin *-phobia* from Greek *phobos* save *taphephobia* from the somewhat pejorative designation *hybrid word*? I discuss that subject in my *Practical English: 1000 Most Effective Words*: "Figuratively, *hybrid* is applied to anything made from different elements. There are *hybrid* words, like *television*: *tele-* is derived from Greek, *-vision* from Latin.") *Taphephobia* brings to mind the superstitious expression *knock on wood* (*touch wood*, in Britain), said after an expression of satisfaction with the way things are going at the moment ("I haven't had a cold for years!"), in order not to tempt fate into reversing the course. It is said that *knock (on) wood* comes from the rather grim picture of a person accidentally interred alive knocking on the inside of the lid of his wooden coffin. After that kind of experience, the disinterred one would certainly be entitled to a lifelong case of *taphephobia*.

taphonomic(al)   See **taphonomy**.

taphonomist   See **taphonomy**.

taphonomy (taf ON uh mee) *n*. We are familiar with fossils and the phenomenon of fossilization, whereby organic material is replaced with mineral substances in the remains of an organism, affording clues of great importance in paleontology and paleobiology. The study of the processes involved in the fossilization of animal and plant remains is known as *taphonomy*, from Greek *taphos* (grave) plus the suffix *-nomia*, from *nomos* (law, custom). It was J. A. Efremov, in *Pan-American Geology* (1940), who coined this word: "I propose for this part of paleontology the name of '*Taphonomy* ', the science of the laws of embedding ... *Taphonomical* research allows us to glance into the depth of ages from another point of view." The March 2, 1974 issue of *The Times* (London) contained the following: "Russian scientists have brought together a team of geologists ... and a group of *taphonomists*: the last belong to a specialty created in Russia for studying the way animals and plants are preserved in their burial sites." A 1981 issue of *Nature* states: "Paleontologists ... are bringing their subject out of the museum through studies of the processes by which the fossil record forms (*taphonomy*)."

tapia (TA pyuh) *n*. In Spanish, *tapia* means "mud or adobe wall, wall fence" as well as a "wall measure of 50 square feet." Taken into English, it denotes a material used for walls, consisting of clay or mud, puddled (i.e., mixed with water to form an impervious mixture), beaten into solidity and dried. Hooker & Ball's *Journal of a Tour in Morocco and the Great Atlas* (1878) speaks of "the remains of massive walls of *tapia*." *Tabia* (TA byuh), probably a modification of *tapia*, is a somewhat different building material consisting of earth, lime and pebbles rammed between forms. It is an extremely durable material, especially in arid regions. Many of the castles in the northern Sahara are built of it and have proved to be long-lasting. Still another building material, known as *tabby* (derived from a number of words of African origin—'*tabi*, *tabax*, *ta'bo* and *ntaba*, all having to do with mud in one way or another) and made of lime, sand or gravel and oyster shells, was once used on the coasts of Georgia and South Carolina. This *tabby* hasn't a thing in the world to do with the noble creatures known as *tabby cats*. Finally, in this category, we have the word *pisé*, the past participle of the French verb *piser* (to beat, pound, stamp) used as a substantive in French meaning "masonry" (*pisé de terre* means "blocks of clay"; *mur en pisé* means "cob-wall," a wall built of cob, a composition of clay and straw); *piser* is from Latin *pinsere* (to beat, pound, stamp); alternative forms are *pisare* and *pinsare*. We use *pisé* to mean "stiff clay or earth kneaded or mixed with gravel" for use in the building of walls or cottages. The mixture is rammed between boards that are removed when it solidifies, a process used in France and in parts of England. *Pisé* can also be used to denote this mode of construction. Edward H. Knight's *Practical Dictionary of Mechanics* (1875) states that "The best material for *pisé* work is clay with small gravel-stones interposed through it." But Lord protect us from *pebbledash*, British for "pebble-coated stucco," which I describe in my *British English, A to Zed* as "a not very good- looking and all too frequent building surfacing in Britain ... and one wonders how in the world this miserable invention ever came about."

tapis (TA pis) *n*. Late Latin took the noun *tapetium* and its variant *tapecium* from Greek *tapetion*, the diminutive of *tapes*, meaning "cloth woven with varicolored figures and designs." *Tapis* is a generic term for any cloth wrought with colored designs, such as tablecloths, curtains, rugs and carpets; it is French for "rug, carpet, tablecloth." The phrase *on the tapis* (from the French *sur le tapis*) means, literally, "on the tablecloth," which we shorten to "on the table," meaning "under discussion" or "being considered." Incidentally, where we use the verb *to table* meaning "to postpone consideration of at the moment," presumably for later action, the British use it meaning "to present for discussion." In my *British English, A to Zed*, I give the meaning of *table* (the verb) as "submit for discussion," with the comment: "This term means exactly the opposite of what it means in America, where to *table* an item is to *shelve* it or postpone discussion of it, perhaps hoping it will never come up again." Another use of *tapis* is in the phrase *tapis vert*, taken from the French, meaning literally "green carpet" but used to denote a grass walk, a long strip of lawn, as used by Mrs. Lyndon B. Johnson ("Ladybird") in her book *White House Diary* (1965) in the sentence "He wants to ... preserve the *tapis vert*, the long green ribbon that stretches from the Capitol to the Lincoln memorial." In Wood's *Practical Garden Design* (1976) we find the phrase " ... on either side of the *tapis vert*— '*green carpet*,'" referring to a grass strip. *Tapis* once meant "to adorn with tapestry" or "to embellish (tapestry, etc.) with figures." It came to mean to "lie low so as to be hidden, to lurk or skulk," or, transitively, "to hide," and in a wholly different sense, "to adorn with tapestry," but those uses are obsolete. However, in the form *tapish*, now dialectal, especially in Sheffield, a city in the English county of Yorkshire, it is used to mean "to languish" or "to be mortally ill." In the 1891 supplement to Sidney Addy's *Glossary of Words Used in the Neighborhood of Sheffield* (1888), *tapish* is defined as "to waste or pine away" and an example is furnished: "He *tapished* and died." It's a long way from rugs and carpets to pining away and dying. Don't get the idea that the words have a common derivation, which they quite obviously haven't.

tapsell (TAP s'l) *adj.* When you think of a gate, you visualize a swinging barrier that closes an opening in a fence, hinged on one side or the other, moving inward or outward as best suits the particular need. Not so with a *tapsell* gate, which turns about a central post and thus admits entrance. It is a type of churchyard gate peculiar to the English county of Sussex, one of the Home Counties, those nearest London. The origin of the word is unknown, and though I have characterized it as an adjective, it might well be a noun, or, for all I know, the name of the inventor used attributively. H. Hall, the author of *Some Sussex Sayings & Crafts* (1957), says: "*Tapsell* gate, this ingenious gate is peculiar to Sussex, but nothing is known of its origin or its designer. Its special use is to prevent cattle entering churchyards, and to make room for coffin bearers to pass through easily ... Today there are only six in the county." However, the March 15, 1979 issue of the magazine *Country Life* tells us: "*Tapsell gates*, which turn on a central pivot, are peculiar to Sussex. It has been suggested that they are so-called after one Tapsell, a Sussex iron-master." In any event, Hall's mention of cattle brings to mind another type of gate that prevents cattle from trespassing, the *kissing-gate*, which I discuss in my *British English, A to Zed*:

> Kissing gates found in rural Britain are gates hung with the side away from the hinge swinging within a V- ... or U-shaped enclosure in such a way that people can get in but cattle can't. You push the gate away from the near side of the V or U, step into the latter, slide over to the other side, and push the gate back. This quaint device acquired its romantic name (or so one is told) because it was often the place where a swain said goodnight to his lady love, and a certain amount of lingering and incidental activity were in order.

Sounds like much more fun than *tapsell gates* and coffin bearing.

tar(r)adiddle (tar uh DID'l) *n., vb.* This rather happy-sounding flippant-seeming word means "fib," or "white lie" and can also, in context, mean "pretentious nonsense." The *-diddle* element apparently comes from the slang verb *diddle* (to swindle, cheat, cajole), of unknown origin, and the whole word is credited with no etymology except that reference to "diddle." In Mrs. Elizabeth Gaskell's novel *Wives and Daughters, an Every-day Story* (1865), we read the amusing passage: "Oh, don't call them lies, sister; it's such a strong, ugly word. Please call them *tallydiddles*, for I don't believe she meant any harm." Mrs. Gaskell came close. *Tar(r)adiddle*, as an intransitive verb, means "to fib," and transitively, "to impose upon by telling fibs." In that sense, it is quite close to the verb *diddle* without the *tar(r)a-*, but that element seems to give it a happy-go-lucky air, rather than a dark, deep, scheming atmosphere. Yet *tar(r)adiddling* may have serious consequences. An 1828 issue of *The Examiner, a Sunday Paper on Politics, Domestic Economy, and Theatricals*, of which Leigh Hunt was the original editor, wrote of a public figure whose enemies " ... squibbed, and paragraphed, and *taradiddled* him to death." So go easy on *taradiddling* your adversaries.

tarantism (TAR uhn tiz'm) *n.* This was the name of a hysterical disease that took the form of an irresistible need to go into maniacal dancing; it became epidemic in Apulia and neighboring parts of southern Italy from the 15th to the 17th centuries. The malady took its name from the *tarantula*, to whose sting or bite it was popularly attributed. The tarantula in question was a large, hairy poisonous spider, named from the town of Taranto, the Roman Tarentum, a seaport town in Apulia where it proliferated. Opinions differed as to whether the maniacal dancing was caused by the bite of the tarantula or was a cure for the disease. A popular form of the dancing was the *tarantella*, a lively, whirling dance native to southern Italy, done in triplets by one couple, and formerly believed to be a cure for *tarantism*. Getting back to the tarantula for a moment, there are several spiders that bear this name. The one discussed above is the wolf spider found in many parts of southern Europe, *Lycosa tarantula*; there are American tarantulas as well, sluggish types, whose bite is painful but usually not venomous. (They are ugly and scary, nevertheless.) An item in *Chambers's Encyclopedia* (1883) reads: "*Tarantism* may be defined as leaping or dancing mania, originating in, or supposed to originate in, an animal poison ... The gesticulations, contortions, and cries somewhat resembled those in St. Vitus's dance, and other epidemic nervous diseases of the middle ages." Apparently, the writer of that article didn't take the connection between *tarantism* and the tarantula very seriously.

taratantara (tah rah TAN tuh ruh) *n.* A lovely bit of onomatopoeia is *taratantara*, imitating and denoting the sound of a trumpet (though one has to indulge in a bit of imagination) and referring figuratively to "pretentious talk, grandiloquent language, flamboyant oratory." A similar word, *tantara* (TAN tuh ruh), sometimes extended to *tantarara, tantararara* and *tantaratara*, means a "flourish" on a trumpet, occasionally a drum roll or a like sound. We didn't invent *taratantara*: It appears in the writing of the Roman poet Ennius (239–169 B.C.) and was taken into Italian as well. Ouida (Mlle. de la Ramée), in *Pascarèl; Only a Story* (1873), wrote this romantic sentence: "Their Tirolean postilions roused the echoes ... with a *tarantarratara* upon their tassellated bugles." A nice elaboration of our word and an evocative bit of *taratantara* in itself, no?

Targum   See **Shekinah.**

targumic   See **Shekinah.**

targumist   See **Shekinah.**

targumize   See **Shekinah.**

tath (TATH) *n., vb.* This is the term for the "dung of cattle and sheep allowed to remain on the field on which they have been pastured, so as to improve the fertility of the land." John Cowell's *The Interpreter: or Booke Containing the Signification of Words*, as augmented by W. Kennett (1701), tells us that in Norfolk and Suffolk (counties of England) " ... the Lord of each Manor had the Privilege of having their Tenants (sic) Flocks of Sheep brought at Night upon their own Demesne Ground [i.e., estate], there to be fouled [i.e., confined?] for the benefit of their Dung, which liberty of so improving their Land is called *Tath*." The term applies as well to coarse tufted grass that grows on land manured in this manner. *Water-tath* has been applied by stock farmers to all grasses that are especially rank and luxuriant. They differentiate between *water-tath*, produced by excess moisture, and *nolt-tath*, produced by dung. (*Nolt* is a Scottish word for "cattle.") A *tath-field* or *tath-fold* is one in which cattle or sheep are confined for purposes of manuring the land. *Tath* is used as a transitive verb in Scottish or other dialects to denote the process of manuring land by confining cattle on it, and *water-tathing* is the flooding of land to improve its productivity. As an intransitive verb, *to tath* is a term applied to cattle meaning "to drop dung upon land and thus to manure it."

tath-field   See **tath.**

tath-fold   See **tath.**

tatpurusha (tat POOHR uh shuh) *n.* This Sanskrit word means, literally, "this servant," from *tad-* or *tat-* (that one) plus *perusha* (servant), and denotes a class of compound words in which the first component is a noun or noun stem that modifies the second component by relating to it as possessor (*horsehide*), thing possessed (*sailboat*), object of action (*lawnmower*), location (*heartworm*) or agent (*manmade*). A related but different kind of compound is the *dvandva* (DVAHN dvah), also a Sanskrit word, consisting of two components related as though joined by the conjunction *and*. The full grammatical name is *dvandva compound*, and here are some examples: *prince-consort, secretary-treasurer, bittersweet*. *Dvandva* means "pair" in Sanskrit, formed by the reduplication of the numeral *dva*, meaning "two," and etymologically related to the English word *two*. *Tatpurusha* (also called *determinative compound* in Sanskrit grammar) and *dvandva* bring to mind another type of compound word, also from the Sanskrit, with the pleasant name of *bahuvrihi*, which swam into my ken in the dark days before the other two did. It has the alternative name of *possessive compound* and is fully discussed in my *1000 Most Challenging Words*. *Bahu* and *vrihi* mean "much" and "rice" respectively; if the words are combined, the compound thus formed becomes an adjective or noun signifying "(one) possessing much rice." Compare, in English, *redcoat* (British soldier in colonial times), *graybeard* or *tightwad*, or in German, *Dummkopf*. Mahatma Ghandi's title meant literally "great soul," from *maha* (great) (cf. Greek *megas* and *maharajah*) and *atman* (soul). (And Rudyard Kipling bestowed the title *Greatheart* on Teddy Roosevelt, in a poem written after his death.) Philologists have gone to Sanskrit for terms like *tatpurusha* and *bahuvrihi*, perhaps because compounds of German-type length and complexity are common in that language, and Indian grammarians are assiduous in classifying them. Perhaps, too, our scholars, like the author (and, I hope the readers) of this book are susceptible to the glamor of exotic words.

tautonym (TOT uh nim) *n.* This would be an easy one to guess if you had a bit of Greek at your command. The prefix *taut-* or *tauto-* comes from the adjective *tautos* (same, identical), which in turn is derived from *to auto* (the same), neuters of the definite article and *autos* (same). The suffix *-onym* is from the noun *onoma* (name). We find *taut-* in *tautological*, *tautophony*, etc. and *-onym* in *homonym*, *pseudonym*, etc. Thus, a *tautonym* is a "name that repeats itself," as found in certain two-word classification terms (known in zoology and botany as *taxonomic binomials*). Examples: *gorilla gorilla*, the common anthropoid ape of equatorial Africa; *mephitis mephitis*, the common North American skunk. In these *tautonyms* the generic name and specific epithet are identical. They are used in zoology to designate a typical form, but they are prohibited in botanical taxonomy (classification) under the International Code of Botanical Nomenclature. The botanists, poor chaps, have to search for another name for the species, the major subdivision of the genus. Sounds like discrimination to me, but there must be a reason. In a *tautonym*, both words must be nouns. *Foolish fool* or *dopey dope* may be *tautological*, but those aren't *tautonyms* for two reasons: The components aren't identical, and the first element isn't a noun. Identical twins can be concocted, like *sage sage*, but that won't do either, because the first *sage* is an adjective, and in any case, if we go along with the dictionary, the term *tautonym* appears to be restricted to biological taxonomy.

taxiarch (TAKS ee ark) *n.* This word has nothing to do with taxis or arches. It was the Greek title for a commander of a *taxis*, a division of the army. In Athens, a *taxis* was a group of soldiers from a *phyle* (FEYE lee), a tribe or a division of people within a state formed at first on the basis of kinship and later based simply on locality. *Taxis* means "arrangement," related to the verb *tassein* (to arrange); *phyle* was taken intact from the Greek for "tribe." The *-arch* of *taxiarch* has the same effect as the prefix *arch-*, meaning "chief," as in *archbishop*, and is the stem of *arche* (beginning). *Taxiarch* is as good a reason as I can think of for ʼy warning: Don't jump to conclusions in matters of etymology!

taxis   See **taxiarch.**

telegony (tuh LEG uh nee) *n.* There is a belief among some, scientifically unsupported, that a previous mate transmits his genetic influence to the offspring of his former mate and a subsequent mate. For example: Mr. and Mrs. A divorce; the ex-Mrs. A marries Mr. B. According to the theory of *telegony*, Mr A's genes have a serious influence upon the children of the second marriage. Some dictionaries (e.g., *WIII*) give the impression that this supposed carrying over of the influence of a former male relates only to quadrupeds, the definition using the terms *sire* and *dam*. Some carry the supposition so far as to include the offspring of all subsequent matings of the female. There is another unsupported theory called *saturation*: the supposed increasing resemblance to the male parent of successive progeny of the same parents. Who dreams these things up? In any event, the term *telegony* is constructed of the familiar Greek prefix *tele-*, the combining form of *tele* (far), and the suffix *-goneia*, from *gonos* (begetting, offspring). The adjective is *telegonic* (tel uh GON ik), which should never be confused with *telegenic* (tel uh JEN ik), meaning "suitable for telecasting; endowed with looks and presence that are attractive on television." If *telegony* were a fact of life, a person whose beautiful mother was formerly wed to a terribly unattractive man and whose father looked like John Barrymore would never qualify for the male lead on a soap opera.

telestic   See **telestich.**

telestich (tel ES tik, TEL es tik) *n.* As opposed to an *acrostic* (from Greek *akros*, extreme or end, plus *stichos*, line or row), a poem or prose composition in which the initial (in a single acrostic), the initial and final (in a double acrostic) or the initial, middle and final (in a triple acrostic) letters of the lines form words, a *telestich* is a type of poem, usually a short one, in which only the consecutive final letters of the lines form one or more words or names. This word is formed of the Greek prefix *tele-* (the combining form of *telos*, end; not that of the other *telos*, far) plus our old friend *stichos*. In the improbable event that you run into the word *telestic* (tuh LES tik), you mustn't think that it's a misprint for *telestich* that dropped the *-h*. *Telestic* is a perfectly good, if rare, word in its own right, from Greek *telestikos*, a verbal of *telein* (to initiate into mysteries or sacred rites) and is an adjective meaning "pertaining to the mysteries," or, more simply, "mystical." If there were any cockneys in ancient Greece, they would have dropped their initial, not their final, aitches.

tenebrae   See **tenebrism.**

tenebrific   See **tenebrism.**

tenebrious   See **tenebrism.**

tenebrism (TEN uh briz'm) *n.* From Latin *tenebrae* (darkness), a noun plural in form but singular in meaning, we get the name, taken intact from the Latin, of certain church services (Matins and Lauds) celebrated in the final part of Holy Week to commemorate the sufferings and death of Christ, with the chanting of psalms and the progressive extinguishing of candles until only one is left burning under or behind the altar—a most impressive and moving ritual that lingers in the memory. Apart from that special use, the Latin word has given rise to a number of terms dealing with darkness: *tenebrific* (ten uh BRIF ik), meaning "gloomy" or "gloom-producing," *tenebrious* (ten EB ree uhs), *tenebrose* (TEN uh brose) and *tenebrous* (TEN uh bruhs), all meaning "dark, murky," and figuratively, "mysterious, obscure" and *tenebrism*, the name given to a school of painting usually associated with the Italian painter Caravaggio (c. 1564–1609?), who submerged most of his forms in shadow and with dramatic effect illuminated the rest by means of a beam of light emanating from a specific identifiable source. The members of the school were known as *tenebrists* (TEN uh brists). Cognoscenti like to use the term *tenebroso* (ten uh BROH soh) as a learned synonym of *tenebrist*, but more modest art historians are satisfied with the latter. W. M. Rossetti, in an article in the *Encyclopedia Britannica* (1886), wrote of the "school of the Tenebrosi, or shadow painters," which seems to me to be something of an oversimplification. An article in the February 1963 issue of *The Burlington Magazine* states: *"The Last Supper* introduces us to a *tenebroso* effect." Your recollection of that masterpiece will tell you much about *tenebrism*: One picture *is* worth a thousand words!

tenebrist   See **tenebrism.**

tenebrose   See **tenebrism.**

tenebroso   See **tenebrism.**

tenebrous   See **tenebrism.**

tenson   See **sirvent(e).**

tenzon   See **sirvent(e).**

thanatism (THAN uh tiz'm) *n. Thanatos* is Greek for "death," and *thanato-* is its combining form. In ancient Greek culture, *Thanatos* was the god and personification of death and the twin brother of *Hypnos*, god of sleep, whence we got *hypnosis* and other *hypno-* words (see **hypnopedia**). According to the eighth-century B.C. Greek poet Hesiod, the twins were born of the goddess *Nox* (Night) by parthenogenesis. *Thanatos* contributed a fair-sized collection of *thanato-* words to our language. *Thanatopsis* (than uh TOP sis) may be familiar to us as the title of the poem of that name by the American poet William Cullen Bryant. *Thanatopsis* means "contemplation of death," from the prefix *thanat-* (omitting the *o* before a vowel) combined with Greek *opsis* (sight, view). *Thanatognomonic* (than uh tog nuh MON ik), "characteristic of death," weds *thanato-* with *gnomon* (indicator). *Thanatography*, an account of a person's death, uses *-graphia*, from *graphein* (to write). *Thanatophobia* should be obvious: "morbid fear of death." *Thanatology* (than uh TOL uh jee), with the familiar *-logy*, from Greek *-logia*, based on *logos* (discourse), is the study of death, its characteristics and causes. To get back to our headword: *Thanatism* is the belief that at death, the soul dies together with the body. Ernst Heinnich P.A. Haeckel, in the McCabe translation of *The Riddle of the Universe*, says: "We give the name of *'thanatism'* ... to the opinion which holds that at a man's death ... his 'soul' also disappears, that is, that sum of cerebral functions which psychic dualism regards as a peculiar entity, independent of the other vital processes in the human body." In the December 1900 issue of *The Academy, a Monthly Record of Literature, Learning, Science and Art*, these words appear: "We prefer to say that even atheism and *thanatism* are speculations." Most things are.

thanatognomic   See **thanatism.**

thanatography   See **thanatism.**

thanatology   See **thanatism.**

thanatophobia   See **thanatism.**

thanatopsis   See **thanatism.**

thank'ee-marm   See **thank-you-ma'am.**

thank-you-ma'am, also **thank'ee-marm** (pronounced as they appear) *n.* Neither of these is an expression of gratitude but simply, in American colloquial usage, a "hollow or rut across a road" that causes the people in a vehicle passing over it to nod involuntarily, the way one might do in acknowledging a favor and expressing thanks. Originally, such ridges were often built as a means of spilling off rain water. Their purpose now is to make drivers slow down as a precaution when they near thickly settled neighborhoods. In *Kavanagh, a Tale* (1849), Henry Wadsworth Longfellow describes a trip in which "We went like the wind over the hollows in the snow;—the driver called them *'thank-you-ma'ams,'* because they made eveybody nod." Oliver Wendell Holmes, in *The Guardian Angel* (1867), quotes a metaphorical use of the term: "Life's a road that's got a good many *thank-you-ma'ams* to go bumpin' over, says he." William Howells uses the alternative term in *The Landlord at Lion's Head* (1897): " ... one of the *'thank-ee-marms* in the road ..." It's a pleasant bit of fanciful usage, like the British road colloquialism "silent policeman," denoting a raised strip across a road put there to slow drivers down as they approach a thickly settled residential or commercial area, a sound device also known as a "rumble strip."

theandric (thee AN drik) *adj. Theandric* is our adaptation of Greek *theandrikos*, from *theandros* (god-man), built on the nouns *theos* (god) and *aner* (man), and means "simultaneously divine and human, partaking of both the divine and human." Edward Irving, in *Sermons* (1828), wrote of "Heretics ... asserting that there was only one operation, *Theandric* or Godmanly." The form *theandrical* is also found. In *A Treatise Concerning the Fulnesse of Christ* (1656), Henry Jeanes gave the following definition of the word: "*theandrical*, that is, divinely human." A closely related adjective is *theanthropic* (thee an THROP ik), with roughly the same meaning: "possessing the nature of both God and man at once divine and human." Here, *theos* is joined with *anthropos* (man) to form the ecclesiastic Greek noun *theanthropos* (god-man), from which our adjective was formed. In *Gleaning of past Years* (1868), the statesman and scholar William Ewart Gladstone pointed out that "the *theanthropic* idea, the idea of God made man without ceasing to be God, was ... familiar ... to the old mythology." The form *theanthropical* (thee an THROP ik uhl) has been used but is rare. *Theanthropism* (thee AN thruh piz'm) is the doctrine of the union of divine and human natures, or God as man, in Jesus Christ. Bishop Lightfoot, in his *Commentary on St. Paul's Epistles to the Colossians, etc.* (1875), made the clear statement that "the monotheism of the Old Testament is supplemented by the *theanthropism* of the New." Apart from that theological meaning, *theanthropism* is used in discussions of mythology. Thus, the same Gladstone, in his *Homer*, a literature primer, speaks of the "*theanthropism* ... of the Olympian system." As you might suppose, there are the forms *theanthropist* (thee AN thruh pist), used both attributively and adjectivally, and *theanthropology* (thee an thruh POL uh jee), synonymous with *theanthropism. Theanthropos*, mentioned above, now obsolete, was once a title given to Jesus. One form that I would not have predicted is *theanthropophagy* (thee an thruh POF uh jee), combining *theanthropo-* with *-phagy*, from Greek *-phagia* (-eating), based on *phagein* (to eat). Jeremy Taylor, in *The Real Presence and Spirituall of Christ in the Blessed Sacrament Proved against the Doctrine of Transubstantiation* (1654), spoke of the Catholics who "deny anthropophagy [cannibalism], but did not deny *theanthropophagy*, saying, that they did not eat the flesh or drink the bloud of a meer man, but of Christ who was God and man," a perfectly logical theological distinction, as far as I can see. As opposed to the doctrine of *theanthropism, ebionism* (EB ee uhn iz'm), the doctrine of the *ebionites* (EB ee uhn ites), a Christian group of the first century, held that Jesus was only a man and that Christians were subject to the Mosaic law. This group developed into a distinct sect in the succeeding century. To *ebionize* was to follow or imitate the tenets or practices of that sect. In a sermon delivered by the Reverend Robert Gell in 1650, he referred to the "*Ebionites*, who denied the deitie of Christ," and Frederick W.

Farrar, in *The Life and Work of St. Paul* (1879), wrote of the "*Ebionite* hatred still burning against St. Paul in the second century." *Ebionite* came from Latin *ebionita*, based on the Hebrew *ebyon* (poor).

theandrical   See **theandric.**

theanthropic   See **theandric.**

theanthropism   See **theandric.**

theanthropist   See **theandric.**

theanthropology   See **theandric.**

theanthropophagy   See **theandric.**

theotokion (thee oh TOH kee on, thee oh toh KEE on) *n. Theotokos,* in Greek of the Christian period, is an epithet of the Virgin Mary, meaning "Bearer of God" or "Mother of God." That word is formed of Greek *theos* (God) plus -*tokos* (bearing), from *tok-,* the stem of the verb *tiktein* (to bear, bring forth). *Theotokos* has its Latin equivalent in *Deipara,* from *deus* (God) plus -*para* (bearing), from *parere* (to bear). *Deiparous* (dee IP uh ruhs) is an adjective meaning "bearing a god." (The Greeks and Romans were deeply interested in the genealogy of their divinities.) Now, as to *theotokion,* that is a "hymn of the Eastern (i.e., Greek Orthodox) Church in praise of the Virgin Mary as the Mother of God." That hymn forms the final *troparion* (troh PAIR ee uhn) of a canonical ode. And what is a *troparion*? That is the term for a short hymn chanted liturgically in rhythmic prose during services in the Eastern Church, specifically a stanza of one of the nine scriptural canticles forming part of the morning service of the Eastern Church on certain designated days of the year. If you want to hear one, consult the calendar of your friendly neighborhood Eastern Church (Greek, Russian, Ukrainian or whatever) and don't be late.

theotokos   See **theotokion.**

Therapeutae (ther uh PYOOH tee) *n. pl. Therapeuein* is a Greek verb with a number of related meanings, starting with "to attend" (generally) and continuing with "to worship" and "to attend medically," which is the basis of our familiar noun *therapy,* meaning "medical treatment" generally but these days commonly taken as a shortened form of *psychotherapy.* It is the senses of *attend* and *worship* that gave rise to the name *Therapeutae,* New Latin from Greek *therapeutai,* the plural of *therapeutes* (attendant, worshiper, medical attendant), denoting a sect of Jewish mystics who lived in Egypt in the first century A.D. The Alexandrian Jewish theologian Philo (c. 20 B.C.–c. A.D. 50) described them as ascetics devoted to meditation and contemplation. The sect resembled the

Essenes, but unlike them, it included women. Their name is sometimes anglicized to *Therapeuts*, by which name they are mentioned in the English translation of David F. Strauss's *New Life of Jesus* (1865). They were taken, says Strauss, as "the Egyptian branch of the Essenes," and Robert A. Vaughan, in *Hours with the Mystics* (1856), called them "a sect similar to the Essenes, [numbering] many ... whose lives are truly exemplary." When I first ran across this word, I mistook it as a term for ancient physicians, but the uppercase *T* made me sufficiently inquisitive to indulge in a little investigation, and the foregoing tells the story.

therianthropic (thair ee an THROP ik) *adj.* This adjective is descriptive of an organism combining human and animal forms, and *therianthropism* (thar ee AN throp iz'm) is the "representation of such forms or the worship of them as gods." *Ther* and *Therion* mean "wild beast" in Greek, and our old friend *anthropos* is "man," as we know from words like *anthropology, anthropoid,* etc. *Theriolatry* (thair ee OL uh tree) is "animal worship," *-latry* being based on Greek *latreia* (worship). *Theriomorphism* (thair ee oh MOR fiz'm) is "belief in gods with the form of beasts." The Egyptians worshiped the deity Anubis in the form of a jackal, Horus in the form of a falcon and other animal gods. The *-morphism* came from Greek *morphe* (form). Getting back to *therianthropism*, the Egyptian goddess Hathor had a woman's body and a cow's head; Anubis was sometimes represented as a man with the head of a jackal; Thoth had the body of a man and the head of an ibis; Medusa had wings, and snakes for hair; and the well-known Sphinx was a winged lion with a human head or at times a ram's or hawk's head. These deities must have made religion quite fascinating (and scary) in the old days and a lot more absorbing than the dry sermons that required the services of a church official who went around waking up little boys by tickling them with a feather in colonial days. See also **manticore** and **theroid**.

theroid (THAIR oid) *adj. Thero-* is the combining form of the Greek noun *ther* (wild beast), which has given us a number of words having to do with the animal form or nature. *Theroid* describes a person brutish in form or nature. The Greek word *theroeides*, combining *thero-* with *eidos* (form), is the immediate ancestor of *theroid*. Henry Maudsley's *Body and Mind* (1870) tells us: "There is a class of idiots which may justly be designated *theroid*, so like brutes are the members of it." Mention has been made in scientific journals of the appearance of animal peculiarities of anatomy in persons exhibiting *theroid* mental characteristics. *Therio-* is the combining form of a related Greek noun, *therion* (wild animal) and has also given us words having to do with animal life and representation. Cf. **therianthropic** and the related words discussed there.

thesis   See **hemiola**.

thirdings   See **heriot**.

thurible (THOOR uh b'l) *n.* A *thurible* is a "censer," a vessel in which incense is burned, as in religious ceremonies. *Thurification* is the "burning of incense," and a *thurifer* is an "acolyte who carries and swings the censer." The Latin source of these words is *t(h)uribulum*, and that is based on the Latin noun *t(h)us* (frankincense—which goes back to Old French *franc encens*, meaning "pure incense"); and there is actually an English noun *thus*, pronounced the way it looks, or THOOHS, if you think that this *thus* pronounced THUS is confusing. Zarathustra never spake incense, just thus. As Macbeth spake in Act III, Scene 1: "To be thus is nothing;/But to be safely thus." And as Artemus Ward says in *Moses, the Sassy*: "Why is this thus? What is the reason of this thusness?" The reason is that who would have thought that *thus* (incense) could ever have been defined thus? Let us discard this *thus*; a *thus* by any other name would smell as sweet.

tombac (TOM bahk) *n.* This word has appeared in a great variety of forms: *tombaga, tambaycke, tumbeck, tombago, tambaqua, tumbanck* and goodness (or the *O.E.D.*) knows what else. The current form, adopted from French, is *tombac*, equivalent to Italian *tombacco*, Portuguese *tambaca*, Spanish *tumbaga* and, adopted from Malay, *tambâga*. Whatever the form, it is the name of an alloy that originated in the East Indies, of copper and zinc in varying proportions, mostly copper (82 to 99%). It is found in the East in gongs, bells, etc., and in Europe (under different names: Prince's metal, Mannheim gold, etc.) it is used in the manufacture of cheap jewelry. There is *red tombac* (more than 92% copper), *yellow tombac* (82 to 90% copper) and *white tombac*, in which arsenic replaces zinc and the alloy. By its various names, *tombac* is mentioned in travel literature over the years from 1608 to 1872. In some of the words, the *tombac* is a mixture of gold and copper, copper, tin and zinc, etc. Whether it is used today or not, it would make a good (if rather easy) anagram in crossword puzzles.

tragelaph   See **hircine.**

triage (tree AZH, TREE uhj) *n. Triage* is French for "sorting, selection," a noun of action from the verb *trier* (to choose, sort, select). Our verb *try* is related in that it comes via Middle English *trien* from Old French *trier* (to pick out, sift). The *O.E.D.* makes short work of *triage*, confining the definition to "the act of assorting according to quality," and quotes examples of its use in sorting fleece and coffee beans. The *Supplement* goes much further, extending the use of the word to the assignment of degrees of urgency to wounds or illnesses so as to determine the order of treatment. A quote from a 1974 issue of *Time* further extends its use as follows: "In the West, there is increasing talk of *triage*, a commonsense if callous concept that teaches that when resources are scarce, they must be used where they will do most good." More specifically, a 1975 issue of the Toronto *Globe and Mail* states: "The concept [of *triage*] should now be applied to countries crippled by food shortages, famine and overpopulation ... ," and a 1979 issue of *The Guardian* (London) carries the use of what by now has become a quite versatile word a step further: "There is (*sc.* in New York) an unofficial '*triage*' system in which teachers and school administrators concentrate their limited resources on helping those students who seem to be capable of succeeding." *W III* describes "the process of grading marketable produce" as a British sense of the word, and adds the definition "the lowest grade of coffee berries consisting of broken material." Its definition relating to "patients and esp[ecially] battle and disaster victims" specifies the purpose of this type of *triage*: "to maximize the number of survivors." If you run into the word, you will have to use a certain degree of *triage* yourself to determine whether you are dealing with broken coffee beans, famine, teachers and students, hospitals or battle and disaster victims. Quite a word. What next? Dating services, marriage bureaus, harems?

trigamy   See **digamy.**

trim   See **trimmer.**

trimmer (TRIM ur) *n.* This word obviously means "one who *trims*," but the verb *to trim* has an unusually large number of meanings (16 in the *O.E.D.*). One of them is "to modify one's attitude in order to stand well with opposite parties; to move cautiously, or 'balance' between two alternative interests, positions, opinions, etc."; in other words, "to sit on the fence," to maintain neutrality on a controversial issue, to act as a *mugwump*, a term originally applied to Republicans who denied support to James G. Blaine, their party's nominee in the 1884 presidential election. Despite the popular belief that *mugwump* came from the expression "to sit on the fence with one's *mug* on one side and one's *wump* [rump] on the other," it was taken from the Algonquian language, where it meant, literally, "great man," and satirically "big shot." From that sense of *trim*, the word *trimmer* was applied to one who *trimmed* between opposing political parties and came to denote any person who performed a "balancing act" between two parties or opinions so as to stay in favor with both sides. There is another angle on *trimmer*. To *trim* a boat is "to balance it so that it doesn't capsize." In politics, this means balancing between the extremities of rival factions that threaten the "ship of state." Such was the argument used by George Savile, marquis of Halifax, to justify his own policy in the British constitutional troubles of the 1680s. In this sense he wrote a pamphlet entitled *The Character of a Trimmer*, published in 1688, which includes an eloquent passage to the effect that the only thing a *trimmer* is *un*compromising about is his patriotic opposition to foreign designs of invasion and the like. Perhaps he was an early advocate of the "extreme center." Savile described the *trimmer* as follows:

> Our *Trimmer* is far from Idolatry in other things, in one thing only he cometh near it, his Country is in some degree his Idol; he doth not

Worship the Sun, because 'tis not peculiar to us, it rambles about the World, and is less kind to us than others [kindly note the 17th-century observation about the English weather with its "sunny intervals" and "showery spells"; there'll always be an England]; but for the Earth of England, tho perhaps inferior to that of many places abroad, to him there is a Divinity in it, and he would rather dye, than see a spire of *English* grass trampled down by a foreign Trespasser.

Shades of Mrs. Thatcher and her pretty rough speeches these days to those at Brussels who would have England cede some of her sovereignty to the say of a tighter E.C.! In an 1872 issue of his *Journal*, Sir Walter Scott spoke of "an attempt to govern *par bascule* [by see-saw]—by *trimming* betwixt the opposite parties." As to the adoption of *trim* and *trimmer* in that sense, I would incline to credit it to the 14th definition in the long *O.E.D.* list: "*Naut[ical]*. To adjust (the sails or yards) with reference to the direction of the wind and the course of the ship, so as to obtain the greatest advantage." To sum up: A *trimmer* is a "timeserver," and that's the long and short (or middle-sized) of it.

tripody   See **prosodion.**

triptych   See **polyptych.**

triptyque   See **polyptych.**

trochee   See **dolichurus.**

troparion   See **theotokion.**

tuft (TUFT) *n. Tuft*, in its common uses, is a familiar word, but one use in British English may come as a surprise. A *tuft* is a "gold tassel" that formerly adorned the top of a mortarboard (the "cap" that is a part of the uniform known as "cap and gown," also called *academicals* in British English) worn by undergraduates at Oxford and Cambridge. Originally, this distinction in dress was a privilege allowed only to the sons of peers having a vote in the House of Lords. Later, this privilege was granted to all peers and their eldest sons, and in 1870 it was made optional. *Tuft* was university slang for a student with that privilege. Thackeray, in *A Shabby-genteel Story* (1840), tells of a "lad [who] went to Oxford ... frequented the best society [and] followed with a kind of proud obsequiousness all the *tufts* of the university." The term *tuft-hunter* was originally applied to those who obsequiously sought the society of the university *tufts*. Later, it included any person who sought to become a familiar of persons of title or rank generally, and eventually it was applied to any toady or sycophant. Thackeray used the term in *The Newcomes; Members of a Most Respectable Family* (1855), in a passage describing a person who "was accused ... of being a *tuft-hunter* and flatterer of the aristocracy." In his *Personal and Literary*

Memorials (1829), Henry Beste wrote of one who "made no disgraceful *tuft-hunting* distinctions in favour of noblemen ... " *Tuft-hunting* is a special brand of *lion-hunting* in the sense of chasing after celebrities and persons of rank, a strenuous activity of certain party-giving social climbers whose names become all too familiar to readers of gossip columns.

tuft-hunter   See **tuft.**

tychism (TEYE kiz'm) *n. Tyche* is Greek for "chance" and with an uppercase *T* was the name of the goddess of fortune. When the gentleman gambler in Frank Loesser's *Guys and Dolls* sang "Luck, be a lady tonight," he *was* addressing a lady—a goddess. *Tyche*, with an upper- or lowercase initial, lent her (or its) name to *tychism*, the doctrine that the element of chance must be taken into account in reasoning, whether cosmological, philosophical or other. The word was coined by the U.S. mathematician and philosopher C. S. Pierce in 1892, who said: "I endeavored to show what ideas ought to form the warp of a system of philosophy, and particularly emphasised that of absolute chance ... which it will be convenient to christen *tychism* (from *tyche*, chance)." In his *Study in Moral Theory* (1926), J. Laird wrote: "The theory that every event ... *must* occur precisely as it does occur I shall call *determinism* ... The opposite theory I shall call *tychism* ... either general or restricted." A 1978 issue of *Scientific American* carried the statement that " ... Pierce's doctrine of '*tychism* ' maintained that pure chance—events undetermined by prior causes—are basic to the universe." In reference to its *chance* discovery, a rare mineral consisting of carbonate and sulphate of magnesium and sodium was christened *tychite*. (I didn't know mineralogists were that well versed in Greek.) There is a series of *tycho-* scientific terms, among them *tychoparthenogenesis* (teye koh par thuh noh JEN uh sis—exceptional parthenogenesis, that term meaning "egg development without fertilization," from Greek *parthenos*, maiden, hence the Parthenon in Athens, dedicated to the virgin goddes Athene, plus *genesis*, origin) and *tychopotamic* (teye koh POT uh mik—occurring occasionally in or near rivers, *potamos* being Greek for "river"), referring to the floating organisms of pools and overflows from rivers). Probably superfluous caveat: Do not confuse any of those *tycho-* words with *Tychonic* (teye KON ik), which describes anything relating to the Danish astronomer Tycho Brahe (1546–1601) or his system of astronomy, or *Tychonian* (teye KOH nee uhn), a disciple of that system. Ignorant of the term *tychism*, and unsatisfied with *randomness*, I coined *randomism* years ago when asked to define my creed.

Tychonian   See **tychism.**

Tychonic   See **tychism.**

tychoparthenogenesis   See **tychism.**

tychopotamic   See **tychism.**

tyrosemiophile (teye roh SEM ee oh file) *n.* I am going to include a second, entirely unrelated word in this discussion: **misapodysis** (mis uh puh DEYE sis). Both words are borrowed from Philip Howard's instructive and entertaining column "Word-Watching" in *The Times* (London). They are chosen as a demonstration that if you know enough Greek roots, you can string selected ones together and invent interesting words that fill a need and obviate circumlocutions. I say "invent" because my search has revealed no lexicographical inclusion of either word. *Tyrosemiophile* : Take *tyro-*, the combining form of *tyros* (cheese); add *semio-*, the combining form of *semeion* (mark, sign); then add *-phile*, from *philia* (loving), and you have "cheese-mark-fancier," a term applied, according to Mr. Howard, to "collectors of the labels on French cheese boxes." (Whence "French" and whence "boxes," Mr. Howard? What about Edam, Gouda, Emmenthal, Jarlsberg, Muenster, Provolone, Gorgonzola, Cheddar, Double Gloucester, Leicestershire, Liederkranz, boxed or unboxed?) A not very useful word, perhaps, but what else would you call a *cheeseboxlabelfancier*? The word appeared in a work by the American writer Thomas Pynchon, who is never timid about coining neologisms. Now *misapodysis*: Take *mis-*, the combining form of *misein* (to hate) or *misos* (hatred); add *apodysis*, from *apodyesthai* (to undress), formed of the prefix *apo-* (away, off) plus *dyesthai* (to dress), and you get *hatred of undressing* (i.e., in public, before someone). An extreme case of *misapodysis* is found in the practice, in some nunneries, of bathing in one's nightie, even in private, or so I'm told. *Apodysis*: how else avoid the cumbersome circumlocution?

tzedaka(h) (tse DOK uh) *n.* You will have found that the great majority of words discussed in this book are of classical Greek or Latin origin, but words of many other origins have been included as well. After all, we are one world, and the nations are dependent on one another for many aspects of life, including language. The English language has long been internationalist; no isolationism in that department. We borrow these foreign words that can't be quite fully translated in a way that conveys all of their subtle connotations. We speak of *Zeitgeist* (German for the "spirit of the age"); *dolce far niente* (Italian for "pleasant idleness"); *entre nous* (French for "between ourselves"); *mañana* (Spanish for "tomorrow—some time in the future"); and *guru* (Sanskrit for "wise leader"). And we have loaned as well as borrowed, when our foreign cousins have seen fit to adopt an English term not quite translatable into their vocabulary. Here, we have *tzedaka(h)*, taken from Hebrew *sedaqah* (righteousness). *Tzedaka(h)* means "charity," and specifically, the "duty to help fellow Jews." Freemasons, Elks, Rotarians and countless other groups, as well as ethnic or national enclaves of co-nationals in foreign lands, feel that type of obligation, but the Jews, against the background of millennia of persecution, feel it especially strongly. Dagobert David Runes, in his *Concise Dictionary of Judaism* (1959), defines *tzedakah* as "righteousness; charity." The 1962 *New*

Jewish Encyclopedia tells us: "The Jewish concept of 'charity' has ... been refined to mean more than the mere giving of alms; it has been considered as '*Tzedakah,*' an act of justice and righteousness." In *The Joys of Yiddish* (1968) Leo Rosten discusses *tzedaka* and its variant *tsadaka* extensively and gives their origin as Hebrew *tzedek* (righteousness). His definition: "The obligation to extablish justice by being righteous, upright, compassionate—and above all, helping one's fellow man." He quotes Josephus (Jewish scholar, first century A.D.): "He who refuses a suppliant the aid which he has the power to give, is accountable to justice." A noble sentiment indeed; and to plunge from the sublime, how about the Yiddish *chutzpah* (unmitigated effrontery, gall, cheek, nerve), *shlemiel* (simpleton, loser), *shlep* (drag, pull), *mavin* (expert, connoisseur), *megillah* (long, prolix account, rigmarole)? These loan words have been naturalized into English and can be found in many an English dictionary. I have occasionally performed an act of *tzedaka(h)* in explaining one of them to an unenlightened *goy.*

Ucalegon (yooh KAL uh gon) *n.* A *Ucalegon* is a "next-door neighbor whose house is on fire." I received a letter from a reader in Lafayette, Louisiana, in which (after words of praise, I am happy to say, about my *1000 Most Challenging Words*), she wrote: "I wonder ... that you could refrain from including the word '*ucalegon.*' This is a splendid word that I have had the opportunity to use once in my life, when my husband called me to say that our next-door neighbor's house was on fire. 'Oh,' I said, 'then we have a *ucalegon.*' I think he has been a little in awe of me ever since." That sent me to the dictionaries, and I found only one that listed *Ucalegon,* but that was with an uppercase *U.* The winning dictionary was good old *W II,* and there I read: "*Ucalegon* (u-kal-e-gon) *n.* ... In Trojan legend, one of the ancient counselors who sat with Priam on the wall. Aeneas speaks of the flames reaching *Ucalegon*'s house, next to that of Anchises [father of Aeneas], before he fled from the city. Hence, a next-door neighbor whose house is on fire." In this delightful *W II* item, the pronunciation parenthesis includes a symbol over the *u* giving it a *yooh* sound, as in *unite,* the accent on the *kal,* and a schwa symbol over the *e,* all resulting in *yooh KAL uh gon. W II* sent me to the *Aeneid,* where I read, in translation, that in answer to Queen Dido's plea, at the end of Book I, to Aeneas to tell her about "Grecian guile, your people's trials," he commences (start of Book II) his recital of the destruction of Troy. Fire is everywhere. "The spacious palace of Deiphobus has fallen, victim of the towering Vulcan. And now, *Ucalegon*'s his neighbor, burns ... " In the beautiful compressed style of the original, the four significant words are " ... *iam proximus ardet Ucalegon.*" (Book II, lines 310/311.) The foregoing translation is that of Allen Mandelbaum (University of California Press, 1971). I find "*Ucalegon*'s, his neighbor, burns" awkward. Such are the demands of prosody, one supposes, but I don't know why this wonderful scholar decided to substitute his iambic pentameter for Virgil's heroic dactylic hexameter in the first place, though who am I to begrudge the excellent man his privilege? So you see there did exist a *Ucalegon*, complete with uppercase *U*, and my correspondent was perfectly correct in her awe-inspiring response to her husband's cry of alarm. I have advised her, however, that she must capitalize the *U* even though the name is used generically, just as we must capitalize the initial in *Sherlock* when we characterize someone as a "regular Sherlock" for having solved a mystery, or the *E* in Einstein when we call someone "an Einstein" because he has an I.Q. of 200+. The generic use of the eponymous original's name doesn't deprive him of his uppercase initial. Getting back to the translation of the Latin, *Bartlett's Familiar Quotations* gives us: "*Ucalegon*'s afire next door," while *The Oxford Dictionary of Quotations* presents: "Already neighbor *Ucalegon* burns," which is most faithful to the original; but alas, in a dazzling display of metathesis, the second (1953) edition index misspells *Ucalegon* "*Ucelagon*," and in the third (1979) edition the quotation has disappeared!

ultroneous (ul TROH nee uhs) *adj. Ultro* is a Latin adverb with a variety of meanings. It shares with *ultra* the meanings "on the farther side, beyond" and is thought to be derived from *ulter*, a supposititious word, i.e., one not found in Latin literature but assumed to be the basis of a derived form, in this case *ultro. Ultro* has many more meanings than the more common *ultra*: "besides, moreover, also" and figuratively, "superfluously, wantonly," but its relationship to *ultroneous* is explained by its additional meanings "spontaneously, voluntarily, of one's own accord, unasked." *Ultroneous*, then, means all those things, but in adjectival use. Sir William Hamilton, in *Discussions on Philosophy and Literature, Education and University Reform* (1852), expressed the opinion that "the exercise of the student in the University classes, should be partly exigible [requirable, non-optional], partly *ultroneous*." A witness who testifies of his own accord without being cited [subpoenaed] is described as *ultroneous* in Scots law; it used to be inadmissible but is now merely considered less credible than that of one who has been required to testify. In *Horae Subsecivae* (Spare Time, Unoccupied Hours—1863), James Brown used *ultroneousness* in a special sense: "The law of personality, of *ultroneousness*, of *free will*, that which in a great measure makes us what we are ... "

upaithric   See **hypaethral.**

usquebaugh (US kwih baw, -bah) *n.* The *O.E.D.* lists 21 variant spellings of this word! It is derived from Irish and Scots Gaelic *uisce* or *uisge* (water) plus *beatha* (life), i.e., "water of life," and in this respect is akin to Latin *aqua* (water) *vitae* (of life—genitive of *vita*). *Aqua vitae*, which today denotes alcoholic liquor, was originally a term in alchemy. The related *aquavit* or *akvavit* is a very dry Scandinavian ginlike liquor flavored with caraway seeds. Well, after all this learned etymology, what do you suppose *usquebaugh* is? Whiskey! Just good old plain old whiskey. In Farquhar's *The Beaux' Stratagem* (1706) we read, "An honest Gentleman that came this way from Ireland made her a Present of a dozen bottles of *Usquebaugh.*" In one of his *Waverley Novels, The Legend of Montrose*, Sir Walter Scott wrote of "a flask of *usquebae*, designed for the refreshment of Lord Menteith." I don't think it would do you much good, in an English pub or an American bar, to ask for an *usquebaugh*, whether straight (or as the British say, neat), or with water or soda. You can give it a try, but I'd stick to *whiskey*, or, in the British spelling, *whisky*, though the Irish retain the *e*.

usucapient   See **usucapion.**

usucapion (yooh zooh KAY pee uhn) *n*. In Roman law, this is the term for the acquisition of ownership of property through long uninterrupted and undisputed use. Such use is known in our legal system as "prescription," and the right so acquired is called "prescriptive." The term under Roman law was one year for personal property (chattels) and two years for real property. The term of possession under our law varies from jurisdiction to jurisdiction. Easements, as well as ownership rights, are acquired in this fashion. *Usucaption* (yooh zooh KAP shuhn) is a variant form. To acquire such title is to *usucapt* (yooh zooh KAPT) it, and one claiming such title is a *usucapient* (yooh zooh KAYP ee uhnt) or *usucaptor* (yooh zoo KAP tuhr). All of these words are derived from Latin *usucapere* (to acquire ownership by length of use, to obtain by prescription), formed of *usu* (by use—the ablative of *usus*, use) plus *capere* (to take). Beware of squatters! They could wind up owning what you had fondly gone on believing was yours.

usucapt   See **usucapion.**

usucaptor   See **usucapion.**

vellicate (VEL uh kate) *vb*. In Latin, *villicare* means "to pluck" or "twitch"; it is the frequentative of *vellere*. (A *frequentative*, which I discuss in my *1000 Most Challenging Words*, is a verb that serves to express the frequent repetition of an action expressed by another verb. In other words, *vellere* means "to pluck or twitch," and *vellicare* expresses the frequency or nervous repetition of that action.) From *vellicatus*, its past participle, we get *vellicate*, a word not much used these days but common in medical usage in the 17th and 18th centuries, meaning, as a transitive verb, "to irritate (body tissues)," referring to the action of certain medications. It meant as well "to tickle" or "titillate." It was so used by the poet and naturalist Erasmus Darwin, Charles's grandfather, in

Zoonomia, or the Laws of Organic Life (1801): "So when children expect to be tickled in play ... by gently *vellicating* the soles of their feet, laughter is most vehemently excited." Intransitively, *to vellicate* is "to twitch or otherwise move convulsively." *Vellication* can be used to denote the act of twitching or tickling, or the twitching of any part of the body, especially a muscle. And in *Letters to and from the Late Samuel Johnson* (1788), edited by Hester Lynch Piozzi (Mrs. Thrale), we read in one from the great S.J.: "These *vellications* of my breast shorten my breath." He used it figuratively in *Prayers and Meditations* (1781): "At night, I had some mental *vellications*, or revulsions." *Vellicative* is the predictable adjective. John Mason Good, in *The Study of Medicine* (1822), wrote: "They [the teeth] are colloquially said to be set on edge ... from jarring noises ... [or] from *vellicative* or acrid substances." (Or, in my experience, from fingernails scraping along a slate blackboard.)

vellinch (VEL inch) *n.* This word has a variety of spellings. The *O.E.D.* lists *valinche, valincher, velinche* and *velincher,* but no *vellinch,* which is vouched for by *W III,* where it is said to be a variant of *valinch,* an alteration of *valentia,* itself a modification of the Spanish noun *venencia,* and that, according to my Spanish dictionary, is a "tube for sampling sherry." As to *valentia,* that is Spanish for "courage, gallantry, exploit, boast, great effort, imagination, and—wait!—a second-hand shoe shop in Madrid." What that has to do with tubes for sampling sherry must remain a mystery. A *vellinch* is a "tube for drawing a sample from a cask through the bung-hole," also known as a *shive hole, shive* being a term for a "thin wooden bung" for a cask or a "thin cork" for a wide-mouthed bottle. (*Shive* has lots of other meanings not relevant here. As Casey Stengel was fond of saying: "You could look it up." And once you start looking ...) A *vellinch* is sometimes called a *flincher,* which is an obvious corruption of *valincher* or *velincher.* This whole comment is a good sample of the sort of thing you get into if you own a lot of dictionaries.

vespertilio (ves pur TIL ee oh) *n.* Bats come out in the evening, and *vesper* means "evening" in Latin (hence, *Vespers* for evening prayers and the adjective *vespertine,* describing evening phenomena). In my *1000 Most Challenging Words,* under *acronical,* I discuss *vespertine* and *crepuscular* and say that they "cover things that happen in the early evening, at dusk, just after sunset," whereas *acronical* "applies to phenomena occurring at sunset." It is not surprising that the Romans chose *vespertilio* as their word for "bat," and that is what it means in English. In a book by Sir Thomas Herbert published in 1665 with the lovely title *A relation of Some Yeares Travaile Begunne Anno 1626, into Afrique and the Greater Asia,* the author writes that "These *vespertilios* ... hang in swarms upon the boughs of Trees." He doesn't add "upside down," the way I've always seen them, but we can infer it. The *Vespertilionidae* are, according to the *O.E.D.,* "a large family of insectivorous bats, including the common British species." The same dictionary lists the tantalizing nonce word *vespertilionize* with the definition "to convert or turn *into* a bat [emphasis is mine]," as used by Charles D. Badham in an 1854 book entitled *Prose Halieutics*. *Halieutics*, according to the book from which I quoted above, "is the art and science of fishing ... " This partially explains the following sentence from the Badham book: "Others ... have *vespertilionized* this skate into the Sea-bat." But good for Badham: It takes courage to coin a word like *vespertilionize* !

vespetro (VES puh troh) *n*. Quite a word, *vespetro*. It is distinguished in a number of ways. First, it is not in the *O.E.D.* Second, it is the name of an extraordinary alcoholic drink: a liqueur with a base of brandy, to which are added anise, fennel, coriander and angelica, the whole being sweetened with sugar. Angelica is an umbelliferous plant of the genus *Angelica* (*umbelliferous* denotes a member of the family known as *Umbelliferae*, which includes carrots, celery, etc., as well as angelica, characterized by being topped by a cluster rising from a given point at the top of the stalk, known as *umbels*, from Latin *umbella*, sunshade; the type of angelica used in *vespetro* being *Angelica Archangelica*, cultivated for its scent, medicinal qualities, etc.). Now—last but not least—comes the derivation. It was taken as is from the French *vespétro*, which, according to French dictionaries and at least one English dictionary as far as I have discovered (*W III*), is based on three French words: *vesser* (to break wind noiselessly; Cassell's French-English dictionary lists the noun *vesse*, elegantly translated as "silent evacuation of wind" but marked "indecent!"); *péter* (to break wind—no mention of silence this time; *Cassell* gives *péter* a string of meanings, including "to fart," and marks this one "vulgar and not decent."); and *roter* (to belch; no disapproval by *Cassell* this time). So the *ves-* of *vesser* or *vesse*, plus the *pét-* of *péter*, plus the *ro-* of *roter* add up to our headword *vespetro*! But nobody says what farting noiselessly, farting noisily and belching have to do with *vespetro*, and one is left to imagine that indulgence in that rather elegant-sounding liqueur produces a series of inelegant bodily manifestations. I'll have *Armagnac*, if it's all the same to you.

vilipend (VIL uh pend) *vb*. From Latin *vilis* (paltry, mean, worthless, base), which gave us the adjective *vile*, plus *pendere* (to suspend, consider, weigh, estimate), which, from the meaning "suspend" or "weigh" in the literal sense, gave us *pend, pendant, pendent, pending*, etc., we got *vilipend*, meaning "to consider as of little value, to despise, to treat contemptuously, to disparage, to vilify, to abuse." Sir Walter Scott, in *Waverley; or 'tis Sixty Years Since* (1814), wrote of "a youth devoid of that petulant volatility which ... *vilipends* the conversation and advice of seniors." In *Vanity Fair* (1848), Thackeray condemned one for "*vilipending* the poor innocent girl as the basest and most artful of vixens." As an intransitive verb, to *vilipend* is "to be disparaging or depreciatory." *Vilis* and *pendere* gave the French *vilipender*, the Italians *vilipendere* and the Spanish and Portuguese *vilipendiar*, so it seems that the vile practice is rather widespread.

virelay   See **sirvent(e)**.

virga (VUR guh) *n. Virga* is a Latin noun with a number of meanings: "twig, sprout, slender branch, rod, switch, scourge, wand, staff, cane, streak, stripe (a colored stripe in cloth)." The one we are interested in here is "rod," for at least two reasons. *Virga* is the term for trails or wisps of water, drops or bits of ice falling from a cloud but never reaching the ground because they melt or evaporate before they get there. If they reach the surface of the planet, the technical name is *praecipitatio,* which in common parlance is *precipitation,* familiar from TV weathermen's lingo. I said there were two reasons: first, because the wisps or trails of moisture or ice in the air do sometimes resemble *rods*; next, because of the British idiom "to rain stair-rods" where we would say "rain cats and dogs," (which they say as well). The British use of *rods* in their (to us) peculiar phrase is the opposite of the wispy *rods,* i.e., *virgae* (plural of *virga*), which never get to the ground. Their *rods* do get to the ground, and how! (Cf. The French *pleuvoir* or *tomber des hallebardes,* literally "to rain halberds," the 15th- and 16th-century shafted weapons with axelike cutting blades, beaks and spikes.)

virlai   See **sirvent(e).**

vomitorium (vom ih TOHR ee uhm) *n.* Since this word is recognizably Latin, and because you have probably read about the ancient Roman custom of resorting to self-induced vomiting during a banquet to make room for the next course (by means of tickling the back of the throat with a feather), you might jump to the conclusion (always dangerous in etymology) that a *vomitorium* was some sort of little room where this rather horrid operation was performed. But no: A *vomitorium* was a "passage in an ancient amphitheater leading to and from the seats." The word was anglicized to *vomitory,* an "opening or passage in a theater allowing the audience to enter and leave." Tobias Smollett's *Travels through France and Italy* (1766), describing the ruins of an ancient amphitheater, speaks of " ... the remains of two galleries, one over another; and two *vomitoria* or great gateways at opposite sides of the arena." In *The History of the Decline and Fall of the Roman Empire* (1776), Gibbon writes: "Sixty-four *vomitories* (for by that name the doors were very aptly distinguished) poured forth the immense multitude." No feathers, no tickling; just entering and leaving the amphitheater with the contents of the tummy intact. Nonetheless, the word is dervied from the Latin *vomitus,* the past participle of *vomere* (to vomit), and the exiting (if not the entering) of the spectators through a *vomitorium* is an understandable if somewhat unpredictable extension of the concept.

vorpal (VOR p'l) *adj.* When Alice, in *Through the Looking-Glass,* held the book "in some language she didn't know" up to the mirror, the words went "the right way again," and she read a poem entitled "Jabberwocky," about that frightful beast, the Jabberwock, and how he (whoever the hero was) "took his *vorpal* sword in hand," and how "the *vorpal* blade went snicker-snack" and "he left it dead." " ... It's *rather* hard to understand!" said Alice, " ... However, *somebody* killed *something*: that's clear, at any rate." Obviously, the blade was very sharp indeed; "keen, deadly," is the definition of *vorpal* given by the *O.E.D. Supplement*. W. H. Auden saw fit to use the word in *New Year Letter* (1941) when he wrote: "Wave at the mechanized barbarian/The *vorpal* sword of an agrarian ... "

water-tath   See **tath.**

woop-woop (WOOP woop) *n*. This is a term heard in Australia and New Zealand (sometimes *woop-woops* or *wop-wop*), thought by some to be sham aboriginal, for a "backwooods town or district." It is sometimes preceded by *the* and sometimes capitalized (as two words). The American equivalent would be "one-horse town" or "whistle stop" for a small town, and "boon-docks" for the backwoods; in Britain, a sleepy little town is a "one-eyed village." *Woop-woop* is said by some to come from the "geelorious town o' Whoop-Up" in E. L. Wheeler's *Deadwood Dick on Deck* (1878), a fictitious American gold-mining town way out in the boondocks. The inventor of *woop-woop* certainly went way out of his way geographically if that theory is to be given credence. Vance Marshall, writing under the pseudonym Jice Doone, in *Timely Tips for New Australians* (1926), defines *Woop-Woop* as "a humorous method of alluding to the country districts used most frequently in New South Wales." Noel Harvey Hilliard's *Maori Girl* (1960) contains this bit of conversation: "'Where do you come from?' 'Up in the wilds, the *woop-woops* ... '" The term *woop-woop* is sometimes used as well to denote a denizen of the backwoods, a country bumpkin. *Woop-woop* sounds perfectly plausible to me: I've been in Walla Walla.

xeniatrophobia   See **xenodochiophobia.**

xenodochiophobia (zee noh doh kee oh FOH bee uh) *n*. A concoction from a group of Greek elements, this means "fear of foreign hospitality," i.e., worry about foreign hotels. We start with *xenos* (foreign; cf. *xenophobia*); add *doche* (reception, entertainment, hospitality; akin to *dechomai*, to receive hospitably); and wind up with the familiar *phobia*. Voilà: *xenodochiophobia*, a common American ailment inhibiting travel abroad. ("Should I bring along soap? Toilet paper? Disinfectant?") In his letter to the *New York Times* of Sunday, March 12,

1989, Mr. Louis Jay Herman of New York City adds "a few more suggested contributions to the Hellenizing of travel language," to which I shall add a bit of etymology: *cacohydrophobia* (ka koh heye droh FOH bee uh), built of *kakos* (bad), *hydros* (water) and *phobia*, resulting in "fear of bad water," or, as Mr. Herman puts it in a loose but effective translation: "Can I drink what comes out of the tap in this joint?" He continues, "This can also be Latinized as *malaquaterror* (which speaks for itself) and, for nonclassicists, *turistaphobia* will do perfectly well." I would even more freely translate *turistaphobia* as "dread of Gyppy tummy, Delhi belly or Montezuma's revenge," but now we're playing fast and loose (accidental but apposite pun). Next: *xeniatrophobia* (zee nee ah troh FOH bee uh), from our old friend *xenos* plus *iatros* (doctor) plus an even older friend *phobia*, meaning "dread of foreign doctors," who suffer not so much from inadequate medical skills as from inadequate acquaintance with the English language, as far as my experience indicates. Now: *xenonosocomiophobia* (zee noh nos oh ko mee oh FOH bee uh), joining *nosos* (mischief), *komion* (carrying off) and our intimate friend *phobia*, meaning "fear of foreign pickpockets," who, in my travels, have proven more adept than our own pros. Finally: *hypselotimophobia* (hip suh loh tim oh FOH bee uh), from *hypselos* (high), *timos* (price; lo! the cascading dollar!) and the by-now Ancient *Mariner*-type clinging albatross *phobia*, adding up to "fear of astronomical prices" (have you had breakfast in Tokyo lately?). There being no classical Greek for *airplane*, I can't manufacture a classical etymology for "dread of plunging airplane," but the English will suffice, unless you prefer *Icarianism* or *Phaethonianism* (see the former in my *1000 Most Challenging Words*).

xenonosocomiophobia   See **xenodochiophobia.**

yarmulke   See **zucchetto.**

zariba (zah REYE buh) *n.* This is an Arabic word, taken over intact, for "cattle pen" or "enclosure," from the root *zarabu* (to shut in). In parts of Africa, especially the Sudan, a *zariba* is an "enclosure, commonly built of thornbush, to ward off attack from enemies or wild animals," but the term is applied generally to any fortified camp. The transliteration of the Arabic has taken a number of different forms. In O'Reilly's translation of Werne's *Expedition to the Sources of the White Nile* (1849) we find: "A shining *seriba* of reeds, the stalks of which ... perhaps only afford resistance to *tame* animals," a description seemingly at variance with the reference to wild animals in the definition given above. The poet Eliza Dook's *Journal* (1852) notes: "The Sultan has planted a *zeribeh*, or circular inclosure, with two issues." Note *planted*, which must refer to thornbush; the *issues* were outlets. Sir Samuel Baker's *The Nile Tributaries of Abyssinia* (1867) tells us: "We employed ourselves ... in cutting thorn branches, and constructing a *zareeba*." The term has also been applied to a troop formation to resist attack and was used figuratively in an article by A. White in an 1898 issue of the *National Review*: "The ... Tsar ... is ... surrounded by a *zereba* of detail and enticed from affairs of State by organized diversions." The word has also been used as a verb. Intransitively, *to zariba* is "to build a *zariba*." An 1885 issue of *The Nineteenth Century* contains the following: "Orders were given to *zereba* ourselves ... The Brigadier ordered the force to *zereba* on the best position that was near." A year later, the *Contemporary Review* described "a large garden, *zarebded* in with aloes and henna." I feel *zaribaed* in myself, with many more obscure words to write about. Good word, though.

zarzuela (zar ZWAY luh, -ZWEE-) *n.* This is the name of a traditional type of Spanish operetta with spoken dialogue, often on a topical theme treated satirically. It gets its Spanish name from the *Real Sitio de la Zarzuela* (Royal Residence of the Comic Opera), a palace near Madrid, where the first *zarzuela* was performed in 1629. Joseph Hergesheimer, in *Bright Shawl* (1922), defined the *zarzuelas* as "operettas of one act, largely improvised with local allusions." A 1973 issue of the *Oxford Times* tells us: "The modern *zarzuelas* are really operettas or lyric dramas, which are a kind of Spanish equivalent of Gilbert and Sullivan and the Viennese operetta, full of tunes which have become part of Spain's popular culture." Back in 1888 *Lippincott's Magazine* mentioned " ... the absurd things ... seen in pantomimes by the *zarzuela* companies at the theatres." Pantomimes are an English specialty, dramatic entertainments produced for children and others in the Christmas season, usually based on fairy tales and legends, with songs, dances, lots of clowning, topical jokes and familiar stock roles. The *Lippincott* reference to "pantomimes by the *zarzuela* companies" may give British readers some idea of the nature of this Spanish entertainment.

zetetic (zee TET ik) *n.* As an adjective, *zetetic* means "investigating, inquiring" or "proceeding by investigation or inquiry"; as a noun, in the singular or plural form *zetetics* (but always treated as a singular), it means "inquiry, investigation." It is derived via Modern Latin *zeteticus* from Greek *zetetikos*, based on the verb *zetein* (to seek). In *The History of Philosophy* (1660), Thomas Stanley informs us that the *"Zetetic* Philosophy" was so called "from its continual enquiry after Truth" (a lofty aim, we must agree!). An 1859 book by S. B. Rowbotham entitled *Zetetic Astronomy* had the subtitle: "A description of several experiments which prove that the surface of the sea is a perfect plane and that the Earth is not a Globe!" The exclamation point is part of the subtitle, not mine, apparently stressing the validity of the conclusion in the face of the established belief to the contrary. An 1853 edition of William Thomson's *Outline of the Laws of Thought* tells us: "[Logic] has been called ... *Zetetic* or the Art of seeking." *Zetetic* also has the meaning "investigator, inquirer," and the term was used more specifically to denote an adherent of the Greek skeptic school of philosophy. Rowbotham's *Dictionary* (1858) tells us that "the ancient *Pyrrhonists* were called *Zetetics* or seekers." Pyrrho of Elis (c. 300 B.C.) was the founder of the first school of skeptic philosophy, which held that it was impossible to achieve certainty of knowledge. He advocated universal skepticism, and the term *pyrrhonism* came to acquire the meaning of "skepticism" generally or "absolute incredulity." His disciples were known as *pyrrhonists*, and it seems wrong to identify them as *zetetics*. To *Pyrrhonize* is to practice *pyrrhonism*, i.e., "to doubt everything." Wouldn't the good citizens of Missouri be astonished to discover that they were all *pyrrhonists*?

ziggurat (ZIG oo rat), also **zik(k)urat** (ZIK oo rat), *n.* Thus we identify an Assyrian or Babylonian temple tower of pyramidal form in which each ascending story is smaller than the one below, so that a terrace is left all the way around. The January 5, 1898 issue of the *English History Review* mentions the "*ziggurat*, or great tower, of which the Tower of Babel was a famous example." Joining the successive stepped-back stages were outside staircases, and the whole structure was surmounted by a shrine. Its name was taken from the Akkadian word *ziqqurratu* (height, pinnacle), Akkad being the northern division of ancient Babylonia and the Accad mentioned in Gen. 10:10, where we read that "the beginning of his [Nimrod, the mighty hunter's] kingdom was Babel, and Erech, and *Accad* ... " Some identify Akkad with Agade, about 18 miles south-southwest of what is now Baghdad, the capital of Iraq, which the Ayatollah would have loved to get his hands on. Ah, history! All the way from the *Ziggurat* of Babel to pal Khomeini.

Zingg (ZING) *adj.* Theodore *Zingg*, born in 1905, was a Swiss meteorologist who specialized in petrology, the study of rocks: their origin, mineral and chemical composition and alteration. He developed a system of classification of pebble shapes (apparently, there's a system for everything) in which two ratios are formed from three mutually perpendicular diameters, and these are used to classify pebbles as belonging to certain fixed shape categories. His system is known to petrologists as the *Zingg system*. Petrologists are concerned about the relation between sphericity and the *Zingg* shape indices. There are four basic *Zingg* shapes: disks, spheres, blades and rods. You and I walk along the beach and admire the pretty colors, and sometimes the shapes, of those millions and millions of pebbles, but I don't think we pay much attention to *Zingg* classification. On coming across a particularly striking little pebble, we might exclaim, "Zing! Isn't that one a beauty!" but that kind of *zing* has nothing to do with friend Theodore.

zizis   See **daven.**

zoanthropy (zoh AN thruh pee) *n. Zoanthropy* is a type of monomania, a form of insanity restricted to one subject, in a person otherwise sane (*monomania*, from the Greek adjective *monos*, single, alone, plus *mania*, madness). The subject in *zoanthropy* is the belief of a human being that he is an animal. The derivation, here too, is elementary: *zoon* (animal) plus *anthropos* (man), both Greek nouns. One form of *zoanthropy* is *lycanthropy*, in which the person imagines himself to be a wolf; from Greek *lykos* (wolf) plus our old friend *anthropos.* We have heard about the werewolf, or wolf-man, a person afflicted with *lycanthropy*, also known as a *lycanthrope* or *lycanthropist. Werewolf*, also *werwolf*, is from Old English *werwulf*, formed of *wer* (man—related to Latin *vir*) plus *wulf* (wolf). There are many legends about werewolves, men who could assume the form of wolves, with the appetite of wolves, who roamed about at night devouring infants. The Greek historian Herodotus (fifth century B.C.) tells us about the tribe of Neuri, who could turn themselves into wolves once a year. A member of the family of Antaeus, the giant wrestler slain by Hercules, was selected annually by lot to become a wolf for nine years. Other legends involved other animals: When wolves disappeared in England, witches often "became" cats. And haven't I read somewhere about enchanted princes who became frogs?

zoetrope   See **phenakistoscope.**

zootrope   See **phenakistoscope.**

zucchetto (zooh KET oh, tsooh-) *n. Zucca*, in Italian, means "pumpkin, gourd" and colloquially "head," or, in equivalent slang, "bean, nut, noodle," etc. *Zucchetta* is its diminutive: "small pumpkin," or what the British call "marrow," a vegetable not seen in America, really a large variety of what we call "zucchini," a plural—one never hears of a "zucchino"—and what the British as well as the French call "courgettes." Enough of this botany: Change the *a* to *o* and you have *zucchetto*, meaning "skullcap" in Italian and English (finally!) and particularly the round cap worn by Roman Catholic ecclesiastics, differing in color according to rank: black for priests, violet for bishops, red for cardinals and white for the Pope. Before we get away from the etymology, the Italian *zucca*, in its colloquial sense, has a synonym, *cucuzza*, and that may go back to Latin *cucurbita* (gourd). *Zucchetto* has a synonym, *calotte*, which has a variety of additional meanings in the field of architecture that have nothing to do with ecclesiastical skullcaps: "small dome, upper zone of a dome, inner dome of a double dome, metal cap for a cupola." *Calotte* comes via French from Italian *calotta*, which in turn comes from Greek *kalyptra* (cover), a word that has itself been taken intact into English as a botanical term denoting a hood that covers a number of botanical features and is related to the Greek verb *kaliptein* (to cover). In J. D. H. Dale's translation of Baldeschi's *Ceremonial*

According to the Roman Rite (1853) certain clerics are advised that "They should take off their *zucchettos* in the act of genuflecting," and in M. J. F. McCarthy's *Five Years in Ireland* (1901) there is the tale of how "[Pope] Leo XIII … took off the *Zucchetta* (sic) he had been wearing and gave it to [one] Father O'Brien." Another type of cap worn by Roman Catholic ecclesiastics is the *biretta*, which is quite different from the small, round *zucchetto*, in that it is square and stiff and has three or four upright projecting pieces that go from the center of the cap to the edges. It is called *berretta* in Italian and sometimes in English and at times is spelled *biretta*. It is derived from Late Latin *birretum* and is akin to *beret*. Another type of religious skullcap is the *yarmulke* (YAR muhl kuh), worn by Orthodox Jewish males most of the time, always during prayer and religious study, and usually by all Jewish males while attending religious rites like Bar Mitzvahs.

zumbooruk (ZUM booh ruk, zum BOO-) *n.* This word, subject to a number of spelling variations like so many words of Hindustani origin, derived from the Hindustani noun *zamburak*, based on the Persian word *zambur* (hornet), is the name of a small cannon mounted on a swivel, especially one fired from a support mounted on the back of a camel. The gunner was known as a *zumboorukchee*. James B. Fraser, in *Travels in Koordistan, Mesopotamia, etc.* (1840) mentions "a large body of *zumboorukchees*," and a 1904 issue of *Blackwell's Magazine* describes "rakish swivel-guns, bell-mouthed *zumbooraks*." From reports in travel books about India in the old days, it appears that the swiftness of camels and the skill of *zumboorukchees* combined to produce a very effective weapon.

zumboorukchee   See **zumbooruk.**

zyme   See **zymurgy.**

zymite   See **zymurgy.**

zymurgy (ZEYE mur jee) *n.* This is a word easy to find in any dictionary, since it's sure to be on the last page. From Greek *zyme* (leaven, ferment) plus *-ourgia*, based on *ergon* (work), *zymurgy* is the "branch of technological chemistry that deals with fermentation processes," as in wine making, brewing and distilling. *Zyme* is itself a word in English, taken intact from the Greek, meaning "ferment" (the chemical reaction, not the psychological kind involving agitation and inner tumult), and its adjective is *zymic*. There is a whole series of *zym*-words having to do with fermentation, but my favorite is *zymite*, designating a priest who uses leavened bread in the Eucharist.